AT ONCE NOTORIOUS and visionary, Edward Gibbon Wakefield and his brothers played a key but controversial role in the early British settlement of New Zealand, Australia and Canada. Once famed as New Zealand's 'Founding Fathers', they have since become the arch-villains of all post-colonial scenarios of the past. Philip Temple, deciding that neither myth made good historical sense, saw that, astonishingly, there was no adequate biography of the family most responsible for the establishment of the Wellington, Nelson and Canterbury settlements.

In stitching together a net of letters and documents, Temple has produced the most comprehensive account yet of the Wakefield family's role in colonial development and self-government across the old Commonwealth. He follows not only the brothers' careers but also establishes the role of the Wakefield women and gives detailed accounts of Edward Gibbon Wakefield's first elopement and his later abduction of Ellen Turner. Temple explores Edward Gibbon's tortuous career through colonial politics from the 1830s to the 1850s and shows how he and his brothers and son strongly influenced, for good and bad, the founding of new nations. This engaging narrative, written in a strong and evocative literary style, relates a story of courage and vision, cupidity and stupidity, high risk and adventure, success against the odds and, ultimately, terrible tragedy.

PHILIP TEMPLE is an award-winning New Zealand author with 40 novels, non-fiction works and children's books to his credit. At various times, he has been the Robert Burns Fellow at the University of Otago, the Katherine Mansfield Fellow in Menton and National Library Fellow in Wellington. His longstanding interest in New Zealand colonial history yielded many books on the history of mountaineering and exploration, in particular *New Zealand Explorers*, which he adapted for television and which first stimulated his interest in the Wakefields. He lives in Dunedin.

A Sort of Conscience

The Wakefields

PHILIP TEMPLE

AUCKLAND UNIVERSITY PRESS

First published 2002
This edition 2003

Auckland University Press
University of Auckland
Private Bag 92019
Auckland
New Zealand
http://www.auckland.ac.nz/aup

ISBN 1 86940 307 X

Publication is assisted by the History Group of the Ministry for Culture and Heritage

Cover illustration: M. T. Clayton, *Settlement of Wellington by the New Zealand Company. Historical gathering of pioneer ships in Port Nicholson, March 8, 1840, as described by E. J. Wakefield*. Chromolithograph. Alexander Turnbull Library, C-033-005. William Wakefield is seated in the waka with the *Tory* behind.

Cover design: Christine Hansen

Printed by Printlink Ltd, Wellington

CONTENTS

Part Three: War to the Knife, 1839–1848

Part Four: A Suicide of the Affections, 1849–1879

INTRODUCTION

IN THE POLITICAL AND SOCIAL climate of the early twenty-first century, Edward Gibbon Wakefield and his family are the villains of all fashionable post-colonial scenarios of the past. Until about 50 years ago, Edward Gibbon was considered at least partly responsible for the British settlement of New Zealand, his brothers and son its active agents and its occurrence essentially a good thing. Wakefield also played a seminal role in the shaping of British colonial policy over two decades from the early 1830s, had a direct influence on the settlement of South Australia and assisted in the creation of a Canadian constitution. This arguably positive work was always overshadowed by the notorious cases of fraud and abduction that had led to his earlier imprisonment. Yet many of Wakefield's notable contemporaries, and historians and economists over the century following his death, were willing to look past the notoriety to his vision and political achievements.

The decline of the Wakefields in the pantheon of politically correct memory can be judged by the fact that in 1966, when some New Zealanders still thought Home was England, the *New Zealand Encyclopedia* listed no fewer than eight entries under the name Wakefield; by 1990, the sesquicentennial judgement of the first volume of *The Dictionary of New Zealand Biography* allowed only two:* Edward Gibbon, whose influence in planning New Zealand's colonial settlement could not be set aside, and his son Jerningham, principally because he wrote a good book. Notably absent were William, leader of the New Zealand Company's *Tory* expedition in 1839 and then of the Wellington settlement, and Arthur, leader of the Nelson settlement in 1841 and killed by Te Rangihaeata in the Wairau confrontation of 1843.

This official revisionism, and the antipathy the name Wakefield often aroused, alerted me to a vein of prejudice in much educated opinion. I found also that, though there were four hagiographies of Edward Gibbon Wakefield, written in the days when he was seen as a founder of empire or commonwealth, there was no

* Though Edward Wakefield (1845–1924) was included in the second volume.

dispassionate biography of a family that played such a significant and controversial role in the establishment of the larger British colonial democracies. All of this provoked me to set out to discover just who Edward Gibbon Wakefield and his family were, where they came from and what they did. I felt that an understanding of their character and circumstances would contribute towards a better understanding of their motives and actions. It seemed a necessary and useful task, one that would assist in reaching fresh perspectives on colonial history.

As is often the case with biographical projects, this work has taken much longer than expected: I planned to complete it in three to five years, but ended only after eleven. I underestimated the time it would take to research and write about an entire family, even if one was the central figure, and to grasp the colonial, and wider, politics of the first half of the nineteenth century. Also, I became utterly absorbed in the forensics of the project: the piecing together of clues in correspondence, for example, that brought to light previously unrecorded events and actions or newly illuminated character and motive.

I experienced those transcendent moments, familiar to all historical biographers, when the author seems to touch the hand or face of their subject. When, years ago, I travelled wild country to retrace the journeys of early New Zealand explorers, this occurred with positive identification of old campsites or plants that were the holotypes for original scientific descriptions. With the Wakefields, it occurred on such occasions as taking delivery from Admiralty archives of the log of the ship Arthur commanded while chasing West African slavers in the 1820s; or when turning the pages of Eliza Wakefield's diary, reading the last entries before her premature death; or when sitting in the cold parish church of Stoke-by-Nayland, where this scattered family had occasionally gathered together and where they are now forgotten save in the tilt of churchyard gravestones.

The political context was always important, especially for Edward Gibbon Wakefield from the 1830s, but I searched, too, for the people, their characters and relationships. At such a distance in time this proved difficult, for there were often considerable gaps in correspondence or journals and sometimes very little at all – for William until 1839, for example, or for Felix until he returned from Tasmania to England in 1847. I did not fully grasp Edward Gibbon's complex personality until I read archived correspondence in Ottawa that suddenly threw into relief the English and New Zealand material.

I cast wide in an attempt to explain behaviour and motive, paying attention to medical conditions and the effects of personal loss and grief. I wished to discover the role of women – wives, sisters, daughters – on Edward Gibbon Wakefield and his brothers. The influence of grandmother Priscilla had been made plain in the earlier hagiographies, but mother Susannah had always been pushed into the background. Why? Even elder sister Catherine had not been fully drawn, although so much of the surviving correspondence suggested that the book might well be titled, 'My Dear Catherine'.

Although the focus of the book would be on Edward Gibbon Wakefield and his siblings as adults, I needed to explore fully the family circumstances that shaped them and influenced both their careers and their personal behaviour. Grandmother Priscilla and father Edward were deeply involved in reform movements of the late eighteenth and early nineteenth centuries and it seemed essential to look at the people and causes that surrounded the new generation of Wakefields as they grew up. The starting point for the narrative became obvious: Edward the father's marriage in 1791, at a time of great political and social change, and as the eldest son of a family whose financial resources had unexpectedly contracted. In times of general upheaval there was personal upheaval; tensions both creative and destructive governed the future of a family whose reduced income could no longer adequately support the upper-middle-class status and political influence they had come to expect. They became a part of the growing 'uneasy classes' who would turn to emigration in the great wave of British colonisation of North America and Australasia that began in the generation after the end of the Napoleonic Wars.

The chapters have been arranged in four parts that correspond to relatively distinct eras of Wakefield family history in the century after 1791. Part One covers the early years, in which all of Edward Gibbon's generation reached maturity, and ends with the catastrophic fracture of the family caused by Edward Gibbon's and William's imprisonment following their abduction of Ellen Turner. Part Two spans the most active years of Edward Gibbon Wakefield's writing and propaganda in the cause of planned colonial settlement, concluding with William setting out as leader of the New Zealand Company expedition. It also includes Edward Gibbon's journey to Canada with Lord Durham, William's military career in Spain and Arthur's naval career. The first half of the book is located principally in England, although Arthur takes us to the East Indies and all over the Atlantic world.

Part Three deals with the establishment of New Zealand's Wellington and Nelson settlements, and the conflicts they entailed, to the points of both Arthur's and William's deaths. Edward Gibbon Wakefield's second period in Canada is included, as is Felix's life in Tasmania. The final part focuses on the development of the Canterbury settlement, Edward Gibbon's and Felix's migration to New Zealand and Edward Gibbon's part in early provincial and national government. It concludes with the death of all the remaining siblings of that generation and Edward Gibbon's son, Jerningham.

I decided to do the Wakefields the courtesy of attempting to treat them within the context of their own times. They would not escape the reality of who I was, formed in a later period, but I could call on my experience as a novelist and attempt to enter their world. Although the book would be broadly chronological, and drawn from my extensive research in four countries, I decided on a creative narrative that paid attention to story, characters and dialogue, in the form of letters, journals and public writings, which would allow the reader to hear the Wakefields' own voices.

Because the Wakefield brothers became scattered all over the world in the classic family diaspora of empire, it made sense also to follow their careers with a degree of separation, rather than present the reader with a clutter of events connected only because they all happened in the same year. There were different stories to tell: they had strong familial, and usually career, connections but diverged more often than they converged. For example, though Chapter Two centres on Edward Gibbon Wakefield's schooling and the start of his diplomatic career to the point of his mother's death in 1816, his story is suspended at that point so that, in Chapter Three, we may step back chronologically to traverse Arthur's distinctive naval career to a logical suspension point in *his* story, the 1816 Battle of Algiers. These chronological 'meeting points' occur throughout the book, often with physical meetings of the brothers, though the whole family never met after about 1820. From the mid-1830s, however, colonising became very much a family business with Edward Gibbon as its managing director; and there was a final convergence with five of the six brothers ending their lives in New Zealand, the apotheosis of the Wakefield colonial dream.

I have, by and large, left judgements of the Wakefields mostly to their peers and have avoided directing the reader. There are exceptions, where it seems timely to discuss an issue, or where it seems necessary to temper the sometimes extreme views of the Wakefields' contemporary critics. This is not in the cause of revisionism, an attempt to rehabilitate Wakefield character, but to suggest balance. Most of my own conclusions on their personalities, behaviour and achievements are reserved for the epilogue.

In testing all the shibboleths surrounding the Wakefields, I found that they were sometimes much better and sometimes rather worse than I expected – and than past writers have been only too eager to claim. I cannot claim perfect balance and accuracy for this book – there are too many gaps in the record, too many uncertainties – but I have worked hard to justify the facts and statements it contains, and I am content to accept evidence that proves any of them otherwise. As for the book's interpretations, I can only expect some disagreement. The past can never be known perfectly, let alone entirely grasped by one writer. A study such as this finally stands or falls on whether it, in some way, enlarges our knowledge and understanding; and whether it seems authentic both to its subject and to the experience and sentiments of its generation of readers.

Despite distant admiration for that saintly Quaker Priscilla and some affection for that 'flower of the field' Arthur, I hold no brief for the Wakefields. Like most large families, they showed courage and vision; cupidity and stupidity; recklessness and ignorance; passion and compassion; tolerance and intolerance. The book's title refers to this ambiguity of character, frankly expressed by Edward Gibbon Wakefield in an 1821 letter to his sister Catherine, whose religiosity did not dampen her undying affection for her brother; and who considered that his sometimes unscrupulous means always had worthwhile and generous ends.

These Wakefields were a fascinating family, somehow at once atypical and untypical of their times. Like and admire them or not, they undeniably made a difference to their world and remain an indelible part of British colonial history, and of New Zealand in particular. If we understand them better, we may better understand ourselves.

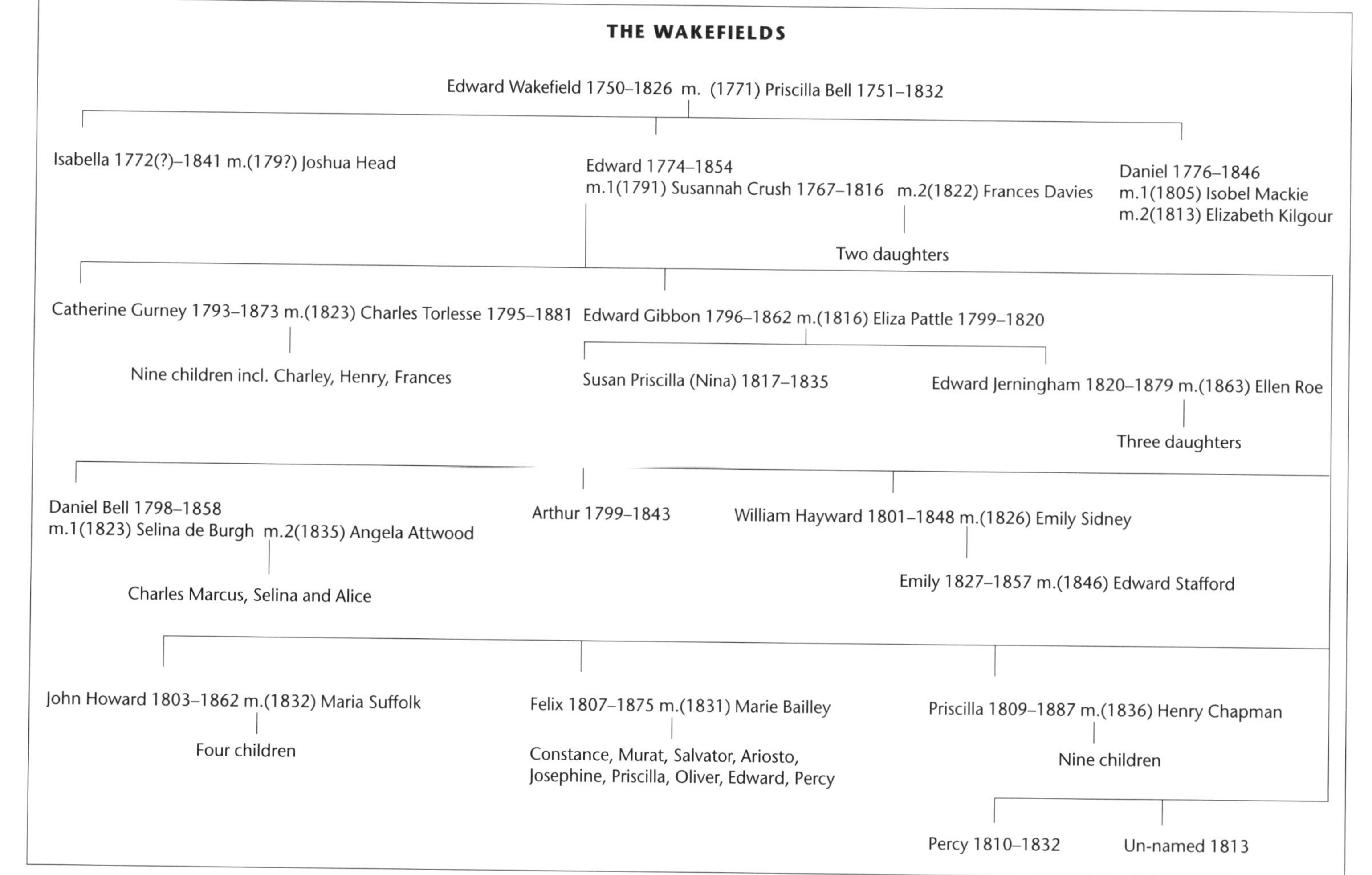
THE WAKEFIELDS
Edward Wakefield 1750–1826 m. (1771) Priscilla Bell 1751–1832
Isabella 1772(?)–1841 m.(179?) Joshua Head
Edward 1774–1854
m.1(1791) Susannah Crush 1767–1816 m.2(1822) Frances Davies
Two daughters
Daniel 1776–1846
m.1(1805) Isobel Mackie
m.2(1813) Elizabeth Kilgour
Catherine Gurney 1793–1873 m.(1823) Charles Torlesse 1795–1881
Nine children incl. Charley, Henry, Frances
Edward Gibbon 1796–1862 m.(1816) Eliza Pattle 1799–1820
Susan Priscilla (Nina) 1817–1835
Edward Jerningham 1820–1879 m.(1863) Ellen Roe
Three daughters
Daniel Bell 1798–1858
m.1(1823) Selina de Burgh m.2(1835) Angela Attwood
Charles Marcus, Selina and Alice
Arthur 1799–1843
William Hayward 1801–1848 m.(1826) Emily Sidney
Emily 1827–1857 m.(1846) Edward Stafford
John Howard 1803–1862 m.(1832) Maria Suffolk
Four children
Felix 1807–1875 m.(1831) Marie Bailley
Constance, Murat, Salvator, Ariosto,
Josephine, Priscilla, Oliver, Edward, Percy
Priscilla 1809–1887 m.(1836) Henry Chapman
Nine children
Percy 1810–1832
Un-named 1813

PART ONE

This Mottled World

1791–1827

CHAPTER ONE

The Matriarch and Her Sons

IN EARLY OCTOBER 1791, SEVENTEEN-YEAR-OLD Edward Wakefield returned to his parental home in Tottenham village, an hour's coach ride north of London, and announced, 'Mother, I am married!'[1] Priscilla Wakefield's reaction is not known but may have been only lightly admonishing, given the long-suffering equanimity of her Quaker disposition and the precocity of recent Wakefield marriages. Her own had been contracted with Edward senior when both were only 20, in 1771; his father had married at 21. Her daughter Isabella caused no grief, but Priscilla's amiable patience was to be battered and tried her entire long life by the unexpected conjugal announcements of her sons and grandsons as they pursued a 'fine irregular genius for marriage'[2] that was finally suppressed only by trial and imprisonment.

Edward had taken up with Susannah Crush, the 'bastard daughter of Robert Crush and Mary Galifant';[3] Crush was a yeoman farmer of Felstead in Essex. Edward described Susan as 'The most beautiful woman I have ever known'. With a cascade of golden hair and 'a soft angelic beauty . . . she was a model for a sculptor'.[4] Gentle, unsophisticated and undemanding, Susan was not a woman of family and brought Edward no land or cash. Physical attraction, and his 'ardent and enthusiastic disposition',[5] seem to have been the motives behind the marriage of the tall, good-looking teenager to a woman seven years his elder.

The connubial and domestic arrangements of Edward and Susan during the first years of their marriage are not recorded, but nearly two years elapsed before their first child, Catherine Gurney, was born in the parish of St Olaves, Old Jewry, City of London on 17 July 1793. Almost another three years passed before Priscilla noted in her journal on 20 March 1796, 'Susan has a boy in London',[6] who was to be named Edward Gibbon. As she entered middle age, the tensions and stresses of coping with the demands and deficiencies of her growing extended family inform most entries in the journal that Priscilla kept for 20 years. 'A plan in agitation for fixing Daniel [son] at Cowes. I fear his stability is scarcely equal to a situation so distant from the advice and counsel of friends' (13 February). A few months later: 'Drank tea with my Father who rapidly declines into the vale of years [70]. Age and infancy demand the attention of all closely connected' (10 April).

Priscilla's husband Edward (EW) 'was a man the interest of whose fortune left him by his father was £3000 a year and his commercial and banking concern rated him as a man of the very first consequence. . . it must have had its weight with her parents and I suppose with herself.' But EW had not inherited his father's skills and luck in business and banking. 'She bore his unexpected failure like a heroine and it has procured for her great respect ever since. . .'.[7]

The family suffered from recurring financial problems, a direct practical burden for Priscilla and the chronic prompt for many of her sons' and grandsons' actions in future years. She found solace, fortitude and life purpose in an enduring Quaker faith inherited from both her mother Catherine, granddaughter of Robert Barclay of Ure, the seventeenth-century Quaker apologist (and progenitor of the famous banking family), and from her father, Daniel Bell. After their marriage at the meeting house in Tottenham High Road, her parents had made a home at nearby Stamford Hill, 70 acres bordering the River Lea where a wharf and warehouse served Bell's lifelong coal business. By 1796, Priscilla saw it as 'Once the place of all my domestic joys, but now, alas! almost stript of all' (22 July). As her widowed father neared the end of his life, she wrote on 25 July, 'Could but age feel the advantage of continuing agreeable: what a delightful task to alleviate its miseries, as it is, it is an incumbent duty.'

Priscilla Wakefield's Quakerism was actively and pragmatically philanthropic. She was no admirer of orthodoxy. At a Friends' meeting she 'mixed with numbers of those who think that extreme plainness of habit and address is essential to rectitude. I admire the simplicity of their manners, and the purity of their morals, but do they not sometimes deviate into mere formality and uniformity of habit?' (6 September 1796).

Priscilla had been brought up in an environment less restricted than that of many Quaker families. Daniel had been fond of shooting, riding and fox-hunting, which were not at all compatible with Quaker practice since Friends were adjured 'not to distress the creatures of God for our amusement'.[8] Priscilla was said to be 'fond of general society and some worldly amusements':[9] in December 1796, she went to London and 'saw Macbeth. Delighted with the combined talent of Mrs Siddons and Kemble.' But her piety and sense of propriety intervened as she added, 'Why are these amusements polluted by dreadful intermixture of vice and profaneness.'

'Her whole life was a devotion to benevolence!' said her brother Jonathan.[10] Already, in 1791, Priscilla's determined kindness had established at Tottenham a charity for lying-in women. This was supported by annual subscriptions for which 'one hundred and twenty poor married women are upon the average annually relieved with the use of linen during their confinement, and small donations of money'.[11] In 1792 she organised the funding of a School of Industry where up to 66 girls could be taught reading, writing, sewing, knitting and some arithmetic. The girls were encouraged to enter domestic service and a guinea was paid each on completion of every three years' continuous work as servants.[12]

Priscilla's good works were unremitting: winter soup kitchens, a meeting to put a stop to the dangers of chimney sweeping, a manufactory to encourage spinning in the parish. But her most enduring philanthropic achievement was the introduction of savings banks. The concept was not new. Savings banks had been set up in Germany in the middle of the eighteenth century and later promoted by Jeremy Bentham, the Utilitarian,[13] and Arthur Young, the agricultural reformer,[14] of whom young Edward Wakefield was an enthusiastic disciple. But a bank in Britain first took practical shape as one of the functions of a Friendly Society for women and children that Priscilla Wakefield helped to establish at Tottenham in October 1798. Its objects included a fund for loans, 'to prevent the use of pawnbrokers' shops', and a bank for the savings of the poor.

Initially, the Friendly Society bank operated only to encourage children to save, without the benefit of interest. As an agent of Providence and a representative of the Christian 'kingdom within', Priscilla's moral purposes were clear: 'It habituates the children to industry, frugality, and foresight; and, by introducing them to notice, it teaches them the value of character and of the esteem of those who, by the dispensation of Providence, are placed above them'.[15] Priscilla's charitable labours would never challenge the existing social and political order; she was a member of a non-conforming Quaker movement which, by the 1790s, 'had prospered too much . . . . their hostility to State and authority had diminished to formal symbols'. Its continuing tradition of dissent 'gave more to the social conscience of the middle class than to the popular movement' for social and political reform.[16]

In 1804 the children's fund was converted into the Charitable Bank, taking interest-earning deposits from adults, too. It was overseen by six wealthy trustees, 'each responsible to the amount of 100 pounds for the repayment of principal and interest'.[17] Priscilla and her son Edward persisted in a campaign to have savings banks more widely established under government guarantee. Edward's association with the Secretary of the Treasury in 1817 helped at last in the passing of a savings bank act that procured government security for the deposits of trustees and managers. Security for all depositors – as savings banks spread throughout Britain – had to wait for Gladstone's reforms 40 years later. (A proposed statue of Priscilla in Tottenham, to memorialise her as the savings bank founder, never eventuated.)

Priscilla's Quaker philanthropy in aid of women and the poor was a late expression of what Pope called the 'strong benevolence of soul' that had gathered strength throughout the Georgian age. Her lying-in charity was one of the fruits of the medical reforms that saw more than 100 new hospitals and dispensaries established during the eighteenth century; her school was set up through the new Sunday Schools movement. Charity was the watchword of the new Puritans and Evangelists, and saw its most famous expression in William Wilberforce's campaign to end the slave trade. 'What pleasure it is,' Priscilla wrote, 'to confer happiness.'[18]

While charity and moral improvement lubricated middle-class consciences of the time, ideas of political and class reform were locked up during the generation-long military struggle with Revolutionary France and Napoleon. Republicanism, democracy and deism, those dangerous doctrines of the American and French Revolutions, stirred the working classes and were rigorously suppressed by the state. Tom Paine, advocating deism, republicanism, the abolition of slavery and the emancipation of women, had his seminal work, *The Rights of Man* (1791), banned and was forced to flee England when indicted for treason.

The friend and feminist counterpart of Paine was that so-called 'hyena in petticoats', Mary Wollstonecraft. Her 1792 book, *Vindication of the Rights of Women*, scandalised English society with its calls for sexual emancipation and equality of opportunity for women. With no political rights or access to power, Wollstonecraft did not need to be indicted for treason. The ridicule and contempt of the male establishment and the wave of disapproval and condemnation from the middle-class members of her own gender were censure enough.

Priscilla Wakefield's commentary on Mary Wollstonecraft soon after her premature death in 1798 reveals how religious conviction and social conformity always informed her own best intentions. Because originality of Wollstonecraft's genius 'was not curbed by any regular cultivation, her faculties were left to expand by their own force'. Although this 'probably contributed to leave her free from the usual fetters of prejudice', it also 'deprived her of the inestimable benefit of an early impression of religious principles' so that she 'deviated from those wholesome necessary restraints which the doctrines of revealed religion impose upon natural inclinations, when they lead beyond those limits which the good order of society and individual happiness require. . .'. Priscilla considered that 'A national energetic education, suited to the different ranks', would offer women 'the sure tho' gradual emancipation from the sensual chains with which they are now so frequently manacled'. For Priscilla there was an 'inestimable advantage to be derived from general improvement. . . the communication of *useful* knowledge to all ranks of people as the best security for orderly conduct and obedience to lawful authority'.[19]

Priscilla's own dissertation on women appeared that same year. In *Reflections on the Present Condition of the Female Sex* she advocated a more rational system of training girls with regard to their physical development, recommending games, outdoor recreation, cold baths and the discarding of stays. A college should be established to educate girls as governesses and teachers of art and science, and she recommended that girls dependent on their 'own exertions' could take up useful trades and even engage in farming 'without detriment to their place in life and chances of matrimony'; women of position could undertake the inspection of workhouses. Women, Priscilla pointed out, were excluded from many trades and occupations for which they were at least as well equipped as men, and they were grossly underpaid. To change this state of affairs she called 'loudly upon women of rank . . . to employ women only . . . procure female instructors for their children . . . frequent no shops that are not served by women . . . . they should reward them as liberally as they do the men who have hitherto supplanted them. Let it be considered a common cause to give them every possible advantage.'

This early feminist cry for equality was muffled by her conviction that 'nature and reason' had decreed a husband's role to be the 'one head or chief in every family'. Self-sufficiency in a wider range of employments and a healthier style of upbringing would make women better wives and mothers, and more useful members of society, and give them the skills to maintain themselves if, for whatever reason, they found themselves without the support of a male's income. Priscilla reasoned from hard experience. Her conviction that upper-class mothers should educate their children, not governesses, stemmed from the example of her 'most excellent of mothers, to whose incessant care and admirable example I owe the foundation of any merit I may possess'.

Philanthropy based on an abiding nonconformist faith and a belief in self-improvement and in the subordinating proprieties of class and gender[20] were to prove powerful influences in the dominating role Priscilla played in the education of her grandchildren. Her educative ideas found an even wider market in a series of sixteen instructional books for children which she began to produce in 1794. Five dealt with natural history; the others, employing different narrative techniques, were designed to convey the kind of *useful* knowledge from which the children of the growing middle class might benefit.

A
Family Tour
through the
British Empire
containing some account of its
Manufactures, Natural and Artificial Curiosities
History and Antiquities
interspersed with
Biographical Anecdotes.
Particularly adapted to the
Amusement and Instruction of
YOUTH

was first published in 1804. Her 'British Empire' consisted of England, Scotland, Ireland and Wales.

In Priscilla's tour of this empire, widowed (but financially secure) Mrs Middleton of Richmond determines one fine morning in May that her children will not waste their summer holidays again at Brighton, a place 'too well adapted to form habits of idleness and trifling'. Instead they will make a journey throughout the kingdom for their health and improvement. 'Imprint it on your memories, that we do not travel for the amusement of the moment, but for the sake of collecting useful knowledge.'

'"That will suit my taste completely," said Arthur, who was just fourteen; "novelty delights me; and when I am a man, I will travel all over the world." "A rambling spirit," replied his mother, "differs much from the laudable curiosity of surveying proper objects." '[21] Told through a general narrative style as well as the children's letters and journals, Priscilla's *Family Tour* was a considerable best-seller, going through fifteen editions.

The Middleton family are the protagonists of most of her travel books. In *Excursions in North America*, Arthur travels to enlarge his education (1806); to augment his completed university education in *The Traveller in Africa* (1814), and to forget his troubles and sorrows as *The Traveller in Asia* (1817). The absence of a husband and father in her tales reinforces Priscilla's belief in the precedence of a mother's role in the education of her children and represents, perhaps, something of an unattainable personal Utopia.

Her successful educative formula was laid out early in the preface to *Mental Improvement* (1794), a two-volume work on the 'Beauties and Wonders of Art and Nature, in a series of Instructive Conversations': 'The art of exercising the faculty of thinking and reflecting upon every object that is seen, ought to constitute a material branch of good education; but it requires the skills of a master's hand, to lead the minds of youth to the habit of observation. . . . The design of the following little work is to excite the curiosity of young persons. . . .' She chose the form of dialogue 'as the best suited to convey instruction, blended with amusement; being desirous that it should be read rather from choice than compulsion, and be sought by my young readers as an entertainment, not shunned as a mere dry, perceptive lesson.' It was a lesson in literary style that her grandson Edward would never forget when he came to propagate his own ideas of empire.

Although the desire to disseminate useful information to the young, in the proper form and manner, was a genuine motive for Priscilla's writing, there were always practical considerations. 'Though EW has more favourable prospects,' she wrote on 16 April 1798, 'there remain sufficient reasons for me to continue writing.' It was a particularly anxious time. Banking crises the year before had contributed, at the beginning of 1798, to the failure of her husband's business ventures. 'One rub after another frequently threatens us with a view of poverty and dependence' (21 January). The next day, Priscilla wrote, 'the affairs in the Old Jewry sent me to bed very low, although not altogether unattended with confidence in the Divine goodness in the future'.

A few days later husband Edward was to become a ship-broker and by mid-February son Edward had established a partnership 'in the factory and underwriting business'. By the end of March a brewhouse and ship-broker's had 'fallen together' into EW's hands, affording 'a prospect of obtaining an independency after having discharged those incumbrances which have so long pressed heavily upon us'. She wrestled with both a desire for relief from financial straits and the temptations of excessive worldly gain: 'Prospects brighten and appearances promise a sufficiency, which with moderation and content may procure everything a wise man may want. I desire the moderation and temperature of my mind may not be disturbed by any favourable alteration in our circumstances. The vicissitudes I have suffered should render me steady' (30 March). Her summary for the year, however, concluded that EW's new business had a 'poor prospect of yielding a profit that will render us independent' and son Dan's new job in the Navy Pay Office was 'wholly inadequate to enable my son to marry and lead a domestic life'.

Edward, like his father, was partly engaged in business in the City but for much of the time lived with his young family at Romford in Essex where he was endeavouring to make a go of a large farm. A third child, Daniel Bell, had been born there on 27 February. Susan was now into the cycle of child-bearing that was to contribute to the ruin of her health: Daniel had been born almost two years after Edward Gibbon and three more boys were to follow at intervals of approximately one year and nine months, suggesting that as soon as each child was weaned Susan fell pregnant again.

In January 1799, Priscilla visited the farm at Romford. 'Edward's plans as usual too wild for the promotion of a sober, uniform system of life. I wish he had fewer occupations, and were more inclined to turn his mind to parental duties, and the regular objects of a chief of a family' (14 January). Now 24, Edward had inherited his mother's philanthropic enthusiasm, if careless of its Quaker disciplines, and his father's peripatetic, Jonah-like career through business. His enthusiasms for prison, agricultural and educational reform were intertwined with often badly judged speculations in business and farming. Priscilla's other son caused her no less anxiety. Dan seemed 'determined to maintain the necessity of being what is called a man of the world or town: in the language of reason a genteel profligate, who breaks every commandment of the decalogue' (18 April). On 9 August, Dan had 'a return of spitting blood which alarms and disturbs me'.

The erratic and self-indulgent behaviour of husband and sons stretched the 'regulation of the temper . . . of all qualities the most useful to conduct us steadily through . . . vexatious circumstances'.[22] Indeed, after a particularly exasperating day with husband and son Dan, 'the exercise of patience was the best work I did'.

Education at her knee had clearly not turned out the kind of boys she had hoped for. There was an impetuous and unreliable strain in her Wakefield men that was past all her instruction. 'Surely this life is a state of discipline preparatory to a better or how can we account for the trials with which it is beset.'[23]

While visiting her daughter Isabella, married to Quaker Joshua Head, at Ipswich in January 1799, Priscilla found relief from family anxieties in meeting 'Mr. T. Constable, a pleasing modest young man – remarkable for a natural genius for painting'. In April that year, Constable visited her at Tottenham. 'Painting, the fine arts, literature and the effects on society were the interesting subjects that beguiled the time and displayed the abilities of this virtuous, diffident young man, so superior and contrary to the young men of fashion, generally admired by the world' – and by her sons.[24]

By 18 June, her eldest son had a new project in mind. 'Edward has engaged in another large farm: distance, situation, encumbrance, uncertainty of success, a stab to underwriting, all concur to render it an event very painful to my feelings.' The next day, at Romford, Priscilla 'found Susan very low, could not offer her any consolation, as I am much hurt at most of the consequences likely to attend their settlement in such an obscure situation as Burnham Wyck [Burnham-on-Crouch, Essex]'. Three days later Priscilla's diary recorded: 'Susan and the children spent the day with me. . . . Susan's natural good sense co-operating with her own endeavours has produced a general improvement in her manners: will not the seclusion at Burnham retard the progress of this improvement?'

Edward's shift to Burnham Wyck and the financial arrangements involved with the new farm precipitated a rift in the family. Priscilla described 9 August as 'A morning cloudy in more senses than one. Ironing with my hands: my mind occupied with the consequences of EW jun. withholding the income by which we have of late been supported. Family dissensions, a large share of anxiety and difficulty for me, and the want of a sufficiency to live upon, are the spectres that at the moment haunt my imagination: some providential turn that human nature does not foresee may soften the harsh features of this unpleasant group.'

On 28 August, Priscilla 'Took courage and went to Romford. Susan, when not under the influence of an irritable temper, is a sensible woman, actuated by the best principles. In this unhappy dispute her behaviour is most truly endearing. I enjoyed the dear children's company, but not without a mixture of apprehension that it may be long before I taste that pleasure again.'

The 'dreaded separation' began on 7 September and lasted three months until, on 12 December, Priscilla could write, 'Am fairly satisfied with respect to Edward: but sorely regret we should be obliged to receive an annuity from him. If even a limited independence could be procured, how preferable!' She bent again to her books. 'Necessity obliges me to <u>write</u> & in the effort I forget them all.'[25]

Edward and Susannah's third son, Arthur, was born at Burnham on 19 November 1799. The day before, Priscilla had written: 'Buonaparte has effected a revolution in France.' The rare appearance in her journal of reference to the momentous military and political events of her time illustrates not only Priscilla's preoccupation with family problems, personal faith and charitable enterprises but also reflects the truth of G. M. Trevelyan's statement that 'The war was in the newspapers, but it scarcely entered the lives of the enjoying classes'. Although Priscilla was hardly enjoying life financially, all her family expected that they should be in positions of comfort, status, influence and even political power. The tension between the expectation and the reality was the Wakefield mainspring to action.

The enjoying classes owed their insulated affluence in time of war to 'The navy . . . who have done so much for us'. Jane Austen's Anne Elliott, moving with resigned irony through the drawing rooms of Kellynch and Bath before the restrained pursuit of Captain Wentworth, knew the right object of gratitude for her lifestyle.

The Royal Navy not only secured Britain from the worst of French intentions; it also preserved its trading links from enemy disruption so that, during the first years of war, Britain continued to turn a trade surplus, which allowed it to subsidise its allies. But when the Northern League took sides with France an export market was lost and key sources of timber and wheat were cut off. Trade surplus turned to deficit. The cost of the war blew out as Britain paid out for subsidies to Continental allies, rising garrison expenses and increased grain purchases.[26]

When Prime Minister William Pitt the Younger initiated the first income taxes, so that the nation would not be burdened with an insupportable national debt, this event, at least, penetrated to Priscilla's journal. On 29 March 1799 she wrote, 'EW much taken up about the tax on income.' No doubt she handled his agitation as she had when an earlier provocation had put 'EW in hysterics after supper. These things require firmness.'

Social unrest and political agitation in England had already been met by a series of draconian measures on the part of Pitt's Tory government. In 1795 the Seditious Meetings Act prohibited meetings of more than 50 people except under licence; and the Treasonable Practices Act redefined treason to include those who devised evil against the king, plotted to help invaders or sought to coerce Parliament. Those who attacked the constitution faced seven years' transportation to Botany Bay. Renewed agitation in 1798, as the war threatened to wreck the economy, brought more suppressive acts. Newspaper publishers were put under the close supervision of magistrates. In 1799 and 1800, Corresponding Societies – groups of artisans and tradesmen working for constitutional reform and a franchise not based on property – were suppressed; and combinations of workmen actively seeking better conditions of work and pay were made subject to punishment by summary jurisdiction.

By 1800, bread was so scarce and expensive in England that the poor rioted. The navy came to the rescue again. Nelson had already scuppered the French fleet in Aboukir Bay in 1798; in 1801, his victory at Copenhagen broke up the Northern League and led to a two-year period of uneasy peace and economic retrenchment.

Although little of the tumult and momentum of social change seemed to impinge directly on Priscilla Wakefield's view of life, many personal and familial difficulties and preoccupations reflected the strains of the times. But if both Priscilla and son Edward were aware of the causes of upheaval around them, their actions showed an interest mainly in dealing with their symptoms. On 1 May 1800 they visited the Ipswich gaol 'and saw many objects that excited pity and deep reflection'. On the 28th of the same month, Priscilla attended a church meeting where she heard 'two solemn addresses . . . both expressive of a belief in the Universality of the Divine Love to all creatures; let the principle teach universal charity'.

By this time the two generations of Wakefields were fully reconciled. At Burnham on 23 March, Priscilla could write: 'The joy of the children at seeing me showed that they had not forgotten me'. She 'Made the most of the time in conversing with Susan . . . her good sense higher than ever in my esteem. I am not sure that the welfare of the whole does not depend on her prudence.' Priscilla was now concerned about 'the effects [Edward's] new line of connections may have upon his character and conduct, as well as upon the future consequences with respect to his wife and children of their present residence'. The situation of the farm at Burnham Wyck was 'low and unhealthy' and family members often suffered from fever and the ague, especially Susan, who was pregnant again before the end of the year.

Now 50, Priscilla began to take increasing responsibility for her grandchildren as Susan's health and state of mind started to deteriorate. Catherine, the eldest, was seven. 'Kitty has been a good deal with me: it seems now pretty well decided that I am to superintend her education for the present at least, an employment which must divert my attention from other objects in a considerable degree; but who has a better claim to my care?' It was the only education that Catherine was to receive. On 4 November Priscilla took her 'dear girl' to London to 'have two strong teeth out; she behaved like a heroine. May she be endued through life with fortitude to support the evils she may encounter with the same courage.'

While at Burnham, Edward prepared his first publication, a pamphlet putting forward his ideas about improving the miserable condition of the poor and alleviating the increasing burden of the poor rates on landowners.[27] Unsurprisingly, Edward's social philosophy echoed his mother's: a place for everyone and everyone in their place. In discussing the merits of benefit societies he wrote, 'whatever tends to encourage among [the poor] habits of industry and economy, and whatever brings them more under the notice of their superiors, and enhances among them the value of good character, will tend to make them better servants and less burthensome on the rates'.

Edward was opposed to 'indiscriminate relief' for the poor, which would 'encourage idleness and extravagance'. There should be a 'distinction ... between the family brought into distress through sickness or misfortune, and the family reduced to want by their own idleness and vice'. Edward was keen for the classes to better appreciate each other: 'The rich do not sufficiently estimate the virtues of the poor; nor are the latter aware of the real and affectionate interest which many of the higher classes in England feel for their concerns'. The higher classes should be *'immediately awakened to the duty of assisting'* the lower to attain a *'superior tone of conduct* .... regular and principled habits of life. . .'. Edward perhaps saw himself as an intermediary, not necessarily bound by the responsibilities of either.

The first years of the Wakefields' new century reverberated to the noise of financial disaster, and family dispute and acrimony reached the point of active litigation. In 1801, EW was 'tricked out of a fine trade, by which we are once more set adrift . . . the small sum of reserve that I have treasured up as a bank against future wants has been appropriated to immediate urgencies and is probably lost for ever'. Life lurched along, Priscilla 'fearing lest husband, sons and brother should all be overwhelmed in one gulph'. From this time, her husband is referred to mostly as 'Mr Wakefield' in her journal, suggesting that relations had cooled after 30 years of marriage, many of which had been under financial strain.

At the height of the next crisis, in February 1804, she took matters into her own hands: 'Went to London and spent a most agitating day, using extraordinary efforts to ward off a bankruptcy, and procure ready money to satisfy these sharks'. A week later: 'At home all day pleasing myself with the pictures of tranquillity when our difficulties shall be finished.'

Barely a month later, son Edward was in 'a contest with John Gurney', her brother-in-law, over a large amount of money. Priscilla pulled out all stops to avert a lawsuit and the matter went to arbitration, taking the rest of the year to settle. Just before Christmas, she exulted, 'We are conquerors though we gain only a paltry £600!! My son's character is unsullied, ought I to repine: yet his just demand is so much reduced. My own sufferings are, I think, more bearable than to see those I love suffer, without the power of helping them.' John Gurney's son Daniel was to write later that Priscilla's sons 'were clever but unprincipled men, and from circumstances owing to a connection with them in business caused my father great anxiety'.

An alternative and revealing view of Edward's character, activities and intentions is contained in a letter written at the time of the dispute by Daniel Bell, Priscilla's eldest brother, to his uncle David Barclay:

> I disapprove very much his having given a public entertainment and attempted a public shew of stock and improvements in agriculture. Such an undertaking may be very laudable and proper with the great and independent, but is totally inconsistent with those who are fettered with pecuniary embarrassments. [He] was induced to do it chiefly from an expectation of profits in the sale of livestock. . . . He had I believe a further view in this coming forward to public notice, which was to create an interest with the great people in the agricultural line by shewing them his abilities as a farmer which he thought a probable means of receiving a stewardship, in case he should be dispossessed of his farm. . . . E. Wakefield's pursuit has been a laudable one – his industry, activity and perseverance have been conspicuous. His error has been engaging in a concern too great for his pecuniary resources.[28]

The Wakefields were now estranged from the Gurneys though Priscilla tried to patch things up soon after by meeting with their daughter, her married niece Betsy, 'hoping that all connection with the family of my dear sister may not be severed'. The Gurney relationship, especially with Edward, remained difficult for years, but it is possible that Priscilla's 24-year-old niece Elizabeth Fry's interest in prison reform was stimulated by the Wakefields. A year after their visit to Ipswich goal Priscilla wrote, 'Prisons and workhouses are his [Edward's] game. May he be inspired to enlarge the sphere of human happiness and virtue!' But it was Elizabeth Fry who was to prove more effective, with her Quaker-inspired reforms among the female inmates of Newgate and other prisons, beginning in 1813.

At the time of the dispute, Elizabeth Fry and her husband visited Priscilla when she was tending Kitty and infant Edward Gibbon at Tottenham. Twenty-five years later, Elizabeth Fry visited Edward Gibbon again, in the hell-hole of Newgate, igniting recollection of that earlier occasion:

> Mrs Fry came to see me the other day, and made me think of you and the old house, and that pond which you used to dread so much. You do not remember, I dare say, so I will tell you that she and her husband being on a visit to you, he gave me half a crown and told me to throw it into that same pond. I, being six years old, thought him a very honest man, and concluded that the money was bad, and that he wished it to be thrown away. Away I threw it therefore, and came back from the pond, quite proud of my share in so honest an action. What I had done coming out, Mr Fry gave me another half crown, which I kept. And at night, as if there could be no good without evil in this world, I went to sleep chuckling over the idea that I had got five shillings out of my father's enemies, as from something I heard during the day I imagined our cousins Fry to be.[29]

A worse family fight soon followed. In 1801 Edward had entered into a partnership with Priscilla's brother Jonathan in order to raise capital to pursue his farming and business ventures. By November 1806 the farm was failing and he was engaged in yet another 'contest', this time with his uncle and other financially interested parties. The fight went badly for Edward and by 14 March 1807 'he had fallen into the hands of his enemies' and ended up in gaol. 'Obeyed a summons [on 16 March] to visit my unhappy son. My bodily health seems inadequate to my trials . . . the prospect dreadful.' As Edward noted the next day, 'The measure was one of those harsh things that can hardly ever be erased from memory.' Over the next days Priscilla argued and pleaded again in aid of one of her menfolk. A week later the farm was gone but Edward emerged from the sale with 'a pretty fortune'.[30] Despite this, Priscilla considered her brother's 'severe unkind treatment of my son . . . has broken all friendship between us'.

There was no let-up. On 7 November 1807, Priscilla recorded that there were 'No less than five suits at stake'. There were two involving Edward and 'Dan's trial', plus 'Two causes for his wife's debts'. On 3 June 1805, Priscilla had received news of son Dan's sudden and clandestine marriage. Neither son had shown any confidence in surviving her scrutiny of their connubial intentions. Dan had been paired in Priscilla's mind with various suitable partners but had never procured an adequate income to support a marriage. After the Navy Pay Office, he had looked at joining Edward in farming and his father in business but finally settled down to the law. At 29, concupiscence finally got the better of him, as it had Edward fourteen years before, or as Priscilla more delicately put it, 'a late domestic connection undertaken apparently from the impulse of feeling, rather than of judgment'. In a letter to Dan in 1800, after scolding him for his 'Budget being empty far too soon' she dissertated on the life of Catherine the Great, who had been debased by 'the indulgence of private vices unworthy of her elevated mind'.[31]

On 8 June, a few days after news of the marriage, 'Dan and his bride came down: embarrassment showed all parties to disadvantage. She is young, rather handsome, unapprehensive for the future, and a child in experience.' Or so it seemed. Isabel Mackie soon charmed her new in-laws with her 'sweetness' and though there was a 'great difference of manners', Priscilla was persuaded that Isabel's character 'may be moulded to excellence'. Soon, she 'gains upon us every time we meet her' though Priscilla, at the end of that year, remained concerned at Dan's 'improbability of being able to support a wife, especially one educated in the lap of luxury, and in habits of expense and elegant trifling'.

The first sign of trouble came in the new year of 1806. On 9 January, 'Dan came down very unexpectedly, and as if for some purpose, but I could not discover his motive.' He had tried, but finally he did not have the courage to tell his mother. It was left to her sister Elizabeth Hanbury to announce that Dan had been conned. Sweet Isabel was an expert swindler, playing the role of a woman of status and fashion to better front fraudulent schemes with her father, mother and cousin. She had fleeced Dan of most of his small income and, with the aid of her mother, had bought linen and other household goods, charged to his name, which they had then sold at pawnbrokers. 'Public exposure, disgrace, enthralment, ruin to my beloved son now stare me in the face,' wrote Priscilla on 12 January. Dan faced debts totalling £5,000 and legal wrangles that threatened his law career.

Priscilla rushed around the relatives to raise funds to fight Dan's cause but found that 'The displeasure of the family seems to take the place of their pity. A mother only can feel with uniform tenderness. I would go through fire and water to re-establish him.' The legal toils went on and on, through 1806 and 1807, Priscilla hoping that the suits to both annul the marriage and settle the debts would go in Dan's favour. 'I wish to feel his dire misfortunes with the tenderness of a mother, and the patience of a Christian, but oh! how difficult!' (29 April 1806).

Against the odds, Dan was called to the Bar on 1 May 1807. Six months later, both suits went against him. To escape his creditors and his wife's claims for alimony, Dan dropped out of sight for almost a year, perhaps to his Uncle Joseph's place in Ireland. When he reappeared in October 1808 it was with the 'usual salutation, saying "All's well!"' By the end of that year he had purchased chambers with the help of a friend: 'His wife's creditors have been wonderfully quiet, his own affairs are well arranged and he quietly pursues his profession'. After a few years, Dan cleared his debts and on 20 August 1813 Priscilla recorded the final passage of the infamous Isabel: 'Edward brought the awful intelligence of the death of a certain unfortunate young woman by poison'. Released, Dan married Elizabeth Kilgour three months later. Nothing is known of her, but the marriage was childless.

For Priscilla there was, at least, continual good news about her books. In September 1803 she 'received a large offer' for *The Juvenile Travellers; containing the remarks of a Family during a Tour through the principal States and Kingdoms of Europe* and in 1805 the first volume of *Domestic Recreations; or Dialogues Illustrative of Natural and Scientific subjects* was published. This could not 'fail of engaging the attention of youth, for whose service they are intended; and must contribute to their instruction and improvement'.[32] In 1806, *Excursions in North America* appeared and the third edition of *A Family Tour Through the British Empire*.

Despite the geographical range of her topics, her books were works entirely of scholarship and imagination. There is no evidence that she set foot far beyond the parish of Tottenham (High Cross), Middlesex, which, in 1801, had a population of 3629. Three hundred and fifty-five families were employed in trade and handicrafts and 181 in agriculture; the rest were placed under the heading of gentry, which included the Wakefields. For the gentry, Tottenham was attractive because it 'lay out of reach of London's smoke cloud'[33] but was within easy reach of business in the City. The district grew food for London markets and its only industry was a corn and oil mill. Most of Tottenham village consisted of houses, inns, alehouses and public buildings along either side of the High Road that ran along the elevated land above the River Lea marshes and formed part of the main coaching route between London and Cambridge. There were many fine country houses in the neighbourhood, notably the 300-year-old manor house of Bruce Castle. Edward and Priscilla Wakefield's house stood close to Tottenham High Road, almost at the top of the hill, not far from the High Cross erected to commemorate the visit of King Edward I in 1290.

The distant margin of Priscilla's world was her daughter Isabella's home at Woodbridge, near Ipswich in Suffolk, 70 miles away. She made the fourteen-hour journey there by coach with an overnight halt at The Blue Mills post inn at Colchester. Often her son-in-law, brewer Joshua Head, met her there in his curricle and she enjoyed a 'sweet drive' in the open air for the remainder of the journey to Ipswich. She found refuge in 'the happy tranquil state' of daughter 'Bell's' family where 'one out of my flock is sheltered from care and want, and surrounded with every comfort that a moderate mind can ask, to which is superadded a disposition to be contented and to enjoy'.

Back home in Tottenham there was some comfort and joy from the increasing visits of Edward's children. These numbered six with the arrival of William Hayward on 8 August 1801 and John Howard, who appears to have been born while Susan was in 'Bell's' care at Ipswich, on 2 June 1803.

Although relieved of a daughter's duties by the death of her father in October 1802, Priscilla now cared for Edward's eldest children at Tottenham for long periods as the family's health continued to suffer in the low, swampy environment of the Burnham Wyck farm: malaria was still endemic to this country in the early nineteenth century. Susan found it increasingly difficult to cope with the bearing and nursing of one new child after another. On 17 January 1803 Priscilla's time was 'almost wholly engaged in nursing, teaching and amusing Kitty and Edward who have the whooping cough, it having immediately followed the measles'.

Edward's deteriorating financial situation on the farm and his erratic involvement with business and philanthropic schemes at the expense of his family contributed to Susan's increasing disaffection. In June 1805, Priscilla recorded, 'Some conversation with Kitty [now almost twelve] made me very uneasy and proved that her understanding and observation are beyond her years.' Young Catherine had begun to understand and observe that her father was 'a great lover of women'.[34] His 'old nurse' said to Susan one day as he rode from the door, 'Ah you may look at him. Hundreds envy you – he was born to make the women's heart ache'.[35] And, by his own admission, to bring about their ruin.[36]

Deepening parental disharmony and family disruption were reflected in the behaviour of Edward Gibbon, now nine years old. As Priscilla wrote on 24 October, 'Stayed at home with the children, find two a much heavier charge than one. Fear my reading and writing must be sacrificed for the next three months at least, but hope to render in that time some essential benefit to my dear little boy, whose extreme habits of liberty at home increase the difficulty of orderly restraint.' The final crisis was only days away.

On 26 October 'Edward arrived in the evening in a high fever with Dan and William: a pacquet of bad news . . . . Susan very bad and left with servants.' By 30 October Priscilla 'Ventured to remove Susan to Tottenham, brought the rest of the children: cannot foresee whether they will ever return to that unwholesome spot'. The next day 'With Dan we have now eleven additional to our family: EW very patient under this accumulation of difficulties, through which I cannot perceive a way'. Then, on 2 November, 'Susan worse, the fatigue almost insupportable'.

Susan and her children stayed in Tottenham but her health did not seem to improve: 'A miserable visit to Susan before breakfast. Her trials and natural dispositions are but ill suited, and increase each other' (15 July 1806). Edward stayed down on the farm. At the end of 1806, Priscilla wrote, 'I cannot even imagine how he will arrange his affairs: no comfort nor advantage to themselves or their poor children can be procured, unless they unite in their sentiments and agree to live together.'

After the loss of the farm in 1807, Edward took a house in Duke Street, Westminster, but Susan and the children remained in Tottenham. Priscilla continued to teach Kitty but Edward Gibbon, Daniel and William had begun to attend Tottenham Grammar School under Thomas Haigh and were joined by Arthur at the beginning of 1807, a year that saw yet another son born, Felix – and the first real difficulties with Edward Gibbon.

On 4 February Priscilla recorded 'An early summons to Haigh's, on account of a great delinquency of dear Edward, almost rendered me incapable of application'. The next day her mind was 'painfully engaged with the perverseness of dear little Edward: his obstinacy if he inclines to evil terrifies me: turned to good it would be a noble firmness'. On 8 February: 'My thoughts much occupied with my little Edward, whom I tenderly love, but whose inflexible pertinacious temper makes me fear for his own happiness and that of those connected with him'. Six days later, 'My dear little Edward still in disgrace. My heart yearns to forgive him: he has some fine qualities, but he is a character that requires delicate handling.' Priscilla handled him delicately enough for dear little Edward to last the rest of the year at Haigh's until, on 12 December, the boy 'left Tottenham, and my protection, for the dangers and temptation of Westminster School'.

With the strains of Dan's trial, the altercations attendant on Edward's loss of the Burnham farm and the stresses of dealing with wayward grandchildren, 1807 was Priscilla's *annus horribilis*. Little wonder that at its end she cried out, 'My bosom is full. I want a friend. Dear Kate is too young. With whom can I repose my sorrows?'[37] The next day, she recorded the death of two infants in a nearby village house fire and 'felt relief at shedding tears for the sufferers & my own sorrows at the same time'.

The domestic conflicts of these years were occasionally interrupted by alarums and excursions offstage. In August 1803, Priscilla reported, 'The dread of invasion causes general alarm and preparations. My Edward a lieutenant-colonel of Volunteers. Sincerely do I pray he may never be called to expose his own life or destroy that of others.' They were difficult times for patriotic but pacifist Quakers – and difficult for Edward to lead his company of volunteers when the government had neither the money nor the organisation to give them weapons or military training. All they received were a few pikes.

The crisis of 1803 followed a year's uneasy peace. The administration of Henry Addington had reduced the army and slashed the navy's strength so that Nelson complained of sailing in a half-manned ship to join the Mediterranean fleet. While Britain used the peace to reduce the armed forces, Napoleon was taking over northern Italy and control of Switzerland and Holland and the French navy was increasing the number of its ships of the line from 43 to 66. Britain attempted to pre-empt France's expansionist plans by declaring war again. Napoleon then concentrated all his forces for invasion but never reached the point where he could confidently launch out against the superior forces of the Royal Navy. Edward Wakefield was able to put his pike away.

The naval end game with France concluded with Nelson's overwhelming victory at Trafalgar. Priscilla wrote in her diary: 'Jan. 8, 1806. Accompanied the children to London to see the Funeral of Lord Nelson by water: a day altogether contrary to my taste, but it seemed a necessary sacrifice to the enjoyment of others.' The combination of victory at Trafalgar and the death of Nelson had been received in London with both 'transport and anguish'. The Wakefield family watched with tens of thousands of others as Nelson's coffin was carried up the Thames from Greenwich to Westminster, escorted by scores of small boats and barges bearing peers of the realm; and on the following day when the funeral procession to St Paul's stretched all the way back to its starting point at the Admiralty. It was the high point of patriotic feeling during the long wars and it was approached only by the celebration of Waterloo ten years later. It was the first brush of the Nelson touch for six-year-old Arthur.

In June 1808, Edward went to Ireland for eighteen months, leaving Susan pregnant again and the care of his children and increasingly incapable wife to 57-year-old Priscilla. His progeny increased to eight on 22 January 1809, when Priscilla junior was born, and her grandmother had two, three, sometimes four of the six boys with her during holidays and on Sundays while the youngest, Felix, came to her full time when Susan was more ill than usual.

Despite her responsibilities for the younger children, Priscilla kept up an astonishing round of domestic, social and philanthropic activities. There were daily lessons for Catherine, visits to the School of Industry, committee meetings of the Charity Bank or Lying-in Charity for both of which she was treasurer; ironing, mantua-making, and writing letters, books and a journal; making or receiving visits most days, especially to friends and relatives who were ill or suffering bereavement; going to exhibitions and taking Catherine to plays; and starting reading parties which met at the houses of members in turn. They read together such works as Edmund Burke's *A Philosophical Inquiry into the Origin of our Ideas on the Sublime and Beautiful* and Isaac D'Israeli's *Curiosities of Literature* ('an improper book'). Privately, she read the *Edinburgh Review, An Improved Version of the New Testament* and such recent publications as Scott's *Lay of the Last Minstrel* and, later, the first cantos of Byron's *Childe Harold.* [38]

Edward's disappearance to Ireland had its origins in his giving evidence before a parliamentary committee, earlier in 1808, when the Irish Chancellor of the Exchequer suggested that he should undertake a survey of the country to ascertain its condition and resources. By this time, Edward's reputation for proselytising in favour of agricultural, penal and educational reforms had attracted the attention of Arthur Young and brought him acquaintance with contemporary James Mill.[39] Edward took credit for bringing royal attention to the pioneering educational work of Joseph Lancaster.

By the end of the eighteenth century, burgeoning urban populations and expanding industrialisation had brought an increasing demand for the workforces of the new factories to be basically educated. Lancaster, a Quaker, sought to meet this by establishing a school for poor children in Southwark, using a 'monitorial system' whereby older children taught younger ones – within a disciplined and carefully graded system – the basic elements of reading, writing, arithmetic and the scriptures.

In 1802, 24-year-old Lancaster visited Priscilla Wakefield, seeking her interest and support and on 20 September, she made 'A most interesting visit . . . to Joseph Lancaster's wonderful school, where I was delighted with the effects of order and regularity' among the hundreds of pupils. Edward wrote, 'At her instigation I waited on my noble friends, the Duke of Bedford and Lord Somerville, and requested them to visit Mr Lancaster and to patronize those efforts, which appeared to her to be so highly deserving of encouragement.'[40]

Following this, King George III himself proclaimed, 'Lancaster, I highly approve of your system, and it is my wish that every poor child in my dominions should be taught to read the Bible.' Despite royal support and the backing of reformers such as William Wilberforce and James Mill, Lancaster's dissenting Quaker views were violently attacked by Tories and members of the Church of England establishment who 'feared that education even in writing and ciphering might elevate above their station those who were doomed to the drudgery of daily labour'.[41] Rival schools under the National Society for Promoting the Education of the Poor in the Principles of the Established Church were established, with methods similar to Lancaster's. These, along with Lancaster's schools, were the forerunners of universal primary school education in England.

Edward Wakefield remained involved with Lancasterian schools until 1814 when, with Francis Place, he founded the West London Lancasterian Association under the optimistic banner of 'Schools For All'. The viability of this association depended on their finding subscribers for 300 shares at £10 each. After ten long days of canvassing, they sold only 76 and the project lapsed. By now the establishment tide was against Lancaster and though his methods survived in various transmogrifications until the end of the century, he abandoned his London work that same year and went to America.

Edward's Irish commission fulfilled entirely his enthusiasm for discovering causes and proposing remedies for reform, as well as providing the opportunity for financial reward and political status. It was also an escape from the responsibilities and stresses of family life.

'I resided in Ireland . . . for the purpose of collecting materials, in which pursuit I passed over the greatest part of the island . . . [and] applied for information to people of every rank, from the nobleman to the peasant.'[42] Edward Wakefield's interests were principally economic, 'to point out the advantages which England might derive from Ireland, were its interests better understood, and its industries properly encouraged by sound and well digested laws'. But his wide-ranging survey was to produce more. His memorial, the massive two-volume quarto work, *An Account of Ireland, Statistical and Political,* published in 1812, demonstrated genuine concern for the social and religious conditions in Britain's unhappy island and was invested with warm good sense and humanity. Arthur Young thought it a 'very able work'. Another reviewer described it as 'lively, dogmatical and disorderly', which might have been as much a comment on its author.

Edward divided his book into 31 parts. Beginning with a detailed description of Ireland, by division and province, he went on to examine its natural and human resources, agriculture and fisheries, communications (down to the times of mail coaches), industry, commerce, administration, politics and government, education, religion, population, customs, manners and habits.

Edward spelled out the dire social and economic effects of absentee English owners exploiting Irish estates through corrupt and inefficient agents. With great foresight, he saw that too great a reliance on plentiful potato crops by peasant families on smallholdings had not only led to a rapid population increase – encouraged by the Catholic clergy – but was also 'fraught with danger' if, as he thought probable, the potato crop one day failed. He supported the recent contentions of Thomas Malthus that there was no advantage to a country in sheer numbers of people and that a statistically backed understanding of the relationship between a population and its use of a country's natural resources was fundamental to economic theory and planning. There was a rapidly growing threat of overpopulation in both Ireland and Britain and the remedy of emigration, not only to the United States, but also to other 'waste lands' of the world, was gathering credence. At the time of Edward's visit, the emigration goal of most impoverished Irish was England and the cotton-manufacturing districts of Lancashire in particular.

Elsewhere in his book, Edward illuminated the condition and enduring character of the Irish with unconscious irony and humour. Such crimes as sheep stealing 'do not stand high in the scale of moral turpitude; and when interrogated, why they do not prosecute those who steal from their flocks, they always reply: "Plaze your honour, would you have us hang a man for stealing a bit of mutton?"' Edward may have approved this humane good sense when British law still prescribed death or transportation for such minor crimes.

In Connaught, he observed, 'When a man sustains an injury, or conceives himself affronted, he calls in to his aid, not only his immediate friends and relations, but his neighbours and fellow parishioners, and sometimes the inhabitants of a barony. Whole districts thus become interested in individual disputes; the combatants marshal themselves under leaders distinguished for their prowess; *shillelas* are their weapons, and when a general engagement takes place, many are wounded on both sides. Bruised limbs and broken heads are the usual consequence of such encounters.'

Prescient, lively and thorough though it was, Edward's book had no discernible effect on the British government's Irish policies. Nevertheless, fourteen years later, a journalist could still refer to it as the 'celebrated work on Ireland so often referred to for the accuracy and interest of its details'.[43] The book raised Edward's standing in the radical and reforming community and, in particular, brought him into friendship with Francis Place, the philanthropic, Malthusian and Utilitarian tailor of Charing Cross.[44] Place had been a leading light in the radical London Corresponding Society in the 1790s, promoting political self-education among working men through meetings for reading, conversation and discussion. Edward Wakefield became a regular visitor to the library behind Place's shop, which had become the centre of moderate radicalism in London.

Place recalled that when he first met Edward, his 'circumstances were by no means prosperous; he was, however, an active, zealous advocate for anything likely, in his opinion, to be useful to mankind . . . remarkably anxious to promote education amongst the poor, and I found him an excellent co-operator for many useful purposes'.[45] Wakefield was not alone: with the rising influence of the Evangelical movement, participation in some kind of philanthropic activity had become something of a fad, as Anna Laetitia Barbauld noted: 'There is certainly at present [1813] a great deal of zeal in almost every persuasion . . . Bible societies, missionary schemes, lectures, schools for the poor are set afoot and spread, not so much from a sense of duty as being the real taste of the times'.[46]

In 1814 Place's and Wakefield's names appeared together with those of Quaker William Allen and James Mill on a 'Proposal for Establishing a London Asylum for the Care and Cure of the Insane, on an improved system of management'. Earlier, Edward had written to bookseller William Hone, 'I am glad to find that there are others as well as myself who have observed the wretched state of the madhouses near to the Metropolis – I have pretty well exposed them in procuring the liberation of the Revd. Mr Chauner.'[47]

In September 1814, with Francis Place, Edward undertook a walking tour from London through the West Country to visit 'celebrated establishments for the insane',[48] gathering information in support of the 400-bed London proposal, which was modelled on The Retreat in York. This Quaker institution had 'a marvellous example of cure and rehabilitation compared to other asylums . . . testimony to the efficacious plan of moral treatment and kindness'.[49] The London asylum's cost was to be met by charges on friends of the inmates – and it seems there were not sufficient friends to take this project beyond its proposal. But having 'minutely inspected' the West Country asylums, Edward was able to bring powerful evidence to bear on the Parliamentary Select Committee on Madhouses in 1815. There he publicised the scandalous conditions of inmates at Bethlem Royal Hospital, London – where he had discovered one patient chained by the neck – and this stirred the committee to insist upon reforms.

Place, who supported Edward in his concurrent opposition to a new bill promoting physicians' interests at the expense of lunatics and their relatives, wryly commented, 'As usual, I was not disposed to make any display, but Mr Wakefield, who was always looking out for effect and very desirous of speaking to great men, went before the committee.'[50]

The pair also fought the iniquitous corn laws that protected the income of rich landowners at the expense of the often impoverished consumers of bread. As Place reported to James Mill, 'Wakefield is in town and has a hankering after the corn law, this is occasioned I suspect by his intercourse with the Aristocratic Whigs & Tories.'[51] Nascent democrat Place directly challenged lapsed Quaker Edward on his fawning to the upper classes. In reply Edward wrote, 'In contempt of Rank and artificial greatness I am at least your equal – but I have experienced – that in every gradation – there is a vast varity [*sic*] – and we must make allowance, for the manner in which these persons have been brought up, equal credit should be given them as others for acts of pure and disinterested benevolence – and there are those amongst what are called the Upper Classes – who are capable of so acting I can assure you.'[52] But tradesman Place's treatment at the hands of the 'Upper Classes' had extinguished any chance of his believing in their 'disinterested benevolence'. Conflict over class, overt or implicit, was to prove the fatal flaw in Place and Wakefield's relationship.

During this same period, Edward also prepared a report on the educational and social condition of the Drury Lane district that was eventually published by

Lord Brougham's parliamentary committee in 1816. In this, he promoted the idea of appointing 'educational visitors' who could make a thorough collection of social statistics, providing a foundation for planning and reform. It is possible that Edward Wakefield's greatest contribution to the reform movements of his time was his pursuit of the information vital to petition, planning and education. He was a prodigious researcher. As the Irish book was about to be published, he wrote to Arthur Young about a new major project: 'a statistical account of Great Britain and of the West Indies'. A few months later he reported back to Young on an 800-mile walking tour he had made, with prisons a particular focus, from Northampton through Derby, Chesterfield, Sheffield, Leeds and Settle to Kendal, returning by Lancaster, Liverpool, Chester, Shrewsbury, Ludlow, Hereford, Monmouth, Chepstow, Gloucester, Cheltenham and Oxford to Tottenham. 'The contrast between the happiness of the peasantry of the highly cultivated agricultural districts and the manufacturing ones . . . was striking.'[53]

This precursor to Cobbett's famous rides, however, produced no major work in written form, probably because of the continuing impecuniosity and disorderliness of Edward's domestic life. In proposing the new project to 71-year-old Young in July 1812, he wrote: 'I would not hesitate in commencing the undertaking were my fortune sufficiently large to well educate and establish in life, nine children – I am preparing them to eat the bread of independance [*sic*], and I mistake their dispositions if they will not eventually feel satisfied with my conduct in pursuing great and useful works, rather than seek the selfish gratification of adding to my private fortune'.[54] On this vain and virtuous note, he solicited Young's help in finding government backing and raising £500 to support his writing.

Edward's offspring had increased to nine with the birth of Percy on 7 December 1810, less than a year after his reluctant return from Ireland, where he had been far from preparing his children for independence. In October 1809, Priscilla had written to him, 'I am . . . anxious to hear that you have determined to return for a time at least to visit your wife and children. If any thing can allure you back surely eight lovely promising children should have that power, how can you reconcile turning your back upon them who have never offended you but have the strongest claims upon your care and protection.'[55] She was especially worried about Edward, who 'requires the eye and the company of a father, to choose associates for him, to form his character & to shelter him from the dangers to which a lad of his age is exposed'.[56]

The well-being of sixteen-year-old Catherine was of particular concern to Priscilla.

> We have begun to give Catherine a monthly allowance of £2 to buy cloaths and pay for her washing in order to teach her frugality and the value of the articles she wears . . . . At present she lives in great retirement associating chiefly with a few of our neighbours

> amongst whom there is nobody to fear – as to keeping her back, it is difficult because her person is formed so as to more look eighteen than sixteen. She is rather of a reserved disposition, but when that is overcome she is very lovely and fine – Your absence sometimes half breaks her heart, many bitter tears she sheds over your letters, she often exclaims what will become of her, still more of her brothers if you remain in Ireland, deserted and without a protector or a guide to usher them into life. [57]

Priscilla threatened her son's reputation – 'Your respectability credit and consequence appears to me to depend upon your return, will not the world say you have abandoned your family, it is likely they will attribute it to some unworthy motive . . .' – and tugged at his conscience: 'Have you no recollection of the tenderness you once felt for her [Susan] – have you no sympathy for her afflictions. . .'.[58]

When Priscilla's remonstrances at last procured the news that Edward would return by Christmas, it was 'joyful news for all . . . . Susan is very thin but I do not doubt but the prospect of your happy return will enliven her countenance and renew her good looks. . . .' Priscilla was both sounding a warning and yet encouraging Edward away from the attractions of his Irish liaisons to resume his relationship with his ailing and exhausted 42-year-old wife. Priscilla was less certain about Edward's decision to take a house in Tottenham. In January 1810 she confided to her journal, 'Edward and Susan become our new neighbours: from which I expect some enjoyments and some perplexities. It is a matter of doubt how far their fixing so near us will be productive of happiness to either. . . . My weak frame is unequal to the struggles of solicitude.'

Edward renewed his conjugal rights with Susan but the consequences were lamentable. She bore her ninth child, Percy, in 'wretched health'. A 'poor little diminutive wretch', he 'never looked like living'.[59]

Priscilla continued 'extremely anxious that Edward should obtain a permanent income.' She considered 'His expenditure large and uncertain: his income much otherwise'. Edward did not earn much from his great book. Although 750 copies were published at £6 the set, sales were slow after half the edition was subscribed in the first six months. Two years after publication, he wrote, 'I laid out in Books paper &c upwards of £200 and whether I shall obtain one farthing I think doubtful.'[60]

Edward later maintained that he spent much of his profit from the Burnham farm in educating his family 'during the expectation of settling down with the Naval Arsenal'.[61] In 1811 he unsuccessfully sought a private secretaryship in the Admiralty and then, until 1813, was engaged in 'maturing plans' for the arsenal at the 'request of the late and present Lords Melville (First Lords of the Admiralty)'.[62] The new arsenal was planned to replace the current naval facilities and yards at Sheerness, Woolwich and Deptford. By July 1813, he gave up waiting for a vacillating government to make a decision on the project: 'I am now determined to find if possible a Cottage and a few acres of land in Suffolk'.[63]

With Arthur Young's help, Edward leased a house at Southgate Green, near Bury St Edmunds, and set up a land agency. In an eight-page pamphlet circulated to landowners from October 1813, Edward took 'the liberty to offer himself to the notice of owners of Estates; 1st. TO AID IN THE MANAGEMENT OF LANDED PROPERTY, BY LOOKING OVER, AND MAKING A WRITTEN REPORT OF THE CONDITION AND THE CAPABILITIES OF THE ESTATE, WITHOUT INTERFERING WITH THE PERMANENT STEWARD'.[64] He also offered his services as auditor, valuer, superintendent and manager for sale.

His practical experience in agriculture, his research into new farming methods and the reputation of his Irish work stood him in good stead. He opened an office in St James, then at 42 Pall Mall the following year. Then Francis Place could report, 'Wakefield has had some success with Lord Shrewsbury, and a further access of business from the other persons, he will do well – but his expenses must destroy his income for some little time longer.'[65] By 1815 politician George Rose, ex-paymaster general and treasurer of the Royal Navy, would write, 'He is in the first employment in his line and steward to many persons of great property; appears extremely intelligent, very conscious of it, and to be just saved from being a democrat by the power of his judgment and integrity over his presumption.'[66] By then, Edward had begun to turn away from active involvement in reform schemes, and he bewailed conservative reactions to his proposals: 'They are lamentable times – I shall pursue steadily my own path and in time I think that I may form a good living. In the meantime my family must live with economy and I am determined to apply myself exclusively to this object . . . no man living has ever looked at money with greater contempt than myself – but I feel that I have carried it much further than I was justified with a family dependant [*sic*] on me for support.'[67]

From 1810, Priscilla's health had steadily declined: the deteriorating handwriting of her journals reflected the unrelenting stresses of her family responsibilities and labours. 'My spirits depressed by the weather, a feeling I do not approve to indulge: why should clouds affect me?' She became increasingly lame. 'Endeavours to recover the use of my legs by friction and exercise', as recommended by doctors in London and Ipswich, were of little help. At the end of 1811 she wrote, 'My health is in a very enfeebled state but with thankfulness I add that as far as I can judge my intellectual powers are unimpaired. I have published "Instinct Displayed" and begun "Travels in Africa".' Writing afforded 'considerable relief from the cares of life', though it did not earn her a great deal: by 1814 some 20,000 copies of her books had been sold, for which she received just £1,400.[68]

Recurrent financial problems had caused removal to cheaper homes in Tottenham and, in 1813, precipitate departure. On 2 April 1813 Priscilla wrote, 'A prospect of pecuniary arrangement of an unpalatable nature. Obliged to consent to take leave of dear Tottenham, and go on Monday to Ipswich . . . My spirits low and confused. Altogether it is too much for my powers mental and bodily.' By now she was largely confined to a wheelchair. Three days later, she left 'the place of my nativity, the scene of so many interesting pursuits, where I have received so many testimonies of esteem and friendship from my neighbours of all classes, that I am attached to the place by no common ties. . .'. At 62, she did not expect a 'very extended continuance' of her life, 'an awful and awakening thought to double diligence, whilst my intellectual faculties are spared'. The character and condition of husband Edward seemed to merit no comment by either Priscilla or any other member of the family.

Priscilla's removal to daughter 'Bell's' at Ipswich, and in July to her own house nearby, was assisted by 20-year-old Catherine. She stayed with Priscilla until the end of October when she was sent for to nurse her mother, who had just shifted to Bury, and to look after her younger brothers and sisters. Susan was in her tenth confinement and at the beginning of December Edward wrote to Young: 'The last week brought me another son – who with his mother is doing well – in my domestic circle this is an event of peculiar interest'.[69] Edward's 'doing well' can only have been epistolary politeness: the child, Susan's last, did not survive long enough to be named.

CHAPTER TWO

Ten Years Too Early

IN 1810 EDWARD GIBBON, NOW FOURTEEN years old, began to cause more trouble. On 1 July Priscilla noted, 'Anxiety from a new quarter. All not pleasant at Westminster.' Westminster School competed with Winchester and Eton for both scholarship and quality of pupils. The education was narrow, based upon the relentless training of memory employing the works of classical authors. Although Edward Gibbon obtained his remove (promotion to a higher form) in 1810, he found this regime painful. Later in life he commented, 'I don't meddle with Greek and am nervous about Latin! So much for Westminster!'[1]

The other kind of training at Westminster was designed to make a man of him: flogging for misdemeanours, institutionalised hierarchical persecutions and humiliations from older boys formed a code of sadistic discipline and order intended to stiffen and train the leaders of the nation. The future Bishop of Adelaide, Augustus Short, went to Westminster soon after Edward Gibbon. When his clergy complained of hardships in the new colony of South Australia he said, 'You should have been a fag at Westminster in my time.'[2] Then there was the bullying. Family tradition has it that Gibbon, though younger than his opponent, fought and wore down a class bully through sheer persistence and stubbornness. If so, this served to sharpen characteristics that later drove his political opponents to submission or pure despair.

In the meantime, he brought these qualities to bear in a refusal to return to Westminster at the start of the 1810 autumn term. Priscilla's journal for 21 September recorded, 'Edward Gibbon returned from an attempt to go to school. His perverseness frustrates his father's views for him.' The boy proved inflexible about Westminster but was persuaded instead to go to the High School in Edinburgh, under the care of Edward's friend, James Gray, 'a clerical gentleman of great literary acquirements, and peculiarly distinguished as a Greek Scholar'.[3] Priscilla trusted that he would be 'instructed in religion and morality as well as in Latin and Greek'.

All was well for six months but then 'painful accounts' reached Tottenham of Edward Gibbon's misbehaviour, which culminated in a request that he be taken home. A school friend from that time recalled that he had a 'reputation for cleverness, marred, however, by want of attention and punctuality'. He was a great practical joker. 'On one occasion . . . he passed himself off as a blind fiddler, and performed his part so well amongst his every day acquaintances, that not one of them discovered the joke; and he drew from them charitable contributions to a considerable amount . . . the bilking [cheating] of police-men was another favourite joke. . . .'[4] It is unsurprising that his hosts found him a complete pest.

Edward removed him from Edinburgh in January 1812. School days were over but he learned much, no doubt, from accompanying his father during his 800-mile walking tour through the Midlands and North between July and November of that year. Otherwise, he remained at home 'without sufficient employment', Priscilla considered, 'to occupy the talents and activity of his mind. Consequently his present state is disadvantageous to himself and troublesome to others.'

There was an attempt to introduce Edward Gibbon into the East India Company, no doubt with the assistance of James Mill, but this 'present state' of affairs lasted until October 1813 when, with the aid of Uncle Daniel, he was admitted to Gray's Inn. The law did not prove congenial either. Finally, in August 1814, Edward found him employment in the diplomatic service as a King's messenger through the offices of the Hon. William Hill, later Lord Berwick, who was British envoy to the court of Turin. Edward wrote to Francis Place, 'His going abroad is an amazing relief to me for although he has many good points he was quite out of my management. He will now I trust feel the responsibility of his situation and the value which character will ever be to him. . . .'[5]

Unruly and unsettled, untrained and unfitted for business or profession, Edward Gibbon at eighteen showed intelligence, energy, fierce independence, and a proclivity to strut and perform, a desire to be the centre of attention. When he later described the behaviour of lads about to take part in the formal ceremony where they were let off the death sentence in Newgate Prison, he recalled his own adolescent feelings: 'They have just the same air of agreeable excitement and self-importance, for days before the scene takes place, as marks a Westminster boy when he is about to be distinguished by acting in public'.[6]

Edward Gibbon's first public role was an adventurous one, carrying government despatches across a Europe in excitement and turmoil following the defeat of Napoleon in the spring of 1814, and on to the diplomatic pomp and circumstance of the Congress of Vienna that autumn. In September, Edward wrote that he 'left Paris, and is either at Genoa or on his way to Vienna. His fate in life depends upon his conduct during the next six months. Should he settle down to business as he ought, he will make a man, but he is very likely to go off at a tangent, and then I cannot tell what may happen to him.'[7]

The new peace had been celebrated across England: 'We are all so much occupied with preparations for the children's feast, that we seem to think and talk of nothing else: what can be more appropriate to the celebration of Peace than the innocency of children'. Priscilla's letter to twelve-year-old Will in June 1814 was tempered by humanitarian reservations about the restoration of the monarchy in France and Spain: 'Did they *know* that the King of France had determined to carry on the infamous traffic in slaves for five years to come, the villages of Africa would have greater cause to mourn than to rejoice. I had hoped that the enormities practised in that wicked trade had nearly come to an end, but to see that renewed, and the Inquisition re-established in Spain is truly grievous and is like groping back into the dark.'[8]

Edward Gibbon's departure caused Edward to hope that his absence would enable him to 'bring up the other branches of my family with much greater regularity and order than had he remained at home'.[9] Bringing up Arthur had amounted to sending him off to sea (see Chapter Three), while William and probably Dan had been despatched to the cosy hearth of Westminster School. In 1814 or 1815 Priscilla instructed William: 'I suppose now you are fagging away at Greek and Latin; try to gain the esteem of your masters by diligence and general good conduct. Never be persuaded by the ill example of others to do that which your conscience tells you is wrong.'[10]

And when she wrote to sixteen-year-old Dan in September 1814, 'I hear that you are a pattern of industry that with common talents will effect more than genius without it', this was encouragement to a boy whose stolidness had gained him the family nickname of Dodo. 'I set my mind on your gaining a prize, dear Will also seems very desirous of success, may he obtain his wish, but I cannot expect you will all get it.'[11] To young Felix, who suffered more than the others from ill health, Priscilla wrote from Ipswich in March 1815, 'I hope by this time you are quite well, and able to go to school, and that you remember the good advice I often gave you, to leave off talking nonsense, to be mild and gentle, and in all things to take pains to be a good boy.'[12]

Little information survives to tell of the academic success or otherwise of the Wakefield boys though, from later writing, it is clear that William got better Latin from Westminster than his older brother. Only Howard and Percy proved to be Oxbridge material. Howard was elected to Trinity College, Cambridge in 1822 but never resided and 'wretched' Percy's academic fame at grammar school seemed to have assured him a place before chronic illness and premature death.

Edward Gibbon was away from home almost a year, spending the winter and spring after the Congress of Vienna as attaché to William Hill in Turin. The foreign service was grossly underfunded and the training of diplomatic staff often rudimentary.[13] Appointments such as Edward Gibbon's were usually by favour or patronage and young men learned the skills of diplomacy through being attached to an ambassador or envoy, living in his family and acting as his clerk or attaché.

Edward Gibbon's patron had spent the greater part of his diplomatic career in Italy, at Genoa, Turin or Naples. Turin was capital of Piedmont or the Kingdom of Sardinia, an important player in the post-war manoeuvrings of the great powers. After the Congress of Vienna, and then Napoleon's return from Elba, its boundaries had been expanded to incorporate all of Savoy and the Republic of Genoa, giving the kingdom control of the Riviera territories from Carrara to Nice. The military state of King Victor Emmanuel became a formidable barrier to any potential future attack by France over the Plain of Lombardy towards Central Europe. Hill handled British liaison with the Piedmontese court skilfully enough to remain of value in the post for at least a decade.

Sociable, hospitable to travelling English intellectuals and poets such as Byron, William Hill was a bachelor who grappled Edward Gibbon to him as a son. Francis Place saw them together in London at the end of 1815:

> Mr Hill will not allow him to be away from him for an hour even, and endeavours to detach him from his family, telling him his father has 8 other children, and can spare him, he laughs at him for writing to any of them and hints that he will be good for little until he divests himself of all affection and feeling for any of them – Mr Hill is right – to be an accomplished man in his employment, one must stifle humanity and destroy all the kinder emotions of the heart – must be capable of doing all manner of actions with the same sang froid, chuckle at cheating the multitude and feel a horrid satisfaction at observing what are called our nearest and dearest friends, constantly deceived by us, and as constantly attributing our actions to motives which are any but the true ones.[14]

Edward Gibbon wrote eloquently of his first long sojourn abroad: ' I passed a miserable winter at Turin, amongst one of the ugliest races of women in the world. In March, whilst the plain of the Po was still covered with deep frozen snow, and all things above the snow were enveloped in dense, chilling, choking fog, I removed to Genoa.' Following the old track over the Apennines,

> three turns of a wheel carried the traveller from the climate of the Baltic, as it were, to that of the Mediterranean. The contrast was most delightful, not to the sight only, but to every one of the senses. . . . I beheld, suddenly and at one view, a long range of mountain steps clothed with vegetation, partly of the dark evergreen, partly of the bright green of spring; and, winding through those wooded hills, the narrow vale of Polcevra with its clear stream and brilliant gardens; and beyond these, Genoa the Magnificent, with her lighthouses, domes and marble palaces, glittering in the sun; and last, the Mediterranean itself, rising, apparently to me who looked down upon it, into a huge bank of blue, which formed the background of the picture. Was this not a sight for eyes just thawed? . . . I breathed highly rarefied air, and felt the soft breeze pass over my face. I listened, doubting; but it was true – the music of the chestnut groves had begun. Presently there were violets by the roadside; and at Campo Marone, the first post-house

> on the sunny side of the Apennines, I received strawberries from a group of girls, with bare arms and necks and fresh flowers in their hair. I was mad with animal joy.[15]

There is a flair of Byronic romanticism in this writing, echoing lines from the Third Canto of *Childe Harold's Pilgrimage:* 'And peasant girls, with deep blue eyes,/ And hands which offer early flowers,/ Walk smiling o'er this paradise'. Although written some fourteen years after the event, the passage reveals the 'ardent and enthusiastic disposition' Edward Gibbon had inherited from his father and evokes the acute sensations of the young explorer of a wild, rustic and ancient world that might have provided the perfect setting for one of the romances of his favourite author, Walter Scott. Edward Gibbon was one of those post-war English travellers who brought an 'atmosphere of freer life' to a land whose people had begun dreaming of united 'Italy' and chafed under the repressive police state that had returned with the restored royals.

'My dear Edward Gibbon arrived greatly improved in body and mind, his aspect and manner pleased me, but what most delighted me was his noble independent spirit,' wrote Priscilla in her journal on 20 July 1815. The next day, 'Our dear visitor took his leave to go to Paris, a city torn by contending factions. May Heaven preserve him in the midst of so many dangers.'

Edward Gibbon had arrived in London with despatches less than a fortnight after the Battle of Waterloo. Francis Place told James Mill that he was

> much improved in appearance, and somewhat softened, though not much in his manners, this has been produced by the contrasts his journeys have presented him, and to the visible superiority of the English over all the nations of the continent has made him like them better than he did, his conduct has however been very ambiguous and his tales have contradicted one another so that his father who has more of feeling than of solid judgment in his composition, has been distressed beyond any thing you will be able to imagine, I have not allowed him to trifle, but have plainly and fully told him of his follies, and, as I think, with some effect – he has left Mr Hill, but not with disgrace.[16]

There is no other reference to the 'follies' that so distressed Edward and inspired Place's disparagement. His strong reactions to the nineteen-year-old do not suggest only a puritanical tradesman's disapproval of wild and immoral actions from the son of impecunious but aspiring gentry; they are also the first unfavourable extra-family responses to a powerful, magnetic and seemingly irresponsible personality whom one either rejected outright or engaged with regardless of risk. To most who encountered him, Edward Gibbon Wakefield promised ruin or reward, and a frightening or exhilarating ride to either; there seemed no chance of compromise.

At this young age, feeling his oats, let loose without direction or a developed self-discipline on to the tumultuous roads of post-war Europe, any folly was not only possible but likely:

> You remember that Genoese girl before whom you trembled, and I became faint, though she only handed us some grapes? Do you remember that, having recovered ourselves, we measured her eyelashes? Do you remember how long they were, and how she laughed? Do you remember that bright laugh, and how I patted her cheek and told her that it was softer than her country's velvet? And how she blushed – do you remember that? – to the tips of her fingers and the roots of her hair?[17]

In response to a request for news, Place wrote another letter to Mill before the end of that July: 'His conduct is wholly inexplicable, he despises his father's advice, and laughs at his opinions he talks largely of being on his own hands, and independent of his father . . . I wish his father could make up his mind to see only a common man in him and to leave him to himself he would then be comparatively at ease'.[18] Earlier, Edward had written to his mother, 'I cannot say how much I lament the manner in which he conducts himself towards us – for an intimate constant and unreserved communication between such near connections is certainly one of the greater sweeteners in life.'[19]

Demanding to be his own man, Edward Gibbon was, if possible, more unbiddable than he had ever been. With that callousness peculiar to youth, he rejected the vacillating, emotional and unconvincing entreaties of his father. What a pitiful example Edward may have seemed to the overweening son – a failure in business, a failure in farming, a failure as a husband, a father and a son, cadging money to get by. And in his reform schemes, his achievements were faddish and ineffectual alongside those of Place, Young and Mill on whose coat-tails he rode. Despite his son's contempt, Edward never lost faith that Edward Gibbon possessed some kind of genius. To use Place's words, he always remained 'in raptures with him, ridiculously so'.[20]

Although Edward Gibbon had temporarily left William Hill's employment, he obtained a minor commission from the Foreign Office and set off for Paris after just three weeks in England. Louis XVIII had just returned, again, after the defeat and exile of Napoleon. France was plunged into new elections which produced La Chambre Introuvable, an assembly dominated by royalists intent on punishing those who had supported the Revolution and Napoleon and reduced France to humiliation. The victorious allies had confined the country's borders still further, burdened the French with war reparations and established a pillaging occupation force of 150,000 soldiers. Although a general amnesty for Republicans and Bonapartists had been declared by the government, La Chambre Introuvable demanded blood and eighteen prominent men were executed, including Marshal Ney and the Comte de Labédoyère who had both largely contributed to Napoleon's resumption of power.

On 27 August, Edward Gibbon reported on the popular resentment and outrage at the execution of Labédoyère. In a letter that eventually found its way into the press, he described the atmosphere of Paris in the turmoil of the Second Restoration. This, the first published example of Edward Gibbon's writing, was colourful and politically driven, hinting at the volumes of propaganda to come.

> A caricature has been published in which, on one side, the King is represented as kneeling to the sovereigns and requested them to withdraw from his private room – on the other he is seen running to the window – and begging with extended arms that they will return for that he hears a noise in the closet – This is a very, very just picture of the present policy of the King's government – and there is a noise in the closet – the fermentation is extreme but admirably concealed . . . I know a National Guard – who relates a Plan of his own invention by which the Allies would infallibly be destroyed – I have twice heard him finish his relation – with these – words 'Union and Force – we shall see whether six millions of Frenchmen will be enslaved by one million of Calvinist tartars – Austrian bears – Prussian Monsters & English shopkeepers'. . . .
>
> Labédoyères 'Murder' has done an immensity of harm to the Royal Cause – . . . Why choose out of 500-000 equally guilty men – the one who has a young wife and five children. – His trial was a mere matter of hasard. It was done without motive and the cold-blood refusal of the King to Mme. Labédoyères kneeling prayer has made a wonderful sensation against him – To make it worse he had just done dinner and was puffing & blowing with a red face & full belly towards his 'Satin lined Loafer' at the moment she fell at his feet. . . .

Edward Gibbon went on to describe the political manoeuvring that took place to mark the Fête of St Louis on 23 August. Police officers 'invited' all Parisian householders to 'illuminate magnificently' in the evening though King Louis, as a 'good father of his people', had prohibited such expense. After the 'very general illumination' took place, the press cried, 'Let the foreigners see this . . . and they will be convinced that our beloved King is the sole object of our present pleasure and future hopes.'

'This little ruse de politique has succeeded to admiration,' he continued, '– Englishmen and Russians agree today that the illumination was universal and that the King is beloved, the Austrians and Prussians grumble for their hopes of future commotion and plunder are lessened. A little enquiry would have let them into the secret of the Officer of Police on the morning of the fête – but soldiers never enquire.'[21]

This lesson in manipulation and propaganda was not lost on the precocious King's messenger. His vanity considered it would do him no harm, either, to have his account published by London's *Statesman* newspaper: it appeared anonymously, though he let it be known it was his work. Francis Place was furious. 'I would have paid £100 rather than that letter should have been printed. Should it ever be known at the Foreign Office that he wrote it, all his prospects in the line of life he has chosen, and the only one he is fit for, would be blasted in an instant. . . .'[22]

But nothing untoward came of it and when Edward Gibbon returned to London in December, Place commented more calmly that the young man was 'no doubt permanently provided for, and that too in the line in which he is most likely to continue – and Wakefield who expected him home without a shilling and without employment – and without the means of providing for him has much to rejoice at'.[23] The provision had come in the shape of William Hill, who had returned to London from Turin, taken a house in Princes Street, off Hanover Square, and made Edward Gibbon his secretary. Place thought it 'a rascally employment, but the world does not treat it as disreputable, and Edward cannot be spoiled by it – Edward's manners are far more agreeable than they were his knowledge of diplomacy has shown him the necessity of this'.[24] The dishonest and mischievous rascal was beyond redemption, though acquired manners made him more bearable.

Were there any other views, besides those of the peevish Place, the distracted but devoted father, the disapproving but forgiving grandmother and Hill the enthusiastic employer? Brother Arthur's comment to Catherine in September 1815 reveals that most of his immediate family probably thought Gibbon's personal behaviour difficult and, in some degree, reprehensible: 'I long to see him, for I think he will be much improved in every way'.[25] But by then both Arthur and Catherine had got religion, and a tendency to be sanctimonious.

Edward Gibbon, never more than a nominal believer, attacked them both on this count early the next year. Writing to his sister, Arthur said: 'I am very glad to hear that Edward's bravado has had no effect upon you it is more than I can say if I tell the truth, though I hope it is growing up again, he used no good arguments, not enough to shake any one of firm sentiments but my opinion was not guarded against, it never has sustained an attack of the kind before; practice makes perfect.'[26] Yet Arthur's mention of receiving a 'very good letter' from Edward Gibbon soon after this event and Gibbon's intimate confidence in Catherine in later years are evidence of the unwavering affection and loyalty between the Wakefield siblings.

If Place was the first among many to count him dishonest, to Catherine six years later, Edward Gibbon revealed his judgement of his own character with both candour and pathos: 'I shall never be offended at your speaking out and giving me the benefit of your advice – by which you ought to believe that I will benefit if I <u>conscientiously</u> can. This, you will say, is an odd word for me; but I have a sort of conscience; such a one as I should like my children to have, a <u>good deal</u> less injured than mine perhaps has been by beginning life ten years too early.'[27]

What conflicts and what experiences – what injury – did he undergo or witness as a small child in the isolated, stressful and unhealthy environment of Burnham Wyck, and share with Kitty, whose understanding and observation had been beyond her years? Did his later cavalier rejections of his father's advice derive from a sense of being abandoned when he was farmed out to Priscilla? Did he feel left out of sight and out of mind when Edward went to Ireland for two years and was continually absent from home chasing elusive reforms? As the eldest boy of nine children, he would have been aware early that much was expected of him; his sense of responsibility for his brothers remained with him for life, perhaps reflecting the emotional burden his afflicted mother placed upon him in the absence of an unreliable husband.

Edward Gibbon had no bad word for his grandmother, though the springs of his agnosticism may have lain in his observation that Priscilla's obdurate faith in all things 'working together to produce universal good, which will triumph finally over apparent evil, and endure for ever' did not overcome the realities of emotional deprivation, wider family enmities and an endless shortage of money. His experience of this last condition set his face against having a large family of his own, as he told his grandmother: 'I know you think a numerous family a great advantage. That is, I believe, the only opinion of yours in which I cannot agree with you. What should I do, for instance, with six? Why, they must eat each other for I could not keep them. But to show you that I do not altogether disagree with you, I will add that I should like to have forty daughters with as many thousands a year to divide amongst them at my death or their marriages. I know you would quote the bundle of sticks; but if all the sticks are rotten, that is poor, what becomes of the argument?'[28]

At nineteen, Edward Gibbon wanted life in his own hands: to be free of moral stricture, free to find affection, a fortune and his own fame, whatever that might be.

Francis Place's (and James Mill's) interest in the Wakefield family was not confined to Edward's co-operative activities in philanthropy or to commenting on Edward Gibbon's character and prospects. In late 1815, seventeen-year-old Dan became Place's next concern. The boy stayed and worked with Place as he neared leaving school. It was decided that, in the new year, he should learn bookkeeping, conveyancing and practical farming before entering Edward's office. 'There he may be both usefully and profitably employed – he is a hard working, plodding fellow, with the vice of lying about him, and a good deal of sly cunning, which I shall endeavour to drive out of him. In doing this I shall encounter some of the absurd notions of respect for the great which his father still cherishes, but I shall not be turned aside, for the boy is capable of being made a good man – a clever one he will never be.'[29]

But, by Christmas, Dan had disgraced himself by some unexplained 'folly' and it was determined to send him to a merchant's counting house in Amsterdam. Place wrote Mill, 'He tells me . . . he will fag at the business until he has gone through it and is master of a set of books . . . he is both sulky & lazy and cares little for any body, he is by no means an agreeable fellow to have with one, but this I disregard for his sake, and the sake of his father the worst he has no confidence in me nor perhaps in no one, he has told me he can understand my intentions to serve him as arising from my friendship for his father, plainly at the same time insinuating, that more could be done for him. . . .'[30]

In August 1815, Edward wrote to Place for a loan of £100 and to ask him to pass on an 'inclosure . . . I consider it most important to the welfare of my family – and all my future plans – it is a subject upon which I am most uncomfortable'.[31] The 'inclosure' was a letter that Edward wanted Place to deliver in person to physician Sir William Blizard. Edward sought his advice and help in recommending to Susan that she go to a 'watering place' for her health.

A few days later, Place wrote to James Mill,

> Mrs Wakefield is in town, we have had her 3 times with us, she is in a strange way, her intellectual powers are almost all obliterated, and she is rapidly sinking into a state of inanity. She is reasonable one minute, childish the next, and laughing like an idiot the next, she cannot put her own clothes on, will lie in bed for days, and cry for many hours continuance, it is a dreadful misfortune for them all, but most so for the children, she is utterly unable and unfit to manage her house in any way, and yet is so tenacious of her authority, that she will allow no one to manage for her. Wakefield himself wants resolution, and instead of having the family with him in London where he could compel obedience to his wishes, he flies from the annoyance of his wife, and leaves both her and the family without any wholesome advice or restraint, it fills me with vexation and regret, he is constantly asking my opinion, which the anxious state of his mind prevents him from hearing – ever.[32]

When he sent Edward the loan, Place wrote, 'Your family occasions an unceasing solicitude and repeated conversations in mine.' He explained that he and his wife had agreed that Susan should not be at home 'since she is incapable of managing her house and can no longer command the respect of her children, than which nothing can be more pernicious to them'. Place had 'no hopes from medical aid except as a temporary relief, which must not however be neglected', and stressed that 'the estrangement from her family will not be for three months only, it will probably be for ever and appalling as this consideration is, you must screw up your mind to its serious contemplation'.[33]

Edward's reaction was to be, in Place's words, 'miserably intimidated by the Bugbear, <u>Public Opinion</u> – "what would the world say" he has replied, turning himself in an agony on his chair, and looking vacantly through the window. . .'. Place feared that his friend's 'unceasing and anxious desire to be taken notice of by the great, his expectations of providing for his sons by these means, and his dread that the Honbl and Noble Gentlemen, should no longer nod or wink at him' would prevent him from taking a 'right course'. 'I sympathize so much with him respecting his family that it causes me constant vexation to see him distress'd in mind by causes which he makes for his own annoyance . . . he really has enough to occupy him seriously without any need of inventions.'[34]

Susan's health had deteriorated markedly after her last confinement at the end of 1813. She had visited London from Bury for medical advice but had returned 'still a great invalid'. Edward was to reveal later that Susan had 'a confirmed liver complaint', probably a consequence of past malaria. Self-pityingly, he wrote that this and 'attention to children absorbed every thought, by degrees all my pursuits were abandoned and it was either in a sick room or a nursery I had to have my wife, many was the day that I dined alone and many the night that I slept alone and by degrees I sought companions at a distance and knew little of domestic life'.[35]

Edward denied Place's implication that Susan had taken leave of her senses and that the three children likely to still have been at home – Felix, Priscilla and Percy – were without proper care; Catherine had taken over much of the maternal role. A few weeks later Place admitted to James Mill: 'It is true, as Wakefield says Mrs W. has no delusions, *i.e.* she does not take a Church for a Playhouse, but she is incapable of doing any thing beyond crying and complaining, and refusing both advice and assistance'.[36] Mill replied, 'All that is threatened in this case is a little more of that misery to which his family are used – & which will produce the right resolution in the end. It would answer the same purpose if he could find a steady private family, in which she might be boarded cheaply.'[37]

With Sir William Blizard's support, Edward sent Susan to Margate. On 18 January 1816, Place reported to Mill: 'Mrs Wakefield can scarcely be said to be better, and Mr Finch who seems to understand her case gives no hopes of her recovery'.[38] She was now with Edward at Exeter and a return home to Bury was planned for the following week. But in early February 1816, at the age of 48, she died at Salisbury on the uncompleted return journey, 'full of charity and love', Edward said, 'her last breath lisping blessings on me and on her children'.[39] On 10 February, Priscilla received 'the afflicting and lamented news of poor Susan's death, which unfitted me for all employment. . .'.

Blessings were all that Susan had been able to give her children for years. For 22-year-old Catherine, her mother's death was a formal confirmation of her dual role as housekeeper for her father in London and surrogate parent to her several siblings. She had begun a long journey. For the rest of her long life she was to provide the only stable hearth and home for her entire generation. In Ipswich, she shared care of the youngest, Priscilla junior and Percy, with grandmother Priscilla and aunt Isabella Head. But since her grandmother's shift to Ipswich in 1813, Catherine had learnt increasingly to cope with her responsibilities alone. In this, she was closest to brother Arthur who had been coping alone since his eleventh year. Both were to find the only certainty of comfort and support in the rod and staff of religion.

CHAPTER THREE

The Best Boy in the World

IF EDWARD GIBBON WAKEFIELD COULD complain of beginning life ten years too early, Arthur Wakefield could have complained of not beginning life at all before he was thrust into a separate universe. But Arthur was never a complainer: 'the great thing in this world [is] to make ourselves contented with whatever fare we may meet – discontent is the origin of many wrongs'.[1] But he had no option when, at the age of ten and half, he was enlisted in the Royal Navy as a volunteer 1st class. For pacifist Priscilla this was 'a line of life I entirely disapprove. To part with him on such an errand is no small trial.'[2] Arthur had been proving the most tractable of Edward's boys, pious and obedient to her schooling, and was becoming her favourite.

Why Edward chose Arthur for the navy, over the other boys, is unclear, though Gibbon would probably have refused, and eldest boys were not usually sent away. Dan was, perhaps, considered too old by the time Edward returned from his Irish expedition and Will, in 1810, was still too young.[3] Perhaps Arthur's sponsor Captain Philip Beaver, Edward's 'old and intimate friend',[4] simply took a shine to the lad one day on leave and offered to take him off Edward's hands and into a profession that not only had potential for advancement and material reward but also 'fashion on its side'.[5]

Arthur shipped with Beaver on the *Nisus,* a frigate of the Lively Class which had just been launched and fitted out at the Plymouth Dockyard. One hundred and 54 feet long, it displaced 1072 tons and was armed with 28 18-pounder cannons, four 9-pounders and 14 32-pound carronades.[6] The *Nisus* carried a crew of almost 300, mostly volunteers since, because the ship was a fifth-rater and fleet commerce raider, there was the chance of good prize money. Arthur joined the *Nisus* on 10 June 1810, his big sea chest filled with clothing, medicines and tonics, books and portable soup, and sailed for the Cape of Good Hope. He would spend little more than two of the next 30 years on shore in England.

The navy was school, profession and family. 'The quarterdeck of a man-of-war may justly be considered as a national school for the instruction of a numerous portion of our youth: there it is that they acquire a habit of discipline and become instructed in all the interesting minutiae of the service. Punctuality, cleanliness, diligence and dispatch are regularly inculcated, and such a habit of sobriety and even of self-denial acquired, that cannot fail to prove highly useful. By learning to *obey*, they are also taught how to command.'[7]

It was a hard school below. Arthur would have slung his hammock in the midshipmen's mess on the orlop deck, a dark and evil-smelling space just above the bilges, and there run the risk of being 'thrashed all day long, and fare very badly; the weakest goes to the wall there'.[8] The horseplay was rough in a service which, despite the steady reforms, still collected seamen with press gangs and disciplined them with flogging for minor infractions and death for major crimes. As the Articles of War, drawn up in 1749, made clear, 'Every person in the Fleet who through Cowardice, Negligence, or Disaffection shall forebear to pursue the Chace of any Enemy, Pirate, or Rebel, beaten or flying . . . shall suffer Death . . . If any Officer, Mariner, Soldier or other Person in the Fleet, shall strike any of his superior Officers, or draw, or offer to draw, or lift up any Weapon against him . . . shall suffer Death. . . . .'[9] Death 'rang through and through the Articles; and even where the words were utterly incomprehensible the death had a fine, comminatory, Leviticus ring, and the crew took a grave pleasure in it all; it was what they were used to. . . .'[10]

Arthur's hammock would have been cut down, his possessions and food stolen, and he would have had to fight for his place under the rule of the fist. As part of his first day aboard the *Nisus* he may have been sent, like Marryat's Peter Simple, with chits to obtain his cocked hat from the main-top, his officer's dirk from the butcher and to fetch the captain's monkey from the goose-neck. In the nauseous gloom below he would have eaten unpalatable slops at a table that doubled as the surgeon's bench. If he was seasick, he might have been treated to a 'good basting [beating], which was a sovereign remedy'.[11] If he had committed a misdemeanour, he would have been 'mast-headed' for some hours to cool off.

All the bullying, fagging, japes and summary justice were among the rites of passage of this sail-driven extension of the English public school. As a fledgling officer, Arthur was expected to endure, survive and be strengthened by the college of nautical hard knocks so that he might endure and survive the far greater hardships and punishments of storm at sea, privation in small boats, tropical disease and injury, wounding or maiming by gear failure, rogue cannon or enemy action. After withstanding the bastard watch in a North Atlantic gale or the raking grapeshot of a French frigate, a cuff round the ear from a shipmate was almost a mark of affection.

It is likely that Arthur would have gained some protection from the worst excesses of older midshipmen who had lost all hope of promotion and vented their envy and bitterness across the back of a raw young newcomer with evident intelligence and good prospects. A master's mate or young lieutenant would have cast an eye of tough benevolence over him as he learned the ropes; and his sponsoring captains carried ultimate responsibility for him. The Articles of War provided for that worst exploitation of a young boy: 'If any person in the Fleet shall commit the unnatural and detestable Sin of Buggery or Sodomy with Man or Beast, he shall be punished with Death'.[12]

From the rigours and stresses and humiliations of the naval life, Arthur found solace and strength, like his beloved grandmother, in the faith that Edward Gibbon was unable to shake five years later. His older brother underestimated the white heat of danger, physical hardship and emotional deprivation in which Arthur's belief had been forged. At fifteen Arthur wrote to Catherine:

> Though I am a sailor and condemned to rough out the fatigues and horrors of a man-of-war, I can not forget entirely my maker, who gives me more reason to thank Him, than any of you. He saves me from such perilous situations. Still so many go through the world, from one week's end to another & never deliver up a single Prayer nor Thanks for all the benefits they have received, but on the contrary go on swearing, & you would think, trying who would go the farthest down. It is very rarely you meet with a Sea-faring man that thinks of Religion, it is very remarkable, because they have certainly the most need of its existence. They who never can trust ten minutes, for life, who are thrown up by one wave & down by another, who ought always to be prepared, do not know when they may come into fight, and still they never think of it, least the generality of them. Does it not stand to reason that a man that fears nothing from the Almighty must be a brave man, and a brave man is so necessary in this kind of life.[13]

Arthur began learning to be brave as the *Nisus* sailed south to the Cape in the summer of 1810. He also began learning the skills of almost every man aboard, from topmast to magazine, from bowsprit to spanker boom; mastering the intricacies of navigation, log-keeping and bookkeeping, beginning an education that would eventually give him French, Spanish and Italian and all the technical skills he needed to command a ship of his own. After a year of this he officially became a midshipman. At the great age of eleven, he was granted many of the privileges of an officer and had absolute authority over the ordinary seamen, no matter how old they were. 'Many a brave and brawny tar was forced to submit to shrill obscenities and stinging slaps from some smooth-cheeked young tyrant. There was no recourse to higher authority. "By the god of war," one officer roared to his seamen, "by the god of war, I'll make you touch your hat to a midshipman's coat, if it's only hung on a broomstick to dry!"'[14]

After Trafalgar, the main British and French fleets in Europe merely fenced with each other in the coastal waters of the Mediterranean, English Channel and North Atlantic. Napoleon had 56 ships of the line in commission by 1811, but none of them ever went out of sight of their harbours. Further afield, however, the French and the British continued a running colonial war in West Indian, African and East Indian waters. On 14 December 1810, Priscilla wrote in her journal, 'An alarming account of the squadron destined for the Mauritius. The "Nisus" said to be in safety. Alas! to what anxiety does dear Arthur's profession expose his friends.' The *Nisus* had sortied into the Indian Ocean, carrying the flag of Admiral Bertie, and after rendezvous with ships and troops from India, had participated in the capture of French Mauritius. This action cleared the way for an unimpeded attack on the rich prize of Java, part of the East Indian empire controlled by France's Dutch allies.

The six-month campaign to take Java began in April 1811 and the *Nisus* was part of a 34-ship British fleet that included four third-rate ships of the line and fourteen frigates. A military expeditionary force of almost 12,000 officers and men was transported from India and the bulk of it landed on Java in August to attack a similar Dutch force entrenched in a fort outside the chief town of Batavia (Djakarta). A brigade of 500 seamen and Royal Marines joined the siege of the fort, which was protected by more than 280 guns. Arthur was ashore with Captain Beaver when the 'breaching batteries sustained a heavy cannonade' the day before the fort was stormed and captured on 25 August.[15] British losses on Java for the month were given as 'only' 156 killed, 788 wounded and 16 missing compared with 1000 Dutch dead.[16] The British Empire came cheap; and Arthur was unscathed.

The action was not yet over. Beaver sailed east along the north coast of Java, commanding a three-frigate squadron to confront the garrison at Cheribon (Tjirebon). Beaver's approach to its commandant was direct: 'Sir . . . . My force is sufficiently strong to make all attempts at resistance futile and vain. I therefore summon you to surrender . . . . Five minutes are allowed for your decision; after which time . . . hostile operations will commence. . . .' If he did not comply with Beaver's various conditions then 'a dreadful retaliation will await not only the town, but the whole kingdom. I am, &c.' In the face of this, the commandant gave up without a fight. Since most of the garrison were 'natives', Beaver 'desired them to go home, and remain there quietly; assuring them, that if any were found to act afterwards against the British, they would be immediately hanged: they seemed grateful and departed'.[17] Pax Britannica.

Captain Beaver thought that it had not been in his power to 'do any thing brilliant' except contribute to the 'speedy reduction of this important colony' and come away with large quantities of arms and general stores, 250,000 Spanish dollars' worth of coffee and nine wagonloads of money (silver and copper). From this would come the prize money that had proved such an incentive to action and of which Arthur would in due course receive a share to augment his pitiful wages of £2 a month.

Arthur had to wait another three years before sailing again with Dash, Valour and Plunder. During the years 1812, as Napoleon trekked to Moscow and back, and 1813, as Wellington fought his way through Spain to the edge of France, Arthur and the *Nisus* carried out unremarkable Cape Station duties in southern seas, ranging from India to Brazil. Whether or not this suited his taste completely, like the eponymous fourteen-year-old hero of Priscilla's bestselling Middleton family travel books, Arthur was making his own tour through the real empire and becoming a man in the process.

Post-Captain Philip Beaver died in the service in April 1813 and the *Nisus* was taken over by Captain Charles M. Schomberg. When he brought the frigate back to England, Edward sought to have Arthur transferred to the more promising command of Captain Brenton in the *Spartan*. But in the halls of the Admiralty Schomberg told Brenton: 'You shall not have him. As long as I have a pendant flying, Arthur shall be one of my midshipmen.'[18] Unfortunately for Schomberg, the *Nisus* was paid off at Spithead at the beginning of May 1814, whereupon Arthur joined the *Hebrus*. Although he had been away from his family for four years, he would have had the opportunity for only a short trip home before his new ship sailed for the North Atlantic Halifax Station. The *Hebrus* was a 'fir-built' 1812 Scamander class frigate, a little smaller than the *Nisus*. Four guns lighter, she put to sea with a crew of 274 officers, men and boys.

Captain Edmund Palmer took charge of the *Hebrus* at the time of its fitting-out in October 1813. Palmer had been in the navy throughout the wars, making the rank of commander in 1804 and being advanced to post-captain in 1807 following his role at the 'reduction' of Alexandria. At the time Arthur joined the *Hebrus* Palmer had just been awarded an honorary medal from the Board of Admiralty for his capture of the French frigate *L'Étoile*[19] after a pursuit through the Race of Alderney. When Arthur joined, the *Hebrus* was refitting after suffering heavy damage in this encounter. In Palmer's affections he was to replace 'a most promising young gentleman, Mr P. A. Crawley, who fell early in the action';[20] as Palmer's protégé, Arthur's career came to depend on his captain's good opinion.

In June 1812 President Andrew Madison of the United States had declared war on Britain. Although not all the states had enthusiasm for it, war to remove British influence from North America was seen as a way of countering British arrogance in persisting with maritime blockade and search during their prosecution of the war with the French, and impressment of seamen aboard American ships. But American forays into Canada in 1812 and 1813 achieved nothing. They burned public buildings in York and Newark and the British retaliated by burning Buffalo.

In the summer of 1814, Vice-Admiral Sir Alexander Cochrane took command of the British fleet blockading the east coast of the United States and in August sailed for Chesapeake Bay with a squadron of seven frigates, including the *Hebrus*. Smaller craft accompanied the squadron plus transports carrying a small army of 3000–4000 men under Major-General Robert Ross. The first object of the expedition was to destroy a flotilla of American gunboats in Chesapeake Bay which, under Commodore Joshua Barney, had been harassing ships of the British blockade. If this was successful, the army was intended for an attack, no less, on the capital, Washington. Cochrane issued an order for the navy (but not the army) to lay waste any towns and other property it could successfully attack. The excuse was retaliation for the American destruction of Newark, though this had been avenged at Buffalo and the miscreant American commander responsible for Newark's burning had been court-martialled.

The British forces were split: two frigates and four smaller ships moved up the Potomac and another frigate was sent north to create a diversion at Baltimore, while the *Hebrus* and three remaining frigates escorted the main force up the Patuxent, driving Barney's flotilla before them. The frigates and transports could move up river no higher than Benedict, about 50 miles from Washington. Here the army was disembarked on 19 August, along with a marine battalion, a detachment of seamen and the rocket corps. Two days later, the army advanced to Nottingham, 'the armed boats and tenders of the fleet . . . making a corresponding movement in communication with the troops ashore, and in pursuit of Commodore Barney who, with his flotilla of 17 gun-vessels, retired before them'.[21] The next day, Barney put his crews and cannon ashore and blew up his ships before the British could reach them. Ross's force now prepared to march on Washington, joined by naval parties from the frigates under the command of their captains. Palmer chose Arthur Wakefield to go with him as his aide-de-camp; after four years of training he had become a dutiful midshipman, presentable, efficient and, above all, brave.

On the morning of 24 August, labouring in the humid 100°F heat of a Maryland midsummer, the British forces reached the village of Bladensburg, about 5 miles from Washington. Here they 'encountered a huddle of seven thousand American militia . . . . It could not be called an army. A few companies were in uniform. The rest were clad as they would have been clad in the fields, except that they had muskets. They were under two or three worthless generals . . . and various members of the cabinet . . . accompanied President Madison in riding or driving aimlessly about among the troops.'[22] Only about 1500 British had arrived on the scene, including the *Hebrus*'s party, but General Ross decided to attack at once, sensing the Americans' lack of preparation. Within an hour the American militia were routed and Arthur, brandishing his cutlass, 'had the good fortune to secure one of three flags taken from the enemy'.[23] He seems not to have drawn blood. He then accompanied Ross into Washington, where the general's horse was shot from under him, as the militia retreated across the Potomac into Virginia. The president, his cabinet and their households took off for Baltimore. Monroe had arranged the removal of state records and Dolly Madison collected up her husband's presidential papers, curtains and silver from the President's House. A local mob pillaged the interior before the British soldiers arrived.

'When our officers entered Washington city, they found the table laid at Mr Madison's palace for a *grand supper;* the champagne was in coolers – a fine dessert on the side-boards – little did they dream who would be their guests! The unexpected visitants took the liberty of ordering the supper to be served up – and the health of His Majesty was drank at the head of the President's table!'[24] Before they set fire to it.

After their sumptuous supper, General Ross sent for glowing coals from a nearby tavern and Arthur, with the other British officers, supervised the burning of the President's House, the Capitol, the Treasury and the War Office.[25] The British completed their destruction by spiking hundreds of pieces of cannon at the foundry in Georgetown. The public buildings of Washington were saved from complete destruction only by the sudden intervention of a violent and torrential rainstorm. Fifteen years in the building, they were to be four years in repair. 'The American papers state that the stores destroyed at Washington cost the United States *seven* millions of dollars! *The loss is irreparable,* at least, during the present war; the last, perhaps, that ever will be waged by the *United States*.'[26]

It was, at least, the last war waged by the United States against Britain; and the sacking of Washington, together with the stalemate in Canada, brought about negotiations that led to peace by the end of the year. Neither country had gained any ground or advantage by the conflict. There was a kind of fraternal regret about the Washington fiasco. Commodore Barney and his gunboat crews who had been captured, some wounded, on the field at Bladensburg had been treated 'as if they were brothers'.[27] When they marched back to their ships, the British left behind most of their 185 wounded to be cared for by the Americans and, perhaps, to tend the graves of their 64 dead. The Americans lost many more on the battlefield and the British figures did not include a greater, unknown, number of losses from infected wounds and dysentery – and desertions.

Edmund Palmer put Arthur in charge of a prize of 280 tons, which he sailed from Chesapeake Bay to Bermuda, a distance of about 700 nautical miles, a voyage of several days. Even at this distance in time, it is easy to engage with the pride this fourteen-year-old must have felt, his sense of confidence and triumph after the hot heady days of ordeal and adventure, fear and exultation.

Arthur was mentioned in despatches that reached the Admiralty at the end of September and the boy became the Wakefield household's hero. At the beginning of October Edward Wakefield, who was with James Mill and Joseph Hume MP at Ford Abbey, wrote excitedly to Francis Place in London: 'Arthur will be made a lieutenant which certainly would not be more extraordinary than his name appearing in the Gazette'. He enclosed a letter from Hume to the Admiralty, asking Place to forward it and make enquiries on Arthur's behalf. 'I do not flatter myself much about it. At the same time – it is but fair to the boy, to give him every chance.'[28]

A few days later Edward wrote again to Place with details from Arthur's letter which told of spending nine days and nights without taking off his clothes and marching under the burning sun. 'During the battle the shot fell thick as hail stones, he has been placed in an extraordinary situation for a young boy.' Reflecting the embarrassment in liberal circles about the excesses of the attack on Washington, Edward added, 'I dislike the work in which he has been engaged'[29] and lamented the bad effects the sun may have had on Arthur. Writing to young Dan, Priscilla thanked God for his preservation: 'Your father and mother must be highly gratified. His conduct and success is like a bright sun that I hope will revive them both.'[30]

After the American peace, the *Hebrus* returned to the Home Command and Arthur had a chance to visit his grandmother, before Napoleon's return from Elba in March 1815 called him back to duty: 'Depressed at parting with Arthur from the very uncertain prospect of when we shall meet again, and my conscientious abhorrence of the hostile profession in which he is engaged'.

The *Hebrus* was involved in one last action before the conclusion of the long European wars. In June 1815, Arthur accompanied Captain Palmer when he was sent to Bordeaux in command of a small expedition to organise French royalists. Palmer directed the dismantling of four forts and the destruction of heavy artillery before helping to maintain order in the city and oversee the dispersal of Bonapartist troops following the armistice.

Despite his exploits, there was no promotion for Midshipman Wakefield. He was too young and he had not served the requisite six years. Besides, the wars were at an end: the fleet in commission was in the process of being reduced from 700 to 130 ships, 120,000 men were paid off and, of the 6000 officers in service, nine out of ten would be put ashore on half-pay. Opportunities for promotion were now rare and would depend on personal preferment and influence.

In September, Arthur wrote to Catherine from Sheerness: 'We were paid off yesterday, & all the men sent away, and I am I believe to be kept on the Ship on the Peace establishment. I received £19 pay, & I hear that the Prize Money for Java is due, & amounts to £42 the first payment & something like that the second which will help. Thank God I am not out of employment to be a burden to my Friends as I was afraid of.'[31]

After more than five years observing them at close quarters, he had a priggish, even contemptuous, view of the sailors beneath him: 'Directly they hear anything, a little proper but uncommon to them, they set [a religious man] down for a

Methodist Parson . . . . Sailors are . . . the most uncouth set of beings. They are the most ignorant of all the human race, besides.' He did not approve of the conduct of his colleagues in the midshipmen's mess either. A few months later, he wrote to Catherine, 'We have a very good pious man on board in our berth who contributes much to my comfort by stopping many of them from their noisy amusements. We have raised a subscription, for the Naval Bible Society, through his advice. I am very sorry I had never read any of the Revelation when Edward was down for I think there is something of great consequence there, I intend to do it.'[32]

If Arthur disapproved of his shipmates, ashore everyone approved of him: 'Arthur has been with us, he is an open hearted good boy whom every body loves, he begins to feel the want of school instruction, and has taken to reading – he is the flower of the flock'.[33]

If Arthur had 'taken to reading' the Revelation, he would have taken heart from the words 'He went forth conquering, and to conquer' (6:2) when the *Hebrus* was ordered from the Irish Station in August 1816 to join Admiral Lord Exmouth's expedition to bring the Dey of Algiers to reason; to give this 'semi-civilised state . . . [a] serious lecture on the subject of international courtesy'.[34] During the Napoleonic wars, Moorish pirates had roved the Mediterranean with relative impunity, though admirals St Vincent and Nelson had taken time off from the real business to 'check their insolence' on more than one occasion. The Algiers-based pirates clearly did not know, however, when to refrain from attacking stray merchant ships, and were also holding more than 1000 Christian slaves; ransom money of 382,500 dollars which they had extorted from Naples and Sardinia and, worst of all, had imprisoned the British consul. It was time to teach them a sharp lesson.

Exmouth raised his colours in the 100-gun first-rate ship of the line *Queen Charlotte,* leading a fleet that included four other great wooden walls, five frigates and ten smaller warships; the Dutch, now allies, contributed six more ships. Altogether the combined fleet was manned by nearly 8000 men, bringing to bear 1000 guns. It was estimated that the Moorish batteries contained a similar number of guns, though these – and the gunners – were probably not of the same quality as those on the British ships. Algiers had a garrison of about 40,000 men.

On the morning of 27 August, as the *Hebrus* drifted into Algiers under light airs, Arthur was probably apprehensive about the violent prospects of the day. A message had been sent to the Dey with a list of demands and Captain Palmer anticipated the response. At 10.40 a.m. the *Hebrus*'s cutter returned from the transport brig 'with 8 cases of Shells. Beat to Quarters and Cleared for Action'.[35] By afternoon, the messenger had returned to the flagship empty handed. As signals midshipman for the day, Arthur at 1.20 p.m. 'Ans^d^ signal to bear up and prepare for Battle'. It was the only great fleet action in which he was ever engaged.

The admiral in *Queen Charlotte* took 'his Station off the mole Head within half a cables length of the Enemy'. More than 200 of the Moorish guns were on the mole and, in the port beyond, lay four frigates, five large corvettes and 30–40 other armed vessels. At 2 p.m. Captain Palmer anchored the *Hebrus* 'on the Queen Charlottes Larb^d Quarter about a Cable and half from the Mole Batteries and Commenced firing fore and aft'. A 'Merry Midshipman' on board the *Queen Charlotte* wrote to friends in London two days later: 'Well, just as the old lady was going to let fly her broadside, the Admiral, I suppose, had some pity on the poor devils; for he stood on the poop, and motioned with his hand for them to get out of the way – but there was such a crowd that this was impossible, even if they had wished; but I don't suppose they understood what the Admiral meant – at last, Fire! fire! fire! – and bang: I think I saw 500 or 1000 of them bang down in an instant.'[36]

The mole guns were silenced and the town, arsenal, storehouses and ships within the mole were soon burning as the allied fleet fired 50,000 round shot from its 1000 guns, 2755 of them from the *Hebrus*. At 3.50 p.m. the log of the *Leander* recorded that Arthur, 'an officer of the Hebrus, came from the commander-in-chief, with orders to cease firing, to allow the enemy's frigate moored across the Mole to be set on fire, which was done in gallant style by a boat from the Queen Charlotte'.[37]

The 'Merry Midshipman' continued, 'The short and the long of the story is, that in six hours we knocked all their batteries and castles about their ears and eyes, like the last scene in *Timour the Tartar.* When we come home, it would save the public some cash, and give us a little employment, to hire us to clear the way for the new street [John Nash's Regent Street in London]: we should have St. James's Market down in a twinkling. . .'.[38]

By midnight it was over: '12, light Breezes with heavy Thunder and Lightning. Adm^l and Squadron standing out'. The next morning Palmer recorded in the *Hebrus*'s log that a midshipmen and three men had been killed on board, another midshipman and sixteen men wounded. In the entire fleet 141 were killed and 722 wounded, many maimed for life. The proportion of casualties was the worst of any Royal Navy major fleet action, even for that of Trafalgar or Copenhagen. The number of Algerian dead and wounded was estimated at between 4000 and 7000. The Dey of Algier gave in to British demands: 1083 Christian slaves were freed, a promise given to cease slavery, the ransom monies returned and peace made with the Netherlands.

On 29 August, as the decks of the *Hebrus* were being holystoned free of powder, blood and soot, and as shot holes in its hull underwater were being stopped, Captain Palmer wrote a short letter to accompany the battle despatches that were about to leave for London. 'E. Palmer to Edw. Wakefield. Hebrus, Algiers Bay, Aug 29 1816. My Dear Sir, I cannot suffer the Dispatches to go without assuring you of the safety of Arthur. He is the best boy in the World and will one day do you and the Service great Honor. ever Yours truly, E. Palmer.'[39]

CHAPTER FOUR

It Might Make One in Love with Death

PRISCILLA WAKEFIELD CONSIDERED HER grandson Edward Gibbon's £150-a-year position as secretary to the Hon. William Hill 'a respectable and luxurious situation, but unfavourable to principles and morals'. Barely 20, Edward Gibbon circulated at the fringe of Regency society in the spring of 1816, the first he had known without war or the threat of it. Anxious to be seen in the right fashions and conducting himself with the correct etiquette as he visited opera or theatre, took a turn or two in Bond Street or a stroll along Piccadilly, he would have considered himself at least at the second level of Pierce Egan's gradation of London society:

> The NOBLE (high birth; on such good terms with himself that if a *commoner* accidentally touch him in crossing his path, he looks down, with a sort of contempt, muttering, *'D—n you, who are you?'),* the RESPECTABLE (the merchant &c., their *stilted* place in life acquired by talent, or from lucky circumstances, with more *upstart* pride than the former character, and fastidiously squeamish in mixing with any but *upper* customers), the MECHANICAL (honest, industrious, merry, and happy, if not more so in London, perhaps, than the other two classes put together, and so independent in mind as to *chaff* 'win gold and wear it'): and the TAG-RAG and BOB-TAIL *squad* (who do not care how the *blunt* comes or how it goes. *Togs* or no *togs!,* but, nevertheless, who must live at any price, and see a *bit of life*. . . [1]

By a mixture of talent and lucky circumstances and a little upstart pride, Edward Gibbon turned a chance encounter and a glance through a window into love and a fortune. Attracted perhaps by their signs of mourning, he first saw them as they were returning home, the recent widow, Mrs Eliza Pattle, and her beautiful sixteen-year-old daughter, also Eliza, who lived in the house opposite Mr Hill's.

Mrs Pattle, intensely aware of Eliza's charms both physical and financial, rarely let her out of her sight; but Edward Gibbon managed 'by signs from the windows' to introduce himself to the young woman. Mrs Pattle later deposed that Edward Gibbon 'never was invited or admitted into her house with her knowledge'.[2] But almost certainly, before she took her daughter away from London for the summer seclusion, and presumed safety, of Tunbridge Wells, Edward employed the tricks of disguise and persuasion he had perfected in Edinburgh to arrange clandestine meetings with Eliza. He was 'mad with animal joy' at the sight of her. 'Love, they say, is blind. I may be so to her defects, but I cannot bring one to my recollection.'[3] His ardour and interest were returned. And he learned that she was a ward in Chancery: her father, a nabob or East India Company merchant who had made an uncalculated fortune, had died in Macao the previous November.

When the Pattles shifted with their retinue to Tunbridge, Edward Gibbon determined to follow. William Hill saw what he had in mind and cautioned him about the impropriety and dangers of eloping with a ward of Chancery. He also, however, recognised the impossibility of diverting him from his infatuation. His affection for Edward Gibbon and his honed experience as a diplomat combined to produce a solution: he gave him a year and half's salary, plus some arrears – about £250 all told, more than enough to support his enterprise – and waited, on hand as a respectable sponsor to ameliorate the consequences.

Edward Gibbon used some of the money to suborn three Pattle servants: the cook, the manservant and the coachman. Legend has it that Mrs Pattle 'had her suspicions and apprehensions, and to avert the dreaded consequences, hurried her daughter from place to place, trusting, full surely, that the stranger would, losing the scent, abandon all further pursuit'.[4] But however elaborate Mrs Pattle's precautions, they failed. On the morning of 13 July, Eliza, the cook, the manservant and the coachman were nowhere to be found. Mrs Pattle implored two of her husband's old friends to set off in pursuit of a chaise in which other servants insisted they had seen Eliza depart with the young man from London. But these were the manservant and cook in disguise; the coachman had furnished a gig for the elopers to head off in the opposite direction.[5] It was Edward Gibbon's best practical joke so far.

Two days later Mrs Pattle received a letter from Eliza, post-marked Brompton, which also betrayed the Wakefield style:

> Calais. July 14, 1816. My dearest Mother, Trusting the almost unwarrantable step I have taken has not occasioned me entirely to forfeit your affection, I hasten to inform you of my safety, also ere this reaches the dear hand for which it is destined I shall be a wife, whose I need not say. . . . You perceive by my date we are across the water but do not write to me till I do so again as we are still moving, our destination is uncertain. This will be a great privation to me but it must be so for a short time, therefore for God's sake do not let my hope of your forgiveness prove deceitful for till then I must

> remain your unhappy but affectionate daughter Eliza. P.S. . . . Oh! for heaven's sake forgive me and then I shall be quite happy. It only rests with you. . . . [6]

Mrs Pattle went to London to see Hill, who confirmed the elopement and his role but who presumably did not know, or did not let on, where Edward and Eliza had gone. Hill mollified Mrs Pattle's fear and outrage, spoke so highly of Edward's qualities and prospects, the sincerity of his ardour and good intentions that she was already half conciliated. And she knew of her daughter's responding passion and the good chance that by now Eliza's 'I shall be a wife' meant at least *in copula*.

Edward and Eliza, ignorant of William Hill's successful blandishments and fearful of being overtaken by the Lord Chancellor's agents before a legal marriage had taken place, took a circuitous route north, travelling as brother and sister. Edward Gibbon was reputed to have turned up at his Aunt Bell's house in Ipswich in the middle of the night asking for a boat in which he rowed Eliza up the River Orwell 'to a place of safety'.[7] Priscilla Wakefield's journal confirms that they passed through: 'July 14. The excellent Sermons of Dr Watson, Bishop of Llandaff interrupted by the news of the arrival and departure of two fugitives in whose welfare I am deeply interested!'

They were headed for Edinburgh, a 500-mile journey from Tunbridge which would have entailed travelling for the best part of a week when macadamising of the turnpike roads had scarcely begun and the best post-chaises did not average more than 5 to 6 miles an hour. The attraction of Edinburgh was twofold: Edward Gibbon had friends there and, from school days, he knew that a marriage in Scotland 'could be proved valid if the consent was merely heard by any one witness who was prepared to say so later in a court of law – "the ostler, or the chambermaid, or the post boy"'.[8] There was no need even to go through a ceremony.

But Edward and Eliza wanted to do things properly. Arriving in Edinburgh about 20 or 21 July, they took lodgings at St Leonard's Hill and Edward went to see the hosts of his Edinburgh High School sojourn five years before, Mrs and Mrs James Gray. 'The worthy lady, mindful of the former frolics of the young man, reasonably entertained some doubts as to the character and merits of the female' Edward Gibbon had with him and sent her son David to the lodgings, where he found 'the most beautiful young creature he had ever beheld, and her language and accomplished manners were such, as at once convinced him that she was a virtuous young lady of rank and education. She was . . . so dejected by fatigue and anxiety of mind, that he hastened with the welcome report to his parents.'[9] On 27 July, at St Cuthbert's Church and with the Gray family as witnesses, Edward and Eliza were wed by two Scots ministers.

There is no word or evidence to indicate that Eliza Pattle was other than a willing party to the runaway marriage, nor that she ever regretted it. It seems certain that Eliza was swept away by Edward's passionate and worldly plausibility, the determination and ingenuity with which he carried out the entire enterprise. She was pliant, willing to become his 'own creature, whose mind would in time take just what impressions I pleased'.[10]

Edward Gibbon's initial actions may have been motivated by hopes of a fortune – later he certainly became obsessed with making the most of it – but the unwavering evidence of his private correspondence attests to his utter devotion to a wife who swiftly lost all her past identity, even her name, for 'my dear Nina was perfect'.[11] And as Tennyson wrote, in an age when wife and property were sometimes indistinguishable, 'Thou can love thy lass and her money too.'

The couple returned to London immediately. At first, 'her mother refused to be reconciled to her',[12] until Edward Gibbon exerted his charm and persuasion. Seeing their mutual devotion, unable to annul the fact of a legal Scottish marriage and probably learning from her daughter that it had been consummated, Mrs Pattle acquiesced – provided they repeat the marriage directly in Church of England form, around the corner at St George's, Hanover Square. This ceremony took place on Friday 16 August.[13] Soon after the wedding, Priscilla wrote to Catherine: 'I am charmed with your account of Eliza, and pleased that she has been introduced to our Tottenham friends', adding with unconscious irony, 'but am hurt that Edward does not repose the most tender confidence in a father that has done so much for him'.[14] Except for Felix, who was to have little option, no Wakefield boy in either generation reposed any confidence in their fathers over questions of marriage.

For Francis Place, the elopement was almost the last straw: 'Wakefield is an ass, he went to Brooks's and then . . . began boasting of his [Edward Gibbon] being a fine young man, of his wonderful feat and still more wonderful character which got him through with the Chancellor, and got for himself more than he bargained for . . . .' And the wedding caused more vituperation:

> Wakefield has brought up all his family [for the wedding] and is hiring beds &c for their use, he is mad – stark raving mad, Edward must borrow £1000, no matter at what loss – they have no money, Hill is off, numerous demands are made, and they must have food and clothes, according to their real or supposed rank, here is comfort and happiness, the produce of order and regularity and morality with a vengeance, how few are the people who ought to be allowed to have children, and what a fine display of divine wisdom in permitting such things.[15]

James Mill tried to calm him down – 'You must treat Wakefield [Edward] on this subject a little gently who chiefly fails through an infirmity of your own of blabbing out whatever visions form themselves in his brain – those which form themselves in the hard part as well as those which form in the soft part'[16] – but Place's concern for the Wakefields persisted a little longer. Two months later he told Mill, 'Wakefield will be with you in a few days . . . . you must put your hand to the work, so long as his head is wrong his conduct cannot be right, and when one sees a large family in imminent danger of being ruined, it becomes a duty not to be neglected to endeavour setting him right'.[17] Appealing to philosopher Mill's belief in the efficacy of education on character, Place told him that Wakefield was a 'believer in innate propensities' that would break out regardless of any kind of training. Place considered this 'pernicious' belief simply a way of Edward Wakefield finding an excuse for his children's follies and saved him 'the labour of thinking . . . . I have given his notions a racking and if you will but work a little at the ram, they will soon fall into a heap of rubbish.'

Place severed connections with the Wakefields about 1822 but in October 1817, in his last reference to them in a letter to Mill, he had already lost patience.

> Wakefield – I did not intend saying any thing of him . . . But as you will not be satisfied without something more, let me tell you that the older he grows the foolisher he grows – You – yes You – cannot [know] how ridiculous he has been making himself appear to all my family – laughing at his own folly & crying from mere childishness (as we say of the children) 'all in a breath' – Edward & Dan – Dan & Edward – and Mrs Pattle – and Edwards wife . . . and his want of a wife for himself – but she must have money – and be young – and handsome and one who has these recommendations will not have him . . . then for a climax inordinate exultations at 'Edwards luck' in marrying a fortune – and little less at his having inspired all his boys with the same notions, all are intent on getting women with fortunes.[18]

By this time Place, who had worked for seventeen years from 7.30 a.m. until 9.30 p.m., six days a week, to put together his fortune of £30,000, would have learnt that Edward Gibbon, EGW,[19] who had used trickery to run off with a nubile heiress, had manipulated £70,000 from her father's estate.

Little more than a fortnight after EGW's London marriage, the Lord Chancellor had made 'the most liberal settlement on his ward's husband that had ever been remembered in the records of Chancery'.[20] An income of £600 a year had been settled on EGW, from the late Thomas Pattle's estate; this would be paid out twice a year, with the first instalment due the following February. Further, he was invited to make his own suggestions for a proper settlement when he came of age on 20 March 1817 and these would be taken into account once the full extent of the Pattle estate had been proved. Pattle himself had believed himself to be worth £90,000.[21] The unheard-of speed with which the first stages of the marriage settlement had been made must be attributed to the good offices of William Hill, the affectionate persuasions of a loving daughter and the flattering promises EGW made Mrs Pattle.

In September the newly-weds departed for Italy, with Mrs Pattle a fixed and dependent member of the new ménage. EGW was to be attached to the Hon.

Algernon Percy at the British Legation in Turin. Before they left they had time to visit Priscilla. Soon afterwards she wrote to them jointly that 'the tenderness she had felt for Edward Gibbon in his infancy had "ripened into a mutual friendship not very frequent between grandmothers and their grandsons", and continued with assurances of loving regard for Eliza herself, from whom she had already "experienced every mark of tenderness" '.[22]

The removal to Piedmont got off to an almost fatal start. En route in Avignon, around mid-September, Eliza 'was very near dying of a miscarriage'.[23] While EGW went on to Turin, Eliza stayed with her mother in Genoa for two months to recuperate properly. Conflict developed between the separated households which threatened the stability of the new marriage and to imperil the right settlement outcome for EGW. Much of this was fomented by the extraordinary behaviour and influence on Mrs Pattle of her servant, apparently caused by both jealousy and drug addiction. On 11 November EGW wrote to his father, 'Nothing can be effected while such a bitch as Miss Lawes remains. She is the plague of our lives from her folly, vulgarity and dreadful paroxysms of passion.'[24] A few days later he added, 'She took poison . . . because I would not introduce her at Court and she told Mrs P. she did it to make her unhappy . . . . Luckily she is accustomed to immense quantities of laudanum, which she drinks as I do water and as she does brandy.'[25] By 23 November EGW was reporting that 'My wife is impenetrable to all the shafts of Miss Lawes's malice and entirely sacrifices her mother for me; but no insignificant disagreements take place between Eliza and her mother upon various subjects, particularly in consequence of Mrs P's reproaches and sarcasms about duplicity etc. at Tunbridge Wells'.[26]

At the end of November EGW crossed the Apennino Ligure to escort his extended family to Turin, in time for the Carnaval, leaving Miss Lawes behind. Another three months passed before she was sent on her way to England, and it took almost as long for EGW to rid himself of the *bête noire* in his own household, his manservant Clouting, who was proving 'an ungrateful scoundrel. . . . He steals wine and other things, swears till he is black in the face that another servant is guilty . . . He builds upon his knowledge of different circumstances which took place at Tunbridge Wells and thinks I dare not discharge him. I tell you all this that his lying complaints in England may not be attended to on his return.'[27]

Despite his lack of 'tender confidence' in his father before the elopement, EGW now depended entirely on him as a trustee to negotiate favourable marriage settlement terms in London. But early in the voluminous correspondence between them that now ensued, EGW stood on his dignity as a married man. In October 1816, Edward reprimanded his father for writing to William Hill in Turin, his second trustee, in paternalistic terms: 'I beg that I and my wife may not for the future be the subject of any correspondence between you and Mr Hill. I am sorry, very sorry to use this sort of language to you . . . . but I cannot have this nonsensical interference in my affairs. Why am I to be looked upon as a fool or a baby because I have been wise or foolish enough to marry?'[28]

Insecurity, anxiety and some petulance characterise most of EGW's surviving letters at this time as he tries to adjust to marriage and cope with his mother-in-law, an unwelcome but unavoidable player in the settlement negotiations: 'The difference between my marriage being a good thing for me and a very indifferent one depends upon the temper of Mrs. P. . . . I am determined not to live in purgatory upon the hopes of what she may leave me, but I will treat her well in proportion to what she gives me.'[29] By December he could almost see his 'way clear to the possession of £100,000',[30] but settlement, and adequate cash flow to live on and to minister to the needs of Mrs Pattle, plagued him for another eighteen months. 'I am at the whole expense of the establishment and I cannot treat Mrs P. as I would my wife who would gladly live upon a bone with me.'[31] He ascribed his indebtedness entirely to her 'usual expensive habits', upon spending 'a great deal to amuse a certain person and prevent her starting for India'.[32]

A 'natural' Eurasian child of Nathaniel Middleton, a Bengal civil servant, Mrs Pattle yearned to return to the pleasures and high life of her youth. Now a 'healthy woman of forty', she had begun to think of remarriage after a year's widowhood. The memories of an old flame waxed warm: 'Heat kills her, and yet she pants for India. The smooth-faced fellow whom she does not expect perhaps to find much changed will grievously disappoint her matrimonial expectations when she sees his yellow bilious face and hears the hollow voice which the ravages of 20 years' heat and bile have given to his almost rotten carcase.'[33]

EGW's unreliability and duplicity are revealed in a letter he wrote to grandmother Priscilla on the subject of Mrs Pattle in February 1817:

> I thought I should never like her, but a week's stay in her house greatly altered my opinion. Since then, her great and admirable affection for her daughter – I may call it devotedness – has quite gained my heart; independent of her many other good qualities, which I never heard her allowed her by her relations in England . . . . I do all I can to make up to her the want of friends she now experiences, and I am in hopes that her daughter's marriage will not turn out, what she first supposed it, a lamentable event.[34]

Yet six months later, when EGW wrote to his father, Mrs Pattle had 'but one passion, and that is vanity'.[35] She 'forms friendships with nobody. Conversation is irksome to her . . . She . . . does nothing but dress herself three or four times every day. All this feeding of ennui I was obliged to destroy in order to get the settlements signed and it cost me God knows what.'[36] Notwithstanding, 'we are on the best possible terms, but she has never forgiven me at bottom'.[37]

In that same February letter to Priscilla one can almost see his slyly affectionate smile as he writes with a flourish, 'I was very sorry to hear by my father's last letter that you were so unwell; but I am in great hopes that he has frightened himself without much cause. I was going to say, "as usual." "Fie, for shame," you will say, "to discredit what your father says." But then you know I do not always mean what I say or write, and this I may clearly apply (rather advantageously to myself) to many of my many tirades against him.'

While EGW was engaged in domestic manoeuvring with his mother-in-law, he pleaded with and exhorted his father to get the settlement fixed to his best advantage. He cursed what he saw as attempts by Mrs Pattle's half-brother and the other executor of her husband's will, Hastings Middleton, to influence her in favour of the Middleton and Pattle families. He became paranoid about his letters being opened in London by untrustworthy clerks and beseeched his father to use no lawyers other than his Uncle Daniel.

In the midst of all this, in April 1816, he badly injured the muscles and tendons of his right leg while horse riding. Doctors ordered him 'cataplasms – hot baths and bed for two months at least. I am to be lifted in and out of bed by servants . . .'.[38] His work prevented such a régime and he hobbled about lame for three months. Soon after, in July, he took off for Venice until the settlements arrived, a journey he insisted later was 'absolutely necessary' and without which they would 'never have been executed'.[39]

The reasons are now lost but the entire affair of the settlements reveals how well developed, at an early age, were EGW's complex and unscrupulous methods of intrigue, manipulation and cajolement to gain his own ends – and at whatever cost to his health and sanity. The trip to Venice brought on a violent bilious attack that laid him up again, for a month. 'I will one of these days enter into an explanation of all the circumstances which led to my anxiety about the settlements,' he told his father, 'but at present I am too weak, and I don't know whether the whole had not better be buried in oblivion as it would only make you change a favourable opinion you have formed.' But he had 'never done any thing without the best advice and that I have had to do with the devil'.[40]

At last, in September, the settlements were signed to EGW's great advantage. The late Thomas Pattle's estate had been proved at £163,769. From this, the large sum of £70,000 was settled on him in the form of a trust fund from which he was entitled to the interest and dividends for life, provided he supplied Eliza with £200 a year pin money;[41] she would inherit £30,000 herself when she reached 21. Mrs Pattle had already received £20,000 on her husband's death and would now also receive £2,000 a year.

The trust fund could be used to buy property, enabling him to further his ambitions which, by the end of 1817, had become focused on a parliamentary career. But,

> I shall not find anybody inclined to put me into Parliament for my £70,000.[42] Even if that could be done I should not think of bringing my family to England, for till I have more fortune I can take advantage of but few of the benefits attending a seat in Parl$^{t.}$;

> but as a single man. You will perceive this when I write that single word Society, for without proportionate fortune I cannot introduce my wife . . . I feel confident of a certain power of speaking in public if my lungs are strong enough, and look forward to a seat in Parliament as the only thing to raise me and my family to anything like what my ambition proposes for them.[43]

He admitted the colour of his politics from Genoa soon after his twenty-third birthday and, not unexpectedly, they had been hued by his most important mentor, 'a regular Church-and-State Tory':[44] 'Mr Hill's political sentiments (or party sentiments, if you please) are so well known that no doubts can be entertained as to those of his secretary, who has lived with him for five years and who never thought of politics till he saw him'.[45]

For nine years from the time of his marriage settlement EGW, with the unremitting assistance of his father, sought to somehow buy into the favour of a borough. There is no trace of any Wakefield backing for the great parliamentary reform movement that steadily gained momentum from this time, bringing about the Reform Bill of 1832. The Wakefields supported the establishment status quo and EGW's stated allegiance to William Hill's politics was by way of giving his father the assurances he needed when negotiating for purchase of a Crown property in Radnorshire. As a land agent and estate steward, Edward Wakefield was in a good position to assess promising properties, though his suggestion of an East Anglian estate did not find favour. Remembering the feverish horrors of his childhood, EGW wrote, 'For God's sake don't place me in the fens.'[46]

Although EGW's earliest views on English politics were reactionary, or at least conformed with the views of his employers and sponsors, he was more independently clear-sighted about the political state of Genoa as part of Piedmont. In early 1818 he advised his father that he had almost finished writing 'an account of the political state of the Duchy of Genoa since its cession to the King of Sardinia',[47] which he estimated would fill a book of 'from 250 to 300 pages octavo'. He wanted Edward to find someone who would publish it anonymously since his views would undoubtedly be diplomatically controversial. The manuscript was never published and has not survived, but he stated that, while supporting the cession after the Congress of Vienna, 'we have allowed the King of Sardinia to pursue such a system of government as will inevitably make the Genoese more inimical to us, and more friendly to the French, than they would have been if the ancient Republic had been reestablished'. And, he continued, 'You will find it difficult to believe the history of all the stupid and abominable regulations (for there are no laws) by which this country is governed . . . .' He sent a duplicate of his letter separately since he feared it would not pass through the post office unscathed. Earlier, he had written, 'We are not amused here by political squabbles of any sort. Everything proceeds in the well beaten track of silent despotism. All public measures are enveloped in a cloud of mystery which none even attempts to dissipate. The most bold sometimes parody the Scripture by exclaiming "Good Lord, deliver us". The having written unpublished such a sentence would in this country infallibly condemn the author to the galleys.'[48]

After March 1817, the Wakefields spent most of their time in Genoa, avoiding the cold and sober upland Piedmont capital of Turin in favour of the warmth and light of the Riviera. And whatever he thought privately about the local politics, EGW and his Eliza were well distanced from their realities as they moved with ease and enjoyment through an enclosed world governed by diplomatic protocol and furnished with all the social graces and niceties. Although he complained about the cost of pandering to his mother-in-law, EGW did not reduce his own household below the level that William Hill's expectations or his own dignity allowed, and was consequently always in debt. Not only Mrs Pattle needed pampering: Eliza – Nina – also could not manage without somebody to wait on her at table.[49] In October 1817, EGW rejected his father's suggestion that they return to England because of the increased expense: Eliza could not 'in England enjoy half the luxuries which I now obtain for her'.[50]

EGW had to have the right dress for his position and pestered his father for months after his arrival in Piedmont to despatch his uniform from Weston's of Bond Street and his helmet from Wagner's. The young English peacock was then properly togged out to be a regular arbiter of diplomatic taste. In December 1818, this almost led to the loss not only of his job but also, potentially, his life. At a function in Genoa for the Grand Duke Michael of Russia, EGW drew the attention of a visiting Welsh linen draper to that fact that he was improperly dressed for the occasion. Insulted by his tone, the Welshman challenged him to a duel. EGW's aristocratic betters laughed at the idea of his giving satisfaction to a mere linen draper, but the Welshman then insulted him publicly and there seemed no alternative for EGW but to resign his post and meet the man somewhere outside Genoa. When all seemed lost, the Welshman withdrew, just as William Hill rushed over from Turin to settle the matter. In Hill's formal letter to the draper, he described EGW as someone 'who has long had my entire confidence, [and] who, when Mr Percy and myself have been otherwise occupied, has sometimes conveyed my wishes and sentiments even upon important affairs to persons of the highest rank . . .'.[51]

William Hill thought as highly of Eliza. In 1823 Edward Wakefield wrote, 'She lived with him for four years as a daughter, and he thinks of her just as I do, describes her excellent acute sense, and yet the kind, reserved way; she never forced it on you, but left it to you to find out; he talks of her gentleness, relates the impression which she made upon all his friends. . . .'[52]

The young couple were devoted to each other and for EGW, his dear Nina had 'the right position of her heart'.[53] Eliza's submission to EGW's role as master of the house and marriage was unquestionable: 'What a lovely thing it is to marry and be so happy as to wish for nothing. Edward, too, is happy in seeing that he has made me completely so. . . .' She was more than content to be a 'happy wife and mother, quite convinced that I have but to look on the being I love best to find a happy smile ready for me'.[54]

Eliza became pregnant again in February 1817 and by September EGW could announce to his father, that expert in pregnancies, that she had 'grown large enough to satisfy even you'.[55] They were in Turin at the time, and EGW was anxious to remove Eliza to the better climate of Genoa before her confinement. At the beginning of November he escorted her as she was carried over the mountains in a sedan chair and their daughter Susanna (for his mother) Priscilla (for his grandmother) Wakefield, forever known as Nina, was born on 4 December without complications.

Within a week EGW reprimanded his father 'that as a father of a family I must maintain my dignity and demand attention to my wishes in what at least regards my own affairs. I dare say you call to mind what you were at my age.'[56] Yet, in some ways, he was 'sorry to have children: it will cripple half my schemes for my younger brothers'. Six months earlier, he had written, 'I am more anxious than ever for the well-doing and well-being of all my brothers.'[57]

The *gravitas* of becoming a father was more than for the immediate child. Although EGW willingly employed his father as agent and adviser, his respect for him as head of the family had long been diminished. His high opinion of himself, reinforced by Edward's 'raptures' about his ability and destiny, pressed him to increasingly taking over this role. It accorded with his new-found wealth, his seniority among his brothers, and their need to also find fortunes to fulfil their expectations of social status and influence.

A vignette of the condition of three of EGW's brothers, not long before the elopement and their mother's death, is included in a letter to Catherine from Arthur, written at Sheerness in February 1816. Their shared stoicism, equanimity of character and faith in Providence stood in calm but clear relief to the impetuosity and amoral opportunism that often governed the behaviour of their brothers. In 1816 Catherine, already an experienced mother of her siblings, would have taken serious note of the opinions of that sixteen-year-old man of the world, Arthur: 'I heard not a very good account of William [now fourteen and a half] before I left Town. I think the way to govern him is difficult, but the right way in my opinion is gentleness not alone in action, but in words – speaking to him civilly – and as little about his great Fault Passion as possible, I mean at the time he is in it, not that I think talking to him coolly would have no effect, on the contrary.'[58] For Arthur, twelve-and-a-half-year-old Howard had '(a) much better temper, he soon forgives and forgets, that is the way to push along'.

Dan, about to turn eighteen, ' is going on well, I think, learning german, ready to go out in a few weeks. I think he is the least like any of us in disposition, though I do not mean he is a bad one, but a character of reserve, I think (more inside than out). I hope he will do well, and it will be a great comfort to us all . . . . believe me your ever Affectionate brother.' There might be expressions of doubt or reservation, frustration or even disapproval among this Wakefield generation, but there was always a steadfast affection, a sense of sharing a difficult life – a common enterprise for family betterment that, in its self-interest, sometimes served to enlighten that of others.

Soon after his arrival in Turin, EGW suggested to his father and grandmother that Arthur should come to stay with him. 'I could give him employment here and good society' – as a decoration he could be proud of – 'and he might easily acquire Italian, besides – all that is necessary for his profession . . . .' But felt that this would be a bad thing unless he was 'quite idle at home and without a prospect of employment'.[59] The memory of his recent combat of faith with EGW still loomed in Arthur's mind and it is possible that he decided against travelling to Turin or Genoa between 1816 and 1819 because he wished to avoid his older brother's overweening influence. EGW regularly complained of Arthur not coming to stay in Piedmont and dryly commented, 'Arthur often writes to me very proper letters.'[60]

This was an uncertain time for Arthur. The crew of the *Hebrus* was about to be paid off after its return from Algiers, preparatory to the decommissioning and sale of the frigate in 1817. There was no immediate chance of a posting for him and, though he had completed six years' service with distinction, Captain Palmer lamented he was still not old enough to get a commission.[61] It is unclear how he was employed for the eighteen months from November 1816, but it seems he undertook some shore training and it may have been during this period, his longest sojourn on dry land, that he undertook a 'thorough examination of the French naval arsenals of St Servan, L'Orient, Brest and Cherbourg',[62] and gained a better understanding of the language, perhaps in the employ of Captain Schomberg of the *Nisus*.

Palmer, though now on half-pay himself, continued to do what he could to further Arthur's career. When the number of the fleet's actively employed officers was being pruned to no more than 600, advancement in the navy still depended on recommendation and preferment, and Arthur, despite his manifest ability and courage, had neither title nor money. Palmer wrote to him in Paris in February 1818:

> Much pleased to find you are going on so well & with so much profit to yourself: you must continue to make the best use of your time and Sir G. Campbell will, I trust, assume the Portsmouth Command ere long which will call you over. It is impossible you can have a stronger recommendation to Sir George than that of Lord St Vincent

> and I am persuaded you will lose no opportunity of cultivating his good opinion.[63] Sir George is one of household of the Prince Regent, & if a Royal visit is paid at Portsmouth, a small promotion may arise out of it, of which the Admiral will have the nomination.[64]

Three months later, Campbell did assume the Portsmouth command and Arthur was posted to the *Queen Charlotte,* the first-rate flagship veteran of Algiers. On 15 May, just before taking up the post, he was baptised into the Church of England, a sincere expression of faith that also did him no harm in seeking a commission. He was joined that day by Dan: both had followed the example of Will who had been baptised in January.

In December Arthur finally passed his lieutenant's examinations, causing EGW to both rejoice from Genoa and express disappointment that he still could not find the opportunity to visit him.[65] For Arthur had consequently received a posting to the *Superb,* a 74-gun third-rater bearing the broad pennant of Commodore Sir Thomas Masterman ('Kiss me') Hardy and bound for the South American Station in July 1819. In diplomatic and consular activities, Arthur attended Hardy as his flag midshipman; he had to wait two more years, until his majority, for formal promotion to lieutenant.

From Turin in November 1816, EGW also thought that Dan should stay with him for a month or two because it 'would be most beneficial to him, and particularly in what he greatly wants – a brushing up, vulgarly speaking'.[66] He could also be of use. He intended making Dan 'work hard . . . and at accompts too. I can give him some that will puzzle him and do him a great deal of good' before he forwarded him, like a package, by 'some courier to Frankfort'.[67] If Arthur thought Dan reserved then EGW, like Place, seemed to consider him something of a plodder and decidedly rough round the edges. When Dan arrived at the end of November he thought him 'much improved in some things, but not in point of manners. He has associated with low clerks at Amsterdam and all his leisure time has been spent with them at Coffee Houses, bawdy houses etc. . . .'[68]

Dan was not to be so easily packaged and, after a short stay at Turin, decided that travel came before work. But his first attempt to set off for Naples was delayed: 'Dan . . . has not yet left Genoa . . . he has been very ill owing to a kick from a horse – for I have been teaching him to ride and he comes off but badly'.[69] When he did get away, he fell off a cliff at the Pozzuoli caves of Nero near Naples, 'a distance of above a hundred feet',[70] according to EGW. He bounced off a rock on his descent, which fortunately deflected him into deep water, and he was able to swim ashore; there he passed out and was carried to safety by local fishermen. Back in Genoa at the beginning of May, EGW reported, again, 'He is much improved', though whether from the physical or moral consequences of the fall is not clear; and he decided Dan 'has travelled enough. Steady employment is what he wants – or he will be unhinged for ever.'[71]

Dan got his 'steady employment' with William Hill, taking up EGW's routine work during his absence in Venice, and while he remained in bed with his bilious fevers afterwards. In the middle of September EGW wrote to his father,

> He fully expects that he is to return to England as soon as I am well, and to do whatever you choose in order to qualify himself for your office. He has some leisure time but he reads and Mr Hill has a very good library here. He is not by any means idle but he wants energy and activity. Tell him to do any thing and he will do it; but he originates nothing and is too indifferent about what he does; but he is afraid of Mr Hill and exerts himself for him. I have told you the worst of him and I fully believe that his apathy is physical and not habitual. I consider heavy but not weak, and Mr Gray Bennett who is both heavy and weak has by industry worked himself into a very distinguished personage, so that I have no real fears about Dan.[72]

No physical illustration or description of Dan has survived but EGW's and Arthur's assessments of their brother, and Dan's apparent physical ineptitude, combine to give us a picture of a deliberate, undemonstrative and well-meaning character, capable but quite lacking in flair and, if Place is to be believed, prone to 'sly cunning'. The one letter of his which survives from this period is so banal as to be virtually unquotable, responding only to others' requests or dealing in domesticities: 'Give my love to every body and remember me to Mrs Place. The weather is amazingly hot and disagrees with me most mightily. Do now make Howard stick to learning French. Remind me to Catherine in particular. . . .'[73]

Although barely two years separated them in age, EGW and Dan circulated in different intellectual universes. They could never be close and though EGW might write, 'I will not neglect him, you may be sure',[74] there remained a stubborn edge of resistance in Dan, and fear of his brother's determinations for him: a dull boy trying to find his own place in the glare of the glittering accomplishments of an older brother. Dan lingered on in Turin until February 1818 when he returned to London and, presumably, began working with his father.

In March 1819, EGW was daily expecting seventeen-year-old William to arrive from Paris when he reported to his father, 'Nina, her mother and children are quite well. The boy prospers and some fancy him very like you.'[75] But Edward Wakefield was never to check for himself the purported resemblance of this grandson, another Edward, born in the last quarter of 1818. The infant died before his first birthday and was buried in the Protestant cemetery at Genoa on 1 August 1819. It was the first event in the long trial of tragedy and misadventure, providential or self-inflicted, that was to blight the lives of all the brothers.

It seems certain that the death of baby Edward (and Mrs Pattle's illness) precipitated the Wakefields' return to England two months later. Catherine was called upon for help and from Dijon in October, en route from Genoa to Paris, she wrote to her father, reporting the party's halting progress and giving instructions for their arrival. Her letter provides a rare insight into the character of the family and Catherine's domestic efficiency:

> We are thus far on our way to Paris, which we expect to reach in a week. We are all tolerably well: that is, Mrs Pattle is lame but still better than we expected; the child [Nina] is not the least hurt by the travelling; and William, I think, is better – indeed, he calls himself quite well, though I know he is not so strong as one could wish.
>
> I write this letter to give you a few instructions with respect to preparing for our return:–
>
> In the first place, have Mrs Pattle's picture put in the dining room.
>
> 2. Have the best bedroom prepared for Mrs Pattle and have a tub put into it for her to wash in: this she is very particular about.
>
> 3. Edward and Nina will sleep in the room next to mine, but the little room by the drawing-room must be prepared for Edward to dress in: it will want a washing stand and looking glass.
>
> 4. Make Yateman change the looking glass in Mrs Pattle's room.
>
> 5. Order the young woman named Sainsbury to be ready to come directly as Mrs Carter will not go to our house at all. If the cook does not manage pretty well with respect to the cooking Mrs Rich must get another as Mrs P. is very particular and also not in good health . . . . Little Nina is a delightful child and will be no trouble to us.[76]

The Wakefields found a house in Westminster but at New Year 1820, the family was gathered in Ipswich. Eliza had received at Christmas *The Ladies Complete Pocket Book*, replete with tables and cab fares, lists of public offices and times of opening, dreadful little poems, short sentimental stories, charades, enigmas and fashionable songs and dances. During the first three weeks of January she recorded events and her feelings:[77]

> I hope that I am a year wiser than in 1819. I find that I am very weak and never restrain myself from giving pain to those dearest to me and in retrospect what would I give to wipe away the ungrateful blot . . . . Dear Edward! Would that I could make thee as happy as I desire and as thy kindness to me deserves!
>
> 4 January: I feel myself much flattered by the attention of such a person as Mrs [Priscilla] Wakefield. One feels oneself much raised by the estimation of persons of strong minds and powers . . . .
>
> 6 January: Dined *en famille* – a large party. Grandmother been married 49 years and still happy . . . if providence gives us such a spell of happiness . . . God grant it may be so . . . .

> 10 January: I believe that I am not so very blameable in longing for my dear Boy . . . Little soul rest thee in peace – I trust that all is for the best . . . .
>
> 20 January: My dear Baby have I forgotten thee . . . I think not for I cherish thee and shall look for thy dear features in the little stranger . . . .

Eliza was pregnant again, the conception having taken place in the consolation of grief soon after little Edward's death. But Providence was not to be so easily outmanoeuvred. On 25 June her second son was born. Three days after he was baptised Edward Jerningham on 7 July, with Catherine as witness, Eliza was buried in the Parish of St Margaret's, Westminster. 'Dear Nina', who had sublimated her entire young adult life to her husband and children, died just four months short of her twenty-first birthday.

A few months later, EGW was finally able to express his feelings to Catherine, who had taken the motherless boy into her care:

> I could not have conceived that returning to London after a short absence would have affected me so much . . . for the four last years nearly all my journeys have conducted me to poor dear Nina's arms, where her augmented fondness has been a full recompense for a disagreeable absence . . . . nothing but a dreary blank presents itself in the place of those endearing caresses and tender enquiries with which my darling Nina always greeted me.
>
> All this is selfish – I know it now, as I foresaw it before. At first I could look back with calmness and even complacency on the past. She, poor soul, had been extremely happy and a retrospect of our connection could not be otherwise than pleasing to me; but now that I begin to suffer deprivations of all kinds from the want of my happy home, the future presents itself in dismal colours and absorbs what little satisfaction I have hitherto derived from a mental recapitulation of past happiness.
>
> These uncomfortable feelings unsettle me extremely: indeed I feel unable to form any plans of life because each view of my future existence presents the same dreary prospect, the same hourly recurring want of that cheerful happy face, lightened up, as it was, by a temper, manners and habits so exactly suited to my taste and inclinations . . . my poor Nina's devotion to me was so great that in some instances my faults became hers from imitation, although her pleasing manner of committing them often gave them the appearance of virtues. . . .
>
> I have had some pleasure in the recapitulation of my poor darling's virtues, and yet the recollection of them adds to the bitterness of my misfortune. Time our oldest enemy will, I suppose, prove my best friend.[78]

CHAPTER FIVE

By Hook or by Crook

CATHERINE WAKEFIELD WAS 'PASSIONATELY attached to her brothers, especially the eldest'[1] and their bonds of sympathy and sorrow deepened after Eliza Wakefield's death. Catherine, at 27, now became the only mother Edward Jerningham was to know; and in 1821 she also took charge of three-year-old Nina, when EGW's tragic household finally broke up. At first, he and Nina had shared a house with Mrs Pattle at Walton-on-Thames, outside London, but within six months she had taken up with Major Alexander Robson of the 19th Foot Regiment. By August 1821 Mrs P. had become Mrs R.[2]

EGW wrote to Catherine: 'I have heard without astonishment that Mrs R. is going abroad. In case she should wish to see the children I positively desire that it be in your presence and never out of it . . . I shall be very glad to hear that she is gone.'[3] For the time being, he no longer needed to humour his mother-in-law, who had refused to co-operate in any adjustments to the marriage settlement that might have given EGW ready access to the £30,000 due to Eliza on her twenty-first birthday. This would now rest in trust for a further 21 years until Jerningham attained his majority, and could not be used to advance EGW's schemes.

Although glad to see the back of her, EGW continued to need Mrs R.'s help in prosecuting a suit in the Prerogative Court to overturn her late husband's will. If this could be proved invalid then he and Mrs R. both stood to benefit at the expense of the other legatees, EGW by raising his settlement sum to £100,000. They joined in mutual self-interest.

As early as December 1819, EGW had sent a long interrogatory letter to the lawyer who, alone, had written out the will at Thomas Pattle's dying dictation in Macao. By this dubious action, EGW hoped to acquire sufficient evidence to show that the will was improperly drawn up and the lawyer was unreliable. He put forward Mrs R., the widow, as the prime mover of the case, but EGW was 'from the very beginning, the effective party opposing this will'.[4] It was to be a drawn-out case with, ultimately, a farcical and expensive conclusion.

No matter how far he was from home, EGW expressed a detailed interest in the care and welfare of his 'Dear little Nina'. During the second half of 1821 he spent some months in the Presteigne district of the Welsh border country, seeking a likely estate and new connections. From 'the solitude of a dirty Welsh inn' he wrote to Catherine in London, where she was caring for his children at father Edward's house in Pall Mall: 'She is beginning to fill up the terrible void created by her mother's death and I feel that I shall not be able to live without her . . . . I must have my dearest Nina with me, by hook or by crook. I cannot make myself at all happy without her. I know that this is a selfish feeling, because she cannot be so well with me as with you; but its very force is a guarantee that I shall do all that a man and a father can do.'[5]

At times, his directions to Catherine for Nina's welfare were desperately over-anxious: 'Let her have her best as well as common clothes, a sufficiency of strong and thin shoes and let some of the latter be of silk or jane with sandal like strings to tie crosswise round her ancles – teach the nurse how to tie them and how to put on and adjust all her clothes neatly and prettily.'[6]

His dependence on Nina had become extreme, reflecting his emotional isolation and disillusionment. After the stress and disjuncture of his childhood, he had found direction, control of his fortunes and unimagined happiness in his four years with Eliza, only to have it all capriciously destroyed. Save for those few years, he seemed afflicted with a kind of congenital unhappiness that could engender neither faith nor trust. Nina now was his emotional life-raft. With prescient fear he wrote, 'She is a dear little soul and I love her so much that I am sure almost that I shall be deprived of her. If that were to happen, good bye to my philosophy. I should think even worse than I do now of this incongruous, contradictory, mottled world.'[7]

There were some points of conflict between EGW and Catherine, especially regarding Nina's religious education. After her grandparents' removal to Ipswich in 1813, Catherine had come under the influence, with her Aunt Bell, of the Reverend John Thomas Nottidge, the evangelising vicar of Halsted, who had drawn and baptised her into the Church of England. 'This was a tremendous crisis in her life. In the acceptance of the Creeds and the Liturgy she found satisfaction for her deepest spiritual needs . . . To her, forms of prayer, whether of supplication or praise were the actual expression of her heart's desires, and this gave an unusual power to all that she said and taught on religious subjects.'

Catherine had found her refuge from the family; a place where she could define herself against the dominating interests of her father and brothers and, in the house of religions, a room on a different floor from her grandmother's. In churchly faith and devotion she could also find some resolution of inner anguish and conflict: as a plain young woman who matured early, her lack of money and status severely constrained her marriage prospects. In a journal she kept during the first half of the 1820s, Catherine revealed 'a true "agonizing" in her effort to live out in daily life the highest aspirations of her soul' – and perhaps in finding a way to sublimate her emotional and sexual needs. Throughout the diary 'there is an unswerving trust in her Heavenly Father, an absolute confidence in Christ as the deliverer from sin, and a practical reliance on the Voice of the Holy Spirit as her guide through innumerable perplexities'.[8]

Catherine coped with much during her growing years. She shed 'many bitter tears' when her father was away in 1809 and the restraining hand of her grandmother may have produced the outbursts of temper that prompted Priscilla's admonitory letter to her in February 1810: 'Every thing in its place is easier than seeking for what ever is wanted. The neglect of attention to order causes loss of time and vexation. – Make those allowances for the faults of others, especially those of temper, of which you often stand in need. – We must not expect too much when we ourselves are liable to offend . . . . Above all, let a sense of duty activate your conduct. . . .'[9]

By late 1817, Catherine was torn between the demands of family in both London and Ipswich. Grandmother Priscilla wrote to Edward, 'Your children are all well, Catherine had need to be divided between us, I do not know how to spare her, nor you to do without her. . . .'[10] She pointed out, a month later: 'Hitherto your girls have cost you scarcely any thing, it is high time to begin to think of them, by industry and good management, Catherine has contrived to clothe herself & the two little ones, but her small income is insufficient to admit of her making a trifling allowance for her sister's board . . .'. By the end of 1817 Catherine's spirits were 'much broken, & not likely to be soon restored to their former equilibrium. . . .'[11] It was perhaps at this time that she gave herself up to Nottidge who was her 'gift of God – a pastor after his heart, who fed his people with knowledge and understanding!'[12]

Catherine's diary revealed the contrast between her life at Ipswich, where she lived in an 'atmosphere of religious thought and habit' under the influence of the revered John Nottidge and his wife – 'My dear Uncle and Aunt', and the atmosphere of her father's house in London where he, EGW, Dan and William showed little interest in religion: 'this was a constant grief and distress to her'.[13] It was both sad and ironic that the two brothers with whom she could most share a spiritual communion – Arthur and, much later, John Howard – were almost never in England. Apart from her journey to Genoa in 1819, she was never to leave it.

Catherine's character, in such great contrast to EGW's, would forever reflect the ingrained influence of Priscilla. As a close friend wrote after her death, 'An abiding and very strong sense of duty produced strictness in her government of all who were under her charge, but to none more than herself. Her character was essentially a strong and matter-of-fact one, thus lacking the charm of a more imaginative disposition, and by many people she was not understood, but to those who once came under her influence and knew of the unselfish pains she took for the good of others, a very deep respect and affection remains.'[14]

The deep bond between Edward Gibbon and Catherine, therefore, seems all the more remarkable. Catherine's unwavering love for her brother endured all the outrage and tragedy that he was to bring upon the family and he, for his part, demonstrated not only abiding affection but also a humble respect for a sister who was his only rock of moral certainty in this mottled world. Despite their disagreement over aspects of Nina's education and governessing, EGW knew where Nina's spiritual sanctuary lay, a refuge perhaps from his own amoral inclinations: 'I shall consider it my duty towards her to let her be a great deal with you . . . . Independently of my wishes that she should continue to love you next to me in the world I shall hardly find any body whose example I should so much wish her to follow as yours or from whom she would be so likely to learn virtuous principles and happy inclinations.'[15]

After five pages about Nina in this January 1822 letter, EGW added a few lines, almost as a footnote, about nineteen-month-old Jerningham: 'I long to see Master Edward for my pride is alarmed at the possibility of his legs being crooked by injudicious walking etc. etc. which are only the phantoms of my imagination. I shall love him bye and bye, I suppose, as much as I do his sister.' If Nina was the substitute for his beloved wife, Jerningham was the agent and living symbol of her death. Many years were to pass before EGW came to love his son and then, perhaps, never without reservation.

EGW's grief did not long prevent an attempt to remarry for practical gain. His interest in the Presteigne district was to acquire an estate large enough to give him a seat in Parliament, probably by making the purchase in favour of one of the great landed families. In the same year that he spent so much time in this Welsh border region, his father was travelling in Wales on estate management business.[16] Presteigne attracted the Wakefields because property prices were low, the local population was small and the area was relatively distant from any urban influences. But though £70,000 might gain EGW a seat through an estate, it would not provide sufficient income – after his obligations to Mrs R. were fulfilled – to maintain an appropriate lifestyle for an MP. The solution was to marry the extra cash.

EGW knew that Catherine could hardly approve, but he was at great pains to explain to her his *genuine* reasons for planning marriage to an unnamed gentlewoman in the autumn of 1821: 'Whilst I continue to pay this tribute to the memory of the only woman whom I ever really loved, or ever shall love in the strictest sense of the word, I can tell that it would be unwise in me to forswear marriage whilst my motherless children, my own pecuniary situation and my inclination to a domestic life lead me to seek for a mother for them and an increase of fortune and a home for myself.'[17]

Catherine would have been most easily persuaded by his concerns for his children: 'they will receive the utmost attention' in a home where 'my will will be a law, not negatively but actively; for I am certain that the lady would at once fall in with my views and that she would do her utmost to carry them into execution'. The woman in question was ideal for his purposes, 'well informed, perfectly ladylike in her manners and has been educated with the utmost strictness .... her principal recommendation with me is that her mildness, submissiveness and tenderness are remarkable'. She was very fond of children and had a 'very large fortune'.

He found it necessary to justify repeatedly his behaviour in relation to the dead Eliza, not only to Catherine but also, it seems, to himself: '"Take her for all in all, I shall never see her like again"'. As evidence that he was not in love EGW explained that 'nothing but perfect coolness could have carried me thus far over the difficult and stormy sea upon which I am embarked'. Because this letter is isolated, without surviving preamble or sequel, it is not clear what or who had embarked him on which stormy sea. Did he attempt to elope again but this time encounter an intransigent father? Did the woman in question prove less mild and submissive than he expected? Did she decline his persuasions once it became clear to her that he did not love her and wanted only her money and mothering? Whatever the case, nothing came of this enterprise and no more is heard of Presteigne. Within a year, Edward purchased for EGW a 220-acre property at Cugley near Newent Woods in Gloucestershire. There would be rents, at least, if no marriage or borough.[18]

EGW's attempted remarriage and his mixture of candid confession and self-interested justification provide another insight into his motivations. Even in a time when property and women were still inextricably linked to the exercise of paternalistic authority and power, EGW's attitude to wives, real or potential, seems to have been unusually chauvinistic and domineering. He was driven by vanity, ambition and an unfailing sense of self-importance: essential ingredients, it could be said, for a successful politician but not for a good husband. Behind the protestations of his letter to Catherine slides the cool conniver willing to employ whatever manipulation or flummery is necessary to achieve his ends. If one loved EGW or admired his ideas, he could be forgiven his foibles; he was hardly the worst in a world still comprising mostly the bought and the sold. But it was also an age of gathering reform and rectitude whose apostles counted moral gain at least as important as the material. If not wholly reprehensible, EGW nevertheless represented a moral ambiguity between the old and the new; to some, he seemed the crippled offspring of his family's philanthropic tradition.

EGW's marital manoeuvrings must have been difficult for Catherine to cope with when she was not only responsible for his children but also beginning her own courtship with a theological scholar. She met Charles Martin Torlesse, two years her junior, at a ball in Bury St Edmunds sometime in 1821, and they renewed their acquaintance at Ipswich when he visited his parents and she her grandparents. They became engaged in 1822, probably at the time he was ordained priest in June.

Charles Torlesse was the youngest son of John Torlesse, an East India Company circuit judge who returned to England in 1784, 'having amassed a considerable fortune in India'.[19] Charles had the Latin and Greek grammars flogged into him at a Chiswick preparatory school that was later used as a lunatic asylum. He often said that he 'should not be surprised if some of its inmates as lunatics might have been there as boys, "with their senses flogged out of them"'.[20] He went on to Harrow, ending as captain of the school, and then Trinity College, Cambridge where he graduated well in divinity in 1818. Steeped in the classics, he seems to have been an amiable, pious and unadventurous man, a creature of habit and tradition. 'He used some of the furniture of his Cambridge rooms as long as he lived, especially . . . an armchair which he always said was so comfortable that when once in it he forgot all his troubles.'[21] Given the character of her father, grandfather and most of her brothers, Catherine could perhaps only have married a clergyman who promised to be utterly dependable and predictable.

Just before Christmas 1822, Catherine went off to Woburn Vicarage in Bedfordshire, with Nina and Jerningham in tow, to observe the work in a parish under the charge of Charles's sister Harriet and brother-in-law, Charles Bridges. In writing to her fiancé, she shared the details of her journey, her thoughts on studying scriptures and told how the reverend couple spent an hour each morning looking out biblical references (providing him with a long list). But her practical and domestic preoccupations soon emerge from the piety: 'I do hope (at least, if I have anything to do with it) that you will not have such a large parish as this; it seems to me an almost overpowering charge . . . . Now I shall tell you, as they are to be your model, a little of what strikes me about their establishment, and I quite think with your mother, that the outfitting for a house as this . . . must cost £500, and nothing short of this perhaps could ensure the comforts you have been accustomed to.'[22] At that rate, it would be at least a cosy, if not a rich, living.

In April 1823, Charles Torlesse became the curate at St Mary Key, Ipswich, but within six months took up the curacy at Stoke-by-Nayland in south Suffolk. On 7 April, Easter Monday, he and Catherine, now almost 30 years old, were married by John Nottidge. Fresh from the ceremony, Edward Wakefield described the occasion: 'She is languid and looks poorly – but has gone through the ceremony really well – when she took my arm to walk up to the Communion Table she trembled badly, but she repeated that part of the service which she had to do, with great firmness, and was with us at a pretty large party at breakfast afterwards. . . .' He went on to talk of his relationship with his oldest child:

> I have formed my Catherine's mind and created an intense intimacy with her long before she became the entire substitute of her angel mother – an event which cloathed her with duties – that she has discharged with cheerfulness and infinite credit to herself – perhaps you may think that the same intimacy may continue in her married state . . . intimate as we shall no doubt continue still, the same intimacy which has been the

> comfort of my life is this day dissolved – this is the painful part of the matter to me, but . . . what a responsibility must I have been – had I by driving away Mr Torlesse condemned her to a life of celibacy and thus deprived her of all the duties and the pleasures and the honors of domestic life. . . .[23]

After two or three weeks of honeymoon at the tiny bathing resort of Felixstowe, Catherine and Charles Torlesse went on to the Lake District (with introductions to Wordsworth and Southey).

Edward reported that the wedding party included his father, sister 'Bell' and family but 'My mother is extremely feeble and we were fearful of exciting her feelings – and therefore did not say one word of it to her until it was all over'. She could now 'do little more than smile'.[24] There were Torlesse relations but no other Wakefields: 'My immediate relations being evangelicals or quakers I have little inclination to cultivate a great intercourse with them.'[25]

The only one of his other children to attend the wedding was 'sweet and tractable' Priscilla, now fourteen years old. The youngest, Percy, whom Edward still considered would 'never live to be an object of much anxiety', was soon to be 'very near the head of Bury school and there never was so small a boy yet so high . . . should he carry an exhibition he would go from Bury to Cambridge with great eclat. . . .'[26] King Edward VI Free Grammar at Bury St Edmunds records a Wakefield, probably Percy, on its roll until 1826. The calamitous events of that year were almost certainly instrumental in his never reaching Cambridge. This poor 'diminutive wretch' lingered on another six years until he was carried away in the first cholera epidemic, soon after he reached his majority.

At the time of the wedding, John Howard was about to go to India. In 1812, Priscilla had dubbed him 'a clever fellow'[27] and after two years at Westminster he had gone on to the Kings Grammar at Bury from where,[28] after four years, he was elected to Trinity College, Cambridge in 1822. But he never attended university, deciding instead, at the age of nineteen, to become a soldier in the employ of the East India Company, probably through the good offices of James Mill. He arrived in India in August 1823 and was posted as an Ensign to the 17th Native Infantry Regiment of the Bengal Army.

John Howard was the only one of the siblings to break ranks, rebelling against family attempts at instruction and guidance. In August 1821, EGW wrote to Catherine, 'Pray persevere incessantly in your present treatment of him. There is no other chance of saving him from ruin.'[29] And in January 1822, 'He must in the long run be turned over to us and I am well pleased at treating him as I have done for he cannot but fear, though he does not love, me and it has been pretty well proved that he will do nothing from affection.'[30] John Howard was perhaps the first to decide that the only way to deal with EGW's domineering behaviour was to 'thoroughly hate him'. There is no record of communication between them again.

Felix had finished at the grammar school and, aged sixteen at the time of Catherine's marriage, would soon be under training as a surveyor and civil engineer with the Ordnance Survey. In 1823 he spent time working on estate management with his father to whom he was 'a most delightful boy, quite the flower of my family'.[31] Edward had in mind that Felix and Dan, who was probably working with Edward full time in 1823, would eventually take over most of his business. William's activities are hard to trace, largely because he was 'so dilatory in writing'.[32] 'Will never answers,' Edward complained.[33] The one letter that does survive from this period shows that he, too, worked for Edward but spent more and more time in Paris.[34] Increasingly he became confidant and assistant to EGW who, after Presteigne, had returned at least partly to diplomatic work.

EGW was in Paris when he performed another role in the theatre of elopement that engaged the Wakefields in the decade from 1816. In the Bois de Boulogne on 26 September 1823, he acted as second to a family friend, Robert Mills,[35] in a duel with the married captain of dragoons who had made off from Exeter to France with his sister, a 'lovely and fascinating lady of high connexions'.[36] In the autumnal mists of the Parisian woods both parties presented and Mills fired but missed. 'Mr De L—sle then discharged his shot in the air, declaring to his second, that "although the measures resorted to by Mr M–lls had compelled him to demand satisfaction, yet considering himself, as he ever must, the original aggressor, he never intended to fire at him nor ever would."' The fate of the young woman is unknown; Edward confided, 'It is a bad affair what must become of the girl.'[37] For EGW, there were fruitful consequences to the duel. He received the 'handsomest letters . . . to thank him for the part which he took',[38] and he was invited to be attached to the British Embassy as 'secretary general and attaché ad libitum'.[39]

Within weeks Edward was writing, 'I fancy Dan will ultimately succeed with Miss De Burgh' and, at the end of November, 'arrangements are making for Dan's marriage'.[40] But, like much of Edward's correspondence at this time, this served to thoroughly embroider the truth. The dénouement came three months later. In February 1824, ten months after Catherine's wedding, six-year-old Nina wrote to her from Hinde Street, Marylebone. 'Papa told me that you are going to have a little baby. I hope you will like it. What will be its name? If it should be a girl, will you name it after me, Nina?' (The child was a girl, named, of course, Priscilla.) Nina also announced to Catherine, 'You have got a new sister called Selina. She is aunt Selina to me. She is very kind and I think she would like to go to Stoke and take walks with you and uncle Torlesse.'[41]

If Dan had not always taken instruction from EGW, he had at least learnt by example. At the beginning of February, having failed to make any headway by regular means, he had eloped with Selina Elizabeth, youngest daughter of Godfrey de Burgh of West Drayton Hall, Middlesex. De Burgh was not amused. He wrote to Edward Wakefield that the first he had learned of Dan's intentions was 'by a letter he addressed to me during the period she was on a visit to a relation at Hampstead; and but a very short period before she came into Somersetshire; in my answer to that letter, I fully and candidly stated my sentiments, and the line of conduct I meant to adopt', which was clearly disapproving.[42] Dan's subsequent conduct had reinforced De Burgh's position (all the following words underlined): 'The marriage has I understand taken place, & in violation of a solemn assurance given me in his letter from Bath wherein he states having given up all Idea of a union with my family etc etc etc notwithstanding which he came at the Dead Hour of the Night, and Eloped with my Daughter; such has been his conduct and by it he must Abide [triply underlined].'

Whether Dan was motivated by love or money, or both, is not known and if he eventually acquired a marriage settlement from De Burgh, it was not of great consequence. But, like all the Wakefield marriages of this generation (except Catherine's), it ended in tears. By 1828 Selina lay buried in the De Burgh vault under the chancel of West Drayton Church with her infant son, Charles.

Edward had not only, to Francis Place's disgust, 'inspired all his boys' to emulate EGW's elopement feat but, as example, had surreptitiously secured for himself a new wife who fulfilled his long-stated requirements that 'she must have money – and be young – and handsome'.[43] The recipient of the long and intimate letter Edward wrote on the day of Catherine's wedding was Frances Davies, daughter of Dr David Davies, headmaster of Macclesfield Grammar School. 'As a wedding letter is not like one upon ordinary subjects I shall think it most proper to inclose this to your father . . . if my expressions are warm – I am sure that both your father and you will attribute them to my ardent and enthusiastic disposition – which directs my pen this morning, upon a subject as to which I am so deeply interested.'[44] He was alluding not to Catherine's wedding but their own.

The date of Edward and Fanny's secret wedding has never been determined, but biographer Richard Garnett, who received family information more than a century ago from the ageing daughters of Catherine, Dan and Felix, states that it took place in 1822 at the British Embassy in Paris and, therefore, probably with the collusion of EGW and perhaps William.[45] An undated letter from Edward to Fanny at the Hotel Montmorency in Paris reveals his attempts to overcome her initial refusal by waxing vainly and extravagantly on his noble connections and income: 'I have spent at least £3000 a year but I now make a great deal more.'[46] This letter is among the first in a voluminous clandestine correspondence between the pair which continued over the following few years as Fanny, after the marriage, was kept moral hostage at home in Macclesfield by her disapproving father and Edward roved England on his estate management work.[47]

By 1823, Edward was 49 and Fanny in her mid-20s. The responses and protestations in Edward's letters show that Fanny was torn between the bonds of her precipitate union with him and her love for and duty to her father. She often keenly regretted the marriage and, with egregious snobbishness, lambasted

Edward for being socially beneath her and seeking to augment his income from her father's resources. To the latter accusation, Edward replied with details of the sums of money with which he was entrusted on behalf of various clients (including more than £6,000 on behalf of economist David Ricardo), totalling more than £76,000, and promised that in two or three years' time he would draw £2,000 out of his business 'for our purposes'.[48] Elsewhere he wrote, 'I think that £1500 a year does nothing in London, a great deal in the country . . . I think that you and I should not spend £250 a year in eating and drinking, this would leave £500 a year for Clothes, pocket money and travelling but this is exclusive of House Rent if any were to be paid.'[49]

Edward urged her to love and respect her father. Ingratiatingly, he wrote, 'Could he ever be brought to let us live together it would be the study of my life to afford him pleasure.'[50] He cautioned her not to leave her father abruptly and advised her to 'throw her arms around her father's neck and beg his forgiveness'– and then talk about settlements later, when he had calmed down.[51]

Edward had also found a partner capable of shocking even his flexible morals. She suggested that it would have been better to have been intimate with Edward without marriage and on another occasion that he should take a mistress while they were separated. Edward replied in the manner of an ingénu: 'I am doubting whether the steps I have taken in marrying you may not make me a very bad person'.[52] 'I could not kiss a woman whose lips I fancied polluted by anothers breath . . . . however painful I am determined to restrain myself . . . I am in this respect perfectly moral.'[53]

When she wrote that she did not love him, Edward declared, 'I believe you do it in the greatest degree and were you with me one week you would enjoy what you call the passion of love to a degree of extacy and madness of which you have not a notion, this is my firm belief and I think that you may do it with perfect modesty.'[54] He began to conclude that they were

> remarkably alike but I can assure you that I am vain enough to believe myself in almost every respect greatly your superior. I have been thinking it over for miles today as I rode in the corner of the coach.
>
> There is I think a strange mixture of mind in you but it is deeply stained with pure womanish weakness which would disgrace a milliners apprentice at the same time . . . you can assume a manly tone of thinking . . . . but this eternal dwelling upon the grades of society is so unlike a person who has lived in the best that I often doubt you. I admire your ambition and to gratify it feel young enough to do wonders . . .[55]

But not as young as EGW whose capacity to attempt wonders would soon disastrously conflate Fanny's ambitions with his own.

In November 1823, Edward told Fanny, with typical vaunt, 'There is little doubt but that Edward will gain his suit which will make his fortune £7000 a year.'[56] EGW's case in the Prerogative Court to overturn the Pattle will was nearing its conclusion and to Nina's letter to her Aunt Catherine in February 1824 he appended a footnote: 'My father will have given you a most melancholy account of me – incorrectly, however, for I do not care about my late apparent defeat in as much as any attack was only a feint. We have appealed and the whole question yet remains open.'[57] These sentences may have mollified Catherine's alarm but they were charged with delusions of hope and defiance. For the judgement had gone badly against him and appeal was hopeless.

Sir John Nicholl, summing up and making judgement in 'a case of some weight and novelty',[58] concluded that no proof was offered that the will of Thomas Pattle was a forgery or that the lawyer who had processed it, or anyone else, had acted fraudulently: 'An instrument is not forged without some inducement; nor can there be a conspiracy without conspirators.' EGW, seeing that the case was going against him, asked 'to let in fresh evidence' of a later will which significantly changed the bequests and would have seen him entitled to at least £100,000. He said that, after receiving a series of letters from an anonymous correspondent, he and his brother (William) had travelled to Paris where a letter proving the later will had been given him by this mysterious benefactor – but only after a solemn promise and written engagement had been given 'neither to disclose his name, nor to give any information which may lead to its disclosure, under any circumstances'.[59]

This story had other improbable curlicues and, though there were transcripts of the key letter, the original had disappeared: 'Mr Wakefield, who always carried it about his person, went one day into the city to his banker's – then walked about the streets – then dined at an hotel; then went to the play; and, at last, discovered that he had lost it!'[60] Judge Nicholl found that EGW, in collusion with Major and Mrs Robson, had produced slight, if any, evidence to prove fabrication and forgery and awarded considerable costs against them for proceedings that had continued for more than eight years. It is likely that EGW and Mrs R. fell out finally over this fiasco. Smarting at the cost but undaunted by the results of the suit, EGW cast about for another way to restore and augment his fortune, with William as his faithful squire.[61]

Failure in the courts, and thus continued shortage of cash, were coupled with EGW's continued failure to find a political place. 'Parliament and office are his first objects,' Edward puffed nevertheless. 'He will go in to support Mr Canning with the full expectation of holding a considerable official situation.'[62] George Canning became Foreign Secretary and Leader of the House in September 1822, after Castlereagh committed suicide. With an election due, he was seen as a likely prime-ministerial candidate to succeed the Earl of Liverpool, whose government had now been in power for ten years. Edward fondly anticipated a place in the

House himself. He told Fanny he was being pressed to stand for Honiton in Devon: she could help him a great deal as an MP by 'getting up facts' for him.[63]

Sometime in 1823, EGW prepared a political article in the form of a letter to the Marquis of Titchfield, a Member of Parliament independent of the Tories and the Whigs, but a sympathetic associate of Canning. Through this article, EGW intended to publicly invite Lord Titchfield to become leader of a new party that would supersede the worn-out older political groupings and genuinely have the confidence of the entire nation: 'the passage of political power from the few to the many is assumed throughout as self evident'.[64] This epistolary manifesto was never published, possibly because Titchfield sickened and died in March 1824, but it seems as if EGW was picking up on a new democratic mood in England.

Continuing repressive anti-Jacobin methods of government, which had brought controls on public meetings and the press after the Peterloo Massacre in 1819, began to ease with the death of Castlereagh and the arrival of reformer Robert Peel at the Home Office. Although Byron could satirise the death of George III in 1820 and say 'the angels all are Tories', they were slowly becoming Conservatives, adapting to the need for constitutional and social reforms, which were driven by the agitation and demands of the working and artisan classes. The divided Whigs represented the interests of the landed magnates and were still a long way off from being Liberals, a pejorative term in the early 1820s. By and large, as William Hazlitt remarked, the Tories and the Whigs were like rival stage coaches which splashed each other with mud but went by the same road to the same place – protecting the vested interests of the ruling classes, short of provoking a popular revolution.

If the use of 'liberal' indicated contempt, 'radical' had become the familiar term for reformers such as Francis Place and Joseph Hume MP who manipulated parliamentary committees in 1824 and 1825 to bring about the repeal of the Combination Acts, thus allowing the legal formation of trade unions. There is no indication that either Wakefield, father or son, supported this key piece of reform or that EGW early demonstrated democratic sympathies beyond what was politically useful.

His attitude towards what was praiseworthy in a society can be gleaned from the letter he wrote to Catherine from Presteigne in August 1821: 'There are no great fortunes in the country, so that there is little or no attempt amongst people of small fortune to rival their betters and all make a point of maintaining a pretty strict equality . . . The farmers and yeomen are obliging, sensible and industrious and are habitually fond of a sober life. The common people appear to be simple and well conducted, having no communication whatsoever with large towns.'[65] The underlined 'equality' is embedded in a description of class order – everyone in his place and a place for everyone – where the 'common people' and their 'betters' have found an acceptable balance for order and stability, away from the radical rumours of the growing 'large towns'. This view fitted well with the providential image of society EGW had learnt at Priscilla Wakefield's knee some 20 years before, and his father's deference to rank. EGW's rush of 'democratic' fervour in (unpublished) support of Titchfield was the first clear sign of his astuteness in recognising the political future, of picking up on power trends that any politician ignored to his peril.

Another unpublished EGW essay from this time expresses an overwrought patriotism that was, nevertheless, genuine. As Francis Place had caustically observed in 1815, EGW recognised the 'visible superiority of the English' well before his majority, and if there was one immutable belief in his political and social thinking, enduring all his life, it was in this 'superiority' of British civilisation and its power for good in the world. In this he was scarcely remarkable, feeling and expressing the overwhelming conviction of the greater part of his countrymen, even those who demanded radical reform. His application of this conviction was destined to lie not in attempting to reform Parliament or the entrenched British class system but in influencing the character of the great diaspora of British civilisation that was soon to take place. But in 1823, when he wrote the following jingoistic effusion, such an idea had not yet entered his head.

> We defy history to show us a country like England where all classes of people have been advancing together in knowledge, prosperity, virtue and happiness. If it be true that our nobles are luxurious, is it not also true that our peasants and mechanics have learned to read? If it be true that we take more pains than formerly about what is ornamental, is it not also true that every day produces some new useful invention? Have not our merchants, manufacturers, farmers and tradesmen made as great a progress in knowledge and virtue as any other class of people in the arts of luxury? Is there not more sterling sense and virtue amongst the people at large than at any period of our history? The attainment of knowledge, virtue and happiness are so many arts, and they have been practised in England, for the first time in the history of the world, by all classes of the people, with equal success. History can furnish us with no materials for the discovery of what may happen to the English people. They may (and, if those who conduct their public affairs do but assist them, they will) reach that point of perfection which shall enable a good patriot to say without extravagance 'See England and die.' Perish then the miserable despondency of those who contend that the decline and fall of England have commenced, and that her bright day of prosperity, virtue, happiness and glory has passed away for ever![66]

In this piece of hyperbole, EGW had again picked up on what was currently moving and shaking English society, industry and commerce. It was an early and crude example of the work of a skilled publicist. He had long shown an ability to persuade with the pen, developed and honed by influencing and instructing members (or potential members) of his family, and in polishing diplomatic missives and despatches. His gift of the gab, his power to attract and ensnare those sympathetic to his temperament and views had also been well practised in the demanding social milieux of Genoa, Paris and London. He had learnt how to charm most birds out of the trees.

Although these years of economic depression and political restlessness were often marked by a miserable despondency among the thinking classes, there were also many, though less extravagantly than EGW, who considered that Britain was on the up and up, or at least capable of reform, improvement and, above all, Progress.

At the first official national census in 1801, when EGW was five years old, the population of England, Scotland and Wales had been just under 11 million,[67] and of London, 960,000. Twenty years later, the population of this united kingdom had increased by 27 per cent to 14 million and of London to 1,250,000; in the next 30 years to 1851 the nation's total jumped 50 per cent to 21 million and London's population doubled. By that year, the city had become the world's first metropolis and Britain the first country in which more than half the population lived in cities and towns.

In the first part of the century, this rapid population growth caused many to fear Thomas Malthus's dire predictions that increasing productivity in agriculture and industry would encourage the feckless to breed faster and – since the growth in human numbers was geometrical but in the means of subsistence only arithmetical – famine, war and disease would prove the only effective checks on overpopulation. Malthus advocated 'moral restraint' as a way to manage population growth. Later, others began to pay earnest attention to the question of birth control, including Francis Place who was involved in propaganda on the subject after about 1823 (and after producing ten living children himself).

From his own peculiar experience of family, EGW was instinctively sympathetic to the idea of personal control but was yet to witness, and fully appreciate, the inequities, miseries and narrowing of hope, created by burgeoning population growth. Malthus's prediction of geometrical growth in Britain proved correct, but this was caused by a decreasing death rate rather than an increasing birth rate. Also no war came to reduce numbers and widespread disease had no marked effects. Even the arrival of cholera in 1832, and typhus epidemics later, brought about effective public health measures such as improved sanitation. Malthus's retribution of famine came to scourge Ireland's population in the 1840s, bearing out Edward Wakefield's 30-year-old warning, but the consequence seemed the final evidence that, if a country's population outgrew its resources, some of it must go elsewhere.

There was Progress, above all, in science and technology which, for EGW, 'every day produces some new useful invention'. Out of coal and iron had come the power of steam and the machine which, in the mid-1820s, was about to become mobile in the railway revolution. Through military victory, its corollary of trading dominance and the well-capitalised self-confidence that these spon-

write, it is so long since I have heard from any of you however your . . . no news good news I will suppose everything [well] . . . I have two Cardinals, or red headed sparrows from Buenos Ayres for Mrs Pattle. You must send directives what is to be done with them. . . .'[72] He sat in a cramped cabin of the *Superb,* moored at Spithead after a 'very tedious passage' home from Rio de Janeiro, admitting, 'I have no idea how things stand'. Clearly, he did not know that Mrs Pattle was remarried and gone abroad. He had been away almost three years: he had been absent when EGW and Eliza had returned from Italy, absent when Eliza had died. He even had a 'box of things for Place', who had cut off relations with his father Edward.

Arthur was preoccupied with the problems of his own world. The *Superb* would be out of commission in less than six weeks and 'The great object is to get employed, but not so much to be merely employed but advantageously – to do this we must not run our heads into the fire, but go coolly to work. Captain Palmer must be consulted first. . . .' There was a little security in half pay when he had no posting, but even on full pay he was desperately short of cash to pay his bills as a new lieutenant: 'The first year is always the most expensive – but otherwise it is a most difficult thing to manage without a considerable sum besides this pay', to cover messing, clothing and equipment costs. And the naval diplomacy of South America had produced no prize money.

As he assisted in the decommissioning of the *Superb,* Arthur attended a public dinner of the Merchant Seamen's Society where a government minister praised the shipbuilding quality and efficacy of the merchant marine. Arthur wrote to his father that he had never heard such a nonsense for 'the fiscal regulations by which the builders of trading vessels were tied down rendered them, as a fleet, the worst craft in the world'. Edward encouraged Arthur to write a paper and present it to Lord St Vincent, his chief sponsor in 1819, who was still alive (just) and now Admiral of the Fleet. St Vincent was convinced and advised publication as a pamphlet, 'the appearance of which,' according to Edward, 'is said to have originated those alterations in the specified build of merchant ships which have since so materially improved them'.[73]

The pamphlet assisted Arthur's career. After the *Superb* was paid off Arthur was appointed, with the continuing support of Captain Palmer, to be St Vincent's aide-de-camp when he attended King George IV at Greenwich. This led, a few months later, to a post on the *Brazen,* a 26-gun sixth-rate sloop under Captain George Willes. Arthur sailed back to South America on courier and escort duties for a year and then returned to the Channel Station to chase smugglers at home. During the second half of 1825, the *Brazen* sailed for Africa.

Although Britain had declared slaving illegal in 1807 and put a squadron of ships on patrol off the West Coast of Africa in 1811, slave trading still thrived. Other countries were slow to come to the party and, even when they did, the conviction and fining of apprehended slavers was made difficult by a maze of maritime and treaty law. Slaving was a lucrative business for those supplying the still active markets of Cuba, Brazil and the southern states of America and vested interests in those countries did their best to legally obstruct the operations of the Royal Navy. The anti-slavery patrols were to continue for half a century, not ending until the Cuban slave market was closed in 1869.

The navy's was a task against formidable odds. First, there was the tropical climate and its diseases: *Beware and take care of the Bight of Benin / There's one comes out for forty goes in* went the old sea shanty. Fifty years later, Trader Horn would memorably describe the equatorial coast of West Africa as 'the most pestilential and fever-stricken coast in the whole world, and has received the well merited name of the White Man's Grave'.

Then there was the strenuous and monotonous task of handling a sailing ship in the fickle airs and calms of tropical seas; of patrolling an almost featureless coast, trying to locate among the mangrove creeks slaving ships that were well armed and often faster than the navy vessels. The latter were heavy, dank, hot and unhealthy, designed principally for service in the fresh winds of colder, northern waters. And there were never enough of them: the African Squadron in Arthur's time comprised just two frigates and three or four sloops and brigs to patrol the 2500-mile coastline from the Gambia in the north to the Congo in the south. Their officers and crews struggled on in the knowledge that 'Neither mountains, river nor deserts will prove barriers to the slave trade, as the black chiefs will bring their slaves from every extremity of Africa as long as there is a nation that will afford them a slave market.'[74]

Yet, like most of his colleagues, Arthur did his best with what he had been given and, while under Willes, he had one notable success. When they came upon a Spanish slaver armed with four guns, Arthur was put in charge of the ship's boats with 25 men and overtook and surprised the ship at a distance of 9 miles from the *Brazen.* Cutlass in hand, he led the boarding party, overcame the 48 crew and freed 420 slaves.

The sight that would have confronted Arthur after overcoming the slaver's crew would have been very similar to that vividly described by the Commodore of the African Station, Charles Bullen, who captured a Brazilian brig in May 1827 with 525 slaves on board: 'I have to assure your Lordships that the extent of human misery encountered, as evinced by these unfortunate beings, is almost impossible for me to describe. They were all confined in a most crowded state below. . . . The putrid atmosphere emitting from the slave deck was horrible in the extreme . . . . all were crowded together in a solid mass of filth and corruption, several suffering from dysentery, and although but a fortnight on board, sixty-seven of them had died from that complaint.'[75] Arthur's Spanish capture was equivalent to about 10 per cent of all the slaves liberated in 1826 but only a token victory when it was estimated that about 125,000 black Africans were slaved across the Atlantic to the Americas each year in the late 1820s.

He may have made a little income from this action. Each freed slave was prized at £10 headmoney. Half of the £4,200 bounty would have gone to the Crown and the other half split between officers and crew at rates set by Prize Regulations, after a percentage had been deducted for the funds of Greenwich Hospital. Then there would have been pay-offs to his agent and probably his commodore. For the Spanish capture, Arthur would have received about £100 plus a small percentage of the value of the ship if that had been taken as a prize. He would make no fortune when such successes were few and far between. In May 1826 the *Brazen* detained another slaver but this time the outcome was less fruitful in every sense: of 245 slaves liberated, half did not survive their ordeal and were 'buried prior to condemnation' of the ship.[76]

It may have been the Spanish capture that prompted Commodore Bullen to give Arthur his first command in September 1826 when the gun brig *Conflict*'s captain was invalided home. The *Conflict* was a fourteen-year-old square-rigged two-master, 84 feet long, weighed 180 tons, carried a crew of 50 and was armed with two 6-pounder cannons and ten 18-pounder carronades suited for close action. A scan of the *Conflict*'s log for the following year shows that, on his anti-slaving patrols, Arthur ranged almost the full length of the West African slaving coast from Sierra Leone in the north to Annobon Island, below the equator in the south.[77] He also ventured out to Ascension Island in the mid-Atlantic where, his log prosaically reports, he buried one of his crewmen and took on fresh water. Often he returned to a base of the African Squadron at Prince's Island (now Principé) in the Bight of Biafra, chosen because of its healthier climate, 100 miles off the death coast, and its plentiful supplies of fresh water, food and wood.

Arthur did not free any more slaves but in February 1827 Bullen gave him the task of taking 21 'Fantee' natives from Sierra Leone – where they had been stranded, half-starved, for four months after being liberated – to their home at Accra.[78] And he was successful in capturing two vessels, empty of slaves, but loaded with goods for their purchase at an estimated value of £40,000. From this, as the brig's captain, he must have collected a tidy percentage, perhaps as much as £4,000.

At the end of 1827, still healthy, Arthur was ordered to take the *Conflict* home after more than two years on the pestilential slave coasts. He may not have been as successful as some more dashing officers in capturing slaves and ships, but he had pursued a tough and honourable assignment with efficiency and purpose and beyond reproach. When he signed off at Plymouth in February 1828, in the refreshing frosted air of England, Arthur set out again to catch up with family affairs. His first task was to travel up to London to visit EGW who, on 27 February, wrote Grandmother Priscilla that she would soon see Arthur who would give her 'a pleasing account of Sierra Leone'.[79] Arthur would also give her an account of how his eldest brother was faring in Newgate Prison, where he had now served the first nine months of a three-year term.

CHAPTER SIX

To Pick the Father's Pocket

FRANCES DAVIES PERSUADED HER FATHER that they should visit Paris for the vacation at Christmas 1825. They would have the company of the Wakefield brothers, attached to the British Embassy and circulating among the 'first society in Europe'. Dr Davies still disapproved of Edward Wakefield's secret marriage to Fanny. The social charms and connections of EGW and Will might ease the way for a reconciliation, although EGW had insisted that he would not agree to communicate with Fanny until she showed his father proper wifely affection.

William had spent most of the past two years in Paris, infatuated with Emily, the daughter of Sir John Sidney. In 1824, Edward Wakefield had told Sidney that he 'deprecated the growing attachment which I observed growing between these young people'. As he could not keep his son away from Paris he recommended that, unless Sir John wished for the union, he should immediately place his daughter under his own protection. 'I daresay your son is a gentleman,' Sir John replied, 'perhaps it is only a little innocent flirtation.'[1]

On hearing of this exchange, William had cut communication with his father and 'two years of uncontrolled intimacy' had led, by early 1826, to the point where 'the world was beginning to say that the intimacy was so great and had lasted so long that marriage ought to take place'.[2] As family friend Phyllida Bathurst wrote to 24-year-old Will ('dearest little Willy O'), Emily had an 'excess of . . . affection' for him: 'Perhaps it would be better for both [of you] if she were less ardent in her attachment; but so it is, and I never saw one creature more devoted to another than she is to you.'[3]

Phyllida Bathurst, widow of the British ambassador to the Court of Vienna, had known EGW and his family since Turin; her late sister had been the 'intimate friend' of EGW's diplomatic colleague and friend, Algernon Percy. In Paris, she had begun to care for EGW's Nina and Jerningham[4] and 'set herself to work most disinterestedly to find rich wives for both EGW and William'.[5] She saw them, accurately, as part of a 'most loyal family at the Shrine of the saffron coloured mantled God [Hymen]'.

EGW was already coupled with a mistress and a marriage prospect but in the overheated salons Fanny Davies would have quickly learnt that 'those who know Paris believe nothing that is said, and say nothing of what is done there'.[6] Phyllida Bathurst's prattling to Willy affords an insight into the preoccupations of her social set: 'Cuthbert is gone. I should have preferred him, and so would she, but he is so enveloped in the icy bands of the little white Countess, that it were in vain to hope that Em would have been really attached, but with the other she has played until she has a little burnt her fingers . . . You alarmed me, I can tell you for she was inclined to you. . . . '[7]

Fanny Davies was exhilarated by the fashion and form, the matchmaking of sex and status. On EGW's immaculate arm in salon and opera foyer, she was overcome by his effortless command of language and etiquette; and by a fresh surge of ambition to raise herself, her socially deficient husband and this fine stepson higher in the 'grades of society'. As talk in the Bathurst drawing room revolved around matches for EGW and William, despite the latter's attachment to 22-year-old Emily Sidney, Fanny lightly tossed in the name of Ellen Turner, only child and heiress to William Turner, the Sheriff of Cheshire, who was just building a new house on the estate he had bought at Shrigley, near Fanny's home at Macclesfield. Turner had made a 'very large fortune by Trade' [silk] which he had discontinued to become 'all at once, a "County Gentleman"'.[8] Ellen was also heiress to her Uncle Robert's fortune; there was half a million there at least, probably more.

EGW was immediately interested. There was an election due about mid-year – his father was planning to stand for Reading – and he could take advantage of the fact that William Turner, as sheriff, probably had a Cheshire county seat under his influence; Fanny's father, as a clergyman and headmaster of Macclesfield Grammar School, was a distinguished figure in the district and this could only help to raise his own credentials; and then there was a local radical issue in which he could take an interest: the 'distress' of the silk weavers. Here, after a decade of frustration, was a real opening: money, a seat in the House, a good cause, a mother for the little ones, a nubile young woman ready to become his 'own creature, whose mind would in time take just what impressions' he pleased.

Phyllida later chortled at Will, 'Little did I think when we laughed with Miss Davies about Miss Turner and I desired her to get her for you or him, that Edward would in 2 or 3 days time [within only two or three days] woo wed and carry her off, but he is born for odd adventures and certainly had he been a general would have carried everything by des coups de main'.[9]

EGW would have crossed paths with Balzac who, from his observation of the Parisian salons at that time, wrote for his character Vautrin:

> You seduce a woman that you may set your foot on such and such a rung of the social ladder; you descend, in short, to every base action that can be committed at home or abroad, to gain your own ends. . . . That man with yellow gloves and a golden tongue commits many a murder; he sheds no blood, but he drains his victim's veins as surely . . . walk off with something or other belonging to somebody else, and they exhibit you as a curiosity in the Place du Palais-de-Justice; you steal a million and you are pointed out in every salon as a model of virtue . . . . Do you believe that there is any absolute standard in this world? Despise mankind and find out the meshes that you can slip through in the net of the Code.[10]

William became formally engaged to Emily Sidney in Paris at the middle of January 1826. Soon afterwards, he travelled to London to attempt a discussion with her father about the 'terms of a Settlement to be made on the said projected marriage'.[11] But he was unable to make any headway and asked EGW to come to England to act as go-between Sir John Sidney and his father. EGW arrived in London on 20 February but talks, or an attempt at talks, with Sidney did not go well and, six days later, EGW and Will went to see Edward at Reading. Edward wrote to Sidney's lawyer on 26 February, putting the case for the marriage and inviting Sidney to a meeting.

In the meantime, Fanny Davies had returned to Macclesfield with her father after the Christmas–New Year holiday in Paris and prevailed upon a common acquaintance to introduce her to the Turners at Shrigley, 'that the first time she made a visit there, she might have the pleasure of accompanying her in her carriage'.[12] Fanny met Mrs Turner but not, alas, her daughter Ellen, who had returned to school in Liverpool only the day before. She would mark her fifteenth birthday there in a few weeks, on 12 February. As the daughter of a headmaster, Fanny asked knowledgeably about the workings and staffing of the school, the quality of its education for young girls of the better classes.

EGW and William stayed only a day with their father at Reading before going north to Macclesfield. In his affidavit sworn a year later, William stated that his father asked him to go with EGW to settle 'certain other pecuniary arrangements' with Fanny's father on which would depend Edward's agreement to Sidney's marriage settlement proposals. William declared that when he departed Reading with EGW his 'sole motive . . . was a disinclination to leave' the person on whom his marriage settlement depended. EGW, in his affidavit, said that he had 'always possessed over the mind of [William] a remarkable and almost unlimited influence' and did not tell him of his intention to marry Ellen Turner until they reached Macclesfield. He pressured William to help him with the 'elopement' against his 'deep and exclusive interest' in his impending marriage to Emily Sidney.[13]

Although William's reluctance to become involved in EGW's 'elopement' is believable, the flimflam in the affidavits verged on a perjury intended, at the eleventh hour, to lessen William's punishment for his collaboration in a carefully planned abduction. It was simply a lie that Edward's approval of the 'proposals of the said Sir John Sydney [*sic*]'[14] depended on the outcome of arrangements with Dr Davies. There *were* no proposals from Sidney. On 4 March, Sidney's lawyer replied to Edward, 'Without a suitable provision for Miss Sidney and any children she may have, he cannot consider even the propriety of the proposed union. Sir John desired me to observe that he cannot estimate on the Talents and acquirements of the young gent as he hath not yet applied them for his advancement in life. Under the circumstances Sir John hath desired me to say further that he does not wish to trouble you to call on him or on me on the subject.'[15]

In his publicly circulated *A Statement of Facts Regarding the Marriage of Edward G. Wakefield Esq., with Miss Turner*, EGW wrote that the idea of marrying Ellen Turner came to him as he was disinterestedly defending her father, whom he had never met, against vicious Macclesfield gossips who considered Turner a vulgar nouveau riche.

> My friend Dr Davies, who is one of the most noble-minded persons I know, was near me at the time. I asked him with a look and manner that begged him to say 'Yes' whether he would join Mr Turner's procession [as High Sheriff to the Chester Assizes]. He answered, 'Yes, that I will, if only to shew that I do not share these people's pitiful jealousy.' God knows why! – I cannot tell – but I exclaimed, 'So will I!' A thought, a wish, a determination, just then entered my head. It was that I would marry Miss Turner myself before the Chester Assizes, and get up such an escort for her father, as must have driven the most bilious of his detractors mad.

EGW's final decision to attempt the runaway marriage may have been spur of the moment, but this was a nice piece of fiction to mollify the outraged father, after the event and as EGW faced imprisonment.

At the end of February 1826, Fanny Davies waited for EGW and Will at Macclesfield with all the intelligence she had gathered about the Turners. At Reading, Edward must have decided that, with EGW's developing designs on Ellen Turner and Will's wedding and settlement in the balance, it was time – after more than three years of secrecy – to complete his own 'pecuniary arrangements' with his reluctant father-in-law. He saw EGW, skilled in the deceits and manoeuvrings of European diplomacy, and experienced in all the manipulations required for marriage settlement, as the ideal agent to bring all three marriages to a successful conclusion. A couple of years before, Edward had enigmatically written to Fanny: 'We are in an awkward scrape and are in that state of risk – that in my opinion it justifies something being risked – and I think parliament the least risk if it can be attained.'[16] Now was the time to take the big risk. Such a scheme had worked before, with the Pattles. And the rewards would be immense: marriages with money beyond their expectations, Parliament within the year. Still in raptures with the genius of his eldest son and drawn on by Fanny, Edward, no matter how nervous, saw that the triangular plot would make the social and political fortunes of them all. Two of the women involved were willing parties; the unsuspecting third, the key to the whole, would be charmed into the gilded cage.

The Wakefield brothers arrived in Macclesfield on 28 February and stayed with the Davies. On 2 March, Thursday, they went riding with Fanny and, after a brief conversation with Turner's solicitor, Grimsditch, visited the estate at Shrigley as part of their excursion. On the following Saturday morning, Grimsditch encountered Fanny, who elicited from him details about Mrs Turner's sudden illness, 'a determination of blood to the head', and the information that both he and Turner would be travelling to London on the Monday. The next day, without her father's knowledge, Fanny sent for her banker who supplied her with £150 that she said was for her cousin; both Wakefields were witness to the transaction. As Fanny signed the necessary papers EGW jokingly asked her if she were signing her will. Afterwards, they went over the details of the plan that the money would fund. 'The apparent impossibility of the thing urged me on,' EGW recalled, 'and I pursued its execution with reckless activity.'

Early on Monday 6 March, the Wakefields travelled to Manchester with EGW's French manservant, Edouard Thêvenot. Here they purchased a green carriage with £40 of Fanny's money and waited until seven in the evening at the Albion Hotel until some minor repairs had been made to it. Twice, Thêvenot was sent back to Macclesfield via the post to check that Turner and Grimsditch had both gone to London. While they waited, EGW concocted a letter from a fictitious 'Doctor Ainsworth', dated half past midnight on the Monday night, advising Elizabeth Daulby, the head mistress of Ellen Turner's boarding school, that her mother was seriously ill and had called for her daughter: 'Though I do not think Mrs Turner is in immediate danger, it is probable she may soon become incapable of recognizing any one. Mrs Turner particularly wishes that her daughter should not be informed of the extent of her danger' so that she would not be unduly alarmed.[17]

At two in the morning on Tuesday 7 March the Wakefields and Thêvenot set off in their carriage for the Liverpool school. Will was dropped off at Warrington en route and EGW alighted from the carriage just short of the school. Thêvenot, drilled in his role as Turner's new servant, directed 'Dr Ainsworth's' carriage and delivered his letter, carrying his part off to perfection: young Ellen Turner was delivered to him with expressions of concern and care from Elizabeth Daulby and her sisters. Thêvenot then ordered the carriage back to Manchester and, in the tension of the moment, completely forgot about EGW. When the carriage pulled up at the Nag's Head at Warrington to change horses, William rapidly gave him instructions to take Ellen to the Albion in Manchester, where she must be told to wait for her father. At the Albion Thêvenot, with great presence of mind, dissuaded Ellen from visiting her uncle, who lived just a few hundred yards down the road, on the pretext that she would miss her father. She tucked into a tart and a custard while she waited. Will hired a chaise and four horses, went back down the road to Liverpool, found EGW and the pair rattled into Manchester at speed just an hour or two later, soon after midday.

Composing himself, EGW entered the Albion parlour and introduced himself to Ellen Turner.

> I thought of the passion of Hatred towards myself that would probably take possession of him [William Turner], of the apparent impossibility of success, of the great danger of the attempt, of the world's reproaches, and of every thing that would have deterred me, had I been in my senses, from committing the act of a madman.
>
> Still, I had not entirely lost my senses; for my determination to marry Miss Turner was clogged with three very reasonable conditions. They were, first, that I should find her to be a sort of person whom I could love and cherish for her own sake; secondly, that I should bring her to believe that she would be happy in marrying me; and, thirdly, that I would not use force, or the shadow of force, nor even put the slightest constraint upon her inclinations, in any part of the adventure.

Instead, a 'consummate master . . . of all the arts of dissimulation and treachery',[18] EGW told the ingenuous, unsuspecting young Ellen that he was a business associate of her father. She had been taken away from school, not because her mother was ill, but rather because of her father's 'embarrassed state of affairs'. Employing all the information about Macclesfield, Shrigley and the Turners that he and Fanny had gathered, EGW referred to local bank failures at the end of the previous year and the difficulties this had caused for Macclesfield business people. Ellen remembered how one of her friends had been withdrawn from her school because her father could no longer pay the fees and how her own father had jestingly said that he might have to withdraw her, too, for the same reason. And now this seemed to have happened and he, EGW, had undertaken to convey her to her father who was waiting for her, somewhere in Yorkshire, where he was attending to further pressing matters.

Ellen Turner must have been apprehensive but EGW declared, 'She was not in the least alarmed, but answered me cheerfully and aptly upon every subject. In ten minutes the carriage was ready. She held my arm whilst I stood in the hall talking to a Waiter, joined me in wishing the Landlady good day, and entered the carriage amidst a crowd of idle gazers, whom my hurried arrival had collected round the Inn.' EGW opened the blinds of the carriage, fearing that 'an appearance of concealment might excite curiosity'. They drove off to Delph, the stage on the road to Huddersfield, with William and Thêvenot outside on the box, and EGW alone inside with the girl.

EGW found Ellen 'tall of her age, and her voice and manner . . . very commanding; her countenance [was] pale, but . . . enlivened by two piercing eyes, and a finely shaped mouth, with teeth extremely well formed and white as to form a fine contrast to her ruby lips'.[19] He had to work fast.

> My great object was to draw her out; to see what sort of mind she had; to learn what had been her education . . . . I soon discovered . . . that she had a vivid Imagination, and a Judgment beyond her years . . . . she felt no alarm in my company because her Judgment enabled her to see and feel the great pains that I took to treat her with the delicate and respectful, yet tender kindness, that her extraordinary situation demanded . . . . A state of high excitement caused my spirits to overflow. She was almost equally elated. We talked and laughed incessantly. Never in my life did I say so much in the same time . . . . Her quickness, imagination, and good sense, astonished and delighted me . . . . She was gratified to discover that I enjoyed the display of natural Wit and keen Sense of the ridiculous, with which she is gifted. Marriages, it is said, are made in Heaven. Ours was made by the first two hours of our conversation.

If EGW's *Statement of Facts* can be believed – and it was a document contrived for his defence – Ellen Turner fell in with the spirit of the enterprise early on. 'I asked her whether she knew where she was going. She said, "No, but I suppose *you* do? and I do not wish to be told. I rather enjoy the uncertainty."'

EGW averred that if he had found Ellen 'ugly, ignorant, and vulgar' he would have seen her safely back to the school, counting on her father not to take the matter further for fear of exposing his daughter to ridicule and prurient curiosity. If she had objected, then he would have sent her home with a chaperone: 'I should neither have appeared nor have written; and I had, by many precautions, taken care to conceal the real Actor in what would have been called "an unsuccessful attempt to run away with Miss Turner".' So, at first, EGW either did not disclose his name to her, or offered the alias of Captain Wilson, which he had used in purchasing the carriage.

EGW prepared Ellen for the fact that her father might not be at Huddersfield: so difficult were William Turner's circumstances that he must be careful in his movements. They might have to travel on together into the night and through the following day to meet him. After Ellen found that her father was not at the George Inn in Huddersfield, 'my supposition of her regret at the thought of our separation was confirmed by her high spirits . . . she *did* continue the journey . . . with every mark of delight at our incessant conversation, and at the hurry and excitement of the whole adventure'.

Most of Ellen Turner's education had been in preparation for the right kind of marriage. According to EGW, she was well acquainted with the marriage service, having 'often read it, little thinking . . . that she should want it so soon'. Here, for the first time and in the most exciting circumstances, she was the complete object of a charming and accomplished man's lavish and flattering attention. 'He is a gentlemanly man, of rather a slender form, light hair and eyes, and is what the

French would call a *bel homme*. His dress betrays a touch of dandyism.'[20] Still with the trust of a child, perhaps stimulated by a frisson of abandon, she was swept on in the exhilaration of the adventure.

At Halifax, the next stage, Thêvenot, 'on whom fright and fatigue had brought on a fit of the gout', remained behind. In French, EGW told him to go back to London and book family rooms at the Brunswick Hotel. 'Do not tell any body than I am married, and go to bed and stay in bed, ill or well, till you see me three days hence.' He spoke to Will in French, too, about Ellen and the next stages of the journey. She knew French and told them not to 'tell secrets' unless they wished her to understand them. Although she must have now half-guessed what was happening, she was probably fearful of the consequences of an attempt to escape – and, perhaps, intoxicated by the growing fantasy of elopement. When the party arrived at the Devonshire Arms in Skipton at ten that night, the keeper assumed, from their laughter and high spirits, that it was a 'runaway match' and invited them to stay on their way back.[21]

Over the moors they rattled and lurched through the night, stopping only to change horses, to snatch a hot drink or gingerbread, at Settle and Kirkby Lonsdale before they pulled up for breakfast at Kendal in the first grey light of Wednesday, 8 March. EGW dismissed the idea that, now *'She had passed one whole night with me!'* he could use this to press her to become his wife without delay. He was aware from beginning to end that sexual intercourse with Ellen would seal their union both legally and in the considerations of the family. Had this not been the case with Eliza?

But here some sense and sensibility governed his actions. Ellen was fifteen years his junior, literally half his age, and utterly unknowing. He had a daughter of his own. He would not be forgiven by anyone of his acquaintance, let alone Ellen, if he did not treat her with the greatest care and delicacy, did not bring her to love him, 'render her the happiest of women' before the ultimate conjugal connection. 'I behaved to her as I would to a beloved Sister . . . with intimacy without familiarity, and with the greatest . . . kindness, but with no more tenderness than any man of feeling would display to a helpless woman, accidentally placed under his sole protection.' There was another consideration: if in the midst of the dishonour of the abduction he could show that he had behaved impeccably towards Ellen, and demonstrate that he had genuinely won her heart, he might also win over the family and society at large.

The problem he faced at Kendal, and on which he had no doubt brooded during the 'dangerous rapidity with which the Yorkshire post-boys drove through the darkness', was how he could 'honourably' persuade Ellen to marry him within the next 24 hours. He decided to tell her that her father was not at Kendal but that a letter had been left for them at the post office. William and he affected to read it near the carriage window. William seems to have said no word worth remembering during the entire escapade, keeping his counsel as was his lifelong habit – though at six o'clock on a winter's morning in Westmoreland, after a day and a night clinging to the carriage box, he was probably incapable of offering anything that made sense.

EGW told Ellen the letter was from the solicitor Grimsditch and that he was now in a position to describe exactly her father's plight. Some time before, Ryle and Daintry's bank at Macclesfield had failed and her father had been almost ruined. He had been saved by an uncle of EGW, a rich Kendal banker, who had lent him £60,000.[22] That had relieved him for a while but now the Blackburn bank had failed, too, and his affairs were worse than before. EGW's uncle was demanding the estate at Shrigley as security for the loan. There was one way out of the predicament which, he said, Grimsditch had outlined in the letter: 'Why, that you should marry me! and then my uncle, if you do, will settle matters between you and me, and it will save your father from being turned out of doors, and all your family from destruction.'[23]

Exhausted from travelling non-stop for 24 hours – and from the endless emotional game-playing with EGW; sobered by fear for her father and mother's well-being; stunned at the prospect that marriage, real and full of unknown complications, might lie only hours away, Ellen tentatively agreed to consider it, but on condition that she see her father before the matter was finally settled. EGW ordered the carriage on to Penrith and Carlisle where, he assured her, Turner would be waiting. William joined them inside.

Arriving in Carlisle about midday, the brothers got out and disappeared inside the Bush Inn for a few minutes. A maid at the inn considered that Ellen seemed distressed but EGW would not let her out. The head waiter had no doubt what was happening and confirmed with EGW that he wanted horses for Gretna Green, less than two hours' drive away, across the border to the north.

As EGW knew from his trip to Edinburgh with Eliza in 1816, English marriages had required the publication of banns since the 1753 Marriage Act but in Scotland they needed simply a declaration before a witness. Since Gretna was the closest place in Scotland to the major population centres of England, a brisk marriage trade had developed in the village. Three 'parsons' had established themselves there with connections to inns in Carlisle. The Bush had an arrangement with Gretna Hall and the old parson-blacksmith David Laing and provided a regular shuttle service along the road skirting the sands of the Solway Firth. The high and the low availed themselves of the Gretna service. John George Lambton, later Lord Durham, had married his first wife there and, eight years before, old Lord Erskine, ex-Lord Chancellor, had tied the Gretna knot with his housekeeper.

EGW ordered the carriage on in a hurry, telling Ellen there was no time to waste. William climbed out on the dickey again while EGW spun the last part of the story to Ellen. He told her that William had found her father with Grimsditch concealed in a small room at the back of the inn; they had tried twice that day to cross the border but the sheriff's officers – the men she had seen about the carriage door – prevented them coming out. Ellen Turner recounted, 'Mr Grimsditch had intreated that Mr William Wakefield would not stop in the room, or they should be discovered . . . . he had taken him by the shoulders and turned him out . . . He said that my papa requested, if I ever loved him, that I would not hesitate.'[24]

EGW continued: 'I swore . . . to make her, as a devoted husband, more than ample reparation . . . . this tenderness from me, and the caresses to which it gave rise, soon restored our cheerfulness . . . . on the Border it was impossible to think and speak of anything but Waverley and Walter Scott, and the last hour of our journey to Gretna was occupied in telling stories of the hair-breadth 'scapes of run-away couples, and in all but boisterous mirth at the anticipated surprize of her Cheshire friends. . . .'

At Gretna Hall, EGW 'in order to gratify another romantic whim, took care that the ceremony should be more formal and solemn, than is either necessary or usual at Gretna'. According to 74-year-old Laing and the other witnesses to the wedding, Ellen was composed and decisive and embraced EGW willingly afterwards. The old parson had put a ring on her finger that was too large and a certificate was signed by him and the innkeeper as witnesses to the couple's signatures. EGW paid Laing £30 and Ellen gave him 20s as a gift to buy the traditional 'pair of gloves'. She was cheerful at the dinner afterwards, as they celebrated with Laing's recommended 'shumpine'.

Whatever his satisfaction, EGW must have realised that his problems had only just begun. He had to get Ellen back to Paris without hindrance, present her father not just with the *fait accompli* but with an explanation and a settlement proposal that would bring him round to acceptance of the marriage. Most difficult of all, he had to convince Ellen that he genuinely cared for her, once she realised that the reasons for their marriage were a complete fraud – that she had, indeed, been kidnapped.

Later on 8 March, as they shuttled back into Carlisle, Ellen was bursting to be able finally to 'throw herself into her father's arms, and to congratulate him on the salvation that she had bestowed on him'.[25] But EGW informed her that the post-boys had carried the good news ahead of them and her father, now at liberty, had rushed home to attend urgently to his affairs. They travelled on as far as Penrith where the three slept in separate rooms. At first, EGW promised that they would go on to Shrigley the next day but then announced in the morning that he had pressing business in Paris to attend to and would arrange for Ellen's father to meet them in London.

EGW and Ellen arrived at the Brunswick Hotel in London about 11 p.m. on Friday 10 March after another two days of constant travel. William was dropped off at Leeds, to go to Shrigley and explain all to William Turner before bringing him on to London. And this is where the plot began to unravel. William could not have reached Macclesfield before the early hours of Friday morning when he discovered that Turner and Grimsditch were still in London. William gave all the details to Fanny Davies and then left Macclesfield on the Friday night. His whereabouts for the next ten days remain unknown, but letters to him from EGW in Calais and Phyllida in Paris during this period indicate that he was lying low in England, perhaps at his father's house in Reading. As William went south, Turner left London for home, conceivably passing EGW and Ellen's carriage on the turnpike as they rattled in on their way to the Brunswick.

Edward Wakefield had visited the Brunswick earlier in the day, to see Thêvenot, who was staying in bed as ordered. With him was a man posing as one of EGW's brothers: none other than Robert Mills, returning EGW's duelling favour. Mills came back later and waited until the couple arrived, telling EGW that his father 'desires that you won't remain in London a single hour, for that you are liable to be apprehended and brought to justice'.[26] This must have been Edward in a typical panic because, to that point, no one outside the Wakefield group knew what had happened.

EGW then told Ellen that Mills had brought the news that her father had gone on to Calais on urgent business and they must follow him there. He ordered another chaise and four to leave in the middle of the night for Dartford. It was this, most likely, that caused Ellen to drop on to a bed and burst into tears, an event witnessed by a Brunswick waiter. The next day, they crossed the Channel from Dover and finally came to rest at Quillac's Hotel in Calais, after five days of continuous coach travel in which they had covered the length and breadth of England.

Either Mills or Edward Wakefield inserted a marriage notice in Saturday's London papers. For the Turners, this was the first news that anything was amiss with their daughter. EGW's forged 'Ainsworth' letter and Thêvenot's part at Liverpool had so convinced the Daulbys that they had seen no reason to enquire further after Ellen.

On Saturday 11 March, before William Turner arrived back at Shrigley, Fanny told her father what was going on and prevailed on him to visit Turner's sister. Fanny wrote to William: ' [She] seems very kindly disposed, but she did not know what her brother's feelings would be. Perhaps Edward [EGW] or *Madame* [Mrs Bathurst] ought to write to her, touching *tender chords*. The old uncles have been written to by her wish.' In a postcript she added: 'You must not let a foolish account of the affair get into the paper; it would much annoy Turner, I am sure.'[27]

On receiving a note from a Turner niece, Elizabeth Daulby came from Liverpool with the forged letter. William Turner probably demanded of Fanny her account of events and by the Monday morning, 13 March, the picture was complete. At that moment, EGW in Calais was writing a contrite letter to Turner:

> I have done you an unpardonable Injury; and I feel, that in your Situation I should be furious with the Man who had dared to marry my Daughter without my Consent; still I hope that in a similar Case I should suspend my Judgment till I could learn *all the*

> *Facts*, and till I could ascertain whether my Child's Prospects of Happiness had been seriously affected by such an Event. It is with this Feeling that I have ventured to beg that you will take the Trouble to *know* me, and to learn from all my Friends whether or not your Daughter has made an unhappy Marriage. I trust in God and firmly believe, that she has *not*; and if I shall succeed in making her completely happy, you must be satisfied . . . . I acknowledge the full Extent of the Wrong that I have done you, but I may be able to *repair* it, unless you put Reparation out of my Power . . . . At all Events, I have incurred towards your Child the most sacred of Obligations; and I feel sure that, come what may, even though you should entertain towards me the most unrelenting Hatred, she has a Claim upon my devoted Tenderness. . . .[28]

EGW had left such an address far too late: if it were to have worked at all, it should have gone with William at Leeds. Perhaps he did not write earlier for lack of time, fatigue or, as he admitted, because he had at first not known what to say. Did the onset of remorse and gathering apprehension cause even EGW to be, temporarily, at a loss for words? Whatever the reason, by the time this letter reached Shrigley, the nemesis of William Turner's agents had reached him.

Turner went post haste to London again on Monday the 13th, taking with him his brother and brother-in-law. They turned Grimsditch out of his bed in the early hours of Tuesday morning; as soon as he could, he obtained a warrant from Bow Street and a despatch from Foreign Secretary George Canning to Lord Granville in Paris, asking him to render assistance. William Turner was too distressed to go on, but Grimsditch set off in pursuit of EGW with Ellen's uncles, another lawyer and a Bow Street officer. They arrived in Calais on the morning of 15 March.

Why was EGW waiting for them? He had written to Phyllida Bathurst, entreating her 'support and protection for [Ellen], on her arrival at Paris and presentation in the world as a bride. . .'. She 'gave all the orders to the Governess of his Children for the reception of his bride; the little ones prepared flowers and nosegays for their young mother and all Mr Wakefields friends were prepared. . . .'[29] EGW told her, 'If her parents are reconciled towards our union, I shall have nothing to desire; but if on the contrary they are inexorable, I shall look upon myself as doubly bound by honour, affection and gratitude to be her fond protector through life, and in supplying to her those ties I have severed her from, never give her cause to repent the sudden and even rash step I have caused her to take. . . . So help me God.'[30]

For public consumption, EGW declared that, as he waited at Calais, naturally anxious to know the outcome of William's representations to Turner, 'I was so fully occupied in teaching, dressing, caressing, and amusing, the high-spirited and affectionate girl, whose happiness, whatever might be the conduct of her family, I now considered as the first object of my existence, that I was indifferent to almost every thing, but the actual enjoyment of the moment, of which no one can imagine the intoxicating nature, who has not, by rare good fortune, been the first object of a young heart's legitimate tenderness.'[31] EGW had not physically taken Ellen Turner's maidenhead but, like Balzac's golden-tongued society 'murderer', had as surely drained away the blood of her innocence. There were two other more cogent reasons why EGW did not press on to Paris. First, he knew that his old friend Algernon Percy was due in Calais from London, on his way to Paris and Switzerland as British Ambassador to the Swiss Cantons. It made good sense to wait and travel on under his diplomatic protection. 'Clothed with such patronage' he might 'evade any attempt to take him or his prize'.[32]

Second, it seems likely that Ellen refused to go on – that EGW faltered in his excuses and cajolements before her pathetic insistence at meeting every Dover packet, so that she would be the first to greet her father. EGW entertained her and treated her as the 'earthly idol of a passionate and romantic Husband', but he was paralysed by his inability to tell her the truth, by waiting on the judgement of her family. The last traces of his irrational daring drained away; remorse began to erode his overweening self-confidence. The contempt he had shown for the society he had just raided began to turn on himself.

Algernon Percy arrived a day too late, travelling to Calais on the same packet as the five-strong Turner party. EGW, walking the pier with Ellen on his arm, spied the enemy in time to take her back to Quillac's Hotel and to have a discussion in the courtyard with Percy, who told him that he could do nothing in the face of the Bow Street warrant and Canning's despatch. When he was finally confronted by his pursuers, EGW made sure that Ellen was confined to the room of their suite. Grimsditch demanded to see Ellen and EGW replied, 'with some agitation, "Is it intended to prosecute me?"' Grimsditch told him that he had 'stolen Miss Turner; that he had got Possession of her by Means of a forged Letter, and that the strongest Measures would be resorted to. . . . He had struck a Blow at the Peace of the Family, the effects of which he could never repair; and that I thought it would be the death of Mrs Turner, if she were not dead already; and that we had left Mr Turner in London broken-hearted, and unable to go another Yard after his lost child. I told him that he deserved to be shot.'

'Your Animadversions are very severe,' EGW answered, 'but they are very just; I do not attempt to justify my conduct; I have a Daughter, and if any Man were to take her off in the same Manner, I believe I should send a bullet through his head.'[33] Nevertheless, EGW argued for the legality of the marriage, saying that neither the Bow Street warrant nor the Canning despatch would avail in France. Grimsditch forcefully pointed out that he had carried Ellen away by deception and fraud and that under English law the marriage was void and he was subject to a heavy penalty.

At last, under the pressure of Grimsditch and Ellen's uncles, EGW gave way to their demand to see Ellen in private. When, after 20 minutes, EGW was called into her room and he continued to claim her as his wife, Ellen 'clasped her uncle, Mr Critchley, round the shoulders in wild agitation' and cried, 'I am not your wife, I will never go near you again – you have deceived me'.[34] Another report had it that Ellen cried out, 'Oh! He is a brute! He has deceived me! and I never called anyone a brute before!'[35]

EGW's letter to William, written the following day, conveys the most authentic account of his views and feelings:

> I soon knew what they were come for, but would not attempt to avoid the Question. – Shortly – I saw them, found that *with Ellen's Consent* they could take her away; they insisted on seeing her; I could not object; she told *all*, and was anxious to leave me when she knew all. I expected as much, and therefore made a Merit of Necessity, and let her go. They tried to take *me*, but for *that* they were on the wrong Side of the Water, as I well knew. However, I offered to go with them, but begged Mr Critchley to believe that I would be in England to answer any Charge as soon as I had seen my Children and settled my Affairs.
>
> Nothing could be more hostile than the whole Spirit of their Proceedings. I could readily have escaped *with Ellen*, but their Account of Mrs and Mr Turner's State, made such a Step impossible.
>
> I made, and gave in Writing, a solemn Declaration, that she and I have been as Brother and Sister. How this may affect the Validity of the Marriage I know not, nor could I raise the Question. I was bound, and it was wise to give some Comfort to Mr Turner. I am now in a Stew about *you*, and wish that you were safe. There can be no doubt that the Law can punish us. For myself, *I will meet it* come what may; but if you are able, pray get away as soon as possible. I do not care a Straw for myself. The grand Question now is, Is the Marriage legal? They all said no, and quoted William and Mary upon me, 'till I was tired of their Majesties Names. – Pray let me know *that;* but I wrote to Nunky.[36] Do not stay; you can do no good. I shall go to England as soon as possible; upon this you may depend. I shall not write again till I hear from you, for fear of Accidents . . . . Pray write, but say nothing to any body. I am the Person to speak.[37]

At the same time, EGW wrote to Emily Sidney in Paris, preparing her for the worst. Mrs Bathurst, writing to Will on 19 March, recounted that this 'threw her into a state, that had we not been here to soothe and support her, I really think the Poor Child would have sunk under her anxiety. She came to us on Edward's message – half dead, and thinking that you were dead and we had to break it to her'.[38] By this time, EGW had arrived in Paris to arrange for Nina and Jerningham to be placed under Mrs Bathurst's care when he went to England to face prosecution. And only a day or two later, without warning, William turned up. On 23 March at the British Embassy, he and Emily were married.

The trial of EGW, William and Frances Davies for the abduction of Ellen Turner was to last more than a year, involving three hearings at Lancaster Assizes and the judgement in the Court of King's Bench, London. At first, EGW was charged with a capital felony,[39] meaning that he would be executed if found guilty (though the old act providing for this had just been repealed). 'I was urgently requested to escape to America.'[40] But he was as good as his word, returning to England in May. In April, it was reported that he was in Switzerland,[41] perhaps still attempting to enlist Percy's support, but he spent most of his time preparing a defence and writing his *Statement of Facts*.

William returned to England as early as 28 March, when he was taken into the custody of the prosecutor's attorney and a Bow Street officer who had shadowed both brothers in France. He was committed to Lancaster Castle on 5 April but released eight days later on bail sureties to a total of £2000, pending trial at the August assizes.

EGW surrendered himself 'unexpectedly' on 23 May to a Macclesfield magistrate. At the magistrates hearing, which was held in the small village of Disley over the following days, Ellen Turner, schooled by the Turner lawyers, said that she had understood the marriage certificate from Gretna to be a sort of quittance that would save her father from financial ruin and this was the sole reason she had entered into the union. EGW could find no reply to this legal logic save a weak, 'That was not the answer that was given.'

Any feelings for him that Ellen might have developed during their week together had been driven out by her sense of betrayal and humiliation. 'Not a single glance was exchanged between them. He sat lolling with his hand to his head, and she cast her eyes upon the ground all the time she gave her deposition . . . . While walking before the door with his friend Dr Davies, Miss Turner watched him from the window for some time, but no act of recognition took place.'[42] At the beginning of the hearing, it was reported that EGW conducted himself with 'great sang froid' dressed in a 'blue surtout, buff waistcoat, blue trousers, Wellingtons and a hat which might possibly be <u>one</u> inch in breadth; of course the last Parisian cut'.[43] But when he was committed into custody at Lancaster Castle to stand trial on a capital charge, his 'air of perfect indifference' was replaced by one in which 'he seemed considerably agitated'.[44]

In London before his surrender, EGW had seen to the publication of his *Statement of Facts*. This was designed partly to put his own case[45] but also to counter the prurient sensationalism of the stories appearing in the 'public prints', the tabloids of the day, which fastened onto what one lawyer described as 'a novel and extraordinary case, which did not occur more than once a century'.[46] EGW wrote, 'I am impelled to make this statement . . . in order to remove from myself some of the most injurious, and from my Wife the very mortifying, imputations, which have been cast upon us both.[47] It may be well to pursue me vindictively, but it is cruel to make her suffer for my sins . . . . a public Laughing-Stock, and the object of everlasting Newspaper curiosity and comment.'[48]

On publication of the 'Statement' EGW attached an open letter to William Turner dated 6 May in which he pointed out that the first of the bad reports had appeared in a Macclesfield paper published by Turner's own agent. There is no record that Turner responded to this or any letter from EGW other than through his lawyers. Or to the entreating letters of Phyllida Bathurst to him and his wife:

> Had Mr Wakefield selected my own and only child as the partner of his life I should have been perfectly contented and have esteemed her a most fortunate woman. If . . . through your gentle influence Mr Turner be induced to extend the hand of conciliation instead of persecution towards Mr Wakefield I feel convinced that you will by such a step secure your daughter's happiness for ever . . . . Her treatment I am told was gentle and most affectionate indeed knowing him as I do it could not be otherwise and the proof of forbearance he gave by abstaining from motives of delicacy from making her his beyond the possibility of discussion speaks at least to a mother's heart most highly in his favour.[49]

The prosecution proceeded with a vengeance that seemed careless not only of cost – to the tune of £10,000 – but also of the public exposure and humiliation of Ellen Turner. Prosecuting lawyer Sergeant Cross averred that EGW's sole object had been 'by the hand of the daughter, to pick the father's pocket',[50] but the ferocity of the prosecutors shows that they understood his ulterior motive very well. Even after his arrest, EGW still wrote and spoke of being returned to Parliament with the influence of his reconciled father-in-law. Was this mere self-delusion – a belief that hope, as he wrote in *A Letter from Sydney,* is more grateful than reality – or a considered tactic to win sympathy through his platform of reforming working conditions? Whatever the case, his prosecutors were determined to destroy any chance of a Wakefield presence in Parliament. Edward Wakefield's radical reputation was well known and EGW's expressed concern for the depressed condition of the Macclesfield silk weavers was directly opposed to Turner's business interests.[51] Edward's peripheral involvement with the abduction had become quickly known when, on Fanny's indictment, he declared their marriage so that he might work for her defence. Although his prospects had been utterly ruined, Edward still, hopelessly, put himself forward as a candidate for Reading in the election later that year. At least one handbill containing a damning letter from Turner was used against Edward in the Reading contest.[52]

The drawn-out trial process and endless publicity of the case not only destroyed Wakefield reputations; it also broke EGW financially. He was obliged to spend £6,000 on his defence: the first £3,000 he raised as a loan 'upon terms ruinously extravagant' and the second by selling a 'reversionary life interest of £1500 a year, for less than two years' purchase'.[53] In his last self-defence before the judgement he implied that the prosecution knew full well they could not sustain the first, and most serious, charge of felony but were determined to break him. It can be convincingly argued that if William Turner had been chiefly concerned to rescue, protect and rehabilitate his daughter then pursuing EGW through the courts at such length and with such determination did little in aid of those objects and simply enlarged the case to the Great Scandal of 1826–27.

But though political motives were clearly present, the prosecution lawyers would have also convinced Turner that the only way to procure an annulment of the marriage was to convict EGW on the gravest charges they could make stick. There were too many other legal 'Scotch marriages' in England for them to easily find another way to overturn the union. Whether by EGW or her father, and whether in the name of protested familial or connubial affections, Ellen was used as a pawn in the game of property and politics.

EGW spent three months in Lancaster Castle before the first hearing at the Lancaster Assizes in August 1826. His letters to Fanny from this time convey a tone of monastic resignation and lonely martyrdom that might have provoked another reference to Walter Scott had the castle been closer to the Scottish border. On 26 May, his first day in gaol, he wrote: 'You ought to know how little I care for personal luxuries. Air, exercise, water, privacy and books are all-sufficient for any man of common sense and courage. I have all these, so I give you my word that, could I forget what others feel for me, I should at this time be as much at my ease as I ever was in my life.'[54] It was an opportunity for retreat, for rest and recuperation after the hectic business of the previous three months.

On 30 May:

> I have got to myself a room twenty-four feet square and a yard fifty feet long. I have a fire, a table, two chairs, plenty of water, which to me is the same as plenty of air, plenty of books, pens and paper. I am locked into my cell at seven, but have candles, and I am obliged to attend chapel every day; when, however, at my own request, I sit alone, unseen, in the *condemned pew.* (Ominous!) My confinement is solitary at my own request, but I and myself could always make company. At present we walk, talk and laugh together, without a moment's lassitude during the day.

During these periods of self-dramatisation, he may have worked out at what point in February common sense had left courage in favour of irrationality and then where he had miscalculated. It says something for his resilience that none of his experiences of the four years from March 1826 dented his belief in his ability to manipulate and change the public world to his own ends.

The walls of Lancaster Castle incarcerated a sentimental celebrity, as he explained on 5 June: 'Some of my unknown correspondents write law to me, some consolation, some love, and one an offer of marriage!' Because, without something to love 'I should be very unhappy', he had a cat, 'with one woolly draggle of a kitten, and a root of grass which grows in a hole in the wall, and which I watch and nurse as if it were a cutting from the Tree of Life . . . The magistrates come to stare at me, so I compel them, by standing and staring formally with my hat on, to be regularly introduced by the turnkey.'

The charge of felony was withdrawn and at the muddled, crowded and inconclusive August hearing, EGW was held over in bail until the following assizes where he would be tried for a misdemeanour. Frances Davies (now revealed as Wakefield) pleaded not guilty to a charge of conspiracy and was held to bail of £2,000; William pleaded not guilty to misdemeanour and conspiracy and his bail was continued until he was to be brought up for trial three days later. Then the whole case would be tried even though the principal, EGW, would not be in the dock. A court reporter at Lancaster described EGW as a 'gentlemanly-looking man. His countenance, though pleasing, is wanting in expression. He was fashionably dressed, but seemed considerably embarrassed by the situation in which he was placed. The brother is a very young man, in whom levity seemed the prevailing characteristic.'[55]

Whether of his own volition or on the recommendation of the others, William promptly absconded to Paris so that the trial could not be held. His Emily was already three months pregnant. William's 'levity' had extended to leaving Lancaster 'in female attire, and in the company of two ladies'.[56] A bench warrant was issued for his arrest, but Will had a vital twelve-hour start on the police. A broadsheet ballad of the time sang, 'Postponed is Gibbon Wakefield's trial,/ And William Wakefield now is "fly" all/ He's gone and fixed his recognances,/ With lots of ugly Law expences. . . .'[57]

William had left in the lurch two men who had stood surety for him: Dr Davies who, by now, must have bitterly rued the day he ever set eyes on a Wakefield, and another friend, John Cuthbert of Broadstairs, Kent. Both were estreated for £500 and £1,500 respectively though, by January 1827, they were given to understand that, if William presented himself for trial at the next Lancaster assizes, these sums would be refunded.

The movements and activities of the Wakefields over the following six months are unknown, though EGW undoubtedly worked at his defence (and witnesses for the defence) and even attempted to contact Ellen Turner. In September, it was reported that he would 'move for a writ of *habeas corpus* to bring up his wife (if Miss Turner may be called by that name) to the Court of King's Bench, in order that she may be delivered up to him'.[58] This did not occur, but later in the year he was said to have been 'haunting the neighbourhood' of Shrigley before Ellen received, in December 1826 a parcel 'containing a copy of Ackerman's "Forget-Me-Not" for 1827. The work was not new to her, as her father had presented her with a copy a few days previously; but she could not conjecture from whom she had received a second. At length, on looking it over . . . there was discovered . . . a portrait of Edward Gibbon Wakefield . . . placed directly opposite' verses from Ariosto's 'The Praise of Love', which began:

Let others praise it if they please,
And call that life a life of ease,

Free from the bonds of Cupid;
I hold that heart most surely dead,
Or buried in a breast of lead,
Which is so cold and stupid.

And finished with:

For me, whatever be my lot,
I still will love; when I do not,
Why let me die and perish.[59]

Ellen Turner (strictly, Wakefield) was apparently unmoved at the prospect.

The main trial of EGW and William was finally held at Lancaster on 23 March 1827. Frances had been given leave not to appear but Edward was there, counselled by brother Daniel, now a leading barrister in the Court of Chancery. William had travelled back to England in February, Emily giving birth to their daughter at Dunkerque en route. On 15 March the child had been baptised Emily Charlotte at St Margaret's, Westminster, in the presence of Sir John Sidney. A few days later, William was arrested for the bail debts he had left behind and put into Lancaster Castle.

On the day of the trial 'every avenue leading to the Castle was thronged . . . The rush was immense, and in a few minutes every spot of the Court which could command a view of the proceedings was occupied with the greatest avidity.'[60] The throng had come to see the dénouement of the year's great *cause célèbre*, the final fall of the dastardly dandy whose 'face and figure' had become 'familiar to those who have at all frequented the fashionable lounges about town'.[61] No one cared much for William who was often unremembered by witnesses except as the shorter of the two brothers.

The throng had come to hear the execratory ring of the indictment against the prisoners who 'unlawfully, wickedly, and injuriously; and for the sake of lucre and gain, did conspire, combine, confederate, and agree together, with divers other persons whose names are unknown, by divers subtle stratagems and contrivances, and by false representations, unlawfully to take and carry . . . the said Ellen Turner, then and there being a maid, unmarried. . . .'[62]

The throng had come to see the careworn, injured father, but above all the daughter, 'an uncommonly fine young woman' whom the prosecution pointed out had 'developed' considerably over the year since the crime. Two days earlier, *The Times* had strained to describe the suffering this 'young lady of delicate constitution' had undergone in agitation at the approaching trial.[63] In the court, 'she appeared to labour under considerable apprehension at first, but she recovered her self-possession, and gave her evidence in a mild, but firm and collected manner, and with the greatest clearness. Mr Wakefield sat directly opposite to her, but she kept her eyes fixed upon the jury box, and scarcely moved them during the whole of her examination.'[64] How they all watched for that – any little wrinkle of distress, of doubt, of lingering affection. And they were entertained by the procession of witnesses – ostlers, post-boys, maids, innkeepers and all – who said she had been laughing and happy or distressed and crying, depending on who had brought them to the stand.

The most entertaining of all was David Laing, the parson-blacksmith, though he never admitted to smithying. Now 75 years old, he had been dressed up by the defence in clerical fashion to reinforce the fact that he had been marrying people for 48 years. Before that, he admitted to being a gentleman and when asked 'What do you call a gentleman?' he answered shrewdly, 'Being sometimes poor and sometimes rich.' Laing

> leaned forward towards the counsel . . . with a ludicrous expression upon his features, and accompanied every answer with a knitting of his wrinkled brow, and a significant nodding of his head, which gave peculiar force to his quaintness of phraseology and occasionally convulsed the Court with laughter . . .
>
> 'What did you get for this job besides the *Shumpine?* Did you get money as well as *Shumpine?*'
>
> 'Yes, sure I did, and so and so.'
>
> 'Well, how much?'
>
> '£30 or £40, or thereabouts, as may be.'
>
> 'Or £50, as it may be, Mr Blacksmith?'
>
> 'May be, for I cannot say to a few pounds. I am dull of hearing.'[65]

David Laing was to conduct no more marriages. He caught a bad chill on the way home from the trial and died of it.

The prosecution made much of the fact that the only reason EGW and his associates were not being tried for a felony was that the marriage had taken place in Scotland, beyond the jurisdiction of English law. Sensationally, Sergeant Cross alluded to abduction being a capital crime though he must have known full well that the law had been recently changed, altering punishment to transportation or imprisonment with hard labour.

The defence was led by the best 'verdict-getter' of the day, James Scarlett. He made no attempt to deny or qualify the abduction but concentrated on proving that Ellen Turner was treated without force or intimidation and had been a generally willing and happy partner to the whole adventure – and that the Scottish marriage was entirely legal. While EGW could be convicted under English law for conspiracy to carry off an heiress under sixteen without her father's approval, Scottish law allowed for any girl over the age of twelve to validly contract a marriage without parental consent. Misrepresentation of circumstances or fortune did not invalidate any marriage freely consented to: 'Although it should afterwards turn out that the pedigree was assumed – the boasted riches a fiction – the beauty mere paint and padding – and the air of virtue gross dissimulation, the law of Scotland will not interfere.'[66]

Judge Baron Hullock was extremely reluctant to accept Scarlett's evidence and argument for the marriage's legality, though he could not deny it, but in his summing up he attempted to influence the jury in favour of Frances Wakefield. He did not think the evidence justified them in reaching the conclusion that she 'was a party to the criminal proceedings'. But after retiring for only 45 minutes, the jury found all three guilty. The marriage remained valid.

'Every age does not produce such a Quixote as Mr Wakefield,' proclaimed one legal commentator, 'nor is every heiress, especially if she is a "clever" girl, and "well educated," so credulous as to believe any cock-and-a-bull story told to her by an utter stranger . . . or so exceeding pliable as in a few hours to consent to marry him, on the strength of his mere statement as to her father's wishes . . . . how many ages may elapse before such a Quixote . . . shall stumble on such an heiress . . . and how many thousand chances to one are there against the completion of the scheme. In short, in all human probability, such a case will never occur again.'[67] Nor such a Quixote have such a Sancho Panza as Will? Although such a case never did occur again, it proved to be a kind of Wakefield prototype for the credulous being persuaded by the plausible EGW, with the aid of his enigmatic brother.

Judgement in the case was made at the Court of King's Bench in London on 14 May. Employing the affidavits sworn that day by EGW and William, the attorney-general attempted to mitigate William's punishment by using the argument that EGW had always had undue influence over William. But that did not wash with Mr Justice Bayley who committed him to Lancaster Castle for three years.

In his elaborate last ditch self-defence speech, EGW was perhaps persuasive in deterring the court from imposing a heavy fine which would have seriously affected his children's care, education and inheritances. They took him at his word and sent him to Newgate for three years. Frances was let off: as EGW had arranged with Sergeant Cross, on the understanding that he would plead guilty to one charge at Lancaster. Although the prosecution had subsequently ignored this at the trial, Judge Hullock's favourable summing up in her behalf led to the prosecution later entering a *nolle prosequi* against Frances and she was not brought up for judgement.

Now the marriage must be overturned and this could be done only by legislation. A fortnight later, EGW was escorted from Newgate Prison to the House of Lords to attend the second reading of 'An Act to annul and declare void an alledged Marriage between Ellen Turner, an Infant, and Edward Gibbon Wakefield'. The entire evidence was gone through again; EGW could bring no defence nor call witnesses, protesting that he had not been given enough notice. And he was out of cash. After a last fruitless attempt to establish his innocence, to declare that Ellen had married him for love, that he had 'never been fairly tried',[68] EGW withdrew his opposition to the bill and was taken back to prison.

Ellen Turner's honour was restored and she was now of an age, mind and situation to marry a man of worth. Her father was once again in control of his fortune and the Wakefield miscreants' hopes, fortunes and social and political ambitions were destroyed.

Francis Place was hardly surprised that it had come to this. He had foreseen that for EGW 'to be an accomplished man in his employment, one must stifle humanity and destroy all the kinder emotions of the heart – must be capable of doing all manner of actions with the same sang froid'.[69]

Catherine's daughter, Frances Torlesse, wrote late in life, 'I do not think any words can be found to describe the grief caused to [my mother] by his conduct, or how keenly both she and my father felt the social stigma attached to his name.'[70] Otherwise, there is scant record of family feelings about the abduction and trial and the extent to which shame and odium blighted the lives and work of all except Arthur, out of sight at sea, and John Howard, out of sight in India.

Of grandmother Priscilla's reaction there is no record, but the calamity fulfilled her long-held fears about EGW's tendency to 'perverseness' and his capacity for 'great delinquency' if his energies were not directed to some 'noble' purpose. She was undoubtedly forgiving, but also much preoccupied with grief at the death of her husband of 55 years. EW died in 1826 after a long period of ill health and it seems more than likely that the abduction delivered a final blow. Stress, shame and distraction among the family during this time may also have had some bearing on the early death of Dan's wife Selina and, in particular, on the death of Dr Davies in January 1828 at the age of about 72.

Edward Wakefield had long known that EGW could 'very likely go off at a tangent'. Yet his enthusiastic aiding and abetting of his son's often dubious schemes and ambitions, his soft-headed rapture before EGW's talents, had brought down on him a devastating retribution. If, as Francis Place had written, Edward had moaned 'what would the world say?' about Susannah's 'madness' in 1816, what did he say eleven years later, 'turning himself in an agony on his chair, and looking vacantly through the window'? His 'dread that the Honbl and Noble Gentlemen should no longer nod or wink at him' had been fulfilled with a force and ignominy he could not have imagined. His reputation and business were ruined, as were the immediate careers and income prospects of Dan and Felix. Edward soon removed to France with Fanny, that convicted conspirator, whose snobbery and unscrupulous social ambition were punished by exile. Despite EGW's efforts to save her from sentencing, she blamed him for her disgrace and misery – and the circumstances of her father's death – and kept father and son apart; a generation was to pass before her reconciliation.

What of the other two young women involved in the triangular plot? In June 1826, after the marriage dissolution, Ellen Turner returned to crowds of welcome in the villages around Macclesfield: 'the bells of Shrigley church rang merrily, flags were displayed in various directions' and the people 'evinced their exultation by loud and hearty cheering'.[71] The year before it had been reported that Thomas Legh of Lyme Hall 'who possesses immense estates in Cheshire, which lie contiguous to those of Mr Turner, was on the point of paying his addresses to Miss Turner when she was carried off'.[72] Legh now felt no constraint in pressing his suit and the pair were wed on 14 January 1828.

Two great capital estates were united and 'Wakefield may bid adieu both to her and her fortune'.[73] It was an occasion for great celebration. A half-day holiday was granted local workers, 'two fat beasts and twelve sheep were slaughtered, and distributed in suitable proportions among those who had gathered with each a quart of beer from the hall'.[74] The 'youthful and lovely bride . . . was elegantly but plainly attired in an Esterhazy silk dress, with a white hat and veil and looked remarkably well . . . after the ceremony, the happy pair set off for Lyme Hall . . . where they will probably remain till Mr Legh's Parliamentary duties call . . .'.[75] After three presumably happy years of marriage, Ellen died in childbirth in January 1831, a month before her twentieth birthday: it was a ghastly echo of Eliza's fate.

Long before that, in August 1827, the following obituary notice had been published :

> DIED. On Sunday last [12th] at Quiddenham [Norfolk], the Seat of her uncle the Earl of Albemarle, to the great affliction of her near relations . . . Mrs William Wakefield. This accomplished and beautiful young lady has fallen victim to a broken heart, in consequence of the distant imprisonment of her youthful husband, who, in an inadvertant moment, joined his elder brother in the mad prank of taking away a young lady to Gretna Green . . . She left an infant daughter six months old.[76]

PART TWO

Forward, Forward Let Us Range

1828–1839

CHAPTER SEVEN

This Black Place

IN 1834 CHARLES DICKENS, AS BOZ, PAID 'A Visit to Newgate'. On his tour of the prison he guided the reader to the chapel and the condemned pew: 'Imagine what have been the feelings of the men whom that fearful pew has enclosed, and of whom, between the gallows and the knife, no mortal remnant may now remain! Think of the hopeless clinging to life to the last, and the wild despair, far exceeding in anguish the felon's death itself, by which they have heard the certainty of their speedy transmission to another world, with all their crimes upon their heads, rung into their ears by the officiating clergyman!'[1]

By his own admission Dickens had Edward Gibbon Wakefield's Newgate book, *Facts Relating to the Punishment of Death in the Metropolis*, on his shelf and as a cub reporter at Parliament he may well have heard EGW, this new reformer, expound on the iniquities of the current prison and punishment system to its 1831 Select Committee on Secondary Punishments. As yet unable to match its veracity and flair, the young journalist had been impressed by EGW's first-hand account of condemned men in a pew that Dickens could people only from his imagination.

For Dickens's 'officiating clergyman' was, in EGW's masterly report, 'an orthodox unaffected Church of England divine, who preaches plain homely discourses', addressing himself to the 'congregation at large, who listen attentively – excepting the [condemned] clergyman and the burglar, of whom the former is still rolled up at the bottom of the condemned pew, whilst the eyes of the latter are wandering round the chapel, and one of them is occasionally winked, impudently, at some acquaintance amongst the prisoners for trial.' EGW goes on to describe the priest's sermon, delivered 'in a deep tone, which, though hardly above a whisper, is audible to all':

> he talks for about ten minutes of crimes, punishment, bonds, shame, ignominy, sorrow, sufferings, wretchedness, pangs, childless parents, widows and helpless orphans, broken

and contrite hearts, and death to-morrow morning for the benefit of society. What happens? The dying men are dreadfully agitated. The young stealer in a dwelling-house no longer has the least pretence to bravery. He grasps the back of the pew; his legs give way; he utters a faint groan, and sinks on the floor. Why does no one stir to help him? Where would be the use? The hardened burglar moves not, nor does he speak; but his face is of an ashy paleness; and, if you look carefully, you may see blood trickling from his lip, which he has bitten unconsciously, or from rage, or to rouze his fainting courage. The poor sheep stealer is in a phrensy. He throws his hands far from him and shouts aloud, 'Mercy, good Lord! mercy is all I ask. The Lord in his mercy come! There! There! I see the Lamb of God! Oh! how happy! Oh! this is happy!' Meanwhile, the clergyman, still bent into the form of a sleeping dog, struggles violently, – his feet, legs, hands, and arms, even the muscles of his back, move with a quick jerking motion, not naturally but, as it were, like the affected part of a galvanized corpse. Suddenly he utters a short sharp scream, and all is still. . . .

EGW's account concludes with the dispersal of the congregation: '. . . and then the congregation disperses; the condemned returning to the cells; the forger carried by turnkeys; the youth sobbing aloud convulsively, as a passionate child; the burglar muttering curses and savage expressions of defiance; whilst the poor sheep-stealer shakes hands with the turnkeys, whistles merrily, and points upwards with madness in his look'.[2]

This powerful piece of reporting, this cogent appeal to a reader's compassion, was a flowering of style and acuity that had first shown itself in EGW's *Statesman* letter from post-Waterloo Paris and had been subsequently exercised in the lost Italian manuscript. In its combination of vivid reportage, management of statistics and didacticism, EGW's *Facts Relating to the Punishment of Death* was in the centre of the Wakefield literary stream flowing from Priscilla and Edward. But, as Ellen Turner had testified, EGW had a flair for imaginative expression and invention far exceeding theirs. Had he been possessed more by literary than political ambition, had he perceived that his talent for persuasion was best leather-bound, then Dickens might have faced a considerable, if more romantic, rival in the production of Newgate and social novels. Indeed, EGW's critics would have it that much, if not all, he was to write over the next 20 years was fiction anyway.

The culmination of three years in the hell-hole of Newgate, *Punishment* reveals not only literary skill and deeply engraved experience but also a baring of social concern of which Edward and Priscilla were doubtless equally proud. This and the other work deriving from the Newgate period, *A Letter from Sydney*, contributed much to EGW's redemption within his family and established the base from which he could attempt social and political rehabilitation.

As always, EGW's motives were mixed. Only the most hardened cynic would distrust his 'principal motive' in writing *Punishment*, 'for publishing what he has seen. Incredible scenes of horror occur in Newgate. Is it to be desired that such evil should remain unknown? By the answer to this question the writer must be blamed or excused for doing what, to those who do not ask themselves the question, may seem like ministering to a vulgar appetite for horrors.'[3]

EGW wished to demonstrate beyond doubt the evils visited upon the condemned and the horrible inefficiencies of the irregular application of the death sentence for a wide range of offences. In appealing to the evangelical mood of middle-class consciences he could influence the process of reform. If there was some drama in the telling, was that not the nature of the subject? His concern was genuine and this would also go far in confirming EGW as a compassionate man, misunderstood as a result of temporarily misguided actions for which he had thoroughly and sickeningly paid his dues.

EGW was not alone in advocating reform of capital punishment and had arrived late to the debate. Aristocratic missionary Thomas Buxton, Elizabeth Fry's brother-in-law and Wilberforce's parliamentary successor in the fight against the slave trade, had published his *Inquiry into Prison Discipline* in 1818, based on an inspection of Newgate, and had become a focus for advocates of capital punishment reform. But, like Fry, 'Elephant' Buxton's attitude was permeated with do-gooding condescension: an aristocratic missionary, he and EGW would always be at odds in either cause or method.

Punishment, which appeared after EGW's anonymously published *A Letter from Sydney*, would also serve to legitimise the latter book's new theories for alleviating the terrible plight of the hopeless poor and improving the prospects of the 'uneasy classes' which, to a degree, would always encompass members of his own family. In tandem, both books might begin to legitimise EGW's credentials as social theorist and political thinker, so that some who mattered might regret the circumstances that precluded such a figure and mind from contributing in a normal parliamentary way to the governance of the nation. They might then be prepared to accept him in a less obvious but no less influential role. But what had EGW seen and experienced that engendered such effective prose?

Newgate Prison was on the way to the abattoirs of Smithfield, at the corner of Old Bailey and Newgate Street, a site now occupied by the Central Criminal Court. 'How dreadful its rough heavy walls,' wrote Dickens, 'and low massive doors, appeared to us – the latter looking as if they were made for the express purpose of letting people in, and never letting them out again . . . .'[4] In *The Chronicles of Newgate* Arthur Griffiths described it thus:

> The whole place except the press yard was so dark that candles, 'links or burners,' were used all day long; the air was so inconceivably disgusting, that the ventilator on the top of the prison could exercise no remedial effect. That malignant disease, the goal fever, was chronic, and deaths from it of frequent occurrence . . . . Evil was in the ascendancy

> throughout; wickedness and profligacy prospered; the weakest always went to the wall . . . Into these filthy dens, where misery stalked rampant and corruption festered, unhappy prisoners brought their families, and the population was greatly increased by numbers of innocent persons, women, and even children, to be speedily demoralized and utterly lost . . . .[5]

In the dozen years preceding EGW's incarceration in 1827, there had been some improvement in the excessive overcrowding of the noisome gaol, but the only significant reforms had been brought about by Elizabeth Fry. After she had first visited the women's wards in 1813, she related, 'All I tell thee is a faint picture of the reality; the filth, the closeness of the rooms, the ferocious manners and expressions of the women towards each other, and the abandoned wickedness, which everything bespoke, are quite indescribable.'[6]

Facing much scepticism from prison authorities Fry, with a committee of Quaker helpers, worked daily in Newgate for the benefit of the women prisoners, establishing a school and work programmes that were discussed, voted on and disciplined by the women themselves. Although Fry tended to regard her wards as 'erring servants', she wrought a transformation through offering the women prisoners a way to self-esteem and dignity and her work became a model for the improvement of women prisoners' conditions in gaols everywhere.

Among her helpers in the 1820s was EGW's sister Catherine. She went with Elizabeth Fry to Newgate, and also 'on to the convict ships, and has often described to me Mrs Fry's wonderful reading of Psalm 107 to the women'.[7] Probably more appreciated by the prisoners were Catherine's and Elizabeth Fry's efforts at practical relief. There is no evidence that Catherine visited her brother at the prison; by the end of 1827 she was pregnant with her fourth child, was still responsible for young Priscilla, now aged eighteen, and carried a heavy load of household and parochial work at Stoke. But Elizabeth Fry did visit EGW, in February 1828, and her example is likely to have spurred his own involvement in prison reform, now that he had settled to his dark incarceration.

Whereas the condition of women prisoners had been improved by Fry's work, nothing had been done for the men. The prison had become principally a place of detention for those awaiting trial, but there were up to 50 or more awaiting execution in a public hanging by 'Jack Ketch' at the gallows erected in Newgate Street.[8] A number awaited transportation to Botany Bay and there were smugglers, various short-term offenders and a few prisoners, like EGW, who had been committed by Parliament, the commissioners of bankruptcy and taxes and the Courts of King's Bench, Common Pleas and Exchequer.

Corrupt governance of the prison meant that the convicted and the untried, the felon and the petty criminal, the sane and the insane, the old and the young were crammed in together. Living conditions were abominable: the men slept on rope mats on the floor, huddled under unwashed stable rugs to keep warm; the food supply was uneven, pumps in the yards were the only source of water for drinking or ablution and almost all the prisoners were 'ragged and ill-clad, squalid and filthy in the extreme; many without stockings . . . . The days were passed in idleness, debauchery, riotous quarrelling, immoral conversation, gambling . . . instruction in all nefarious processes, lively discourse upon past criminal exploits, elaborate discussion of others to be perpetrated after release.'[9] Add torture, endless fighting, prostitution, rape, sodomy (and anything else that comes to mind) and the picture of this egregious sewer of humanity is complete.

This was the condition of the common prisoners. But, as the Inspectors of Prisons found in 1835, Newgate prisoners were 'permitted to purchase whatever his own means or the means of his friends in or out of prison can afford'.[10] This meant that the better class of prisoner could buy anything but his freedom. EGW would have 'rented' a room of his own, perhaps in the keeper's house at the main gate. He had a servant, had meals brought in from local taverns and newspapers and books delivered.

Above all, there were no restrictions on visitors. In September 1827, nine-year-old Nina Wakefield wrote to her Aunt Catherine, 'Papa et moi sont très heureux, et nous sommes beaucoup ensemble, car j'y vais à dix heures et demi jusqu'à 2. Le Dimanche j'y vais depuis 4 1/2 jusqu'à 8.'[11] Living near the prison with a governess, Nina visited her father every day for schooling; seven-year-old Jerningham, then with Catherine, was due to join them soon.

EGW sought Catherine's advice and help to find the *right* governess for them 'during the years of danger'. 'I was afraid that my children might either be left in the streets or tormented past endurance. That immediate pressure is over; but I live upon thorns, knowing that I am not giving Nina a fair chance and having my mind quite occupied in guarding her from evil, instead of actively promoting her good.'[12] He told Catherine 'strong religious principle and habits of strict regularity' were the first criteria in choosing a governess. These attributes did not conform with his own character but they were essential in the person responsible for the security of his children. A governess's ability to instruct them came last because 'I have nothing to do but to attend to their education which is proceeding to my heart's content. Their progress during the last six months surprises even me, who am bound to think my own children prodigies.'[13]

EGW proudly reported their attributes. To their great-grandmother Priscilla he wrote, 'My boy, upon reading your letter, became very red, sprang towards me and exclaimed, "Why great-grandmamma wants me to be a *sloth*, and I want to be a general or a prime minister or something of that kind!"' Jerningham, of an 'aspiring nature', was clearly his father's son. 'Nina, on the contrary, quite approved your peacable sentiments, but then she is a little old woman in good sense; and, to speak quite seriously, she has the tenderest heart in the world.'[14]

Despite EGW's exertions, the Torlesses feared for Nina and Jerningham's welfare. In February 1828, EGW wrote to his grandmother of Charles Torlesse's visit 'for the sole purpose of advising me to send my daughter abroad – upon which subject he did not open his mouth. His silence did him honor; and I hope he was not blamed for the fruitlessness of his journey. If he were, it was unfairly; for had he talked till now, he must still have gone back to report no progress.– If any one were to ask me for my teeth or half my limbs, I might perhaps part with them – but my daughter! What could have put it into their heads?'[15]

Although EGW was clearly concerned for the well-being of both his children, his voluminous letters to Catherine were dominated by a preoccupation with Nina's delicate temperament. When she was about to make arrangements with a new governess he advised Catherine to mention

> having been struck by Nina's great sensitiveness, which amounts almost to a disease, and say that it requires the utmost care and judgment in those who surround her .... Nina's disposition is so affectionate, even to excess, as to cause her a great deal of pain .... mention the subjects or points which most readily excite Nina's feelings. 1. Anything like a doubt of her affection for those whom she likes. 2. Any reproach which conveys a reflection on her truth or honor. 3. The belief that she has hurt the feelings of those whom she likes. 4. Seeing anyone whom she likes offended with her. 5. And most particularly, any lasting but silent displeasure in . . . anyone to whom she is much attached.[16]

The siblings were close and the stress caused by their father's confinement was demonstrated in unexpected ways. Later that year, when Nina returned after a stay with Catherine, she and her brother

> met in tears, and were both speechless for some time. He, to my surprise, was pale and almost faint from emotion. I took no notice of them, and after a time Edward left us. She then talked at a great rate; but I observed that her spirits were artificial. At length, about seven o'clock, in the midst of an indifferent conversation, she burst into tears and threw herself into my arms, saying, or rather sobbing, "I didn't half take leave of aunt, we parted in such a hurry!" I consoled her as well as I could. She said that she very nearly cried at getting into the coach, but that, fearing the strangers, she conquered herself till she got to Nayland, where she put her face into the corner of the coach and cried heartily. She said that she liked Stoke much better than she expected, and that she loved aunt more than she expected, and that she could not believe in the pain she suffered in coming away. . . . Were I an ass I should say you have stolen her heart; but I rejoice at the feelings of affection for you which have been renewed and strengthened by this visit; and I well know that she does not love me a bit the less for loving you so much. In fact, I know her tears and sobs were caused by a double excitement, that of losing you and finding me. What a beautiful, yet what a dangerous character! . . . now I am Tom Fool enough to cry myself.[17]

In the dread fortress of Newgate, Nina's visits were 'a short time of sunshine coming in the midst of a dreary season. Your [Catherine's] basket was very acceptable to some of the liquorish mouths that surround me, and as its contents were distributed in Nina's name, they have raised her in the esteem of some of her fellow-creatures. My cook, slut and butler, who is an Irishwoman, said on receiving some cake and fruit, "Sure she's a sweet cratur, sir, and it does my heart good to see her in this black place".'[18]

Other visitors were Arthur between ships, who would have found conditions in Newgate only a small improvement on those of a slaver; Dan grieving for his lost wife and son, and now turning to the law for sustenance; and Felix coming of age with a family so dispersed it could not help him celebrate.

The most frequent caller at Newgate was Uncle Daniel. EGW reported to his grandmother, 'His disinterested, generous and most friendly, I may say more than paternal, conduct in all my late troubles is far above any praise. . . . I never, I am sorry to say, gave him any cause to wish me well. Yet when I was in need he chose to become my friend.'[19] Uncle Daniel's generosity of spirit resembled his brother Edward's but, rather than general schemes of reform, was directed towards advising and assisting those who by bad luck or bad judgement had lost their way in the law. At the time of his death in 1846 he was in 'very embarrassed circumstances, a result which may be wholly ascribed to his benevolent disposition. He has on many occasions been known to refuse money, and return fees for holding briefs on ascertaining that his clients were in distress.'[20]

Uncle Daniel undoubtedly had some fellow-feeling for EGW following the indiscretions of his own youth and the consequences of his disastrous marriage to Isabel Mackie. Also, though he and his second wife Elizabeth Kilgour had adopted a daughter, he had no son of his own to distract his paternal affections. His country home at Hare Hatch, between Reading and Maidenhead, was to became a favourite haunt for his nephews and their families during the 1830s and early 1840s. Soon to be appointed a King's Counsel, Daniel undoubtedly advised EGW on the letter and processes of the law informing *Punishment*. Also he had a reputation for pamphleteering on political economy and was in touch with the reform movements of the day; it is likely that he was one of the chief agents supplying EGW with political information and ideas during his time in Newgate.

Movements for parliamentary and electoral reform; Catholic emancipation; law, prison, poor law, industrial and financial reforms were all twined together, conjuring up increasing unrest and uncertainty. The fifteen-year Tory administration of the Earl of Liverpool was replaced in April 1827 by George Canning's hybrid cabinet, which lasted only until his death five months later. The succeeding Goderich government survived just four months and by the beginning of 1828 the Whigs and Tories were so divided that no party leader would take office. The

Duke of Wellington, now 58, had no sense of party politics but, as the country's paramount military chief and hero, he felt it his iron duty to carry on the king's government. His confused administration continued for almost three years. Catholic emancipation was achieved in Ireland with threats of civil war but nothing was done to meet the rising demand for reform of Parliament and the franchise.

The labouring poor, suffering from the effects of the commercial depression of the late 1820s and their exploitation by the new breed of capitalist factory owners, were beginning to come together in the first organised union actions. In the countryside, the abject poverty of agricultural workers was about to lead to the arsonist 'Swing' movement. Britain was moving inexorably to the point of revolution.

It is within the context of incipient revolution, a ferment of ideas and visions, influenced increasingly by scientific discoveries and their technological applications, that the commentaries, theories and proposals put forward by Edward Gibbon Wakefield must be placed. It should be remembered, too, that all ideas and theories are the product of reordering the known, of assembling disparate, often neglected, parts to find a working whole. This is neither to damn EGW with faint praise nor to excuse his endless self-regard but to suggest his frequent effectiveness in exposing problems, proposing workable solutions and, above all, resourcefully promoting them, sometimes beyond their usefulness.

EGW had become, by circumstance and character, a transitional man. Partially educated in values by Priscilla, that doyenne of eighteenth-century conforming philanthropy, he had been brought up in a middle-class family environment that reflected the revolutionary disturbances and military conflicts of the early nineteenth century. As a Regency man, his behaviour had been reinforced by the vain pomp of a diplomatic world operating within the reactionary protocols of the restored European monarchies. Yet, alerted to changing values and responsibilities by his father's reforming propensities, he faced the new capital-labour constructs of an industrial age and the moves towards political reforms. EGW revealed the conservative influences of his grandmother and father in wishing to preserve the stability of class and tradition – coloured by his own romantic cast of mind – but also recognised the need to make room for new models of capital and industry. His attitudes would always be qualified by a humane concern for the plight of the hopeless and the poor. Politically he was a misfit, neither Whig nor Tory, perhaps a new liberal but not a genuine radical. And he was to associate with other political misfits who were often in revolt against a society to which they could not or would not adapt. A good measure of contempt (and envy) for that society had been an essential ingredient in EGW's abduction of Ellen Turner.

In *Facts Relating to the Punishment of Death in the Metropolis*, EGW saw Newgate as 'the greatest *Nursery* of capital crime' and from its inmates had 'the opportunity of strictly examining more than a hundred thieves, between eight and fourteen years' from which he learned that 'London abounds with smaller nurseries of petty offences' where nineteen out of 20 of his subjects had been seduced into a life of crime.

> A practised thief often spends as much as £10 in the course of a few days for the purpose of corrupting a youth, by taking him to playhouses and other shows, and allowing him to eat and drink extravagantly at pastry-cooks, fruit-shops, and public-houses. The inevitable consequences of such indulgences is the victim's discontent with his previous mode of life; and when this feeling predominates, he is considered ripe for receiving without alarm the suggestions of his seducer. Very often a still more effectual means of seduction is applied, viz, the precocious excitement and gratification of the sexual passion, by the aid of women in league with the thieves, and to whom is commonly entrusted the task of suggesting to the intoxicated youth, that robbery is the only means, and a safe means, of continuing to enjoy a life of riotous debauchery.

In Newgate, more practised boys were visited daily by their 'sisters', women they paid to appear in 'a frill and a pinafore . . . at the bar of the Old Bailey' in their defence.

EGW's interviews of inmates allowed him to describe the processes of crime in the metropolis. He wrote of the 'lodging-houses' with up to 50 beds which were 'kept generally by receivers of stolen goods, and resorted to by none but thieves or those who are on the point of becoming thieves'; and the way in which a boy, 'becoming an expert thief, deserts his original seducer, with whom he is no longer willing to share the fruits of his plunder, connects himself with a gang, probably takes a mistress, and is a confirmed robber on the high road to Botany Bay or the gallows'. EGW knew the addresses of such lodging houses and other dens of crime, including that for Ikey Solomons, who was soon to follow him into Newgate and to achieve immortality as Dickens's Fagin.

EGW lamented the lack of effective law to break up the receivers' dens: 'Where is the Police?' The new Peelers or Bobbies might increasingly harass the thieves but did little to stop them. He recommended the 'appointment of a body of officers specially charged with *the detection of criminals*' – in other words what would, more than 40 years later, be known as the CID. He also called for a 'measure of *espionage*' in the form of undercover agents in Newgate who could winkle out the criminals and their sponsors. EGW also suggested a public prosecutor. Few robberies were ever brought to the notice of a magistrate because the onus for prosecution lay on the 'cost of money, time and peace of mind' of the robbed; and criminals operated in that knowledge. The criminal body would be 'greatly alarmed at the prospect of a system of steady certain prosecution'.

The chief value of *Punishment*, however, was the way it cogently reinforced, from first-hand observation, the 'doctrine of Romilly, Buxton and Bentham' – the need to reform capital punishment. Before Newgate, EGW concurred with the popular belief that execution was a deterrent; that it was necessary to hang a few now and then *pour encourager les autres*. But upon witnessing the arbitrary and cruel application of the death sentence, he became convinced not only that it was inhumane but also that it had little or no effect as a deterrent.

In December 1827, EGW witnessed the execution of 23-year-old John Williams, convicted of 'stealing in a dwelling-house'. On the morning he was to die, Williams tried to escape by climbing the pipe of a cistern in the Newgate press yard. He fell and badly broke his leg which was dressed 'with the same care as if surgical skill could have preserved the use of those limbs for years'. He was then carried to the public scaffold and hung, blood flowing from his wounds in 'the struggle of death'. This sanguinary spectacle so shocked the consciences of Londoners that it was to deter not thieves but many law-abiding citizens from bringing prosecutions for robbery. Inside the prison, 'a sentiment of ferocious anger and desperate recklessness was created, such as, if frequently aroused and generally prevalent, would be the cause of innumerable and horrid crimes'.

During the 1820s, Robert Peel at the Home Office had made some reforms to the justice and penal system and instituted the London metropolitan police force which EGW found wanting. He had also carried five statutes exempting about 100 felonies from the death penalty.[21] Yet the sentencing system still decreed execution for crimes as trivial as sheep stealing and fourteen years' transportation for misdemeanours as minor as stealing two blacksmith's hammers.

Juries were becoming increasingly reluctant to send petty criminals to their deaths for minor crimes and this uncertainty about the application of capital punishment weakened its deterrent value still further. Added to this were the tortuous and unpredictable proceedings of the trial and appeal system which condemned Newgate convicts to an agony of waiting: 'I have seen brown hair turned gray, and gray white, by a month of suspense . . . the smooth face of a man of twenty five becomes often marked with decided wrinkles on the forehead, and about the eyes and mouth . . . . [it] causes a great diminution of flesh over the whole body.'

EGW excoriated the use of 'religious ceremonies in conjunction with the punishment of death . . . . the palpable absurdity of mixing a religion of charity and forgiveness with acts of irreparable vengeance . . . . the preacher of the Gospel comes to be considered as an adjunct of the executioner . . . to break the spirits of capital convicts, so that they make no physical resistance to the hangman'.

The callous vagaries of sentencing and the random savageries of imprisonment and execution created a 'lottery, of which the blanks are death . . . an attempt to foretell the result in any case would be mere guesswork'. Thieves understood from this that their trade was a 'game of hazard, in which . . . the player always wins until he loses all' and that the average period during which a player would always win was two years. EGW was sure that any gaming house offering those kind of odds would find plenty of takers.

For the Newgate condemned, the brutal procession towards public execution, authorised by law and religion, had become a ghastly theatre. Criminals inside and outside the prison were morbidly fascinated by a drama of life and death in which they were both players and audience. They took the 'same sort of delight in witnessing executions as the sportsman and soldier find in the dangers of hunting and war'. 'For some days after an execution a common amusement of the boys is to play the scene over again; one boy acting the convict, another the Ordinary, a third the Sheriff, and a fourth the hangman . . . on one occasion before the bodies of the men just hanged had been removed from the scaffold.' Boys also rehearsed the parts they should play in the rituals of reprieve. When the names of the spared were announced, 'Instantly, the boys fall on their knees, and recite a thanksgiving to God and the King for the mercy graciously vouchsafed them . . . . this sight . . . is, in truth a mockery. The whole scene is got up betwixt the Ordinary . . . instructing the Schoolmaster, and the Schoolmaster instructing the boys, as to the part these last are to play in the farce.'

Whether farce or tragedy, EGW was persuasive that the punishment of death, especially public execution, was no deterrent to habitual criminals. Rather, it was a positive incitement to crime through its brutal arbitrariness, provoking a reckless fatalism and an impulse of savage retribution among the convicts to match that of their oppressors.

EGW's *Punishment* met some criticism for its loose use of statistics and often colourful style. But the new liberal *Athenaeum* magazine commented, 'Out of evil comes good, for to Mr Wakefield's three years' imprisonment in Newgate we are indebted for this judicious, sensible and serviceable publication. Mr Wakefield has laboured wisely and diligently to atone for the wrongs he committed, and every good man will be content to forget that he ever erred.'[22] EGW could have not wished for a better opinion but given that, as was usual, the reviewer published anonymously, it is safe to assume he was a Wakefield friend or promoter. But the *Examiner*, too, lauded EGW for a 'masterly exposition of this subject'.[23]

EGW followed up *Punishment* with evidence to the parliamentary select committee in 1831 and a powerful, almost savage, sixteen-page pamphlet in 1833 in which he laid the responsibility for brutalising the people through the spectacle of public executions squarely at the feet of the judiciary. In a fictional letter from the mythical Jack Ketch to Mr Justice Alderson, EGW described the 1832 hanging of a small boy 'for killing with malice aforethought':

> When I began to pull the cap (not yours but mine) over his baby face, he pressed his small hands together . . . and gave me a beseeching look; just as a calf will lick the butcher's hand . . . 'Pray, sir, don't hurt me.' 'My dear,' answered I, 'you should have

> spoken to my master: I'm only the journeyman and must do as I'm bid.' This made him cry, which seemed a relief to him; and I do think I should have cried, myself, if I had not heard shouts from the crowd: poor lamb! shame! murder! Quick, said the sheriff; ready, said I; the reverend chaplain gave me the wink: the drop fell: one kick, and he swayed to and fro, dead as the feelings of an English judge.[24]

This dramatised documentary of the 1830s worked powerfully to sustain the campaign against capital punishment, the wave of reform on which EGW had become a prominent rider. In 1832, house-breaking, horse-stealing, sheep-stealing and the coining of false money ceased to be capital offences. After 1838 no one was hanged except for murder (or attempted murder up to 1861). But the belief that public executions worked as a deterrent persisted and prevented their abolition for another 30 years. It was 1868 before Jack Ketch launched the last criminal into eternity outside Newgate Prison.

CHAPTER EIGHT

A Castle in the Air

THERE WAS APPROBATION FOR EGW'S penal propaganda; a stirring of rehabilitation. But there was no career in it, no real opening for advancement. It was another facet of prison life, another fruit of convict interviews, that would provide him with an unexpected way forward.

As, in the desolation of his early days of imprisonment, EGW contemplated life after Newgate, he may have bitterly recalled the advice he had received in March 1826 to escape to America. He had long disapproved of the excesses of rude democracy in America, but perhaps there, or in one of the new colonies, he could leave the odious part of his reputation behind and make his remaining capital go further than it would in England. He was also aware that although, courtesy of Robert Peel, execution had been ruled out as a penalty for abduction, only his Scottish marriage to Ellen Turner had saved him from transportation to Botany Bay. In Newgate he met convicts awaiting transportation, often after their sentences of death had been commuted; and sometimes for a second time after they had taken more than a ticket of leave from their sentence.

For most of these convicts, he thought, the prospect of 'transportation to the colony offers them prospects of wealth and happiness far beyond any that they could indulge if destined to remain' in England.[1] Botany Bay was their great escape. During 1828, he got Uncle Daniel and other friends to bring him all the literature they could find. He read 'with care every book concerning New South Wales and Van Diemen's Land, as well as a long series of newspapers published in those colonies'. He declared that for convicts who had been 'men of station', the antipodean penal colonies were the 'only place on earth, where misconduct in other places does not subject men to the ill-opinion of society'.[2] The climate was better, too.

Turning the enforced discipline of incarceration to good advantage, EGW also read the literature on the theory of population, emigration and colonisation; the proceedings of parliamentary committees on emigration; reports of private colonisation ventures; and pored over maps. With Uncle Daniel's prompting, he chewed on economic theory, starting with Adam Smith. And then like Priscilla, without travelling further than the confines of his dark university, he concocted what she might have called *The Traveller in Australia* but which he titled *A Letter from Sydney, The Principal Town of Australasia.*

Unlike Priscilla's work, this was no mannered didacticism aimed at children but a racy account of life in the penal Antipodes, mixed with economics, political puffery and moral purpose leading to the explication of a theory of planned colonisation. Since it came from EGW, no one should have been surprised to discover, eventually, that it was a double hoax. First, it skilfully purported to be – and was readily believed to be – the writings of a genuine resident of Sydney. Second, it was published under another's name, to avoid detection of its real author and, therefore, instant discrediting of its thesis.

EGW's sudden enthusiasm, his enduring and energetic devotion to the subject of colonisation, cannot be explained entirely by his interest in personal emigration or because it seemed like A Good Idea. As populations continued to burgeon, emigration became a recurring issue of the times, and EGW's sharp intelligence picked up on the earlier stumblings and failures of emigration and colonial policies. He saw that in the great and overpowering debates on parliamentary reform, from which he was thoroughly disenfranchised, colonisation – organised emigration – had become a political side issue. Natural but thwarted politician that he was, he saw that it offered an uncrowded platform.

Planning and promoting colonisation would provide a kind of employment: if he was successful he might obliquely gain political status as thinker and expert – a philosopher almost – and perhaps in the long run it might offer a way to improve his financial fortunes. Powerless to influence the greatest political events of the moment, he exploited and brought dynamism to a gathering social and political movement. And, if nothing else, emigration and colonisation provided him with a way to express himself, to be *taken notice of*. There was also a certain romance to conjuring up utopias in the sun. Reading and writing about them was a way to escape his grim environment, to give release to imagination and trapped energy.

His economic arguments and proposed practical methods of planned colonisation would change or be modified in the face of experience, but EGW's basic philosophy of colonisation, as set out in *A Letter from Sydney*, never altered. In the face of a 'present redundancy of population', when '*All trades, pursuits and professions are becoming more and more overstocked; and multitudes of persons, of all degrees and ages, are moving about, without employment, useless to themselves, and a burden to the public*', EGW found 'most extraordinary . . . the small degree of public attention attracted to our colonies, which exceed in number and value those which any state in the world ever before possessed'. Until now, the poor had been 'maintained by their parishes at home', and the rich had 'been brought up too indulgently to sit down willingly as settlers in a new country', but now necessity would 'overcome all repugnance'. Although '*No pains should be spared to teach the labouring classes to regard the colonies as the land of promise*', many of the children or grandchildren '*of the highest families in this land*' must also consider emigration '*unless they resolve to drag on a life of dependence and indigence here*'. It was unfortunate, EGW continued, '*that these establishments should so long have been regarded as fit only for the residence of convicts, labourers, mechanics, and desperate or needy men.* THE GREEK COLONIES CONTAINED A MIXTURE OF ALL CLASSES OF SOCIETY. Regularity and subordination were thus encouraged and preserved in all stages of their progress, and they rose to wealth and eminence much earlier than they would otherwise have done.' If both '*enterprising young men of rank and connections*' and '*young men and women, in the intermediate ranks of life*' could learn to look to the colonies '*as the most certain means of obtaining a comfortable settlement*' and if the poor could be persuaded that it '*would be better for them to purchase a passage, by binding themselves to serve as bondsmen a few years after their arrival in the colonies, than to wear out an abject and hopeless life at home*', Britain might be 'materially relieved of the useless population by which it is likely soon to be encumbered.'[3] And of its 'superabundance of capital'.

And EGW had a dream.

> The colonists, being an instructed and civilized people would be as well qualified to govern themselves as the people of Britain . . . . they might either take a share in framing the general laws of the empire [or] they might frame their own laws, in a Colonial Assembly . . . . At all events, they must be governed, by whatever machinery, with a view to their good and contentment, which is the greatest good, instead of to the satisfaction of their governors only . . . . Mutual dependence would prevent oppression on the one part, and on the other a wish for independence; reciprocity of interest would occasion mutual good will; there would no longer be injurious distinctions, or malignant jealousies, or vulgar hatred between British subjects, wherever born; and Britain would become the centre of the most extensive, the most civilized, and, above all, the happiest empire in the world.[4]

Priscilla's 'British Empire' of 1804, enclosing just the United Kingdom, had become for her grandson, a generation later, one that encompassed the world. Yet it was still an empire with a small 'e', an aggregate of colonies acquired by various, often dubious, means to serve the demands of trade. A century before, John Gay had rhymed with the spirit of the age: 'Be commerce then thy sole design,/ Keep that, and all the world is thine'.[5] Now the territorial fruits of victory from the 'Great War', the industrial pre-eminence of Britain and the power of the Royal Navy as the world's policeman were combining irresistibly with the 'idol of commerce' to generate visions of Empire with a capital 'E'.

This 'happiest empire' could call on the moral precepts of Christianity and 'civilisation' for legitimation, but it was essentially a merchant and middle-class dream fuelled by the hard practicalities of creating new markets for the investment of excess capital, the sale of manufactures and the disposal of surplus labour. And an opportunity for the aristocracy to extend their existing land empires and born-to-rule privileges overseas. There would, too, as EGW observed, be outstanding side benefits for Britain's mercantile marine.

Neither the British working class nor the people who already inhabited the 'waste lands' of North America, South Africa, Australia and New Zealand were or really needed to be consulted: after all, an expanding British empire could only be good for them. Although the humanitarian lobbies in the Colonial Office and missionary societies espoused the sovereign rights of aboriginal peoples, even they never doubted the superiority of British civilisation and the pre-eminence of its unique and splendid political and religious institutions.

They would have agreed with EGW's comment that 'Any people, no doubt, must be the better for communication with the most civilised people in the world'.[6] Whig Lord Palmerston, about to become an almost permanent Foreign Secretary and seen as the personification of a 'high-spirited and over-confident' England, 'considered that all foreigners, at some time or other, might benefit by English advice and English examples'.[7] The worldwide evangelising of missionaries, for all their self-proclaimed virtue and disinterest, played a vital 'secular role as ambassadors of the British Empire and advocates of its expansion'.[8] Any form of humanitarianism – almost by definition a reactive force – would be always playing catch-up with the entrepreneurial enterprises of capital and commerce. And any that advertised colonisation as a form of philanthropy would be difficult to resist.

Emigration was a fact of life; the long British experience of colonisation had already created an entire, new English-speaking nation. Voluntary emigration, mostly to the United States, saw more than 30,000 a year leaving Britain by the end of the 1820s. But with almost 100,000 people on parish relief by 1827, the pressure for a general emigration, an economically driven British diaspora, was becoming intense.

There had been much emigration discussion and a number of public and private emigration schemes in the decade or more before EGW's discovery of the subject: schemes of assisted emigration to Canada; a settlement of 3500 people in South Africa which had become dispersed after much suffering and hardship; Lord Durham's 1825 New Zealand Company investigated colonial trade with that country but decided the prospects were not good enough. Until 1827, Robert Wilmot Horton at the Colonial Office had used government money to 'shovel out paupers' to the colonies and then pushed for a scheme that would allow parishes to raise loans against the poor rates so that the impoverished could be sent on one-way trips abroad. But crude mechanisms for getting rid of unwanted people were not enough.

There was no enthusiasm at the Colonial Office for the idea that Britain's colonies should be increased or that they should be anything much more than a source of trade and a depository for paupers, convicts – or missionaries. The colonies were part of the Secretary for War's portfolio until 1855 and most of the ministers who held the post saw it either as a stage to higher things or were well-intentioned nonentities. Few had a sure grasp of colonial theory or issues.

The real power at the Colonial Office for more than 20 years was James Stephen, who became permanent counsel to the office in 1825 (at the age of 36), assistant under-secretary in 1834 and permanent under-secretary from 1836 until 1847. Son of a master in chancery and a brilliant graduate of Trinity College, Stephen gave up a lucrative private law practice for the opportunity that the Colonial Office post gave him to help destroy the slave trade. This, despite Wilberforce's act of abolition in 1807 (and the Royal Navy's hard work), was still thriving. Like Wilberforce, Stephen was a 'saint', an evangelical Christian, and was a committee member of the Church Missionary Society. The austerity of his character may be judged from the tale that smoking his first cigar gave him so much pleasure that he vowed never to smoke another. Stephen was a reluctant colonialist, viewing Britain's far-flung possessions not as the material for permanent empire but as historically acquired liabilities that should be managed in trust, protecting the rights and welfare of indigenous peoples, until they were able to become self-governing. By the time Edward Gibbon Wakefield came to discover the colonies, they already had a formidable patron saint to whom he might seem the very devil.

None of the emigration planners had adequately thought through the real costs and consequences of their schemes: how they could be self-financing – profitable even – and how new settlements could survive as effective social and economic, let alone civilised, communities. EGW, from his cloistered course of study, came up with a theory of colonisation that depended as much on his vivid imagination as on the facts and the writings of others who had gone before him. His 'arrival on the scene may be compared to the descent of some gorgeous tropical bird among the sober denizens of a respectable farmyard'.[9] No theory concocted by one man in a prison cell ever affected so directly many members of his family, and tens of thousands of others, including 'better, wiser and more cultured men [who] admitted with a candour that did them justice, that his faith made him their master'.[10]

EGW's theory rested on what he saw as the essential requirement to ensure the proper balance of land, labour and capital in a new colony. In the past, he decided, colonial lands had been given away or sold too cheaply, encouraging the accumulation of too much land in too few hands, dispersing settlers, ensuring a chronic shortage of labour and poor investment opportunities and resulting in a wild frontier society. In Australia, he wrote, 'We are in a barbarous condition, like that of every people scattered over a territory immense in proportion to their numbers; every man is obliged to occupy himself with questions of daily bread;

there is neither leisure nor reward for the investigation of abstract truth; money-getting is the universal object; taste, science, morals, manners, abstract politics, are subjects of little interest, unless they happen to bear upon the wool question; and, what is more deplorable, we have not any prospect of a change for the better.'[11] The answer? 'CONCENTRATION would produce what never did and never can exist without it – CIVILISATION.'[12] The concentration of capitalists and labourers was necessary because 'colonisation means the creation and increase of everything but land'.[13] To achieve that vital concentration, the price and disposal of land must be managed.

EGW built on the ideas of Robert Gourlay who, in *A Statistical Account of Upper Canada* (1822), had suggested that waste land should be sold and not given away and the profits used to finance emigration. In *Letter*, EGW decided that 'the object in view may be attained by fixing some considerable price on waste land. Still, how is the proper price to be ascertained?' He eventually developed the idea of a 'sufficient' price for the sale of land that would vary and be regulated according to each set of colonial circumstances. This price should be low enough to attract the small and large capitalist but high enough to prevent excessive speculation; and at just the right incentive level for labourers to work for landowners in the hope that, after a few years, they would accumulate enough capital to buy land themselves. A chief object of the sufficient price was to prevent labourers from turning into landowners too soon.

Regulating the balance between capital and labour by the manipulation of land prices would, EGW reasoned, concentrate colonial settlement and raise agricultural productivity. A planned settlement would have both town and country sections of land for sale. Liberal philosopher and economist John Stuart Mill, the son of Edward Wakefield's friend James Mill, became a devoted supporter of EGW's colonial theories. He wrote that EGW's 'system consists of arrangements for securing that every colony shall have from the first a town population, bearing due proportion to its agricultural, and that the cultivators of the soil shall not be so widely scattered as to be deprived, by distance, of the benefit of that town population as a market for their produce'.[14]

Profits from the managed sale of land would be used to pay for the regulated immigration of labourers. Young immigrants, married couples of good character especially, would be given preference so that the social barbarism of frontier settlements would be avoided and the new societies would be founded on fruitful and multiplying families.

But the new colonies would not be made up only of capitalists and labourers. To bring that essential, civilisation, to a colony EGW opined that there should also be a 'gentry class', a 'higher order' of emigrants.

> They may become landowners in the colony, or owners of capital lent at interest, or farmers of their own land, merchants, clergymen, lawyers or doctors, so that they may

> be respectable people in the sense of being honourable, of cultivated mind, and gifted with the right sort, and right proportion of self-respect. The most respectable emigrants . . . lead and govern the emigration of the other classes. These are the emigrants whose presence in the colony most beneficially affects its standard of morals and manners, and would supply the most beneficial element of colonial government. If you can induce many of this class to settle in a colony, the other classes, whether capitalists or labourers, are sure to settle there in abundance: for a combination of honour, virtue, intelligence and property, is respected even by those who do not possess it; and if those emigrate who do possess it, their example has an immense influence in leading others to emigrate. . . .[15]

The socialist Labour League, in September 1848, criticised Wakefield-inspired systematic colonisation as simply a 'facsimile of English society, with its classifications'.[16] EGW never disguised it. From the outset, he wrote that the new colonies would be 'so many *extensions* of an old society. Pursue that idea, and you will see that emigration from Britain would not be confined to Paupers, passing by the free bridge.' There would be 'farming bailiffs, surveyors, builders, architects and engineers; mineralogists, practical miners, botanists and chemists; printers, schoolmasters and schoolmistresses, booksellers, authors, publishers, and even reviewers; merchants to supply us with English goods, and to take our surplus produce'.[17]

J. S. Mill concurred. 'If to carry consumable goods from the places where they are superabundant to those where they are scarce, is a good pecuniary speculation, is it not an equally good speculation to do the same thing with regard to labour and instruments? The exportation of labourers and capital from old to new countries, from a place where their productive power is less, to a place where it is greater, increases by so much the aggregate produce of the labour and capital of the world.'[18] Free trade would burgeon to the benefit of the great mother country of civilisation and those new countries of the happy empire created in her own image.

Although hostile to his theories, Karl Marx paid EGW the compliment in *Das Kapital* of describing him as the most notable political economist of the 1830s. 'It is the great merit of E. G. Wakefield to have discovered not anything new about the Colonies, but to have discovered in the Colonies the truth as to the condition of capitalist production in the mother-country.'[19] His colonisation theory, Marx said, was essentially a servant to capital, a proposal to manufacture wage workers in the colonies who, for the freedom to own land themselves, paid a ransom through the sufficient price to capitalist landowners. In paying this, they also funded the immigration of more labourers who would then be exploited by their old capitalist masters. An incipient democrat, however reluctant, EGW was never a nascent socialist; he was ever the middle-class entrepreneur with a collection box for charity.

Marx delivered not only a socialist critique of EGW's colonial capitalism; he also pointed to its contradictions. EGW criticised the barbarism of open frontier American settlement: 'Ignorance which promotes conceit and mean pride, is a result of dispersion; the original cause of it in America being not democracy . . . but the low price of new land.'[20] Yet elsewhere in the same book, EGW wrote,

> In America, notwithstanding high profits, individuals seldom accumulate large fortunes. Though the produce divided between the capitalist and the labourer be large, the labourer takes so great a share that he soon becomes a capitalist. Under this most progressive state of society, therefore, the increase of capital is divided, pretty equally, among a number of capitalists increasing at the same rate as the capital; so that while none are compelled to work as servants through life, few, even of those whose lives are unusually long, can accumulate great masses of wealth. Moreover, in such a state of things, the independence and self-respect of all begets a love of equality . . . . in this state of things, there is no idle class, no spending class . . . no adoration of wealth, no oppression of the poor, no reason for political discontent. This appears to be the happiest state of society consistent with the institution of property.[21]

These *were* early days in America and EGW said his colonial theories could be valid for only about 50 years.

This commentary was remarkably reflective of the sentiments in EGW's 1821 Presteigne letter to Catherine. But the contradiction that Marx pointed to was EGW's failure to realise that the ideal capital balance he perceived in America came not from systematic colonisation serving the interests of groups of offshore capitalists but from free, unorganised settlement driven by a belief in democracy. EGW's adherence to class and the 'great law of subordination' was always in conflict with his instincts for philanthropy and equality of opportunity. His sense of democracy was always qualified by the need to recognise the interests of the ruling oligarchy. He would both manipulate and be captured by the owners of capital who alone could make his colonial schemes work.

Initially, at least, EGW saw the fantasy in his theories, the spinning of utopias, one of which would one day inspire *Erewhon*. 'My castle in the air is finished. View it only as a structure of the imagination. Still, does its foundation appear solid? Are its ideal proportions just? Does it seem to unite the chief properties of a good building – usefulness, strength, beauty? If you answer, yes, then I ask, though this plan be too magnificent for execution, may we not really construct a smaller edifice upon this model? In plain English – if the principles here suggested be correct, why should they be not reduced to practice, upon whatever scale?'[22] EGW's thinking was nothing if not audacious, but this can be seen as no more than an individual response to the condition of the times, best expressed by his young contemporary, Robert Browning: 'Ah, but a man's reach should exceed his grasp, / Or what's a heaven for?'

The concept was astounding: to manufacture kitset Little Englands, complete down to every nail and knock-down frame house, and ready to assemble after three – or four-month voyages round the world to lands that Captain Cook had first sighted only 60 years before. Astounding, or absurd. Because EGW's colonies in the air not only took no account of aboriginal peoples in waste lands for which Britain had no sovereignty, they also overlooked the fact that they had never been explored or surveyed, and paid no real attention to geography and climate or the practical, technical difficulties of translating theory into action.

More importantly, like all ideologues, EGW never considered the infinitely unpredictable behaviour of the people who, by and large, were motivated to go to the colonies to escape their old constricting or impoverished environment for a better one where there was the hope, the chance, of Improvement, of Getting On, of going up a notch or two. As Dickens would write in *David Copperfield*, 'Mr Micawber is going to a distant country, expressly in order that he may be fully understood and appreciated for the first time. I wish Mr Micawber to take his stand upon that vessel's prow, and firmly say, "This country I am come to conquer! Have you honours? Have you riches? Have you posts of profitable pecuniary emolument? Let them be brought forward. They are mine!"'

It was one thing to postulate a theory but another to disseminate it and then to convince and galvanise. Because if it were to work at all, enough men who mattered would have to believe in it. In a great burst of creative writing between 1829 and 1835, EGW worked to attract and influence a wide audience with a series of entertaining, sometimes dramatic, books, articles and pamphlets which persuasively channelled into print a deluge of fact and argument.

The first agent for his work was Robert Gouger, a Robert Owen-influenced radical from Lincolnshire who came to London in 1829, attracted by the Swan River colonising project. After meeting with EGW in Newgate, he was enthused by his theories and abandoned the badly conceived West Australian scheme which, as predicted by EGW, ended in dispersion and failure.

In June 1829 Gouger arranged for the printing and distribution of EGW's anonymous pamphlet, *Sketch of a Proposal for Colonising Australasia*, which was later incorporated as the appendix to *A Letter from Sydney.* Two months later, EGW completed writing *Letter*, which was published in nine instalments in the *Morning Chronicle* between 21 August and 6 October and then issued as a book edited under Gouger's name in December. Thorough and single-minded, Gouger placed the pamphlet where he thought it might make an impression and began enlisting support for the formation of a colonisation society founded on the 'main principles of selection, concentration and the sale of waste land for the purposes of emigration'.

One can imagine how it was for EGW when he emerged from under the stone of Newgate and into the spring sunshine of May 1830, flinching a little as he joined the press of humanity beyond the walls. After three years of dark exile, he could stretch his legs beyond the confines of the press yard; his nocturnal company beyond the condemned and the depraved; his daily visitors beyond his children and family and those who had come clothed in prurient sympathy. He had greeted those, as he always would, by 'standing and staring formally' with his hat on.

He had probably prepared himself well for his departure; sent out for a new hat, coat and cravat, brought in a barber that morning. Now he squinted in the unobscured sunshine, wrinkled his nose at the forgotten smells of free streets and stumbled over their cobbled unevenness. The future was uncertain, threatening, too large. But the small soft hands of Nina and Jerningham tugged him on towards the carriage where his Uncle Joshua Head was waiting to drive him home. He tipped the turnkey who loaded his trunkful of books and then turned his back on the low massive doors of the jail.

In his pocket he had a theory, in his valise he had a plan and already he had at least one charmed disciple. For all the disapproval and humiliation, he still had it in his hands to make that world his own, no matter how long the voyage towards it. He had confidence still in his power to persuade, to influence, to enthuse, even to inspire; and to give and gain affection. But it would be always an affection short of the rare kind of intimacy that now lay well behind him, beyond the deep moat of imprisonment. No matter what his enemies might accuse him of, he knew he still had a sort of conscience.

CHAPTER NINE

Life as Propaganda

WHILE EGW LEFT NEWGATE IN SEARCH of social and political promotion, Arthur continued to find none at sea.

> *Halifax, Nova Scotia: 5 October 1830:* My dear Father, As I rather anticipated, I have joined the Winchester as second Lt. but I have not had a word from the Admiral nor do I expect one. What his intentions are in doing it I can not tell, in fact nobody knows his plans many hours before their execution. We shall sail in a few days for Bermuda & the West Indies. There is a prospect just now of two Admiralty vacancies but of course from what the Admiral has said I stand no chance of either. Capt Jacksons is one of them, he has been very ill & must go home. I shall know about matters when we get to Bermuda as the Spanish proverb says 'to know a man you should either sail with him or gamble with him'.[1]

The plaintive tone of Arthur Wakefield's letter reflected the wretched lack of influence that had, twice in recent times, stymied his chance of a merited promotion to commander and captaincy of his own ship.

In July 1828 he had joined the *Rose* at Portsmouth, relieved to embrace naval certainties again after navigating the turbulence and chaos of family affairs. He was ranked senior lieutenant to Commander Eaton Travers in the eighteen-gun, 398-ton sloop when it patrolled on the Cape Station and then sailed north into American waters. At Halifax, in February 1830, he had jumped overboard 'in very severe weather, when I assisted . . . the purser of the *Rose*, who had also jumped overboard, in rescuing a corporal and private of marines'.[2]

Six months later, he repeated the performance but was unable to save his new captain, Commander J. G. Dewar 'who was drowned on the coast of Labrador'. Extracts from the *Rose*'s log[3] tell the story: '15th [August] 6 p.m. Mr Wakefield came on board and reported Captain Dewar drowned, trying to ford an arm of the sea at upper part of bay. Fruitless search for the body. 16th – sent boats in search. 5.30 returned with body found in 9 feet of water'.[3] Given temporary command of the *Rose* while he fulfilled Dewar's orders 'for the protection of the fisheries in the Gulph of St Lawrence', Arthur was soon superseded by a junior officer.

When Arthur wrote to his father in October 1830, Sir Edward Colpoys, commodore of the station, had just taken Arthur on to his flagship *Winchester* as a kind of consolation: he was to serve 'a great part of the time' as senior lieutenant on this large, Java class 62-gun fourth-rate frigate. But Sir Edward soon died and Arthur 'lost the prospect of that promotion which, if he had lived, the senior lieutenant of his flagship might have expected and which, on that account, is so frequently bestowed on senior lieutenants of flagships when their friends in command happen to die on a foreign station'.[4]

Colpoys's great-nephew, a midshipman – later admiral – who served with Arthur in the *Winchester* and later in the *Thunderer*, wrote that he was the 'man of all others in the service that I had the greatest regard for. He was good all round, as a sailor, officer, gentleman and also was an excellent linguist . . . My Grand Uncle . . . gave him acting commission as commander which was superseded by the Admiralty in favour of Pilkington, I believe his junior who, to use a phrase well known in the Navy, could not hold a candle to him. However, in those times no one was insane enough to suppose he could get on otherwise than by personal favour.'[5]

For nearly three more years in Canadian and West Indian waters, Arthur served four captains on the *Winchester* and had to wait until June 1832 before being promoted to first lieutenant. Perhaps jumping overboard at Halifax again had finally prompted it. He tried to save a sailor's life but though he 'picked up the man before he had been two minutes in the water, life was unfortunately extinct'. The navy recognised, at least, that Arthur Wakefield was indestructible and knew what he was about, but merit in middling class men was not nearly enough for rapid promotion.

It might have been the case, too, that courageous, efficient and dutiful though he was, Arthur's piety and self-righteousness rose rather strongly up the noses of upper-class admirals. Arthur had scarcely put a nautical foot wrong but he was not above introducing the odd religious tract into the officers' mess and these did not always go down well between the claret and the port. An abstainer himself, Arthur did take to snuff.

Arthur's loftiness informed his October letter to father Edward: 'I am sorry but not surprized at your account of domestic affairs, to tell you the truth I do not think much about those who have gone headlong into ruin when their education and talents might have placed them [among favourable] situations if they had only been contented with one half of what their imaginations (but not their efforts) lead them to expect. One might moralize for a month & not come to any other conclusion than worldly wisdom is but folly. So many strange things have come to pass . . . public & private.'[6] Arthur was laying up much credit for the next life. Whatever he did in this, it seemed there would be no promotion.

To save paper and postage before the advent of penny post and envelopes, some early-nineteenth-century correspondents perfected a calligraphic habit apparently designed to infuriate future researchers. They wrote both ways across the page: that is, between the words and lines sideways. Faded ink, foxing and tattering have left many surviving letters written this way tantalisingly half-decipherable. Arthur's October letter is such a one. It was addressed to his father in Blois, Loir-et-Cher, but overwritten lines appear to come from Catherine: 'I have had a painful letter about Mrs Brown's money. Cannot you in any way procure the means of discharging that. I send you a budget of disasters but I cannot alter the Truth. I had a letter from William lately: they were all well. Priscilla was here last week & quite well. Mrs Dykes wants to have a pupil to educate with her daughter and Priscilla wishes it extremely if you could hear of such a person. The terms would be 100 pounds per annum including music and everything. Let me hear from you directly.'

It is possible that Edward had sent Arthur's letter on to Catherine at Stoke, who was now passing it on to EGW in London. But these added words and others, scribbled anxiously in the margin, asking how to deal with mortgagees and suggesting the possible loss of an estate, open a small window on to the tangle and stress of Wakefield 'domestic affairs' that occasioned faultless Arthur to express no surprise.

Edward and Frances Wakefield had taken up self-imposed exile at Blois where, eventually, he managed a silk manufactory, and she gave birth to two daughters, Frances, who 'died young', and Laura. In many of the years after EGW's trial they travelled extensively throughout central, eastern and southern Europe. One surviving journal shows that, in the summer of 1830, Edward and his new family travelled from Linz to Vienna and then north to Berlin via Prague and Dresden. A more extensive journal, from April to November 1836, describes a journey from Marseilles to Genoa, Pisa, Florence, Rome and on to Naples where they spent three months. Undated notes reveal that Edward at one time planned a book on France like his Irish tome and he is reputed to have completed a history of Hungary that was never printed.[7] Although no further work under Edward's name was published, he continued to be free in sending advice to British politicians, drawn from the vast amount of information he accumulated during his peregrinations.

Felix followed his father to Blois. Edward's 23-year-old 'flower' had completed his training as a surveyor and civil engineer with the Ordnance Survey, but had lost all opportunity to advance in his father's lucrative estate management business when Edward abandoned it to go to France. It is not known if Felix was with Edward in the years after 1826 but he was in Blois by 1830 where he gathered some expertise in irrigation techniques, became fluent in French and learned some German. His understanding of French language and custom was accelerated by bedding a servant girl in Edward's house. When Marie Bailley became pregnant, it is easy to imagine how pressure from Edward and Frances, in particular, would have pushed him into marriage well before Constance was born in July 1831. If this should have got back to England so soon after EGW and William's release from prison! Continued pressure from his father and stepmother may well have been behind Felix's emigration to Tasmania. He arrived in Hobart in April 1832 with Marie and the daughter, named with unwitting irony, who would prove the only constant factor in Felix's family life.

He began work as a 'temporary assistant surveyor marking out sections that were being offered for sale, but he was then seconded to the Roads Department supervising road building and surveying routes for new roads. It was not long before he was in dispute with senior officials over his demand for an increased forage allowance.'[8] This was the first station of a disputatious, self-destructive life. More than any of his brothers, Felix had been deprived of a regular upbringing, his life overshadowed, distracted and disrupted by their doings. 'He could not write decent English, or rather was incapable of writing a letter upon any matter of business that would be fit to be seen, and he was so devoid of the sense of the value of money as to be capable of independence.'[9] In temperament, Felix had become 'excitable, self-assertive and resolutely bent on pursuing his own erratic course'.[10]

In October 1833 Felix and his family shifted to the Launceston district. Arthur in England received the news that 'Felix has got the situation of surveyor from the Governor & I shall write to him giving him a little advice as I know in these colonies it requires very good management not to become compromised by the settlers who are in quest of good grants or lots . . . it is a great chance for him if he keeps it. There are hundreds of officers capable & willing to take such a situation & many of high rank applying for similar ones.'[11] While EGW scribbled and orated colonial theory in London, Felix was already in colonial practice – the first of the brothers to arrive in the Antipodes – and Arthur had a grasp of practical colonial land settlement problems from his first-hand knowledge of conditions in South Africa and Canada.

In his exile from England, father Edward left the direct management of his estate interests to agents but ultimate oversight to Catherine and son-in-law Charles Torlesse. Even Arthur was saddled with Edward's problems during his brief sojourns ashore. Between ships in July 1833, he wrote to Blois from London, 'I shall be glad to assist you here in any way I can, but I do not pretend to be a good hand at interview with lawyers & rogues, & I must not [incur] any expence or I shall be on the pavée.'[12] Earlier, he had written, 'If I do not see any immediate prospect of [employment] I will go over to see you, but my funds are wearing out & I am afraid of the expence.'

The reasons for Arthur's continued bachelorhood are plain. Apart from the lack of opportunity caused by his monastic life at sea, he simply did not earn enough to set up a household or to think of maintaining one. He would have to reach the rank of post captain if he were to take a wife to sea and, at the age of 33 and in such a peaceful world, the chances of that had begun to recede. But he did not stop trying.

He wrote his father, 'My gun machine is under inspection by order of the Admiralty at Sheerness and I have been down there about it. I left it in very good hands & am now waiting the report of Capt. Chambers . . . . As soon as that is received at the Admiralty I shall make one more effort for promotion.'[13]

Arthur had become an inventor, too, responding to the latest developments in the service. His 'machine' was for the 'imitation of shot practice' and the inspection report was favourable enough that it was put into use on the gunnery training ship *Excellent* at Portsmouth. Established in 1830, the *Excellent* was an experiment, becoming 'the repository of gunnery ideas, and even inventions',[14] and represented the first move in the Royal Navy towards the specialised training of officers.

In aid of promotion, Arthur's last captain's report would have been favourable, too, telling how, as senior lieutenant, he oversaw the decommissioning of the *Winchester.* During a period of nine days, the frigate had been 'dismantled and paid off without an accident during the dismantling, or an irregularity, or the omission of a single formality'.[15]

Arthur could not be passed over. A few anxious months later, he went down to Sheerness again and took up an appointment as first lieutenant on the *Thunderer*, which was being fitted out for a tour of duty in the Mediterranean. Less than two years old, the *Thunderer* was an 84-gun ship of the line; half of its armament comprised massive 32-pounders. Although Turkish and Greek questions had been settled for the moment, the presence of such a smart and formidable vessel would assist to deter any Infidel plans for refighting Navarino.[16] And who better could Captain Furlong Wise have to master the *Thunderer* and its 700-strong crew than Arthur Wakefield, that gun specialist who could also 'safely declare', without a trace of swagger, that he was known to have 'paid especial attention to the management and discipline of men'.

Catherine's terse lines of October or November 1830 referred to both William and Priscilla. After release from Lancaster Castle five months earlier, William would surely have hastened to Quiddenham to be with his infant Emily and then taken her for a time to Catherine's at Stoke. How he had dealt with his grief over his wife's death must be imagined: William left nothing on paper to guide an understanding of how he had hoped to reconstruct his personal life and make a career.

Arthur had once wondered how to cope with a younger William's 'great fault Passion'. By now this had become veiled in reticence. 'No one who had an interview with [him] knew what he thought and what he meant to do. His manner was attractive and, in outward appearance, sympathetic, but the inner man was out of sight and hearing.'[17] William's character may have been completed by the trauma of trial, imprisonment and guilt at being responsible for his dear Emily's heartbroken death. It may have seemed, after the first sweet months of freedom, that not only were his opportunities for employment and social rehabilitation severely circumscribed but also that there was nothing except his daughter worth living for; and that, for her, a better future lay mostly without him, in the care of the Sidneys or Torlesses. He did not have the flair, the imagination, the sheer gall of EGW. There was no ideal or ambition to be pursued; there never had been.

He travelled on unexplained missions to Austria,[18] Russia and Lapland before, in 1832, going south to the sun in Portugal and a career as a mercenary soldier. This was another environment where, for 'men of station', misconduct in other places did not subject them to the 'ill-opinion of society'. He could test his courage, honour and resourcefulness on the battlefield: it would be a way to restore himself or to die in the attempt.

In 1830 Priscilla, 'young Priss', turned 21. The youngest surviving member of her Wakefield generation, shadowed at first by Percy, she had spent almost her entire life in the care and tutelage of Catherine and her grandmother, for whom she was the companion of her last years. In 1823 there had been a tussle for her. Edward had written to Frances, 'She shall leave the Torlesse's immediately. I never blamed Edward [EGW] for removing his children approved it, there was nothing else left for him to do . . . . do not alarm yourself as to any children of yours being brought up under my mothers influence. . . .'[19] But the problem was not so much the senior Priscilla, who now could do 'little more than smile', as the sanctimonious Torlesse household over which 'that bigot' the Reverend Nottidge 'as a gentle Pope exercised an unquestioned influence'.[20]

Edward removed Priss to the care of a governess in Bath at the end of 1823 but this arrangement did not last long. She was baptised at Stoke by Charles Torlesse in 1825 and was found employment as a teacher, partly at a small orphanage in Ipswich established by his mother. Arthur reported to Edward in 1833,

> I have placed Priss very comfortably with Mrs Torlesse and so far independantly that I am to pay 20 pounds a year for her rooms etc. . . w. I have done. I told you I should write to Fanny about making an allowance to Priss, & she sent me an order for 10 pounds on Jones & Lloyd, but upon presenting it they said they had not the funds. I suppose money w. she expected to have been paid in had not been. I do not at all understand how you & she get on with money matters but unless she speaks to you about it perhaps you had better not mention it.[21]

Any business to do with Frances had to be handled carefully. As evidenced by her correspondence with Edward ten years before, she was a volatile and 'unprincipled woman'.[22] She nurtured a 'fury' at EGW over the Turner affair which was, at times, contradicted by solicitous enquiries after his health and condition, prompted perhaps by the recollection that EGW's plea bargaining had saved her from prison.[23]

Frances Wakefield would have been curious to know of EGW's actions and state of mind after his release from Newgate. At first, in the shelter and comfort of Joshua Head and Aunt Bell's home at Ipswich, he would have had the company of his 79-year-old, infirm grandmother Priscilla, 'verging towards the close of her long and useful life. Her admonitions and benediction, we may be sure, were not wanting.'[24] He soon went to stay at the Torlesse home, fifteen miles away at Stoke though, as his involvement with colonisation politics increased, it was necessary to set up house in London with a governess for Nina, turning thirteen, and Jerningham, just ten. But home for EGW and his children – and for William and Arthur, too – would now always be the Stoke-by-Nayland vicarage where Catherine was to spend 50 years of her life.

An epistolary account of this generation of Wakefields would surely be entitled *My Dear Catherine*. This eldest sibling, settled and secure, increasingly mindful of her position as the matriarch of the family, stored away the letters despatched to her at Stoke from brothers scattered all over the world. But she also fulfilled a Priscilla-like role for her extended family and the parishioners of her South Suffolk neighbourhood. Catherine had none of the intellectual strengths of her grandmother but her concern for the local poor was expressed, with vicar husband Charles, in establishing and running a school for girls and, stirred by the example of Priscilla's savings banks, the Stoke and Melford Benefit Society. A schoolroom was built and teacher installed though 'the farmers and their wives as a rule strongly objected to the poor girls being taught. The education was scanty enough, but they learned to read and write, and to repeat the Catechism, and the whole of the afternoon was given to needlework and knitting. . . .' Later a school for boys and girls was started in a nearby hamlet where the boys were taught to knit. 'It was not considered at all derogatory to their boyhood to knit their own worsted stockings in the odd times between minding sheep and scaring birds; for it must be remembered that the boys, as a rule, went out to work when about eight years old.'[25] A boy could earn sixpence a week bird-scaring; women and girls worked at stone-picking and a family might glean enough corn after the harvest to last until Christmas.

Suffolk agricultural labourers, like those elsewhere in Britain, were paupers throughout life and the Torlesse benefit society encouraged the poor to make quarterly contributions to the fund that insured its members for payments in sickness and for funeral expenses. The society was a great success and lasted well into the twentieth century. A 'feast' was held each Whit Monday. The club members assembled on the village green, marched to church and, after a short service, repaired to a 'neighbouring barn, where dinner was served, consisting in the first place of puddings and gravy followed by mighty joints of beef, and finishing with plum pudding; a certain amount of beer brewed for the occasion was served, and pipes and tobacco handed round'.[26] For the impoverished labourers of the district and their families it was an occasion for a year's dreaming.

Charles and Catherine's primary responsibility was the spiritual welfare of the community, centred on the Plantagenet-towered Church of St Mary the Virgin, a building that dated in parts to the early fourteenth century.[27] The living was in the gift of squire Sir William Rowley, who gave the appointment to Charles Torlesse in 1832 after he had served eight years as curate. On Sundays, 'In the early days, Holy Communion was administered but ten times in the year, always after full Morning Prayer . . . the Sermon . . . was half an hour long at least. Special sermons . . . were expected to be much longer.' For moneyed people, 'The high square wooden pews were strictly appropriated to the different houses, and were looked upon as private property by the respective families. The Tendring pew had a small fireplace in it, and a large table in the middle . . . when the squire thought the sermon had lasted long enough, he poked the fire vigorously; if that hint were not sufficient he came and rattled the door handle.'[28] Torlesse, a great enthusiast for church music, raised money for an organ and he and his eldest daughter Priscilla in 1862 inaugurated the first village choral festival held in England.

This was the rural idyll recollected by Catherine's youngest spinster daughter Frances (Fanny) in old age. Of her mother, she wrote,

> Besides her work in the parish schools and clubs, there were girls always being trained in her house for service . . . . Remembering that she had a large family of her own to train and to provide for, the amount of work accomplished is really astonishing. Many and great were the sorrows and trials of her life, but I never knew her fretful, and well do I remember . . . when for some good reason we were all most anxious for fine weather, her saying that she never concerned herself about what was entirely out of her own power, finding always enough work to employ all her capacity where it could be useful.[29]

If her grandmother's life had been a 'devotion to benevolence', Catherine's could be characterised more as a deeply pious and practical devotion to duty within the expectations of her husband and the parish. The virtues of uncomplaining work and selfless charity provided measures for her life's worth and certain ways to manage the world's sorrows and trials.

When EGW came to visit her again with Nina and Jerningham in the summer of 1830, Catherine had five of her own children, four of them girls, the eldest only six; she was just pregnant with her sixth child and three more would come. Catherine would always keep the month following the birth of a child in strict seclusion. She said, 'God has given me that month that I may have more time for quiet thought and prayer for the children.' The haste to produce a large family may have been prompted by Catherine's relatively late age at marriage. Most of her children suffered poor health and one of her sorrows was to be that few survived to old age.[30]

From the time tiny Jerningham was left in her care, Catherine treated EGW's children as if they were her eldest. On and off during the next 20 years or more, EGW would visit Stoke to rest, to recuperate, to write. He would rent a cottage near the vicarage with enough space, at first for his children and later for a litter of enormous talbot hounds and beagles that he would take on early morning rambles over a Suffolk countryside rolling about the valleys of the Box and Stour: a striding and bucolic John Bull with a retinue of baying and yapping hounds to startle and impress the local yokels. He got to know the neighbourhood and the neighbourhood him. From the tower of St Mary the Virgin on autumn nights in 1830, he watched the flare and pulse of hayrick fires, and heard the sound of distant alarms.

EGW had come back into the world at a tumultuous time. George IV died a month after his release, precipitating a general election that was to prove the beginning of the end for the Tories who had ruled for most of the previous half-century. The election was held in the glare of a revolution across the Channel in July when the French 'drove away a mischievous Bourbon king to take a harmless Bourbon king'.[31] The combination of these events formed the catalyst that stirred Britain's long-gathering brew of political, social and industrial discontent to the edge of its own revolution. In the countryside, pauperised agricultural labourers revolted by secretly burning hayricks, after threatening letters were sent to tenant farmers and landowners under the fictitious signature of 'Captain Swing'.

EGW gathered information about the phenomenon at first hand in Suffolk and in 1831 published a pamphlet, *Swing Unmasked or the Causes of Rural Incendiarism*. It was a radical, signatured polemic that took the part of the downtrodden peasant as fiercely as he took the part of the Newgate condemned in *Facts Relating to the Punishment of Death*, published the same year. Another 1831 pamphlet, *Householders in Danger from the Populace*, completed a salvo of publications with which he endeavoured to stake out a place in the turmoil of reforming debate. Their combined effect with *Letter from Sydney* and his other colonisation propaganda confirmed a philanthropic heart but sent mixed political messages.

EGW's account of rural life in *Swing Unmasked* explodes the soft glow of Fanny Torlesse's Victorian nostalgia:

> The privileged classes of our rural districts take infinite pains to be abhorred by their poorest neighbours. They inclose commons. They stop footpaths. They wall in their parks. They set spring-guns and man-traps. They spend on the keep of high bred dogs what would support half as many children, and yet persecute a labouring man for owning one friend in his cur. They make rates of wages, elaborately calculating the minimum of food that will keep together the soul and body of a clodhopper. They

> breed game in profusion for their own amusement, and having thus tempted the poor man to knock down a hare for his pot, they send him to the treadmill, or the antipodes, for that inexpiable offence. . . . Every where they are ostentatious in the display of wealth and enjoyment; whilst in their intercourse with the poor they are suspicious, quick at taking offence, vindictive when displeased, haughty, overbearing, tyrannical and wolfish; as it seems in the nature of man to be towards such of his fellows as, like sheep, are without the power to resist.[32]

In trying to outdo the polemic of old William Cobbett,[33] EGW used the plight of the oppressed agricultural labourer to savage those who had oppressed him. The name Swing was a metaphor for the rural arsonist; *Swing Unmasked* was a metaphor for EGW's resentment and contempt for the classes who had humiliated him and were determined to shut him out, just as they were determined to exclude the peasant from a decent life. The pamphlet was also a demonstration of the strength of analysis and reason against ingrained class ignorance and prejudice. In these, he could consider himself his enemies' superior.

EGW effectively described the miserable condition of the rural poor, unchanged for centuries. 'The important difference between past times and the present is, that whereas, in past times, the misery existed without being known, – we now know all about it. The modern press, with its myriads of eyes and tongues, penetrates into the hovel of the peasant, even pries into his heart, and every day disturbs the peace of fat warm men, by some fresh picture of physical want and mental suffering.'[34]

EGW saw that the new power of the press – not only to convey the condition of the poor but also to convey to the poor news of distant revolution and reform – was crucial to an understanding of the rural revolt. EGW knew all about the influence of the 'public prints' from their coverage of his trials. There were now about 300 newspapers in Britain, the larger ones generated by steam-driven printing presses. The growth of literacy and newspaper reading can be gauged by the fact that the circulation of *The Times* increased from about 6000 in 1815 to around half a million in 1850. EGW's acute awareness and use of the influence of papers and magazines on middle-class opinion explain much of the success of his propaganda. On the question of literacy, he recalled the work of his father: 'About thirty years ago, the education of the poor became a fashion in England' and, though disapproval of the ruling class meant this became only a half education, it was enough to allow the poor 'a knowledge of their own debasement, a discovery that they are slaves'.

He described how the burning of ricks was the peasant's most effective method of revolt. It could be accomplished with some safety under the cover of darkness and it would hurt most of all the 'peasant-hated rural aristocracy'. After canvassing ways of suppressing Swing, from hanging to raising wages, and dismissing all as inhumane or impractical,[35] EGW concluded: 'By no means can the peasantry be made to forget the little they have learned; and to confer on them such instructions as would much improve their moral sentiments, is evidently impossible whilst they constantly endure physical want. Political excitement, assuredly, will not subside until the nation, which has outgrown its laws, shall have obtained other laws in accordance with public opinion.'[36]

This was written in December 1831, as the third Reform Bill was introduced into Parliament and soon after the late October Bristol riots had marked the Lords' rejection of the second. In *Swing Unmasked*, EGW deferred to Francis Place in order to understand the consequences of increasing wages or taxing 'landlords and parsons' for the support of rural paupers at a time of such intense political unrest. In February 1831, Place had printed his own pamphlet on Swing,[37] after circulating a draft for comment to, among others, Jeremy Bentham, John Stuart Mill, Joseph Hume and EGW.

Place might have cautiously approved EGW's pamphlet, but they diverged markedly in their response to the reform crisis and the Bristol riots. In November a National Political Union was established with Place in the chair. Its proclamation stated: 'The Riots, Conflagration, and Bloodshed at Bristol, have at length been arrested. By whom? By the *Bristol Political Union*, to whom the Magistrates have delegated their authority, and whose Members have been sworn in as Special Constables. . . .'[38] Huge crowds were gathering in London which '*may* be exposed to the horrors of Bristol'. A national union was needed 'to obtain a full, free, and effectual representation of the Middle and Working Classes in the Commons House of Parliament . . . to preserve peace and order in the country, and to guard against any convulsion, which the enemies of the People may endeavour to bring about . . . to watch over and promote the interests, and to better the condition of the Industrious and Working Classes'.

Widowed Dan Wakefield, still working towards admission to the Bar, was active in the union from the first meeting. (William, briefly in England, also attended.) On 18 November, as a member of the committee of management, Dan put forward a clutch of resolutions to the union council that would 'disabuse the public mind concerning stigmas . . . cast upon the Political Unions – that they endeavoured to coerce public opinion by animal or numerical power, rather than by moral force . . . . it wished to induce and invite all classes, of every denomination and rank, having moral influence and integrity, to join their standard, and enlist themselves as compatriots under their banners. . . .'[39]

Dan's participation in the union was part of his endeavours to construct a political career. In March, he had called on Place and told him that 'it was intended to publish a list of persons who for various reasons ought to be returned to Parliament'.[40] Undoubtedly, he intended that, reform permitting, he would be on it. This led to the formation of the Parliamentary Candidate Society, of which Place was treasurer and Robert Gouger secretary. Among the committee members were Daniel Wakefield, Bentham, Hume and Charles Buller. Membership of the reforming 'club' was close-knit and it spread its energies across the field of radical issues.[41] Buller, in 1831 was 'six feet three inches in height, and a yard in breadth, but though of great bodily strength he was often ailing'.[42] He had entered Parliament in 1830, aged 23, taking over his father's borough of West Looe in Cornwall, but had voted for the extinction of his constituency by supporting the first Reform Bill. After being temporarily out of the House, he was returned for Liskeard in 1832, following the passing of the second Reform Bill, and in the interim had been called to the Bar. Since his days at Trinity College, Cambridge, Buller had had a reputation as a brilliant debater. 'Everyone who came within Buller's presence was amused by the keenness of a wit which never wounded, and impressed by the sincerity of his purpose for good.'[43] Buller and EGW, from this time, became the most steadfast of friends.

While Francis Place chaired the union, and Dan helped manage it, EGW published *Householders in Danger from the Populace*. 'If events similar to the Bristol riots should occur in the capital . . . who will say that we shall escape a revolution?' The upper classes would be safe, simply retiring to the country, but middle-class householders whose business or profession fixed them in London were in most danger. From whom? The government only had 'vague and uncertain' ideas about who was the enemy within. But EGW's own 'concurrence of favourable accidents [i.e. imprisonment in Newgate] has bestowed upon me, with hardly any exertion of my part, what I believe to be accurate information concerning . . . the London populace'. This populace, 'bent on producing a state of anarchy, with a view to plunder and the destruction of the rights of property', could be subdivided into three classes. 'First, COMMON THIEVES. Secondly, persons whose extreme poverty, frequent unsatisfied hunger, and brutalizing pursuits, render them as dishonest as thieves . . . the RABBLE. Thirdly, a body, principally work-people, though of the working-class they form but a very small proportion – disciples of Owen and followers of Hunt[44] . . . these I shall call DESPERADOES.' EGW described the Huntites as having a 'naturally weak intellect; having deficient foreheads and a sinister expression; being noisy, egotistical, boastful; yet given to lamentation, and afraid of their own shadows. They are addle-headed. I once asked a thorough-going Huntite what was his object. He answered – a republic, with Henry Hunt for president, by means of universal suffrage, annual parliaments, and vote by ballot . . . . They wish, indeed, for a state of things which would give importance to noisy tongues in empty heads, and they urge others to rebel. . . .'

EGW warned that the 'desperadoes' would take advantage of the general insurrection of the 'common thieves' and 'rabble' to get rid of their opponents and impose their new fanatical ideas. A reform bill would not be enough to counter this grave danger; barricades and police would not save the day; soldiers would be reluctant to shoot at a mob partly composed of prostitutes, their intimates, their 'molls'. There would be no insurrection 'IF EVERY HOUSEHOLDER WERE KNOWN TO POSSESS A GUN' (twenty shillings each from Birmingham).

'The householders must be in danger from the populace, unless this precaution against anarchy and rapine be adopted.'

This sensational piece of writing reflects the atmosphere of alarm and apprehension that enveloped middle-class London in November 1831 as mobs surged through the streets, whipped on by orators like Hunt.[45] The fear of riots and worse was real, but where the political unions sought to bring order by pressing for reform and co-operating with existing law-enforcing authorities, EGW's suggested remedy was impractical and absurd. In straining for impact, to achieve a salutary influence in the debate, EGW exposed his political impotence.

Cast out from genteel society by his imprisonment, EGW could not lend his name to any public body such as the National Political Union or the Parliamentary Candidate Society, and brother Dan acted as his surrogate. The frustration of his social rejection, the canker of his wounded self-esteem, consequently acted as goads to his energy and ambition. His adversaries were to make the cardinal political error of keeping him out, leaving him without a job. Officially answerable to no one, he would follow only the dictates and motives of his own political agenda and self-interest, whether enlightened or not. If EGW had been, somehow, tactically drawn into a parliamentary or diplomatic role, the Colonial Office and its ministers, in particular, might have been spared much draining struggle, abuse and financial entanglement over the next 20 years. But the opinion of the ruling class largely echoed the sentiments of that saint at the Colonial Office, James Stephen, who 'deliberately preferred' to have EGW as a declared enemy. 'I saw plainly that the choice before me was that of having Mr Wakefield for an Official acquaintance whose want of truth and honour wd render him most formidable in that capacity or for an enemy whose hostility was to be unabated.'[46]

A later enemy would aptly describe the role that EGW was now nearly always forced to adopt: 'He may be the screw under the stern, but he wont do for the figurehead.'[47] He must pull wires at closed meetings and have the right kind of people round 'for a chop', for it was said that EGW 'was a master in the art of persuading. He seldom failed if he could get his victim into conversation.'[48] He was archetypically machiavellian, his political techniques appropriately matured in Italy, and his passion for ends would always triumph over the moral niceties of means. He had been indulged and undirected in youth; in maturity his frustration and envy were to flare at times into malice and vituperation against his political enemies, deeply marring and detracting from his real achievements as a thinker, planner and propagandist – and bearing no relation to his unwavering generosity to his family and friends.

Above all, to have influence he must continue to write – letters by the hundred, magazine and newspaper articles, prospectuses, pamphlets and books. This would be life as propaganda, of both doctrine and personality, and like all propaganda, it would veer erratically between the prescient and sane and the improbable or fantastic.

CHAPTER TEN

A Long and Sore Trial

IN LATE AUGUST 1834, FROM LONDON, sixteen-year-old Nina wrote to her Aunt Catherine in Stoke: 'The fact is, that in common with Papa and Dodo, my mind has been so completely engrossed for the last six months with the old subject of a New Colony that I have never been able to think of anything besides.' Reminding Catherine 'how hot we were about it at the time when we last enjoyed seeing you (which is now two and a half years ago)', Nina went on to explain their disappointment when 'our sanguine hopes of success were upset by His Majesty's Government; (to the great damage of our loyalty). . . .' But Catherine would 'easily imagine our joy, mingled with eagerness and anxiety, when, after another trial, the plan has at last met the approbation of the Colonial Minister, has been made Law by the parliament, and certain of being carried into effect immediately'. Nina had written to her aunt in the spring of 1832, telling her that the 'colonists were soon coming to the "practical part" of their scheme, and expressing the warmest wish of our all emigrating to Spencer's Gulph', but she had been 'wrong in thinking the termination of our toil was at hand. We had to go through two more years of tedious expectation, harassing procrastination, uphill labour and chilling disappointments, the very thoughts of which make me feel sick; but at length we have triumphed over all our open and hidden foes, we are within an ace of the goal, nothing but a miracle can wrest the prize from us. . . .'[1]

The 'old subject of a New Colony' had first emerged early in 1831. In January the government, influenced by the National Colonisation Society's propaganda (mostly the work of EGW), imposed a uniform system of pricing for land sales in New South Wales. It was a direct reflection of EGW's theory. Also, an Emigration Commission was set up to collect and diffuse emigration information related to British colonies and to render 'any such assistance as may be in [its] power' to help people emigrate. Eventually, the commission and its successors became responsible for regulations governing the seaworthiness, management and condition of emigrant ships and the oversight of emigration practice.[2] Again reflecting EGW's theories, these organisations would come to vet the character and suitability of prospective emigrants who were taking advantage of free passages to New South Wales and Tasmania, funded by the proceeds of land sales. Encouraged by their influence on government policy, EGW and his supporters 'resolved to try and establish a fresh colony, in which both our economical and political views should obtain a fair trial'.[3]

News had recently arrived in England of the discovery of 'a magnificent river falling into the sea at Gulf St Vincent' in South Australia. 'At that time the extensive country now known by that name was a nameless desert about which nothing was known by the public or the government.'[4] Undeterred, and employing scant information but large imagination, EGW and Society members prepared a plan for submission to the Colonial Office. The final version, *Proposal to His Majesty's Government for founding a Colony on the South Coast of Australia*, was printed and circulated in August.[5] This comprehensive settlement proposal incorporated the key Wakefield principles of a sufficient price on land to achieve concentration, with most of the land sale profits to be used to fund the immigration of young people of both sexes. Representative local government was envisaged, with a Legislative Assembly eventually administering all the new colony's affairs. There would be no convicts. But this first proposal foundered on a chicken and egg dilemma in which the Colonial Office would not approve the scheme until the proposed company's capital of £500,000 had been subscribed, and city capitalists would not invest until the Colonial Office approved.

In December 1831 the colonisers tried again by establishing the South Australian Land Company, with a prospectus that was a freshened-up version of the August *Proposal*, and sought a charter from the government. Approaches to the Colonial Office were led by company committee chairman W. W. Whitmore and Colonel Robert Torrens, both MPs, but EGW was the power behind planning and promotion, as Torrens admitted.[6] Torrens, who had long advocated emigration as a solution to overpopulation, had, along with Wilmot Horton, initially opposed EGW's theories on the grounds that the regulation of land sales was inimical to the freedom of individuals to buy, sell and use land as they chose. But he had been won over by EGW's broader vision of settling the world's waste lands not just by facilitating emigration but by *colonising* according to managed economic principles and civilised values.

The timing of the company's proposals could hardly have been worse: in the middle of the great parliamentary reform riots and debates and the changing of the guard in government from Tory to Whig. James Stephen, at that time permanent counsel to the Colonial Office and Board of Trade, damned the charter proposal in a long memorandum of 39 foolscap pages: 'This project is wild and impracticable. There is no reasonable prospect that it would be sanctioned' by the government. He asserted that the Crown was being asked to give up all in return for nothing so that the company could secure 'a lucrative employment connected with great patronage, little labour and no risk'.[7]

EGW saw the chief stumbling block as political: 'The part of our South Australian-plan to which the Colonial Office most objected, was a provision for bestowing on the colonists a considerable amount of local self-government.'[8] Stephen appeared to confirm this in his statement that it was never the intention of a British government to 'settle a republic'. The company committee reworked their proposal and returned to the Colonial Office, offering to drop everything from the charter except land sale and emigration fund proposals and a long-term provision for a legislative assembly. In August 1832, negotiations with the committee were cut off by the Secretary for War and Colonies, Lord Goderich, with the caustic response that 'as the committee were so ready to abandon essential provisions of their scheme, he had serious misgivings as to the maturity of their knowledge and counsel'.[9]

Prospective settlers with a combined capital of £200,000 and 6000 poor people who had applied for assisted passages were left in the lurch. The government's rejection 'broke up and scattered the first body of South-Australian colonists; many of whom, though till then without any turn for politics, now joined the rebellious Political Unions of the time, whilst others sailed for the United States, where they have prospered, though they resemble Irish Americans in their feelings towards England'.[10] This had been the worst of Nina's chilling disappointments.

A more personal disappointment and grief marked the following month when matriarch Priscilla died in Ipswich on 12 September 1832 at the age of 81. Her infirmities had long circumscribed her participation in family affairs and limited the application of her didactic pen, but her very presence had remained a moral touchstone to inspire her granddaughters, to irritate her eldest son and to chasten her eldest grandson. EGW had begun work on his seminal *England and America*, and at her funeral he might have contemplated the wellspring of his writing, both in the constructive example of Priscilla's own books and in the long hours at Tottenham, listening to her read, when his mother was absent in sickness and his father absent in care.

Priscilla's death marked a breathing space for EGW, a time of reflection and reconsideration after a hectic two years dominated by the hullabaloo of parliamentary reform and his strenuous attempts to help launch South Australia. The first election under the new franchise was due and there was nothing more to be done about South Australia until the next parliamentary regime was established. The winter should be given over to writing, to starting another book, which would set out the condition of England, the nature of the reforms that had taken place and what lay in store politically and economically. In particular, he would explicate at length the 'art of colonization' with a view to cogently making his case in preparation for another assault on the Colonial Office.

England and America was substantial in size (about 150,000 words), sprawling in construction (twelve 'Notes' or chapters, with various sub-notes and appendices) and digressive in style. 'Have you read Papa's "England and America", the third chapter especially?' Nina demanded of Aunt Catherine. 'If not, get it, read that part carefully, and then reflect on the happy opening formed by a new colony for a man of small fortune and large family.'[11] The tone and authority of the instruction reveals how much Nina had become her father's first confidante and amanuensis, and been moulded by his view of the world. Thirteen years on, his daughter, now the same age as his first Nina when he carried her away, EGW could have paraphrased for Catherine what he had written in 1820: 'my poor Nina's devotion to me [is] so great that in some instances my faults became hers from imitation, although her pleasing manner of committing them often [gives] them the appearance of virtues'.[12]

The 'third chapter' promoted by Nina was memorably entitled 'Uneasiness of the Middle Class': those who, 'not being labourers, suffer from agricultural distress, manufacturing distress, commercial distress, distress of the shipping interest, and many more kinds of distress' and who were not fortunate enough to belong to the privileged, 'spending' class who could be distinguished as those who, 'whenever they are wronged, or would injure, can buy law without depriving themselves of any other costly luxury; those, in short, who, be their rank what it may, have more money than they know how to spend'. There was a superabundance of farmers, retailers, lawyers, curates, doctors, 'a swarm of engineers, architects, painters, surveyors, brokers, agents, paid writers, keepers of schools, tutors, governesses, and clerks', but not enough work, only cramped opportunities, not least for those young women who were not of, or able to marry into, the spending class. 'There is not in the world a more deplorable sight, than a fine brood of English girls turning into old maids one after another; first reaching the bloom of beauty, full of health, spirits, and tenderness; next striving anxiously, aided by their mothers, to become honoured and happy wives; then fretting, growing thin, pale, listless, and cross; at last, if they do not go mad or die of consumption, seeking consolation in the belief of an approaching millennium, or in the single pursuit of that happiness in another world, which this world has denied to them.'[13]

Nina had steered Aunt Catherine past the second chapter which told of the 'Misery of the Bulk of the People'. In affecting detail, EGW wrote again, as he had in *Swing Unmasked* and *Punishment of Death*, of the pauperish mass of the English people and their dire circumstances, adding another layer to his social improvement polemic. He was writing at a time when the novel was about to replace the poem as the chief vehicle for the literary imagination. Instinctively, EGW used character and dialogue to make his case:

> Now watch the child. Trembling he draws a black bag over his head and shoulders; the master grasps him by the arm and guides him to the fireplace: he disappears up the chimney. Now watch the master. He is motionless, his head on one side, listening attentively. Ask him a question: 'hush' is the answer, with his finger on his lips. Presently a low, indistinct moaning is heard in the chimney. 'William', says the master, putting his mouth to the edge of the fireplace, and speaking in a brisk, cheerful tone, 'that's right, William.' Another moan: and then 'I say, William – brush it well out, I say." Down comes a quantity of soot, and the child is heard scraping the sides of the chimney . . . . This time the master shouts to him, 'Billy, I say, Billy, how do you get on?' . . . . whenever the child cries, or is silent, his master shouts to him, 'Billy, I say, Billy, my lad' . . . . 'We always speak to 'em when they're up the chimney, for fear they should run sulky and stick.'[14]

Into the mouth of a Spitalfields weaver he put an eloquent plea for food and employment: 'The more gin we drink, the more we want; but also the less we drink gin, the more we feel the want of something else. Give us bread, meat, beer, and fire; then we should feel warm without gin. I am not begging: we are all ready to work . . . work, work, work, we have plenty of that. If we did not work we should die outright. But what does our work bring? work and hunger, work and cold, work and sorrow. . . . life such as ours, without gin, is worse than death. . . .'[15]

Thomas Malthus was addressed too: 'Not vice and misery, Mr Malthus, but misery and vice is the order of checks to population. Charity, virtue, happiness! these are English words still, but the meaning of them appears to have settled in America. I wonder that emigration is not more the fashion. . . .'[16] This was, after all, the point of *England and America*, reached after EGW's writing on the relation of capital and labour that caused Marx to pronounce him the leading political economist of the 1830s. And after a political discourse on the recent reform bill which 'was carried by physical force; and those who compose the physical force know this, are proud of it, boast of it, and will never forget it. Did they approve of the bill? As a step, yes; but merely as a step . . . . Universal suffrage was, is, and will be the object of the working classes.'[17]

EGW was now in step with the political times. 'In England, it is no longer a speculation whether democracy be consistent with high civilization. This is the experiment which the English are about to try. Who is there who does not wish them success? If they should succeed, then all the talk about the difference between old and new countries will go for nothing, anywhere; and, in time, the greatest happiness of all will be everywhere secured.'[18]

He had travelled a long way from being the reactionary protégé of Tory William Hill and, more recently, from labelling democratic Owenites as fanatics and desperadoes. Like every good pliable politician, EGW knew when to move on. Yet his acceptance of a widespread future democracy was also influenced by his own outsider status and sympathy with the underdogs of society.

EGW remained a conditional democrat: 'The misery and ignorance of the bulk of the English people render them unfit to enjoy, or rather fit them to abuse, a great extension of the suffrage.' The people had to be educated and made fit for democracy. In the meantime 'there appears but one way of postponing universal suffrage; namely, by preventing the demand for it'. The people would need 'Prudence, wisdom' before being given democracy, and the means to this end were 'high wages, leisure, peace of mind and instruction'.

The first step was to raise wages for those 'millions of people . . . called into existence by machinery'.

> In order to raise wages immediately, the field for the employment of English capital and labour must be enlarged; whereby profits, and the rewards of many services not called labour, would be raised at the same time as the wages of labour. The whole world is before you. Open new channels for the most productive employment of English capital. Let the English buy bread from every people that has bread to sell cheap. Make England, for all that is produced by steam, the work-shop of the world.[19] If, after this, there be capital and people to spare, imitate the ancient Greeks; take a lesson from the Americans, who, as their capital and population increase, find room for both by means of colonization. You have abundance, superabundance of capital; provide profitable employment for it, and you will improve the condition of all classes at once. Instead of lending your surplus capital to foreign states, or wasting it in South American mines . . . invest it in colonization; so that, as it flies off, it may take with it, and employ a corresponding amount of surplus labour.[20]

An approving reviewer of *England and America* suggested that its central arguments, which required the 'instantaneous repeal' of the Corn Laws, meant that the book should have been 'more appropriately called an Essay on Free Trade and Colonization'.[21] In EGW's vision of British free trade, 'Made in Birmingham' or 'Made in Sheffield' would become worldwide trademarks of manufactured quality.

The political and economic discursions of the first two-thirds of *England and America* led inevitably to its disquisition on colonisation. This included the publication of part of the correspondence between the South Australian Land Company and the Colonial Office – plus acerbic footnotes. In one, EGW cited a government insider's comments on the company's 1832 proposal to the office: 'If you want the sanction of government, you must put a great deal of patronage into your plan: this plan is too cheap, altogether too good, ever to be liked by our government. Instead of £5000 a year for governing the colony, say £20,000 a year; and give all the appointments to the Colonial-Office. If you do this, you will get a charter without trouble: if you hold to the present plan, you will never get a charter, except by appealing to the House of Commons; and not then until there shall have been two or three elections under the reform bill.'[22] These and other attacks by EGW on the venality and hypocrisy of politicians and bureaucrats had substance but were often malicious and hypocritical[23] – his wounds ran deep and he could never resist the opportunity to strike at those who worked to prevent him getting his own way.

Given that EGW had already published other works under his own name, the marginally actionable nature of some of his comments in *England and America* may have been behind his decision to publish anonymously rather than his self-deprecatory excuse that he did not have a 'name which should give to every statement or suggestion the weight of authority'. Abuse might still attach to his name, but it is hard to picture EGW as a shrinking violet.

The book's agreement was signed on 18 October 1833 between the publisher and R. S. Rintoul acting on EGW's behalf. But if there were any legal proceedings then the author was to 'come forward and hold the publisher free from all pecuniary and other damages'.[24] Scotsman Robert Rintoul, who had been made editor of the *Spectator* on its reincarnation in 1828, had become EGW's staunchest press ally. He had been publishing his articles since the Newgate period and his review of *Punishment* in 1831 averred, 'If ever a man redeemed the wrong he had done society, by conferring on it a vast benefit, it is Mr Wakefield.' Where the Whig (Tory from 1835) *The Times* was forever EGW's opponent, the new Radical *Spectator* was the unflagging supporter of his ideas. EGW publicly and privately recognised Rintoul as the 'person to whom I am especially indebted for having been able to propose with effect recent improvements in the art of colonization'.[25]

England and America was a success and renewed interest in planned colonisation. Robert Gouger had failed to resurrect the South Australian Land Company earlier in the year but the impact of EGW's book and his unrelenting enthusiasm and persuasion encouraged him to try again. By December, Gouger had gathered together a new provisional committee, abandoning a profit-making joint stock company for an association to secure a charter to found a South Australian colony belonging to the Crown but administered by the committee acting as a board of trustees. The new committee included Buller, Torrens, Sir William Molesworth and other Members of Parliament. Negotiations resumed with the new colonial secretary, Lord Stanley. The sticking point was still the question of political control. Stanley wanted a colony that would be chartered as far as the money, the work and the responsibility were concerned, but still reserved all legal powers to the Crown. EGW was certain that if this question could be addressed, there would no trouble raising the capital because of the high level of interest in the scheme shown by bankers and merchants. EGW decided that a new bill was needed to create a hybrid colony, part Crown, part chartered, to satisfy both government and association interests. In March 1834, he called on brother Dan to turn his dictation into law. It was the beginning of colonisation as a Wakefield family business.

Dan had been called to the Bar in January 1832 and, following his involvement with the National Political Union and Parliamentary Candidate Society, stood as an independent liberal at the first election for the reformed Parliament in December. Dan presented a list of pledges to the electors of Lambeth, avowing that in the new kind of Parliament they deserved to know exactly where their MP stood on key questions. 'He who flatly refuses to pledge himself is evidently fit . . . to *represent* nothing but his own breeches pocket. The candidate . . . who volunteers a full and *plain* declaration of his views . . . is probably an honest politician . . . . I offer pledges as a candidate in order to feel comfortable as a member. If you accept my pledges, you will bind yourself to let me vote as I please.'[26] Among Dan's pledges were taxation reform, continuing parliamentary reform, abolition of tithes to support the clergy, the abolition of slavery and the 'repeal of all trading monopolies', particularly in such necessaries as sugar, tea and bread.

His campaign was damaged when Lord Mahon, mistaking him for EGW, vilified his character after Dan gave an address in Hertford at the end of October. Although it was clear who Mahon was referring to, Dan sought satisfaction and obtained a public withdrawal.[27] Some mud must have stuck, but this was not the only reason why Dan was not elected.

Despite his fine intentions, he was probably underfunded compared with his Tory and Whig opponents when, despite reform, traditions of treating still lingered. At the nomination meeting just before the election, Dan declared to the crowd on Kennington Common that 'whether in or out of Parliament he would always use his best exertions to effect that which the majority of the people considered best calculated to promote their benefit'.[28] On a show of hands for the four candidates standing for the two Lambeth seats, a Mr Tennyson and Dan received an overwhelming demonstration of support. But when the final results came in four days later, Dan ran a distant third. He formally 'protested against the election of Mr Hawes [second place to Tennyson] . . . inasmuch as he and his agents had been guilty of bribery and corruption in procuring votes. (Cries of name, and cheers) . . . . He felt confident that had the ballot prevailed he would have been elected as one of [Lambeth's] representatives. . . . whatever might happen . . . he would appear among them again at the next election. (Cheers).'[29]

There was no mention of emigration in Dan's election pamphlet; but in the South Australian Association he soon saw the chance of a different kind of political career. A month of negotiations and modifications of the Wakefield bill followed before Stanley promised to put it to the government. After much compromise, the association anticipated success and moved into high gear, publicising and promoting the new British province in the Antipodes. But by late May nothing had happened. 'Over fifty intending colonists signed an appeal to Gouger pointing out that unless some immediate move was made it would be too late to proceed to South Australia that year . . . some had already sold their property and were ready for instant embarkation. One family had actually purchased a schooner and refitted it for the southern adventure.'[30]

Stanley resigned from cabinet at the end of May and the association moved quickly to capture his successor, Thomas Spring Rice, before Stephen caught his ear at the Colonial Office. Gouger and Dan Wakefield travelled to Spring Rice's home at Cambridge where he promised to recommend to cabinet a new bill if it included specific provisions covering the amount of land sold and capital raised before the scheme came into operation.

The association organised a meeting at Exeter Hall on 30 June, attended by 2500 people and lasting six hours, where the principles and plans of the scheme were laid out and questioned. 'The speeches, for the most part, were based on Gibbon Wakefield's *England and America*. They vaunted the abounding opportunities awaiting the respectable man of small capital and the emigrant labourer.'[31] Personal odium was still too recent for EGW to be confident of speaking in public, but Dan was his surrogate when he waxed eloquent on the prospects for self-government for the colony once it had reached a population of 50,000. This would be one of the greatest checks ever devised to counter the bad government of colonies – that is, at the direction of the Colonial Office. Dan had been well schooled by EGW. One Thomas Lovett asked whether there would be any fixed rate of interest on capital and whether the association did not intend to grind the people down to the lowest possible wages once they got them out to Australia; and whether poor immigrants would have a chance to acquire land, to make and alter laws and be given an equal opportunity for political power. Dan's reply was a lawyer's yes and no. No money would be lent to migrants, all land would be put up for open and public purchase and he did not believe that there would be any possibility of sinecure places since the colony's income would be small.[32] In other words, capital still counted.

The South Australia bill went to its second reading in the House of Commons on 21 July. It survived attempts to throw it out and attacks in committee before it arrived in the Lords in early August. Many suspected it was a get-rich-quick plan for its promoters, another bubble to be floated on the South Seas. The Duke of Wellington at first described the association's project as 'a speculation'. When pressured to retract this, he stated it was not something for hasty legislation and could wait for another session. The association's offices were now thronged with intending colonists seeking office in the new colony and preparing for the first expedition; ten days of intense lobbying followed to try to push the bill through.

At the height of the lobbying, Robert Gouger wrote to the Duke of Wellington, seeking to persuade him that the bill was based on humanitarian principles and was not a party issue, appealing to his apolitical sense of honour and duty.[33] But EGW was the most active proponent, working underground 'like the mole, in out-of-sight obscurity'.[34] After the bill was made law on 15 August, he wrote to Rowland Hill,[35] an active and persuasive member of the association's committee, that in order to save the bill he had made friends with Wellington, implying that, if he supported the legislation, South Australia's capital city would be named after him. EGW pressed Hill to use his influence to see that this was done though 'I heartily dislike him, and never call him by any other name than Old Wooden Head; but the military colonists do respect him, and a colony is of no party'. [36]

Although the bill was passed, the Colonial Office could still undo it all with delays and regulations. EGW's agitating style of manipulation entertains in this excerpt from another letter to Hill that followed close on the heels of the first: 'After passing the Stanley Bar, escaping the Sands of the Commons, steering thro' the dangerous rocks of the Lords, the colony is in danger of being drowned by arriving, if not within, still close upon the rainy season. Every day lost now is worth a month, considering the vast difference between summer & winter during the weak infancy of a nation. . . . it is shameful that such a delay should occur without an object, but, at the Colonial Office, Right and Wrong have nothing to do with it, The only rule for getting on there, is Importunity, which includes a good deal of impudence.'[37]

EGW's sense of urgency to see South Australia through disguised his anger at the association's increasing propensity to stray from his principles of colonisation. There had been too many compromises: 'We struck out this provision because it displeased somebody, altered another to conciliate another person, and inserted a third because it embodied somebody's crotchet'.[38] In April, Gouger had already recorded, 'Saw Edward Wakefield [EGW]. We disagreed materially on the mode of going to work after the Act of Parliament should be brought in, and this led to much unpleasant talk between us.'[39] In May, Gouger added, 'Edward Wakefield thinks I have lost sight of the principle of colonization in allowing the introduction of any clause making the immigration fund applicable to any other purpose than the conveyance of labourers.'[40] EGW's disagreement with the association's direction – and deepening conflict with its principals – probably explains his reluctance, after the bill was passed, to commit to his own emigration to South Australia. But Nina was working hard on it. . . .

'I have not changed my mind as to emigration,' she wrote to Catherine late in August 1834.

> I still wish very much to go out, especially if you were going . . . Dodo [Dan] expects to obtain the appointment of Judge-in-chief in South Australia, in which case he turns colonist immediately. William also, who, now peace is restored in Portugal, has got nothing to do, and finds it hard indeed to get paid for his former services, talks of leaving the Queen's service, and emigrating to South Australia, in which case, as Felix is already there [i.e. Tasmania], and Howard is sure to join them from India presently, there will be a nice party of our family at our Antipodes. The more I think of it, the more I wish that Uncle Charles would give up his poor living and turn South Australian with you, and all yours, including dear Priscilla; for then I think Papa might be persuaded to go too, and then what a nice party we should make! – flying from straitened means and anxiety for your children in future, to plenty, large profits

> for yourself, and easy, happy prospects for all your family . . . I wish I were at Stoke, for I am sure I could persuade him [Charles], and then if I succeeded, we should have nearly the whole family of us joined together in South Australia, for I take it for granted that if you went, Papa would go too, with both his chickens.[41]

Nina's letter to Catherine bloomed with adolescent fancy but was full of her father's fantastic hopes and his belief that propaganda, no matter how overdrawn, was a legitimate means to a desired end. A fortnight later, from her Great-uncle Daniel's home at Hare Hatch, Nina wrote another letter, even more fantastical, to her intimate friend, thirteen-year-old Rosabel Attwood, daughter of Thomas Attwood MP, the Birmingham businessman and reformer. 'I hear there is a possibility of your family all turning South Australians at once, in which case, as I am trying hard to persuade my father to the same thing, and feel pretty sure of success, we may calculate on the chance of meeting again very soon, and probably all going in one party. . . .' Nina reminded her friend of her wish to step 'on a shore on which no one had been before yourself, but unfortunately for that idea, there have been so many navigators, sealers, runaway convicts, etc., on that coast that you cannot feel sure of treading an unbeaten track, and the only way of standing where white man never stood before is to be one of the exploring party which will be sent, immediately after the landing of the people, up the country to discover and survey it'. She continued enthusiastically:

> The explorers travel through forests, across rivers, and over vast plains, which have never been seen before; making maps and taking sketches as they go along. . . . An exploring expedition is like a donkey excursion on a large scale, but you have the extra satisfaction of knowing that you run the risk of some little danger, and that you are enjoying a pleasure which cannot be enjoyed by anybody in England. Think of standing on a high hill and looking for leagues in every direction without seeing a human being, or any animal except a few quiet kangaroos and emus, and hearing no noise but the rustling of the trees and the bubbling water of the little cascade at the foot of the hill, or the bustle of your party pitching their tents for the night on the hillside, and preparing for supper a fat Wallabee kangaroo which one of the sportsmen of the party shot that morning as they were traversing some beautiful grass plains. . . . After supper . . . the captain of the expedition proposes that the hill on which you are going to pass the night be called after you; all present instantly assent; a glass of wine is poured on the grass at the entrance of the tent, the party rise and give three hearty cheers, and the captain proclaims that henceforth the hill shall be called Mount Rosabel. . . .

Nina hoped the Attwoods would decide quickly about emigration 'as I am almost sure of going with papa in October, we shall not have the pleasure of forming one party on the voyage unless you make very great haste in your preparations, which, by-the-bye, are different in their magnitude when you are going to the other side of the world to when you are taking a trip to a watering-place. But I hope that you will be ready by the 20th of October, and we will all sail together, singing merrily, "The deep, deep sea!"'[42]

Rosabel replied to Nina's letter. On 18 October, two days before the date Nina had adjured her to be ready for the long voyage, EGW wrote to her mother.

> Though I do not like to leave Rosabel's letter unanswered, I cannot write to her. She is too young to be told of my wretched feelings, and I cannot hide them. Besides, my dear Nina talks of her very often with a strong affection, which you will see is natural when I tell you that she was never intimate with any other girl at all near her own age; and thus I am unmanned only by thinking of her.
>
> My dear child is declared to have a mortal complaint of the lungs. Two or three months is all the time that I can expect to keep her in England; but a vague hope is held out to me that a warm climate may save her. Of course I am on the point of removing her; but of giving her even that poor chance I am not sure, so great is her weakness, and rapid the sinking of all her bodily powers. She is reduced to a skeleton, but is patient, cheerful, rational and fearless. Heartbroken myself, I am obliged to laugh and play with her as when she was quite well. You will see why I cannot write to Rosabel, and will excuse me for indulging, while writing to you, in these expressions of grief. It is a sort of comfort to me to imagine that you will feel with as well as for me. Yet what right have I to give you the pain of sympathising with me? None, nor can I tell why I inform you of my misery, unless it be that my only present consolation is the number of people who have shed tears at the thought of never seeing my darling again.
>
> I have but just left her at the seaside,[43] and am hurrying to make arrangements for our departure – to what distance must depend on her state. . . .[44]

It would be a voyage shorter and more conclusive than any to the land of the 'fat Wallabee kangaroo'.

At a crucial time, EGW was now distracted and removed from any effective participation in South Australian activities. Before the new act could come into effect, a Board of Colonisation Commissioners, acceptable to the Colonial Office, had to be appointed and it had to sell £35,000 of land and deposit a guarantee fund of £20,000 with Treasury. Then a political crisis in November led to a change of government and a brief return of the Tories under Sir Robert Peel. The composition of the board was not completed until the Whigs returned under Lord Melbourne in April 1835 and the appointment of Lord Glenelg as Secretary for War and the Colonies. EGW, ministering to the failing Nina, took little part in the events of this critical period.

In a letter to Catherine from Portsmouth, late in November, EGW could report that he and his daughter were 'about to take the only chance that remains': they were sailing that day for Lisbon.

> The change will be great and sudden, with all the advantages of being at sea, and without most of its ordinary inconveniences. But I have next to no hope. She is sadly reduced, and the cough is very bad. Yet the Drs still declare that the lung is not incurably affected, and that the change may do wonders for her. With so uncertain a result before me, I cannot, of course, say much of the future. I start all of a sudden, having been offered the passage only yesterday; no delay being possible on account of the Captain's orders, nor any desirable, since the Drs say 'don't lose an hour; in a few days more it may be too late'. Thus, I depart without seeing Edward [Jerningham]. He does not know that Nina is ill, and I am unwilling to tell him. But I write to him by this post, saying that I am obliged to go to Lisbon on urgent business. If possible, he shall join us there at Xmas, unless my worst fears (or my hopes, however faint) should be realized.

Nina, 'delighted at the prospect of the voyage', sent her dearest love to Catherine and her family. 'It will comfort you to know that I continue well in strength and spirits, being strung for a long and sore trial which, I know, must be borne. . . .'[45]

After the shock of the first bout of bloody coughing, and then weeks of desperation at trying to find a cure for Nina or, at least, a favourable diagnosis, there was now relief in decision: a chance in the sudden sailing of a ship; the healing prospects of sea air and sun. In saying nothing to his son, EGW expressed every father's obdurate hope for a failing child. Edward Jerningham did not join his father and sister in Lisbon for Christmas. As companion for Nina, EGW found a Portuguese girl of her own age, Liocadia di Oliveira; together they shared the 'long and sore trial' of caring for her, of easing her steady decline, of coming to terms with the inevitable.

Seven weeks after arriving in Lisbon, EGW sent two letters by the packet to England. 'My Dear Mrs Attwood, – Yesterday my dear child, becoming aware of her danger, wished to write to several friends by dictating to me. A letter to her brother so much exhausted her that she could proceed no further, but she desired me to write in her name to those whom she could not but neglect, and amongst them to Rosabel. It is only to keep my promise to her that I send this scrawl, so that I may tell her when she wakes that I have done what she desired. She is sinking fast. All hope has been at an end for some weeks.'[46]

To Catherine, EGW wrote, 'I make an effort to write one line for the purpose of warning you of a misfortune which now seems inevitable. Poor Nina is still alive, but that is all I can say. . . . The next packet will probably take an account of her death. I write by this one, doubting whether I shall be able to write when all is over. Hitherto, you will be glad to hear, I have been well and cheerful; but I know that the strain on my spirits, or mind, is severe and that I shall have to pay for the effort by and by. God Bless you . . . I shall not lose a day in getting to Edward.'[47]

Seventeen-year-old Nina died about a week after Catherine received this letter, on 12 February 1835. Almost three months passed before EGW could write to her again, after he returned to London.

> I should not have got courage to do so now, if I had not promised to convey to you the kindest expressions of regard which were uttered by dear Nina on the very last day of her life. It was only then that she became entirely conscious of her situation. She desired me to give you a lock of her hair, and to tell you that in her last moments she thought of you with the tenderest affection. Indeed the prospect of dying seemed to strengthen the strong love which she bore to all whom she loved at all . . . . Of you she spoke frequently and made for you with her own poor starved hands, a little packet of her hair, which I shall send you when I am able to open the box that contains it. I have nothing more to say. As you did not know her when she was no longer a child, when she had become my friend and partner in every thought and object of interest, you cannot sympathise with me: you cannot estimate my loss. The vulgar notion of death has no terrors for me; but I feel more than half dead myself, having lost her for whom alone, of late years, I have lived. . . .

Nina had died of tuberculosis, all too common at the time, but it had struck suddenly, ' almost without a parallel and not to be stopped'. Although everything possible had been done, the illness 'lasted just four months, and life was preserved for the last six weeks merely by carefulness. The change of climate had no effect whatsoever. . . . It appears certain that the disease had existed for months, perhaps years, before it declared itself. I make a comfort of not having to blame myself. But then, on the other hand, it is an even chance that Edward will be attacked in the same way. . . .'[48]

Although Nina had been susceptible to coughs and colds, and suffered whooping cough early in 1820, there is nothing to suggest that her constitution was exceptionally or congenitally frail. EGW's words betray his uneasiness at the knowledge that, during the Newgate years, he had subjected his children to severe physical and mental stress. Their unstable and variable living circumstances had inevitably exposed them more to disease. Almost certainly, sometime between the ages of nine and twelve, Nina had picked up the tuberculosis bacillus that had then lain dormant, focused perhaps in a lymph node, to become virulent during her involvement in the South Australian crisis.

EGW would be forever haunted by the possibility that his own reckless behaviour had been at least partially responsible for Nina's death, by exposing her to the 'filth' and 'closeness of the rooms' during the three 'years of danger' in Newgate.[49] Although grief stirred him to write these last words in his letter to Catherine, they also contain a sense of guilt: 'The subject is one on which I never talk or write when I can help it.'

Thirty years later, towards the end of his life, he was never heard to 'mention his wife or Nina'. He said then, 'I should have been in a lunatic asylum before now if I had not been able to put a subject out of my mind.'[50] His ability to shut out trauma, to suppress his grief, gave EGW the emotional armour to go on. Nina's death had meant 'good bye to my philosophy', confirming for him beyond doubt the capricious nature of an 'incongruous, contradictory, mottled world'. He would never again trust himself to engage in an intimate relationship. The recollection of pain was bad enough; the danger of more was too much to contemplate. His behaviour towards those who crossed or opposed him in the years from 1835 must be interpreted in the neurotic context of EGW's hidden despair; and in the absence of a wife or daughter able to draw out and neutralise its poison.

At length, EGW sent Catherine the lock of Nina's hair and a fragment of her unfinished cross-stitch embroidery, 'the needle stuck in just as the little tired hands left it'.[51] It was said that Catherine could never again speak of Nina without tears. They would have been tears not just for Nina but also, like her grandmother Priscilla, for herself; and for her brother and all that had been lost.

CHAPTER ELEVEN

Down the Ringing Grooves of Change

On his return to England in the spring of 1835, EGW moved to renew his life with 'other objects of interest. To make a beginning, I intend that henceforth Edward should live with me . . . . [He] is grown into a little man. I hear [from school] a very high character for abilities and good conduct.'[1] Edward Jerningham, or Teddy, was almost fifteen. The effect on him of Nina's death, of his only and elder sibling, is undescribed but it cannot have been less than intense. The children had been close. A year or two before, when Teddy had been home from school, the two – probably cued by EGW's tales of his own schooldays – 'skilfully disguised themselves to impersonate a young married couple, and in that character audaciously called on Wakefield himself to request information about a house which he had advertised as being to let . . . . Wakefield did not discover the deception . . . and the youthful couple departed in great glee at having secured excellent "terms" from their prospective "landlord". To their delight that evening their father told them of the visit he had had from a "charming young couple" who had agreed to take the house. . . .'[2]

Teddy's grief was complicated by the onus of EGW's expectations of him as his only child. He could have had no doubt about the superior place Nina had held in his father's affections – or the incomprehensible reserve EGW showed towards him. Jerningham's experience of his father had been limited to time during holidays over the previous four years. EGW had sent him off to boarding school but, conscious of his own experiences, at Westminster in particular, and showing radical views consistent with the beliefs of his father and grandmother, chose the innovative Bruce Castle School, the most progressive of its day. His decision would have been further influenced by sentiment – Bruce Castle was the old manor house at Tottenham – and by his association in South Australian affairs with one of the school's founders, Rowland Hill. Hill, with his father and brothers, had established an experimental school at Hazlewood near Birmingham in 1817 and ten years later bought Bruce Castle as a 'branch establishment' for the London area.

Bruce Castle offered a broad curriculum compared with public schools still restricted to teaching the classics. The Hills included modern languages, science and even technical subjects: 'Several of the pupils have thus become expert carpenters, and, for their age, tolerable machinists'; they printed the school magazine on their own press. Even more remarkable was the school's governance. There was no corporal punishment and the 'pupils are regularly admitted to *a share of its government*'.[3] 'Each pupil was trained to be a gentleman, and to put a check on another pupil's ungentlemanly conduct . . . This was carrying out the old Saxon system of the Hundreds, where each section was responsible for the behaviour of persons within that section.'[4]

EGW took Jerningham away from Bruce Castle to have his company and assistance at his King's Bench Walk home in the Temple and when he travelled to France. Later, Jerningham was enrolled for a time at King's College nearby, a university institution opened in 1831 in direct opposition to the Bentham and Hume University of London, founded in 1826, which was seen by the clergy to have the 'fundamental defect . . . of . . . the entire omission of every thing connected with Christianity'.[5] The 1828 inaugural meeting for the college was chaired by the Duke of Wellington and had two archbishops and seven bishops on the platform. It was planned that the new university would have as 'an essential part of the education imparted, to imbue the minds of youth with the principles of Christianity', according to the Church of England. It seems inconsistent for EGW to have sent Jerningham to the religiously driven King's after Bruce Castle, and when the Benthamite London University was more in accord with his ideas and connections. But EGW may have been more concerned with impressing potential supporters of his colonisation schemes than with the character of Jerningham's education – and of using this as a way of slighting Rowland Hill.

For a brief time after returning from Lisbon, EGW also had the company of Nina's last young friend, the peasant girl Liocadia di Oliveira whom, for Nina's sake and at her request, he had promised to educate and look after, if her parents consented to give her up. Perhaps her presence was too much a reminder of Nina's last days because EGW soon placed Liocadia at a ladies' school in Twickenham. He continued to provide for her education and maintenance, and occasionally took her with him to Stoke, but she would never become part of his household. Also, about the time Jerningham began to attend King's College, it seems EGW contemplated adopting a child. But slowly, his deeper and deeper involvement with colonial enterprises absorbed his energies and distracted his loneliness.

EGW soon began to break with the South Australian Association. Superficially, the argument revolved around the proper application of the sufficient price for the new colony, but EGW would certainly have felt that he was not being afforded proper notice and influence in the association's affairs. He would have been piqued at being overlooked as one of the government's new commissioners for South Australia though, even at five years' distance from Newgate, he remained *persona non grata* for any official position. 'A dilettante Commission,' he called it, 'an amateur Commission, a sort of fancy Commission', downplaying both the competence and attention to duty of its unpaid members.[6]

In his four-month absence from England, the South Australian reins of power had been firmly grasped by Torrens as commission chairman, Rowland Hill as secretary and Gouger as South Australian Colonial Secretary. EGW was to vent his vexation, the spleen of his powerlessness, on all three. He had decided that £2 an acre was the proper sufficient price for South Australia but the association and the commission considered that 12s was the highest price at which land sales would move. On 25 May, EGW told Gouger that at 12s South Australia would become another West Australian fiasco. 'On your own account I long to add to some of the arguments by which, just this time six years ago, you were induced to abstain from going to ruin at the Swan River.'[7] A few days later Gouger noted in his diary, 'Rowland Hill has to-day received a long letter from Edward Wakefield, still urging the old topic [of £2] and speaking of me as his mere delegate in the previous Committees! This gentleman will not let me get away without a downright quarrel with him, and Hill himself thinks he wishes to quarrel with him.'[8]

In early June, EGW attacked Gouger for not supporting a high enough sufficient price: 'How do you know that nobody will buy land at a sufficient price? That experiment has not yet been tried. That experiment may be tried here without risk to anyone. We wholly disagree, you see, on what you call principle . . . . I am obliged to you for having spoken to the Commissioners, as you have thereby saved me and my plan of colonization from all responsibility as to the success of this undertaking. My firm belief is that, if the Commissioners should act in agreement with you, the first expedition will prove a lamentable failure.'[9]

He wrote also to the commissioners, staking out his pre-eminent role in the South Australian project:

> The plan has been defended in so large a number of pamphlets and books that a list of them would surprise you. Now all those books were written by me or by friends of mine; while I also composed nearly the whole of the advertisements, resolutions, prospectuses and proposals, and of the applications, memorials, letters and replies to the Government, and other documents of any importance adopted by those three associations [the Colonisation Society and the South Australian companies of 1831 and 1834]. The draft of a charter submitted to the South Australian Association, and the Act of Parliament which was substituted for that proposed charter, were drawn by a near relative of mine under my immediate superintendence . . . . By entering more into detail I could readily satisfy you that in the steps which led to the passing of the South Australian Act I have had even a more constant and active participation than appears by this general statement.[10]

EGW repeated his objections to Torrens and threatened to withdraw his support for the entire project. Conscious of EGW's power to deter investors and cause political problems with adverse propaganda and manipulation of sympathisers, Torrens compromised by agreeing to lift the price to £1, but he had to threaten resignation from the commission board before the increase could be carried.

The first land regulations for South Australia, incorporating the £1 price, were issued on 19 June. The following day Torrens attempted to reconcile Gouger with both EGW and Dan Wakefield, who trailed faithfully at his brother's political heels. Gouger recorded, 'I told Torrens that I never again would meet them as friends; if I met them in public life for the furtherance of a public object, well and good; but I would not meet them in private life.'[11]

EGW had lost the confidence and friendship of an effective ally of six years standing, the man who had made possible the first publication of his colonial theories. This rift can be ascribed not only to EGW's grievance at being left to loiter in the corridors of power but also to his inflated sense of his own indispensability and his anxiety at Gouger's enlarging role. As the new South Australian Colonial Secretary, Gouger now had an increased influence on association affairs and was marked out to be a key figure in running the new colony. Excluded from any such role, and jealous that Gouger would be carrying his principles into actual practice, EGW could exert power and gain kudos only by attempting to maintain proprietary rights over the principles themselves.

Temporarily satisfied with the turn of events, EGW took an active part in selling sections at the association's Adelphi offices when land went on sale in mid-July. He was also preoccupied with another book project. On his return from Lisbon in April he had contracted to prepare a new edition of Adam Smith's *Wealth of Nations* with his own commentaries, to be issued serially in six volumes. The first appeared in autumn 1835 and in the preface to the series, EGW wrote that though he considered a good deal of Adam Smith's writing irrelevant to current economic conditions, much remained that was worth commenting upon, adding to, correcting. 'My last object has been to apply the doctrines of Adam Smith and others to some new circumstances in the economical state of our own country . . . . There are no means now for stopping the democratic movement: after a halt, it only proceeds more rapidly. But the popular discontent may perhaps be removed. What are the causes of that discontent, and the means of removing it, are questions in political economy; and questions too, as it happens, which have been to some extent examined by Adam Smith.' EGW felt that Smith's 'sagacity' allowed him to 'foresee in speculation that rare coincidence of low profits with low wages, and of both with rapidly increasing national wealth, which has actually occurred in Great Britain, and has lasted for years, without being so much as perceived, till quite lately, by any of the economical writers under whose eyes it took place. My last object, then, has been to ascertain, with the aid of the text, the causes of our peculiar economical troubles, and the means of removing them.'[12]

EGW's commentaries on *Wealth of Nations* pointed out the continuing relevance of Adam Smith, and his debt to the economist's ideas in his own formulation of political and economic theory, despite the fact that his colonial approach was distinctly different. EGW understood, like Smith, that though the creation of wealth was the major goal of economic enterprise it should always, in the best traditions of the Scottish Enlightenment, remain 'subordinate to a belief in civilisation'.[13] At every stage, this belief informed EGW's plans and dreams for his antipodean colonies.

In February 1839, with the issue of the fourth and final volume, the publisher felt obliged to publish an apology and a disclaimer, pointing out that though EGW had been paid a £200 advance for his commentaries he had, in fact, provided them only for Book 1 and the first five chapters of Book 2. 'After every mode of entreaty and of remonstrance has been resorted to in vain, during the course of the last three years' nothing more had been forthcoming. 'The publishers feel that they cannot any longer remain silent under what appears to be a fraud . . . . They therefore submit this statement of facts to the public, and, in publishing this Volume, . . . complete, as far as they are able, their engagement with the subscribers.'

This professional notice was a public reflection of what friend and foe alike had privately experienced of EGW's entrepreneurial enthusiasms. A year later Sir William Molesworth, one of his most ardent supporters, wrote to a colleague, 'I can't put reliance on Wakefield because he has too many projects afloat.'[14] While admiring of his ideas, energy and persuasive felicities, even his closest friends were wary of the volatility of EGW's moods, intentions and opinions.

By the end of August 1835 fewer than half the South Australian sections had been sold at the £1 price. Pressed by committed and anxious emigrants, the association had to keep up the momentum. Without reference to EGW, they dropped the price to 12s for five months from 1 October. This opened the way for shipowner, merchant (and resigning commissioner) George Fife Angas to float a new South Australian Company which, by January 1836, had bought up 13,700 acres at a 40 per cent discount and raised other funds to meet the financial conditions of the South Australia Act. The governor was gazetted on 21 January; his letters patent and the order in council establishing the province of South Australia were issued on 19 February. Three days later, the first shipload of settlers left London.

EGW's reservoir of influence with the Association had been used up; he had left himself no friends in the key positions of control in South Australian affairs. Gouger would continue to propagate the Holy Writ of the sufficient price and the emigration fund but the establishment of the colony would be governed by Angas's business-like evangelism and Torrens's belief that the proceeds of land sales should be used for covering all colonial costs – not just emigration – in a 'self supporting system'. Torrens moved to try and amend the South Australia Act to accommodate this, but EGW forestalled him by publicly accusing the Colonial Secretary, Lord Glenelg, of trying to subvert the primary intent of the act. The premium paid by land purchasers under the sufficient price, he wrote, was intended purely to pay for the emigration of labourers. 'It is the "fundamental law" . . . the Directors say – "The Company will have all its labourers conveyed out by means of this fund; and consequently will *receive back again the money it has paid for land, in the shape of passage money for its servants*".'[15] The concentration of landowner, capital and labourer was essential to EGW's colonial vision which not only sought the most effective means of transferring capital and people to new lands but also foresaw the re-creation of the best attributes of British society and civilisation.

Torrens and Glenelg drew back when EGW provoked enough paid-up colonists to protest that any change to the principle of the emigration fund would be a breach of contract. But Torrens simply bided his time. The future management of the South Australian colony was now out of EGW's control. Despite telling Catherine in December, 'I have half a mind to go myself, for a year, to tell the tale of the beginnings',[16] he was left fulminating on the quayside. And in the perverseness of his unrelenting disagreement with Gouger and Torrens can be detected EGW's tacit belief, since Nina's death, that he really did not have the heart for South Australia.

Dan was out of it too, marginalised again by the behaviour of his older brother. Since EGW had drawn him in to draft the South Australia bill, Dan had been closely involved with promoting the project and developing plans for the colony. He was on the committee of the South Australia Association and from August 1834 had been a member of the management committee of the South Australian Literary Association. This had the object of 'cultivating and diffusing useful knowledge' among colonists and tackled such subjects as natural history, the Aborigines, a police system, internal water carriage, a land bank, labour regulations and religious provisions. 'Lists of equipment for the voyage were prepared, and useful devices exhibited, such as a steam cooking apparatus and a tea kettle heated by a mixture of turpentine and spirits.'[17]

Following his prominent part in the drafting of the South Australia Act, Dan had been frequently spoken of as the colony's first judge. He pursued this post by seeking the support of John Shaw-Lefèvre, the Colonial Office's appointee as a South Australian commissioner and, earlier, Lord Stanley's under-secretary at the Colonial Office. After the accession of Melbourne's second government in April 1835, Dan reminded Shaw-Lefèvre that Spring Rice had 'all but promised the appointment' to him when the act was passed in 1834, and sought his influence with the new Secretary for War and Colonies, Lord Glenelg. Expecting to procure the judgeship, Dan made a second marriage on 1 September to Angela Attwood, sister of Nina's friend Rosabel and the eldest daughter of Thomas Attwood.

The Wakefield-Attwood connection can be traced back to Dan's involvement with Place's National Political Union in 1831. Thomas Attwood was one of the great heroes of the parliamentary reform movement. In 1830 he had co-founded the Birmingham Political Union and, at a series of extraordinary outdoor meetings in 1831 and 1832, had attracted crowds of up to 200,000 people. 'Remember, my friends,' he orated, calming riot but infusing hope, '*our* weapons are PEACE, LAW, ORDER, LOYALTY and UNION. Let us hold fast to these weapons, and I tell you that the day is not distant when the liberty and prosperity of our country will be restored.'[18] In May 1832, when it was rumoured that the Duke of Wellington intended fresh opposition to the Reform Bill, Attwood threatened to assemble a million men on Hampstead Heath in protest, an action that the government knew was within his power. This broke the last opposition and the bill received the royal assent a few weeks later.

Attwood's return from London to Birmingham was in the nature of a grand royal progress. The most popular man in the Midlands, he was returned to Parliament for the new two-seat borough of Birmingham but, by 1835, he was becoming increasingly disillusioned at his limited ability to effect reform in a Parliament which, though more representative, remained under the control of the moneyed and the powerful.

It is said that Dan lost interest in South Australia when EGW withdrew and that this was 'much to the relief of his wife's relations'.[19] 'I am very anxious about my dear Angela,' Thomas Attwood wrote to his wife. 'I should not like her to go to Australia, and I take it for granted that Mr Wakefield will not go. With his talents and connection I hope he may do well in England.'[20] Attwood family pressure may have played some part in Dan's withdrawal of interest, but other factors were much more influential. Before putting forward Dan's case for the South Australian judgeship to Lord Glenelg, Shaw-Lefèvre had canvassed the opinions of colleagues in the law and they were all unfavourable. One had reported that the 'general recommendation is against him . . . . I have heard a great deal of him but nothing good . . . . [there is] a general unwillingness to have anything to do with him. The notoriety of the Family may have something to do with this.'[21] Dan had also written at length to MP Joseph Parkes, soliciting his sympathy and support, presumably unaware that Parkes was one of a group of MPs who had agreed to support the South Australia bill only on condition that EGW held no office in the settlement association or company. Shaw-Lefèvre wrote even-handedly to Glenelg, saying that there was 'certainly an impression against [Dan], but I cannot trace any adequate grounds for it'.[22] He pointed out Dan's contribution to the South Australian project and suggested Glenelg make further enquiries himself. But clearly Dan had little chance.

Finally, when EGW severed his connection with the association at the end of 1835 he would have, effectively, forbidden Dan to take any further part in the enterprise – for Dan, not Gouger, was EGW's cypher on the committee – and EGW's domination of his brother was complete. Unable to stake out his own place in EGW's empire, Dan's interest in South Australia was expunged. He dropped out of colonial and political consideration, probably to his own relief as much as his wife's relations', and went to live in his father-in-law's house near Birmingham, planning a return to the law.

EGW's dissociation from the South Australian scheme allowed him to avoid the blame for anything going wrong. When reports came back in succeeding years of inadequacies in the survey, squabbles over land sales, speculation, political conflicts and disputes over the principles governing the colony, EGW had the perfect told-you-so evidence of his June 1835 letter to Gouger. Had he not warned that the 'first expedition will prove a lamentable failure' if the colony was not established strictly according to his principles? There *was* no thoroughgoing attempt to establish South Australia consistent with his colonisation principles; but the colony's problems were not attributable only to disregard of his advice and the conflict of intractable individual interests.

The hybrid South Australia Act, which he and Dan had largely constructed, was compromised and flawed, inadequate for constitutional direction. And the application of the sufficient price, while theoretically ideal in providing for concentrated, civilised settlement, took no cognisance of the varying quality of the land sold – whether this was governed by a town section's favourable or unfavourable location within the new city plan or by the varying fertility of rural sections. Sections were drawn by ballot – literally a lottery – and the real value of the land was determined after settlement by its genuine commercial or agricultural worth, thus encouraging both speculation and discontent.

The sufficient price also took no account of the economic imperatives of pastoralism. In *A Letter from Sydney* EGW had railed, 'Here we have nothing but wool, wool, wool,'[23] and dismissed sheepfarming as the enemy of civilised colonial communities. This ignored the concomitant truth that, in the early stages of settlement in Australia, woolgrowing was the chief way to ensure a colony was economically self-supporting. Australia's vast savannah lands were ideal for large-scale sheep and cattle grazing on the station principle. Tightly knit new towns with surrounding farms providing agricultural produce for local consumption were not enough.

Nearly seven years after *Letter*, as the first ships were on their way to South Australia, EGW admitted the importance of pastoralism, but attempted to fit it firmly with the sufficient price. When giving evidence before the House Select Committee on the Disposal of Land in the British Colonies in June 1836, EGW agreed that 'The right of pasturage is a very important item in Australia . . . . As the object of a fixed price for all freehold land would not be served at all by any restriction upon the use of pasturage, I should allow the utmost possible liberty of use . . . subject to such conditions as would secure the use.' He suggested a nominal rent, or none at all, but with pastoral leases subject to the adequate, verified stocking of the land.[24]

Before the same committee Torrens argued that it 'would involve great difficulty to ascertain in such an extensive district the quantity of stock kept upon the land',[25] and considered that a high enough rental would ensure pasturage was used. Torrens grasped something of the difficulty of trying to fit pastoral squatters, ranging into South Australia from adjacent states with roving flocks, into planned 'civilised' settlements created from the regulated sale of freehold land. It was like 'trying to control Arabs'. Neither EGW nor Torrens came up with any solution to what proved to be a fatal flaw in the Wakefield system of colonisation: how to control pastoral and other speculators who simply moved outside the surveyed boundaries of the settlements.

But at the time of the select committee hearings, the practical test of EGW's system was yet to come and his submissions received a largely sympathetic hearing. EGW was both careful and measured in his language, refrained from personal attack and impressed members with the authority and cogency of his arguments. The chairman was Henry George Ward who, along with committee members William Hutt and Bulwer Lytton, were members of the South Australian Association; Hutt was also a commissioner and had been a member of the National Colonisation Society since 1830. Sir Francis Baring and William Ewart Gladstone were being converted into long-term EGW supporters.[26] His only real critics on the committee were Poulett Scrope and Colonial Under-Secretary Sir George Grey.

The hearings turned out to be a benefit for EGW. A third of the evidence heard came from him and the committee's resolutions endorsed all the key parts of his theory such as a uniform and fixed minimum price for land, the nett proceeds from land sales to be employed as an Emigration Fund. In its final resolution, the committee entirely endorsed the central tenet of EGW's political economics: 'The transfer of . . . labour to the Colonies, by enabling them to turn to the best account the advantages of soil, climate, and great natural fertility, which they possess already, cannot fail to open new channels of industry, and commerce, both to them, and to the Mother Country, and thus to enhance, incalculably, the prosperity of the United Empire.'[27]

The lessons from South Australia, the first attempt at systematic colonisation, would take time to be identified and learned. But the incontrovertible fact remained that an organised settlement was being planted in a distant wilderness with, in a time of *laissez faire,* the Crown's direct participation in questions of sovereignty, government and management. Although the sufficient price principle proved to be flawed in the actual practice of land sales and provision of labour, the principle of a self-funding emigration scheme by a tax on sales proved sufficiently effective to attract enough hard-nosed investors and emigrants to make the colony work. EGW's achievement was the initiation of a new culture of planned migration with a considerable degree of government intervention entailing high standards in emigrant selection, and this went a long way towards ensuring a balance in the population of agricultural, trade and professional skills as well as a high level of literacy. Tens of thousands of emigrants set out for Australia in the years that followed the first settlement of South Australia in 1836 and, 'As a consequence of the Wakefieldian programme, Australia joined the big league of emigrant destinations'.[28]

EGW was a prime instigator in the movement of a culture, the extensions of British society and values, which led Britain to become the 'centre of the most extensive, the most civilized, and, above all, the happiest empire in the world'.[29] Civilisation and happiness would, as always, be judged through the lens of self-interest. But for most British settlers, as the rising star of Britain's poetic firmament, Tennyson, was writing,

> Not in vain the distance beacons. Forward, forward let us range,
> Let the great world spin for ever down the ringing grooves of change.
> Through the shadow of the globe we sweep into the younger day
> Better fifty years of Europe than a cycle of Cathay.[30]

News of South Australia did not filter back to England until 1837 and any difficulties reported would be put down by the commissioners to teething troubles; picked off by EGW as the consequence of transgressing his sacred dogma, or thoroughly obscured by continuing propaganda for the promised land. But for EGW the evidence that he had lost all influence with the South Australians came when Torrens was able to amend the South Australian Act later in 1836 to allow the Land Fund to be used for colonial costs other than emigration. The final insult came in July, soon after the select committee hearings, when King William IV's secretary sent a note to the new governor 'signifying His Majesty's pleasure that the capital town of South Australia should be named Adelaide'[31] after his consort. EGW was mortified at the betrayal of his undertaking to 'Old Wooden Head'. Amends would have to wait.

EGW's success at the select committee hearings and the prominence he had now achieved through his writing as a colonial theorist and political economist encouraged him to try re-entering public life. He was also encouraged by the support of a number of radical MPs whose friendship he had gained through their involvement in colonial politics.

He moved to find a seat in Parliament in December 1836 when he prepared an address 'To the Electors and Other Inhabitants of Birmingham', anticipating that his new Attwood connection would help win him the second seat there in the forthcoming general election. Thomas Attwood was becoming increasingly democratic in his ideas, allying his Birmingham Political Union with the ultra-radical Chartist movement, but this alienated his more moderate supporters. EGW's address was a counterfeit of Attwood's position: 'The House of Commons was reformed by its own members – by their ignorance, frivolity, laziness and selfishness – their callous indifference to the sufferings, and their haughty disdain of the petitions of the people.' His 'one subject', he wrote with electioneering hyperbole, was the 'means of preventing Distress, or, in other words, of securing a state of uninterrupted Prosperity'. He would work for laws 'calculated to benefit the bulk of the People . . . . I should rejoice to see the People obtain Universal Suffrage, Vote by Ballot and Annual Elections.'[32]

A cynic might have asked whether this could be the same Edward Gibbon Wakefield who, five years previously, had labelled supporters of such ideas as desperadoes. But if a week in politics is a long time, five years was in the nature of a millennium. EGW would have argued that he was hoist not so much by his own propagandistic petard as by the changing demands of the time.

The list of his other planks, however, revealed his expediency. He supported reform of the currency, an Attwood obsession, and legislation for Ireland and the claims of the Dissenters, other Attwood enthusiasms. The only original Wakefield plank was reform of the criminal law, 'more especially as regards the punishments of death and of transportation'. On the last question, his staunchest ally was Sir William Molesworth MP, who would soon obtain a committee of inquiry into transportation and write its report; he campaigned against it unceasingly until his death.

Molesworth, a committed Wakefield disciple, was fourteen years younger than EGW and came of a family that had been settled at Pencarrow, near Bodmin in Cornwall, since the time of Elizabeth I. Weak constitutionally, Molesworth had been disfigured by scrofula in childhood and persecuted for it at boarding school. Like EGW, Molesworth went to Edinburgh High School, then Edinburgh University and finally Cambridge where, in 1828, he was expelled from Trinity College after a quarrel with his tutor. This was resolved by a duel fought in Calais. He survived this and took off for Rome and Naples for two years where he indulged in 'youthful follies' and Arabic studies.

At his majority in 1831, the demands of family duties called Molesworth home and news of the accelerating parliamentary reform movement enthused him to play a part. At Cambridge he had been influenced by Charles Buller's utilitarian propaganda and he became one of James Mill's utilitarian faithfuls after gaining the seat for East Cornwall in the first reformed Parliament. Molesworth was introduced to the committee of the South Australian Association at the end of 1833 when he came under the influence of EGW's personality and ideas. His family fortune enabled him to be a 'trustee responsible for the safety of considerable funds belonging to that colony'.[33] EGW had got him young.

Like EGW, Molesworth had suffered personal trauma and disappointments. His closest sibling and younger sister Elizabeth, who took the 'keenest interest in his political work', had died young from influenza. His interest in Islam, his professed agnosticism and his radical political views led to his being disappointed twice in attempts at marriage, being described by the young women's guardians as an 'infidel' and 'unbeliever'. Molesworth was embittered by his personal disappointments and for some years withdrew from Parliament and society, taking refuge in studies for his definitive edition of the works of Thomas Hobbes, published between 1839 and 1845.

Molesworth attached a letter of endorsement to EGW's Birmingham address and EGW wrote to Rintoul about organising a political meeting in Birmingham on suffrage issues, especially the secret ballot. But the Birmingham attempt came to nothing, most likely because electioneers attached to the Attwood camp would have wanted nothing to do with EGW's lingering notoriety and the inevitable uproar that would have been attached to a Wakefield nomination. In January, William Wakefield wrote to Dan, 'I see no more of E.G.'s proposed trial at Birmingham than from [your] father in law's letter which seems to me a closer.'[34] This suggests that Attwood himself doused EGW's hopes.

Disappointed politically, EGW returned to a new project that had increasingly engaged his attention. It had gathered momentum following a simple question from the chairman of the Select Committee on Disposal of Lands in the British Colonies. On 27 June 1836, H. G. Ward asked EGW: 'Are there any parts of the world, subject to our dominion now, in which you imagine that new colonies might be founded advantageously under this proposed system?'[35] The question smacked of a set-up.

'Many,' EGW answered imperiously. 'I consider that in Australia at present there are no colonies . . . . they call the keeper "His Excellency", and the chaplain "Right Reverend"; but the real truth is that they are nothing but gaols. Then South Australia is not yet founded.' There were other potential colonial sites in Australia, and also,

> Very near to Australia there is a country, which all testimony concurs in describing as the fittest country in the world for colonization; as the most beautiful country, with the finest climate, and the most productive soil; I mean New Zealand. It will be said that New Zealand does not belong to the British Crown, and that is true; but Englishmen are beginning to colonize New Zealand. New Zealand is coming under the dominion of the British Crown. Adventurers go from New South Wales and Van Diemen's Land, and make a treaty with a native chief, a tripartite treaty, the poor chief not understanding a single word about it; but they make a contract upon parchment, with a great seal: for a few trinkets and a little gunpowder they obtain land. After a time, in these cases, after some persons have settled, the Government at home begins to receive hints that there is a regular settlement of English people formed in such a place; and then the Government at home generally has been actuated by a wish to appoint a Governor, and

> says, 'This spot belongs to England; we will send out a governor.' The act of sending out a governor, according to our constitution, or law, or practice, constitutes the place to which a governor is sent a British province. We are, I think, going to colonize New Zealand, though we be doing so in a most slovenly, and scrambling, and disgraceful manner. That country appears to me to be open to colonization.

EGW went on to speak of South Africa, Ceylon, the west coast of North America and South America, but New Zealand was the focus of his lengthy reply. Clearly, he had been thinking about it for some time, perhaps after his disappointments with South Australia, and had shared his thoughts with Ward. Both he and committee member Sir Francis Baring, banker and currently joint secretary of the Treasury, let it be known after the hearing that if EGW intended going forward with a New Zealand scheme, he should keep them informed. William Hutt nodded his agreement.

EGW left the select committee elated at his success. He knew he could count on a number of radical MPs, but first he would have to recruit Lord Durham, still nominally chairman of the dormant 1825 company, before any new enterprise to New Zealand could be activated; Durham had briefly tried to resurrect his company in 1834. EGW popped New Zealand into his portfolio of projects. There could be something in it for all of them.

CHAPTER TWELVE

Strangers to their Family

THE FOURTH TIME ARTHUR WAKEFIELD JUMPED overboard it was into the comfortably tepid waters off Piraeus in the recently independent kingdom of Greece. This time, in 1834, he had 'the satisfaction of saving a life',[1] which made a change from the holystone and polish routines of showing the flag of the *Thunderer* throughout the Mediterranean, and overseeing the protocol of on-board receptions for grateful Greeks, less grateful Turks, self-consciously haughty French, intriguing Spaniards, anxious Italians and dubious North Africans of all nationalities.

The Mediterranean was the theatre for a great deal of diplomatic game-playing as the various great powers represented both their presence and self-interests with naval squadrons. In the summer of 1835, for example, there was Trouble in Tripoli and Tensions with the Turks. 'It is reported that the Russians have managed to put a stop to the intended augmentation of the French squadron in the East, and something is said about a threat to take possession of the Dardanelles, if Great Britain does not reduce her present force, or draw it out of the Archipelago . . . .' The Austrians had 'been very active', as had an American squadron off Malta and a Turkish flotilla of ten sail 'supposed to be the Tripoli expedition returning to Constantinople'.[2] During this period, the *Thunderer* was part of the nine-strong squadron cruising the Greek archipelago that so provoked the Russians.[3] As the day-to-day commander of the frigate, Arthur sometimes had his practical hands full: 'The winds have been very boisterous, and the *Thunderer* lost her main yard, main sail, and fore and main topsail, in a sudden squall.'[4]

From his time in South American waters, Arthur was practised in the post-war Royal Naval arts of 'cruiser' diplomacy. But he possibly took most personal pleasure in squadron competitions such as the full de-rigging and rerigging of ship – down to half masts and back again – or target gunnery, all to be undertaken with speed, accuracy and the least loss of life and injury, and within sight of the maximum audience. Arthur even had time for another spot of inventing. Sir Josias Rowley, his Commander-in-Chief, 'after witnessing and approving my invention for facilitating the fishing of anchors with a double hook, officially submitted the same to the Lords Commissioners of the Admiralty, and . . . this improvement has been in constant use . . . on board the greater part of the Mediterranean squadron'.[5]

There was the occasional pirate, smuggler and slaver to deal with; but during the 1830s there was no serious exchange of hostile fire over the placid waters of the great middle sea and the Mediterranean squadron had the easiest of all assignments in pursuing the British imperial aim of keeping the sea lanes open for Free Trade. Arthur was serving in an executive arm which, in the most direct and practical manner, secured and protected both freedom of the seas and the interests of British citizens wherever they might be. In post-colonial times, it is routine to dismiss nineteenth-century cruiser or gunboat diplomacy as the height of imperialistic arrogance yet, in different forms, this has always been a great power tactic, right up to the present day. Britain's keeping the sea lanes open was to the advantage of all trading nations, not least the United States. British naval power brought about the independence of Greece as a consequence of the Battle of Navarino and prevented French interference in Garibaldi's expedition to unite Italy in 1860.

Arthur, as one of the élite officer class of the Royal Navy, was directly serving the interests of his elder brother. Colonial plans were a nonsense without the naval securing of sovereignty and protection of Britain's rapidly expanding mercantile marine. Some considered it just as well that the navy had turned from warrior to policeman as ships and manpower were run down in the long hushing years of peace on the high seas and the service became increasingly sclerotic in command, tactics and techniques. The 1830s were the long lazy days of a late summer for sail and Arthur must have grown frustrated at dwindling opportunities for both action and promotion.

Despite this, the fact that Arthur made first lieutenant of the *Thunderer* at the age of 33 was an achievement in itself. In 1832, just 776 Royal Naval lieutenants were actively employed and about 300 of these had entered the blind alley of service in the small ships of the Coast Guard. Service in a leading ship of the line still gave Arthur the chance of a way up. The parallel career of an officer of the same age, and possibly known to him, illustrates not only Arthur's advanced skills and leadership qualities but also his relative good luck. Michael Turner, born in 1799, was said, like Arthur, to have had 'quite good Interest'.[6] He also served in the Anglo-American War, was at the Battle of Algiers and, again like Arthur, passed his lieutenant's exams in 1818. But then, during the next 20 years, Turner found employment in only one commission and ended his naval career as Admiralty agent in a contract mail steamer.

Arthur's appointment on the *Thunderer* concluded with the end of Rowley's term as Commander-in-Chief Mediterranean and the ship's return to England in

February 1837. In January, William Wakefield wrote to Dan that Arthur's friends in the service 'cry out much at his not being included in the late promotions'.[7]At Plymouth a bitterly disappointed Arthur dutifully oversaw the paying-off of the *Thunderer* and its crew of 700 and, again, 'no accident or irregularity occurred, although during ten days of that disorganizing period the ship was without marines, and had no other than blue-jacket sentries'.[8] Thomas Attwood recorded that he had dinner with Arthur in London on 18 February, in company with Dan, Daniel Senior, EGW and Jerningham.[9] This family gathering would have encouraged Arthur to prepare the extensive memorial of service he completed ten days later and sent off, with numerous captains' testimonials attached, to the First Lord of the Admiralty, Lord Minto. Arthur's concluding appeal was unconsciously poignant: 'Indeed, my Lord, I have become a stranger to my family; I have no home but in the service; no tie, or enjoyment, or wish, or serious thought apart from it; nor any hope consequently, except in your Lordship's justice, of that distinction which I know not how to seek, other than by respectfully asking your Lordship to reconsider whether I have deserved it.'[10]

Although EGW had excited Arthur's interest in his new New Zealand project, he was distracted from it first by his promotion, just two months later, to the rank of commander,[11] and then decisively, two months after that, to command of Her Majesty's steam vessel *Rhadamanthus*. Yet it was a half-hearted kind of promotion. As first lieutenant of the *Thunderer,* Arthur had been fulfilling the position of commander without the rank's title or pay. Although this was now recognised, and he was one of only 150 commanders employed by the navy, he was eligible for command of nothing more significant than eighteen-gun ships and this carried little social consequence. And he had been given command of a paddle steamer. Although the naval world was beginning to turn from sail to steam, status was still borne forward not by smutty smoke-stacks but by cloud-white billowing sails reflected in polished brasswork above decks 'earnestly washed or sanded at all hours of the day and night'.[12] After the brief euphoria of being given his first ship, Arthur must have become aware that, unless the opportunity occurred for distinguished action or service during the *Rhadamanthus* commission, his line of promotion was coming to an end.

But first there was excitement and pride in his novel command. He wrote to Catherine in September: 'I had a letter yesterday from my father congratulating my steam appointment at which he is delighted and I must say that I am also. It is quite a superior way of moving and at this moment it is in very great progress. I hope to do well with it although I have one of the original vessels which is several years behind the present ones in advancement.'[13]

Progressive Arthur was deprecatory of a ship that had already performed well. Launched at Plymouth in April 1832, the *Rhadamanthus* was described as a wooden paddle sloop, almost 165 feet long, armed with two 18-pounders and two brass 6-pounders, and powered by a steam engine generating 220 horsepower. The *Rhadamanthus* had been present at the siege of Antwerp in December 1832 and in 1836 was one of only thirteen steamers in a fleet of 172 ships. It held a unique record: in 1833 it became 'the first [steam] warship and indeed the first British steamship to cross the Atlantic, to the West Indies . . . five years before Brunel's more famous *Great Western* inaugurated the Atlantic ferry service'.[14] Behind the times or not, the *Rhadamanthus* was to remain in service for 30 years, three of them under Arthur's charge on the Mediterranean Station.

It was prosaic work as Arthur employed his paddle steamer in its various roles as mail packet, tug, freighter and ferry. The 18-foot deep hold of the *Rhadamanthus* was filled with all manner of cargo, from ropes to ammunition, as he served bases around the Mediterranean where he was often called upon to tow ships of the line out from windless harbours. He had accommodation comfortable enough to transport senior officers and their families, as well as diplomatic couriers.[15]

In the days before the Suez Canal, *Rhadamanthus* was one of the Mediterranean steamers that provided a vital link for the swift relay of despatches along the mixed sea and land route between England and India. On one of these missions, Arthur almost came to grief. In January 1839, while entering the harbour of St Tropez with 'the Indian despatches in charge of a special messenger',[16] Arthur put the *Rhadamanthus* aground on a shoal of rock, a calamity he attributed to a lack of large charts. *Rhadamanthus* was grounded for one and a half hours and only refloated by lightening ship, which meant 'blowing out the boilers, throwing shot overboard, getting the pinnace out etc. . .'. Part of the keel needed extensive repairs and the entire false keel replacing. Refloating and repairing the steamer generated expenses that would not have gone down well at the Admiralty.

William's concern for Arthur's promotion in January 1837 included more than passing on the dismay of his fellow naval officers. Now colonel commanding the 1st Regiment, the 'Reina Isabel' (Lancers), of the British Legion, wintering at San Sebastian, he told Dan in London to 'advise him to ask for a command of a brig. It will make him to a certainty and the Commodore Lord John Hay would give him every chance in case of any thing going on.'[17] Hay commanded the Royal Naval squadron supporting the anti-Carlist forces in northern Spain. But Arthur, with his memorial to Minto, chose a more orthodox route to promotion than the bloody, confused and rather disreputable route to status and honour that William had followed as a mercenary in the Portuguese and Spanish wars since 1832.

They met just once in these years when Arthur, on his way to the Mediterranean with the *Rhadamanthus*, called in at San Sebastian in late September 1837 with mail and ammunition for the legion.[18] The sight of the vessel's funnel and paddles was not unfamiliar to William because the 'armed steam frigate' had been part of Hay's squadron in spring of the previous year. Arthur, the stranger to his family, had probably last seen William in 1828 when he visited him at Lancaster Castle, after seeing EGW in Newgate. William may have found Arthur little changed – hale and energetic, ever the ideal of the upstanding naval officer loved by his peers. But Arthur would have found William much altered. He was no longer the pale, enervated prisoner, the grieving young widower, the 'young gent' who had not yet applied his talents for 'his advancement in life' or seemed likely to have the chance of doing so. After five years as a cavalry officer in Portugal and the Basque Country, William sported the tan and the medals, the dash and the cheroots of a mercenary who had given and ridden with death, had witnessed plague and peculiarly Spanish barbarities. He had become as astute a politician as a soldier through learning to manage the machinations of military tactics and politics, which often changed daily, and which were overarched by the intrigues, treacheries and jealousies of chronic Iberian royalist feuds.

William enlisted in the Portuguese service on 19 September 1832 as a 31-year-old captain. He had not served in the British Army and there is no evidence that he undertook any military training before becoming a soldier of fortune, but from his days in Paris he would have learnt how to use a pistol and a sabre and become a capable horseman. When joining up, William may have been among those described by Colonel Charles Shaw, who fought and commanded through Portugal and Spain in those years: 'The generality of officers are composed of men who are totally unaware of the dangers and privations; and who are led away by the gaiety of the uniform, or the thoughtless, joyous appearance of the officers of a garrison town'.[19] One observer at his trial had remarked on William's levity of countenance, but now he was no longer a young man and though there may have been an apparent carelessness and bravado in his decision to join he knew, like those other volunteers in the future British Legion – and in the newly formed French Foreign Legion – that he could find forgetfulness and even oblivion in the exile of a mercenaries' war.

William was one of some hundreds of British officers and men who had entered the service of Dom Pedro, anointed Emperor of Brazil after its independence in 1822. His father, the King of Portugal, died in 1826 and Pedro's seven-year-old daughter had become queen under the regency of his younger brother Dom Miguel, a move sponsored by the Duke of Wellington. But Miguel then claimed the throne for himself, whereupon Pedro abdicated the Brazilian throne and sailed to Europe in 1832 to fight for his daughter's inheritance. Politically, liberals and radicals supported Pedro and monarchist absolutists sponsored Miguel; the French and the British, now under Palmerston's foreign policy, supported Pedro.

In June 1832, Dom Pedro sailed from the Azores with a force of 7500 and took Portugal's second city, Oporto, without opposition. Then began a year-long siege of the city by Dom Miguel's army, his 30,000 besiegers against Dom Pedro's 11,000 defenders. William joined Pedro's service on the eve of the most serious Miguelite assault, the Battle of St Michael's Day on 29 September. William survived this baptism of powder and blood, although 2000 on either side were killed or wounded, largely because cavalry in a besieged city 'were never of the slightest use'. The lancers during these 'hard and dangerous times had plenty of sleep, and little or no exposure to musketry'.[20] Almost a year later, after the repulse of what proved to be the final assault on Oporto, William was rewarded with his first decoration: he was made Knight of the Tower and Sword, 1st Class, which suggests that he had begun to distinguish himself in action.

After this, in July and August 1833, Dom Pedro's forces broke out of Oporto and the lancers proved their worth in open battle. It is not clear if William accompanied the small expeditionary force that sailed south under the dashing British Admiral Charles Napier, now in command of the Pedroite fleet, or followed later with the larger force under Portuguese General Saldanha. Napier defeated the Miguelite fleet, which carried double his own firepower, off Cape St Vincent and this opened the way for Saldanha's occupation of Lisbon and the final defeat and exile of Dom Miguel in May 1834. William was made an Officer of the Tower and Sword in January to acknowledge his contribution to the new queen's cause.

Medals were no advance on cash. He returned to England soon afterwards where, according to Nina, 'he has got nothing to do, and finds it hard indeed to get paid for his former services, talks of leaving the Queen's service, and emigrating to South Australia'. The latter must have been *all* talk, cut off by the terrible interregnum of Nina's decline and death in, of all places, Lisbon – an event made even more poignant by William's delighted renewal of his own relationship with daughter Emily, now seven, at Stoke and Quiddenham.

In the year following the end of the Portuguese war, William found no useful employment or prospects in England and when the call came for volunteers for the new British Auxiliary Legion to fight another infant queen's cause, in Spain, he was among the first to enrol. Regular army officers were deterred from enlisting in the legion by the obdurate opposition to intervention in the new war from the Duke of Wellington and the Army Commander-in-Chief, Lord Hill. Most of the legion's eventual 400 officers had no previous military experience and were accepted without scrutiny of character or capabilities. Among these were men seeking a cheap glory, 'Captains who merely [go] out to get dubbed colonels, and pick up one of the diffusely distributed Spanish orders'.[21] William was one of only 40 officers who had seen service in the Greek, Colombian or Portuguese armed forces. He proved to be made of sterner stuff, one of the few to see out the legion to its extremely bitter end.

The cause of the Spanish Carlist War was depressingly familiar. In September 1833, King Ferdinand died leaving an infant daughter Isabel and doubt as to whether the law of succession allowed a woman on the throne. Ferdinand's brother, Don Carlos, decided it did not but his widowed queen decided it did. Palmerston, trying for a solution to both the Portuguese and Spanish succession disputes, engineered the Quadruple Alliance between Britain, France, Spain and Portugal in April 1834, which bound the Spanish and Portuguese regents to compel Don Carlos and Dom Miguel to leave their respective countries. It worked with Portugal but not with Spain. Don Carlos was soon back in Spain from English exile, precipitating a long and savage war. Neither the British nor French governments wished to officially intervene but the alliance opened the way for the volunteer legions and, later, the support of a Royal Naval squadron in the Basque theatre of operations where the British Legion was exclusively engaged. Don Carlos pronounced the legionaries rebels against the constitutional cause, who would be summarily shot if captured. Forty-seven were to die this way; but this was as nothing compared with the barbarity of Spaniard towards Spaniard. Carlists threw 170 loyalist Barcelonan prisoners from the ramparts of a fortress, 'firing at them as they fell. Those who were not shot were dashed to pieces on the rocks below.'[22] The people of Barcelona retaliated by shooting or hacking to death 107 Carlists held prisoner in the city.

The first of the British Legion arrived in San Sebastian on 10 July 1835. It was a 'day and scene worthy of the ancient times of romance and Spanish chivalry . . . . the battlements of the over-hanging walls swarming with fair dames who waved their handkerchiefs and fans, while two splendid military bands, stationed in one of the bastions, played the beautiful air, the Hymn of Riego, and the whole shore up to the gates of the city, glittering with military uniforms and gorgeous trappings, resounded to the cry of *Viva Isabel Segunda!* and the wild cheering of our men'.[23]

By the time the commander of the legion, radical MP Lieutenant-General George de Lacy Evans,[24] arrived in August there were 10,000 officers and men ashore, including William who was heavily engaged in drilling and training his lancers. A skirmish with hardened Carlist guerrillas had quickly shown up both the military and the physical deficiencies of the rag-bag regiments. Evans countered his critics in the English press by declaring, 'In one month I shall have a force equal to anything in this country or nearly so.'[25] But so ineffectual was his force that Evans was lucky his men were not seriously tested in battle until after the 1835–36 winter. And by the end of that, 1000 of them had been wasted by fever.

William, now promoted to major, took his lancers into winter quarters with the rest of the legion at Vittoria. Irishmen in the regiments were followed by 'tribes of shoeless Moll Flaggons from the Green Isle . . . with a pyramid of babes on their backs and a couple trotting on each side . . .'.[26] There were scarce rations and pay for the men, none at all for their women and children, and how many of them died along with their men when the typhus struck is unknown.

As Colonel Charles Shaw recalled, 'Entering a small room in a corner, I was nearly knocked down by the effluvia. Here nine men had been for four days without surgeons . . . . I suppose they are now all dead . . . . seventeen men had been for forty-eight hours abandoned, all suffering from severe dysentery.'[27] Soon, 'from dawn of day till set of sun, the streets re-echoed to the melancholy sounds of the fife and drum playing the Dead March as the departed soldier was borne to his last home'.[28] By April 1836, the legion was leaner from death and desertion, the survivors toughened by the rigours of a winter of impoverishment and harshness, extreme even in the experience of local Basques.

On 5 May, with the aid of effective bombardment from the Royal Navy's steam frigates in the bay, the legion's foot regiments drove 3000 Carlists from positions they had been consolidating for months at San Sebastian and made a valuable haul of rifles, ammunition and supplies. Spanish medals were indiscriminately strewn on officers and other ranks alike. Three weeks later, William earned his own decoration, Knight of San Fernando 1st Class, when another successful assault was made on the Carlist forces before San Sebastian. On 28 May, after the legion, with the assistance of Royal Navy sailors and marines, had thrown a pontoon bridge across the Urimea River, artillery and infantry were swiftly followed by the English Lancers, who were soon 'hot at it. They charged the enemy on the Ametza Hill, assisted by the Royal Marines; clearing the way there, they galloped forward, came up on some of the Carlists who were retreating on Passages, and drove them helter-skelter into the water, stabbing, cutting, shooting, and drowning them in mingled slaughter.'[29] William's gallantry brought immediate promotion to lieutenant-colonel. By September he was in command of the 1st Lancers.

Since Vittoria, the officers of the regiment under its first commander, Colonel J. Kinloch, had earnt a reputation for meting out sadistic punishments in response to often trivial misdemeanours. One corporal, Deana, was given 100 lashes on the indictment of a vicious captain for failing to obey an order when incapacitated by a serious injury that had followed a fall from his horse while in action. The captain's motive was to bring about his death so that he could commandeer his possessions, which included a particularly valuable watch. After the flogging, Deana 'fell into a fever, and became insensible for twelve days'.[30] But he survived to become one of the so-called ringleaders of a mutiny that came close to destroying the legion.

In July 1836, the first year of the volunteers' engagement to the legion came to an end and this brought dispute and disturbance in the ranks over pay, conditions and command. Kinloch called upon those men of the 1st Lancers who wanted to go home to put down their names. 'Sixty of them did so: their horses, arms, and accoutrements, were then taken from them; they were marched into San Sebastian . . . allowed to go about at liberty, until all at once four companies of the 10th regiment were brought in, and marched them out . . . to be tried by court martial' for mutiny. Deana and three others, marked out by the sadistic captain, were arraigned before a court martial attended, but not participated in, by William Wakefield. Two men were sentenced to 500 lashes each, Deana and the fourth to 300.

The 8th Scotch Regiment was in a genuine state of mutiny. Upon hearing of the course of the court martial, the men of the 8th, who had been told by the lancers that they '*depended on the 8th for getting justice.* – turned lawlessly out, armed themselves, rushed into where the Court was assembled, overset the tables and put a stop to the proceedings. . . .' After most of the members of the court had disappeared, just one man remained who, 'when the mob rushed out and tumbled over the tables, chairs and papers, stepped back a pace, pulled out his cigars, picked the best one took a look of what was going on, lighted a lucifer, touched the cigar – folded his arms across his breast, and puffed out his smoke.'[31] This officer is not named but the cigar and attitude give him away: it was almost certainly William.

The mutiny began to spread as the 10th Regiment threatened to join the 8th, and only a mixture of cajolement, concession and selective punishment brought the rebels round. Men were paid, new clothing and equipment issued and regular training resumed. In the 1st Lancers, some justice was served. Kinloch resigned and William took his place. Following the next battle near San Sebastian, William saw to it that the infamous captain was cashiered for cowardice, and Corporal Deana promoted to sergeant for gallantry.

In this battle, the 1st Lancers were led into action for the first time by William, 'an officer who was strict in discipline, though not as tyrannical as Colonel Kinloch . . . but every whit as brave and efficient before the enemy. Kinloch was a tyrant, but at the same time a clever officer and a hero in courage. Wakefield on the other hand was as clever, less tyrannical, and distinguished, nay almost reckless in courage.' His Lancers were made up of 'men carefully selected – principally of those who had been in British cavalry regiments, or men likely to make good dragoons'.[32]

> On the morning of the 1st of October, the Lancers had been . . . early called out by the sounds of '*boot and saddle*', from their trumpets. We saw them charge in gallant style on the south-east side of the Ametza Hill . . . . the Carlists gave way, until they came behind their breastworks, at which it was rendered impossible for the cavalry to follow farther, and necessary for them to retreat, being exposed to heavy fire. The sight of horses going back without riders, and men without horses showed too plainly what they were exposed to. The Lancers went through their evolutions in beautiful style; some of their charges, wheeling and retreating, were as regularly performed as ever the same has been seen with any cavalry regiment on a field-day.[33]

It could have been a rehearsal for the 'gallant six hundred'.

The one letter from William that has survived from his legion days conveys the character and perspicuity of a gallant and respected colonel now accustomed to command. In January 1837 he wrote to Dan from San Sebastian,

> The aspect of affairs here is variable as the wind. A few days ago we were all in high spirits at the probable immediate arrival of 6000 men with whom we were to have

> commenced a campaign. Evans had decided on remaining and there appeared a prospect of putting an end to the war in a few months. Today arrived the intelligence that it is very doubtful whether any reinforcements will be sent to us. Espartero [Spanish general] is, it appears, jealous of our doing any thing and therefore would rather begin the offensive preparations against the Carlists at the Ebro than from the coast. The mistake which has hitherto crippled the Queen's army and which the recent failure of Gomez has but more strongly exposed. Nothing can describe Spanish pride and folly better than this decision of Espartero. He was utterly lost before Bilbao but for the assistance of Wylde and the British Navy & Artillery, but now he holds up his head and will take no co-operation. The consequence will be that you will hear of his being beaten by the Carlists if he dares to attack there. . . . The legion never was in finer order or better spirits. The men are well fired, fed and clothed. The officers 10 months in arrears & much in debt.[34]

The legion's campaign was completed successfully in the spring of 1837. One of William's comrades in arms later wrote, 'I well remember the brilliant charge you made at its [cavalry's] head in the early part of the action of the 16th of March 1837 in which you captured the commanding officer of the Carlist cavalry.'[35] Time was now up for most of the volunteers, whose two-year term of service expired in June. De Lacey Evans left promptly to get back to the House of Commons, exhorting his men to re-enlist in a New Legion under the command of Colonel M. C. O'Connell.

To the surprise of the rank and file, they were paid up by the Spanish government and this encouraged some to stay on, especially those robbed of these wages or entrapped while drinking them away. All in all 120 sergeants and 1500 men re-enlisted and 120 officers, including William, who was promoted to a full colonel in charge of the cavalry (and made Knight of San Fernando 2nd Class). 'Many of the officers remained from strict principles of honour, being determined that they would not return to their own country where they knew they would be branded with reproach, until they had seen the last of the war. . . .' There were some who had 'no situation having gone out . . . on the unhappy equality of not knowing what to turn themselves to should they come home . . . . These last . . . I venture to say were few, compared with those who remained from an honourable wish to . . . carry out the military credit of the expedition they were engaged in.'[36]

William's motives were a mixture of both honour and employment. What could he do back in England? His legion colonelcy was worthless to the staff of a regular army who had nothing but contempt for the mercenaries whose motives and actions had been both bitterly criticised and grossly misrepresented in the public prints. William might as well stay, see the task through and make sure of collecting his arrears in pay.

The New Legion lasted only six months. Like its predecessor, it was systematically starved and neglected by the Spanish government, and mauled by the

Carlists. In a retreat from failure at Andouin, it was said that William received credit for gallantry that others deserved since 'Wakefield was not with his regiment of Lancers that day, nor the days immediately following on which there was slaughter, which has occasioned a variety of free remarks to be made on his professional character; all of which are however sufficiently balanced by the many proofs which he at other times afforded of unquestioned bravery'.[37] William's reasons for being absent from the field that day must have been good ones: when O'Connell wound up the New Legion in December 1837, William was left in command of a residual force of 400 lancers and artillerymen who, along with a detachment of Royal Marines, continued to render support to the anti-Carlist forces.[38] There was, still, nothing for him to go home to. William stayed on in Spain until the spring of 1838 when the steamer came down to San Sebastian from England with mail from EGW. He was planning to resurrect the Swan River settlement in Western Australia along the proper lines of the sufficient price and there was a post in it for William.

William returned to England to join again with his elder brother's ambition; but EGW's Swan River scheme soon dissolved into the great lakes of his Canadian enterprises[39] (see Chapter Fourteen) and by year's end William was without employment or prospects. He turned to his legionary colleagues for help. On 16 December, De Lacey Evans, replying to William's request for a testimonial, wrote: 'I should be unjust if I hesitated a moment . . . in assuring you of the high sense I entertain of the decided efficiency and ability with which you discharged your duties both as an officer and Gentleman . . . your distinguished conduct in quarters and before the enemy justified me in recording my approbation on several occasions in public orders . . .'.[40] Evans wished William 'all success', but no one pressed forward to offer 'a responsable employment' to this 37-year-old mercenary officer. William might be a capable Colonel Courageous, skilled and reformed, but he remained well outside the English social pale and his 'diffusely distributed Spanish orders' served to accentuate rather than to disguise his dubious past. There were few sources of cheer for him in England as the festive season approached.

CHAPTER THIRTEEN

The Ingenious Projector

'EVERYWHERE WERE BRIDGES THAT LED nowhere; thoroughfares that were wholly impassable; Babel towers of chimneys, wanting half their height; temporary wooden houses and enclosures, in the most unlikely situations; carcasses of ragged tenements, and fragments of unfinished walls and arches, and piles of scaffolding, and wildernesses of bricks, and giant forms of cranes, and tripods straddling above nothing. There were a hundred thousand shapes and substances of incompleteness, wildly mingled out of their places, upside down, burrowing in the earth, aspiring in the earth, mouldering in the water, and unintelligible as any dream . . . . In short, the yet unfinished and unopened railroad was in progress, and, from the very core of all this dire disorder, trailed smoothly away upon its mighty course of civilization and improvement.'

Dickens's *Dombey and Son* was published a few years later, but these words from the novel's opening pages could be describing the construction of the London and Birmingham Railway, built between 1833 and 1838 and employing 20,000 labourers; it was the 'largest public work ever to be undertaken in the whole history of man, with the possible exception of the Great Wall of China'.[1] The huge new foundries and workshops servicing the railway boom 'drew thousands of men away from the country into the towns, and meanwhile the railways, and later the steamships, were equipping themselves to bring in food and take away all the multifarious manufactures of the new urban industrialized society into which the application of steam power to the movement of men and goods was carrying the nation at express speed'.[2] As Arthur Wakefield put it in September 1837, steam was 'in very great progress'.

The railway is the metaphor for the condition of Britain at the beginning of the Victorian age, exemplifying the explosion of industrial technology into business, workplace, home, town and countryside. Railway building demanded the employment of vast amounts of capital and mass labour, organised within new management and work disciplines. The resulting industrial and social change, and the increased 'distress' it caused to the burgeoning working classes, were fully evident by the time young Victoria succeeded her uncle, William IV, in June 1837. The political reforms that had been a response to the social and economic distresses of the 1820s were insufficient to cope with the stresses and strains of industrial change. Chartists demanding more and more democracy maintained a sense of revolution in the country. Reforms in church and government were driven by both the Benthamite test – 'What use is it?' – and an evangelical puritan ethos generated by the nonconformist sects. Morality was no longer left to the pulpit. Increasingly, moral purpose was expected in political action as well as in individual and family behaviour. The excesses and eccentricities of the age of George III and his sons were gone; the new queen and her consort came to represent precisely the changes in public and private morality and the slow but steady shift of power from aristocratic privilege to democratic choice.

Within this climate of industrial change and social stress, Edward Gibbon Wakefield, after his short-lived attempt to stand for Parliament in Birmingham, turned his energies towards his new colonising project. For all the capital and labour being drawn into the 'dire disorder' of railway construction, the economic distress of the nation was far from resolved and would remain so until the full transition to an industrialised society during the boom of the 1850s. There was still a superabundance of capital and labour to be accounted for. Colonisation that promised investment profits and employment of labour appealed strongly to business entrepreneurs, especially those with interests in shipbuilding and ownership who were bound to gain advantage from any successful colonial enterprise.

In conformity with the new spirit of the age, moral purpose should accompany any capital career; and it was this tension between profit and morality that characterised EGW's new plans. He sought fulfilment of his utopian ends by juggling the means of business with his colonial theory. Investors and emigrants must be attracted and satisfied but the philanthropic ideals of his theory, at least in part, must be preserved; and the moral imperatives of the Colonial Office, buttressed by the evangelising zeal of the missionary societies, must be acknowledged and managed. And there was that other enduring imperative: EGW's determination, still undimmed after 20 years, to see to the 'well-doing and well-being' of his brothers. He had Arthur by his side, and Dan not far away, when he began serious work on his New Zealand project. But he could not have anticipated that it would end by consuming them all, including himself and his son.

'Starting to work in earnest this morning,' begins the letter that EGW scrawled to Dr Samuel Evans on 10 May 1837. Evans was a schoolteacher and lawyer, marked as secretary for the new association. The letter conveys an impression of nervous haste, of a half-formed scheme.

> I have done the plan part of the pamphlet . . . . But I have another object in writing. The facts relating to 1. the proportion of unoccupied land 2. the inclination of the natives to sell land & encourage English settlers 3. the evils which they suffer through the permanent or temporary residence of lawless foreigners should be classed under separate heads and it is most desirable that your labour should produce, not a mere mass of facts, but a well selected collection & digest upon each point . . . . Any satisfactory proofs of conversion to Christianity . . . should appear under the head of capacity for civilization. I dare to say that other points will occur to you as you proceed.
>
> At your leisure, pray think of settlers – emigrant Founders. The first questions asked by the great men will be – Where are the colonists? Where are the funds? With a good body of intending settlers, all will probably go well from the first. This is the lever with which every move is to be effected.[3]

The letter EGW wrote two days later to Charles Torlesse was of a wholly different tone. Gone is the sense of plotting, of manipulating and in their place are authority and principle – and pure illusion. 'I have set on foot a new measure of colonisation on principles similar to those which have worked so well for South Australia. The country is New Zealand – one of the finest countries in the world, if not the finest, for British settlement.' He explains that a New Zealand Association is being formed, which will 'comprise a more influential body than that which founded South Australia'. Although 'the body of capitalists who will first emigrate – is already considerable . . . [w]e have no clergyman. The New Zealanders are not savages, but a people capable of civilisation. A main object will be to do all that can be done for inducing them to embrace the language, customs, religion, & social ties of the superior race.' The missionaries had already begun this process and 'We want a missionary at heart, to be placed at the head of a system for operating on the minds of the natives – a man of high feelings, great zeal, & superior talents – a sort of Mr Nottidge, but young & strong . . . . he must be a superior man; & if he have a wife, she must be superior too.' Proudly, he reported: 'Captain Arthur thinks of commanding the first expedition, & my own thoughts are turned in that direction. For me, all will depend upon the manner in which the foundation shall be laid – if it be very good – superior to any other thing of the sort – then I become one of the builders of the superstructure.'[4]

Of all his brothers, Arthur was ideally suited to command the first expedition. In handling ships and men he had few peers; morally he was without stain. His piety and evangelical propensities completed the image of the ideal leader that EGW could present to investors, settlers, missionaries, politicians and bureaucrats alike.

Arthur was currently with EGW at Hans Place, Brompton and added a coda to the letter to Charles. 'You will recollect that I mentioned to you at Stoke that Edward had his eye upon N. Zd. I am so far interested about it that I fancy I see an opening for useful & active employment – I have made up my mind to go into the preliminaries, and to go, if not previously employed – I have been reading a great deal on the subject and am delighted with the accounts of the country . . . . The influence will be great wh. will be brought to bear in establishing the settlement, & I fancy it may become a very grand undertaking.' Arthur, always circumspect with EGW before, had become infected by his splendid vision, and willingly represented the new New Zealand Association's aims over the following two months until the *Rhadamanthus* came steaming over the horizon.

EGW called the first meeting of the New Zealand Association on 22 May, the only time he chaired any meeting of the several colonising bodies of which he was the progenitor. Three years later, in public and political retrospect, he declared, 'The first principle which we laid down was that the society should be rather of a public than of a private character; and that at all events no member of it should have any pecuniary interest in the object in view. The only object of the society was to bring the subject before the public and Parliament, and not to take any part as individuals in what might be the result.'[5] He retreated to his role as puppet master the following week when a committee was elected including ten MPs led by Wakefield stalwarts Hutt, Baring and Molesworth. The committee's chief task was to frame a bill to give effect to the objects of the Association as described in EGW's rapidly compiled pamphlet, *A Statement of the Objects of the New Zealand Association*. 'As the Association had been in existence for little more than a fortnight [*sic*], this implied considerable confidence in the author of the *Statement* and its elaborate plans for the present and future inhabitants of New Zealand.'[6]

The extraordinary position of EGW as the association's keeper of the mystery of the grail, its revered mentor without official office, is observed in the diary of an intending colonist, Edward Hopper, who attended a meeting of the association in July. 'I was surprised at the deference paid to Mr Wakefield's opinions upon various points of the subjects by the gentlemen present . . . . Mr Wakefield is a man of middle stature, fair complexion, fine skin, fine intellectual forehead, apparently of fixed and decisive character equal to bearing out his own views with a masterly hand. It was from his incarceration for three years in a certain College that he became a thinking man . . . he is at present looked up to by many eminent political characters.'[7] Hopper assessed other members present at the meeting according to the newly popular science of phrenology: 'Lord Petre has a most miserable head. Is much better calculated for a fox hunter than a Philosopher. The intellectual department is very deficient . . . Wm Hutt Esq has a fine head. Good intellect. . . .'

EGW's powers of persuasion have sometimes been put down to the hypnotic quality of his 'brilliant blue eyes, indescribably tender when in gentle mood, but frequently blazing with passion and excitement. The great charm and impressiveness of his personality, notwithstanding, were incapable of definition: they lay in that mysterious magnetic power which excited feelings of intense devotion among those who came fully under its spell, detained unwilling listeners within hearing, and often subjugated them at last, but, by the law of compensation, frequently aroused violent antipathy among the unsubdued.'[8]

The Wakefield Hypnotic Theory is not without foundation. By 1837, EGW and Jerningham had become exponents of mesmerism at 'magnetising soirées'. Their efforts at putting the ladies under are well recorded.[9] In 1840 EGW almost came to grief when he successfully mesmerised a girl but was unable to revive her and spent several frantic hours searching the streets of London for a doctor friend who was finally able to bring her round.[10]

Whatever the power of EGW's magnetism, his theories, plans and enthusiasms would never have gone beyond soirées if they had not spoken to the condition of the men who came within earshot. The prospect of EGW's ideal colonies, distant from England's distress and dark satanic mills, bewitched prospective colonists among the uneasy classes. 'There was a feeling among them that they were moving with, and not away from, the civilized world.'[11] Before he left for New Zealand in 1842, William Fox wrote, 'The Wakefield system is one of those discoveries which is so simple that its truth must be apparent to the meanest apprehension.'[12] Like every other ideologue who has since used New Zealand for political or economic experiment, EGW had his congregation of devoted true believers. They may have been drawn by EGW's vision of a new and better Britain or inspired by the altruism of saving the British disadvantaged and the Maori benighted.[13] But they were equally enraptured by the implications of EGW's statement that 'No part of the world presents a more eligible field for the exertion of British enterprize, or a more promising career of usefulness and satisfaction to those who love to labour in the cause of human improvement.'[14] Despite the declared disinterest of the association, this was code for profit from land bought cheap and new openings for trade, as well as attendant opportunities for political and social status denied in the old country. But then, in an age of free trade and *laissez faire*, could the provision of such opportunities not be seen as a kind of commercial philanthropy?

All this was not lost on the Colonial Office and the missionary societies who not only wished to manage the British settlement of New Zealand in their own self-interest but also held genuine humanitarian concerns for its potentially fatal impact on the native inhabitants. This was the year of the Report of the Commons Committee on Aborigines, a high point of 'nineteenth-century humanitarian idealism towards indigenous peoples'.[15] Among the report's recommendations were that the sovereignty of indigenous peoples should be recognised and that large-scale colonisation schemes should be opposed until Parliament had properly considered the matter. An Aborigines Protection Society was formed by members of the committee 'to watch over and protect the interests of the natives'.

This all accorded with the views of the lobbying missionaries. Only two days after the second meeting of the New Zealand Association the lay secretary of the

Church Missionary Society (CMS), Dandeson Coates, gained a promise from the Colonial Office that the society would be given every opportunity to lay objections to any colonising plan laid before it by the association. On 6 June, EGW sent Arthur and Dr Evans along to see Coates, to try and gain the CMS's co-operation, if not its blessing. Coates was obdurately hostile and the CMS summarily rejected the association's advances, scorning the ignorance behind such comments in EGW's *Statement* as 'a great proportion of the surface of New Zealand is unoccupied and waste, and . . . . the natives are strongly disposed to sell land'. The CMS resolved to use 'all suitable means' to defeat the objects of the association on the grounds that European colonisation was inevitably injurious to indigenes, Britain had no sovereignty over New Zealand and the association's scheme would conflict with and defeat the society's plans for the Christian civilisation of the natives. Tartly, in a letter to the Colonial Office, EGW wrote, 'At present (I say it with unaffected seriousness) Mr Coates is the English bishop of New Zealand. But neither a bishop, nor any other chief, can exercise perfect control over subordinates at an immense distance. . . .'[16]

Arthur was likely chastened but not deterred. A week later he accompanied EGW in a deputation to see the Prime Minister, Lord Melbourne, and Secretary at War, Lord Howick. It was judged expedient to bypass the hostile Colonial Office which the association knew would be a political stumbling block and which it also considered was under the sway of the missionaries. James Stephen, now Permanent Under-Secretary at the Colonial Office, had well-known connections with the CMS and, along with Lord Glenelg, Secretary for War and the Colonies and his Parliamentary Under-Secretary, Sir George Grey, strongly sympathised with the findings of the aborigines report.

This meeting was more successful: Melbourne bestowed his 'general approbation' on the association's scheme and Howick promised to examine it in detail. But Melbourne had already sent the draft bill to Glenelg – and therefore Stephen – for comment. Promptly and scathingly, Stephen reported '1st. It proposes the acquisition of a sovereignty in New Zealand which would infallibly issue in the conquest and the extermination of the present inhabitants. 2nd. These suggestions are so vague and so obscure as to defy all interpretations.'[17] 'Stephen's first objection was in line with orthodox humanitarian and evangelical thinking; his second was merely accurate.'[18]

It is difficult to assess how much EGW's role in the association conditioned Stephen's and the CMS's reactions. The enmity between EGW and James Stephen was open for all to see and would continue until 'King Stephen' or 'Mr Over-Secretary', as EGW described him, left the Colonial Office in 1847. EGW's criminal history made him a leper to Dandeson Coates. Stephen and Coates might have been more impressed by the association's intentions towards the natives if they had not been able to discern EGW's hand in such statements as, 'the Association are desirous to express at the outset of this undertaking their sense of the injustice and cruelty of leading savage or semi-barbarous men into engagements which they do not perfectly comprehend . . . a main object of the Association would be defeated, if any kind of injustice were committed towards the natives'. Even so, regardless of its author, any proposal that contemplated settlements which should be treated not as regular provinces or colonies, but as commercial enterprises like East India Company posts, was a positive incitement to rigorous opposition. Such a proposition showed how far EGW's fancies had wandered from current political realities: magnetism did not work so well on paper. A deeper provocation for Stephen and Coates would have been reading that each association settlement would be ruled by persons 'selected from amongst the originators and most zealous patrons of the undertaking'. EGW protested his pecuniary innocence but here, they saw, was a more powerful motive for his involvement in the scheme.

The association pressed and pressed, attempting to use Howick and Melbourne to push the bill on, but the death of William IV and dissolution of Parliament halted all progress, saving the government from any commitment. Stephen continued his scathing attacks within the departments and Howick told the association that a much better structure of governance would be required before a bill could be considered.

Whatever their objections, both the government and the missions had been galvanised by the association's proposals into trying to solve the growing problem of what to do about New Zealand. British settlement was proceeding in an unregulated way, the population of whalers, traders, seamen and other actors at the edge of empire increasing from just 300 to 2000 during the 1830s. The missionaries had been exhorting the Colonial Office to bring law and order to the rough frontier settlements. In 1831 the CMS organised and presented a letter from Maori chiefs begging for British protection from lawless European renegades and in 1837, with the Wesleyans, a petition from 213 British nationals praying for protection from the Maori. Missionaries regularly used spurious threats of French settlement in an effort to push Britain into taking control of New Zealand.

The missionaries piously declared that the association's plans would bring about the destruction of the aboriginal people and that 'barbarous nations need to be enlightened and elevated, before they can be brought to recognise and act according to the rules by which civilized communities can be regulated . . . . The Gospel is the only means for accomplishing this important object. . . .'[19] Such sentiments did not disguise the moral imperialism of their wish to eradicate those abhorrent heathen practices that did not concur with British social values. As much as EGW, they wanted to make the Maori British. There could be no disagreement between the association and the missionary societies about the superiority of British culture and the need to civilise the Maori. The disagreement was on method – and mission hostility was based as much on losing power and influence as on humanitarian conscience.

James Stephen was aware and distrustful of the self-interest in missionary representations to the Colonial Office and was inclined to resist these as much as those of the colonisers. But the government's responsibility for British citizens and their interests, wherever they were in the world, and its humanitarian concern for aboriginal peoples affected by haphazard British settlement, had already forced it to appoint a British resident. James Busby, who arrived at the Bay of Islands in 1833, was expected to be the arbiter of frontier disputes but, without supporting staff and jurisdiction, he soon proved to be an emperor without clothes or arms. By 1837, it had become clear that the Busby experiment had failed; the problems with uncontrolled settlement were increasing and the association was intending to colonise. The CMS solution of stopping the association and increasing the powers and resources of the resident were clearly impractical wishful thinking. Busby, like the missionaries, survived only under the sufferance of Maori chiefs who could easily defeat or compromise such half-hearted measures. Something else had to be done short of taking full sovereignty of New Zealand.

While Baring and Ward harried the government, EGW broadcast with his message. The Colonial Office and the missionaries would never be won over and, though some ministers and MPs could be manoeuvred and manipulated, the association needed as much publicity as possible to generate the influence, the money and the migrants that would be necessary to tip the balance of power.

Alerted by Adam Smith and Grandmother Priscilla, EGW had lately published his conclusion that, 'Thinking, to those who are unused to it, is a very disagreeable process; most people can be induced to exercise their reason, only by some enticement addressed to their imagination. How do the doctrinal parts of Scripture become familiar to a child? By means of the very entertaining stories which accompany them. In all ages and countries, the most successful teachers, whether of truth or error, have appealed to the imagination. In order to instruct it is needful to amuse.'[20] EGW had, perhaps, also observed Lord Petre's forehead.

With John Ward, EGW began work on an attractive and entertainingly instructive book about New Zealand, culling freely and selectively from previous publications on the subject. A folio book of engravings of Augustus Earle's New Zealand drawings appeared soon after. These were the first of nearly 200 books and pamphlets on New Zealand that came out over the following fifteen years, largely sponsored by Wakefield-initiated colonising associations and companies. Although these often received trenchant criticism from missionary and newspaper reviewers, they cumulatively established a propaganda image of New Zealand as a green, pleasant and fertile land, sparsely populated with friendly natives and ideally suited for the foundation of an antipodean Britain.

EGW also arranged for Robert Burford to paint a panorama of the Bay of Islands, based on Augustus Earle's 'on the spot' drawings, and this was opened for public viewing at Burford's two-level rotunda in Leicester Square at Christmas 1837. In the days before photography and cinema, 360° panoramas and three-dimensional dioramas were the principal form of visual entertainment and illusion in transporting viewers to distant, exotic locations or re-created historical events such as the Battle of Trafalgar. The explanatory pamphlet to the Bay of Islands scene drew attention to the virtues of the New Zealand Association and the inevitability of New Zealand becoming a prosperous marine colony. Thousands paid their shilling to see EGW's promotion of paradise and the panorama was later exhibited in New York. When Ensign Best arrived in the Bay of Islands in April 1840, he wrote, 'I was never more enchanted by any scenery, but everybody has seen the Panorama in Leicester Square so that discription is needless.'[21]

Arthur, as he once again bade farewell to Catherine, the association and England, neatly touched on another of EGW's public relations techniques: 'You would have liked to have been present last Sunday at Islington Church where a sermon was preached by Mr Hawtrey on behalf of the Church Missionary Society at which EGW and his two N. Zealanders assisted. The N. Zealanders held the plates and an excellent collection was made in consequence. The colonisation of NZ was recommended by the Revd. gentleman who is to go out as the principal clergyman with a large family. Charles will be amused at EGW, Mary Oliverra[22] and the two N. Zealanders going to hear a missionary sermon, and sitting in the Vicar's pew. . . .'[23] Arthur betrays familial indulgence of EGW's impudence in stalking the lion in its own den, piously attending to a magnetised CMS parson preaching his very own doctrine and presenting a picture of philanthropy with his ward by his side; and flanked by two native New Zealanders who were living and exotic advertisements for the association's cause.

The two young Maori had been brought to London at EGW's instigation when he heard that they had been stranded at Le Havre. Edward Jerningham wrote, 'As I took them in a hackney-coach to my father's house in Chelsea, I pointed out the shops, the crowds of passengers, and the public buildings which we passed. They gazed for some minutes in mute astonishment on the bewildering sight, and then, by an apparently unanimous impulse, covered their faces with their hands, and leant back in the coach, as though they could not conceive, and refused to be forced to see, any more of such perplexing things.'[24]

The Maori had been conned by a whaling captain into working their passage to France with the promise that they would be granted an audience with King Louis Philippe. One of them, 'Jackey', took ill and soon died from consumption but the other, Nahiti, was to play a prominent role in progressing EGW's schemes. EGW took him into his own home and displayed him to curious Londoners as proof of the malleable, friendly Maori. The Duke of Sussex invited Nahiti to assemblies and gave him a medal engraved with Queen Victoria's portrait. He was taken riding in Hyde Park, skating on the Serpentine and, judiciously, to church and meetings of the New Zealand Association.

Nahiti figured prominently in the New Zealand book where EGW used him to introduce the character of the Maori, their environment and their capacity for adaptation to civilised ways. Nahiti 'is a younger son of an inferior chief of the Kapiti tribe who possess both sides of Cook's Straits . . . . the chieftainship of the tribe is at present vested in Raupero [Te Rauparaha], a very old man . . . [whose] own countrymen talk of him with aversion for his many ferocities and cruelty . . . . Nayti [*sic*], his young kinsman, speaks of him as "Very bad man, bad New Zealander, – not like young men." Meaning to ascribe to him the ferocious habits of a past generation, and in opposition to the softened and altered customs of his countrymen of the present day.' Fear not, dear emigrant, cannibals are now rare. 'Nayti has resided with one family for more than three months, and his behaviour has been uniformly gentle and decorous. He has adapted himself with surprising facility . . . has made great progress in learning English . . . [and] now behaves as if he had passed years with his new friends.'[25]

None too subtly, EGW attempted to appease the missionaries. Nahiti 'ever since hearing a sermon preached at Islington Church . . . has been struck by the disinterestedness and generosity of missionary labours, saying, "English people very good, – speak good for New Zealand man, – give money for send missionary to New Zealand, to teach New Zealand man no fight, – me tell my people, English people very good" . . . . all useful objects, or objects which *he* thinks would be useful in his own country, gain his eager attention . . . .' If EGW sought advantage from Nahiti, Nahiti sought advantage from being lionised in London. Neither was quite what he appeared.

On publication of the book, *British Colonization*, in October 1837 EGW urged Catherine to buy a copy through a bookseller in Colchester since an order would 'aid in distributing it'. He praised the 'beautiful appendix' by the Reverend Montague Hawtrey, a fantastically patronising view of how the Maori might be civilised into British ways. It incorporated, however, an idea of which much philanthropic capital would be made: 'What benefit can we grant him [Maori chief] more suitable to his circumstances, with more ease to ourselves, and more in accordance with our own principle of colonization, than a portion of that land which has so greatly increased in value by the mere circumstance of our possessing it?'[26] Was it this that EGW found beautiful or, as a devotee of Walter Scott, Hawtrey's suggestions that Maori should be introduced to the concept of feudal chivalry, complete with the trappings of heraldry, as a way of 'softening and improving' their character?

EGW was now in thrall to his romantic New Zealand imaginings: 'I am still bent on New Zealand & shall, I think, surely go. Tell Charles that we have reason to hope that a Bishop for New Zealand <u>will</u> be appointed. We project, therefore, not a wooden church merely, but a cathedral of stone, as the chief religious edifice of the great Polynesian Antipodes. He may smile but I am in earnest.'[27]

EGW also praised Hawtrey's appendix when he sent a copy to Sir William Molesworth, urging him to write a 'favourable article on New Zealand in the Plymouth or Devonport papers'. EGW could rely on Molesworth not only to write a piece for a Cornwall paper but also to frequently raise New Zealand issues in the House of Commons in favour of the association. They worked, EGW hand in Molesworth glove, not only on New Zealand but also in the fight to abolish transportation. Molesworth had been appointed to chair a select committee on the issue in April 1837, steering it through 38 meetings before it came down with its report in August 1838. EGW had been concerned about the evils of transportation since Newgate, and he attended many of the early meetings of the committee, where he was seen in 'open and perpetual communication' with Molesworth and to have a 'profound intellectual influence' on his ideas and findings.[28]

Molesworth, Buller and those other Trinity radicals, William and John Hutt, formed the loyal core of supporters of the Wakefield colonial crusade but Molesworth was also a link to Lord Durham, whose participation in the New Zealand business had now become vital. Social and political outsiders, Molesworth, Durham and EGW were temperamentally drawn to each other. Durham would have echoed Molesworth's comment, when reproached for his unsocial habits, that he 'preferred to be disliked'.

Born John George Lambton, Durham had been a cantankerous, reforming Whig Member of Parliament since he entered it in 1813 at his majority. He earned the soubriquet 'Radical Jack' from opposing the Corn Laws, denouncing the government for its part in the Peterloo Massacre of 1819 and from bringing forward a motion for parliamentary reform as early as 1821. In 1825 he had become chairman of the unsuccessful New Zealand Company, his first brush with colonisation. Lambton was elevated to the peerage in 1828 and created an earl five years later. As Lord Privy Seal from 1830 he prepared the first Reform Bill and was the most forceful and vital Lords protagonist in seeing through parliamentary reform. His conflicts with Whig leadership and policies brought about his resignation from office in 1833. An election committee was formed to promote the return of candidates who favoured his leadership – he was seen as the head of the radicals in his party – but his 'complete want of tact . . . his irritable temper and overbearing manner made him a most undesirable colleague'[29] and the manoeuvre failed.

There was 'an intimate connexion between [Durham's] physical state and his violent temper . . . . At what time the terrible pains in his head began we cannot tell. We hear of them first in his early twenties. From then to his death there was hardly a month when they did not plunge him into days of agony. From the age of thirty there was scarcely a year that he did not experience a breakdown.'[30] And during the twelve months from December 1831 he suffered devastating personal losses with the deaths of his son, mother and two daughters.

Apart from the colonial question, Durham shared another propensity with EGW. In the new year of 1812, at the age of nineteen, he had made a runaway marriage at Gretna Green with the 'natural' daughter of Lord Cholmondeley after his guardians had refused to countenance the match. Three years later she had died of consumption, leaving him in a state of grief that EGW would have acutely recognised. Unlike EGW, Durham was in a position to make a powerful and devoted second marriage, at the end of 1816 to the daughter of Whig chieftain Earl Grey, that was to sustain him through the following years of tormenting physical pain and political turmoil.

The first meeting between Durham and EGW took place after Durham's return from a two-year stint as ambassador to the Russian court at St Petersburg. He arrived home just two days after Queen Victoria's accession and his investiture as Knight of the Bath was her first ceremonial act. The importance of bringing Durham on board and settling matters between the old New Zealand Company and the association was evident in William Hutt's terse letter to EGW on 9 August 1837, asking why he had heard nothing from him on the matter and urging him to act.[31]

Three weeks later, EGW sailed for Newcastle and visited Durham at Lambton Castle, near Washington. EGW must have been at his persuasive best, flattering the haughty and temperamental earl with suggestions that his own liberal economic and political ideas, underpinned by patriotic sentiments of empire and deference to class and capital, had long owed much to Durham's example. Indeed, had not EGW's ideas about New Zealand been first inspired by Durham's 1825 efforts? EGW brought a letter from Durham back to London which concluded, 'I shall be happy to support a measure which has for its object the civilization of a savage people, and the acquirement of so fine a field for the employment of British Industry.'[32]

Over the following months, an understanding was reached with the old New Zealand Company and Durham became Governor of the New Zealand Association. The association continued to press the government for movement on their bill and the missionaries continued to attack it. Under Glenelg, considered by Howick to be weak and dilatory, the Colonial Office dithered on New Zealand, distracted by more pressing problems elsewhere in the empire. In November, James Stephen wrote in exasperation to his wife, 'Such puttings off, such dawdlings, such panics, such endless & unprofitable talkings, such a paralysis. . . .'[33]

A month later, New Zealand could not be put off or dawdled with any longer. The pressures and demands of the association and the missionaries compelled the government into a series of meetings with them during the ten days before Christmas. Although the decisive steps that would forever alter the state of New Zealand were still some eighteen months away, the nexus of politics and personalities that would bring these about was wrought during the 1837–38 midwinter wrangles.

Across the overburdened desk of the harassed James Stephen, as Glenelg vacillated in the doorway, Dandeson Coates and the Wesleyan John Beecham attempted to face down EGW and his association followers. Although rational and humane in argument, the missionaries were inflexible, blind to their blatant self-interest and sufficiently unpolitical to believe that persistent moral propaganda would achieve their goals when they could offer no practical alternatives to the association's plans. They were no political match for the van of MPs and merchants, led by a volatile EGW rendered unscrupulous by avowed enemies who attacked him personally in order to bring down the association. EGW had also become utterly frustrated at the indecision and prevarication of those whom he saw as bureaucratic bumblers or religious bigots. From the gallery above the cockpit, Howick and Prime Minister Melbourne wearily watched the adversaries, acutely conscious that a major player lurked outside. In these politically unstable times, 'Radical Jack' Durham, again making his presence felt in the House of Lords, was someone to be watched and sweetened lest he become a rallying point for Whig rebels. The players that no one seriously considered consulting, except perhaps Stephen, were the sovereign inhabitants of New Zealand, the Maori. The game was strictly imperial.

The wrangles began when EGW, with a revised but fundamentally unchanged bill, led a deputation of eighteen association members to meet Melbourne and Glenelg on 13 December. The deputation complained that they had been 'rather hardly treated' by the government, that some had given up professions and disposed of property in anticipation of emigration to New Zealand and that one in particular would suffer seriously if the scheme did not proceed. Melbourne opined that this gentleman must have been mad to take such a risk whereupon the individual in question sprang up and declared angrily that he was, therefore, a 'madman'. The meeting ended in disarray.

EGW increased the pressure, calling on Melbourne on 15 December and again on the following day with a memorial from 40 merchants and shipowners 'engaged in the whale fisheries which described remedies for New Zealand's ills, and opportunities which could be opened up only by the colonisation of the country'.[34] The next day Melbourne, who had also told Howick that the association people were 'quite mad' to go to New Zealand, added that he did think, however, that they had 'a right to an answer and I hope you will make up Glenelg's mind on the subject'. Melbourne went presciently to the essence of the debate when he concluded that the problem of New Zealand was 'another proof of the fatal necessity by which a nation that once begins to colonize is led step by step over the whole globe'.[35]

Two days later, reports and recommendations sent from New Zealand six months before by Resident James Busby arrived on Glenelg's desk. They crucially damaged the missionary case, for Busby described the haphazard increase of British settlement and purchase of land, often by criminals and desperadoes, and the ravages of introduced diseases that affected all Maori, whether under missionary care or not.

Plainly, Glenelg could dawdle no longer in attempting a solution to the New Zealand problem. The missionaries' proposal to limit and control settlement under their purview was being overtaken by events, but Busby's proposal for a protectorate, with British power exercised through a government of Maori chiefs, was also dismissed as unworkable. Another of his suggestions, however, was heavily underlined at the Colonial Office: that a charter be granted to the colony of British subjects. With Stephen's prompting, this was the straw that Glenelg finally grasped. Despite the objections of Dandeson Coates on 19 and 20 December, he presented to Durham the offer of a charter for the New Zealand Association.

Immediately, EGW saw that a key term of the charter – the requirement that it become a joint stock company – was unacceptable to the association. Durham promptly told Glenelg that his committee had 'expressly stipulated that they shall neither run any pecuniary risk nor reap any pecuniary advantage'.[36] The government could appreciate the association's high-minded philanthropy, but properly expected that it take some responsibility for its actions in a project as momentous as establishing a colony on the other side of the world. The government rested on its offer, despite Durham's (and Coates's) objection, and the attempts of the Wesleyan missionaries to head off the charter in a meeting with Glenelg on 27 December.

Now two other factors had come into play. Just before Christmas, the startling news reached England of rebellion in Canada. The Tory opposition lambasted the government with it and radical opinion, of which Molesworth was a leader, held that the solution was to emancipate – to let Canada go. Melbourne turned to Durham. Would he cross the Atlantic as an ambassador with extraordinary, dictatorial powers and settle the constitutional crisis in a way that kept Canada within the empire? It was not only that he was the best man for the job. Melbourne would feel much more comfortable with Durham off the Westminster stage and his appointment would placate the radicals. Durham was uncertain and Melbourne renewed his appeal on 29 December, the day of the charter offer, which he may have presented as a lubricant.

Also on the eve of Christmas, EGW dramatically suspended the business of the association and called members to a special meeting at its Adelphi rooms on 28 December to discuss a serious difference of opinion that threatened the association's 'very existence'. It was a difficult time of year for attendance, but 23 turned up, including seventeen-year-old Jerningham and acolytes Hawtrey, Evans and Rintoul (and Nahiti). The small association committee of six was dominated by Molesworth, Ward and Hutt. EGW opened the meeting's proceedings by outlining the history of the association and his first serious moves with the project when he approached his brother Arthur and Dr Evans. From that time, he said, 'the whole of the business of the Association had been transacted by him with scarcely a single exception'.[37]

Some historians have employed this statement as further evidence of EGW's overinflated ego, but it was substantially true – how else could EGW have had the power to suspend the association's business? – and the expenses of running the organisation were being met entirely by EGW and Evans. The next year EGW refused compensation for his considerable personal expenditure of about £1,000.[38] Financially, despite his high expenditures at the time of his trial, EGW was now comfortably independent. Two years before, he told his father that he had sold his Norfolk estate 'at a very considerable profit . . . sufficient . . . to put me out of all difficulties'.[39] He might profit in the long run, but EGW was not directing the association solely for personal monetary gain but for the propagation and implementation of his colonial theories and the *political* status and social acceptance that might result. This was the crux of the special meeting.

EGW explained that a crisis of confidence had occurred following remarks over dinner with Lord Durham and Major John Campbell. Campbell had been planning a military colony in New Zealand but had been persuaded to throw in his lot with the association on the understanding that he would become the chief military authority. During the inevitable discussion about New Zealand, Durham had said over the port, 'Lord Grimsby informs me, Major Campbell, that you are to be the Governor.' Campbell had simply smiled and bowed and, after he and EGW left Durham, offered no explanation. This account of events was all according to EGW. A day later EGW pressed Campbell, who then explained to him that this was Durham's diplomatic way of saying that, because of the unfortunate events in EGW's past, he could never aspire to such a post. EGW told the meeting that since 'the sole ground of objection to him was that he was a proscribed man' – and when he discovered Campbell had been speaking on the subject with a great number of people – he had decided to cut him and bring the matter urgently before the committee.

To submit to Campbell's judgement, EGW averred, 'was to confess that he ought forever to be shut out from honourable distinction and from public life; but suppose that he had submitted, how could the business of the Association gone on?' Campbell had 'represented him as a man proscribed on grounds the most painful and offensive that could be alledged and therefore before he could retire forever into obscurity, he desired the judgement of the Association on a question that to him was dearer than life'. On this tragic and pathetic note, EGW threw himself on the mercy of the meeting. His affecting address soon brought the desired result. Campbell had decided not to attend the meeting but had sent a letter with a representative who declared that Campbell had the 'most sincere respect and friendship' for EGW and had never had any intention of obstructing his appointment as governor. But Evans stood up and destroyed Campbell's credibility by recounting that Campbell had told him the government would not 'sanction any scheme for colonization of which Mr Wakefield was to be placed at the head' and that as a consequence he felt free to be available for the position.

Hutt declared that he had travelled 300 miles at great inconvenience to deliver a testimonial and launched into a long and eloquent eulogy of EGW which even included notice of his contributions to literature and science. It was prefaced by his admission that 'Mr Wakefield has been under a prejudice in consequence of the events referred to which took place twelve years ago. But it is a prejudice, I believe, fast wearing away. I believe the world is fast coming round to an opinion I myself entertain that Mr Wakefield has more than atoned by a long period of proscription and most patient suffering.'

Molesworth strongly supported Hutt's speech – and EGW for governor – and the committee thereupon passed a resolution that endorsed EGW's actions, urged him to continue with his work for the association and expressed 'the opinion that Mr Wakefield is eminently qualified to fill any office in the proposed Colony of New Zealand which may hereafter be at the disposal of the Founders'.

The committee's resolution was a fine emollient to EGW's damaged *amour propre* and he would have left the meeting satisfied that the pretender had been destroyed and his position within the association secured. But it was a temporary and hollow victory. Even in his state of denial, EGW must have known that Campbell had spoken only the truth and a thousand endorsing resolutions from the committee would not change it. Campbell's crime had been in exposing and puncturing the protective bubble of delusion that EGW had created around himself. The committee, in its nice wording of the resolution, had implicitly recognised the reality of EGW's position: appointment to positions of real importance in any Crown-sanctioned colony would not be 'at the disposal of the Founders'.

The meeting served only to arouse EGW's enemies and make new ones. One member at the meeting, the Reverend William White, a missionary who had been banished from New Zealand under charges of 'immorality with native women', professed himself appalled at the revelation that EGW's real motives were not philanthropy but personal power;[40] he became an unwavering critic. EGW could hardly have expected, either, that Campbell would take the meeting's outcome lying down and he both fomented criticism of EGW and his plans and later moved to establish his own New Zealand colony.

A month later, *The Times* produced several slashing articles and savaged EGW directly:

> [I]n the gorgeous fancy of Mr Edward Gibbon Wakefield and the minor magicians by whose wand it has sprung into existence, [the association] doubtless conjures up a state of things resembling, as near as may be, a moral and political paradise. To what extent the enchanting vision has for some months irradiated the steps and beatified the pillow of that ingenious projector is more than we can tell. That his talents are to be unnapkinned as Governor of the proposed colony, – that just before setting sail he is to be knighted . . . . that Sir Gibbon shall have a government-house, with a handsome conservatory, garden, and pleasure grounds . . . that the Governor's salary, though at first only a few thousands a year . . . must present the unremote prospect of a realized

> competency and a retiring pension – all this is only a vague outline of the agreeable adjuncts (subordinate of course to the higher objects of religion and philanthropy) which induce Governor Wakefield to sacrifice his home comforts for the sake of the New Zealand population.[41]

EGW may have considered that to be savaged by *The Times* was a kind of flattery, but he must have recognised his grave tactical mistake: by calling the extraordinary association meeting he had allowed his sense of personal injury to overcome political discretion. Now he was being badly and publicly mauled, despite the loyal support of the *Spectator* and the *Colonial Gazette*.

EGW was an easy press target; his sins were more public than most and he could not afford to buy legal protection. The ruling classes covered their domestic violence, adultery, rape, incest and cruelty by closing the ranks of privilege, buying off enemies and launching lawsuits at the scandal sheets that ferreted out salacious morsels of truth. To missionaries and middle-class moralists, EGW's crime had been abduction; to the spending classes it remained the upstart's offence against class and property.

No innocent himself, Lord Melbourne must have known of the increasingly close association between Durham and EGW but needed to be indulgent in his urgent need to coax Durham into tackling the Canadian constitutional crisis.[42] Financial collapse in the United States in the summer of 1837 had led directly to a savage depression in Canada that was worsened by crop failure. Hundreds of farmers, small traders and businessmen were pushed to the edge of ruin and the calls of Les Patriotes for reform in French Lower Canada quickly led to mass protest meetings and rioting in Montreal by November. Louis-Joseph Papineau, speaker of the Lower Canada Assembly, retired from the town, believing that his presence would lead to further violent insurrection. Knowing his sympathies for the reform movement, governor Sir John Colborne interpreted this as a move to gather armed support in the countryside and sent military detachments to the chief Patriote centres. In the fighting that followed, scores were killed and Papineau and several supporters fled to the United States.

In Upper Canada, news of the Montreal rebellion provoked reformer William Lyon Mackenzie to issue a call to arms: 'Canadians! The struggle will be of short duration in Lower Canada, for the people are united as one man . . . . if we rise with one consent to overthrow despotism, we will make quick work of it. . . .' It was quick work indeed. In the one encounter between the governor Sir Francis Bond Head's loyal volunteers and Mackenzie's followers, the 'rebellion' was promptly routed. Mackenzie followed Papineau south of the border. 'Yet, disheartening as was the story of the rebellions, they none the less made their point. It was no longer possible for the British government to believe that reports from imperial appointees sent out as governors and from the little colonial oligarchies reflected the true condition and needs of the Canadas.'[43]

In early January 1838, as Durham vacillated, another player moved on the Canadian question. Long-serving Whig politician Edward 'Bear' Ellice was related to Durham by marriage and political alliance – both had married Earl Grey's daughters. An intensely private man, Ellice was a mover and shaker behind the scenes in the Whig hierarchy as a member of the House for 45 years from 1818. He held together competing factions of the party and had immense and lasting influence on colonial policy. Ellice was a business and banking tycoon whose family had made its pile from the Canadian fur trade. His nickname 'Bear' likely came both from that association and the kind of commercial success that earned him the considerable annual fortune of £20,000 from his North American investments alone during the last 25 years of his life. Although Ellice only twice set foot in Canada, this 54-year-old 'fur baron' had assumed a directorship and major shareholding in the Hudson Bay Company and inherited 450,000 acres of land in Canada and New York state. This included the Beauharnois seigneury, a large estate on the south bank of the St Lawrence, west of Montreal. In 1822 he had been the prime mover in London behind the Union Bill but his efforts to slide it through the house with minimal debate met unexpected opposition and only minor parts of the bill had survived. Ellice was labelled an evil *conspirateur* by the French Canadians, but the episode served to make him aware of the difficulty of governing Canada from London. As early as 1828 he urged some form of self-government for the Canadas, but careless colonial ministries let the problems drift until the 1837 rebellions forced the government's hand.

Early in January 1838, 'Bear' Ellice presented a new proposal for federal union of the two Canadas, with limited ministerial responsibility. This provoked a new approach to Durham from Melbourne with Ellice acting as broker. When Durham finally accepted the task of special high commissioner to Canada in mid-January, Melbourne agreed that he need take up the appointment only for the term of the crisis and, crucially, gave him complete freedom of action and 'unstinted appointment of all civil officers'. He promised to give Durham the 'firmest and most unflinching support'.[44] Durham had still accepted with great reluctance, knowing that cabinet would never give him a share of power at home and that Melbourne simply wanted him out of the way.

EGW had barracked for Durham's appointment: 'Send a *man* to Canada, and only *one,* with carte blanche – that is, without instructions. . . .'[45] Durham had told him that if he must go, he would need his expert counsel as Commissioner of Crown Lands and Emigration. EGW grasped – nay lunged – at the opportunity for an official appointment in which he could display his wisdom and skills in the colonial field. There was mutual admiration: EGW had become personally devoted to Durham, the lonely and tormented aristocratic radical who, in turn, was now the complete disciple of EGW's colonial theories. EGW would give Durham the expertise he needed to successfully complete his Canadian mission and a successful Durham would be the powerful political sponsor that EGW had always lacked. EGW's devotion and self-interest freed Durham from the circumspection of his peers, who feared EGW's 'predilection for methods that were devious, a desire to over-reach no matter what degree of trickery was resorted to, and a cool and sometimes heartless disdain for the moral code'.[46] In the current climate of public hostility towards EGW both knew better than to broadcast their intentions. Best to wait until they had arrived in Canada, when Durham could gazette EGW's appointment, distant from enemies at Westminster.

Durham and EGW's new and absorbing involvement with Canada partially explains their unwillingness to compromise with the government over the New Zealand charter proposal. EGW perhaps persuaded Durham that, with the government loath to upset his acceptance of the Canadian commission, it would eventually endorse the association's bill but, just as EGW miscalculated the scope and effectiveness of the missionary crusade against him, he also underestimated Glenelg's adoption of Stephen's resolve to obstruct and delay it.

Now another player arrived on the New Zealand scene. At the beginning of February, Glenelg received a report on New Zealand, from Captain William Hobson of HMS *Rattlesnake*, that would have a significant bearing on government thinking. Hobson's report, which had been commissioned by New South Wales Governor Richard Bourke, recommended the establishment of factories (trading stations) at the key points of British settlement, such as the Bay of Islands, based on cession of sovereignty over the sites by the Maori. The Maori would guarantee protection of British property and subjects; British nationals would have to register themselves and their assets with the factories, paying fees that would cover the cost of the system, which included factors (trading company agents) presiding over magistrate's courts, with the chief factor acting as consul to the 'United Tribes of New Zealand'.

Both Governor Bourke and Glenelg were impressed by Hobson's plan because it appeared to solve the key problems of how to bring law and order to the frontier and protect the interests of British citizens without taking sovereignty of the whole country. Neither the Maori nor any adversary power – the French and the Americans in particular – could be seriously disturbed by it and the Maori could be introduced slowly to a form of civil government. Its chief flaw was that factors would be unable to control the activities of distant settlers and traders and these might mean creeping expansion and assumption of wider sovereignty.

Glenelg mentioned the significance of Hobson's report when he wrote to Durham on 5 February 1838 to advise him that, in view of the association's decision, the government was withdrawing its offer of a charter and would remain neutral if the association introduced its bill into Parliament.[47] Powerful missionary lobbying throughout January and the mounting press attacks had now left EGW and the association in a seriously weakened position. There is no record of what EGW thought about the factory plan, though clearly it was antithetical to his proposals for organised emigration and free purchase of land.

EGW was now beginning to withdraw from the New Zealand enterprise. Although Campbell resigned from the Association in mid-February it was after EGW tacitly acknowledged the success of his enemies by declaring that 'he no longer considered himself open to any offer from the Association of such office as might be in their gift'.[48] But he was behind Molesworth's motion of no confidence in Glenelg which he put to the House of Commons on 6 March. Molesworth accused Glenelg of procrastination, inertia, vacillation – to all of which James Stephen could have happily testified – and of obstructing colonisation and settlement of New Zealand's problems. 'What has the noble lord, who should have been most conversant with this evil and this danger, what has he done, either on behalf of the natives of New Zealand, or of our shipping in the South Seas? What has he proposed? What has he thought of? He has done, proposed, thought of absolutely nothing: if it had been a matter in the moon he could not have been more careless about it.'[49] Molesworth's criticisms were largely correct,[50] but his words were as coins in a wishing well. His devotion to EGW and his role in the association were too well known.

Molesworth's motion did, however, remind the House of Glenelg's weakness and put added pressure on the Colonial Office to take some action about New Zealand at a time Stephen later described as the busiest and most anxious of his career. A fortnight after Molesworth's motion, the government employed a time-honoured delaying tactic by appointing a select committee of the House of Lords to inquire into 'the present state of the islands of New Zealand and the expediency of regulating the settlement of British subjects therein'. It would meet during April and May. This stalled any immediate movement on the association bill. Politician that he was, EGW sensed that the association was a lost cause. There were bigger fish to catch in Canada. Also, he was still trying to make something of the failed Swan River settlement, as well as advising Molesworth on preparation of the transportation committee report. EGW congratulated Molesworth on the committee's final report in August as having dealt a death blow to 'an unclean thing'. But he would have congratulated himself more on the report's recommendation that, to solve the labour shortage the abolition of transportation would create in the Australian colonies, the Wakefield system of colonisation should be introduced. There was more than one way to achieve his goals.

EGW did not take part in the House of Lords committee hearings on New Zealand, clear evidence that he had withdrawn most of his energy from the association. Evans stood in for him, speaking on New Zealand from the information that he and EGW had gathered for the association book and with especial confidence on the spurious claims of the 1825 company to ownership of 1,000,000 acres of land. EGW had coached Nahiti to speak approvingly of the idea of more English settlers going to New Zealand: 'I like it. I do not know what my countrymen would like. I think they would like it too, because they like even the bad people now. I think they would like gentlemen.'[51] The weakness of the association's case was thrown into relief by the informed and rational submissions of missionaries Coates and Beecham and the statistically authoritative contribution from the government's Agent General for Emigration.[52]

The committee's report, brought down in August, was the final, brutal blow to the association. It incorporated just one resolution, 'that the Extension of the Colonial Possessions of the Crown is a question of public Policy which belongs to the Decision of her Majesty's Government but that it appears to this committee, that support, in whatever way it may be deemed most expedient to afford it, of the Exertions which have already beneficially effected the rapid Advancement of the religious and social Condition of the Aborigines of New Zealand affords the best present Hopes of their future Progress in Civilization'.[53]

Before the report appeared, the committee's work had been done. On 1 June, the association had introduced its 'Bill for the provisional government of British settlements in the islands of New Zealand'. On the evening of 20 June, Howick recorded in his diary, 'we in the end threw out the most monstrous proposition I ever knew made to the House by 92 to 32'.

EGW was not around to comment on either the bill or the report. Durham had sailed for Canada on 24 April, taking a month to reach Quebec through storms and head winds. EGW, taking Jerningham, not yet eighteen, as his private secretary, slipped away a couple of weeks later to join him. He left both England and New Zealand behind for the prospect of a new Canadian career. But he was unable to abandon his reputation. He had spoken too loudly about his intentions, his departure was reported and the unforbearing enmity of his opponents sailed with him.

CHAPTER FOURTEEN

'I would die in your service'

IN 1840 RETROSPECT, DURHAM'S CHIEF ADVISER in Canada, Charles Buller, wrote of an 'error most injurious to the success of the mission. This was the delay that occurred before we entered upon it. . . [it] took off the bloom of the Mission: the Insurrection was to all appearance wholly suppressed before we started: the danger began to be thought less urgent: and the general impression of the necessity for great powers and unusual measures was gradually weakened.'[1]

Louisa, Lady Durham, writing to her sister-in-law Mary, Countess Grey, put the delay down to ice. Safe navigation up the St Lawrence River was not possible until April and the alternative route to Canada via New York would have been diplomatically most undesirable. There was also the question of the poor health of Lambton, as she called her husband, never secure and frequently debilitating. If the Canadian danger had become less urgent, as Buller averred, this may have been so because the rebels and reformers behind the 'Insurrection' knew that Radical Jack was coming and there was a general confidence that Durham would find a solution to the constitutional problems of British North America.

On disembarking from the *Hastings* at the end of May 1838 Durham, attired in his most splendid vice-regal uniform, rode a fine caracoling white charger through the streets of the Lower Canadian capital of Quebec to launch a truly imperial progress. As he held audiences, levées, balls and dinners through the provinces, his top tables groaned with glittering plate, crystal and fine linen, the packing of which may have been another major contribution to the late departure of the mission.

In Lower Canada, the constitution had been suspended and Durham governed through a special council made up of members of his own staff. Charles Buller, at his right hand, had strong ideas about responsible colonial government and wished to go further than 'Bear' Ellice's proposals, favouring an executive council or cabinet that was responsible not directly to the governor and his self-interested advisers but to a majority of the legislative assembly. This would allow a high degree of autonomy in the governance of local affairs while preserving loyalty to the British Crown. Radical Jack was sympathetic to this proposal, though the problem remained as to how a governor appointed in London would balance responsibility to both his local legislature and to imperial authority. But responsible government was an idea whose time had come and had been frequently propounded by local reformers such as Upper Canada's Robert Baldwin.

The other key members of Durham's retinue during his right royal progress were 'Bear' Ellice's son Edward as his private secretary; EGW, whom he intended to appoint Commissioner of Crown Lands; and legal adviser Thomas Turton, who had worked with Durham on the Reform Bill. Sixteen years before, Turton had been the subject of a divorce scandal after an affair with his wife's sister. Prime Minister Melbourne's initial indulgence of Durham's freedom to appoint whomsoever he wished soon became a political embarrassment when the Melbourne government's opponents, and Durham's many reactionary enemies, got wind of his intention to gazette both Turton and EGW on arrival in Canada. Melbourne decided he could not afford to have the mission or his ministry compromised by the resurrection of old scandals.

Glenelg was instructed to write to Durham, requesting him not to give Turton or EGW any official position. Melbourne followed with, 'Beware of scamps and rogues . . . whatever their ability may be. If you touch [E]G.W. with a pair of tongs it is utter destruction, depend upon it.' Later, in an almost pathetic entreaty, Melbourne wrote: 'Only consider how you injure the Queen, whose age [nineteen] and character demand some respect and reverence . . . . I rely . . . upon your assurance that you will not give Mr Wakefield any public appointment whatever and that his name will not appear in any public document.'[2] Glenelg's letter arrived two days after Durham had appointed Turton. He refused to rescind his decision and proposed also to gazette EGW, who had arrived later in Quebec, after travelling by packet to New York. In keeping with his devotion to Durham, EGW offered to sail home again. Turton also offered to resign but Durham would not hear of either, whereupon EGW volunteered his unofficial services.

On 15 June, Durham replied to Melbourne, advising him that Turton would stay on officially, adding,

> As for Mr Wakefield, your letter arrived before him, and I have therefore been able, without compromising my own character and independence, to comply with your desire. He holds no employment or official situation whatever, nor will his name appear before the public at all. 'Oh no, we never mention him; his name is never heard.' Really, if it were not very inconvenient all this would be very ludicrous. But I am placed in a very painful situation. I am called to perform an almost superhuman task. You provide me with no – or at least inadequate – means from yourselves,[3] and you then interfere with the arrangements I make to supply myself with the best talent I can find . . . The

colonies are saved to England, as far as I am concerned, but you must be firm. Don't interfere with me while I am at work. After it is done, impeach me if you will. . . .[4]

Durham knew that impeachment over the case of Turton's adultery would threaten half the cabinet's reputations. Melbourne himself was open to accusation and Lord Palmerston's long liaison with Melbourne's sister had only just been formalised.

Later, Durham's brother-in-law, Lord Stanley, chimed in: 'I'm also sorry to say that Wakefield talked quite openly to all men of his having been offered an appointment in Canada by you, & that he was leaving England for the purpose of filling a distinguished office'. EGW had not been able to resist broadcasting his triumph after his tribulations with the New Zealand Association and the press earlier in the year. At least Stanley sanctioned making private use of EGW's 'ability & information in framing any system for extensive emigration'.[5]

Attacks on EGW came from other quarters. 'Bear' Ellice, who had been trying to ease the political frictions caused by Durham's controversial appointments, wrote to his son Edward that hiring Turton had been a disaster but 'worse still' had been hiring EGW. One of the most damning letters came from the pen of Henry Samuel Chapman, a 34-year-old journalist who, in 1833, had founded in Montreal the first Canadian daily newspaper, the *Daily Advertiser*. The paper had supported French Canadian aspirations and, though influential, had failed financially after one year. When the paper closed down, Chapman was appointed the paid agent in London for the Special Committee for Correspondence, chaired by Louis-Joseph Papineau. Chapman's role was to liaise with radical MPs and to do whatever he could to further the French Canadian cause in London. On 19 May 1838, Chapman wrote to Papineau's exiled right-hand Patriote, Edmund Bailey O'Callaghan, telling him that EGW was accompanying Durham, outlining the Turner abduction and his colonial settlement schemes which he described as 'speculative jobbing'. Chapman wrote, 'Wakefield's character may be summed up in two words, he is a clever scoundrel . . . . On the whole I look upon him as a dangerous man because of his unscrupulous dishonesty . . . Try and get him thoroughly exposed in the Tory papers.'[6] Later, Chapman was willing to use Wakefield favours when it suited him.

O'Callaghan apparently had no ready access to Tory papers and, though the trans-Atlantic rowing about Turton continued for months, EGW's work for the mission continued discreetly. In his 1840 'Sketch of Lord Durham's Mission to Canada in 1838', Buller wrote that Durham had 'completely entered into all his [EGW's] views of Colonies and Emigration. On the 18th of June he issued the Commission for an enquiry into the state of the Crown lands in all the North American colonies.' Because EGW could not be 'employed publicly', Buller added, 'I was nominally placed at the head of the Commission. But my other avocations entirely prevented me from taking any part in the work: the details of it were accordingly left to my Assistant Commissioner Mr [Richard Davies] Hanson: but the real direction of the whole business was entrusted to Mr Wakefield. . . .'[7]

During the month before Durham's establishment of the commission of inquiry, he and his staff were preoccupied with gaining a full grasp of the political situation in Lower Canada and meeting community leaders. According to Lady Durham, 'He' (as she also referred to her husband) 'had every day a large dinner' with forty or more guests on the 'great days'. It was hard work for Lady Durham and the other ladies of the party and gruelling on a sickly earl who had begun to survive on willpower alone, and on his determination to continue the effect of an imposing vice-regal presence, both in honour to the importance of his mission and out of respect to the Canadians.

To bad health and social and political pressures in Canada were added the continuing political attacks from home. Durham had deflected any problems over EGW by keeping him out of sight, but the charge against Turton continued all summer, led by Lord Brougham, the man who had prosecuted EGW at Lancaster. By August, Lady Durham in Quebec complained to Countess Grey that she was 'very much vexed at this business of Mr Turton, & cannot help thinking Ld. Melbourne is shabby about it'.[8] Yet, though Brougham worried away at the Turton issue, he could not seriously damage the mission until he had a more substantial weapon.

Before his de facto appointment as Commissioner for Crown Lands and Emigration, EGW undertook discussions with Patriote leaders, mostly at his own instigation, to gain insights into French Canadian thinking as Durham addressed the problem of what to do with the 1837 rebels. As Durham's private secretary, Edward Ellice, wrote to his father, Durham consulted only Colonel Simpson of Coteau du Lac and EGW over his decision . . . 'no other person connected with Canada, not even the Atty. General, was consulted . . . Wakefield and Simpson I know went to Saratoga a few days previous to have an interview with Papineau. . . .'[9] This meeting was reputedly abortive,[10] but EGW certainly had discussions with politician Louis-Hippolyte La Fontaine who, after representing the French Canadian interest in London and Paris, visited Papineau in Saratoga before arriving back in Montreal on 23 June. Since Durham announced his so-called Bermuda Ordinance on 28 June in Quebec, the nexus of discussions between the key French Canadians and Durham's immediate circle seems obvious.

Durham's ordinance decreed that eight of the key 1837 Patriote rebels who had been caught and pleaded guilty were to be exiled without trial to Bermuda. Fifteen others who had escaped across the border, including Papineau, were forbidden to return to Canada on pain of death. All others involved were amnestied. The decision brought common sense to the case of the rebels: lives were spared and a lid was put on violent political agitation. But Durham could not presume the rebels' guilt nor condemn them without trial: his ordinance was illegal and this was just the political carrion that Brougham needed.

At the beginning of July, the vice-regal party moved on from Quebec to the Upper Canada capital of Kingston via Montreal. A high moment of the tour came when Durham conducted a ceremonial review of British regular soldiers and Canadian militia and crossed under the Niagara Falls. He followed this with a banquet for 200, with many American guests, south of the border. Charles Buller wrote that a 'million of money would have been a cheap price for the single glass of wine which Lord Durham drank to the health of the American president'.[11] Durham was fulfilling another purpose of his mission – to foster warm relationships with official America.

Now Buller fell ill and stayed at Niagara while Durham went to Toronto. On the return north and east both men were sick enough to take two days' rest at 'Bear' Ellice's seigneury at Beauharnois. The strain of constant travel, diplomatic high socialising and political negotiation was telling on both men. On 14 August, Buller wrote that he was so sick that he felt incapable 'of any communication requiring thought or care'.[12]

There is no information to confirm or deny whether EGW accompanied Durham and Buller any further west than Montreal. He did not appear to suffer from any impairment to his own energies. At the end of July he prepared a seventeen-page report for Glenelg, under Durham's signature, which examined and rejected claims for special treatment by the British North American Land Company. Official letterbooks for July, August and September show that EGW was deeply involved in a variety of land, settlement and timber cutting issues with correspondents as diverse as the Bishop of Montreal and the Chief Justice of New Brunswick. With the help of Assistant Commissioner Hanson, EGW was making a thorough investigation of Crown lands across settled Canada – Quebec, Ontario, Nova Scotia, New Brunswick, Prince Edward's Island – examining witnesses and collecting statistics. By the beginning of September, he was almost ready to write his part of Durham's huge 'Report on the Affairs of British North America'. And while Durham was too sick to go to the theatre, EGW and Jerningham held a magnetising soireé at Charles Buller's residence producing 'sleep, real or assumed, upon several women present'.[13]

At the end of July, Lord Brougham began his deadly attack in Parliament against the illegality of Durham's Bermuda Ordinance, declaring that though Durham had been permitted to make general laws, his commission did not empower him to sentence men to banishment without trial and declare them guilty of death if they returned to Canada; this was 'utterly at variance with the known and just and established law' of England. Here was a powerful legal argument he could use to attack Melbourne, the favourite of the queen, who had left him out of the Whig administration, and to destroy his old Radical foe Durham. Damn the consequences for Canada. Melbourne and Glenelg struggled to cope with the mounting attacks against the legality of the ordinance. Faced with defeat in Parliament and the collapse of his ministry, Melbourne sacrificed

Durham, and advised the queen to disallow the ordinance. On 24 August, *The Times* said: 'True to their base and selfish instincts, the time-serving Whigs, in deference to whom the noble Earl had at great personal sacrifice placed himself in the van of their Canadian conflict, have at the first shot deserted, dishonoured, and dismissed him . . . .' Brougham was winning on both counts.

Durham had popular support both at home and in Canada. But in bypassing the old ruling hierarchies, and by an increasing inclination to regard the French Canadians as a complaining, ungrateful race who would benefit if Lower Canada were made thoroughly British, he had made his task of completing his reforms increasingly arduous. By the end of August, Edward Ellice was writing to his father on the question of constitutional reform: '. . . the only person I now have trust in is Gibbon Wakefield – His opinions & views all tend to republicanism, & there we are safe'.[14] 'Bear' Ellice must have had a fit.

At the beginning of September, Lady Durham recorded in her diary that the stress of his mission had caused Durham to be for 'many days confined to his room' and that even after he went out 'he was still often ailing'. The chronic neuralgia that afflicted him with migraines had been joined by a more insidious, still undiagnosed, disease which steadily diminished his strength and deepened his depression.

EGW and Buller became alarmed at the signs that Durham was declining physically and mentally in the face of all his political and personal difficulties. On 27 August, Durham wrote to a colleague in England, 'I am tired to death of my task and wish it were over.' Soon after this, he must have indicated to EGW and Buller that he thought to abandon the mission. On 7 September, they sent him a remarkable letter of support. It bore Buller's signature, but both EGW's handwriting in the draft and the language and tone of its contents show that much of it was his inspiration:

> Day after day I have gone to you with the intention of making you acquainted with the view of affairs which all those, who have your interests most at heart, concur in taking and expressing among one another; and every time I have been turned away from my purpose either by that despair of the ultimate success of your mission . . . or by getting alarmed at the effect which what I said seemed to have produced on your health . . . . be your bodily disorders what they may, the real cause of your sufferings is in your mind . . . . you have no chance of recovery without raising yourself from your present morbid state of feeling . . . .
>
> You seem to think that if not properly supported at home or here, you have nothing to do but resign . . . the public . . . know nothing of the real nature of your difficulties . . . You have undertaken in time of danger, the maintenance of one of the most exposed defences of the Empire . . . . Why then do you suddenly abandon the post of honour and of danger? . . . in proportion to the high hopes which a nation has formed of you . . . will be the fearful recoil of its unexpected disappointment, and the

> terrible downfall which you will experience from the noblest position ever occupied by any public man in England since the first Pitt. . . .[15]

The letter continued in this passionate, panegyrical tone, urging Durham to ignore his enemies at home and in Canada and 'to pay no attention to the press', but reminding him of how much worse its taunts would be if he resigned.

EGW's and Buller's assurance of undying loyalty and support must have heartened Durham, but such encouragement was almost immediately overtaken by events. Three days later, Durham received his first news of Brougham's attack on the ordinance and on 13 September more details of the parliamentary debate, causing Lady Durham to write to Countess Grey: 'I have not words to express what I think of the wickedness of Ld. Brougham's conduct, in gratifying his malicious spite. . . .' Lambton had 'suffered most severely & I have never seen him so reduced in strength'.

On 19 September, the mail steamer arrived at Quebec with post and newspapers that perfectly demonstrated the pusillanimity and lack of faith which characterised the Melbourne government's handling of Durham's mission. Letters written by Melbourne and Glenelg at the end of July, just as Brougham's attack began, praised Durham for his ordinance and effective handling of Canadian affairs. 'Go on and prosper,' wrote Glenelg. But also in the steamer was a New York newspaper with later news that the ordinance had been disallowed. 'Lord Durham sent for me,' wrote Buller in his 'Sketch', 'told me the news, and almost more by manner than words, let me know that his mind was made up to resign his government.'

There was outrage across the Canadas at the home government's actions and, with the dumping of the ordinance, fears of rebel-organised attacks from across the border and the collapse of the reforms that Durham had been bringing to government, the bureaucracy and judiciary. Durham received messages of support from all quarters, including erstwhile opponents. Public protest meetings were held in Toronto, Montreal and Quebec and effigies of Brougham were burned in the streets.

On 29 September, EGW wrote to Molesworth, 'Lord D resigns. . . . He is . . . coolly and mortally offended at everything Whig but . . . stifles all feelings of personal anger and acts with admirable calmness. He has won the respect of these people and the hearts of all America. No other man can settle these affairs. He *must* (who can doubt it)? May you be men enough to enjoy the prospect!'[16] But by this time, Buller had changed his tune. On 7 September he and EGW had urged Durham not to resign. In his 1840 'Sketch' he maintains that, just twelve days later, he approved of Durham's decision to resign because of the state of his health and also because he would not be able to govern effectively without the support of the home government. Colonel Charles Grey, brother of Lady Durham and Durham's emissary to Washington, confirmed in a letter to his father on 30 September that if Durham stayed, 'I really think it would kill him.'[17]

On 9 October in the Lower Canada House of Assembly, Durham issued the proclamation required of him by the home government that both disallowed the Bermuda Ordinance and indemnified anyone who had acted illegally under its auspices. But he used the proclamation to justify his actions to the Canadian people, to explain his resignation and to regret that he had been rendered incapable of seeing through the reforms he had planned for all Canada's governing and administrative institutions. EGW's key role in Durham's thinking was revealed when he concluded, 'Above all, I grieve to be thus forced to abandon the realization of such large and solid schemes of colonization and internal improvement as would connect the distant portions of these extensive colonies, and lay open the unwrought treasures of the wilderness to the wants of British industry, and the energy of British enterprise.'[18] He promised to keep working for Canada and intended that his final report would yield great results.

His speech was received with great acclamation in Canada – and with anger by the Melbournites in England, including Edward Ellice. Charles Grey wrote his father that Durham 'has not been able to avoid spiting the Government by making the embarrassment caused by their act as great as possible'. The character of Durham's proclamation 'was the doing, I believe, entirely of Mr Wakefield and Charles Buller, of the latter of whom particularly I have not the slightest opinion'.[19] At the end of June, Grey had described EGW as a 'very agreeable man'. But a few months later, after reading John Stuart Mill's public support for Durham's actions, Grey wrote from Montreal,

> The object is too apparent – to get Lambton to put himself at the head of the Radicals, in which case they are quite prepared to give up any sympathy for the 'suffering Canadians'. . . . I know this was Wakefield's sole object in this Country. . . . Wakefield the morning after the Proclamation had been settled . . . could not contain his exultation, boasted of the share he had had in getting it, and said he had now accomplished all he wanted. That Lord Durham had quarrelled with the Government beyond the possibility of reconciliation and that he should now write to the leading Radicals in Birmingham, etc. to ply him with addresses on his return and 'that he was their own'.[20]

John Stuart Mill was, of course, part of the Radical circle and had been in close touch with Buller and EGW while they were in Canada. He had written to the *Spectator*'s Rintoul that Buller and 'Wakefield appear to be acting completely as one man, speaking to Lord D. with the utmost plainness, giving him the most courageous and judicious advice, which he receives both generously and wisely'.[21] A few days after Durham's proclamation, Buller wrote to Mill, 'Wakefield has been of the greatest service to us. He is very clever, has a great view of things – but one must be on one's guard against his rashness & fancy.'[22]

EGW's next great service for Durham, following his resignation, was to sail ahead to England and take the pulse in London so that he might properly describe for Radical Jack the political lie of the land immediately upon his arrival. Durham set sail from Canada on 1 November, on a ship appropriately named *Inconstant*, just as fresh rebellion broke out, which he promptly ascribed to the government's failure to support him. The *Inconstant* almost went aground on the Scilly Islands shoals before arriving off Plymouth on 26 November. Durham did not go ashore for four days, ostensibly because of bad weather, but this did not prevent the relay of despatches across the stormy sound. The measured delay gave him time to gather intelligence and decide on his course of action.

EGW wrote to him from Hatchetts Hotel in Piccadilly on 24 November. During the two weeks he had been in England he had travelled as far as the Midlands and Liverpool to gather information and proselytise Durham's case. 'If I had written immediately on my arrival,' he told Durham, 'it would have been in very gloomy terms.' All the newspapers, without exception had been against him; but now 'the tide has turned' as the press began to perceive that Durham's case had been 'misunderstood'. And 'Your coming straight home to face your foes has had the effect that pluck always has with Englishmen'. He said that the government 'people especially are puzzled and alarmed by this evidence of your resolution and self-reliance. They will submit to your terms – they feel that they are at your mercy. . . . party Tories & Radicals are confounded at the most unexpected dangers which declare themselves in the colony & they will do you justice. I am sure of it. I would not deceive you or mislead you for the world. You took me by the hand when I was proscribed: & I would die in your service . . . I said that you would, and you do now, fill a larger space in the politics of the world than any other man.' EGW told him that the government's tactics would be to undermine his position by saying that all his acts in Canada were really the work of his advisers – 'Turton, Buller, & myself' – and so depreciating them all. He advised Durham to be 'patient & cautious – anything but hasty and confiding. The fright at your returning is increasing every hour.'[23]

The tone of EGW's letters to Durham at this time was almost feverish, conveying a feeling of excitement, conspiracy, of great deeds to be done. It was in accord with his lifelong sense of adventure, outrageous enthusiasms and the 'rashness & fancy' of which Charles Buller had recently written. But his passionate devotion to Durham and his radical causes bespoke not only ambition but also the reforming ideals that had been with him all his life. His means were often dubious but his ends lay in a radical heaven. His astute counsel to Durham was rarely off the mark. Radical Jack was to inscribe in a book he gave EGW, 'I never went wrong so long as I followed your advice.'

Although he knew that Durham would agree with his sentiments, EGW had risked his censure by writing a letter to the *Spectator*, published that same day, in reply to criticisms from MP and agent for the French Canadians, John Roebuck.

EGW wrote that he had been a strong French Canadian sympathiser before his time in Canada but after an extensive acquaintance with them had changed his views. As he had written to Molesworth from Quebec two months before, they were 'a miserable race, and . . . . this country *must* be made English by one means or another'.[24]

EGW wrote another letter to Durham on 27 November, before he knew of his arrival, and its chief intent supported Charles Grey's judgement of EGW's political hopes. In urging Durham to take great care before he took 'any step, public or private', he stated that the fortnight after his arrival would be 'far & far away, the most important occasion of your life; not to yourself alone, but to your country. . . . If you act in perfect consistency with your Proclamation, you may be the means of saving this country, as you have saved Canada, from terrible evils.'[25] On the 29th, EGW wrote, 'My dear Lord, I have just heard of your arrival, & shall go to Plymouth by mail tonight . . . . I have a most important piece of information for you which I will not trust to a letter. Till you have it you should do absolutely nothing – not even decide whether or not you will receive the Plymouth & Devonport address in public. . . .' Since Charles Buller was still in Canada, EGW was now working with William Molesworth in the cause of bringing down Melbourne and installing Durham as premier of a Radical government. 'I have a remarkable & admirable letter from Molesworth wherein he says that he . . . will follow you through thick and thin.'[26]

On 1 December, Molesworth chaired a Devonport public meeting at which addresses of support from Devonport and Plymouth were presented to Durham, who boasted of his success in Canada and declared that in respect to the crisis, '. . . every faculty of my mind is engaged in the task of providing here for the security and advancement of those important national interests'.[27]

That day also saw the publication of the first issue of the *Colonial Gazette*, which EGW had persuaded the *Spectator*'s Robert Rintoul to bring out to propagate Durhamite and Wakefieldian opinion. It lasted until 1847 and had an influence far beyond its small circulation suggested since its contents were freely reprinted in colonial newspapers around the world. The master propagandist was at work again.

EGW told Durham that he had written an account of his Devonport address for the papers, titled, 'Durham Manifestations in the West of England' and continued to stir up support among the Radicals. 'They say – "Now we have got a man who can, and will, go through with Reforms . . . . Those Reformers who are in earnest – who are not content that the Reform Bill should be a final & fruitless measure – are roused . . . . Your return, in circumstances which lead them to hope that you will act independently of the Melbourne Whigs, gives them heart; & they will support you through thick and thin if you are true to yourself.'[28]

EGW went back to London, ahead of Durham's stately vice-regal progress towards the capital, as he attended public meetings at Honiton, Ashburton and

Above: Edward Wakefield senior, painted about 1775 with his wife Priscilla (seated), and her sister Catherine Bell, who was the mother of Elizabeth Fry. FROM IRMA O'CONNOR, *EDWARD GIBBON WAKEFIELD*

Far left: Priscilla Wakefield in 1818. ATL F-79215-1/2

Left: Catherine Wakefield as a girl, painted about 1800. FROM IRMA O'CONNOR, *EDWARD GIBBON WAKEFIELD*

Right: Te Rauparaha, the great Ngati Toa fighting chief and the most powerful man in the Cook Strait region at the time of the *Tory*'s arrival in 1839. Drawing by John Alexander Gilfillan in 1842.
ATL 114-023

Below left: Te Puni, the Ati Awa chief who signed William Wakefield's deed of settlement in Wellington Harbour in September 1839 and welcomed the first New Zealand Company settlers. Charles Heaphy lithograph.
ATL PUBL-0011-02-2

Below right: Ngati Toa warrior chief Te Rangihaeata, nephew of Te Rauparaha and indomitable opponent of land ownership by British settlers. He executed Arthur Wakefield at the Wairau in 1843. Charles Heaphy drawing from 1840. ATL C-025-022

Exeter en route. EGW, caught up in the gathering wave of demonstrations around the country, acted as Durham's most loyal spy, visiting the earl's house at Cleveland Row to report on visitors and letters.

Durham reached London on 7 December to find a copy of Glenelg's despatch to him in Canada about the ordinance which, 'shamefully', also incorporated the young queen's disapproval as a consequence of Melbourne's influence. The next day, Durham told Melbourne's emissary that the government had acted towards him with ill will and that he had been made an object of persecution. On the 10th Lady Durham, on her own initiative, resigned her position as lady-in-waiting to Victoria. The mounting popular support for Durham seemed ready to lift him to the prime ministership; there was speculation about who would hold various offices when he came to power. EGW, and Buller when he returned just before Christmas, urged him to accept the Radical leadership and overthrow Melbourne. Charles Grey was right: they were prepared to sacrifice the Canadians for the sake of ultimate power in England.

But Durham was not and was 'counted a fool by his best friends'.[29] While he had been formulating his report, Durham, aided not least by Buller and EGW, had developed a vision of a British Empire bonded in loyal autonomy by responsible government; of the independent and free association of British-settled colonies, joined by the same civilised institutions, working and growing together for the benefit 'of British industry, and the energy of British enterprise'. Durham knew that most of the radicals who wanted him to lead them into government would never subscribe to his vision of empire. It would be difficult enough to persuade Melbourne's Whigs to accept the recommendations he planned for his report. But he could still do it and, no matter how much he despised them for their behaviour, he must use his now powerful political standing to see his report – his Canadian and Empire mission – through to a successful conclusion. From the middle of December, he declined to speak at any public meetings or accept any addresses – and to meet any members of the Melbourne cabinet – as he shut himself away at Cleveland Row and laboured on the report. It is tempting to think that, although the disease that would soon kill him remained undiagnosed, he had a sense of his own 'abbreviation of time', and knew that completing the report, and procuring its acceptance and application, would do more for his country and its empire than any temporary accession to power.

Durham worked at his report from the time he reached London on 7 December until the end of February 1839 when he signed off its appendices. He presented proof sheets for the printing of the main part to the government on 31 January and completed copies were officially presented to the Colonial Office on 4 February. For the following century, there was unresolved debate about who actually wrote the Durham Report. Early on, Brougham savagely commented to MP and historian Thomas Macaulay that 'the matter came from a swindler [EGW], the style from a coxcomb [Buller], and the dictator only furnished six letters –

D.U.R.H.A.M.'.[30] The *Dictionary of National Biography* 60 years later stated that the report was written by Charles Buller with the 'exception of two paragraphs on church and crown lands', written by EGW and R. D. Hanson. Durham's later biographers made the case for Durham writing it mostly himself. The only sensible conclusion that can be drawn, given the intimate co-operation of the three men in Canadian affairs over the previous year, is that they all had a strong hand in it, with Durham having the overriding editorial mandate. They all subscribed to its findings, from their investigation, analysis and discussion of Canadian affairs at first hand, and it seems logical that EGW and Buller contributed draft sections and paragraphs which were incorporated or modified by Durham – and equally likely that he sought their opinions throughout its preparation.[31]

One key part of the Durham Report, Appendix B on Public Lands and Emigration, was clearly EGW's construction, drafted before he left Canada – even though Buller and Durham may well have tinkered with the wording. We have this on Durham's own word (and Buller's), despite the attempt by some historians since to diminish EGW's role. When he submitted the appendix to the Marquess of Normanby, the new Secretary for War and Colonies, Durham sent a long covering letter, admitting, 'I cannot do this without acknowledging my obligations to Mr Wakefield, whose name does not appear in connection with it, but who has rendered the Commission valuable assistance.' Durham outlined the reasons why he had asked EGW to accompany him, his expertise and the dispute that meant he could not be officially appointed. Nevertheless, EGW 'devoted himself to this extensive and laborious task, for which he has in no shape received any remuneration . . . . If the inquiry shall be judged to have been as efficient as I deem it, – if the conclusions of the Report on Public Lands and Emigration shall be rendered productive of the signal benefits which I anticipate from them, I am bound in fairness to take this means of ensuring to Mr Wakefield the chief share of the merit.'[32]

When Parliament met for the first session on 5 February, Durham rose to ask when his 'Report on the Affairs of British North America' would be laid before the House. Melbourne replied that his ministers needed time to consider it and that he would table it as soon as possible. Two thousand copies were being printed but the government intended to manipulate the public release of the report to suit its own political ends. Yet Melbourne had to keep Durham on side to fend off the Tories and Brougham.

At this point, EGW decided to force the government's hand and, on 7 February, leaked a copy of the report to *The Times*: Melbourne opened his copy on the 8th to discover thirteen columns given over to it. More instalments appeared over subsequent days, other English papers picked it up, and over the following months it appeared in whole or in part in newspapers all around the world. EGW wrote to Durham at the end of the year, 'It seems to have made almost as much impression in the Australian colonies as in Canada. It has now gone the round, from Canada, through the West Indies & South Africa, to the Australias, & has everywhere been received with acclamation.'[33]

It was no ordinary state paper: 'lucid, spirited, forceful [it] was as remarkable for an easy and natural eloquence as it was for an absence of forced sentiment . . . . Its faith and patriotism were as sane as they were inspiring. The common people received it the more enthusiastically because it was the work of one of their heroes. Britishers overseas adopted it as the corner-stone of Empire.'[34] The Durham Report not only led to Canadian democracy and self-government; it was the 'great watershed of British imperial history', providing the matrix for structure and governance of a British Empire whose legacy can still be seen today in the Commonwealth association of sovereign nations whose parliamentary, judicial and civic systems remain rooted in the British – and Durhamite – models. EGW's major contribution to this is incontestable.

The arrival of the report helped to hasten the demise of Lord Glenelg. It encouraged Durham's allies, Lord Howick and Lord John Russell, to threaten Melbourne with their resignation unless the incompetent Glenelg was removed from the Colonial Office. On the day *The Times* published the report, Glenelg announced that he had been offered another position in the cabinet but had refused it. EGW wrote to Durham, 'Below the bar of the Lord's yesterday, Ld. Glenelg's resignation was considered a great triumph for you. It was said "The Report has shot him; who'll be the next?"'[35]

At this point of Durham's triumph, and EGW's widely known part in it, the time seemed ripe to find a political role for EGW under Durham's sponsorship. The opportunity seemed to present itself in the May Bedchamber Crisis, when Melbourne was bounced out of office and then back in again by the efforts and affections of the young Queen Victoria. As the crisis developed, EGW and Buller conferred over the opportunities for Durham. EGW wrote to him, stating that the government's aims in recent times had been to 'keep him quiet' and urging him to again render himself 'formidable' as he had been at critical times over Canada. He would be 'neglected' unless he made a 'thorough union' with none other than Lord B[rougham]'. He and Brougham were the 'two men who had got the greatest hold on the Liberal mind of this country. . . . it would be a bold stroke, to be sure; but is not boldness the first quality in politics and who has been more indebted to boldness than Lord Durham?'[36]

About the same time, William Molesworth wrote a remarkable letter to Durham about EGW's future: 'The best way to give him the position in the world which he ought to hold, and to render his colonial and economical views useful to the country, would be to get him into Parliament, where his talents would soon acquire for him that weight and respect which he deserves to possess, would open to him a field for active exertion and honorable ambition, and ultimately would secure to him the reward which is due for his great discoveries.' Molesworth felt that overcoming the difficulties surrounding EGW's past would not be insuperable and that an appropriate seat could be found for him. 'If you should agree with me . . . no time should lost . . . as I am inclined to think a dissolution must be near at hand . . . . For myself . . . I will contribute a thousand pounds towards his election expenses . . . . I have had no positive communication with him on the subject of his getting into Parliament for a long time, but I believe that he would be most delighted if such an event could be brought about.'[37] Durham responded warmly and the pair met to discuss the matter at Cleveland Row.

But Melbourne stayed in, there was no immediate election and the consumption that had killed Durham's father, his first wife and four of his children was at last diagnosed in him. The disease now struck hard, driving him south to Cannes for several months in the hope of a recovery. He made his last address to Parliament in July 1839 and a year later was dead, five days after Queen Victoria signed the Act for the Union of the Two Canadas. On his deathbed, he is reputed to have said, 'Canada will one day do justice to my memory.' Durham's early death, at the age of 48, ended EGW's chances of a political career in England. But his part in Durham's mission had created the opening for a political career in Canada.

CHAPTER FIFTEEN

Possess Yourselves of the Soil

By March 1839, the New Zealand Colonization Association was in trouble. The colonisers, revivified after sloughing off the skin of the old association six months before, had continued to be thwarted and fobbed off by Colonial Office bureaucrats and Whig ministers, opposed by missionaries at every turn and undermined by competing colonisation enterprises, to the point where they decided to call a meeting to consider a winding up.[1] But they felt bound to take account of the position and views of EGW whose star was now at its highest following the Durham Report. Preoccupied with Canada, he had had little active involvement with the association for the best part of a year, but it was essentially his creation and was structured according to his theories. It could hardly be wound up without his sanction or, as William Hutt and Samuel Evans would have certainly advised, without giving EGW the opportunity to pass judgement on the situation. At the least, their 'ingenious projector' might have some life-saving ideas. It should not be a formal meeting, of the association or of the board of directors. Opinions and options would be best sounded out in discreet, convivial and well-lubricated circumstances. Banker John Wright took up the proposal of EGW's friends that he arrange for a private dinner party at his Hampstead home on 20 March, the occasion of EGW's forty-third birthday.

There was much to discuss and EGW would have relished not only being guest of honour but also the chance of being brought up to date with all the gossip, rumour and political intrigue. The old New Zealand Association members had responded to the defeat of their bill the previous June by reforming themselves into a private joint-stock body which they titled, confusingly, the New Zealand Colonization Association, often referred to from the start as the New Zealand Company, its eventual name.[2] At its second meeting, in September 1838, it was resolved, 'That in consideration of the great services rendered by Mr Edward Gibbon Wakefield, in promoting colonisation, especially with respect of

New Zealand, it is unanimously resolved that the option of taking one of the redeemed shares of £500 in this association be offered to Mr Wakefield.'[3]

Six weeks later, William Wakefield was in town and attended a committee meeting at Wright's bank in Covent Garden, but he was not present the following week when a sub-committee was set up to investigate the 'necessary measures' required to send an expedition to establish a settlement in New Zealand.[4] At the end of November 1838, from director and shipowner Joseph Somes, it had been decided to buy the 382-ton *Tory* for £5,250,[5] even before sufficient subscribers had been secured to officially establish the company. On 10 December, when 20 'bona fida' subscribers had been found, a sub-committee was formed to 'superintend the fitting out of the Tory, the purchase of the necessary provisions for the voyage and the purchase of the necessary goods to be exported to New Zealand'.[6] The company pressed on with the fitting up of accommodation on the ship in early January 1839 and the recoppering of its hull.

Born the son of a lighterman, Joseph Somes had become, by the end of the 1830s, a ship-owning millionaire. The *Tory* had been built to his order in 1834. A three-masted barque, it was an 111-foot two-decker with a draught of 15 ft 6 ins and armed with eight guns. The *Tory* had sweet lines and a reputation for fast passages though the only previous voyage to survive on the record was to the Cape in 1838.[7] The name was a direct reflection of Somes's political sympathies: he was, for a time, a Tory MP.

The steady preparation of the *Tory* gave the company a sense of purpose and progress when nothing else was falling into place. The company was a long way from reaching its paid-up capital of $25,000, it had no offices or manager with promotional energy and some of its directors were distracted by other entrepreneurial opportunities. Settlement plans were delayed for months while the company negotiated with Lieutenant Thomas McDonnell, an ex-assistant of the British Resident in New Zealand, James Busby, over his alleged land holdings and interests in the north of the country.

The company also competed with others for the attention and approval of the government. After the dissolution of the old association had broken its arrangement with the 1825 New Zealand Company, Robert Torrens, one of its original directors, proposed new settlement schemes to the government under the guise of the New Zealand Society of Christian Civilisation and publicly touted his company as the *real* New Zealand Company, confusing and inhibiting investment in the Colonization Association. Torrens still plied his own version of Wakefieldian principles, which had led to his conflict with EGW in 1835. The government was not impressed and the Colonial Office told the society in February 1839 that it had its own plans for New Zealand.

By December 1838, after months of torpor, even the dilatory Glenelg felt the need to take action. He had other colonial problems on his mind but New Zealand continued to contribute, as Brougham had acidly put it, to his having 'many a sleepless day'. At last, he made up his mind to replace Busby and on 1 December advised Governor George Gipps of New South Wales that he intended to appoint a New Zealand consul with Admiralty support. On 28 December, Glenelg offered Captain Hobson the position and asked him to put forward his own suggestions for British governance in New Zealand. Late in January 1839, Hobson responded that the factory plan he had devised in 1837 – and which had drawn so much approval from Glenelg – should be seen only as a minimum step. He considered that isolated factory settlements would leave much of New Zealand exposed to foreign intervention, lawlessness and shady land deals. All this and the inevitability of increased emigration would make it necessary for Britain to take sovereignty of all New Zealand. Prudently, he included a developed form of his factory plan if that proposal proved unacceptable.

Inevitably, Glenelg preferred the half-measure and also ignored James Stephen's recommendation – surprising to his enemies had they known – that once governorship of ceded parts of New Zealand had been established, there was scope for the operation of a 'New Zealand Company' to handle land sales and emigration under a charter of incorporation. But there was no mention of chartering a company in Glenelg's eventual consular instructions, which stated that the aim of the exercise was simply to protect both the natives and existing settlers. Large-scale colonisation would not be encouraged and sovereignty belonged to 'the chiefs of New Zealand'.

Glenelg, after flirting with a charter of incorporation for the New Zealand Association at the end of 1837 – because of Howick and Melbourne's need to persuade Durham over Canada – had finally allowed his sympathy for the evangelical humanitarianism of the CMS and the Aborigines Protection Society to prevail. The New Zealand Company directors must have rued the day they turned down the charter a year before, under EGW's insistence that they reject the joint stock provision, and been enraged when, having fulfilled this, Glenelg turned firmly against them. By February 1839 the missionaries seemed to have won, saving the Maori from the company's land exploitation plans. But Glenelg, who could have acted on his consular scheme at any time after the defeat of the association bill, had left his run too late. As James Stephen was to later complain, New Zealand could have been colonised in a manner controlled by the government long before the New Zealand Company existed, but 'Lord Glenelg hesitated'.[8]

Or was it Prime Minister Melbourne who hesitated? Howick had been trying to eject Glenelg from cabinet since December 1837. Molesworth's continual attacks on the minister, characterising his policy as 'doing nothing reduced to a system', had seriously injured his reputation. But it was only Howick's and Russell's threatened resignations that finally forced him from office in February 1839.

William Hutt demanded of his successor Lord Normanby, on the day he was appointed, that the government grant the company 'in accordance with the ancient precedents, a Charter of Government for the Islands of New Zealand', as offered in December 1837. The gentlemen of the company had 'exerted themselves with success to raise the necessary capital, the want of which was the only real difficulty last year . . . . After waiting two years and upwards they have felt themselves so irrevocably committed to the project that they have purchased a vessel, and are determined to proceed to the land of their adoption, even in the absence of that protection which was never, in former times, denied to Englishmen extending, at their own risk, the dominions of the Crown.'[9]

Normanby dismissed this threat and agreed to meet members of the company only if they accepted that the charter offer to the old association could not be transferred to a new and differently constituted company. On 14 March, when the company members came away from their interview with Normanby, they chose to believe that the new minister not only favoured the general objects of the company but also encouraged it to proceed. In fact, the government's encouragement extended only to the company's activities *after* Britain had exerted sovereignty in New Zealand. Despite Stephen's continued recommendation, the day after the meeting, that the government consult with colonialists to ascertain the best way to establish a Colonial Corporation, Normanby adopted Glenelg's consular plan without change.

Disquiet, resentment and utter frustration at the government's prevarications and delays conditioned the feelings of John Wright's eleven guests at Hampstead on the evening of 20 March.[10] After dinner, he spoke for all the stalwart New Zealand projectors when he said that it was now time 'some decided step should be taken either in advance or to give up'.[11] William Hutt told them Normanby had gone back on his word because the Colonial Office had just informed him that no New Zealand bill would be introduced that session. Hutt 'express'd his opinion that even if Govt should bring in a bill at once it would have more of an injurious tendency than otherwise because they would introduce a clause to the following effect – "That no land should be purchased in the Colony of N.Z. after the passing of the bill except from the Govt." The consequence of this clause would be that the Compy would then have to pay the Govts price, instead of the Natives's which would in all probability amount at least to 500 pr. cent more than what they can purchase for now.'[12] Dejection, groans of dismay. The whole basis of their enterprise was threatened: land bought cheap to sell dear was the key to funding the scheme.

'Mr Wright then ask'd Mr Wakefield for his opinion of what had best be done. Mr Wakefield then s'd, send off your expedition immediately – acquire all the land you can – & then you will find that Govt. will see the absolute necessity of doing something. untill something has been done by the Compy or a Compy the chances of success to americans – the french or the missionaries – are equal – either one or the other may colonize in their own way – there is no power to dispossess them. possess yourselves of the Soil & you are secure but, if from delay you allow others to do it before you – they will succeed & you will fail.'[13]

This was Phyllida Bathurst's General Wakefield speaking, proposing his *coup de main*. It was of a piece with decisions taken thirteen and 23 years before – when any other course of action was to admit defeat, when noble if ambitious ends qualified any manner of means, when possession was nine tenths of the law and when, with luck, dash and magnetism, you could (almost) always talk your opponents into handing over the vital missing tenth. It was what the assembly at Hampstead wanted to hear; it was why EGW had been invited – to give them heart, hope and direction. The consequences of his advice, the ethics of it, were overlooked in the excitement of the idea, in the flush of brandy, port and cigars. One can imagine the tone of the conversation: Damn the government: hadn't the company been badly dealt with – money down the drain so far – idle ship sitting there costing more by the day – no prospects in waiting for Normanby – Colonial Downing Street had let them down again – the worst thing . . . someone else might get there first . . . damned Frenchies . . . .

Wright asked EGW about his 'own intentions towards the present project' – did he still plan to give it his 'cordial support & would he consent still to take the lead?' If EGW were involved, Wright would 'immediately engage 5 shares more on acct of his great confidence in his able management of such affairs'. EGW said he could not take 'any active part' because of his 'engagements in other quarters, & unless he could give his sole & undivided attention to the affairs by working at them not only every day but all day long he did not think he should be of any service'. And because the company was 'an individual speculation of Land & Commerce, differing entirely from measures he had advocated – on the broad principles of Colonization on the new system. he understood nothing about companies & shares, he was therefore unfit to manage such matters.' He would, though, 'pledge himself to raise 5 shares immediately the 1st expedition sailed – but not a single one untill something had actually been done'. After EGW spoke, several others 'express'd their entire satisfaction at the prospects of the company and strongly urged the policy of really acting instead of talking. . .'.[14]

It would be naive to believe that EGW had no inkling as to the import of his dinner invitation and of what was expected of him, and gullible to accept his disingenuous protestations of commercial innocence. Spare drinking EGW had the clearest and coolest head in the aftermath of dinner and knew that playing hard to get and flattering the commercial acumen of his colleagues were the prerequisites to being talked into involvement under his own conditions. The New Zealand Company remained his child, by vision, labour, argument, publicity, even expense. How could he let it down? He would have already made up his mind but allowed himself to be cajoled and persuaded, despite all his 'engagements in other quarters'. In the end, he would have said it was his duty, and the deferring members of the dinner party would have been grateful. They had their galvaniser.

The very next day, all the members of the dinner party (bar one) and six other members of the company, including Molesworth, met at Wright's banking house in Henrietta Street. For the purposes of the minutes, EGW's hard-nosed advice of the night before was translated into a resolution, moved by William Hutt, 'That the report of the delegation appointed to confer with Lord Normanby is satisfactory, and holds out an assurance that the objects of this association will be attained if immediate steps are taken by the association to form one or more settlements in New Zealand'.[15] The meeting went on to decide that a preliminary expedition should be despatched as soon as possible, that the capital of the company should be enlarged by offering shares to the public, that emigration to New Zealand should be promoted and either a royal charter or act of Parliament obtained. A five-man committee of management was appointed: Lord Petre, Hutt, Somes, J. B. Gordon and EGW.

No one could say that EGW did not think of his brothers first. He would have warned William of what was in the offing; indeed it is likely that William was staying with EGW at Hans Place, Brompton, keeping abreast of every detail. EGW would have regretted Arthur's absence but he owed William more, and now there was a job to which William's experience of command, administration, field diplomacy and negotiation was well suited. The company needed, immediately, a principal agent and commander for its crucial first expedition to the Antipodes. The timing was tight: the fitting out of the *Tory* had to be completed, officers employed, supplies purchased and stowed, land-buying plans settled and the expedition started on its four-month voyage in a matter of weeks. Concurrently, legal and financial preparations were being made to launch the New Zealand Land Company with a sale of shares (4000 at £100) and the setting up of an office to manage the sale of land and recruitment of emigrants. The haste with which the company now moved could not have been seriously generated by fear that the government might act to stop them – legally and politically that would have been difficult – or because rival companies, on hearing of their preparations, might pre-empt them. Or because the French might soon take over New Zealand. The urgency resulted principally from the fact that Hobson would soon be on his way and it was essential that the company complete its land purchases – and set first settlers on the far shore – before any form of British sovereignty was exerted.

EGW told his brother to gather up his testimonials. William obtained another fulsome tract from De Lacey Evans on 25 March, the day before the management committee's first meeting, in which he stated his 'unequivocal opinion' of William's 'fitness & aptitude in keeping together, controuling and maintaining order and discipline amongst such body of men as may be placed under your orders'.[16] On 26 March, after reading such testimonials, the directors unanimously resolved to place the 'entire and absolute control' of the expedition in his hands at a salary of £500 per annum with a 'suitable outfit'. In the three-page document presented to William that day, the directors stated that they were led 'to this determination by a knowledge of the arduous nature of the duties to be performed at the extremities of the Globe, beyond the pale of Law, where order will have to be maintained among bold and adventurous men, chiefly by the personal qualities, the temper, firmness and discretion, the mutual resources and, not least, the reputation founded on past conduct in trying situations of the commanding officer. . .'. They were certain that William was the perfect choice because of 'your coolness and self reliance, and quick resources in sudden emergencies, your singular humanity towards the peasantry of the countries in which you have served, and your talents for negociation and the business of civil life, as well as your knowledge of the scientific principles of Colonization and your zeal in this enterprise'.[17] Although it was signed by Evans, the company's secretary, one wonders how late the previous night EGW had worked on the document, testing phrases on William as he smoked a cigar by the drawing room fireplace.

William began work at once, attending all directors' meetings, liaising with EGW, Evans and Somes who, as a 'regular dictator', took an active role in the expedition preparations. Evans was especially anxious to see the enterprise succeed because he had 'relinquished . . . a school in the vicinity of London, under the expectation held out to him by the Association . . . that he would be appointed to the office of Judge' in the colony.[18] William caused some alarm only two days into his task when he declared that the *Tory* was 'too large and drawing too much water' for a preliminary expedition and a ship of about 200 tons would be more appropriate. Somes undertook to search for another ship but reported a week later that no other available vessels were suitable and, besides, the *Tory* was big enough to pick up a useful cargo that would defray some of the expedition's expenses.

On 8 April, William reported that the *Tory* would be ready in about a fortnight but two days later, after news of a proposed Scottish colonising venture to New Zealand, Somes said the ship could go in 48 hours if necessary. William demurred and the meeting resolved on a sailing date of 25 April. The compressed timetable did not cause problems. Fitting out had been under way for months and Somes's expertise ensured that the *Tory* was well-found. Similarly, the expedition subcommittee had been attending to provisioning needs and a trading cargo since the end of the previous year. Technically, as a sea-going venture, the *Tory* expedition was well prepared.

But the press and clamour of day-to-day expedition preparations – and the work of establishing a new company – meant that there was simply not enough time to properly advertise, attract and choose the best qualified expedition officers. William had the skills for managing an expedition, or at least an expeditionary force, but no one involved had first-hand experience of the realities of colonial settlement, and only one or two members of the company had any direct knowledge of New Zealand.

Worse, the haste to beat Hobson precluded a genuinely exploratory expedition with adequate time to determine the best sites for colonies, to thoroughly survey topography and resources in an imperfectly known country on the other side of the world, and to negotiate properly for land with people of whom the company knew little and understood nothing. All this should have been done before settlement plans were drawn up and emigrants despatched. But plans were made up as they went along, mostly by EGW, and based on the 'peculiar system of colonization which has proved so eminently successful in South Australia'.[19] Bad news of the land and financial problems of the South Australian colony had begun to filter back but EGW counted on this not being widely disseminated: his claim of South Australian success was close to false advertising.

William's instructions for the expedition, first read out in draft by EGW at a directors' meeting on 24 April and later published as a 24-page pamphlet, *Instructions from the New Zealand Land Company to Colonel Wakefield*, also gave a misleading impression of informed planning and considered action. The company's written expectations of William were almost impossible to fulfil. They laid out the best intentions of the company, or at least of EGW: the document was as much a piece of propaganda as a set of practical guidelines.

William was given 'sole and unqualified direction' of the expedition and its officers and instructed that its objects were divided into 'three distinct classes:– 1st, the purchase of lands for the Company; – 2ndly, the acquisition of general information as to the country; – and, 3rdly, preparations for the formation of settlements under the auspices of the Company'. Half of the *Instructions* were given over to the first object: 'You will constantly bear in mind that the profits of the Company must, in great measure, depend on the judgment which you may exercise in selecting places of future location'. Because, it was assumed, so much fertile land was available, in choosing settlement sites, land was a 'far less important consideration than natural facilities of communication and transport', a safe harbour, extensive rivers and 'falls of water' that could be used to power industry. The main colony should also be the centre for commerce and trade. Since Cook Strait was on the 'shortest route from the Australian Colonies to England' the best harbour there should be given priority and this appeared to be Port Nicholson, at the toe of the North Island.

William was told to treat Maori 'with the most entire frankness', to make them fully aware as to why the land was being bought and of the 'nature and extent of the intended settlement, so that they may not be surprised at the subsequent arrival of a large number of ships'. He was not to complete any purchase of land until it was 'thoroughly understood by the native proprietors' and that all owners should be 'approving parties to the bargain', with each receiving their due share of the purchase money or goods. He was to make sure that the goods used for purchase should be of such a 'quantity as may be of real service to all owners of the land'.

The *Instructions* assumed that 'the object of the natives is to attract English settlers, by means of whose capital they may obtain goods in exchange for their labour and the natural productions of the country'. And the company was certain that much of New Zealand was 'Wilderness land . . . worth nothing to its native owners . . . and can become valuable only by means of a great outlay of capital on emigration and settlement'. Somehow, William had to quickly educate Maori in the principles and values of capitalism. Then they would understand how much capital appreciation they would realise by the company's generous proposal to reserve one-tenth of all land in the new colony for the 'chief families of the tribe by whom the land was originally sold'. These families would, 'Instead of a barren possession with which they have parted . . . have property in land intermixed with the property of civilized and industrious settlers, and made really valuable by that circumstance . . . . The intended reserves of land are regarded as far more important to the natives than anything which you will have to pay in the shape of purchase-money.'

Although EGW admitted that 'If the advantage of the natives alone were consulted, it would be better perhaps that they should remain for ever the savages that they are', justice demanded that the consequences of land sale and settlement be explained to the Maori and the 'superior intelligence of the buyers should also be exerted to guard them against the evils . . . of finding themselves entirely without landed property . . . in the midst of a society where, through immigration and settlement, land has become a valuable property'. Pains should be taken to ensure the 'relative superiority' of Maori chiefly families. 'If these can be made persons of consequence in the settlements established by a civilized race, they will be able to protect and improve' the rest of their countrymen.

At this eleventh hour, neither EGW nor his colleagues demonstrated any slackening in their belief in the unquestionable superiority of the values and social structures of their 'civilized race'. Maori could be naturally drawn, to their benefit, into a class system founded on private property. It would not have occurred to EGW to question the philosophical validity of his *Instructions*. But while his carefully expressed concern for justice in dealing with the Maori was certainly written with 'Mr Mother Country' (James Stephen) and the 'Bishop of New Zealand' (Dandeson Coates) in mind, there is no reason to think that EGW did not believe in fair and philanthropic treatment of the native New Zealanders.

The *Instructions* also stated, 'It is impossible that you should furnish the Company with too much information' about the natural resources of the country. Yet from the beginning, it was decided to send off the first ships of colonists *before* there was any chance of receiving reports from William. A rendezvous was arranged for the *Tory* with emigrant vessels at D'Urville Island in Cook Strait on 10 January 1840. By then, it was projected, William would have had four or five months in which to locate and buy land for the new colony. But he had no time at all to adequately survey land sections, taking into account the local topography and climate. All this seems inexplicable in an enterprise being run by the sons of Edward Wakefield, surveyor of Ireland, and scientific estate manager. Unbelievably, there was no contingency for the failure of the *Tory* expedition, through shipwreck, misadventure or hostile encounter with the

Maori, which would have left six shiploads of emigrants – more than 1000 men, women and children – to their fate when they arrived in New Zealand.

The idea to settle a new world was visionary; transforming the vision into a pioneering voyage was daring and courageous. But the New Zealand Company's precipitate decision to despatch the *Tory*, and its failure to professionally prepare the way for a new colony, was opportunist, irresponsible and, as far as the Maori were concerned, enormously condescending.

Yet it is easy to forget that, for most aspiring emigrants, life in England in the 1830s not only had few prospects but was also shorter, nastier and more brutal. For many, there was simply nothing to lose, and though they expected to obtain fertile or commercially well-placed, properly surveyed sections in the colony, they knew that they must transport or manufacture their own goods and services, construct their own lives. The earliest settlers might have also expected a storage shed, barracks, jetty, the beginning of a road; but nothing more, other than the opportunity for self-improvement by trade, increasing the value of their land, or through work as labourers that would yield enough income to buy land. For some, the adventure was the thing.

Everyone involved in the New Zealand venture, from EGW down, suffered under the delusion that, though New Zealand had some exotic qualities such as a few cannibals, it was essentially a raw England, fertile, well watered, with a superior, health-giving climate and lots of waste lands to be developed. EGW the arch-publicist has been routinely accused of creating this delusion, of so successfully foisting it on unsuspecting investors and emigrants that thousands of Britons were conned into parting with their money, into abandoning everything for a New Jerusalem in New Zealand's green and pleasant land. The voyage might be long, and usually one of no return, but at the end they would step ashore in a new, sunnier and empty England.

EGW partly created the delusion, believed in it himself, pushed it hard, tweaked what facts there were, in order to sell shares and land and to persuade emigrants – above all to make his theories somehow come true. But EGW's self-confessed 'castle in the air' was built on Arcadian and Utopian foundations deeply embedded in the European imagination. In its New Zealand manifestation, the country was a place of 'great valleys occupied by the most beautiful rivers, their feet washed by the ceaseless south-sea swell, their flanks clothed with the grandest of primeval forests, their bosoms veiled in cloud, and their rocky and icy scalps piercing the clear azure heaven; the fertility of its soil, the amenity and salubrity of its climate, [makes for] the peculiar adaptation of the country for the residence of a great commercial and manufacturing people'.[20]

This contemporary soar was not written by a Wakefield acolyte but drew on an established tradition of New Zealand lyricism. News of the fertile antipodean

Arcadia had first returned with Cook's naturalists, Joseph Banks and Georg Forster and been so increased and embroidered upon that, by 1807, the poetic preface to John Savage's *Account of New Zealand* could glowingly assure that

> Remote in Southern Seas an Island lies
> Of ample Space, and bless'd with genial Skies
> Where shelter'd still by never-fading groves,
> The friendly Native dwells, and fearless roves;
> Where the tall Forest and the Plains around,
> And Waters wide, with various Wealth abound.

EGW synthesised and embellished an image of New Zealand that already existed. The very hyperbole of his colonising propaganda should have alerted all prospective emigrants to a different reality beneath the glossy facade. There were enough contemporary critics, especially in *The Times*, to assist them. EGW's unusually successful puffery cannot be put down to his special genius alone. It could work only insofar as enough people wanted to believe in his dream – *their* dream – of another Eden. In 1839, New Zealand seemed Eden's most likely location, and extensive British (or French) settlement of the country was only a matter of time. EGW cannot be seriously criticised for propelling colonisation; he can even be praised for attempting it within a plausible economic and social model. He can be blamed partially for its over-hasty application, within a wider frame of government dithering and New Zealand Company cupidity and mismanagement. And it was left to slight, inscrutable William to take on, with scant resources and less time, the awesome responsibility of realising the dream. Perhaps EGW and the other company directors recognised that only someone able to follow orders with the kind of blind courage needed for a cavalry charge could conceivably fulfil the task.

On 1 April 1839, the directors' minutes record that there had been many applications for surveyor to the expedition but no suitable captain had been found for the *Tory*. Already, William had seen to the appointment as colonial surgeon of his legion friend, Dr John Dorset, who had been staff surgeon for the 1st Lancers in Spain; and Nahiti had been taken on as interpreter. A fortnight later, a Lieutenant Robson RN was provisionally accepted as captain of the *Tory*, on commander's pay, and asked to report on further outfitting. On 17 April, the directors were told that a suitable military man was unlikely to take up the position of surveyor and they decided to proceed without one; the chief colonial surveyor would sail with the first emigrant ship. But they agreed that the exploratory expedition should have a scientist and, three days later, 28-year-old Dr Ernst Dieffenbach was appointed without pay but with a £100 outfit.

Dieffenbach was probably given the position because no notable naturalist or scientist was available at such short notice or on such miserable terms. Dieffenbach took it because, as a poor political refugee from Giessen in Hesse, the *Tory* expedition presented him with the opportunity for employment with all found and the chance of making a scientific reputation. He was a medical doctor by training but had moved into more general scientific circles by translating German articles on a wide range of subjects. Since arriving in London in 1837 he had met Robert Owen and Charles Darwin and had been recommended to the company by the Royal Geographical Society. Politically, Dieffenbach was a (perhaps token) misfit on the expedition. A revolutionary democrat, he had fled his home after taking part in the abortive storming of the Frankfurt Hauptwache in 1833. In London, as a humanitarian of the J. G. Herder school of philosophy, he had become a member of the Aborigines Protection Society.

On the same day as Dieffenbach's appointment, another Wakefield was accepted for the expedition as an 'amateur'. Edward Jerningham later recounted, 'Such a voyage seemed to offer much novelty and adventure; and I, being then nineteen [*sic*] years old, conceived a desire to be one of the party. My father gave his consent to my departure.'[21] Jerningham was now past all formal education and had absorbed much of worldly and colonial affairs with EGW in Canada and from his continuing role as his father's secretary. What better to round out a young life's training than a year on the ocean main and savage frontier, before his Pattle inheritance at 21 prompted more sober career considerations? EGW would have fondly remembered his own adventures in Europe at the same age and risen to young Teddy's romantic enthusiasm for the voyage. And he could feel comforted that his only child would be under William's direct protection. EGW sent him on his way with the Wakefield literary inheritance, for he exhorted Jerningham to write down his experiences and impressions, as well as assisting in the copying of the expedition's reports. In all this, at least, he could prove himself useful to the company's publicity.

By 25 April, the *Tory*'s outfitting was still not complete and Lieutenant Robson had withdrawn or been deemed unsuitable as captain. Three other candidates were declined and the situation was now considered serious enough to despatch a company member to Devonport on the 26th 'to invite Mr Chaffers to come to London with a view to the command of the vessel'.[22] Also, EGW had yet to complete the company's prospectus and to bring negotiations for a merger with the old 1825 New Zealand Company to a successful conclusion.

Regardless, the directors decided to go ahead with a grand public breakfast for 130 ladies and gentlemen on Saturday the 27th at Lovegrove's West India Dock Tavern, Blackwall, to launch the company and the expedition. The official party was headed by Lord Durham and his son, Lord and Lady Petre and various other worthies who inspected the flag-bedecked *Tory*, which had been towed into the canal by the tavern. They pronounced themselves well satisfied with the expedition preparations before retiring to Lovegrove's tables, heaped with food costing the very considerable sum of £32 10s and liquor worth £51 11s 6d, sufficient to toast the enterprise.[23]

As the *Colonial Gazette* reported, Chairman William Hutt opened the speechifying with the misleading assertion that 'The New Zealand Company had received the assurance of Her Majesty's Government that a bill should be introduced into Parliament immediately, and should be passed as soon as possible (hear, hear), for the purpose of the better regulation of these islands; and this company, following the intention of the Government with no unequal steps, had fitted out an expedition, destined, it was hoped, to lay the foundation of an important colony' in a place which had 'hitherto been abandoned by this country'. Appealing to patriotism and altruism, he asserted that the British settlement of New Zealand would enhance the 'glory of Her Majesty's reign (hear, hear)' and 'redeem from savage life . . . the most oppressed of the aboriginal inhabitants of the globe (cheers)'.[24]

Hutt complimented Lord Durham on knowing only too well 'the true meaning of the good old English cry of "Ships, colonies, and commerce" ' and Durham replied that he supported the enterprise only because it was under 'the new mode of colonization' whereby both colony and mother country mutually benefited. He described the Wakefield system without mentioning EGW, who was either unobtrusive in the general audience or absent. It remained politic to keep him away from the top table.

Lord Petre lent some jollity to the increasingly alcoholic occasion by asserting that, 'He was . . . much interested in the colony for many reasons, the first of which was, that he had a large family which must be provided for (laugh); and notwithstanding the apprehensions that he had seen expressed, that all those proceeding with this expedition were to be eaten up by the natives, one of his sons (who was present), who, however, did not possess more than the ordinary share of patriotism, and, consequently, no more than the ordinary desire to suffer demolition in so unpleasant a manner, was resolved to try his luck, and to proceed to the colony (hear, hear, and laughter).'

William stood up to give thanks for a toast of good wishes and modestly 'expressed his sincere hope that the trust which had been reposed in him would meet with a successful issue'. In conclusion, Nahiti was presented and Hutt 'proposed the health of the chieftain'. Nahiti expressed 'his acknowledgments for the honour which had been done him in a style scarcely intelligible to our ears, but which appeared to be perfectly well understood by those accustomed to hear his conversation'. Amid the costly bunting and bumpers of self-congratulation and facetious insouciance, a whole new world was launched.

On 29 April, Hutt and other New Zealand Company members called on Lord Normanby and, later that day, formally advised him in writing that the *Tory* would sail on 1 May, requesting letters of introduction to the governors of New South

Wales and Tasmania. James Stephen's jaw must have dropped when he read that the company's long advertised intention to send an expedition had become more than bluff. On the back of Hutt's letter, Stephen wrote notes for the 1 May reply, which was sent under the hand of Henry Labouchere, Normanby's Under-Secretary for the Colonies: 'Answer that until the Deputation from this Body waited upon Lord Normanby yesterday his Lordship was entirely ignorant of their intentions and of the objects for which they had associated themselves as a Company.'[25]

Now EGW's jaw must have dropped at Stephen's flagrant chicanery in denying the meetings and correspondence the company had had with Normanby since his appointment more than two months before. But this was the overture to a boycott of the company as the government moved to cover its dragging tracks of the previous two years and to speed up its own plans in response to the company's actions. The letter also advised Hutt that the government knew nothing of the company's plans to set up a colony with an 'independent' government and warned that title to any land bought from the Maori was unlikely to be recognised and would be most likely subject to repurchase by the Crown. Hutt corrected Labouchere with the news that the expedition was purely a commercial enterprise. The records show that Hutt engaged in this momentous correspondence but, in fact, EGW wrote the letters under Hutt's cover.[26] Behind their front men, Labouchere and Hutt, Stephen and EGW politicked, manipulated and lobbed formal missiles at each other.

At the beginning of May, neither the Colonial Office nor the cabinet had the time, energy or ability to take much action about the *Tory* expedition. Melbourne's administration, always shaky, was on the verge of collapse over constitutional issues in Jamaica. In the so-called Bedchamber Crisis, Melbourne resigned but was pushed back into office by an adoring young queen who could not face having her Whig ladies-in-waiting replaced by Tories simply because the country must have a change of government. At the Colonial Office, Stephen and his colleagues were also hunched under a cascade of pressing problems from all around the world. By the autumn he was to write, 'I have been living for the last six months in a tornado.' April to September had become 'the hurricane season in these Downing Street latitudes'.[27]

The *Tory* did not sail on 1 May but a captain finally logged in. Master Edward Main Chaffers had been brought up from Devonport and was introduced to the directors on 29 April. The minutes of 1 May record that, though he had not yet been given leave of absence from the Admiralty, he had accepted command. Chaffers later said that he had given up his naval career at 24 hours' notice. In fact he was ashore on half-pay and, under the naval promotional conditions of the time, faced a residual career on the beach: he would have been more than willing, at a moment's notice, to grasp the opportunity of the *Tory*.

Whatever the circumstances, 32-year-old Chaffers's appointment was an inspired move. He was a seasoned ocean voyager, having been master of the

Beagle under Captain Robert FitzRoy during her famous Darwinian voyage round the world. FitzRoy who, as a member of the New Zealand Association, may even have recommended Chaffers, had put him in command of the tender *Adventure* off the Falklands and South America in 1833, and he had visited the Bay of Islands in 1835. Soon after his return, Chaffers had been awarded a Trinity House certificate qualifying him as master for Her Majesty's Ships of the fifth and sixth rates. The *Tory* was in doubly good hands, for Chaffers had the benefit of mate Richard Lowry's several years of service in the ship. George Robinson had been appointed ship's surgeon and that beautiful essayist, Reverend Montague Hawtrey, its chaplain. But Hawtrey was 'prevented at the last moment by unavoidable circumstances from joining the ship'.[28]

The last moment was the towing of the *Tory* from the City Canal on Saturday 4 May. As the *Colonial Gazette* appeared on the streets with the story of the Blackwall banquet a week before, another celebratory meal was ordered for Sunday. Exclusive to ship's officers and friends, this farewell dinner at Gravesend's Falcon Inn was attended by EGW, Somes, Evans, Molesworth and a 'party of ladies'. This observation from William in his diary marked both the last he would see of English women for almost a year, and the start of a journal and correspondence that now appears all the more copious for the paucity of the written record of his first 38 years.

The cost of £9 11s 10d for 24 dinners plus liquor plus breakages was mere ash on the cigar or another bubble in the champagne of the entire cost of the expedition which was no doubt one of the chief dinner topics of conversation between Somes and EGW. In the report presented to the directors on the next 26 June, expenditure would be detailed as follows: purchase of the *Tory*, equipment for the voyage, advances to officers and crew, insurance and so on £11,093 2s 4d; cost of barter goods, £5,040 2s 10d; cash to William Wakefield for land purchase in addition to barter goods, £1,000; cash to Mr McDonnell for land already 'purchased' in the north of New Zealand;[29] outfits to confidential agent (William), naturalist, draughtsman, maps and instruments £896 14s 5d; advertisements, rents and office expenses, £1,172 0s 7d. The total was £20,202 0s 7d, something like $NZ4 million in today's terms.

Such hefty expenditure demanded a good return and William, through the dinner haze of good wishes and god speed, would have been very aware of the phrase in his instructions 'that the profits of the Company must, in great measure, depend on the judgment which you may exercise'. Despite his chief motives of glory and influence, EGW was not uninterested in the commercial success of the expedition. This manager who knew 'nothing about companies and shares' had a shareholding in the company and would purchase land sections in the new colony. If the enterprise was successful, William, too, would benefit, and Jerningham perhaps. Although it was premature to forecast it confidently on 5 May, there might be a place in the colony for Dan and for Felix, and there was always Arthur. Even more than for Lord Petre, colonisation for the Wakefields was indubitably becoming a family affair.

The pressing hands of farewell between EGW, William and Jerningham on the quayside near the Falcon Inn, as dusk clouded the river, were strong with both affection and apprehension. Jerningham was due to come back in a year or so but EGW could not have been free of fear of what might befall him. He covered it by presenting him with a box of the finest cigars and by repeating his exhortation to write it all down. Somes or Molesworth or Evans nearby might have joked that the Wakefields were pretty good at that sort of thing, in all kinds of ways, and Teddy must be sure to keep up the tradition. Between EGW and William there was a particular poignancy: once again they were involved in a plan together, but neither knew when or if they might sit together again to review and face the consequences.

They waved and waved, as the warps were taken on board and the steam tug *Nelson* eased the *Tory* away from the quay. Three cheers carried over the darkening water and the barque's eight guns were fired in a salute as the waving hats of the expedition supporters disappeared into the gloom. In the night, the *Tory* moved slowly down river and anchored in the estuary. The steam tug 'flitted round us like a firefly till break of day when we weighed but a thick fog and foul wind coming on, we brought up off Margate on the tail of the Goodwin Sands'.[30] By the early morning of 8 May, the *Tory* had made the approaches to Plymouth and anchored in Cawsand Bay, after carrying away a schooner's bowsprit while rounding the breakwater. Late in the day, she arrived in Plymouth Sound in a 'howling gale'.

William recorded that the ship lay in the sound on 9 May, 'getting hands and finishing equipment'. The ultimate complement was 35. The last of the expedition officers to arrive was draughtsman Charles Heaphy, who joined from London on that day. Heaphy was about the same age as Jerningham and his mother, too, had died from the complications of his birth in 1820. Heaphy's father was a well-known watercolourist who had been the first president of the Society of British Artists. Thomas Heaphy's offspring inherited his talent and Charles's first showing was at the British Institute in 1835, the year that his father died. The fifteen-year-old then 'determined to do for himself'.[31] His character and abilities attracted the attention of a London publisher who sponsored him to a school of arts and the Royal Academy, and he also worked for the London and Birmingham Railway. His patron procured him the post of draughtsman to the New Zealand Company expedition when the directors belatedly realised that they needed someone to depict settlement sites and other natural features for Company records and publicity. Heaphy was appointed on 6 May, after the *Tory* left London.[32] He hastened down to Plymouth bearing another, unappreciated, skill that would contribute to the entertainment and well-being of the *Tory*'s crew: he could recite much of Scott's and Byron's poetry from memory.

The hiatus between the *Tory*'s departure from London on the night of 5 May and her departure from Plymouth in the early hours of 12 May provided the scope for myth and drama. Wakefield family tradition has it that 'rumours reached Wakefield [EGW] in London that the Government, angry and possibly amazed also at the discovery that the ship really had started, now meant to stop her at Plymouth. No time was to be lost, and Wakefield immediately hired a post chaise, and, accompanied by his secretary, Charles Allom, set out at furious speed for Plymouth to urge the vessel off without a moment's delay.' It was a 'wild night-drive' but 'Wakefield's energy and resolution achieved their object, the *Tory* sailed without hindrance . . . and thus the first battle for New Zealand was won!'[33] EGW's biographer Richard Garnett, writing with the spectacle of Victoria's Diamond Jubilee in his thoughts, concluded that 'Wakefield's vigorous action was the fitting crown of a series of vigorous actions which won for our Queen as bright a jewel as any of her diadem'.[34]

An overnight coach drive from London to Plymouth (250 miles) was physically impossible but the swift arrival of Chaffers in London from Devonport, and Heaphy's joining at Plymouth within three days of his appointment in London, show that there was ample time for EGW to reach the *Tory* between 6 May and 10 May, when she was originally scheduled to leave England. The question remains whether there was any valid political reason for him to do so. The suggestion that the government ordered a frigate to pursue the *Tory* has no documented foundation,[35] and there is no record of EGW's journey in either William's diary or Jerningham's book. But the convincing assurances of Charles Allom's brother and Jerningham's widow seem compelling,[36] and both William and Jerningham may have deemed it politic not to commit anything to paper. But what could have so disturbed EGW? The government was in such disarray that it was incapable of any action. On 11 May, William noted in his diary, 'The Ministry yet doubtful. We leave England ignorant of who is Prime Minister.'

Any conclusion must be conjecture; but the linking of the frigate *Druid* to the myth of pursuit offers a clue.[37] This was the ship in which Hobson sailed to New South Wales later in the year, on his way to New Zealand. By now, EGW probably had a paid informant inside the Colonial Office. It is possible that he had been given more details of the office's plans for Hobson, after the *Tory* sailed from London, which suggested that his departure was imminent, and EGW raced down to Plymouth to advise William of this, urging him to make all speed.

Whether or not EGW brought the 'final instructions' from London that are said to have reached William on the 8th,[38] he had to wait until the following day for Heaphy, throughout the 10th while the ship rode out a 'violent gale' and for final victualling and crewing to be completed on the 11th. At last, on Sunday 12 May, the *Tory* 'got under weigh 1/2 past 3 a.m. and beat down to the Lizard'.[39] Before the day was done, England was left behind on the heels of a fresh Channel wind. From the outset the *Tory* proved a swift ocean hound and Chaffers showed a good scent for a racing breeze. The hills of Cornwall were soon swallowed by the spring sea haze; for some of them it was the very last sense of home.

PART THREE

War to the Knife

1839–1848

CHAPTER SIXTEEN

'They would extort the masts out of the ship'

FRIDAY, 16 AUGUST 1839: 'I saw LAND on the Southern Island, Tavai Poenamoo, at 12 o'clock, noon, being the 96th day from Plymouth . . . Cook dwells on not having seen land during a voyage towards the South Pole, a voyage of 1098 miles. We have run over 14680 since [sighting land at] Palma, and 16,000 from England.'[1] It was a non-stop, record-breaking run. The *Tory* had fulfilled its greyhound reputation, giving William the extra edge of time he needed to follow out the Company's instructions. Just a week later, Captain Hobson left England on HMS *Druid*, Colonial Office documents in hand, to begin the process of annexing New Zealand to the British Crown.

If William was glad at sighting New Zealand so soon, he was dismayed at viewing it from closer quarters the next day. 'The first appearance of the Southern Island is unpromising – a succession of apparently barren mountains stretching away from the coast 'till they reach those covered with Snow in the interior. . . .' Cook Strait was 'extremely open and easy of access. Entry Island [Kapiti] and the highlands of Terrawhitte [Terawhiti], with a volcanic mountain [Ruapehu], emitting clouds of smoke, are plainly distinguished from Stephens Island but Mount Egmont has not been seen by us. . . .'[2] As Tasman had discovered, it was a 'Land, Uplifted high'. On nearing the coast, William saw that the barren mountains were covered by 'perpetual verdure' but there was little prospect of the hundreds of thousands of gently rolling acres needed for the new colony's farms and towns. But he had neither the time nor the freedom to consider any other region. The company's instructions were that he must purchase land beside Cook Strait's best harbour. He must make the best of what he found.

To pick up fresh water, wood and victuals for the first time since leaving England, Chaffers took the *Tory* into James Cook's favourite anchorage at Ship Cove, within the outer arms of Queen Charlotte Sound. Edward Jerningham waxed lyrical: 'How well Cook has described the harmony of the birds at this very spot! Every bough seemed to throng with feathered musicians. . . . Landing here, I remained for some time absorbed in contemplating the luxurious vegetation of grass and shrubs, and the wild carrots and turnips which remain as relics of our great navigator.'[3] The bird life, too, came in for comment: 'We fell in with plenty of pigeons, parrots, and other birds, which our guns soon made to contribute to the table and to the collection of the delighted naturalist.'[4] Dieffenbach and artist Heaphy took to the hills and islands about the cove, relishing the chance to be among the first to explore and record the exotic flora and fauna for the purposes of British science and commerce. 'Nothing,' Jerningham concluded, 'can be imagined more magnificent than the scenery, or, however, less suitable for cultivation.'[5]

The Maori who lived in the sound greeted the *Tory* as a new source of trade. Accustomed to dealing with whalers who had married among them, and who were entrenched in their evil-smelling hunting and trying bases along the shores of nearby Cloudy Bay, they had boarded the ship as she ghosted in on the evening of 17 August. Fish and potatoes were exchanged for tobacco, the first trickle of the momentous treating and dealing that would change New Zealand forever over the next six months.

William quickly formed an opinion of the Maori from the first visitors to the ship:

> They are a fine race of men, infinitely superior in appearance to those of the northern part of the other Island;[6] very intelligent and capable of being extremely useful to settlers, as labourers, fishermen and sailors. They behave with strict decency and propriety, but are half naked from want of clothes for which they evince a decided preference to powder or ornaments. They have been much spoiled by their intercourse with the numerous Whale ships in the ports in the straight and seemed surprized at my declining the offer of the sojourn of one of their daughters on board during my stay amongst them. With the acquisition of these bad habits they have not lost those of the savage and of the savage of New Zealand in particular. They are suspicious and susceptible to the greatest degree, grasping and importunate, cunning, treacherous and revengeful.[7]

But he was sanguine that the 'rising generation' showed a strong desire for learning and a settled life under the influence of Christianity.

William had come to this view with the help of Nahiti who, at first, seemed the ideal interlocutor between Englishman and Maori. Nahiti was apologetic for the squalid and poor appearance of his kinfolk who appeared, to William, to treat him like a chief. 'He interpreted faithfully their words and intentions and repeatedly cautioned me against either their attempts to steal from the ship or to cheat us in our own dealings. He has greatly gained also in our estimation by juxta-position with his countrymen, amongst whom he assumes the bearing of a smart intelligent Englishman so much so that in talking of him they commonly call him the white man.'[8] The nascent ethnologist, Ernst Dieffenbach, viewed the situation through a different lens: 'Nayti, who was dressed in the best Bond-street style, cut a pitiful figure; civilization had taught him nothing but to be ashamed of his relations.'[9]

In a letter to his parents, dated 10 October 1839, Dieffenbach wrote, 'I feel very much at ease and happier than ever among the wild cannibals; they are a magnificent race, people of a gentle and fine character.'[10] This humanistic view, though written before he and the *Tory*'s supercargo had encountered Te Rauparaha and the mayhem of war on the Kapiti coast, contrasted markedly with William Wakefield's mixture of pragmatic respect and condescension towards the Maori. As the bearer of good Christian-capitalist tidings for a savage race, William was denied the flexibility of thought that might have allowed him to better understand the concepts of kin and land ownership governing Maori behaviour and belief. Dieffenbach quickly understood and accepted the cultural differences, but he was an exception – and a romantic German. No one else aboard would have seriously doubted William's philosophical position, or had the temerity to argue with the company's colonel if they had.[11] As the *Tory* expedition and the tribes about Cook Strait came together, the collision was between trans-ocean barque and coastal waka. In the end, there could be only one conclusion.

The first collision came early. A minor chief, christened 'Dogskin' by the Wakefields for the cloak he wore, demanded utu for the breaking of tapu. A daughter of Hiko, Te Rauparaha's cousin, had been buried at Ship Cove which the *Tory*'s crew had been using for watering, fuelling and recreation. William thought he could settle the utu with tobacco but 'Dogskin' demanded more and carried away the *Tory*'s seine net. Captain Chaffers took an armed boat ashore to demand its return but, outnumbered, returned to the *Tory*, which he prepared for action: 'The guns were shotted, the crew armed, sentries placed at the gangways, and a spring put on the cable so that the ship's broadside might be brought to bear on the beach where the natives were encamped.'[12] A waka came off the beach with warriors armed with tomahawks and mere, but when 'Dogskin' attempted to make the gangway he was met with musket and bayonet. William, pistol in pocket, sent him off, declaring that no armed native would be allowed aboard.

Jerningham considered that the Maori were 'rather puzzled' at this display of force and that it 'excited general respect'. The Maori response was to send a small canoe bearing an old unarmed chief, Te Whetu. William reported, 'He dined with us and after various attempts at extortion of blankets etc. and threats to reporting our breaking the taboo to Raupero and Hiko, he took advantage of a calm night to pursue his voyage across the straight. It is impossible to describe the annoying and irritating manner of these people. They take possession of the deck or cabin, if allowed and would extort the masts out of the ship if any yielding is shown.'[13]

A few days later, visiting white whalers confirmed for William that the Maori demand for utu had been a 'mere extortion', and that they 'were always ready to take advantage of inexperienced visitors in this way'.[14] They were as amused at

William's armed over-reaction as the Maori had been puzzled. Clearly he did not yet understand the rules of dealing and co-existence in this place.

Few Maori had any inkling of what organised settlement would mean and remained secure in their racial hegemony over the land that some called Aotea-roa. Struggles for control over the country's various desirable territories were principally intertribal and not international for, until the arrival of Cook, New Zealand had been the Maori world. The manifest armed strength of the *Tory* expedition, and the attendant resources that it could call upon, would be seen by some Maori as a defensive aid; by others as a milch cow to give them the material upper hand over their enemies and rivals. White men, after all, were only missionaries or traders. Yet the evangelising of Pakeha missionaries had done much to draw the sting of intertribal belligerence, after traders' muskets had exhausted it in unequalled periods of slaughter. The traders' new goods and crops had also begun to affect life and society. 'Instead of an active, warlike race,' Dieffenbach wrote, 'they have become eaters of potatoes, neglecting their industrious pursuits in consequence of the facility of procuring food and blankets, and they pass their lives in eating, smoking and sleeping.'[15]

William, helped by his Spanish experience, was quick to understand tribal rivalries. And before he had been in New Zealand a fortnight, he had some grasp of the land situation about Cook Strait: 'The laws of property . . . are very undefined in this part . . . . neither Raupero nor Hiko possess the power of absolute disposal of any portion of land in the straight – nor can it be acquired by combining the consent of many claimants, or part proprietors as in the northern part of the northern island.'[16] He considered large parts of the region could be easily settled by colonists because of the internecine wars and the desire of Maori to see Europeans among them (though not so many as William had in mind).

The fluid tribal circumstances in the Cook Strait area might work to William's initial advantage but their consequent complexities would plague him forever. He appears to have understood the primitive laws of blood bond that governed kinship behaviour among Maori whanau and hapu; these were, after all, the basic laws underpinning any society. The simple law of ownership through armed conquest and subsequent occupation was also intensely familiar. But William does not seem to have fully understood the implications of tribal land ownership. He could not conceive that a chief had no more power over the disposal of land than one of his subjects. 'No Chief, however high his rank, could dispose of a single acre without the concurrence of his tribe. Without such a law, no tribe could be sure of its integrity, and any number of wedges might be driven into its territory.'[17]

William's journals confirm his fixed belief that he need deal only with chiefs both to secure land and to enable them to lead their people safely into civilisation:

> Explain to the Chiefs the nature and dangers of their situation, the safety of Union [with the Company and missionaries] – the value of knowledge, the importance of the

> rights which they must jealously maintain for themselves against Europeans, & which they must grant to their inferiors. The insecurity of all the uncivilized Aborigines of European colonies essentially depends on their weakness arising from comparative ignorance. This ignorance keeps them without privileges & prevents their deriving any advantage from such rights as their existence as human beings and the good feelings of Individuals of Government may really place within their reach.[18]

He pondered ways of educating the Maori out of their ignorance, enabling them to fit into the new society.

William and the *Tory* expedition spent five weeks on the southern side of Cook Strait, exploring the outer reaches of Queen Charlotte Sound, Pelorus Sound into its headwaters and the Port Underwood-Tory Channel region. The barque was the first full-rigged ship to complete the navigation of the channel and, for part of the time, the *Tory* was anchored off the large Te Awaiti whaling station just inside its eastern entrance. While the *Tory* explorers repeatedly exclaimed at the beauties of their environment and its natural curiosities, and deep-water anchorages were abundant, it was all straight-up-and-down country with no room for more than a minor settlement. From the heights above Port Underwood, Dieffenbach described the sweep of Cloudy Bay and the forested plains of the Wairau Valley, surely just the site for the new colony. But, though he described an overland way from Port Underwood, the proximity of a good harbour to the Wairau Plains was a problem.

Before William could examine the Wairau, the old enemy of the company put in an appearance. News came from over the Strait of missionaries warning Maori not to sell land and that the Reverend Henry Williams of the Church Missionary Society was due in the region soon. William decided to quickly secure title to the great harbour of Te Whanganui a Tara, or Port Nicholson, before this considerable adversary complicated his plans.[19] On 20 September, the *Tory* left Te Awaiti and arrived in Port Nicholson the same day.

William took with him whaler Dicky Barrett as an interpreter. 'Dressed in a white jacket, blue dungaree trousers, and round straw hat, he seemed perfectly round all over; while his jovial, ruddy face, twinkling eyes, and good-humoured smile, could not fail to excite pleasure in all beholders.'[20] Barrett had been in New Zealand for eleven years and was married to the daughter of a Te Ati Awa chief. Edward Jerningham wrote, 'Dicky Barrett promised to be most advantageous to us, as he was related by his wife to all the influential chiefs living at Port Nicholson.'[21] He was also willing to second 'with all his ability' the expedition's aims. 'He was thoroughly acquainted with the feelings and customs of the natives, as well as their language.'

In taking on Barrett as an interpreter, William confirmed that he had begun to lose faith in Nahiti, accusing him of overstating his position among the Cook Strait tribes: it had become clear that his 'brothers' were really 'cousins' and that he had no chiefly status. William may have demonstrated ignorance of complex whanau and hapu kinships, but Nahiti was now in the worst of all possible worlds. He had become a kind of chief from his pumped-up status in London, fulfilling EGW's purposes, accumulating artifacts of civilisation that were, at first, the envy of his Cook Strait relatives. 'The great respect paid in London to his supposed rank of "Chief" or "Prince", had at length induced him to acquiesce in the exaggeration, and . . . we were only undeceived in this respect on our arrival in New Zealand. His fellow-countrymen of all ranks had so ridiculed this somewhat innocent assumption on his part, that he was too glad to bribe their good-will by means of his valuable property.'[22] One Ngati Toa chief had scorned Nahiti as not an ariki but an ariki nono, a chief's arse. Falling into the chasm between cultures, Nahiti was losing face and mana, and soon was no longer trusted by either side as a reliable go-between.

But if Nahiti had no status, did Dicky Barrett really have the language? Or did he speak the kind of pidgin Maori that caused the whalers to corrupt the name Te Awaiti to Tarwhite? And how far did he understand the company's intentions if he 'did not see the whole bearing on our theory of the system of native reserves'?[23] But maybe the interpretative assistance of Barrett's wife and children and entourage would help as they formed a 'sort of colony' in the *Tory*'s ample 'tween-decks when they crossed the strait. And young Jerningham had no doubt about the expedition's noble intentions. In conferring on the Maori 'the great boon of civilisation', 'I felt happy in supposing, that the humblest share in the execution of so great an enterprise might be envied by the most ambitious of men.'[24]

When the *Tory* sailed into Port Nicholson, local Maori saw the arrival of this 'great boon' in quite other terms. They had heard that these particular white men intended to settle among them but anticipated they would do so in a way that brought the material benefits of the distant white culture without diminishing their own mana and dominance. Iron pots, steel tools, blankets and guns were marvellous, empowering things. Maori had already been seduced by earlier traders who brought them the power to shop; the *Tory* expedition promised bigger and better shops in controlled numbers. Just as important was the notion that white men, or Pakeha, would bring peace and security; both through the influence of the Christian ethic of brotherly love and the practical defence of superior weapons. If the Wakefields acted in the conceit of a civilising mission, the Maori acted in the conceit that they could control Pakeha action and settlement – whether via the brotherly spirit envisaged by the old Te Ati Awa chief Matangi who 'almost cried with joy when he spoke of the white people coming to protect the Port Nicholson people from their enemies'[25] or via the threats of Ngati Toa chief Te Rauparaha.

As the *Tory* sailed into Port Nicholson, she was boarded by two chiefs, Te Puni and Te Wharepouri. During the course of their overnight stay on board, William learned that Te Ati Awa bounds of mana in the district had been valid for only a few years since the original inhabitants had 'ceded' this territory to them before moving to the Chatham Islands in 1835. Across the western hills, on the Kapiti coast, other relatively recent arrivals in the Cook Strait region – the Ngati Toa and Ngati Raukawa – disputed territory there and laid claim to the Port Nicholson environs. Other displaced people, such as the Ngati Ira and Taranaki, nurtured claims.[26] According to William, the two chiefs 'betrayed the most lively satisfaction' at his proposal to buy the place. Coming to some kind of treaty with a powerful Pakeha would entrench their mana.

They told him that a schooner had just brought two native missionaries to the harbour who were instructed to build a chapel and houses in preparation for Henry Williams's arrival. But for Te Wharepouri, Te Puni's young nephew, Christianity's 'incessant worship had nearly driven him mad. . . . "What we want", they said, "is to live in peace and to have white people come amongst us. We are growing old," alluding to the numerous aged chiefs on shore, "and want our children to have protectors in Europeans, but we don't wish for the missionaries from the North. They are natives [Pakeha Maori]. We have been long told of vessels coming from Europe. One has at length arrived and we will sell our land and harbour and live with the white people when they come to us.'[27]

This was William's self-serving interpretation of the chiefs' dialogue and the next day their readiness to 'sell' seemed supported by their eagerness to show him around: 'They did not want to talk any more about disposing of it 'till I had seen it'. William was taken up the Heretaunga River, which drained the heavily forested valley at the head of the harbour, and was impressed by its rich soil and 'majestic timber'. On his way back, local Maori 'enquired of my guide, as the canoe glided by down the current, whether the ship contained missionaries. "No,' said he, "they are all devils". Their shouts of laughter betrayed their acquaintance with his allusion and their opinion of the charitable tenet, which had given rise to it.'[28]

These devils disguised in humour negotiated with the Maori to purchase the Port Nicholson district over five days from 23 September. Most of the chiefs seemed enthusiastic but Puakawa, who had visited Sydney and observed the nature of British settlement there, injected a dose of reality into the discussions. He 'objected to the sale of the place on the score of the treatment to be expected by the natives from white settlers and the inexpediency of parting with the homes which they had obtained, after so much suffering, when driven from their native territory. . . . His diction and gesticulation were most vigorous and the most ignorant of the language in which he spoke and the most inexperienced in physiognomy, could not fail of taking the sense of his oration from his expression and action.'[29] Elsewhere in his journal, William denigrated Puakawa as 'the principal CMS missionary' but Puakawa was not to be put off by William's attempt to isolate him. Three days later he exclaimed, '"What then will you say . . . when you find that you have parted with all the land between Rimarassi [Rimutaka] and Turakirai [Turakirae Head] and from the sea to the Tararua! What will you say when many many white men come here and drive you all away into the mountains? How will you like it when you go to the white man's ship or house in expectation of hospitality and he tells you that you have been paid for the land and to be gone, with eyes turned up to Heaven & invocations on his knees to his God?'[30]

The fact that William reported this in his journal, for public consumption, means he saw it as evidence that some Maori understood what selling land meant and that there had been fierce debate over the pros and cons. And the fact that Puakawa finally made his mark on the deed of settlement indicated even dissenters had been persuaded.

> I favored these discussions from feeling assured that the more the affair was debated the more binding would be the bargain, should I succeed in concluding it and in themselves they had nothing disagreeable, for in all seriousness I can assert that I never saw a deliberative assembly conduct its business in a more regular or decorous manner and that the solemnity of the appeals of the speakers and the encouraging applause or earnest dissent of the audience were becoming the importance of the transaction they were engaged in. At the close of the arguments, which ended in a decision in favor of the sale, most of the meeting went away in canoes to the chief village, where another debate was to take place. Indeed in every settlement this floating parliament assembled upon the occasion and formally proceeded to take the sense of its inhabitants.[31]

This was a nice summary of some kind of democratic process but how clear had the company's intentions been made? How well was the deed of purchase, drawn up by Jerningham and dated 27 September, explained to the Maori? And how many had really agreed to sell? Young Teddy's legalese ran to about 1500 words: 'Know all men by these presents, that we, the undersigned chiefs of the harbour and district of Wanga Nui Atera, commonly called Port Nicholson, in Cook's Straits in New Zealand, do say and declare that we are the sole and only proprietors, or owners of the lands, tenements, woods, bays, harbours, rivers, streams and creeks within certain boundaries etc. etc. . . .', which were defined as all the land and water encompassed by the ranges of the Rimutaka to the east, the foot of the Tararua to the north, the 'Rimarap' to the west and Cook Strait in the south. For the goods listed in the deed, the chiefs agreed that they had 'sold and parted with all our right, title and interest' in all the described territory 'unto William Wakefield Esq., in trust for the governors, directors and shareholders of the New Zealand Land Company. . . .' At the end of the deed, it was stated 'that a portion of the land ceded . . . equal to one-tenth part of the whole' would be reserved and held in trust 'for the future benefit of the said chiefs, their families and heirs for ever'.[32]

In a later inquiry into the purchases, Dicky Barrett admitted that 'instead of telling the natives, as the deed set forth, that one-tenth of the surveyed lots should be reserved for their use, he had simply put it that one lot of the alienated land should be kept for the Maoris, and one for the Pakehas, and so on through the whole – that is, that half the land should be kept for their use'.[33] Barrett's interrogator, more than three years later, exposed both the whaler's inadequate grasp of the deed's legalese and his limited fluency in the Maori language. Earlier, Jerningham had already noted Barrett's failure to understand the concept of the tenths. Ill-educated, deferential to the colonel but skilled at safely picking his way through the vagaries of Maori society, Dicky Barrett (Tiki Parete) knew how to tell each party what they wanted to know – just as William Wakefield heard what he wanted to believe.

During the same inquiry, chiefs who had either signed the deed or taken part in the purchase negotiations said they had understood that the blankets, muskets, tobacco, tomahawks, trousers and so on were for the right to use different parts of the harbour – presents in exchange for signatures being collected for Queen Victoria – while the Taranaki people at Te Aro, Pipitea and Kumutoto simply wanted a share and denied giving up land at all. Apparently only Te Puni understood that William wanted land and then only half of it.[34] Clearly, there was confusion among the Maori caused by Barrett's garbled interpreting, but also by their own rivalries and fears, and the constructions they put upon the likely effects and benefits of white settlement. How much of the Maori's confusion should be ascribed to the three usual suspects in post-colonial arraignments? To William's averred cupidity, Jerningham's eccentric sense of mission and Dicky Barrett's ignorance?

To determine that sixteen chiefs of Te Whanganui a Tara were duped, bribed or cajoled into signing the deed of settlement implies, at best, that they were naive and trusting and, at worst, stupid. Too much weight has been placed on the inadequacy of Barrett's interpreting. There were other people aboard the *Tory* capable of interpreting. William recorded that 'Nayti, who had returned yesterday evening from a visit to his relatives, was a subscribing witness and occasionally explained the nature of the deed, as related to the reserve of land'.[35] The often detailed account of Maori statements in William's journal confirms that dialogue consisted of more than pidgin, grunts and sign language.

William's chief motivation was to get a deal done as quickly as possible, before the missionaries or the British government interfered with the company's plans. He was unconcerned whether the Maori understood the legal niceties of selling land to Europeans and knew the hopelessness of trying to explain the workings of a joint stock company with ballots for land sections. He needed a signed document as evidence of land ownership, concrete evidence from a people he felt he could not trust: 'We have had so many instances of misrepresentation and exaggeration, which upon examining, did not appear to be wilful perversions of truth, but the effects of a habit of boasting and colouring, that we now never believe anything coming from these people without due caution and allowance.'[36] As far as William was concerned, whatever the Maori thought was happening, the outcome could only be good for them. And, with their interests at heart, had he not made sure that the tenths were firmly fixed in the deed?

What the Maori thought was happening is best summarised by Ernst Dieffenbach, who was witness to the land purchases in the Cook Strait region, travelled throughout the North Island until October 1841 and wrote the following words in London at the middle of 1842: 'In transferring land to the Europeans the natives had no further idea of the nature of the transaction than that they gave the purchaser permission to make use of a certain district. They wanted Europeans amongst them; and it was beyond their comprehension that one man should buy for another, who lived 15,000 miles off, a million of acres, and that this latter should never come to the country, or bestow upon the sellers those benefits which they justly expected.'[37] Just so. But there was some hindsight in this – as well as Dieffenbach's animosity to the company – and in September 1839 William had to get on. As far as he was concerned, it would all work out in the end.

The deed was marked and signed, the presents of trading goods divided fairly among the inhabitants of the six Maori pa scattered around Port Nicholson and on the morning of 30 September, Jerningham

> observed the natives gathering from all parts of the harbour. Canoes and parties on foot, glittering with their lately acquired red blankets and muskets, were all closing in upon the place of rendezvous; fresh smokes rose every moment on shore as a new oven was prepared for the feast . . . In the afternoon, on a signal from the shore, we landed in our boats with all the cabin party, and all the sailors that could be spared, to take part in the rejoicings. We were joyfully received by the assemblage . . . of about three hundred men, women, and children . . . . it was a high holiday with everybody.[38]

Flags were raised on shore and on the *Tory* to an exciting 21-gun salute from the barque's eight cannon. The Maori responded with peruperu or 'war dance' and haka and when joints of pig were distributed from the opened umu, 'We drank the healths of the chiefs and people of Port Nicholson in bumpers of champagne, and, christening the flagstaff, took formal possession of the harbour and district for the New Zealand Land Company, amidst the hearty cheers of the mixed spectators.'[39]

During the previous week, William had taken possession much more conclusively, claiming title in a symbolic way that made the land British in imagination. He renamed all the main features of the harbour. The Heretaunga River became the Hutt; Matiu Island became Somes. Now there were Lambton Harbour, Thorndon Flat, Baring Head, Sinclair Head, Barrett's Reef, Pencarrow, even Point Jerningham. 'The names of other places were selected from among those most likely to be respected and honoured by the future inhabitants as memorials of the disinterested founders of the colony.'[40] This obliterating of Maori names, this possessive naming, could be described as a terrible arrogance but it was the natural and unconscious act of people confident in their own superiority; the behaviour of conquerors of any kind, military or monetary, Pakeha or Maori. Boards bearing the words 'New Zealand Land Company' were put up in prominent places around the harbour.

The Maori had done a little naming of their own. Just as the whalers could not get their tongues around Te Awaiti, so Maori found the names of the company men difficult to pronounce. The nearest they could get to Edward Wakefield was Era Weke, 'and some wag immediately suggested "*Tiraweke*", the name of a small bird which is very common in the woods, and known for its chattering propensities'.[41] They also condensed William Wakefield to 'Wide-awake', 'after some chief who had been so called by the flax-traders in former times'.[42] In two quick nicknames, the Maori had caught precisely the characters of uncle and nephew.

The *Tory* recrossed the strait to Port Underwood and Te Awaiti where whaler John Guard and local Maori told William that his deals with Port Nicholson chiefs were worthless unless they were 'ratified' by Ngati Toa chief Te Rauparaha at Kapiti Island: 'Raupero' had the real power in the region, by kin and by conquest. William had known from Nahiti, even before he left England, of Te Rauparaha's reputation and his journal shows that he had a detailed understanding of the chief's character, movements and attitudes. It is possible that he had deliberately left an encounter with Te Rauparaha until last, after he had met and dealt with other chiefs, allowing the expedition's strength and reputation to grow through rumour. Firing 21-gun salutes in Port Nicholson had been more than a jolly good show.

As he set out across the strait again, William knew what he had to do: 'In resolving to visit and conciliate the old savage, however strong my repugnance to his character and practises, I am more led by the hope of acquiring his land on which to locate a society which shall put an end to his reign, than by any good wishes to him, and to obtain influence with his presumptive successor, Hiko, who bears a much better character.'[43]

When the *Tory* anchored in the uneasy roadstead between Kapiti Island and Waikanae on 16 October, the expedition came upon the gore and debris of a recent battle in which Ngati Raukawa had attacked Te Ati Awa, encouraged (at least) by Te Rauparaha in retaliation for Te Ati Awa's deal with William. When he was able to get ashore, Dieffenbach the doctor found that sixteen of the Waikanae people had been killed and many badly wounded. 'I was almost the whole day occupied with the latter, who submitted with great fortitude to the operations which I found necessary. Only one man, whose leg was smashed to pieces, preferred death to amputation.'[44]

Te Rauparaha would not visit the *Tory*, fearing that Maori hostile to him would be hidden aboard. William, Jerningham and Dieffenbach were obliged to visit him on tiny Evans Island, off Kapiti, and Jerningham, William and Ernst

Dieffenbach, respectively, remarked on his being 'uneasy and insecure', betraying 'a feeling of insecurity' and, at the least, being 'very restless'. Te Rauparaha denied any involvement in the bloody fracas on shore, but was clearly fearful of retribution through the agency of the white strangers.

Te Rauparaha recognised power when he saw it. His entire career as a fighting chief, from Kawhia down to Banks Peninsula, had depended not just on martial prowess and tactics but on a fine understanding of the uses of intermarriage, utu, treachery, massacre and cannibalism.[45] He was given his first musket around 1812, when he was in his mid-forties, and it was the power of this new weapon that enabled him to move his Ngati Toa tribespeople on a southern migration from the Kawhia region during the early 1820s. His sway over the Cook Strait region since that time had continued to depend greatly on control of the trade in muskets and powder. Here before him was a ship stuffed with weapons and armed with eight loud cannon and a group of Pakeha who wanted to deal for land. Te Rauparaha's 'uneasiness' lay not only in whether these Pakeha could be brought on side but also in how he could control the distribution of their weapons. On being confronted with blankets and soap, he was to say, 'Of what use . . . are such things when we are going to war? What does it matter to us whether we die clean or dirty, cold or warm, hungry or full? We must have two barrelled guns, plenty of muskets. . . .'[46]

Land arrangements with Pakeha had been reached before – for whaling settlements or farming on Mana Island, for example – and Te Rauparaha was aware of missionary activity up north. But no one had come before to deal on the scale proposed by the Wakefields. Te Rauparaha had been to Sydney in 1830 and had some idea of what extensive Pakeha settlement meant. He may not have been averse to the idea of considerable white settlement in the Cook Strait region but he would have certainly intended it on his own terms and, like almost every other Maori, would have seen a land 'sale' as more of a 'lease', with regular tributes of European goods and the owner's right of eviction. His proud nephew, Te Rangihaeata, had for years regarded the white users of coastal settlements in this light; they could only ever have the shadow of the land, never its substance.[47]

Vastly experienced in the ways of war and of negotiating with potential enemies, Te Rauparaha employed a mixture of bluff, threat and bounce in trying to get what he wanted from William Wakefield. But in the slightly built Englishman he had met, perhaps for the first time, a Pakeha who showed no nerves in the face of Maori belligerence: 'If I did not commiserate the mental condition of a wild race just commencing an interchange with civilized people and were not aware of the cruel delusions and dishonest practises of most of the foreigners they have seen, towards them, I should have been angry at their violent and perverse conduct; but I should have been ill fulfilling the task assigned me, if I had shown any want of command of temper or even of countenance. . . .'[48] With his smoking cheroot, William was insouciance incarnate, morally secure in the sense of the worldwide Pax Britannica that Arthur's Captain Beaver had so clearly enunciated a generation before. In physical stature the two men were similar, a change for William after dealing with Maori taller and more robust than almost everyone on the *Tory*. 'His years sit lightly upon him,' he wrote of Te Rauparaha. 'He is hale and stout and his hair is but slightly touched with gray.' Jerningham considered him to be at least 60 but he was much closer to 70.

As negotiations developed, Te Rauparaha and other chiefs came aboard the *Tory* on several occasions. The first time they 'drank ardent spirits freely, repudiating the use of water, and refusing with great contempt anything less than a full tumbler. . . . *Rauperaha* sat for his portrait to Mr Heaphy, and made a noisy demand for a waistcoat in payment as soon as the sitting was over. Indeed, he asked shamelessly for everything which he saw, and he seemed well used to being refused.'[49]

The tussle between Te Rauparaha and William Wakefield was the epitome of the struggle between importunate Pakeha and importunate Maori. William intended to possess himself of the soil. Standing on the dignity of a mana much greater than his own, he was supremely confident of his ability to press the Maori into a bargain, luring them with musket and bauble until he had their signs on the parchment deed. Te Rauparaha knew that William was no agent of government and he also had experience of sharp trading deals. Through his own successful use of deception and fraudulent promise, he recognised another smart operator when he saw one. If William wanted signs on parchment to signify temporary use of Ngati Toa controlled lands, then let him have them, but only after Te Rauparaha had squeezed as many goods out of the *Tory* as he could. The chief probably suspected there was more weight to the deal, but there was nothing strategic in his thinking – and this was where the two men diverged.

Although poor interpreting can again be blamed, this time in the mouth of sawyer Johnny Brooks,[50] Te Rauparaha and his followers would never have grasped, even with the very best of interpretation, the fatal import of the *Tory*'s arrival. At a tense moment of the bargaining, 'They even proceeded to make their customary grimaces at me and the wild fellow jumped about the deck as if to commence the exciting dance previous to an attack. "We will sell our lands to the French and Americans. . . . We do not want your payment; presently there will be plenty of ships here from Port Jackson and to them will give all we possess. We will go to fight at Port Nicholson and kill all your people there."'[51] They could little conceive that part of William's plan had always been to beat the French and Americans and that the peculiar cloth on which they scratched their signs had more power than all the muskets on the ship.

On 21 October, William drew up a plan of both islands in which the chiefs owned 'land by right of conquest or inheritance' and this was 'diligently examined' by men who might not have seen a map or chart before. 'It was repeatedly told them, to their perfect comprehension, that no future sale of these rights or land was to be made by them and that no further payment was to be expected.'[52] They approved of the tenths reservations for chiefs and their families. Jerningham wrote that everything was 'repeated to them over and over again' until 'they showed themselves perfectly acquainted with the bargain . . . and ended by agreeing fully to every provision'. Te Rauparaha 'dictated . . . the native names of all the places on both coasts to which they had any claim, whether by conquest or inheritance' and Jerningham transcribed every name, correctly or distortedly, into the deed.[53] Te Rauparaha would later maintain that his reciting of territories under his control had nothing to do with selling and only with the establishment of mana.

On 23 October, Hiko, Te Rauparaha, Rangaihiro and 'all the chiefs of the Kafia tribes' except Te Rangihaeata came aboard the *Tory* and the full 'cession' to the company was made. Hiko asked for another bale of clothes to be added to the agreed list of exchange goods.

> He had also accepted the Blankets, soap and dresses for the women and had put down the clamor for arms made by all the rest. Nothing remained to be done but to distribute the fowling pieces, of which there were only a dozen, amongst the leaders and for them to sign the deed of conveyance. The guns were brought up and placed on the head of the companion ladder, upon which Raupero, Tunia, usually called the 'Wild fellow' and other fighting Chiefs made a rush at them and each attempted to possess himself of a double-barrelled piece. Hiko, who was busy in arraying himself in a comfortable coat at the time, no sooner saw that the Kafia people were likely to carry off the most valued property by their old habits of violence then calling Rangaihiro and his boat's crew, he threw off his partly-acquired clothes and left the ship in high displeasure at Raupero and his followers. The Negociation was thus abruptly terminated.[54]

William sent all the goods below, provoking the remaining chiefs' wrath, first against each other and then against William. 'To these taunts and threats I returned either laughter or indifference, which together with an occasional declaration that whether we dealt or not they must conduct themselves quietly or leave the ship, soon brought them to a calmer state. . . . In a short time we were as good friends as ever and renewed our conversation . . . as if the treaty were in full progress.'[55]

Although there is never a mention of it, it is likely that the ship's company were discreetly armed, or had ready access to arms, to be used if arguments came to blows. When 'Dogskin' had threatened them in Ship Cove two months before, William had assured the crew that they would be armed if the ship was under threat. But he had 'warned them that, altho' we should always be prepared to resist attacks, the best means to avoid the necessity of using our weapons, was the exercise of the utmost good temper and patience in our intercourse with the natives'.[56]

Not only were the *Tory* and its 'thirty-five souls' potentially at risk from attack but Captain Edward Chaffers and first mate Richard Lowry had their hands and minds full in navigating and safeguarding the ship through the treacherous and unpredictable winds, currents and rocky waters of one of the most dangerous sailing zones in the world. By the time the dispute on 23 October was settled, 'The wind again rising to a gale, it was found adviseable to again shift our anchorage to the shelter of the two small islands. By this time, most of the natives had gone on shore; but Raupero and Tunia remained with a vague hope of obtaining the two guns they had chosen for themselves. Instead of getting immediately to our new birth [*sic*], near the islands, it was necessary to tack several times and at one time we were three miles off Kapiti. The sea ran high and the gale, meeting the flood-tide, caused a ripple in which a small vessel would not live.'[57]

In this heavy tide rip, the *Tory* was hit by some severe squalls and when 'during one of these, the vessel careened over, and the spanker-boom flew in half, *Rauperaha* was in a most abject state of fear; asking me whether we should not turn right over'.[58] As William recorded, 'At this moment poor Mr. Raupero, the King of New Zealand, as he calls himself, was in a piteous fright, declaring that the vessel would capsize and, as Nayti assured me, muttering prayers most earnestly. Some jokes, also, as to taking him and the wild fellow to Port Nicholson, gave him an ill-disguised uneasiness.'[59]

By 25 October the deed was done. In reporting to the company his purchase of land between the latitudes of 39 and 43 degrees south on the western coasts and between 41 and 43 on the east, William wrote, 'you will readily conceive that I have not obtained a title to all the land included within those parallels. It is necessary, in order to properly appreciate the extent and value of the purchase, to know the different possessors and claimants.'[60] He also reported on Maori rumours about the purchase: 'Some said that they had sold land which did not belong to them, alluding to the districts occupied by the Ngatiawas, which I have yet to purchase of that tribe; whilst others betrayed a notion that the sale would not affect their interests, from an insufficiency of emigrants arriving to occupy so vast a space, to prevent them retaining possession of any parts they chose or of even reselling them at the expiration of a reasonable period.'[61]

The Maori appreciation of the 'vast' unsettled spaces in their country underwrote the Wakefield concept of 'waste lands' lying ready for a new productive society that would enrich all. But Maori could not imagine the extent of forthcoming British settlement, the side stream from the flood of British emigration that was annually exceeding the entire population of New Zealand. Or did they simply not believe what William told them? When the first New Zealand Company settlers arrived in Port Nicholson the following year, Te Wharepouri lamented to William, 'I know that we sold you the land, and that no more White people have come to take it than you told me. But I thought you were telling lies, and that you had not so many followers.'[62] Before the 'fatal impact' or 'fatal success' of British settlement there was the Maori's fatal underestimation. Did their own habit of 'boasting and colouring' lead them to consider William's assertions about the size of the forthcoming settlement puffery and Puakawa's warnings the exaggerations of oratory?

Tension and distrust between Te Ati Awa, Ngati Raukawa and Ngati Toa were still intense. William, before sailing back to Queen Charlotte Sound to complete the third and final round of his land purchases, brokered a meeting between Te Ati Awa chiefs and both Te Rauparaha and Te Rangihaeata on board the *Tory*.

> When these came on deck and saw the three Ngatiawa Chiefs sitting down with their faces half hidden in their mats they betrayed great surprise and made their customary warlike grimaces. Then from, I conclude, remembering that the ship was no place to show any hostile demonstrations, they advanced to them and rubbed noses with them in succession . . . Many speeches on both sides succeeded – all in the spirit of peace . . . On the whole, the meeting had the effect intended; many disputes amongst the natives originating in misrepresentations of third parties and ceasing so soon as they have spoken of their grievances face to face, and but for my knowledge of Raupero's duplicity, I should think that he would use his influence to put a stop to further hostilities.[63]

Nothing that had occurred over the previous weeks had changed William's opinion of Te Rauparaha: 'Making every allowance for his condition, and knowing how his intercourse with the refuse of European society has affected him, it is impossible for the most charitable to have any feelings towards this old fellow but those of aversion. It will be a most fortunate thing for any settlement formed hereabouts when he dies, for with his life only will end his mischievous scheming and insatiable cupidity.'[64]

Te Rangihaeata was equally firm in his suspicions of William's motives and in his opposition to land sales or extensive white settlement, but the day after the conciliation meeting he signed the land purchase document simply to procure his share of the trade goods, and while signalling his contempt for the deed's validity.

That same day, Nahiti told William that he wanted to go ashore and stay with his relatives in the Mana-Porirua area until the first settlers arrived. William considered that he had 'little to oppose to his request. Of late he has been worse than useless as an interpreter, having led me into error several times, but I requested him to stay on board as a friend of the party with whom he had made the voyage from England and represented to him the unhappiness he would undergo when stripped of his clothes by his friends and deprived of the comforts to which he had been of late accustomed.'[65] But he would not be diverted and 'got into a canoe full of his friends . . . with all his boxes and goods'.[66]

Four or five months later, when Jerningham returned to Porirua, he discovered Nahiti among the crowd that greeted him. 'He was much ashamed of the wretched state in which I found him. He was wrapped in a blanket and mat, and as dirty as any of his fellow-countrymen around. He tried to excuse himself for not wearing English clothes, by stating that he had been too ill; but a White man at Parramatta had assured me only an hour before that Nayti had given away everything he possessed.'[67] According to Jerningham, Te Rauparaha and Te Rangihaeata had 'bounced' him out of his best possessions and 'the inferior neighbours had not been slow to follow the example, as soon as the great vultures had been satisfied'.[68] Jerningham exhorted Nahiti to find service again as an interpreter with his uncle, but he was a 'sad result of all the pains that had been taken to civilize and educate him', preferring to remain with his own people. Two years later he died of consumption like his friend Jackey, his life and death a paradigm of the fate awaiting many of his race.

Near Te Awaiti in early November, William treated with local Maori to purchase most of the remaining parcels of land about Cook Strait as other buyers began turning up from Sydney. 'Every day brings fresh proof of the speed of our outward journey having frustrated the intentions formed by the New Holland speculators on receiving the news of our departure and destination, as regards this part of the islands.'[69]

The third purchase was problematical. No leading chiefs were present, 'no one of paramount influence . . . to give the people confidence and ensure satisfaction' and to ensure control of the proceedings. More than 200 people came on board the *Tory* to conclude the deal and to take their share of payment. Since they could not look forward to early and extensive white settlement, they 'turned all their attention to obtaining the greatest amount of payment possible'. The division of goods turned into a mob scramble. 'About one hundred and fifty natives were piled above the various heaps of goods, writhing, struggling, stamping, pulling each other's hair and limbs, tearing blankets, shivering whole cases of pipes and looking-glasses, and withal yelling and screaming in the most deafening manner.'[70] Afterwards, shame-faced, the participants confessed to the 'porangi' or madness of their behaviour and assured the Wakefields it had been no fault of theirs. William dryly commented, 'If anyone should wish to take a lesson of patience and controul of temper, let him have a few dealings with a numerous collective New Zealand tribe, and he will find himself proof against any annoying occurrences which he may meet with in the transaction of business in civilized communities.'[71]

Despite this drama, William considered he had done well, gaining possession of most of the Cook Strait lands within three months of arriving. He never lost sight of the warrior instincts of the Maori and an analysis of the goods he rendered in payment shows that he had been able to manipulate the balance of firepower in the region. He had been pushed into giving Te Rauparaha and other Kapiti chiefs some guns and fowling pieces but he gave them only 20 muskets compared with the 120 he had handed over in Port Nicholson and the 60 at Te Awaiti. When he recrossed the strait to Waikanae on 10 November there were more prospects of war. Wharepouri would not talk with William about the future settlement because he was sure he would be killed in a forthcoming fight. William considered that 'nothing short of a great slaughter will satisfy them'. 'For some years it will be necessary, for any settlers in Cooks straights, to be in numbers sufficient to protect themselves, and to form a militia to avoid the outrages to which the caprice or anger of a few Chiefs might subject them.'[72]

When, on 13 November, Wharepouri confronted Te Rauparaha off Kapiti Island, with a superior canoe force, the 'Old Sarpint' protested that he was tired of wars, would go off to live in the Wairau Valley across the strait, out of their way and give Kapiti to Wharepouri as a present. William recorded sardonically, 'Considering how many times he has sold all his interests in the island, the gift cannot be considered worth much.'[73]

Te Rauparaha had the last say. The *Tory* lay becalmed off Otaki on 18 November as the expedition waited for a fair wind to take them north and more land purchases in Wanganui and Taranaki. He came aboard, demanded grog and told William that, because he needed more guns, he would sell some of his land to the men on a vessel that had just arrived from Sydney. After all, he had only sold Taitapu and Rangitoto (Nelson area and D'Urville Island) to the company. 'Colonel Wakefield reproached him instantly, and in the strongest terms, with his falsehood and duplicity; making Brooks, the interpreter, repeat to him several times that he had behaved as a liar and a slave, instead of a great chief.'[74]

Te Rauparaha had judged the situation well. William could do nothing but fulminate and there would be time later to test the validity of the deal. The old chief was shrewd enough to understand that, with the arrival of the company and the deepening influence of Christianity on Maori culture and beliefs, the old world had begun to slip away. If this one Pakeha, Wideawake, carried so many guns and muskets on one ship, how many ships did all the Pakeha have and how many guns and muskets and cannon did they carry? Te Rauparaha could not grasp the entire nature of the technology and power that lay somewhere over the horizon, but he had begun to understand the scale. And he would not hide his eyes against it as Nahiti had done when he first arrived in London. For the short term the Pakeha invasion could be managed with the old ways of cunning and manipulation; the rest of the future was not his to see or understand.

At last a southerly wind came up on the evening of 18 November and took the *Tory* north, out of the Cook Strait region for the first time. The expedition was now two or three weeks behind schedule and William had other land business to complete before the first of the company ships arrived off D'Urville Island in less than two months. He assumed that the first emigrant ships were halfway round the world, though he knew neither how many there were nor how many settlers they carried; he could only guess what the company, EGW and the British government had been up to, but would have assumed that Captain Hobson had set out. The need for urgency remained.

At that moment Hobson, on HMS *Druid*, was still a month away from Sydney and the company's first ship, the *Cuba*, with surveyors on board, was more than a month from New Zealand, despite having left England at the beginning of August. A fleet of six ships carrying nearly 900 settlers had also been at sea for two months. With no communication, the effective and safe conjunction of all these vessels depended on fate and the kind of faith that had prompted the first issue of the company's *New Zealand Gazette* to confidently and correctly aver on 21 August, 'There can be little doubt that the *Tory* has arrived in Cook's Straits by this date'.

Taking just four months to organise the company, sell land, prepare ships, find emigrants and acquire all the appurtenances for setting up shop, home and farm on the opposite side of the world can be viewed either as some kind of lunatic speculation – the New Zealand Bubble – or as an amazing leap of faith. The *Colonial Gazette* of 18 September 1839 asserted, 'None but Englishmen would have ventured on such an enterprise, and Englishmen only had the habits which could insure its success.' Only a churl would have disagreed.

Yet some of the company's directors, when first meeting with the emigrants' Committee for the First Colony of New Zealand, had perceived the danger of haste and recommended a 'great delay' in sending out the first colony. But Dr Samuel Evans, EGW's first disciple, who had moved from secretary of the company to first emigrant as First Colony chairman, represented them all when he told the directors that the committee had 'fully considered all points and was quite determined' to leave for New Zealand before the summer was out. There was some method in the madness. Evans knew that the emigrants needed to arrive in New Zealand well before the end of the southern summer. To delay departure past September would mean delay for another year and then the government would beat them to it. Evans, like many others, had sold up and was risking everything on the venture. There could be no turning back.

There was no stopping EGW either. He was in his element as he concocted the grand design, sold it and left the consequences, often dire, to someone else. 'I have not time to attend to details,' he told his father a couple of years later, 'being only a generalizer or theorizer, and leaving all *the filling-up* of an extensive project to others.' He was engaged night and day in 'the management of people . . . the persuading of all sorts of dispositions to pull together for a common object'.[75] A new phrase that was beginning to enter the English language might have been inspired by the entire New Zealand enterprise under EGW's methods. 'Muddling through' would come to be used with a tone of bemused pride to describe one of those English habits that, in the end, would 'insure success'.

The months of May to September were filled with directors' meetings for finance, shipping and emigration. Agents on 5 per cent promoted land sales across the country and there were willing buyers as the company profited from publishing the success of the South Australia scheme before its shortcomings had become widely known. Advertisements that appealed to those who wished to 'improve their ways and means at a railway pace' in the 'Land of Promise' seemed at odds with EGW's constantly preached ideal of close settlements composed of all the best elements of society. The free emigrants were being carefully selected and vetted but there were no checks on the character of capitalists nor any requirement that landowners should actually go to New Zealand. This was one of those tiresome details that EGW left to someone else. It did not seem to bother him that absentee landowners would mean empty properties all over a settlement and land values distorted by uneven development; that landowners' absence from a colony would create an imbalance between owners and labourers, leading to unemployment of the latter and a distortion of his ideal society.

While capitalists speculated, most of the thousands who sought free passage demonstrated the kind of serious intent that would allow the settlements to muddle through. Benjamin Ironsides, a workhouse bookkeeper from Sheffield, was plain when he made his application:

> Sir, I feel anxious to emigrate to New Zealand in the capacity of agricultural labourer. I was born in 1807 & have this day buried my wife. (I have no incumbrance). I should hope however that this may not be an obstacle to my going out as an emigrant, the fact is there is so large a redundancy of population here, wages generally speaking are so low, that I do unhesitatingly declare that I shall feel thankful to be accepted . . . . Dangers and fatigues I fear not, I rather court them, I am in fact quite tired of working continually for one sum & never perceiving any future chance of bettering my condition.[76]

EGW was everywhere, giving advice to directors and to First Colony meetings, and talking and writing, writing – endless letters, pamphlets and articles. A report in the *Spectator* for 3 August described the high excitement and good cheer attending the drawing of the ballots for the town and country sections. Many ladies were present, 'perhaps the most daring speculators' as they clutched their land orders and waited for their numbers to come up. There were cheers when a 'Natives' tenths number turned out to be a lucky draw, a free opportunity for Maori to benefit from the investors' goodwill. Te Wharepouri, Pouakawa and the rest at Port Nicholson never learned the numbers of their tickets in this London lottery, a game of chance for civilisation.

By the end of August, the cabins and steerage accommodation of the five emigrant ships – the *Adelaide*, *Aurora*, *Bengal Merchant*, *Duke of Roxburgh* and *Oriental* – had been filled and a sixth ship, the *Glenbervie*, chartered to take the emigrants' excess baggage and freight. The official farewell dinner was held on 9 September, marked by the same kind of propaganda puffery that had attended the departure of the *Tory*, but this time with EGW to the fore, proposing a bumper toast to that persistent slogan of Free Trade: 'Ships, Colonies, and Commerce'.

The vessels sailed a week later. As the Colonial Office persisted in its refusal to recognise the company and its enterprise, and aware that the new colony would be beyond the protection of British law, the company prepared its own constitutional code of law and appointed a governing council of fourteen for the colony, with William as its president. The council included Lord Petre's son, Henry; Francis Molesworth, Sir William's younger brother; and Dr Evans, who was appointed resident magistrate at £300 per annum and 'Umpire' of the council. Just before the ships sailed, the laws and list of council members were presented to all male emigrants and they endorsed them with 'enthusiasm and cheers'.

When EGW farewelled the *Adelaide* on 18 September, he fulfilled yet another family duty. He had determined that the best future interests of Liocadia di Oliveira (Mary D'Oliverra), now aged nineteen, lay in New Zealand and he had secured her a cabin passage under the chaperonage of Dr Evans and his family. In the new colony she would be subject to the family's continued protection until her inevitable marriage: she was after all a 'very beautiful and very sweet-natured woman . . . [if] . . . curiously impractical'[77] and had strong Wakefield credentials.

The care of the Evans family proved a signally mixed blessing for Liocadia. All the emigrant ships proved to be hotbeds of dispute either between cabin (poop) passengers and steerage or within each group. But wrangles among the *Adelaide*'s cabin passengers were so bad that they caused a two-day delay at Tenerife in the Canary Islands. The quarrels worsened to the extent that the ship was forced to put in to Cape Town to enable four duels to be fought, one involving the captain, another Dr Evans. 'Umpire' Evans avoided a fight at the last minute by having his opponent bound over by the local authorities.

Another cabin passenger, Sam Revans, was outraged by Dr Evans's 'high-handed' and 'dictatorial' behaviour on the *Adelaide*. 'I thought and have thought how different Wakefield's [EGW's] conduct would have been.'[78] A 31-year-old newspaper man, whose first edition of the *New Zealand Gazette* had so optimistically forecast the arrival of the *Tory*, Revans had bought equipment with a loan from company investors in order to set up the first printery in Port Nicholson, and to continue the *Gazette*. From the *Adelaide*, Revans began writing to his close friend Henry Chapman, with whom he had briefly run the *Daily Advertiser* in Montreal, and who had criticised EGW while an agent for the French Canadians. But both were now Wakefield acolytes and 36-year-old Chapman, who would be admitted to the Bar in 1840, was about to begin editing the *New Zealand Journal*, the company information and propaganda sheet. Revans told Chapman that the Evans family was 'detested'. 'Their conduct to Mr W's little charge, Miss Olivier, amounts to cruelty – but for the power of passing her time in Mrs Smith's cabin – her life would have been truly wretched – Miss Riddiford acts towards the poor little thing in a way she dare not act towards a servant. If Col. Wakefield is lost and Dr Evans takes his place which he has the power to do – the Colony will be in a state of uproar.'[79]

Class ruled, and it seems that the Evanses continued to behave badly towards their charge after arrival in New Zealand. The events and circumstances are now unlikely to be unearthed, but Revans wrote again to Chapman about Liocadia in October 1840: 'Miss Olivvia did write the letter in question, but it was suppressed and the conduct of the Evans' in suppressing that letter and making the girl write one of a different character convinces me that baseness must be added to their list of bad qualities.'[80] EGW would have been outraged to learn of how the Evans family had treated his ward, the last companion of his beloved Nina, and they knew it.

Fortunately, Liocadia had a genuine protector in John Taine, a 22-year-old merchant she had met at one of the emigrants' socials in London before sailing. They were married in Port Nicholson in June 1840, the second couple to be wed there, and in New Zealand, after it became a Crown colony. William acted as best man and Evans, keeping up appearances, gave away a bride eager to leave. The cruel Miss Riddiford deigned to be a bridesmaid.

In November, EGW wrote to Liocadia from London: 'I am truly pleased to hear of your marriage. Colonel Wakefield speaks very well of your husband.' EGW sent boots, shoes and soap and 'I beg you to accept a cradle which I hope may turn out to be a most appropriate present, both in its nature and the time of its arrival'.[81] The cradle arrived in time for the birth of the first of Liocadia's thirteen children, in May 1841.

In coasting north to Taranaki, the *Tory* battled nor'west gales for a week and did not reach its uneasy anchorage off the Sugarloaf Islands until 27 November. William could not wait the week that Dicky Barrett estimated was needed for all the local chiefs to be assembled for a Taranaki land purchase. So he put 'Barrett and his train' ashore to prepare for the purchase. This included whaler 'Worser' Heberley and Negro cook 'Black Lee', both of whom would accompany Ernst Dieffenbach, 'the naturalist [who] also remains on shore here with the view of ascending Mount Egmont'. William considered it a rare opportunity for a 'man of science' to have 'time to examine the most important district as regards geology and mineralogy in these islands'.[82] It is curious that William determined that Taranaki was the 'most important district' scientifically. Perhaps it was the awesome effect of the mountain, that 'most beautiful object from the sea'. Dieffenbach, the most athletic of New Zealand's early European explorers, reached the top of Egmont with Heberley on Christmas Day, discovered many species of flora and fauna new to science, and oil seepages that seemed of only limited use to the prospective colony.

On 2 December, the *Tory* made the entrance to Hokianga Harbour, an established port of call in the kauri trade. The ship was piloted upstream to where sawyers were preparing timber for loading on two barques bound for Sydney. The expedition stayed in the harbour for two weeks while William tried to validate land purchases inherited from the 1825 New Zealand Company and in the deeds of Lieutenant Thomas McDonnell, sometime Additional British Agent in the Hokianga, who had sold his holdings to the company. William's proceedings with Ngapuhi chiefs, some of whom he called over from the Bay of Islands, were as ambiguous as all the land dealings so far but Taonui agreed to go with the Wakefields to Kaipara to show them land also promised for sale to McDonnell. William also purchased from the widow of a Captain Blenkinsopp 'some deeds professing to be the original conveyances of the plains of Wairau by Rauperaha, Rangihaeata, and others to that gentleman in a consideration of a ship-gun. They were signed with elaborate drawings of the *moko* or *tatu* on the chiefs' faces.'[83] Mrs Blenkinsopp was coy about telling William that her late husband had spiked the gun before handing it over. Te Rauparaha had not been amused.

The Wakefields also visited local missionaries, enjoying mutual approbation with Wesleyan Reverend John Bumby. William found him much superior to his disgraced predecessor, William White, who had fallen out with EGW over the special meeting of the New Zealand Association in December 1837. White was now back in the district dealing in land and timber, seeking influence among Maori by wearing the clergyman's habit to which he was no longer entitled.

William also visited the flamboyant self-styled sovereign chief of New Zealand, Baron Charles Philippe Hippolyte de Thierry, godson of unlucky Charles X of France, who was currently engaged in a violent dispute with a young Maori chief over ownership of kauri logs. William felt obliged to send an armed boat up to Thierry's residence to maintain the peace until the dispute was settled. William described Thierry's family as 'exceedingly interesting and well-bred, but suffering from distress and constant alarm'.[84]

Sending a gunboat upriver to solve the Thierry conflict was a positive change for William after months of endless, often inconclusive, negotiations with Maori. On 22 November, he had admitted in his report to the company that he was reluctant to pass on conclusions about Maori customs because he had trouble sorting out the varying and conflicting information he had been given by different hapu. Action was a relief, something he had been schooled in and hardened to during his long years in Spain. Better a charge before citadel walls than constant haggling over blankets and irresolvable arguments over land. If William's best qualities lay in action, he now had a month-long opportunity to display them as the *Tory* left Hokianga to examine McDonnell's 'right of pre-emption' in Kaipara Harbour to the south.

William and Jerningham blamed McDonnell's 'totally erroneous' chart, but on the morning of 19 December the *Tory* went aground on a sand bank a mile or two inside the entrance to the harbour. Jerningham's account still makes exciting reading: 'The usual measures to get the ship off were taken, but in vain. Captain Chaffers and the well-disciplined crew exerted themselves most creditably. Five of our guns, three or four anchors and cables, a deck-load of spare spars . . . and several other heavy articles, were thrown overboard. Kedges were carried out and hauled upon, but with no effect. Some heavy mill-stones and paving-flags were got up out of the hold and rolled overboard. One of them was carelessly sent through our best whale-boat, which lay at the gangway.'[85]

The expedition was on the brink of disaster as the tide began to run out 'like a sluice'. The consequences of losing the ship, or any of its officers, with emigrant ships due in just three weeks' time focused William's mind. Leaving Chaffers and the seamen to do their best to steady and secure the *Tory*, William mustered a volunteer crew to take the second whaleboat in search of help from the barque *Navarino*, said to be loading spars somewhere up the Kaipara. Charles Heaphy, Drs Dorset and Robinson, two Maori and Jerningham plied the oars while William steered. They completely underestimated the power of the ebb and the whaleboat was swept out towards the breakers at the harbour entrance, 'so far to seaward of the ship, that we were invisible to those on board . . . Just as we had given ourselves up for lost, a faint breath of air was felt from seaward; one of the natives' blankets was extended between two stretchers in the bow; and this, with the unremitting efforts of the rowers, kept us in about the same position for two or three hours, till the flood-tide made.'[86]

Even then, they were set to the north among breakers and only the skill of 'Saturday', one of the Maori, at the steering oar saw them through safely. After an excruciating day of danger and hard labour, they came within sight of the *Navarino*, only to be forced ashore by the ebb-tide to spend a night being eaten alive by mosquitoes.

The next day, after they reached the *Navarino*, the captain sent his mate and a crew to assist the *Tory* which had 'forged over the bank into deep water, after being exposed for some hours to heavy seas which broke over her'. The *Navarino*'s mate was able to pilot the *Tory* up the harbour; but the 'vessel was so much injured as to require heaving down . . . . It was plain that she would not be again fit for service for a month or two.'

The *Tory*'s crew began the long and tedious task of unloading all the cargo and ballast so that the ship could be hauled ashore for repair. While this was begun in the entrance to the Wairoa River, William talked again about land with local Maori. They 'laughed at Taonui and the claim of the Ngapuhi chiefs to sell their land for them'.[87] They refused to sell the land allegedly promised to McDonnell by Ngapuhi but offered a different block on another river flowing into the Kaipara.

Just at this time, on 23 December, the *Cuba*, with the company's surveyors led by Captain William Mein Smith, made its New Zealand landfall at the Kaipara mouth. Mein Smith made a quick survey of the harbour from a small boat, somehow missed sighting either the *Tory* or the *Navarino*, returned to the *Cuba* and ordered it to sail on to Cook Strait. On Christmas Day, William decided he could delay no longer his journey south for the D'Urville Island rendezvous.

Leaving Dorset to examine the land offered, and Chaffers to oversee work on the *Tory*, he set off up the Wairoa in one of the ship's boats, bound for the Bay of Islands in order to find a ship that would take him to Cook Strait!

Told the overland journey would take just a day's work in the boat and then a day's walk, William did not reach Kororareka until 29 December after a four-day trek through country infested with mosquitoes. The infamous Bay of Islands anchorage harboured 20 large whaling or trading ships, mostly French and American. Wasting no time, William met up with the skipper of the *Guide*, 'a lazy, indolent old man, fond of grog, and of sleep', and made a deal to charter the brig by the month from 1 January. Mustering a crew was difficult. 'But one method presented itself. A visit to one of the grog shops brought about me plenty of Candidates, who intended to take the advance the Master of the Brig offered and then to ship away from her on the first opportunity. This was prevented by getting them on board hoisting up the boats and, keeping watch that no one swam from the ship as she lay at Paroa Bay, which is six miles from Kororarika, our crew soon sobered down. I forbad all spirits to be put on board even for the Cabin and soon found the usual change that takes place from such a step under similar circumstances.' William concluded with his usual dryness: 'The only feeling that seemed to pervade the ship was that of astonishment that everybody on board was sober.'[88]

Another problem revealed itself after the *Guide* set sail on 3 January and went north about North West Cape, Cape Maria van Diemen and down the west coast of the North Island. There was a problem with the compass and the skipper was 'very good fun with his rough navigation. He had a rickety parallel ruler, a very doubtful quadrant, and a rusty pair of compasses, by means of which he used to make a determined guess at the position of the ship . . . . he would draw a cross of large size on the map, and declare that to be our actual position.'[89] A week later, on the rendezvous day of 10 January, William found himself not in Port Hardy but in Blind Bay (Tasman Bay) to the west of D'Urville Island. The brig beat back and, a day late, William arrived in Port Hardy to find no ships. 'I ascended the highest hill at the head of the port and made a large fire. No answer was returned.'[90]

On the 14th, William sent the brig back to the Kaipara with instructions for Dorset to put goods on the *Guide*, return to Taranaki to complete the land purchases, pick up Barrett and Dieffenbach and make for Port Nicholson. The *Guide* had barely left Port Hardy when William received news from local whalers that the *Cuba* had arrived and gone to Port Nicholson. On the morning of the 15th William resumed his journey in a whaleboat and reached the whaling station at Te Awaiti at midnight. A foul wind held him up for day before he was able to cross the strait. On 18 January he finally met up with the *Cuba* in Port Nicholson, to find that Mein Smith had been there a fortnight and was laying out a town called Britannia on the 'Eritonga' (Heretaunga) flats, behind the Pitoni (Petone) Beach. It was the last frustrating word in a chapter of missed meetings.

CHAPTER SEVENTEEN

'I am half a missionary myself'

WILLIAM INFORMED CAPTAIN WILLIAM MEIN SMITH, Surveyor-General of the company, that he had named the 'Eritonga' valley Hutt and that it was the wrong place to lay out the new settlement's town. Lambton Harbour provided the most sheltered roadstead for ships, which could anchor close to the shore, and there was enough flat or undulating land about Pipitea and Te Aro for the company's town sections; the Hutt could be used for the country settlements. Smith firmly produced his instructions from London which included a plan for the splendid town of Britannia, with 1100 acre sections laid out in a strict geometry. His assistants and labourers had already marked out the first boulevards behind the Petone foreshore. William tried to exert his authority as principal agent but Smith told him that the siting of the town was within his own professional prerogative.

Smith was reputedly a man of strong and religious principle, better suited to the role of teacher or parson than soldier or frontier surveyor, but highly skilled and backed by the credentials of the Royal Military Academy. They confronted each other on Petone Beach in a clash of class and rank. Smith knew of William's Wakefield history and would have held his mercenary colonelcy in some disdain. William saw Smith as an office soldier and, having been in charge of the entire New Zealand expedition for almost a year, would have resented this newcomer's presumption, and his ignorance of people, place and circumstances. But William could bring no moral authority to bear as Smith refused to budge. William turned on his heel, harbouring a resentment that would cause him to harry and vilify Smith at every opportunity.

Leaving Smith to cut survey lines through the swamps and dunes, William turned to korero with the Maori and discovered that, since he was last in Port Nicholson in October, CMS missionary Henry Williams had visited and, as he wrote on 24 January for the benefit of company secretary Ward,

> repeatedly told the chiefs here that the white settlers . . . would drive all the natives into the hills; that they ought to have sold their land at a guinea per foot and advised them to insist upon money being paid them on my return. Knowing, as he did, the solemn cession of this territory to the Company and the large payment made for it; aware also of the reserves made for the native families and other beneficial arrangements for them as well as of the native proneness to suspicion and resistance; he could have been actuated in his doings here; indeed in his visit to the place; only by jealousy and a wish to create mischief and ensure the settlers a bad reception.[1]

It has been said that William was 'not quite sane on the subject of the Church Mission'.[2] Perhaps understandably so. He would have learnt every detail of the unrelenting missionary opposition to EGW's plans throughout the 1830s and the vituperative personal attacks that this had generated. Sensitive to the social marginalisation the Wakefields still suffered, and ever loyal to his eldest brother, William's reaction to Henry Williams was partially the snarl of an underdog at the pious carriers of moral banners. And Henry Williams had indeed set out to frustrate the Company's land purchases and plans. When William left the Cook Strait region the missionary had drawn up deeds covering large tracts of land 'intrusted to him by the Aborigines' – including the whole of the Wairarapa and Taranaki – in order to block or invalidate company purchases. Williams always insisted that he had taken these steps out of concern for the welfare of the Maori, to prevent them being duped by the company or other European land dealers. But this was both a political and a humanitarian act, and one that was not supported by his own mission committee; and though it was small, he did have a personal interest in owning land.

No sooner had William completed his first altercation with Mein Smith, and discovered Henry Williams's machinations, than the first of the settler ships, the *Aurora*, arrived on 21 January. The other five ships arrived at intervals over the following six weeks. Henry Petre on the *Oriental* described how the settlers reached Port Hardy on 22 January to find a 'complete solitude' apart from a few 'natives who came to the ship in a canoe, but with whom none of us were able to hold a conversation'. The ships' passengers rambled about the hills, thinking they were the 'first Englishmen who had trod upon that ground',[3] until a lost surveyor's notebook from the *Cuba* was found and a local whaler, acting as William's messenger, came to send the ships on to Port Nicholson.

When the *Oriental* arrived at Port Nicholson, Petre's fellow passenger Edward Hopper was appalled to find cargo landed from the *Aurora* swilling around in the sea below the high-water mark on Petone Beach and that 'no shelter had been provided for our goods or our persons'. Luckily it was high summer and the lack of preparation for the settlers, William no doubt explained, was that the *Cuba* had taken all of 175 days to make the voyage from England, a month longer than most of the emigrant ships and a full two and half a months longer than the *Tory*.

There were grumbles and apprehension but nothing else to be done but make the best of it. The single men revelled in the novelty and adventure. Tom Partridge wrote to the *New Zealand Journal* on 18 March 1840: 'I am now living in a tent I have bought, for the house is not yet landed; and I am very well contented that I have not yet been obliged to sleep with an umbrella over my head, as most others have done. The climate is so fine that everybody laughs at such things.'

It was less easy for the women, who faced domestic difficulties and the bearing and welfare of children. 'A woman lately confined on board [*Aurora*] died. Another who fractured her skull by falling down the hold is not expected to live. A boy who had both his arms blown off by a Gun on board the "Cuba" and a few trifling cases already occupy part of the Infirmary.'[4]

George Hunter's daughter Margaret wrote on 7 April 1840, 'We are very pleased with the natives, who seem to be intelligent and obliging, but very indolent. They take a great deal of interest in the children . . . Baby is quite well, and likes every thing except the cooking, which we are obliged to do in the open air, over wood fires, laid upon the ground; but we are to get a stove and chimney as soon as possible.'[5]

William observed with some grandiloquence that 'the wand of civilization has been stretched over the land'.[6] Jerningham, exhibiting the literary skills he had inherited from his father and grandmother, created a vivid picture of those early days at Petone:

> The sand-hummocks at the back of the long beach were dotted over with tents of all shapes and sizes, native-built huts in various stages of construction, and heaps of goods of various kinds, which lay about anywhere between high-water mark and the houses. Thus ploughs, hundreds of bricks, millstones, tent-poles, saucepans, crockery, iron, pot-hooks, and triangles, casks of all sizes and bales of all sorts, were distributed about the sand-hummocks. The greatest good-humour prevailed among the owners of these multifarious articles . . . . they pitched their tents and piled up their goods in rude order, while the natives, equally pleased and excited, sung Maori songs to them from the tops of the ware or huts where they sat tying the rafters and thatch together with flaxen bands.[7]

William and Jerningham bunked together in a room partitioned off from a 'large barn-like store' in Petone pa. It was 'anything but warm . . . the only window being a piece of canvass, and the door a rickety and badly-fitted one from a ship-cabin . . . . a "bunk," or wooden shelf, supported Colonel Wakefield's bed. Mine was a cot, placed on the top of a pile of musket-cases and soap-boxes against the partition. The floor consisted of the natural grey shingle which formed the beach; and the roof . . . bent and yielded to every puff of wind. The plan of tying everything together with flax . . . makes these *Maori* houses so elastic that no wind can blow them down.' They had 'plenty of thick blankets, and used to sleep soundly and turn out fresh and hearty at day-break. Then a sea-bath was close to the door. . . .'[8]

Sam Revans, about to set up and print the first Port Nicholson issue of the *New Zealand Gazette*, wrote to H. S. Chapman, 'At present I am so enthusiastic about the place, that I am almost afraid of being guilty of apparent absurdities in my statements.' Revans, whose surviving correspondence with Chapman and writings in the *Gazette* provide an intriguing insight into the development of the new colony and its leading inhabitants, at first had only praise for William. 'Col. W. Wakefield is a good fellow – a great judge of character and admirably suited to the management of such a community as that which he is presiding over. He walks about smokes his cigar and encourages all to go on and prosper. And by an occasional kindness makes & secures his popularity, tho' prepared at any moment to be severe if need be.'[9]

Henry Petre recorded that the first settlers were never short of food since the company's imports of flour, and later cattle and sheep, were supplemented by Maori pork and potatoes. The Maori were friendly and supportive in every way. 'Our conviction was, that we should be received as friends by the natives, if our conduct towards them was just and friendly. Our most sanguine expectations were completely realized.' But, 'Our numbers indeed astonished them, and they used frequently to ask whether our whole tribe . . . had not come to Port Nicholson.' Te Wharepouri had been so shocked by the crowds of settlers arriving that he had begun preparations to take his people back to his old home in Taranaki. But the prospect of work and goods aplenty from association with the hundreds of incoming Pakeha finally persuaded them to stay.

Henry Petre thought that the Maori were 'overawed by our obvious superiority to any physical force that could have been brought against us'.[10] After the last of the emigrant vessels had arrived with the repaired *Tory* on 8 March, William arranged a demonstration of that superiority: line abreast between Somes Island and Petone Beach, '[s]ix large ships, decked with colours, above which the New Zealand flag floated supreme', fired a grand salute. 'A large concourse of those on shore assembled to gaze on the imposing sight.' William stood in the stern of one of three war canoes, Epuni's, as the Maori 'shouted their war-song most vigorously as they passed close to each astonished poop-load of passengers'.[11]

This stirring event marked the end of the first euphoric, make-do summer weeks of the settlement. The idyll of camping on a strange shore, outdoor picnics in lieu of dinner and the novelties of Maori hut building had been dashed by a prolonged southerly storm that caused the Hutt River to flood and wash through the encampments and survey lines. Dr Evans, who had just arrived on the dispute-wracked *Adelaide*, made a quick and shrewd decision to set up house by Lambton Harbour. Earlier arrivals began to press William to shift the town settlement across to that side of the harbour, fearful of the river's unpredictable power and the valley's exposure to southerlies. Only a week after his arrival Evans, 'Umpire' of the settlers law and order council, led a deputation to William requesting that the town site be shifted and followed this with a formal letter which ended by stating that, unless the move was made, 'a very large proportion of the colonists . . . have made up their minds to abandon the undertaking altogether'.[12] This has the ring of a compact between William and Evans to force Mein Smith's hand. More heavy rains and floods in the month that followed left Smith with no option but to concede.

From late March, around the rocky shore of the harbour and by boat, more and more settlers upped stakes and removed to the Lambton Harbour site. The survey had to begin all over again. And though they had no floods to face, there was another problem. Maori living in the area, with pa, gardens and burial sites, occupied the prime several hundred acres. William maintained that he had bought all this land in October, But the resident Maori disagreed: they had never expected to move house for the Pakeha but to share the land. But had Henry Williams not warned them the settlers would come to drive them into the hills?

The very survival of the fledgling settlement was now at risk. It must be resited on the Lambton Harbour site or dissolved. For William, as usual, there was no time to litigate. And was this not what he had been employed for? He remembered his *Instructions*: 'It is only just, in our opinion, that the responsibility which you incur, should be accompanied by the utmost latitude for the exercise of your own judgment as to the means to be employed.'[13] He was also convinced he had fulfilled the order requiring him to ensure that any purchase of land was 'thoroughly understood' by the Maori and that each party to a sale had received a proper share of the purchase money or goods.

William instructed Mein Smith and his surveyors to begin laying off the land 'with as little collision as possible'. But they were also armed with swords and pistols. Colonel William had been conscious all along of the need to take steps to both protect the settlement and advance its interests with armed force if necessary. All parties to the settlers' council agreement promised to 'submit themselves to be mustered and drilled'. Apart from impressive shows of cannon fire from ships on the harbour, William advised the company that he had also 'built a capacious powder magazine and shall mount the four eighteen-pounder guns from the "Adelaide" on the summit of Somes Island'.[14]

The Maori were well aware of the likely consequences of physical confrontation with the Pakeha and what they would lose if the settlers decided to leave the area. So they registered their protest at the survey merely by pulling out the surveyors' stakes and destroying markers. When they did not desist, those settlers eligible to be mustered and drilled put on a show of force to overawe them. The survey proceeded and when sections were finally given out by ballot, the tenths due to Maori were scattered all over the area, often in impossible locations. Six of nine villages at Port Nicholson disappeared. The town was laid out but resentment, dispute and argument over purchase, payment and survey would now plague the settlement, and William for the rest of his life.

It is not surprising that William flew into a rage when Henry Williams returned to Port Nicholson on 19 April, bearing the Treaty of Waitangi for signature by local chiefs, and claimed rights to 40 acres of Lambton Harbour land which he had negotiated with the native missionary Richard Davis in William's absence (at negligible payment). When they met to discuss this, William insisted the land had been included and paid for under the October deal; and when Henry Williams demurred, William swore at him, causing him to leave the meeting. Evans and others failed to persuade Henry Williams to relinquish his claim but his threat to leave the settlement provoked William's apology. When the missionary understood that the company had reserved the tenths for the Maori, he agreed to 'gift' his land interest to the company, reserving an acre for himself and one for Davis.

When the question of Henry Williams's land had been settled, he was 'enabled to obtain the signatures of the Natives of this place' on 29 April. Williams's letter to Hobson on the subject was politic and careful, aware that a deputation of settlers was planning to visit the governor: 'There appeared many strange ideas on our arrival which I hope have now subsided . . . . Upon the opinion and advice of Colonel Wakefield and Dr. Evans I have concluded to proceed to Otako lest the French should be beforehand . . . . I have been highly gratified to observe the great respectability of the parties who have located to this place. . . .'[15]

William's caustic version of events went to the company at the end of May:

> I thought it better to compromise the matter with him, and to ensure the support of the Church Missionaries by giving him an interest in the place; and, therefore, after a candid avowal on his part that he wished 'to have a slice for himself' and other confessions equally disinterested and compatible with his pretended anxiety on account of the native reserves, I agreed to give him one acre of the land he claimed for himself and one acre for the sole use of Richard Davis the Native [missionary]; they, in consideration of the land being surveyed, yielding all their rights to the Company. I cannot express to you the feelings of repugnance entertained by the respectable colonists . . . on account of his selfish views, his hypocrisy and unblushing rapaciousness. He frequently said that finding I had been beforehand with him in the purchase of land in the Strait without consulting him he had endeavoured to do the best for himself and had disparaged the Company and its settlers to the natives. On the whole it was only by a great effort, and in the hope of benefitting the Colony, that I could bring myself to hold any terms with this worst of land-sharks.[16]

William's intemperate and exaggerated report reflected the fact that he had also been warring with Williams over the treaty which, with its Crown pre-emption on land sales, threatened the scope and security of the company's land purchases. William's fury with Henry Williams was fuelled by his belief that missionaries should not meddle in commerce or politics. William was to give much praise to the work of Octavius Hadfield, the CMS missionary now established at Waikanae, 'a single-minded and sincere minister of the Gospel [who] well deserves the estimation in which he is held by all parties', because 'He has always refrained from, and, it is understood, declined any interference in, the secular matters of the natives, other than recommending a peaceable intercourse with their white neighbours'.[17] The missionary's role as a spiritual leader, converting, civilising and pacifying the Maori, served the company's interests best. To each his own in making New Zealand British.[18]

In the midst of the turmoil caused by changing the town site, and from dealing with recalcitrant ship's captains who were not fulfilling their contracts in properly discharging cargo, William found space to write to 'My dear Catherine' on 25 March 1840.

> I have scarcely time to write to my friends, but snatch a moment to let you know that we have accomplished our voyage & object satisfactorily. This country quite equals my expectations & there can be no doubt of the success of our colony. The natives are fast improving amongst us. They like our clothing & observances of the Sabbath. I am half a missionary myself & have perfect control over our tribes here, who have given me the name of Wideawake, by which I am known all over the islands. I have written to Edward [EGW] to send me Emily, but fear he may have left England. If so I trust to you & Charles to look to her, till I can go home for or to her. . . . If you have a son to spare & like to send him to me I can do something for him & he shall not be eaten by the natives. I intend to write to Pris by the first ship to India. I heard from her from the Cape. She & her children were flourishing. . . .[19]

There are signs here of William's homesickness, if not for place then certainly for family, and his firm intention to have his only child with him as soon as possible. Emily was now thirteen, attending a boarding school at Richmond and being cared for in the holidays by either EGW or Catherine and Charles. Their brood at Stoke was now complete with the birth of Frances the year before but, of nine children born alive, most of them girls, Anna had already died at the age of twelve in 1838. It is unlikely that Catherine would have taken too warmly to William's talk of a 'son to spare' not being 'eaten by the natives': Henry was just seven and Charley scarcely fifteen.

'Pris', William's youngest sibling, who had been found a teaching position in Ipswich by Arthur in 1833, had answered the call to teach at Mrs Wilson's missionary school in Calcutta in 1835. Surviving extracts from her banal diary show that, at the beginning of 1836, Priscilla was learning 'Bengalee' from a 'Pundit' and confined to the limited social experience of missionary families.[20] But she had already met Captain Henry Chapman, an older and distant cousin from her father's generation, whom she married later that year, escaping into her own household. William's reference to her children was anticipatory. Priscilla was to emulate Catherine in producing a family of nine, and she was almost as old as her elder sister had been when she first became a mother. At the time he wrote, her first child was two and the second not long conceived. Priscilla was to spend some years in India with her merchant husband before settling again in England. Occasionally she made contact with brother Howard who remained a lieutenant in the 17th Native Infantry and on survey work for fifteen years before being promoted to captain in 1840.

Although William remained 'my dear Kate, yours very affectionately', thoughts of family were only a brief and rare diversion from the almost impossible task he had undertaken as expedition and colony leader, principal agent of the company and 'President' of the settlers' council that had been formed to administer British law and order in the absence of any national jurisdiction. William did not have the skills to cope with all these roles to everyone's satisfaction. For much of his life, he had deferred to EGW, to whom, it was said, he bore 'rather a watery resemblance'.[21] The New Zealand venture was this relationship writ large. But when an exchange of correspondence around the world took at least nine months, and William was essentially left to his own devices, he was bound to be found wanting in some of the attributes needed in a settlement founder.

For William Gisborne, the nineteenth-century public servant, politician and commentator, such a man 'should be intelligent, practical, just, firm, prudent, trustworthy, energetic, patient, persevering and otherwise specially fitted to be a leader of men'.[22] Modern commentators would probably add that he should have been also a paid-up member of the Aborigines Protection Society and a selfless missionary. Although William announced himself half the latter for Catherine's sake, and might have wished himself to be the rest, even he would have agreed that he could not be all things to all men.

What can be deduced of William 'the inner man'? Beyond the early 1820s in Paris, he had been largely isolated from social experience and often separated from his family. His name was never mentioned in connection with any woman after 1827. The heartbreak, guilt and shame over Emily's death appear to have diverted all his affectionate impulses towards his daughter whose upbringing he was, nevertheless, prepared to leave to others. His own upbringing and military responsibilities had taught him formal social skills, and developed a veneer of charm and sensibility, but his personality seems to have been cramped and his emotions suppressed.

Gisborne, whose description of William has generally been relied upon by subsequent writers, may have met him during the last year of his life, when Gisborne was 22 and William was suffering from stress and nervous exhaustion. Otherwise, his description must be a digest of other opinions. Gisborne wrote, 'One remarkable faculty of Colonel Wakefield was his reticence . . . . no one who had an interview with [him] knew what he thought and what he meant to do. His manner was attractive, and, in outward appearance, sympathetic, but the inner man was out of sight and hearing. The feeling of the interviewer was that of taking a leap in the dark. Colonel Wakefield, like the mole, did his work underground.'[23] Only missionaries, apparently, could provoke an outward passion. A lonely, loveless man, William found good company only with fellow military men, some from Spain such as Major David Durie, whose limited but comradely bonhomie he could trust. For the rest, a charming manner and reticence would serve to reserve his judgement, mask his indecision and inadequacies and disguise his political manipulations.

The council and constitution agreed upon by the settlers before leaving Gravesend was intended to provide a temporary but essential system of law and order. When news reached Port Nicholson that Lieutenant-Governor Hobson had arrived in the north to establish British sovereignty, the settlers 'were in daily expectation of being visited either by the Governor in person or by an officer of the Government. In fact we fully expected that Port Nicholson would be chosen for the seat of Government.'[24] When nothing happened after a month, something had to be done. So the council was brought together at the beginning of March and a magistrate and constables appointed. In his first local edition of the *New Zealand Gazette* (18 April) Sam Revans published the details of the council's constitution, which had been 'ratified' by local chiefs. By this time, William had been advised by Ward that the council was illegal but he decided not to reveal this information until colonial government was established in Port Nicholson, probably so that a facsimile of constitutional law and order could be maintained.

One of the first to feel the force of the council's authority was a Captain Pearson, who was arrested for assault but escaped and took his barque, nicely named *Integrity*, to the Bay of Islands and alleged to Lieutenant-Governor William Hobson that the southern settlers were setting up their own 'republic'. Hobson, recovering from a stroke, and anxiously awaiting news that his emissaries had successfully obtained all the necessary signatures from Maori chiefs around the country to validate the Treaty of Waitangi, cried 'Treason!'

Hobson had arrived in the Bay of Islands on 29 January, already appointed Lieutenant-Governor of New Zealand under Governor of New South Wales, Sir George Gipps. He was armed with a variety of instructions and options from Gipps and the Colonial Office – as well as his own opinions – about the best way of placing New Zealand under British sovereignty, with its law and order, while reassuring Maori that their interests would be protected. He carried with him the conclusions of British officialdom that it was not possible to envisage a 'Maori New Zealand in which a place had to be found for British intruders, but a settler New Zealand in which a place had to be found for the Maori'.[25] The actions of the company had been crucial in shaping this attitude.

Within a week of arriving Hobson, with the help of British Resident James Busby and CMS missionaries (especially Henry Williams), had cobbled together a treaty in English and Maori which sought cession, submission and loyalty by the Maori to the British Crown and constitution while safeguarding their customs and property. The Crown had pre-emption on all land sales, which was presented as securing Maori from exploitation by unscrupulous private purchasers. The full import of the Treaty of Waitangi, of becoming British, was never clear to Maori, least of all that the Crown itself would seek to make profits from land sales to pay for the costs of colonial settlement. William Colenso, missionary printer, was the only one at the signing on 6 February to suggest, greatly to Hobson's irritation, that most of the chiefly signatories did not really understand what was going on. In the much touted 'spirit' of the treaty, Hobson and the missionaries placated any Maori misgivings with paternalistic reassurances of trust.

Years later, in 1858, George Selwyn, the first Anglican Bishop of New Zealand, was to say that William Wakefield spent less time on his Cook Strait land purchases than would have been necessary for the 'honest conveyance of a marriage settlement on an encumbered estate'.[26] Had William still been alive, he might have retorted that Hobson had spent even less time putting together the founding document of New Zealand's constitution.

Whatever the intentions, considerations or methods used by any party, the nett effect was the British takeover of New Zealand. William's initiation of the Port Nicholson council caused this to be completed definitively and prematurely. Few treaty signatures from beyond Waitangi had reached Hobson when Captain Pearson brought news of the southern 'republic'. Within hours of his arrival on 21 May, and in view of this 'emergency', Hobson proclaimed British sovereignty over the North Island, based on the 'universal adherence of the native chiefs' to the treaty, blatantly false, and over the South Island by right of discovery, an equally dubious claim. Treaty signatures were eventually collected from around the country but it was this declaration and its official gazetting by the British Government on 2 October that turned New Zealand into a Crown colony.

The wording of Hobson's ringing proclamation against the Port Nicholson council two days later left no doubt about New Zealand's new status. In condemning the council, Hobson described New Zealand as 'part of the Dominions of Her Majesty Queen Victoria' and asserted that the council's attempt to 'usurp' his powers was to the 'manifest injury and detriment of all Her Majesty's liege subjects in New Zealand'.[27] This would have been unintelligible news to most of them.

Hobson thereupon despatched Acting Colonial Secretary Willoughby Shortland with 30 soldiers and six mounted policemen to force the Port Nicholson settlers to withdraw from their 'illegal association'. Before they arrived, a public notice, by William's order as president of the council, had been printed requiring all male residents between eighteen and 60 to be ready for mustering and drill. This was in the interests of the 'protection of life and property, as well as in upholding the power and authority of the British race'.[28] A mustering was pre-empted, three days later, by the arrival of Shortland's party who were 'well received', according to William's tactful report to Ward on 27 June.[29] '[Shortland] holds courts of petty sessions twice a week and is about to build a jail, issue licences etc. . . .'

The 'republic' was dissolved but not without resentment among the settlers towards Hobson and Shortland, who had managed to ignore them for six months, despite their desire for co-operation, and then issued them with heavy-handed proclamations. What else could the settlers have done? Revans made the point on 6 June when he published this notice: 'We would suggest the propriety of giving Colonel Wakefield some evidence of public approbation; for to his kind and judicious management, much of the present quiet and satisfaction is owing.'[30]

Despite the evident hostility of Hobson and Shortland towards the company, William now tried to fulfil instructions he had received a couple of months before, to do his utmost to assist Hobson in establishing British sovereignty over New Zealand, even to offering him the use of interpreters and ships. EGW had privately offered his own sections at Port Nicholson for Hobson's use and the company was shipping out the parts of a house for the governor whom, they assumed, would wish to be based at their principal settlement. 'Just in proportion as you should be enabled to act in concert with Captain Hobson, will be the Company's facilities hereafter in procuring from the Government or Parliament such arrangements as would conduce to the advantage and prosperity of all.'[31] EGW's hand is clear in this attempt to proceed with the best of intentions while getting the government to validate the company's settlement and land purchases.

To ensure that Port Nicholson became the colonial capital, William travelled promptly to the Bay of Islands in July, 'in order to carry to His Excellency an address . . . voted to him at a public meeting . . . and to take his instructions respecting his house and other points'.[32] William's journey with the address of undying loyalty to Hobson and its invitation of residence, presented with all the charm and persuasion William could muster, appeared to establish an amicable relationship between the two men. But it did nothing to divert Hobson from his plan to establish his residency and capital in the north, if only to keep his political distance from the company. His determination to do this, as well as his indifferent health, meant that he would not visit Port Nicholson until August 1841, a year and a half after his arrival.

Tom Partridge, one of the company settlers and a business partner of Revans, was in the Bay of Islands when William arrived and expressed to him the considerable local dissatisfaction with the lieutenant-governor: 'Capt. Hobson I have not yet seen, he is a valetudinarian and seems borne down by the difficulties of his position, which his education does not seem to enable him to reach. – He appears to be in complete subservience to Sir George Gipps and the N.S. Wales faction – and cannot bestow but the most trivial appointments. . . .'[33]

Hobson irritated the inhabitants of Port Nicholson even more when William read out his response to their address at a public meeting after his return in August. Hobson declined their offer to provide him with a proper residence, 'from a conviction of the advantages of fixing the seat of Government in a more centrical position, and one better adapted for internal communication'.[34] Hobson bought land on the southern shore of the Waitemata to establish a capital he called Auckland. Hobson meant 'more centrical' in relation to the larger concentrations of Maori, who then comprised more than 90 per cent of the population. To the Port Nicholson settlers, Hobson's 'centrical' was not only a geographical absurdity but a clear snub to their significance. From this time on there would be little pause in the antagonism between the company's settlers and successive governors and their Auckland establishments which was not settled until the capital finally shifted south in 1865. Nevertheless, William saw that the company kept its word and shipped Hobson's house north to his chosen residence. Appropriately, it was accidentally burned before it could be erected.

The immediate feeling of being under official siege was not helped by the notification by Shortland that the company's land purchases would be subject to a commission of enquiry appointed in Sydney. William wrote, 'I have no reason to think that the titles I have acquired for the Company are exceptionable; but, – the feeling of Sir George Gipps towards the Company, openly expressed, leads me to expect a nomination of Commissioners unfavourable to our interests'.[35] Governor Gipps had called the settlers 'adventurers'.

Revans editorially banged the drum: 'It is true that we are adventurers. We have adventured property and life, our own prosperity and that of our children, in an undertaking which was rightly called by the sagacious Bacon heroic. If this enterprise be successful . . . we shall have realized for ourselves independence, and probably wealth; but at the same time we shall have substituted in this remote region civilization for barbarism, Christianity for heathenism. . . .'[36]

This was all very fine but, in William's absence, the attempt by Mein Smith to allot town sections according to his survey turned into a fiasco, and details of Gipps's New Zealand Land Bill had arrived, creating confusion and panic. On his return, William sorted the sections muddle but there was immediate trouble when settlers tried to take up residence on land already inhabited by Maori. This culminated in violence when Sam Revans began to have his house erected within Te Aro pa. Colonial Secretary Shortland finally discovered that Te Puni had sold the Te Aro land to William without its owners' consent: 'How could I help it, when I saw so many muskets and blankets before me?' he said.[37] Shortland took control of the Te Aro land on the basis that anyone who wanted to take it up before official examination of title must apply to him through William. It was a useful if temporary finesse. And early conflict between settler and Maori was eased by the speculations of absentee owners: there were many vacant town sections on which displaced Maori could squat.

For any problems involving survey and sections, William, in his despatches to England, relentlessly blamed and criticised Mein Smith. But this scarcely disguised the other reality that there were simply not 110,000 acres of agricultural land available near Port Nicholson for the country sections. In this respect, Hobson was right. The Waitemata environs had much more land available for agricultural development – and a better climate. A couple of years later, Lieutenant John Wood observed: 'Auckland, in the course of years, must become the chief colony, for here nature has done what neither capital nor puffery can do for Wellington'.[38] But there was no political or commercial chance the company would concede an inch of that.

In search of extensive farmland, Ernst Dieffenbach and William Deans explored the head of the densely forested Hutt Valley in August 1840 but found no way out of its limitations to the Manawatu or Wairarapa. Although Dieffenbach and Charles Heaphy travelled to the promising Wairarapa via the coast in September William made no company move to explore it for early settlement. He preferred the prospects of the Wanganui region. In May, he had sent Jerningham there who confirmed William's 'purchase' of the land the previous November with goods he valued at £700 (£100 by a missionary observer). In the same mad wrangle that had characterised the Tory Channel purchase, the goods were snapped up by a mêlée of Maori; but few of them were actual owners of land. When William visited the area later he discovered that, yet again, Henry Williams had shadowed him and in December 1839 had given local chiefs a piece of paper saying that he had purchased all the land for the benefit of the Maori, without giving them 'even a fish-hook or a head of tobacco'. Wanganui was turning into as big a mess as Port Nicholson – or Wellington as it had become on 14 November when news arrived of the company directors' May decision. EGW had finally repaid his debt of honour to 'Old Wooden Head'.

According to Jerningham, the settlers took up the directors' name change 'with great cordiality'. But the situation at Wanganui was not helped by his return there at the end of 1840 and his establishment of a kind of baronial residence where he held court wearing an ostrich-feathered hat and a Maori mat for a toga. 'The centre remained an open hall . . .' with a keg of rum at either end of a long table '. . . where all but known bad characters of either race might assemble and be welcome round the ample chimney-corner. But the separated rooms were kept strictly *tapu*, and not even the chief himself ever ventured into them without my permission. In the absence of established laws and usages, I found this sort of feudal system very effectual. I had always a crowd of attendants ready to perform any task. . . .',[39] not least wahine in one of the tapu rooms. Twenty-year-old Teddy had succumbed to the power of an absolute hedonism found only beyond the reach of regular social order and discipline. It was the top of his personal slippery slope.

News of the debaucheries of Teddy and his friends filtered down to Wellington. Revans wrote: 'I hear he is leading a very vicious life at Wanganui . . . a life he knows his friends would not countenance. A wish has been expressed that he should go home, but he is obstinate and will not listen to it. I should be truly sorry that the father should be made to suffer pain by the doings of his son in a place for which he has done so much as EGW has for New Zealand.'[40]

This was just another annoyance William could do without. The brief summer of his new settlement had turned quickly to winter; the fabric of all his designs was threatening to unravel. William had no time for problems with Teddy as he fought an endless war of attrition against an often inept colonial government and, increasingly, settler disillusionment with the company and his own actions, both of which were usually financially constrained.

Some settlers had gone off to Australia, others had been lured to Auckland by Hobson and others had gone Home with tales of hardship and incompetence. Revans was scornful: 'Many leaving will be laughed at when they get home . . . I know nothing that can be said excepting that it is windy; but the wind will not check the progress of the place.'[41] Those who stayed were buoyed by stubborn optimism – 'The colony has gone on (under the unmerited neglect and malevolence of Capt Hobson) beyond my utmost hopes. . . .'[42] – or stoic common sense: 'Although the colony has had some difficulties to contend with, and some real causes of discouragement, I am still of the same mind . . . namely, that the country is excellent, and that the wisest act I ever did was to come out here . . . a man would have been mad to suppose that a body of Englishmen, proceeding to a country inhabited only by savages, and that, too, without the sanction or protection of their own government, could possibly be free from difficulties. They have, however, been very small, and I do not believe we shall have any which men cannot conquer.'[43]

Dealing with the company itself was easier for William with the ameliorating advantages of distance and time. If his carefully crafted reports were sometimes threatened with the sabotage of critical letters sent Home by the disaffected, William knew he could always rely on EGW to set things right among the directors. When F. A. Carrington arrived in December 1839, buoyant with news of the company's improving fortunes and enthusiasm for his task as chief surveyor of the second settlement for the Plymouth Company, this was no Christmas present for William. He sent him off to choose his spot, which became New Plymouth in Taranaki, and resigned himself to more problems. He had lost much heart and enthusiasm: the adventure and novelty had been replaced by politics and business. Although he could have done with Emily by his side, the settlement remained insecure, and she was too young to call away from the benefits of English family and education.

A picture of William at the anniversary of the settlement was drawn by the prolix Revans in his chain of letters to H. S. Chapman: 'The Colonel is generally liked as a companion. We are excellent friends . . . . [he] is no man of business and it is plain he has no pleasure in the pursuit of Company's agent – it is distasteful. How often I have longed that E.G. Wakefield was here . . . . he would have made the place. There is no go in his brother who loves ease and retirement. We want a suggesting mind – a mind with imaginating power like that of which E. G. Wakefield has. . . .'[44]

A couple of months later Revans expressed almost complete disillusionment with William: 'He anticipates nothing but yields to progress reluctantly and with bad grace. He has proved a miserable representative of his brother's daring and energy. All agree that he is the coldest mannered man they have met with. No man ever left him stronger in faith or determination to act . . . . you can understand the mischief of such a character in such a position. Great credit is due to the Colonists for their conduct throughout our trying circumstances and none to the representative of the Company.'[45] Revans could be a contrary character, but his private comments represented a growing body of opinion in the settlement.

CHAPTER EIGHTEEN

Hobson's Choice

THE BRITISH SETTLEMENT OF NEW ZEALAND was marked not only by the usual factors of luck, political cupidity, lack of foresight and self-interest, enlightened or otherwise, but also by desperate failures of communication. The main parties to the establishment of a British Crown colony and the planting of planned settlements were literally a world apart in an age before the telegraph and when steam had only just put to sea. The tortuous progress of around-the-world mail in the 1840s is well exemplified by this extract from a letter from EGW to Catherine: 'We have no letters from Nelson. Those from Wellington came along with a bag from Nelson to Valparaiso, and were there put into a fast sailing schooner. Others, and all the Nelson letters, are on the way in the slower sailor in which they left Wellington.'[1] Via South America was express post; sometimes mail went via Australia and India.

When mail did arrive there were the usual misunderstandings, wilful or not, and there was no possibility for discussion or rapid clarification. The right hand of London often acted before the left hand of Wellington was withdrawn from its pocket, and vice versa. Decisions were made upon instructions or information that were always at least four months out of date; assumption and independent action were normal, often based on belief and conjecture rather than empirical evidence.

So that when William wrote his Despatch Number 20 on 27 June 1840, he would have known that there had been a change in the Whig administration the previous August in which Francis Baring, former chairman of the New Zealand Association, had been made Chancellor of the Exchequer and Lord John Russell had supplanted Normanby at the Colonial Office. Of Russell, that paragon James Stephen commented, '[he] is one of the very few men in the World, who in the exercise of great political power, is filling the precise function for which nature designed, and education qualified him'.[2] But William would not have known that his very first September despatch did not reach London until March; nor that its optimistic news had prompted the company to appoint a political committee, including EGW who was made a director in April, to press the Government 'to adopt prompt and efficient measures for preserving from invasion, or abandonment, the long-established Sovereignty of the British Crown in New Zealand'. William could hardly have predicted the influence of one despatch, though he would have been unsurprised by EGW's amazing use of it.

Such a sovereignty had never existed: the company's averred state of antipodean anarchy was inflated, as was the threat of a French takeover. EGW knew very well that, by this time, Hobson would have arrived in New Zealand and be already advanced in whatever negotiations he had entered into with the Maori. But EGW also knew that, to achieve gains for the company before Hobson's despatches started coming through, he must use the communications gap to advantage. The five-month march gained on Hobson and the government by the early and fast sailing of the *Tory* should be maintained at all costs.

A 'Requisition' presented to the Lord Mayor of London, signed by more than 100 City businessmen, but with no mention of the company, brought about a public meeting on 15 April. It attracted so much interest that its venue was transferred from Mansion House to Guildhall. Resolutions carefully crafted by company members were presented and, despite a few unexpected diversions from the floor, a petition to Queen and Parliament was adopted, insisting on sovereignty over New Zealand from Cook's 1769 right of discovery and that a select committee be set up forthwith to examine the New Zealand crisis, including the so-called threat posed by the French. Russell did not approve of the petition but he could not ignore the political weight behind it and acceded to a select committee which met at the end of the parliamentary session in July.

This was precisely the theatre EGW needed for a well-performed, creative script that served to further his own ideas and the interests of the company. EGW guided its chairman, Lord Eliot, into allowing him to take up more than three of the six days allocated. Even the favourably inclined committee, which included Charles Buller, could not bring itself to write a report or recommendations based on such one-sided hearings and merely allowed Eliot to present the evidence to the house: 73 of 133 pages were EGW's. *The Times* thundered against the company and the entire gerrymander on 27 July in an editorial heavily headlined, 'The New Zealand Land BUBBLE!' The great governor of the bubble had played no part. On 10 May, Lord Durham had resigned owing to ill health, allowing Joseph Somes to take over, and died the day after *The Times*'s peroration.

The company was so heartened by the outcome of events that surveyor F. A. Carrington was sent off as outrider to the associated Plymouth Company settlement, which had been on the stocks in Lord Eliot's West Country since February. By the time a dinner was held to farewell the first Plymouth settlers at the end of October, the influence of the Guildhall meeting and select committee hearing, and the political manoeuvrings that followed, had brought about a remarkable change in the company's fortunes.

'My dear Molesworth,' EGW wrote from London on 26 October,

> Lest you should prepare a speech for the Plymouth dinner which you would not be able to make, I tell you the secrets of a secret committee of the Directors who have been negotiating with Lord John.
>
> Instead of abusing the Government you will have to praise them. They have not merely conceded what we might have gained by continuing the war, but have offered to do all that we could desire. The main points are to be in Lord Eliot's report, with the addition that our Company is really to be the agent of the State for colonizing New Zealand. We are to have a charter for forty years, with an increased capital and great powers. The Plymouth Co. is fully recognized. It will be called an enormous job, but is really a wise settlement of all the questions. We shall have the official announcement tomorrow, I hope . . . . At present this is a secret, and must be kept so till we have the official determination of Government. Lord John has behaved very well. And Stephen excellently . . . . I am very glad to think that your stock in New Zealand shares must now turn out very profitable.
>
> The negociation has lasted for six weeks, and you will now see that I had good reason for not leaving town. The satisfaction of the triumph is almost intolerable.[3]

The start of the negotiation had been largely Charles Buller's doing. Following the habit of his predecessors, Russell had continued to officially ignore the company, in the hope that it might go away. Buller discussed the select committee report with EGW before the middle of September and concocted a plan to change his mind. The first step was a 'casual' encounter between Buller and James Stephen in a London club. Buller employed all his well-known wit and geniality to disarm Stephen, who dropped his guard enough to be gulled into believing that the company, especially its innocent settlers, were in distress and needed more constructive treatment from the government. Russell was approached with similar messages and he asked Stephen to obtain the real views and plans of the company. About this time, Hobson's despatches began arriving from New Zealand and his declaration of sovereignty was ratified on 2 October, three days before the company established its 'secret committee' to continue negotiations.

No sooner had EGW sent Molesworth his letter than he travelled down to Devon to announce the triumph himself at the grand dinner. The company was to be granted a charter of incorporation and, on the basis of all the company's expenditures on colonisation, the Crown would grant four times as many acres as pounds spent, up to 110,000 acres in the Wellington area and 50,000 at Taranaki. All this depended on the assurances of the company that their pre-Waitangi land purchases were valid.

By the time William's Report Number 20 arrived in London on 24 November, in which he expressed fear that Sir George Gipps's New South Wales land commissioners would deal unfavourably with the company's Port Nicholson interests, the world had moved on. The company readily accepted Russell's forecast appointment, on 21 January 1841, of a special commissioner to examine their claims. William Spain did not reach New Zealand until the following Christmas, or begin looking at the claims for months after that. But everyone had William's reassurance – that there was no reason to think that the titles acquired for the company were exceptionable – and considered Spain's investigation would be a formality. When William finally heard about Spain, whatever misgivings he may have secretly harboured, he continued to promote this view, especially since his salary had been doubled to £1,000. And he knew that, with every month that passed, the colonies grew and the settlers' possession of the soil became more secure. Doing nothing seemed the best course of action in this long battle of attrition.

The confidence of the company now knew no bounds. It negotiated the founding and funding of a bishopric for New Zealand in association with the government and with the support of the Archbishop of Canterbury. To celebrate accord with the Colonial Office after so many years of wrangling, the directors put on a widely reported dinner, with Lord John Russell as guest of honour. While the *Morning Chronicle* announced that the dinner 'will serve to remove all apprehension' about relations between the government and the company settlements, *The Times* predictably said it was more a 'significant intimation that [the Company's] pretended purchases from the native chiefs are . . . formally ratified by the Whig Government'.

EGW was unable to share in the evening's glory. 'Edward is not well and was not there, but the mention of his name was received with great satisfaction & applause, I think he will soon get round. He has been bled and blistered for his old complaint in the chest [asthma], I do not think his lungs are at all affected, his complaint arises from getting fat & too much work.'[4] The no-nonsense style of this letter to Catherine betrays the hand of Arthur, back in London to take up what would prove to be his final command.

After his contretemps with the reef at St Tropez in January 1839, Arthur had continued plying the Mediterranean carrying messages, men and merchandise. Commander-in-Chief Mediterranean was Admiral Sir Robert Stopford, who had taken command at the same time as Arthur had been given the *Rhadamanthus*. Stopford was a veteran of the Napoleonic Wars: he had commanded the Java expedition when Arthur was a lad on the *Nisus*. He would soon be described by Foreign Secretary Lord Palmerston as a 'superannuated twaddler' who, though able to cope with the long days of peace in the 1830s, was not, at 70, the man for the major crisis that occurred at the decade's end.

Mehemet Ali, Pasha of Egypt, attacked Ottoman Turkey from Syria in mid-1839. A year of negotiations brokered by Palmerston brought about an alliance between Britain, Austria, Prussia and the Turks, which imposed terms on Ali and led to his defeat with the fall of Acre in November 1840. Although Stopford was in command, all the key operations were conducted by his commodore, Sir Charles

Napier, 20 years his junior and the brilliant commander who had helped defeat Dom Miguel in Portugal in 1834. Napier deliberately disobeyed the old man's orders, almost to the point of mutiny. But everything he touched succeeded brilliantly, earning victory, the government's approval and Palmerston's slur on Stopford.

The details may never be discovered but somewhere in the middle of all this was Arthur, commanding the *Rhadamanthus* off Acre. And in the altercations between Napier and Stopford, he fell foul of the latter. It may have been a case of shooting the messenger; but by Christmas 1840 the *Rhadamanthus* was back at Woolwich, Arthur was no longer its commander and EGW was tempting him to lead a Nelson expedition to New Zealand to follow William's Wellington. EGW probably relished the imagery, the package he could present to potential investors and settlers – a new settlement named for the hero of Trafalgar ('Thank God for the navy!') and led by the best brother of England's colonial genius, a naval hero himself of Washington, Algiers and Acre. For Arthur, just turned 41, the opportunity offered much more than a future in the navy where all his patronage was dead. If Stopford was a 'superannuated twaddler', Arthur would likely become a superannuated nobody.

The disposition of the Wakefield family that Christmas reflected the state of many an English middle-class family at the start of Victoria's empire. Howard and Pris were in India, Felix in Tasmania, William in New Zealand and Arthur just back from defending British interests in the Middle East. EGW was actively involved in creating empire, thinking of Canada, and only Dan, evasive Dan, is unaccounted for, though it is likely he was with the Attwood family at Harborne, near Birmingham.

Catherine would have counted herself fortunate to have two brothers at Stoke for that Christmas, EGW florid and overweight at 44, indulging in rich fare and the cigars he had taken to, while Arthur stuck to his snuff. EGW, the most doting of uncles, was devoted to Charles and Catherine's children as well as William's Emily, said to have had her mother's beauty and delicacy of constitution but also the melancholy of an only child who had grown up essentially as an orphan. The extended Wakefield family gatherings sometimes compensated for this and EGW treated her when he could. Albert Allom, the younger brother of EGW's secretary Charles, wrote of falling in love with her on a weekend outing in Richmond Park.

From time to time, EGW keenly felt the lack of a family of his own. His Nina was now five years dead; Teddy was growing up in New Zealand; Liocadia was gone there and soon married; it would not be long before Emily joined William. He thought seriously again of adopting a child and when he talked to Catherine the old moral debate between them resurfaced:

> I don't know that your objection to me as a teacher is quite valid, since I have brought up more than one person in more than commonly decided religious sentiments. However, that is a point which will hardly bear discussion. I am in no desperate hurry

> about a child, but wish Priscilla & Loui [Catherine's daughters, now sixteen and twelve] to keep a look out for me. I would not confine them to infancy or the youngest childhood if they should chance to meet with one who had been really well brought up so far, & had a very good natural disposition & talents. There are many in the world who should be glad (I say it with vanity) to get so good a berth.[5]

Nothing came of all this, probably because EGW was to be absent from the country for long periods over the following three years.

There must have been talk of the forthcoming Nelson expedition during the Christmas season at Stoke, and the formal charter of incorporation a month or so later confirmed it. But perhaps Catherine had shut out its implications, causing Arthur to write in February 1841, 'You write as if you were surprised at my going to New Zealand. I thought you understood that I had made up my mind .... I am offered the command of the preliminary expedition ... & hope to leave this country in two months. A good body of colonists is forming & I think we shall have such a party that never left Eng. Before. ...' EGW's enthusiasm was contagious, and Arthur was ever mindful of his elder brother's concern to find a place for the Torlesses. 'As yet we have no clergyman, altho' the Church is very much interested about it, I wish we had something definite to tempt Charles with. The Bishopric of New Zealand is settled upon, but the nomination is not made .... It is not unlikely that when the Bishop is nominated he will be allowed to name an archdeacon for the colony. ...'

Other Stoke families soon declared themselves to go with Arthur,[6] and Catherine no doubt twitched when he ended his letter, 'Charlie spent a day here last week, he was very well'.[7] She had seen her fifteen-year-old's eyes light up at Arthur's Christmas tales and the promise of adventure in the Nelson plans. In March, Arthur formally took on Charley Torlesse as an 'improver' or apprentice surveyor on the expedition. Frances Torlesse, Catherine's last born, was then only two years old but in old age she recalled the lasting and disturbing effect of the Wakefields' colonising ventures.

> From that day began the long drawn-out tragedy of my mother's life. In the present day it is impossible to realize what separation meant in those far away days; there was no certainty whatever when letters would arrive, and sometimes a whole year elapsed without news, and in looking back it seems to me that the pivot on which my mother's life turned was 'waiting for the mail' ... The question was often raised that my father should follow his sons to New Zealand ... My mother desired it passionately, my brothers were constantly urging it, but father never saw his way clearly. But the idea coloured our life at Stoke and produced often an atmosphere of marked unrest.[8]

Less than a month after Charley's departure, Catherine wrote to him a letter filled with the import of domestic triviality ('Priscilla is playing and singing Little Bo-

Peep to Frances, who . . . says "more, more"') but admits, 'Stoke has lost its charm for me, and if it pleases God to point out the way I am ready to leave it for New Zealand'.[9]

Charles was never to shift from his favourite armchair but he did buy a section in Nelson and formally saw off the departing expeditioners at Gravesend with a reading from the First Epistle of St Peter: 'Who is he that shall harm you, if ye be followers of that which is good?' If Arthur had anything to do with it, no harm would befall the 27 cabin passengers and 77 emigrants in the barques *Will Watch* and *Whitby*, or their crews. He had thrown all his vast naval experience into planning and equipping the expedition. In telling Catherine of the departure on 27 April, EGW wrote, 'We have not yet recollected to have forgotten anything – which speaks volumes for Arthur's management. I hope that your feelings are, as your reason must be, reconciled to parting with Charlie . . . . I think that you ought to rejoice when you reflect, in the opportunity which Charly now has of making his own way in the world.[10] He cannot be in better hands than those of our excellent brother.'[11]

The company's second major settlement, under Arthur's leadership, at first seemed better planned than the first. The preliminary expedition set out a full five months before the emigrant ships and the second in command and chief surveyor, Frederick Tuckett, had six assistant surveyors, as well as nine improvers, among them Charley Torlesse and Thomas Brunner. The labourers and their foremen were all carefully selected married men, whose wives and families would follow in the emigrant ships to find the settlement fully surveyed.

The mixture of land sections was to be different: 201,000 acres would be sold in 1000 £300 allotments that would comprise one town acre, 50 acres of 'accommodation' or suburban land and 150 acres of rural land. In the flush of their new charter and Colonial Office approval, the company said that these would be laid out at the best site available in New Zealand, probably on the eastern side of the southern island. Of the £300,000 received from sales, half would be spent for emigration, £50,000 for company expenses, £50,000 for public works, £15,000 for religious endowments, £15,000 for a college and £20,000 to 'encourage steam navigation' – surely Arthur's initiative. The price of approximately 30s an acre was expensive but the 50 per cent increase was seen as of no consequence to purchasers who would rush to buy sections once the scheme was advertised.

A New Year letter from EGW to Molesworth superficially suggests that he had become more a man of business. He wrote of yet another new project that 'may be an engine for getting the economy of New South Wales settled; but I wish not to go into it as a company unless satisfied that it will be profitable to shareholders'. But the old puff and hope of the letter's conclusion belies the eternal entrepreneur: 'Let us set about it in earnest. Where there's a will there's a way, and are we not Anglo-Saxons?'[12] Two days later, EGW had changed his mind about New South Wales after he and Arthur attended a dinner with mutual political friends. Now there was enthusiasm for Molesworth to give up the political life, so frustrating for a liberal in England, and become the head of the second New Zealand settlement, which could be named after him. Molesworth would have Arthur for the practical donkey work: EGW considered his brother 'eminently qualified for fagging at such work, having the whole subject at his fingers' ends, with confirmed habits of industry, order, duty-going and with courage and good-temper to boot'.[13]

Molesworth, though only 30, knew both himself and EGW better than to be inveigled into the scheme. He wrote to his lawyer, Thomas Woolcombe, 'I do not feel that either my *health* or *character* qualify me to be the *popular leader* of an expedition. I do not see what position I would hold, or what I should have to do . . . My chief use would be, first, in this country as a great *decoy-duck* to tempt emigrants; secondly, in the colony as a sort of *pigeon* whom every one will feel he has a right to pluck . . . Besides this there is too great an inclination on the part of Wakefield for stage effects, and too much will depend on them to satisfy me . . . lastly, I can't put reliance on Wakefield, because he has too many projects afloat.'[14]

Molesworth was wise to stay out of the Nelson project because there were no ready takers for the new settlement's allotments and it would be sited not where the company chose but where the Crown's representative, Governor Hobson, decided was appropriate. Despite increased advertising, and special offers, by the time the ballot was held at the end of August only 371 allotments had been sold and three-quarters of these were to absentee landowners or speculators. Income was only a third of what had been expected and the new settlement would begin life with a large disproportion of labourers to owners, throwing the burden of the workers' welfare directly back on to the company – that is, Arthur.

Despite the obvious prescription for failure, the company pushed on, sending off the first three emigrant ships without gaining fitness clearances from the government's Emigration Commissioners. This was to prove disastrous for the *Lloyds*, the first ship to leave on 11 September. Unaware of the dire problems unfolding in its wake, Arthur's expedition sailed on with discipline and solemn purpose. Aboard the *Whitby*, he put the improvers to learning the rudiments of surveying and illiterate labourers to reading, writing and arithmetic. Tuckett followed a similar and clearly prearranged programme on the *Will Watch*.

At sea on 17 May the Nelson Literary and Scientific Institute was established by Arthur and the ship's officers to provide a cultural centre for the new settlement. The young gentlemen cabin passengers had about 700 books on board that would form the basis of its library and, when they called in at Tenerife on 19 May, a sum of money was collected and sent back to England to purchase more books and periodicals. The officers started a newspaper and the calibre of the labourers on board was demonstrated by their starting a rival newspaper and making plans to start a Mechanics Institute. Not all the labourers were so sober-minded. Three men were put in chains for stealing grog and clothes; when two of these managed to escape and hide in the main hold to sample the wine cellar they were handcuffed for the rest of the voyage.

The first ship to reach Wellington on 28 August was the *Arrow*, a fast brig carrying stores which had left London a month after the barques. The *Will Watch* arrived on 8 September and the *Whitby* ten days later. The slow passage of Arthur's ship was partially due to the 'Ship making a great deal of water' for most of the voyage that required pumping every two hours.[15] But it was an opportune moment to arrive. Governor Hobson was making his first tour of the southern regions of the colony and the site for Nelson could be promptly and properly decided upon.

On the arrival of the *Will Watch*, William had tried to get Hobson's agreement to establish the new settlement in the South Island on a site that had a good port and 200,000 acres of farmable land. Hobson, exerting the prerogative handed him by Russell, said that he must consider matters other than the company's well-being and that the ownership and availability of the southern lands remained unclear. Privately, he was concerned at a new settlement emerging well beyond the scope of his resources to administer from Auckland. He suggested the new colony be placed near Auckland, on two separate sites, knowing full well that this proposal was impractical and would be anathema not only to William but to the majority of the Wellington settlers who had remained unflinchingly hostile towards him.

William had fostered this conflict in the interests of the company, and as a distraction from its and his own shortcomings. In February 1841, Wellingtonians condemned the governor at a public meeting and in a petition sent to Queen Victoria and both houses of Parliament. At the same time, William had gone ahead with surveys and settlement plans for both Wanganui and Taranaki, bypassing Hobson by dealing with Gipps and then providing Somes in London with the ammunition to attack both Gipps and Hobson at the Colonial Office. Hobson had not helped himself by lauding the properties of Auckland, repeating Shortland's derogatory commentaries on the Wellington climate and soils and encouraging Wellington labourers to leave for the north. It was the foundation of a rivalry and enmity between the centres that has persisted to this day.

Sam Revans worked as chief anti-Hobson propagandist: 'You have the power of annoying us for a time; but it will not be difficult to crush you, and the paltry coterie by whom you are ruled.'[16] In private, Revans described Hobson as '50 years old and 70 in age',[17] an unkind reference to the appearance of a man aged prematurely by stroke and tropical disease and only a year or so away from death.

It is unsurprising, therefore, that Hobson was not enthusiastic about assisting William and the Wellingtonians when he arrived there for the first time on 19 August. The manner of his reception provided the atmosphere for contest rather than co-operation. According to Jerningham, the settlers 'were convinced that they had an enemy to meet, instead of a kind guardian to greet with welcome. An admirable feeling of respect for their own dignity induced all to scout the idea of hissing the Governor on his landing.' Hissing was resisted but Hobson's boat grated on to a 'silent and almost deserted beach'. At a levée held a few days later, only 40 people turned up and the movers and shakers of the settlement declined to pay Hobson attention and give him support until he 'displayed a disposition to make amends for his injustice'.[18]

Among Hobson's staff were missionary George Clarke, Protector of Aborigines, and Te Wherowhero, the Waikato chief, whom Hobson introduced to William as the 'sole owner of Taranaki'. Clarke consulted with local Maori about the company land purchases and consequent disputes. The struggle for political dominance, with its underlying personal enmities, is represented by Jerningham's account of the continuing wrangle over payment for the Te Aro pa site. Clarke was handed a paper in Maori (presumably prepared by a missionary) which stated that payments given to Te Wharepouri in October 1839 had been passed on to his sister as a present and had never been intended as payment for Te Aro land.

> Mr. Clarke, in translating this paper, stopped at the word *tuahine*, 'sister,' and stammered, and smiled, and turned to the Governor, and hummed and hawed, and looked at the paper again, and then looked at Colonel Wakefield, and finished by drawing a long face and being very grave. Upon being pressed by the Governor to explain what he meant, he shuffled, and smirked, and sneered; and then held the paper out, and broadly asserted that it named these goods as the payment which had been given to 'a woman, whom Warepori had let Colonel Wakefield take on board the Tory.' The conception, and the manner of the insinuation, were both such as none but a low-minded man could have been guilty of.[19]

Jerningham would have been hard put to defend any similar imputations towards himself but, as for Uncle William, 'It was well known by every one who had been on the Tory, that Colonel Wakefield had not even allowed the crew to bring women on board.' Jerningham challenged Clarke's translation and, with the assistance of Maori at the meeting, affirmed correctly that tuahine had only the meaning of 'sister of a male'. Jerningham wrote, 'I shall never forget the crestfallen looks of Captain Hobson, who had turned triumphantly towards Colonel Wakefield on the beginning of this accusation, and who now positively quailed before his frank and open countenance. Colonel Wakefield looked enquiringly in the face of the agitated Governor; who seemed much ashamed of the whole affair, and suddenly, without assigning any reason, put an end to the conference.' Jerningham implied that Clarke's subsequent demeanour showed the insincerity of his 'translation'. Giving due allowance in this account for Jerningham's self-interest and colouring, the incident nevertheless illustrates the ingrained missionary prejudice towards the company and the Wakefields, and an inclination on behalf of the governor to support it.

The next morning, Hobson invited William to meet again at Te Aro to settle the dispute and William agreed, provided Clarke was not present. At the appointed time, Hobson walked towards the pa with Clarke and 'Colonel Wakefield got on horseback, bowed to Captain Hobson as he passed the two, and rode to one of the cattle-stations out of town'.[20] Hobson, ineptly, had given him little choice on this question of honour and passed up the chance of a settlement. Politically, William had scored a point not lost on Maori.

Hobson sailed south and returned to Wellington from Akaroa on 24 September. In the meantime, Arthur had arrived and George Duppa and H. C. Daniell had returned from prospecting for William in the south with glowing reports of the suitability of Port Cooper on Banks Peninsula and its nearby plains for a major settlement. William, with Arthur, approached Hobson again and asked him for this site to establish Nelson. Perhaps the mutual understanding and deference likely between Arthur and Hobson, both distinguished ex-naval officers, might help the process. The interview on 26 September, however, was reputedly 'stormy'[21] and unproductive but Hobson asked Arthur to put his case formally in writing.

Arthur objected logically to Hobson's persistent offer of an unsuitable area near Auckland and then proceeded to Hobson's refusal to grant a choice of site in the 'middle island'. In his May declaration of sovereignty Hobson had admitted that island as 'British Territory by right of discovery. Your Excellency, however declares it not yet disposable for settlement in consequence of its not having been purchased from the Natives. The Company proposes to proceed to the purchase of any selected district with the co-operation of the local Government and to defray its expences . . . . The approval of the plan of the 2nd Colony by Lord John Russell and the absence of any restrictions as to the middle island gave the Company every reason to believe that it was open to settlement. . . .'[22]

Hobson answered the next day. If his attitude towards the company had been in any way disguised before, it was now utterly plain. In justifying his decisions, he averred, 'the Company continues to sell towns in England which are beyond the actual wants of the colony, and are used merely as a means of carrying on gambling speculations by persons who never dream of becoming colonists'.[23] Hobson's home truth about speculation was, nevertheless, insufficient justification for his unending obstructionism towards settlement by the organisation which had been officially granted a charter, as long as their land claims were proved. Hobson naysayed Port Cooper on the grounds that other claims had to be examined, including, ironically, those of the French. When the Wakefields asserted that, if they were not granted Port Cooper, they would fall back within the limits of the land William had purchased in 1839, Hobson responded by declaring he would be 'perfectly irresponsible for the consequences' and warned of counter claimants. What Hobson meant by the 'wants of the colony' is unclear but, if he saw his leading responsibility as protection of Maori interests, then discouragement of European settlement was one way of attending to it – as a kind of Canute of the South Pacific.

At first sight, William's same day response to Hobson's letter seems curiously obsequious. He hoped that Hobson would allow for a conscientious difference of opinion and would still grant protection to the new settlers. He added, 'nothing but an imperative sense of duty and obedience to my employers' would have prevented him 'from adopting your Excellency's views on this as on other occasions, without qualification or reserve'.[24] But this was a formal statement in response to Hobson's confidential note, which assured William that the government would 'sanction any equitable arrangement you may make to induce those natives who reside within the limits referred to in the accompanying schedule, to yield up possession of their habitations'.[25] Two days after this exchange, Hobson left Wellington and Arthur and William determined to try placing Nelson in a bay called Blind; the irony was appropriate to all the parties to this discussion.

Before the expedition sailed again, young improver Charley Torlesse wrote a first letter to his mother: 'I never expected to see so fine a town as this, or such a beautiful country, the highest hills are covered with most beautiful trees and luxuriant shrubs, finer than any I have seen in the English green houses. Uncle [William] has a nice large house. The houses are made of wood, & the poorer ones are made of common log frame work & filled up with mud or bows of trees and thatched with reeds. There are plenty of public houses. The people appear universally contented with the place.'[26]

For a few days, there was sense of family in William's house on the rise above the Wellington foreshore[27] as he played host to his elder brother and nephews Jerningham and Charley. A public dinner given to commemorate the arrival of the Nelson expedition, was described by Jerningham as being attended by 'seventy of the *élite* of the colony' most of whom left their glasses upturned on the table when a toast was proposed to the Governor of New Zealand.[28]

Sam Revans neatly summarised the root of the enmity between colony and governor: 'Had Hobson visited us at an early period and appeared kind, the complaints which would have been made to him would have ruined the Colonel. A 93 [*sic*] days' passage [of the *Tory*] and a foolish Governor are advantages which are not experienced by all the world.'[29] Revans was unyielding in his attacks on William's lethargy, scheming and manipulation, although in April, apparently convinced that William had long doubted the company's longevity, he wrote, 'Since the charter has become certain his character has much improved. He is acting with more energy and confidence.'[30] He affected surprise that William began 'saying he does not know why Mr Revans has become his enemy – My answer is I am not his enemy, and possibly his best friend'.[31] Publicly perhaps, but Revans's relentless private criticism of William was cancerous. By October, he had a new Wakefield to analyse. He reported to Chapman, 'Capt. Wakefield is a popular mannered man and has energy but I should say the Colonel is greatly his superior in head. Pity he has not more warmth and enthusiasm.'[32]

At the beginning of October, Arthur set sail with the Nelson expedition to examine Blind Bay at the northern end of the South Island. His feelings were a mixture of frustration at being given Hobson's choice; doubt about the suitability of the site following Carrington's rejection of it in favour of Taranaki for the New Plymouth settlement; and a stoic determination to make the best of it, born of a lifetime of submitting to sometimes incomprehensible orders and coping with the unpredictable stringencies of wind and tide. Diplomatically, he called in at Kapiti to confirm the sale of the Blind Bay (Taitapu) land with Te Rauparaha and Hiko, and made good time to be anchored in Astrolabe Roadstead near Kerikeri by 9 October.

Over the following month, Arthur sent crews along the coastline to prospect for harbours and chief surveyor Frederick Tuckett inland with his assistants, including Charles Heaphy, to explore the Motueka and Waimea Valleys. Kaiteriteri-Motueka Maori, anxious for the expedition to stay at the western end of the bay, did not disclose that there was a harbour behind the long boulder bank at Wakatu in the east, and this was discovered only by accident on 20 October.[33] But Arthur made no decision about the site of the settlement until Tuckett came back at the end of the month with news that there were about 60,000 acres of farmable land in the nearby Waimea. This was scarcely a third of the land needed and Tuckett was not convinced of its quality and extent, but Arthur was sanguine that they would find the balance somewhere in the unexplored interior. Once the *Arrow* proved the entrance of the hidden haven on 1 November, and the other ships followed three days later, Arthur decided that this would be Nelson. He had made the 'best compromise he could between the settlement ideally envisaged in London, and the settlement as it was in fact, with restricted land, a superabundance of labourers, and a deficiency of capital. As for the settlers, they too had to reconcile themselves to compromise. . . .'[34]

Arthur had about three months before the first emigrants arrived in which to survey the new colony, sink wells, build accommodation, make first roads and secure the haven as a navigable port. His expedition knew nothing about the land and its soils or the nature of its forests and laboured under drought, rainstorm, unaccustomed heat and mosquitoes. But Arthur set about his task with his usual energy and efficiency, aided by Quaker Tuckett's team of surveyors; and took prayers every Sunday. The only note of dissension was between the dictatorial Tuckett and his better qualified deputy, Samuel Stephens. Stephens threatened to resign but Arthur persuaded him to remain for the good of the colony.

Stephens, like most who worked under Arthur, developed a deep respect and affection for him. He was to write, 'From his experience of the world his advice was of that kind that I could place confidence in. Their [*sic*] was a sterling uprightness in all his actions both public and private which no one could help admiring, and the execution of his functions as a public officer was always founded on the most rigid notions of justice and impartiality. He was humane, amiable, and kind to all alike, poor or rich, and always accessible to the humblest applicant.'[35]

In giving up navigation and gunnery for survey and colonial management, Arthur revelled in his first enterprise ashore after 30 years at sea. On 23 November he wrote to his father in Blois, 'You will hardly expect that we should have fixed upon a site so soon . . . . All I can say is, that I have realised all my hopes, & have found the most pleasing occupation I could have invented for myself. We have got the wing of one barrack up, & now filled with the stores & provisions. The other is in progress for the use of the surveyors; we are all living in tents, which are very comfortable, except in windy weather, particularly mine, which is pitched upon a hill which overlooks both parts of the site of the town. . . .'[36] He had struck Nelson's famous water supply problem, which 60-foot wells had not solved: 'It is rather strange to want water anywhere in N.Z.' but 'The climate is delightful & everybody is much pleased with the country . . . . We shall have a very compact set of company settlements between Wellington, Nelson, New Plymouth & Wanganui & all we want to unite them is steam. Charles Torlesse is doing very well, & I hope will turn out a surveyor, he is a very active boy.'

Others concurred that Arthur was the ideal settlement leader, but he was not a paragon to all. One of Nelson's first settlers, William Curling Young, would soon write, 'I am not *quite content* with him; only I like him, without altogether *trusting* him. Honest he is, indeed, and generous to a fault – there is no want of openness, and most persons would give him credit for ingenuous simplicity, which is not exactly the [same] thing; but when I say, I do not trust him, I mean that his *thought* of today is not his *thought* of Tomorrow, and so his judgment fails, according to me, and then he squares it to meet expedients.'[37]

Was this evidence of the Wakefield gene of expediency or simply of the straightforward naval commander instinctively adapting, watch by watch, to shifts of wind, orders and enemy action? The 'ingenuous simplicity' that had marked Arthur's character since he was a boy might be an advantage in dealings between individuals, but it might prove a flaw in managing the subtle and sometimes complex politics involved in planting a British colony on a Maori shore. For Arthur seemed to accept without question the rightness of the company enterprise under EGW's vision and William's assurance of land title. His experience was with technical and man management and command protocols. He knew nothing of business or politics. As he had advised his father in 1833, 'I do not pretend to be a good hand at interview with lawyers & rogues.'

Arthur seemed to have suspected both types among the Maori he dealt with after arriving in Blind Bay, and approached them with good-humoured condescension. Before starting the settlement at Nelson, he agreed to korero with several hundred local Maori who came to meet him at Kaiteriteri on 29 October.

Nine chiefs went aboard the *Arrow* where Arthur claimed the district for settlement on the basis of William's purchase from Te Rauparaha and Hiko two years before – but he proposed to give them presents as a mark of good faith and friendship before the survey started. The chiefs saw this as an insult, stating that Te Rauparaha had had no right to sell their land and they had, in any case, never received shares of the 1839 payment. And the fact that Arthur declared his presents equal to these shares seemed to support their stand. He could not repurchase formally, however, because this would upset the new Crown pre-emption on land sales. Eventually, the sight of the blankets, guns, gunpowder, tobacco and biscuits became too much to resist and the Maori reluctantly acceded to Arthur's proposition. Johnny Brooks was again the interpreter and once more there were fundamental misunderstandings about who had sold what to whom.

A week after unloading the ships at the haven, Wakapuaka Maori came and demanded the same presents as the Motueka people. Arthur refused, seeing no end to it, and gave them a third of what they asked, which was agreed to after korero. One of the Wakapuaka chiefs, Paremata, then travelled to Kapiti to consult with Te Rauparaha and Hiko. On Paremata's return at the end of November, Arthur dryly recorded: 'He wished to make out that he & Te Raupero were the only heroes of this country, that they had destroyed the original tribe, and that the Motueka people were interlopers. The fact is one hears a different story from each, the individual interest shewing thro' all.'[38] Two months later, Arthur wrote, 'I have learned from a man from Cloudy Bay that several of the chiefs from that place are on their way here to have a talk about the land, amongst whom is one Tommy Streel, a brother of Te Raupero's. Their object, no doubt, is to get something in the way of "utu" (satisfaction). In practice they have no right, but a very small present to a native gets over at once what might become a knotty point hereafter.'[39]

Then, inevitably, there were the missionaries. After holding Nelson's first Christmas Day service, Arthur reflected on the local evangelists of the faith:

> Epiko, one of the Motueka chiefs told me this evening that the missionary at Cloudy Bay . . . had sent to them not to mix with the settlers but to keep apart in the bush. I put some faith in his statement from having observed the last time the other chiefs were over here they had changed their opinions with regard to coming here to build houses. This short-sighted policy of the missionaries, or of some of them, must eventually fail in its object, that of maintaining an ascendancy over the natives. Their wants, their desire to obtain articles of dress & utility will overcome all the influence of such people, who write most pathetic letters to some of the natives here on Christian matters, but close them by begging them not to forget to send the pigs and potatoes.[40]

On Christmas Day, Arthur inspected the men's houses, mostly toetoe-thatched 'warres' of a 'variety of shapes and modes' although the first more permanent weatherboard houses had begun to arise a fortnight before. Arthur counted 56 but early in the new year Sam Stephens reported nearly 100 erected or in course of erection: imminent arrival of the labourers' wives and children was a spur to industry. At Christmas Stephens drank wine for remembrance: 'A glance through the opening of my little tent at the bright Summer Sun – the Thermometer at 80° in the shade – the shrubs and plants in full bloom – the wood in the foliage of spring resounding with the sweet notes of the Tui and other warblers – soon dispelled the charm and brought home the painful reality that I was alone in a far distant clime . . . .'[41]

Christmas for the labourers was an occasion for drinking after three months of 50-hour weeks. New Year brought more drinking and sports, the first games of cricket, foot, canoe and boat races, fencing and musket drill. January brought even more drinking as 'Great anxiety prevails respecting the non-arrival of a vessel either from England or Port Nicholson'.[42] There was some solace for Arthur in a 'small dish of green peas and a salad' as the first gardens produced vegetables of a quality never seen in England.

On New Year's Day, Arthur wrote to EGW with news of the settlement and offered some sensible advice:

> I repeat to you the caution about – too many labourers in consequence of the expense to the Company and also with respect to selection, every selected man either physically or morally becomes a legacy on the Company as a poor rate payer . . . . We shall be anxious to hear the result of our location in England, I fancy you will then have a demand for your land, do stick to letting it only go to settlers, do not be in any haste to sell it, you must give time for settlers to arrive . . . . The only thing you have to do now to establish permanent fame here is to obtain representative Govt. for the Islands, that will come home to every man's door. It may be got perhaps whilst the shuffling of the political cards is taking place.[43]

At last, on 1 February, the *Fifeshire* arrived but the *Lloyds*, which bore the labourers' women and children, did not turn up for another fortnight. On 22 February, Arthur wrote to William, 'We have got the Lloyds at last but in a sad mess, she has lost 65 children and has been a floating bawdy house throughout the voyage, the master at the head of it. . . . The women are all remarkably well and I have no doubt that if proper means had been used there would have been no unusual mortality.'[44]

Arthur had conducted an immediate inquiry, determining that the licentiousness of the entire crew with the unaccompanied women had been led by the captain, William Green, who was previously accustomed to the transportation of convicts to Australia. The children's deaths were attributed to the carelessness of the unapproved and incompetent ship's surgeon, whom Arthur described as a 'prevaricating vaurien' (good-for-nothing). He refused to pay either and fined the surgeon £1 for each death, putting him in debt to the company. The incident was a disgrace and though the company took steps to prevent it recurring, its inquiry was a whitewash. Only Arthur's rigorous handling of the affair ameliorated what he described to the company as the 'excitement, disappointment, and general spirit of complaint which have been caused in the settlement by the unfortunate results of the voyage'.

A week after the *Lloyds*, the *Lord Auckland* arrived and by the end of February, Nelson township numbered 500 citizens owning three bullocks, a cow and calf, 40 goats, 20 sheep, 200 chickens, pigs, dogs, cats, geese, ducks and turkeys. The invasion of the South Island by alien animals had begun in earnest.

Much more significant for Arthur was the arrival on 6 March of Hobson's newly appointed police magistrate, and chief government representative in the colony. A barrister of the Inner Temple, Henry Augustus Thompson had arrived in New Zealand with recommendations from Lord John Russell. A gentleman used to good society, he was described a few months later by Curling Young as a 'fellow of infinite humour – the richest, raciest, best companion I have ever known'. But he was also eccentric, of unpredictable temper and inclined to panic. On his way over to Nelson from Wellington, accompanied by William who had come to take his first look at the new colony, Thompson had sailed in the company's *Brougham*. To save time on a voyage that could take a week, its captain had decided to take a shortcut through the notorious tidal race of French Pass. Unfortunately the ship went temporarily aground on the reef with 1 fathom of water on one side and 7 on the other. From the impact, four bullocks in the hold fell on Thompson's thoroughbred mare. 'Mr Thompson was the most excitable of all men. Although Mrs Thompson was on board all his thoughts were for his mare. Raving like a maniac he shouted, "Oh my mare." "My mare!" "Where is a hatchet? Cut away the mast!" An old sailor at the helm turned the quid of tobacco he was chewing with a look of stoical contempt and replied – "Cut away my ——." '[45] For Arthur, it was the worst of omens.

CHAPTER NINETEEN

Nursed in Blood

OF TWO ARRIVALS IN WELLINGTON in May 1842, one brought William only trouble, the other great joy.

> My dear Catherine, You will be glad to hear that Emily arrived safely, and in excellent health . . . . On the whole she came to me with much less harm from the voyage than I expected . . . . Many thanks for your kind hints & advice about her, which will not be thrown away. I had rather a fright about her. The 'London' arrived [1 May] two days before the 'Clifford' & I was looking out rather anxiously one evening, when some one brought me word that the 'Clifford' was on the rocks at the heads of the harbour. When I went off it had got dark, and after two hours pulling about in a boat I found the ship ashore in the harbour, but fortunately on the shingle beach & no harm done. All the party on board were in a great way, & very glad to see me . . . . I took Emily home by midnight, doubly rejoiced at having her safely landed. I have happily some friends living close by who receive her every day until I can find some proper companion & duenna. . . .

William went on to describe his recent visit to Nelson and the condition of her 'Charley', 'nearly a man'. 'I do not much like the life of the improvers . . . but I really believe your son gets no harm and has learned a good deal. At any rate he is in the way of being made to work to his own exertions, for Arthur makes him work, altho he watches him, that he escapes mischief . . . . Arthur's steadiness & uniformity of temper, with unwearied attention to his hobby [colonising work] have earned him universal good will.'[1]

New Zealand was becoming a veritable family business but William's warm attention to daughter, nephew and brother were only distractions from the enduring difficult business in hand, and he felt no goodwill towards the other May arrival in Wellington, Land Claims Commissioner William Spain. 'We are in a ferment here on account of a Land-claims Commission, whose uncalled for enquiries, disturb the settlers & the natives, but I hope to pull through it as I have done through worse difficulties . . . . My labours thicken on me. Three large & one small settlement [Wellington, Nelson, New Plymouth and Wanganui] engross my whole time & interest. Habit however is a good school-master & unvaried good health waits on & aids my occupations.' Disingenuously, William wrote as if the ferment was entirely of the government's making. In February, knowing of Spain's arrival and his inevitable hearings in Wellington, he wrote to Ward, 'I calculate on the increased and daily increasing power of the Company. The hostility of the local Government must either give way or be removed.' Now his policy of procrastination and dissemblance, after long delays, had finally met its test.

Spain had landed in Auckland on Christmas Eve 1841, eight months after leaving London. His funereal rate of progress meant that he did not arrive in Wellington for almost another five months. Assigned by Hobson to attend exclusively to the company's land claims, he was assisted by nineteen-year-old George Clarke Jr as a sub-protector of aborigines, both to act as interpreter and to take care of Maori interests. The conflict of interest was not lost on Jerningham, who attended the early sessions of the Land Claims Court hearings: 'It seemed almost impossible that the most well-intentioned man should fulfil both offices together with correctness.'[2]

At the time William wrote to Catherine, the court had been sitting for about three weeks and he realised that Spain was determined to undertake a minute examination of the company's purchase, which included thoroughly examining a range of Maori witnesses, as well as any Pakeha counter-claimants. Dr Evans was the company counsel in proceedings and Crown prosecutor was Richard Davies Hanson, who had worked with EGW in Canada and had voyaged out as William's company deputy on the *Cuba*. He had come to understand the fatal flaws in the Wakefield land ballot scheme as it affected Maori but he had been unable to exert any influence on William, who protested to Ward in February 1841 that Hanson was giving him 'all the trouble he can by protesting almost every step I take . . . . I cannot think what he is about.'[3]

In the same month that the Spain court first sat, Hanson wrote a report for the Aborigines Protection Society in which he explained that providing for Maori by selecting sections at random among white settlers took no regard of traditional pa and garden sites and made it difficult for them to grow their own food and supply the enlarging Pakeha market. He also made clear that land 'purchase' for the Maori meant, at most, 'that within certain specified limits, the party purchasing should be allowed to settle upon the same terms as the members of the tribe owning the land'.[4]

Because of the long-distance communication lag, and bureaucratic delays, it was two years before Hanson's report had any effect. The company simply put it aside. But as the court hearings began, William saw that in Hanson and Clarke he faced unexpectedly determined opponents who threatened to expose his threadbare case. Clarke reckoned his 'clients at some fourteen thousand souls,[5] and knew well that a task of great difficulty and unpleasantness' lay before him. Nothing, he considered, was farther from his disposition than to 'try by any means, fair or foul, to upset the Company's claims': he wished simply to find out the facts of the purchase, make sure Maori were not defrauded and find a compromise in any case where 'disputed ground had been occupied by settlers who had bought their allotments on the faith of the Company at home'. This gave young Clarke 'anxious days and sleepless nights, and inured me to the perils of a peace-maker when both sides were too ready to settle everything by a fight'.[6] Clarke described Spain as a 'man of solid intelligence, but with a good deal of legal pedantry about him. He was somewhat slow in thinking . . . steady and rather plodding in his ways, thoroughly honest in intention, and utterly immovable to threats, though he might have been softened by flattery.'[7]

The court hearing began on 16 May in the courthouse on Lambton Quay, a 'barn of all work' that also served as a post office, police station and church. William fondly thought that producing the purchase deeds, and calling Jerningham, Dr John Dorset and Te Puni as witnesses to his case, would be sufficient to prove the company claims under the terms of the new charter, 'compatible with a declaration which [Spain] had formerly made that he had come to carry out the agreement between the Company and the Government'.[8] But Spain (and Hobson) held that the amount of land guaranteed to the company was 'conditional upon the Company first proving that it had fairly extinguished the Maori title. Spain reasoned that if this had not been the British Government's intention, the validity of the Company's titles would have been immediately admitted.'[9]

Steady and plodding Spain would not be rushed. He requested William to produce more witnesses to prove that the signatories to the company's deeds had had both the right and the intention to sell the land. William considered this 'altogether superfluous' and Jerningham 'made himself rudely conspicuous by interrupting the proceedings with outbursts of wrath, and with open sneers at the preposterous and ridiculous character of the demand'.[10] William told the company directors that in the court, 'The scene gave one more the idea of the progress of a long-nurtured, vindictive family lawsuit, than that of a fair, equitable, and court-of-conscience investigation into the real merits of a treaty between a colonizing body and the aborigines, who are anxious to see its conditions fulfilled on both sides.'[11]

He wrote to Spain: 'I had to satisfy . . . the learned Commissioner; and I should have been well pleased if no one else had anything to do with the question; then two Protectors of Aborigines, one of them interpreter in the same cause . . . as an advocate. . . . I had further to contend against two practising professional men, eager to trip me up, and to fasten on the smallest discrepancy in the evidence, as if this case were to be decided by all the niceties of English law . . . I had also every reason to think that some of the witnesses I might have called had been tampered with.'[12] Spain was entirely unmoved by this bluster and when William would not provide more witnesses, took up Hanson's suggestion of calling in Kumutoto chief Wi Tako. When he gave evidence against the company, William 'retired early from the Court, apparently tired out by the harassing and vexatious nature of the proceedings'.[13] The company case had begun to unravel.

William may not have understood the principles of Maori land tenure in 1839 but he certainly must have grasped them by May 1842. In defence of the company's interests and his own position, however, he could not admit their validity, or the protection of Maori interests afforded by the Treaty of Waitangi, or even the application of British law to aborigines in a Crown colony. For William, Jerningham and their many supporters in Wellington putting Maori rights before theirs was a betrayal of British race and civilisation, applying democracy to savages whose rights to land had, until very recently, depended mostly on force. Yet one of the company's grand aims had been precisely to bring civilised law and society to the Maori.

William decided that his only course of action was to obstruct and discredit the court at every turn. A public meeting on 7 June expressed concern that Spain was not independent of Hobson's government and that, by its delays, the court would injure the settlement. But it was William who was slow in bringing witnesses, took his time attending the court (sometimes not turning up at all) and encouraged attacks on Spain in the *Gazette*. Jerningham accused Clarke in print of helping Maori to concoct false evidence and suggested he was perjuring himself as interpreter to the court. Clarke insisted the proceedings halt until these charges were settled and threatened the *Gazette* with prosecution until Revans retracted and apologised. Hanson was so outraged by William's and Revans's tactics and propaganda that he gathered together a committee of 50 citizens who each contributed £5 to found an opposition newspaper, *The Colonist*. Revans described the new paper's stockholders as 'dupes of Hanson and the Government party' but, for the first time, the Wellington public was receiving an alternative political view.

William's tactics served to delay and make life uncomfortable for Spain, Hanson and Clarke but did nothing to weaken their resolve. Clarke observed, 'The agents of the company could have got more out of [Spain] if they had not begun by shaking their fists in his face, grimacing to their utmost power of contortion, and defying his authority in a very larrikin sort of manifestoing.'[14] Despite Jerningham's contemptuous description of Clarke as a 'gaunt lad of 18 who had evidently got his tail-coat on for the first time' (Jerningham was all of 21) and whose 'tender years and very imperfect education seemed to imply the certainty of his incapacity',[15] the missionary's son soon got the measure of his persecutor. 'Young Edward was very eccentric, and there was a certain strain of rowdyism in his composition that did more harm to himself, poor fellow, than to those against whom it was directed. He could hardly open his lips without uttering some bitter sarcasm against those he disliked, and he was not at all particular in whose presence he did so.' Of William, he wrote, '[he] would have been a master of diplomacy if he had only had art enough to conceal his art, but he always, in any negotiation, betrayed his subtlety in scheming and put the other side on their guard lest they should concede more than they meant to. . . .'[16] While Revans was publicly barracking for the company, his private correspondence supported Clarke's opinion: 'The most striking point in his [WW's] character is his suspicion – it is plain to everybody'.[17]

Spain's court was not William's only concern. He had to deal with growing numbers of unhappy settlers who were now discovering, on arrival in Wellington, that their country sections were not just down the road from the town, or even across the harbour in the Hutt Valley, but 100 miles or more up the coast at Wanganui. Knowing the trouble it would cause, he had resisted calls to construct a road to the potentially rich farmlands of nearby Porirua, though its purchase had been inscribed in the October 1839 deed. It was Ngati Toa country and he knew what Te Rangihaeata's reaction would be to settlement. But the pressure to open a road became too great. Revans wrote in April, 'At last it has been successfully forced on the Colonel and he seems now to ride and witness the progress with pleasure.'[18] Four settlers were granted a licence to build in the Porirua district, despite Te Rangihaeata's belligerence, and, when they did, his men destroyed their work. A public meeting on 20 April voted angrily for Te Rangihaeata's arrest but the Chief Police Magistrate, Michael Murphy, seized on Spain's arrival and refused to take action until land ownership questions had been settled in court. The settlers' ire at Te Rangihaeata's 'outrages', quietly stoked by William, revealed, as Clarke had observed, that they were 'ready to settle everything by a fight'. Edmund Halswell, the company's Commissioner for Native Reserves, travelled to Porirua to settle things down with Te Rangihaeata while Hanson, knowing that nothing would come out in the *Gazette*, wrote a long open letter to Hobson, describing Te Rangihaeata as consistent in his refusal to accept the right of the company to any of the land. For the moment, this issue was calmed but disputes, claims and counter-claims throughout the Wellington region, Wanganui and Taranaki continued to bubble and fizz dangerously.

By contrast, all was sweetness and light in Nelson. Jerningham spent a month there before the Spain court hearings and, bereft of polemic, his writing was at its evocative best when he described the six-month-old colony:

> The little village at the haven was all life and gaiety. Two large wooden stores and a house for immigrants, belonging to the Company, were the centre of business, as labourers came for their rations, or rolled casks and bales into the store. The Lord Auckland was discharging immigrants on the beach; the two Deal boats of the Company were being launched or hauled up by their weather-beaten crews, or making

> trips to the shipping; and knots of whalers, who had come on a cruise to the new settlement, were loitering about on the scattered cannon, ploughs and cart-wheels. Among these beach-combing wanderers, I recognised many old acquaintances. Some of these eccentric characters seemed curiously divided between contempt for the inexperience of the 'jimmy-grants', as they called the emigrants, and surprise at the general industry and bustle prevailing. The cloudless weather, hotter than any I had yet felt in New Zealand, and the vivacity of the scene, made one think that races or a fair was going on, rather than serious settlement. All seemed affected by the bright blue sky and lovely scenery around . . . . every countenance beamed with good humour and enjoyment. The very whalers would now and then condescend to show an awkward clodhopper the handiest way of hauling a package up the sloping beach.[19]

Writing to his father at the same time, William Curling Young confirmed Jerningham's sense of the settlers' mood: 'You would clap your hands if you could see what great things we are doing here . . . . As for coming back to England, I know not what to say. It is something to be here, and to be doing what we are, and to be what we are. I love you all as much as I ever loved you, and should like to see you all again; but my life is in Nelson and my place is here.'[20] Young, the company's immigration agent, would indeed never return to England: he was drowned in the Wairoa River just four months later. Two hundred people attended his funeral and the town shut down in mourning for this well-loved early citizen. They might have also mourned for the end of the optimism he epitomised under the cloudless weather of Nelson's first busy and booming year.

Arthur and his colonists were increasingly beset by problems resulting from too many labourers and too little good land and capital. Ship after ship turned up with men looking for work but few with the capital to provide it. The company had promised to employ anyone out of work at a guinea a week but as the number of unemployed grew beyond expectations, Arthur's duty to find relief work for them building roads put such a strain on his budget that he was forced to reduce relief wages to 14s, plus rations worth about 5s. In April there were 50 men unemployed but this number steadily increased throughout the year until there were 300 in December.

Chief Surveyor Frederick Tuckett and his assistants ranged far and wide, trying to locate sufficient land to fulfil the colony's requirements. By September, it was clear that, including Massacre (Golden) Bay, there was a deficit of 50,000 acres and that much of the land set aside for farms had soils of doubtful quality. Pessimistically, Tuckett considered from his surveys that there were probably not more than 200,000 acres of good land in the whole of New Zealand. But Arthur was determined to have farm cultivation under way before spring and arranged for the first selection of surveyed suburban and rural sections at the end of August. Although almost all the sections were quickly disposed of, not more than a quarter of the 25,000 acres was actually taken up, because there were too many absentee owners and too little capital. The colony's newspaper, the *Examiner*, urged people to go forth and sow – 'It now remains for *all* those who came out to farm to leave the town for their own and its good' – but even from among the colonists who did, many lacked the skills to clear and farm this new country successfully.

Before the survey of Massacre Bay could begin, it was necessary for Arthur, bearing gifts, to visit and parley with local chiefs. He was accompanied by a party of surveyors and friends, including poet and writer Alfred Domett, who reported for October issues of the *Examiner*. In early September, the party visited pa near the Tata Islands and talked with Maori, all of whom – men, women and children – smoked short clay pipes. 'The young women ran about in dingy shifts – bead necklaces in two or three rows round their necks – the shark's tooth, set in sealing wax, fastened in their ears with a black ribbon – giggling like mad, all impudence, fun and ugliness . . . . Among these uncivilised, we civilised (in our own opinion) squatted or stood familiarly . . . . Captain Wakefield with Scotch cap, stick and snuff-box, quiet twinkling eye, and slow smile, nudging the interpreter, in his slow, easy way to ask this question and that.'

A party then visited Takaka, Arthur leading the way up the highest hill within reach 'at a steady and well-maintained pace, characteristic of the man'. From there they obtained a good view of the valley and were encouraged to explore it and establish a survey station. Arthur held discussions with chiefs from Tata, Motupipi and Takaka. 'As much distrust of each other and disregard of the interests of their neighbours was shown by these "children of nature" as could well have been displayed at a congress of European ambassadors, dividing an enemy's spoil among "holy alliances" of selfish sovereigns.' Agreement was finally reached about who had the right to what and the usual blankets, guns, flour, sugar, axes, tobacco and clay pipes were distributed. On 10 September, Arthur's party went ashore at what is now Collingwood and had a quick look at the Aorere Valley. Here they found three shipbuilders using local timber and Pakawau coal for their forge; one recognised Arthur as his old commander, which 'caused his respect to rise to reverence heat'.

Arthur's visit seemed to confirm another 40,000–50,000 acres of useful farmland to the colony and to settle arrangements with local Maori. This encouraged a group of Nelson settlers to form the Massacre Bay Coal Association and they set off in October to open up New Zealand's first mine. Despite Arthur's gifts and blandishments, local Maori knew that the company's claims to land in the area depended on the adjudication of the Spain commission and, when the association investors refused them a share of the new coal trade, they decided to sabotage the undertaking by pulling down landing stages and destroying casks. Chief Puakawa, according to the *Examiner*, 'stamped, ranted, wielded his tomahawk, and foamed at the mouth until he nearly provoked what he richly deserved

– a left followed by a right hander'.[21] Editor George Richardson thought that the Maori should be taught the 'supremacy of the law' before the coal merchants took the matter into their own hands. Magistrate Henry Augustus Thompson agreed.

As one of only two government officials in Nelson, Thompson had been left to his own devices in the realm of law and order. He was also Postmaster, Protector of Aborigines and Registrar of Deeds. Hobson refused to make Thompson a judge until he had proved his worth as a magistrate and he was allowed the assistance of just one clerk and six constables and gaolers. Money was slow in arriving and sometimes he paid costs from his own pocket. These, plus charges to the government for services rendered by private individuals, were often not reimbursed for months, if not a year or more.

Neither Hobson nor a deputy bothered to visit the settlement and for four months between April and August in 1842 no communication of any kind was received from Auckland. Although this was principally caused by shipping delays, and Hobson had severe administrative problems of his own, the settlers soon formed the impression that Hobson cared not a fig for their fate and that they might as well run their own affairs. In Nelson as in Wellington the company fostered an anti-government feeling to explain or distract attention from its own shortcomings.

The government despatches received in August did nothing to alleviate any problems associated with law and order or land tenure. Early in September the *Examiner*, a company supporter, declared, 'Incompetence is stamped upon every act of Governor Hobson. Our interests have been and are being daily sacrificed to the inability, pique, partiality, or indifference of the man whom utter want of consideration for the necessary qualifications for the office has been made Governor of New Zealand.'[22] The paper demanded his immediate recall, echoing the demands of settler groups throughout the country, including Auckland. But the editor of the *Examiner* must have marvelled at his own direct influence on Providence: a week after the editorial appeared, on 10 September, Hobson died of a stroke.

The relationship between the senior company officer and the senior government official depended a good deal on Arthur's patience and tolerance of Thompson's eccentric and sometimes overzealous behaviour. He was accustomed to tearing out his hair when in a rage, which might be occasioned by something as trivial as damage to a gooseberry bush. In April, Arthur wrote William, 'I fear Thompson will get a hornets nest about his ears from his irritability of temper & continual interference in trifles.'[23]

A month later his actions as postmaster were causing Arthur problems: 'Thompson has become very punctilious in one branch of his nominal multifarious duties and seized upon all parcels & letters by the company's bag and made some pay heavy postage for land orders etc, so pray send no more bags let letters go by the Post office or "per favour". . . it was in one of his Excellency's irritable fits that he made these changes & he has I believe written a dispatch to the Governor illustrating his zeal for public service'.[24]

In calmer, more rational mood, Thompson was fine company and, as joint leaders of the settlement, he and Arthur had to find a *modus vivendi*. It is likely that Arthur, as the senior and experienced manager of men, did most to make the relationship work, in his 'slow and easy way'. Thompson could have had only respect for Arthur's organisational skills and Arthur was the first to recognise Thompson's skills as a horseman. On an early ride to view the country sections, astride his own Slyboots, Arthur was 'pleased with the horses not caring about the fern and cantering thro' the flax, Thompson was with me who is no bad pioneer a cheval'.[25]

In one area, they seemed to be in general accord, as were most of the settlers: how to handle the Maori. Four days before the *Examiner*'s editorial on the Massacre Bay coal affair, Arthur wrote to William, 'Our natives in Massacre Bay are beginning to bounce, they have prevented the coal working party from proceeding in their operations. If we can make out a case of assault Thompson is prepared to act, which I think will put an end to it. It is only two of the least civilized of the party who move in the affair.'[26] It seems as if the initiative to punish the Maori at Massacre Bay was Arthur's – not Thompson's as is generally supposed – and that Richardson editorially created the climate for the action from knowing Arthur's mood. In September, however, Thompson had already upset Wakapuaka chief Paremata who, in a shooting incident, had been badly wounded by a lesser chief in a challenge to his authority. Applying only British law, Thompson disregarded Maori protocol and severely damaged Paremata's mana when he declined to take action against the offender, ruling that Paremata had provoked the attack.

The Reverend C. L. Reay, Nelson's resident clergyman, tried to conciliate in the Massacre Bay affair but failed and on 15 November, Arthur, Thompson and 25 men ostensibly sworn in as constables and armed with a 'goodly assortment of most rusty swords and cutlasses', sailed for Motupipi. Clearly, the intention was to show who was now master. A 'court' was established at a landing place up the Takaka River and when chief Puakawa refused to appear to face charges of destroying the lime kiln and casks, he was coerced by a special constable and brought to the bar in handcuffs as the armaments were brought ashore. Puakawa pleaded that he had acted in anger at the Pakeha's refusal to buy coal dug by the Maori, and for this he was fined a total of 10s with 10s costs. His offer to pay the fine in pigs or potatoes was declined and he was not released until his wife produced a sovereign.

When the police business was over, Thompson put on his Protector of Aborigines hat and gave a lecture on the perfect impartiality of British justice. 'It is doubtful whether his audience was impressed, either by the impartiality of the law, or by the dual role of its exponent. Amid a round of promises for good conduct by all parties, Thompson and his escort departed, hoping that their display of court and cutlasses would serve as a permanent deterrent.'[27] Tuckett regarded Thompson's elation at the result of the affair as 'ridiculous' and that only Puakawa's death by drowning six months later prevented his initiating warfare to restore his mana after the humiliation of this 'trial'.

Arthur's excursions to Massacre Bay provided the only diversions from the endless work of managing the new settlement and the construction of his house and garden on the hill overlooking the entrance to Nelson haven. Although Alfred Domett's eulogy of him is necessarily seamed with praise and affection, it affords an insight into Arthur's character, life and work during 1842–43. Early in the morning he would be seen 'chatting with natives gathered round his door, the result generally being a gift of a blanket, or payment of a promised bag of flour or sugar'. On his daily walk from the port to the town Arthur would be

> stopped at every other step; listening, with benevolent aspect, patiently, to all sorts of unreasonable complaints, unreasonable requests; digging his stick in the ground, or taking a pinch of snuff, the only symptoms of emotion shown; now making some little job of work for this man on his own account; putting down another's name for the Company's employ; here advising with a newcomer as to the best employment of his capital; there anxious to learn from a country settler the state of his crops, all the details of his progress; now disentangling with the newspaper editor some puzzling problem of colonisation made a science, with its intricate, ever varying, yet mutually dependent elements; then interesting himself in some old woman's fresh litter of pigs, or cabbage, the pride of her heart; discussing with this man the run of a new boat – with that the practicability of a plan for working the flax plant; – assisting every rational enterprise, dispelling every fainthearted misgiving, with money where possible, with countenance and kindness where not; ever less anxious to lead than to suggest and assist; now at a public meeting, speaking calmly, earnestly, rationally; now helping to organise a literary or agricultural society, or visiting and superintending a children's school . . . .

Francis Jollie confirmed Arthur's 'perfect coolness and self-possession . . . small impressionability . . . . a man of the world [with] a very practical, business-like turn. . . . There was no "beating about the bush" . . . at the same time there was none of that frigidity and want of earnestness of purpose which generally characterise men of similar temperament.' As Domett explained, Arthur followed a simple mode of life, 'In a little house – but an open one; with large hospitality, but plain and unpretending; rising at midnight from the sea-cot he always used, to watch a ship enter harbour, then not so familiar to the pilots – on a boat-excursion, wet through and shivering, yet refusing the dram sent round – setting an example everywhere of indifference to luxuries, of frugality, temperance . . . duty appearing taste or accident.'[28] Although they had scarcely known each other here, indubitably, was Priscilla's grandson.

At the end of June 1842, Arthur wrote to William, 'It is an unheard of position to be in, the government not acting in unison with the settlers with respect to native claims and only canting as to their protection. I wrote to Martin [William Martin, New Zealand's first Chief Justice] some time ago saying that the settlement of the land claims ought to be the next object of the govt. if they wished the islands to advance in the formation of a nation. . . .'[29] William was no doubt heartened by his brother's support but the Spain court hearings were going steadily against him as a succession of Maori witnesses confirmed that their land had not been sold, that the consent of all members of each tribe was necessary for such a thing to take place. Spain considered occupation the only criterion necessary to substantiate a Maori claim.

As the court hearings dragged on, George Clarke Jnr reported, 'Things were in such an inflammable condition in that town [Wellington], that it would have taken very little to bring on serious disturbances at any moment between the settlers and the Maori.' Clarke was pilloried as a 'raw-boned youth', 'a nigger youth' and 'half civilized' for his attention to the Maori. 'There were foolish, hot headed people enough who were bent upon forcing on a conflict between the races. They thought that the natives could be intimidated by demonstrations, or cowed by bullying. . . . There was never a more ignorant, extravagant and dangerous exhibition of the folly of despising your enemy. The native Chiefs on their side dreaded a collision, not from personal fear of an encounter, but because they knew that it would be like the letting out of water from a dam. . . .' Clarke 'went from one side to the other with my life in my hand. I went daily about the town with the feeling that I was a sort of portable fire engine, ready at a moment for the cry of fire . . . . It was a pretty lively experience for a young man's nerves.'[30]

As William was steadily backed into a corner, Spain, too, found himself in a difficult position. He could have easily made a quick decision that the company purchases were invalid but what about the settlers who had purchased their sections in good faith in London? This would not only have raised Maori expectations, it would also 'have been cruel to punish [the settlers] for the sins and blunders of the Company. Mr Spain, therefore, determined to spin out the proceedings, so as to give time for some workable compromise. . . .'[31] It was simply impossible to turn back the clock on a town that now had 3500 settlers, six times the local Maori population. In this sense, William's procrastinations had worked.

Spain judged that the Maori were more interested in obtaining a larger payment than in dispossessing the settlers – though it would be difficult to persuade them that recompense should be closer to the 1839 land value than the 1842 capital value caused by colonial development. William saw Spain's drift and wrote to him on 22 August. He referred to the understanding he had reached with Hobson a year before and offered to compensate those Maori who had missed out in October 1839 and who were unwilling to leave their land without further payment.

The court hearings dragged on and on and a decision on William's offer took months, complicated by Hobson's death. Finally, in January 1843, Acting Governor Willoughby Shortland visited Wellington and announced his approval of the compensation proposal, directing that the amount of payment should be decided upon by Clarke and a company nominee. William decided this should be himself. He had by now received a reply from London to his advice about the September 1841 agreement with Hobson and the company authorised him to spend £500 and allocate 1000 acres of company lands for the settlement of any land disputes. In later life, when a Congregationalist minister and Chancellor of the University of Tasmania, Clarke averred that 'The Colonel was always privately very kind and friendly to me however fiercely we might be opposed in our political contention'.[32] At the time, he privately advised his father that William was designing, crafty and unprincipled.

The opposition between them intensified in February 1843 when Clarke had interpreter Dicky Barrett on the stand and showed his knowledge of Maori to bear 'much the same relation to the real language of the Maoris as the pigeon [pidgin] English of the Chinese does to our mother tongue'. He had long expected that Barrett would expose all the company's 'vile proceedings' under cross-examination. The whaler was an easy target – simple, semi-literate and, in looking after his own interests, he 'ran with the hares and hunted with the hounds'.[33] Clarke thought him very ignorant, though a 'decent fellow enough among men of his class'.

Through his questioning, Clarke made it clear that Barrett had been unable to properly translate into Maori the wording of Jerningham's deed of purchase for Port Nicholson or the concept of the reserved tenths, both of which had always been, at least partly, a mystery to him even in English. But his long questioning in the court revealed confusion on both sides of the purchase fence and the record throws some doubt on the competence of the court's recorder of proceedings. William had clearly been negligent in his choice of Dicky Barrett as chief interpreter during the October 1839 purchase – perhaps relying more on his tribal contacts through marriage than expertise in the language – but William's and Jerningham's extensive reports show that the meaning of the negotiations was much better understood than Clarke and the court were willing to admit. It was one thing to have Barrett in court to clumsily translate the deed and answer questions more than three years after the event; it was quite another to gain a proper understanding of the discussions and korero of the time. In 1839 the negotiating Maori were strongly influenced by personal and tribal fears and interests, and they were equally so in their representations to the court in 1843. And how 'vile' had the company proceedings and intentions been in the racial and social context of the pre-Waitangi period? The company's management and commercial propositions were a mess but William's attitude towards the Maori had never been worse than paternal; condescending but not vicious; self-interested but not vile. William had maintained from the beginning of the hearings that his dealings with Maori had been conducted in a 'spirit of Justice and openness' and were 'perfectly intelligible and satisfactory to the vendors'.

Clarke considered that the company's 'whole transaction had been of a very hasty and hugger-mugger character . . . . my exposure of all this greatly exasperated the agents of the Company, and made even the settlers who had bought allotments on the faith of the Company, look at me as if I was trying to oust them from their possessions . . . but . . . I knew that the occupying settlers could never have peace until the Maori rights were fairly extinguished'.[34]

At the end of February, Clarke claimed £1,050 on behalf of Te Aro, Pipitea and Kumutoto Maori in compensation for land the company had sold on to settlers. William was staggered by this claim, believing it would lead to others and amount to massive compensation payments in the order of £100,000. He had also just been informed that the company was liable for the commission's fees. He refused to pay up and since payment was expected to follow an established claim, Spain closed the court and went up the North Island west coast to investigate other company claims until the deadlock was broken. William was supposed to attend Spain's hearings at Wanganui but went off to Taranaki so that no cases could be settled. From Wanganui Spain wrote to Clarke, 'Wakefield seems determined to put off the settling of this question as long as he can.'[35] Jerningham recounted that he was sent to Wanganui by William to take his place but that Spain, upset at having waited so long, left before witnesses Jerningham called had time to come down river. On his way back from Wanganui, Spain stopped at Porirua where he was joined by Clarke in meetings with Te Rauparaha and Te Rangihaeata. Spain later reported, 'On my arrival I found neither Colonel Wakefield nor any other agent of the Company, and although Porirua is only 18 miles from Wellington, and I remained there for a fortnight . . . he never came near the place, or sent any agent . . . .' He had 'pursued one undeviating system of opposition and annoyance . . .'.[36]

When he returned to Wellington on 23 May, William and Clarke had still not agreed on the Port Nicholson claims, William insisting that he needed permission from London before paying out such a large sum. Both Maori and Pakeha were losing faith and patience in the commission hearings. Settlers were beginning to seize Maori land and farms in Wellington and Clarke told his father that it took his 'utmost energies to keep the Europeans in check and the natives from adopting violent measures in self defence'.[37]

During the discussions Spain had with Ngati Toa chiefs in Porirua, they declared vehemently that they had never sold to William the wide but unpopulated Wairau Valley which ran into Cloudy Bay on the other side of Cook Strait. Jerningham's detailed accounts vividly describe the attitudes of the two chiefs. The previous July, Jerningham had encountered Te Rangihaeata at Thoms Inn at Paremata during a journey north to the Manawatu. He had found him 'very noisy, asking for spirits as usual; and he requested me to buy him a large quantity, in so arrogant a tone that I refused in rather a decided manner'. The chief 'then went on storming about the land; saying that Wide-awake and I should not have any more; that Porirua was not paid for, and that he would never let White people come and live there. He asked whether we wanted it all, that we were so greedy; and said that he would never sell it unless he received "money gold" in casks as high as he could reach.'[38]

In early March 1843, Jerningham was again on the Kapiti coast and 'had occasion to go in a boat from Otaki to Rauperaha's islet near Kapiti, in order to fetch some goods' and found both Te Rauparaha and Te Rangihaeata there, conferring with Ngai Tahu chief Karetai who had come north from Otago to settle old enmities between the tribes. Jerningham had begun to develop a flax business on the coast and spoke to Te Rauparaha about its benefits for the local people. He replied that 'it was only a plan . . . to make the natives slaves to the White people . . . . he then began to talk about the land with much violence. Te Rangihaeata, too, as usual, excited by drink, ran up and down for a little while using very violent language on the subject. . . .' Te Rangihaeata retired to his hut whereupon 'Rauparaha then pursued the subject in a conversational style, as I lay on the shingly beach close by him, among his basking train.

'"Do you mean to take all the land?" said he; "you are driving the natives first from one place and then from another; are you and Wide-awake to have it all?" . . . and he declared he would stop it. . . . I told him . . . that it was no affair of mine, and that I had no control, over it; that the Governor and Wide-awake would settle between them what he had really sold and pay him for the rest . . . . [he] repeated that he would stop the White people: he didn't care for Wide-awake or the Governor either. They shouldn't have Porirua, and they shouldn't have the Hutt; and they shouldn't have Wairau', which had not been paid for.

Jerningham said that they would always disagree on that point, there was no use discussing it and added jokingly that the 'White people would creep on and get their right at last. I remember being struck by the hyena-like scream with which he said, "Then we'll fight about it!" But I still laughed at his obstinacy, and showed him how unequal a battle it would be if he trusted to force instead of justice. He said, however, that he did not care; "it must be one for one, till either the Maori or the pakeha were kuapo", or "exhausted".' As Jerningham left, Te Rauparaha said that he and Te Rangihaeata were shortly going to Nelson 'to tell the Wide-awake of that place [Arthur] not to survey Wairau, as it had not been paid for'.[39] And Jerningham approved, considering that more talk and more presents from Uncle Arthur would settle the matter.

By the close of 1842, Arthur's problems in Nelson had deepened. Unemployment among the labourers was reaching crisis point and there was still a severe lack of capital. Much of the surveyed land remained unsold. This, along with the lottery system that allocated sections at random to absentee owners, meant much of the best land lay idle. Empty areas between farms that were being developed created all kinds of roading, fencing, drainage and weed problems. And most of the land taken up could not be brought into production without considerable investment in buildings, machinery and stock. Above all, despite the Massacre Bay accession, there was still not enough good pastoral land available to yield the quantity of wool and sheep by-products that would earn the colony a living. As the company's agent, Arthur came under increasing pressure from disgruntled settlers to find solutions. He held out to them the hope that new farmable country would be found somewhere in the unexplored regions to the south. At this time, the only other parts of the South Island known to Europeans were harbour regions on the east coast, such as Banks Peninsula and the Otago Peninsula, and the northern and southern coasts frequented by sealers and whalers. The entire west coast region and the interior of the South Island remained a mystery.

In November 1842, Arthur sent off surveyor John Cotterell to probe south-east beyond the Wai-iti and Motueka Rivers. From their headwaters, Cotterell found a pass (Tophouse), which led east to the Wairau Valley. Over a journey of three weeks, he travelled down the Wairau to Cloudy Bay; went east into the Kaiparatehau (Awatere), past the present Lake Grassmere and as far down the coast as the Clarence River. He returned to Nelson with the news that nearly 200,000 acres of empty land were available in this Wairau-Awatere region (Marlborough).

Cotterell's news brought excitement and relief as the settlement prepared to celebrate its second Christmas. Settler Francis Jollie wrote to a friend, 'Our country lands may yet, in the great bulk, be looked forward to as of some tangible value . . . land for the greater part, that we shall be able to get upon, and at once make contributory, in the shape of pasturage . . . to the permanent prosperity of the settlement.'[40] The fact that the Nelson settlers were able to make light of the long and difficult land access to the Wairau; that it was in a region distinct from Nelson; and were able to ignore the persistent statements of Maori that the Wairau had not been sold, were all evidence of their desperation to find a solution to the settlement's problems. The Wairau became the golden panacea. When he heard of Cotterell's expedition and report, Te Rauparaha's older brother Nohorua, the leading chief of Cloudy Bay, visited Arthur and voiced his opposition to any settlement of the Wairau. But Arthur could not afford to pay heed, and relied unquestioningly on the belief that it had been included in William's purchases. He asked Chief Surveyor Tuckett to go with farmer and JP Captain Richard England to make a more thorough inspection of the area in February 1843.

More persuasive than Nohorua's warning had been a labourers' strike. On 16 January, Arthur wrote to William, 'We have had a strike to day of all our road party demanding the guinea a week which I have refused to accede to. I suppose they will return to their work by & bye, but there is literally no employment for our people except the company's works. . . .'[41] Opening up the Wairau would give them even more.

Tuckett and England came back from the Wairau on 5 March, 'well satisfied with the district and describe it as fit for any purpose, that is to say 40,000 acres of superior soil and 50,000 more of good grass land & in all including Kapari-ti-ha round the white bluff, about 200,000 acres'.[42] Tuckett advertised for tenders for the land's survey. It was this that prompted Te Rauparaha and Te Rangihaeata to travel to Nelson from Porirua to tell Arthur 'not to the survey Wairau, as it had not been paid for'. They arrived on 11 March with Hiko and a band of Ngati Toa warriors and held 'violent koreros' with Arthur, Tuckett and Thompson. During the first, according to Tuckett, 'Rauparaha spoke with all the blandness and suavity of an artful woman. Rangihaeata on the other extreme at once denied and defied and never opened his mouth but to breathe forth threats and defiance'. When Te Rauparaha was shown the survey plans in Tuckett's office, he regarded them with open contempt as 'gammon humbug'. Te Rangihaeata declared that if any Pakeha went to the Wairau he would drive them away and that they would not have it 'until we had killed him'. At the beach he harangued his followers about killing all Pakeha who would go.[43]

Te Rangihaeata's antipathy towards the Pakeha and their land demands was, by now, obdurate. He had sensed from the beginning that any concessions to the Pakeha would bring a reduction of mana: that they did not want use of Maori land but its complete possession, which would finally extinguish Ngati Toa power and thus his own. He had also developed a contempt for the power of Pakeha law to administer justice or to inhibit his actions. The reach of English law over Maori was still unclear. Six weeks before, Chief Justice Martin, dealing with a charge of felony against Te Rangihaeata for his belligerence to the Porirua surveyors, had ruled that, under the current circumstances, natives could not be bound by English law. Any expectations Te Rangihaeata may have had that Pakeha law would sensibly protect Maori interests were dispelled in April when the Supreme Court ruled on the rape and murder of Kuika, daughter of a Ngati Toa chief, at Port Underwood. The Maori wife of ex-convict Richard Cook told her people that he was the murderer and Maori were determined on immediate utu but were persuaded by missionary Samuel Ironside to let Cook go to trial in Wellington. In a farcical application of English law, Mrs Cook's evidence was ruled out on the basis that a wife could not testify against her husband. Cook fled the country and the need for utu burned unassuaged in Ngati Toa hearts.

During the visit to Nelson in March, Te Rauparaha's behaviour was, as usual, ambiguous, alternating between threat and a willingness to co-operate provided the price was right. In this case, a 'very big' cask of gold would have induced him to hand over the Wairau, whether it was his to sell or not and, with some of this in mind, he suggested the Wairau question be referred to Land Commissioner Spain.

On 12 March, Tuckett recorded that 'another interview took place at the agent's office; Rangihaeata equally violent and intractable as before; Rauparaha less complaisant, having no further presents to hope for; the agent [Arthur], firm to his purpose, calmly replied to his threats by informing that if they did molest or interrupt the surveyors, he would take three hundred constables with him to the Wairau and make them prisoners; they parted, Rauparaha affecting courtesy; Rangihaeata sincere, but implacable, refused with contempt, all presents which we carried out of the store for him'.[44] In the street, they insulted Tuckett and Cotterell, telling the latter they would kill him if they ever caught him in the Wairau and would 'bung-a-bung' or shoot Arthur Wakefield.

Arthur appears to have been unimpressed by both Te Rauparaha's and Te Rangihaeata's statements and behaviour. He wrote to William on 17 March,

> Te Raupera and Rangaieta have been here bouncing about the Wairau, I maintain that it is in your deed & also in Mrs Blenkinsop and that I shall only give presents upon settling as in the case of the Motueka etc. . . . He [Te Rauparaha] declared we had a right to all these districts and that we might shoot any of the natives who disputed our title, but claimed the Wairau as unsold. He is a terrible old villain – I gave him a present nevertheless upon his visit as well as Rangaieta & Hiko – Te Raupera said he would not allow the surveyors to proceed, Hiko says it is all bounce. I promised to make a [prisoner] of Rangi if he committed a breach of the peace.[45]

That very same day, Nohorua's three Christian sons turned up in Nelson from Cloudy Bay, anxious to stop any Wairau survey and suspicious that Te Rauparaha had made another sale. Rawiri Puaha, the eldest, said the alleged 1839 sale was a fraud in which his people had been deceived. They turned down all offers of presents in order to let the survey proceed, including a schooner which Puaha coveted.

By this time, it should have been plain to Arthur that Ngati Toa were serious about their opposition, but he was blinded by a combination of factors: the pressure for more pastoral land; his conviction that William's purchase was valid; his belief that the Wairau was largely unused by Maori; his certainty that the settlers were bringing the benefits of civilisation to a savage race; and his confidence that the problem could be dealt with as Motueka or Massacre Bay had been managed. He did not deny prospective difficulties, as he made plain to Acting Governor Willoughby Shortland on 2 May: 'I fear Te Raupera and Rangihaeata will give us some trouble, as they are drunken travelling disturbers of the peace. There can be but little sympathy with them as (the self called) dispossessed of their fathers lands.'[46] Arthur revealed no sign of respect for the mana and power of these senior Ngati Toa chiefs.

During the three months from 12 March to 12 June, there was a sequence of altercation and skirmish as Nelson surveyors pressed on with surveying the Wairau and groups of Ngati Toa tried to disrupt the survey and see them off. Cotterell's ranging rods were pulled up and another surveyor had his sawpit destroyed and his whare pulled down. Cotterell went back to Nelson at the beginning of May and returned to the Wairau on the 13th with instructions from Arthur that, in the meantime, the surveyors must make peace with the Maori as best they could. They would, though, be indemnified by the company for any loss and 'in case of actual injury to property the magistrates would take immediate measures to apprehend the offender'.[47]

In Porirua, meanwhile, Te Rauparaha and Te Rangihaeata waited on William Spain. On 12 May they exhorted him to go at once to the Wairau and settle the claims. Plodding Spain cogitated overnight and then informed them that he could not go until after the June session of his court in Wellington. He said that they should stay away from Cloudy Bay and not disturb the survey until that time. Urging Spain, 'Be quick, be quick!', the two chiefs decided to take the law into their own hands. On 1 June they landed in Cloudy Bay with two dozen armed warriors and proceeded to round up the surveyors, escort them to the beach and send them off to Nelson. Keeping their promise to Spain not to harm any Pakeha, or to steal or damage any of their possessions, they simply destroyed those objects made from the 'products of the land, which they regarded as rightfully theirs, such as ranging rods and survey pegs of manuka, and whares of poles, raupo and toetoe'.[48]

By 12 June the Wairau was empty of Pakeha and a group of, eventually, 125 Ngati Toa men, women and children moved up river to establish potato gardens, a confirmation of ownership. Only John Barnicoat and his assistant Robert Crawford were left at the beach to look after an accumulation of provisions and equipment until a boat turned up from Nelson. On 14 June Barnicoat recorded, 'Two canoes arrived with potatoes for the Maoris . . . . They informed us . . . that Mr Spain was coming over to Cloudy Bay in a fortnight's time to settle the Wairoo land question. I was very much pleased to see the entire confidence they appeared to feel in the Government Commissioner.'[49]

The Nelson settlers did not share this confidence. They were already at sea, bound for Cloudy Bay to teach the Maori a lesson. Before their departure, Arthur had written to William on the 13th to say that he had heard on Sunday that 'Te Rauparaha and Rangi had commenced operations on the Wairau', and had burnt one of the surveyor's houses. 'The Magistrates have granted a warrant on the information; and Thompson, accompanied by myself, England, and a lot of constables, are off immediately in the Government brig to execute it. We shall muster about 60; so I think we shall overcome these travelling bullies. I never felt more convinced of being about to act right for the benefit of all, and not less especially so for the native race.'[50]

A week before, Arthur had told William that 'The natives have offered very little resistance' and that he was planning to go to the Wairau with the 'usual presents' for the Cloudy Bay people.[51] But Cotterell's arrival on the 12th with news of the burning had caused Arthur to urge Cotterell to lay a complaint with Thompson. As well as remaining Police Magistrate, Thompson had been appointed a county judge and there were now six other magistrates in the Nelson settlement.

The magistrates had felt uneasy about bringing Te Rauparaha and Te Rangihaeata to trial for obstructing the survey on land still under adjudication but they considered the new information was sufficient pretext to arrest them for arson.

Thompson decided to go to the Wairau immediately to execute a warrant and, within 24 hours, assembled a party of gentlemen, constables and labourers, armed with the same kind of motley collection of muskets, cutlasses and pistols that had been used to 'make a show' at Massacre Bay. The group of gentlemen included almost all the leaders of the settlement: Arthur, Thompson, George Richardson, editor of the *Examiner* and Chief Prosecutor; Thomas Maling, the Chief Constable; Captain Richard England; William Patchett, the company agent for absentee owners; John Howard, the company storekeeper; and surveyor John Cotterell. Johnny Brooks the interpreter was taken along, and about 30 labourers, constables and other surveyors. While en route in the government brig *Victoria*, the expedition met evicted Chief Surveyor Frederick Tuckett at sea and he and his men were persuaded to return with the arresting party to Cloudy Bay. By the time the expedition was all ashore at the mouth of the Wairau on 16 June, and had met up with Barnicoat and Crawford, it numbered 49 men: 33 had muskets, a few had cutlasses and nearly all had pistols.

When the expedition had first come together in Nelson, the feeling among the gentlemen was that they were off on a bit of lark. But it was recorded that, as Arthur packed up in the early hours of the 13th, he was 'deeply anxious'. By the time the party landed at the Wairau, any high spirits had been dampened. Although most of the gentlemen remained convinced that their show of strength would settle the matter, Captain J. H. Wilson, a passenger on the *Victoria*, declined to join the party, convinced the chiefs would not surrender. For the conscripted labourers, 'nor was their honour or their interest in any way engaged . . . . They had nothing to fight for. The New Zealand Co. had been their greatest enemies and deceivers.'[52]

The arresting party made their way up the west bank of the Wairau, expecting soon to meet up with Te Rauparaha and Te Rangihaeata. Instead they encountered Puaha. 'He seemed extremely concerned when Mr. Thompson informed him on what errand we had come and when he saw the armed party. He proposed that we should return to Port Underwood and pledge himself on the part of Rauparo and Rangiharta that they should come there. . . .'[53] He considered that the two chiefs, ensconced further up the valley, would certainly consider that such a large group of armed Pakeha had come to fight. Thompson was unmoved and said the chiefs must come aboard the *Victoria*. The expedition camped for the night after crossing the river to the east bank.

Thompson, as senior magistrate and judge, was the chief government representative in the party and responsible for executing the warrant. The other gentlemen of the party might seek to advise or influence him, but he had the ultimate legal authority. If they could not agree with his decisions then their only recourse was to withdraw, like Captain Wilson, although Quakers Tuckett and Cotterell could decline to bear arms. Under the implicit authority of class, the surveyors, constables and labourers must largely obey orders.

By the time of the encampment on the night of 16 June, Arthur found himself in an invidious position. He was the recognised leader of the Nelson settlement, and he had instigated and shown himself eager to support Thompson's execution of the warrant. Like everyone else, he had had enough of the 'travelling bullies' and considered they should be brought to account. It is what would be expected of any decent Englishman. But beside the campfire under the kahikatea that night, his training, long experience and instincts as a naval commander all told him that the expedition had become extremely risky. In gunnery parlance, it had become a long shot. As a manager of men, he was sensible to the morale of the labourers and knew that very few of them had handled firearms before. In short, it would be impossible to exercise any kind of controlled military action. By contrast, he had noticed that Puaha's followers were well armed and had learnt that the number of Maori upstream considerably outnumbered the Pakeha. Puaha's demeanour and exhortations – 'we do not want a fight, we do not want a fight' – confirmed that Te Rauparaha and Te Rangihaeata were prepared for one. The situation had become more serious than Arthur had anticipated. Twice that night he tried to persuade Thompson to abandon the expedition. Twice that night, the adamant, cantankerous magistrate refused.

Arthur was torn. If he made public his position and announced that he was withdrawing, then this would split the expedition and leave the stubborn Thompson with few followers and in an extremely dangerous position. Even if Thompson also felt compelled to withdraw then, either way, the political consequences for the settlement would be immense. There was, too, the question of losing face before Te Rauparaha and Te Rangihaeata and it is likely that even Arthur would have found this difficult to stomach. He had little choice but to continue on, consider the welfare of the men around him and try, as he always did, to manage the outcome and make the best of the circumstances. As he lay in the camp that night, his mind perhaps wandered over the many difficult and life-threatening situations he had encountered during the past 30 years, and wished for a 50-gun frigate offshore and a party of marines. The words of Captain Beaver may have come whispering down over the years: 'My force is sufficiently strong to make all attempts at resistance futile and vain. I therefore summon you to surrender . . . hostile operations will commence . . . a very severe example . . . and a dreadful retaliation. . . .'

The arresting party left camp before sunrise on 17 June and proceeded upstream, first by boat and then on foot, until they came to the Maori encampment near where the north-south-flowing Tuamarina Creek met the Wairau.[54] Puaha had forewarned Te Rauparaha and Te Rangihaeata of the Nelson party's intentions, arms and numbers by Puaha and, as vastly experienced warriors in the New Zealand terrain, they had chosen the most favourable ground for an encounter.

The Maori were largely concealed among bush and scrub on the flattish west bank of the Tuamarina. Of 80 or 90 warriors, half were armed with muskets and the rest with hand weapons of various kinds, including steel tomahawks. Some of the muskets and tomahawks had been among the payments made by William in the October 1839 purchases. In approaching the Tuamarina from the east, the settlers had to descend a bank beneath a steep spur; the creek itself was too deep to wade but narrow enough for a long canoe to act as a bridge.

Short of the creek, on sighting about a dozen Maori, Thompson halted the party and divided the armed men into two groups under Captain England and Howard, giving them orders to remain out of sight and not to fire unless ordered. This arrangement indicates most clearly that Thompson appreciated the potential for violent confrontation.

Thompson went down and crossed over the canoe bridge, accompanied by Arthur, Richardson, Tuckett, Cotterell, Patchett, Maling and with Brooks to interpret. Te Rauparaha appeared and Thompson flourished the warrant, saying that he had come to arrest ('make a tie of') him and Te Rangihaeata for burning Cotterell's whare and they must come at once aboard the government brig. It was scarcely credible to the 'Old Sarpint' that such a force would have come such a way for such a trivial reason and he guessed accurately that this was simply an excuse to remove the two chiefs and take control of the Wairau. Reasonably, he said that Spain and Clarke would be coming over from Wellington soon and the matter could be settled then. Thompson quickly lost patience, saying it had nothing to do with the Land Court but was a case of arson and if Te Rauparaha was not guilty he would be freed. The argument intensified, and Brooks could not keep up an accurate interpretation. Barnicoat, within earshot on the opposite bank, was sure the Maori could not or would not understand the legal points Thompson was trying to make. As Thompson became more and more excited and Te Rauparaha more and more stubborn, Puaha, clutching a Bible, tried to intercede, but Thompson told him 'roughly to hold his tongue'. He had grown 'very excited and talked loud'.

Finally, Thompson ordered Te Rauparaha to come with him. According to Tuckett, Thompson said, 'There is an armed force, and they shall fire on you if you don't go.'[55] Twice Thompson asked Te Rauparaha to come and twice he refused. At this, Thompson had Chief Constable Maling produce handcuffs and made to take hold of Te Rauparaha's arm. Brooks called out in alarm and Richardson exclaimed, 'For God's sake, Thompson, mind what you're about!' There was confused shouting from both sides and a group of Maori warriors raised their arms. Alarmed that Thompson was about to be attacked, Tuckett urged that all the party be brought together on the west side of the creek. There is no record that Arthur said anything or took any action to this point.

Te Rangihaeata suddenly appeared from the bush shouting, 'What do you want with Rangihaeata? Does he come to make a tie of you? Does he go to England to take your land? Has he destroyed your tents or anything belonging to you? Who is your Queen? I am all the same as Wickitoria!' This 'excessively exasperated' Thompson, who ordered Captain England to 'bring on the men'. Puaha's people rushed to the canoe to prevent the Nelson men crossing the creek but Thompson grabbed it, shouting 'In the name of the Queen!' Arthur helped Thompson straighten the canoe and gave the command, 'Forward, Englishmen, forward!' The Maori rapidly withdrew and took cover as five or six men with muskets crossed and Thompson ordered them to fix bayonets. Te Rauparaha called out, 'Don't fire!' as he sought refuge, taking Thompson's earlier threat to heart.

At this point a musket went off. Maori said the Pakeha fired on them first and the Pakeha witnesses offered three different accounts: that it was impossible to tell who fired first; that a musket went off by accident as one of the untrained men blundered across the canoe; or that it came from the Maori side, particularly from a man who had been suspected of stealing a boat. Barnicoat's judgement was that the Nelson party was the first to attack, in making the advance across the creek, 'but no one can say which was the first to fire'.

Now everyone began firing, Ngati Toa in response to Te Rauparaha's cry, 'Farewell sun and light! Welcome darkness and death!' On the Maori side, about half a dozen were killed in the exchanges of fire and the first to fall was Wanganui chief Te Ahuta and then Te Rangihaeata's wife, Te Rongo, from a stray musket ball in the head. The Pakeha on the west bank scrambled back through the creek, using the canoe for assistance. Patchett was mortally wounded as he scrambled up the east bank and Constable Bernard Gapper shot a Maori who was aiming his musket at Arthur. John Barnicoat's first-hand account tells what happened next.

> There then began to be a general move up the hill. The shots were whistling by very numerously, and we could not see where they came from. Our men loaded and fired very deliberately but after loading were at a difficulty in finding an object to fire at, and were obliged to fire very much at random. Seeing two or three killed and several wounded and being unaccustomed to scenes of bloodshed and . . . not being able to see their foe . . . the men retired up the hill. Several shots came among us while ascending. On getting up into clearer ground there was another stand made. Here too the Mouries had a cover of manuka bush and we still retreated. By this time Captn. Wakefield, Mr. Thompson, Mr. Tuckett and others had joined us.

Thompson was wounded. 'We at last gave way till we fell back on a brow seemingly very defensible. Here Captn. Wakefield called on the men to stand their ground. One man pointed to eight or ten that were walking away over the plain and said he would stand if all the others would.'[56] Although Howard tried to rally them, more men saw discretion as the better part of valour and took to their heels, firing aimlessly as they ran.

This behaviour was later described as cowardice and claims were made that if all the men had stood together and faced the Maori they would have prevailed. But

Barnicoat noted, 'All things considered there appeared to be a great deal of courage shown by our party . . . . I saw several of the men loading and firing with the greatest possible coolness. But they were still undisciplined and unaccustomed to meet bloodshed to meet men almost nursed in blood. The Mouries were old and expert warriors and fought in exactly such a situation as they could have desired.'[57]

Arthur and Howard retreated to the next brow of the hill and, seeing that there was now no hope of gathering together the scattered men, Arthur decided that their best hope of survival was surrender. Thompson waved a white handkerchief and Brooks called out, 'Kati! Kati!' ('Peace! Peace!). One Maori emerged from the scrub, holding out his arms in a gesture of peace but Pakeha further up the hill, not hearing Brooks's call, continued firing and the exchange continued. At that moment, according to Barnicoat, Quaker Cotterell 'stood back from the rest and said "This is no business of mine. I don't approve of this. If there are any men of mine here let them follow me". Captn. Wakefield turned round and said very earnestly, "For God's sake Cotterell don't run away. You are sure to be shot if you do". Cotterell waited a little while and then came among us again . . . . Captn. Wakefield saw that the only chance of safety was for all to throw away their arms and lie down. We then all lay down on the short fern. I had not been on the ground half a minute before three shots had entered the ground close by me.' One killed Constable Maling. At this, Barnicoat decided he was off. Tuckett and another man joined him. Soon they were in flight, leaving a remaining dozen on the hill.

As a group of about 20 Maori advanced with Te Rangihaeata, Cotterell went down the spur, appealing to a man he had earlier been friendly with. He was grabbed by another and Te Rangihaeata tomahawked him in the head and back.[58] He had delivered on the warning given to Cotterell when he was in Nelson. Brooks gave a final call of 'Kati!' and then tried to escape but was overtaken and butchered so savagely that he could later be identified only by his clothing.

The warriors advanced to meet Arthur, Thompson, Richardson, Howard, Captain England, one constable and three other remaining men. They all gave up their weapons and were taken down a short distance to face Te Rauparaha, Te Rangihaeata, Puaha and their followers. Glaring at Arthur, Te Rangihaeata cried, 'Let the white people be killed for our sister [Te Rongo]. They have meddled and without cause have killed a woman in war.' Arthur called for Brooks to translate; but poor Johnny had forever lost his tongue.

The three chiefs then sat down and argued about what to do. The Christian Puaha still wanted peace, arguing that the lives of the prisoners should be saved, that Ngati Toa had killed three times more Pakeha than Maori had been killed. Te Rauparaha also thought it would be a good idea to keep the prisoners as hostages for a New Zealand Company barrel of gold. Te Rangihaeata was outraged at this idea and Te Rauparaha was silenced by his vehement reminder that the Pakeha had killed Te Rongo, Te Rauparaha's daughter and his wife. For that, there could be only utu in kind. Te Rauparaha could have no answer to this.

The coats of Arthur, Thompson, Howard and the constable were removed. As the Maori prepared for their execution, one of the men, George Bampton, managed to move away on the pretext of urinating and then slipped off and hid. He heard sounds of chopping and, when Richardson and Howard attempted to run but were caught, Howard saying, 'For God's sake if we are to die, let us die together.' Te Rangihaeata killed Arthur first with his greenstone mere, Te Heketua, and then Thompson who, typically, tore out his hair in his death agonies. Others killed England and the three remaining men. When the Ngati Toa had finished the executions, they fired their muskets and cheered.

On 21 June, Arthur's body was discovered by the Reverend Samuel Ironside who had come from Port Underwood, now deserted by Maori fleeing from the expected retribution. 'Captain Wakefield had no gunshot wound; his head was dreadfully cut about the forehead by a tomahawk, penetrating into the brain.'[59] A piece of damper bread had been placed beneath his head as an insult; his watch was missing, reputedly buried by Te Rangihaeata with Te Rongo. Two days later, William arrived at Tuamarina as Ironside was burying the bodies of the more than 30 Nelson settlers killed. William wrote to Charles Torlesse a week later, 'Arthur, tranquil in his last moments as during life, died calmly, with scarcely a change of countenance & in an attitude of resignation and repose, tho' not of cowardly submission. His wounds were all in front & his pistol which had missed was in his hand.'[60] William knew that this is what they would want to hear. It was also appropriate to write to the man of the Stoke-on-Nayland household, so that he might find the right way to break the awful news to Catherine, and then to their father Edward in Blois.

William also knew where the blame should be laid: 'I consider that poor Arthur's life has been sacrificed by a hot-headed, inexperienced man [Thompson] who exasperated the natives by gesticulation & threats when they might have been subdued by firmness & calmness'. William would not – could not – admit any responsibility arising from all the prevarications, delays and enmities he had been responsible for during Spain's hearings, and his earlier dealings with the chiefs. The power of his grief, and perhaps his sense of guilt, were not to be publicly expressed for almost four years. After a toast for the Wairau fallen at a public dinner in Nelson in 1847, 'Those present were awed by the grief of Colonel Wakefield, who seemed "as though in an agony of recollection and retrospect" from which he only gradually recovered.'[61] The image of Arthur, that best boy in the world, with his head savaged, open to the brain, would haunt William until the end of his life.

CHAPTER TWENTY

Cui bono?

EDWARD GIBBON WAKEFIELD'S APPENDIX to the 1839 Durham Report was replete with his theories of planned settlement, sufficient prices and assisted emigration. But settlement based on controlled land prices for a country as vast and various as Canada, with its still unsettled legislatures and its uncertain borders with the free-for-all United States made little sense, either geographical or economic. In the months following the publication of the report in February 1839, EGW's energies were mostly devoted to New Zealand, the floating and promotion of the company and the despatch of William on the *Tory*. But his work as proxy Commissioner of Crown Lands in Canada with Durham, and the hospitality of Durham's private secretary, young Edward Ellice, at the Ellice seigneury upstream of Montreal, had created an opportunity for both a circumscribed application of his theory and the bonus of a tidy income.

Throughout the nineteenth century, the building and control of canals between key rivers and the Great Lakes were central to the thinking of all Canadians who sought better communications, improved trading opportunities, development of the west and secure defence lines against cross-border raids by the radically democratic Americans. The St Lawrence-Great Lakes east-west waterway link, between the Atlantic Maritime provinces and the wild western lands, ran close to the American border. For 120 miles between Upper Canada (Ontario) and New York State, the St Lawrence River *was* the border and the danger of American aggression seemed real enough in the early 1820s for British military engineers to construct a canal-lake link that allowed ships plying above Montreal to bypass the St Lawrence entirely, via the Ottawa River, en route to Kingston on Lake Ontario.[1] The American threat was, as ever, also commercial, as by 1825 United States developers had completed canals linking Buffalo on Lake Erie with the Mohawk-Hudson River system running down to New York, providing an American transport system for Canadian produce. Four years later, Canadian engineers finished the Welland Canal, bypassing the Niagara Falls. There was now an uninterrupted waterway between Montreal and Lake Erie, but the Ottawa section was tortuous and limited in capacity. Canals to bypass the rapids of the St Lawrence along the American border became an increasing priority and source of speculation. Not surprisingly, Edward Gibbon Wakefield spied the canal that was needed for more than just the political union of the two Canadas.

EGW had learnt from Edward Ellice that his father Edward 'Bear' Ellice wanted to sell Beauharnois, 270,000 acres of settled farming country on the south bank of Lake St Louis and the St Lawrence River. It was less than 20 miles upstream of Montreal, a growing metropolis of 30,000 people, and within relative coo-ee of the New York State border. 'Bear' Ellice had bought it from the Lotbinière family in 1832 for £50,000 but now the land was somewhat run down, properties had been pillaged during the rebellion and there were boundary and rent disputes with some of the French Canadian settlers. After making an inventory in 1838, Edward advised his father that, though the estate might be worth up to £150,000 if it were improved and Canadian prosperity restored, he would be lucky to get half that in its currently dishevelled state.

But the £150,000 figure stuck in 'Bear' Ellice's mind when, in January 1839, EGW first wrote him, acting on behalf of the North American Colonial Association of Ireland (NACAI), which sought to buy the seigneury. The NACAI had been incorporated in 1835 but until now had made no effective entry into colonial settlement. EGW soon began playing a double hand, 'acting for both parties' as Ellice later admitted, when he privately agreed to take a 5 per cent commission on the proceeds if he could persuade the company to meet Ellice's price. To the NACAI, EGW reinforced Ellice's claim of his estate's value by pointing out that the Beauharnois land held a premium as the logical location for a canal bypassing the Cedar and Coteau Rapids of the St Lawrence River between Lakes St Louis and St Francis. For EGW the deal meant 5 per cent of £150,000 or nothing and he was at his most persuasive. The EGW-Ellis deal, later widely known in Canada as a 'notorious jobb', reveals EGW's (and Ellice's) cupidity at its worst. It also exposes how disingenuous had been EGW's protestations of commercial innocence at the New Zealand Company dinner on 20 March of that year. But as his brief Canadian career ran its course over the following five years, EGW showed himself constant to his past eccentric and ambiguous behaviour as financial self-interest became inevitably intertwined with political motivations, pure and impure.

The directors of the NACAI refused to meet Ellice's price but EGW was able to persuade the association's banker, Colonel Henry Kingscote, to take entire responsibility for the purchase. But Kingscote could not raise enough even for Ellice's required down payment so EGW went back to the directors and persuaded them to accept Ellice's price if Kingscote provided most of the money that was needed immediately. A deal was made in August 1839, though both EGW and Ellice probably foresaw that the full £150,000 might never be raised. Ellice received £20,000 down payment and offered EGW £1,000 as a first instalment on his commission.

On 16 August, EGW visited Ellice's lawyer, Joseph Parkes MP, and told him that he wanted his full £7,500 on signature of the agreement. Parkes refused and reported to Ellice, 'However he is greedy I see, & did not prove himself early in life very nice about getting money. Probably he wants you to buy his remaining commission. But I advise you to hold firm on this point.'[2] Ellice would pay no more until he had actually received his money and the two arch wheeler-dealers wrangled until Ellice refused to deal further with EGW except through Parkes, to whom he raged, 'He is a most dangerous man . . . like the Bull in the China shop, ready to shatter any thing round him to pieces. And yet, he has a great Durham tame completely in his hands! What ingratiation!'[3] There is no record of EGW's opinion of Ellice.

Parkes reported to Ellice on 4 September that EGW had visited him again on the 'old subject' of the commission and 'as usual was full of projects . . . . he is the type of the French book on . . . the Eternal Restlessness of Man. He has a highly gifted intellect, bad morality, & an insane physical tendency.'[4] This last phrase, married with Ellice's 'Bull in the China shop' comment, throws a rare light on the question of EGW's emotional stability and fits with Buller's estimate of his rashness. They all seem to reinforce the picture of EGW – and his view of himself – that he was temperamentally unfit for any role other than theoriser and entrepreneur.

As theoriser, EGW now began to develop the NACAI's plan and prospectus for colonisation of the Beauharnois, contriving to be made a director of the company, which he made contingent on Ellice settling the commission. Parkes reported to Ellice on 3 January 1840 that EGW said

> he cd not & should not harness to the car till he & you were agreed fully . . . . Wakefield requires to be a Director – and Kingscote showed me a letter Wakefield has written to him from – quoting one from Lord Durham in which Lord D. agreed to be a director if required provided he [Wakefield] took command . . . . Kingscote between ourselves fears Wakefield's name in the Directory. . . . he did not so much fear the Miss Turner dirt as the Will Cause [the 1824 case]; and that he must consider seriously before he & others tacked his name with Wakefield's in a Public Body . . . .

Parkes went on to reveal that when the battle to pass the South Australia Bill was taking place in the house in 1834, thirteen MPs agreed to support the bill only on condition that EGW held no office in the settlement company. Parkes advised Ellice that neither he nor his brother should be associated with EGW in any company. 'Use him and pay him to get afloat any company; that is another matter, but one of his paramount objects is to "get over his errors" by his name being mended in company with his betters. If he ever succeeds out will be poured his history by the Turners or some enemy, with all its injurious consequences.'[5]

The next day, in the City, Parkes saw Kingscote, who said he had advised EGW that some 'straitlaced men' such as Lord Fitzwilliam, governor of the NACAI, would object to his being involved prominently, and that EGW was 'more reasonable & would work underground' in some secondary capacity 'being of course properly remunerated'. Parkes considered that in this way EGW

> will get up & work a successful company.
>
> His full character however you ought to know, and its effulgence is only known by the Will cause – a perfect stench with the Bar, of all the courts & those who know the case.
>
> I do Lord Durham the justice to believe that he is ignorant of that case, or I cant believe that he would put himself in the power or in confidential communion with such a man . . . . it was no business of mine to make an enemy of Wakefield by informing Lord Durham, nor in fact had I the most remote idea that he intended Wakefield to join him in Canada.[6]

Many of his colleagues and associates, even Durham (and all earlier writers on Edward Gibbon Wakefield) had been distracted by EGW's use of the Turner abduction as a blind to draw attention away from the earlier will case. He would never find sympathy and rehabilitation following perjury and forgery but there would always be a sneaking sympathy for someone who had appeared to suffer so much at the hands of society for something so youthfully rash and quixotic as running away with a young heiress. After all, had he not behaved as a thorough gentleman and then given himself up, faced the consequences? Had he not, as William Hutt had put it two years before, 'more than atoned by a long period of proscription and most patient suffering'? But how much had Hutt known?

Joseph Parkes obviously did not tell the dying Durham the truth about EGW in January 1840 either. And he had underestimated both the skill of EGW's tactics and Ellice's 'habitual and well-known confidence in his own judgment'[7] in the face of good legal advice. During the course of 1840, EGW moved steadily towards his full commission, got a place on the NACAI directorate with Durham and prepared the prospectus for 'Colonization of the County of Beauharnois'. Ellice was paid partly in cash and partly in shares and strongly influenced the restructuring of the company, which included the appointment of his brother Russell and City friends as directors, in particular Sir George Simpson, governor of the Hudson's Bay Company. But there were also the usual investors associated with EGW's schemes of this time: George Fife Angas, William Hutt, Lord Petre, John Abel Smith and Joseph Somes. While Ellice was pleased with himself, EGW was well placed to win.

Although the Beauharnois prospectus was under the signature of the secretary of the company, its language leaves no doubt as to its author. The methods of colonising consisted of a 'combination of the means requisite, not merely for placing people, but for *permanently establishing society* in a new settlement'. With the exception of a small portion, 'The superior fertility of the county of Beauharnois may be said to be notorious throughout the neighbourhood . . . . The climate is the same as that of the parts of North America whose progress in numbers and wealth is the most remarkable.' EGW puffed the importance of Montreal but also asserted that the French Canadians had impeded communications development with Upper Canada, and were antipathetic to the American get-up-and-go attitude of 'making war on the wilderness'. The impending union of the two Canadas would change all that and one of the 'main objects' of those advocating the union was to improve navigation on the upper St Lawrence. Across the Beauharnois land a ship canal was projected, to overcome the impediment of rapids whereupon the 'only interruption in thousands of miles of water communication would be removed'.[8]

The Beauharnois scheme called for the sale of 'triple orders' of land made up of a 100-acre farm lot and two town lots. A prospective purchaser had to deposit £200 before he could be entered into a ballot for the lots. Even if all the lots had been sold, the yield would have been £200,000, scarcely enough to cover the purchase from Ellice and the improvements promised, let alone a profit, although a tenth of the lands was reserved to the company. The NACAI was not rushed off its feet by investors. The real attractiveness of the scheme depended on the canal and, as usual, EGW had oversold it. The Beauharnois Canal project had not been officially approved and landowners on the northern Soulanges side of the St Lawrence were equally anxious for profit from a canal and were pushing an equally valid case.

Canadian governor-general Lord Sydenham had begun steering the two Canadas towards union and had set up his capital at Kingston at the Lake Ontario end of the Rideau Canal. Although Durham's union proposal had been accepted by the British government, his recommendation of self-government had not, despite 'Bear' Ellice's support as a Whig grandee. Ellice rightly saw that a local government with self-interested autonomy would be more motivated and better equipped to compete with the economic and political pressures of a dynamic United States. But the road to responsible self-government would be gradual, and Sydenham acted more in the capacity of a prime minister, making his own appointments to an executive council that was a coalition of English interests, ensuring majority support in the new legislature.

Sydenham had a low opinion of land companies, especially when he saw that 'scamp E. G. Wakefield' involved in promoting the Beauharnois scheme through the pages of the *Colonial Gazette*. In January 1841 he had written to Colonial Secretary Lord John Russell criticising the NACAI's plan 'which might have done very well for Australia or New Zealand but had been ridiculed by everybody in Canada'.[9] Probably aware of Sydenham's views, John Abel Smith, one of EGW's key supporters, organised joint meetings of all the land companies with an interest in Canada in early January 1841. This resulted in a memorial to Sydenham, written (but not signed) by EGW, urging the governor-general's support of a 'great body of the colonists, who ardently desire that no time may be lost in adopting measures to promote public works and emigration'.[10]

On 6 April, Sydenham dismissed the memorial in a despatch to Russell, before he had received Russell's own despatch of 26 March which strongly supported the memorialists 'amongst whom are some persons of considerable wealth and commercial eminence' who sought to invest in the improvement of navigation of the St Lawrence. He could not dictate to Sydenham, but Russell commended his attention to their projects and advised him that the 'memorialists propose to despatch some person as their agent to communicate with your Lordship on this subject'.[11]

Sydenham's reaction to this was private warmth and official dismissal. On 6 May he wrote Russell that he would have none of it because he had just completed a financial scheme of his own and did not wish to have it menaced. But only three days earlier he had completed two interviews with Sir George Simpson on Hudson Bay Company matters during which Beauharnois had been raised. Simpson reported to 'Bear' Ellice on 3 May that Sydenham had changed his thinking about the NACAI scheme, because he wanted to improve his estranged relationship with Ellice in order to encourage British investment in Canada. He had told Simpson that he would 'forward the views of the Association by every means in his power'. Simpson wrote, 'measures will be concerted immediately for carrying either a ship canal or railroad through Beauharnois, for establishing the company in a land agency business under the sanction and protection of the government. . .'.[12] What was Sydenham up to? Did his own financial plans involve Beauharnois opponents, or did he just wish to exert his political authority with the Colonial Office? Sydenham had kept indifferent health for much of his life and he had only just recovered from a 'very distressing illness' that may have affected his behaviour. An unmarried 'sensualist', he ran an establishment said to 'acknowledge . . . the sway of at least one mistress'.[13]

On the back of Sydenham's 6 May despatch James Stephen noted, 'It gives little reason to expect that the projectors will be very successful.' Under-Secretary Vernon Smith wrote for Lord John Russell's attention, 'Might not Mr. J. A. Smith see this? It certainly is a strong opinion for the seductive power of Mr. Wakefield to overcome.' On 12 June, Russell replied, 'This may wait till the [Canadian] assembly meets, and Mr. Wakefield has detailed his scheme.' At least Russell did not underestimate EGW's chances of bringing it off.

On 2 May, less than a week after seeing Arthur off to New Zealand, EGW had left England for Canada in the company of another NACAI director and supporter, John Auldjo. Sydenham wrote to Russell on 25 May, 'So Wakefield has arrived after all. I have not yet been able to see him, but I am told he is determined to support my Govt. – it cannot be for long tho', as I can do nothing for that horrid swindle of Beauharnois even if I were ever so much inclined. However I shall try to keep him out of mischief at all events.'[14] It seems that Sydenham's comments to Simpson three weeks before had been diplomatic oil.

EGW had to move fast. The first session of the Legislature of United Canada opened on 14 June and he had to present a convincing case before then if he was to achieve legislative support for the Beauharnois scheme. By 9 June he had completed a detailed six-page 'Memorandum Relating to Navigation Improvements' for the benefit of Sydenham and his executive councillors. In another Wakefield sales *tour de force*, EGW admitted and nicely diminished his self-interest. He exhorted the new government to show that it could work in harmony, to prove opponents of the union wrong. 'Confidence in the stability of the new order of things will thus be produced in England; and in this way legislation for improvements may provide the means of carrying into effect, by disposing British capitalists to advance the requisite funds.' Following legislative harmony, 'public improvement should be begun & completed as soon as possible . . . . The noise of the breaking of stones for the roads in the Island of Montreal is more agreeable to every order of British colonists, than the finest words of promise. . . .'[15]

He then proposed a grand plan, 'facile communication *all the way* from the Ocean to the further Lakes'– building canals not bit by bit, frittering public funds, but as a considered whole that would generate confidence in Canada's future and thus encourage large-scale investment. Beauharnois was a key part of the project: 'The personal pecuniary interest which I may have in promoting an outlay of money in the Beauharnois district is so very small, that it need not deter me from urging the superiority of the south side of the St Lawrence for the works. . . .' The chief reasons were the scheme's supposed cheapness and the encouragement it would give NACAI's investors to promptly provide funds on favourable terms and to undertake other improvements in the area. Currently the NACAI's charter allowed it to operate as a bank so it would be making a loan to the provincial government which, EGW suggested, could augment the funds by taxing unimproved wild lands in the hands of 'the great land-owners who are the principal bane of this country'; and from revenue raised from the sale of waste lands, following the principles which 'form the creed of a new colonizing public at home that is now carrying all before it'. It is doubtful if Sydenham, who had now been deeply embroiled in Canadian affairs for a year and a half, would have set any store by EGW's land sales and tax theories.

On 14 July, a month after the first Legislature of United Canada opened, J. W. Dunscomb, member for Beauharnois County and EGW's political proxy, moved that the petition of the NACAI, praying for leave to make roads and loan money for public works, be referred to a select committee. Despite immediate opposition the motion was carried and five days later a bill was brought in from the committee giving the required permission. After its second reading the bill went into committee on 26 July. It was fiercely debated and its opponents managed to adjourn discussion from week to week, postponing its return to the assembly.

Also on 26 July, Sydenham sent a despatch to Russell: 'I have been happy to avail myself of the presence of Mr Wakefield' in order to learn the intentions of NACAI, and that 'the objects which the association at present have in view and the proposed mode of carrying them into effect are likely to be attended with great advantage to the Province'. He supported the Beauharnois scheme provided the Association's charter was changed 'to put an end to the [association's] unlimited power of holding land in the Colony and to any Banking privileges'.[16]

In London on 17 August, Vernon Smith noted on the despatch, 'Mr. Wakefield has won.' He had, perhaps, also heard EGW's triumphant noises in the city upon his recent return. But Lord John Russell saw Sydenham's clever handling of the affair and added, 'I am glad to find Mr. Wakefield proposes to restrain the powers of this Company within proper limits.' On 20 August Sydenham sent the Kingston Legislature his full proposals for public works, knowing that improved navigation of the St Lawrence was a priority approved by most parliamentarians, especially the dominant Upper Canadians. Involving about half all projected public works expenditure, his canal programme was backed by a £1.5 million imperial loan. Sydenham tried artfully to include the Beauharnois scheme as an integral part of the navigation improvement but the assembly did not want to be bound and voted for an unconditional completion of the St Lawrence system.

On 30 August, the bill was passed empowering NACAI to lend money but the way forward was now uncertain and all seemed to depend on Sydenham's continued support. How much this had depended so far on Sydenham's proclivity to stay in favour with Simpson and Ellice and how much on EGW's persuasiveness will never be known. Sydenham's health had begun to deteriorate and in July he had submitted his resignation. A few days after the loan bill was passed, and after he had dissolved the legislature, he fell off his horse, the wound became infected and he died in agony of lockjaw on 19 September. By this time there was also a new government in England, Tory Peel replacing Whig Melbourne, and Lord Stanley had replaced Russell at the Colonial Office. EGW's win was now looking like a loss, but in his long and appreciative obituary of Sydenham in the *Colonial Gazette* he signalled a new approach, another way of ensuring the canal.

Before his first visit to Canada with Durham, EGW asserted that he had been sympathetic to the French Canadian cause but had come to endorse Durham's opinion. 'A miserable race,' he had told Buller. 'This country *must* be made English.' The Anglo-Saxon racism of Durham's report and the expectation that the new union would render English Canadians dominant heightened French Canadian hostility towards the new governance. English had been made the language of the legislature and this also encouraged a patriotic unity among the French members of the assembly.

During his two-month stay in Canada, EGW had noted the close connections between French Canadian leaders and the promoters of the competing Soulanges

Canal, particularly two Roebuck men whose brother, J. A. Roebuck, was a radical MP in London. He had been agent for the old Lower Canada assembly and a confidant of Papineau. During the 1841 debates, French politicians had not actively opposed the Beauharnois project but they were antipathetic to land development companies and there was bad blood from past dealings with 'Bear' Ellice. With Sydenham dead and the new governor, Sir Charles Bagot, probably less amenable to the needs of the NACAI, there was a danger that the Soulanges camp might use their French connections to gain majority support in the next meeting of the legislature. EGW's obituary of Sydenham was written after Bagot's appointment and he noted that, for all the dead governor's constructive policies, he had failed to accord French Canadians their rightful role in the political life of the country. Although self-interest was again a motivator, EGW's brief summer visit had prompted a philosophical change of mind: he had reverted to his pre-1838 position.

The NACAI decided that EGW should go back to Canada as soon as possible. But there was the matter of the outstanding commission. On 30 October, John Abel Smith wrote to 'Bear' Ellice,

> Thinking as I do of the importance of Wakefields present journey to Canada both to the company and yourself and considering the disadvantages as well as the annoyance of any dispute between you and him I think it will be wise in you to close with my proposal which is that you should allow the association to pay Wakefield at once all the claims from you [taking] that amount off the balance due from the association to you.
>
> The association is quite ready to do this and Wakefield will not go unless something is finally settled on this point.[17]

Whatever the ethics of the EGW-Ellice arrangement, Abel Smith and others on the directorate were convinced of EGW's value.

Ellice agreed, replying via Parkes. He cynically noted that he could not have advised the NACAI directors not to be 'befooled by W – without putting them on their guard', presumably against the double dealing. 'I hope, rather than expect,' he went on, 'his commission may be of use to them – He has no knowledge of the country – no patience for the every day requirements of the management of such affairs – and if he does not succeed in some great speculation, like his Lottery scheme – for the conversion of the property – he will raise some flame in the smoke of which he will escape from his engagements – having got the oyster – (a literally fat one £7000) and leaving the shells to his Employers, and to me. Recollect my forebodings, and say nothing at present about them.'[18]

EGW set out for Canada again in December 1841, after seeing Emily off to Wellington, and arrived at Montreal, via New York, about 20 January 1842. He stayed in Canada for the entire year but there is limited evidence, other than from EGW's own published writings in either the *Colonial Gazette* and later books and pamphlets, as to the extent and nature of his work, meetings or political involvements. His influence over the extraordinary political changes in Canada that took place during 1842 is variously rated as non-existent,[19] part of his need to 'attract attention to his own talents in parliamentary politics, something he could never hope to do in England';[20] or seminal in that 'He planned the stroke that pushed the Coalition into office' and 'wrote . . . the despatch which announced the victory'.[21]

EGW's deportment exhibited his character. Out of a black Canadian night in the winter of 1842 he arrived in Brockville, Ontario to deliver a letter from Charles Buller to Major John Richardson. Following a loud knock at Richardson's door, his servant brought in two gentlemen:

> One was a stout and portly man, with a full face and florid complexion. His dress I do not particularly recollect, but it was neither extremely fashionable, nor was it put on the burly form of the wearer with any extraordinary nicety of arrangement. A large handkerchief was tied around his chin, after the fashion of the . . . driver of an English stagecoach. A huge stick was moreover in his right hand and a lighted cigar between his lips.
>
> The *premier abord* of this gentleman . . . was certainly not of a nature to make me feel quite at my ease. However, the next instant set everything right. He introduced himself to me as Mr Edward Gibbon Wakefield . . . and his friend as Mr Colville. . . .[22]

On being urged to stay, EGW complained first of having nearly broken his neck in the dark and then of having to be off, with no time to lose. The incident was a metaphor for his entire career.

EGW had fostered his connection with John Richardson when, as *The Times* Canadian correspondent, Richardson had supported Durham's views and decisions during the mission. He had been sacked by the paper's Tory owners for his trouble. EGW had other more useful connections from 1838. Executive councillor Dominick Daly was Provincial Secretary for Canada East (Lower Canada). An Irishman educated in Montreal, he did not always see eye to eye with English members of the council but had good French Canadian links. T. W. S. Murdock had arrived in Canada as Colonial Office representative in Durham's retinue and later became civil secretary to subsequent governors. He had been a close adviser to Sydenham and Bagot now heavily depended upon him for information and advice regarding all those, politicians or otherwise, seeking the vice-regal attention. EGW used both these vital contacts, and the pages of the *Colonial Gazette*, to further both the ends of the NACAI and his views on Canadian government which, though assisting favourable outcomes for Beauharnois, became increasingly focused on his achieving a position of political influence.

Before Sir Charles Bagot could gather his skirts, EGW prevailed on Daly to put the Beauharnois project to the Board of Works and on 15 February its chair announced that the project would go ahead. In his 'letter' to the *Colonial Gazette* a few weeks later, EGW averred that Bagot had been 'quite decided' on the necessity of completing the canal. The canal survey was completed before summer and on 13 June an executive council committee approved the start of work. EGW's direct involvement in the proceedings is confirmed by Bagot in his letter from Montreal to Colonial Secretary Lord Stanley the day before: 'Gibbon Wakefield is here – or at least always between this place and Beauharnois, where he is busying himself much to get the canal made . . . . I am told that he is in pretty good humour with me.'[23]

On 14 June Bagot announced the decision to the Montreal Board of Trade as Beauharnois MP J. W. Dunscomb, a director of the Montreal City bank, advanced £50,000 for the scheme. On 25 June, an article appeared in the *Montreal Gazette* that gave the detailed technical and economic arguments in favour of the Beauharnois scheme and adduced opposition to it as the vested interests of Soulanges seigneurs and a customs officer who was unwilling to see his office shifted.

The first ground was broken for the canal on 20 July. The day before, Bagot sent a long despatch to Lord Stanley justifying the Beauharnois decision with exactly the same arguments that had been used in the *Gazette* and appending a personal letter detailing the vested interests of those individuals who opposed it. He noted, 'By the intervention of the Agents of the Beauharnois Compy [i.e. EGW and Dunscomb] who have of course a strong interest in the Work, the land necessary for its execution has been given up gratuitously and funds have been advanced for the first expenses.'[24]

EGW had assessed Bagot as being without guile and had seen that the best way to bring off the Beauharnois scheme was to press it with the aid of influential vice-regal advisers. The speed with which the canal was agreed, surveyed, financed and started also caught EGW's opponents off guard, doubling their outrage and leading to a formal investigation of the scheme in October. Despite rigorous questioning of executive councillors and Dunscomb, EGW's role in the affair could not be uncovered. All appeared above board, yet it seems almost impossible that Hartley Killaly, Chairman of the Board of Works, never spoke with EGW on the topic and it was well known that Dunscomb was nothing more than EGW's agent. Only a week after the select committee's report was presented, EGW stated publicly that he had been 'engaged at Kingston during the whole session of Parliament in assisting . . . Mr. Dunscomb, in the exertions by which he defeated what he justly terms "a combination of private interests and political animosities" in their attempt to put an end to the Beauharnois canal'.[25] Bagot closed the issue when he sent a copy of the report to London: 'I cannot but believe and express my opinion that the superiority of the south side is fairly established, and that the Board of Works was fully justified in its recommendation. . . .'[26]

There had also been considerable debate about which side of the St Lawrence was most suitable for the canal. Both lines of investigation, about patronage and engineering, were equally inconclusive. The experience of the next century or more was to prove the question. The Beauharnois Canal, 11 miles long with nine locks giving a lift of 82 ft 6 ins, was constructed between 1842 and 1845 and served St Lawrence shipping for more than half a century until superseded by the technically superior, seven-lock Soulanges Canal on the north side in 1899. Both were superseded in 1959 by the Beauharnois power and shipping canal of the great St Lawrence Seaway, constructed about 3 miles south of the old canal. The smug ghost of EGW might have said, I told you so.

Concurrently with his managing of Beauharnois, EGW began a political campaign that took him into the assembly by the end of the year. Keeping the French Canadians on side was good for business but he left all the details of the Beauharnois project to others. Now that the canal had been achieved there was the more pressing object of progress towards responsible self-government for the new Canada.

EGW began writing 'Letters from Canada' for the *Colonial Gazette* barely a week after arriving in Montreal. His consistent message was the injustices inflicted on French Canadians as a consequence of Sydenham's politics of exclusion and the arrogant policies of Stanley at the Colonial Office. He insisted on the need to reconcile the political interests of both Canadas if there was to be a way forward for stable and responsible government. There were four broad political groupings in the assembly: the Lower Canada French, currently excluded from government; the Lower Canada British, who had taken control of the predominantly French province following the Patriote rebellion and the Durham mission; the Upper Canada British Tories – the minority 'Family Compact' group which had provoked the rebellion in Ontario; and the Upper Canada liberal reformers. In his second letter, dated 22 February (published in London on 30 March),[27] EGW accurately foresaw the solution. The French Canadians could never find an alliance with the British Tories of either Upper or Lower Canada. But if they could find common cause with the Upper Canada reformers then they would achieve more control over their fate and political justice would be served.

Bagot began by following his instructions from the Colonial Office, which were to continue Sydenham's policy of assimilation of French Canada into a British system, but he was urged to be more active in winning acceptance by appointing more French Canadians to bureaucratic and judicial positions. The steps that he took reassured the French that their educational and legal systems would be preserved but he fell short of including them on the executive, let alone as party to a move towards self-government. And yet in concert, it seemed, with EGW's propaganda campaign, Bagot steadily changed his mind.

Later in the year Bagot told the Colonial Office that he had no direct contact with EGW except at a levée towards the end of May, and then a few weeks later over a question of land tenures. Yet EGW in his 'Letters' to the *Colonial Gazette* seemed increasingly to be at the governor's right hand. He predicted with astonishing accuracy Bagot's plans, intentions and policy, boasting: 'Mark my words; have I not almost a right to give myself the airs of a prophet in speaking of Canadian affairs?'

Items that also appeared in the *Montreal Times* and the *Montreal Courier* caused Bagot in early June to ask Dominick Daly to investigate how matters of great delicacy could be 'divulged with such remarkable accuracy. . . . There is somewhere or other a faux frere dans le camp of whose indiscretions or treachery I have not now to complain for the first time.'[28] If Daly did investigate he produced no results. Only a week later, on 12 June, Bagot wrote to Stanley, 'I have some reason to think that [EGW] is in correspondence with Lord Eliot upon Canada matters; and also that he has immediate and very accurate information of whatever passes in your [Colonial] office in regard to them.'[29] It has been argued that Bagot was too distracted by ill health, the exigencies of his new position and the difficulties presented by an unstable political situation to work out what was going on; but it is remarkable that he did not connect the two cases of leaking and suspect EGW as at least the associate of the 'faux frere'.

After reading a Wakefield 'Letter' exactly prophesying ('rumour says') a group of Bagot appointments to the executive council, the *Montreal Gazette* on 10 August asked how 'some weeks before such rumours were current in Montreal this ubiquitous writer was enabled to prognosticate' the appointments 'with all the confidence of assurance'. When an article by an 'English Traveller' appeared on the front page of the Kingston *Chronicle and Gazette* on 24 September, Bagot wrote in agitation to Lord Stanley that this revelation of recent events 'had a most curiously correct report of the history and course of all my late negotiations, of the state of parties, and questions which led to them'. The article was clearly written by EGW, but Bagot continued to miss the connection and insisted 'it was by another hand'.

EGW considered Bagot was a 'kind, true, and honourable Governor . . . shocked at the injustice of the exclusion of the French-Canadians from all part in the Government', but also that he himself had 'taken a very active part in promoting that change under Sir Charles Bagot which admitted French-Canadians to a share of power'.[30] Bagot's diplomatic record and character were impeccable and it seems impossible that he was capable of privately employing EGW as a political adviser over such an extended period of time while disavowing it. Clearer evidence of such a role would have emerged. Above all, EGW himself would have boasted about it.

Circumstantial evidence appears to confirm that neither Dominick Daly nor T. W. S. Murdock could have been in a position to directly collude with EGW in keeping him intimately abreast of Bagot's discussions and correspondence. The conclusion has been drawn that EGW was paying a mole, a minor official, to copy papers for him.[31] Yet if this remained possible for almost the entire year of

1842, with Bagot aware of leaks from at least May and Daly instructed to investigate, then it seems Daly must have been involved. Murdock was described as a man of integrity and loyalty but Daly was seen as indiscreet and perhaps venal. A minor official probably did the copying (and was paid), but under the protection of Daly whose motives were both money and assisting a powerful campaigner for the French Canadian cause.[32]

EGW's motives were dual. There was self-promotion as an astute political commentator, which served to enhance the reputation of all his writings and theories, and there was his usual enthusiasm for what he saw as a worthwhile cause that led to a deepening political involvement. Later, he grasped the opportunity for a political career that he was denied at home.

By July, the Sydenham method of maintaining a majority without French participation had begun to fail under Bagot, who increasingly admitted the injustice of it. By mid-1842 he was, like Sydenham before him, also suffering from the effect of a 'combination of maladies' made more debilitating by the increasing stress of trying to hold the government together. As the uneasy coalition of English Canadian interests threatened to fall apart, several executive councillors urged Bagot to come to terms with the French Canadians before the assembly met in September. On 28 July Bagot wrote to Lord Stanley asking for permission to make a deal with their leader Louis-Hippolyte La Fontaine, admitting that he did not have the 'political courage' to make the decision himself. Aware of this, EGW wrote to Lord Eliot on 6 August,[33] explaining the state of affairs in the hope that Eliot might have influence with the Colonial Office whom EGW knew would be opposed to Bagot's pressing need to include the French Canadians.

Eliot passed the letter on promptly to Lord Stanley at the Colonial Office, who sent it on to Bagot on 3 September, so quickly that he had no time to make a copy. Stanley wrote, 'I think that my sending it to you is as strong a proof as I can give that there is none of the want of confidence of which he [EGW] speaks – and a belief in the excitement which I have reason to know that he has been labouring to establish. I hope I need not give you any proof that while, as I am sure you would wish, I shall always unreservedly give you my opinion such as it is, I shall always be ready to defer to your much ampler means of information and judgement . . . .'[34]

Bagot replied on 26 September: 'Wakefield's letter to Eliot, which I return . . . is undoubtedly a very able paper, and though radicalism peeps forth in many parts of it, it is a very exact picture of the state of things in the Province up to the moment at which it was written – All the substance, and much of the wording of it is to be found in an article which he must have sent to the Colonial Gazette. . . .'[35] Indeed, EGW had written his last 'Letter from Canada' on the 12th and it had appeared in the *Colonial Gazette* on 31 August.

Despite Stanley's reassurance, EGW was right and Stanley's swift action in sending the letter on to Bagot shows how seriously he regarded EGW's power to influence events. The British government was, in fact, extremely disturbed by

Bagot's letter of 28 July and just a day after Stanley's reassurance, he and Prime Minister Sir Robert Peel urged Bagot not to give way to the French faction led by La Fontaine, whom they still presumed guilty of treason from the 1837 rebellion. They told Bagot to carry on as before, completely ignoring the true state of affairs in Canadian politics and the crumbling support for the governor from other factions. EGW never referred to Bagot in other than the warmest terms and his motive in writing both the letter to Eliot and his last 'Letter from Canada' was to back Bagot, both publicly and privately, at a crucial time. EGW had earlier attacked Stanley for the kind of 'arrogance and self-confidence' upon whom 'Mr. Mother-country [James Stephen] would know how to play for the purpose of meddling in everything here'.[36] EGW's war on the Colonial Office, and on Stephen and Stanley in particular, was unending and in this context, at least, his judgement was correct.

EGW's next move was to do what he could to encourage the French Canadians into coalition with the Upper Canada reformers. When he wrote to lawyer Jean-Joseph Girouard on 20 August, he stated, 'I shall certainly return home in November next, with but little prospect of ever seeing Canada again.'[37] This was intended to reinforce his political disinterest but now EGW had begun to think about a place in the assembly and saw that, to achieve it, he should follow his prescient February judgement and back a French Canadian-Upper Canada reformers' coalition.

EGW had been cultivating his contact with Girouard since his return to Canada. The *patriote* had been one of Papineau's chief lieutenants in the Lower Canada assembly between 1834 and 1837 and had spent six months in gaol in Montreal as a rebel, released only after the disallowance of Durham's Bermuda Ordinance. In June, EGW had called on Bagot with Dunscomb to persuade him to appoint Girouard to a royal commission considering changes to the tenure system in Lower Canada. Girouard was a conservative and EGW saw him as an ally in preserving the semi-feudal system at Beauharnois which yielded the NACAI £4000 a year in rents and a potential £140,000 if all the seigneury's tenants bought their freeholds. Although Girouard had withdrawn from politics since the rebellion, he held considerable influence with the French Canadian party in the assembly and EGW now put forward the persuasive arguments for the coalition of French Canadian and Upper Canada reform interests that he had employed with Eliot and in his 'Letter' to the *Colonial Gazette*.

EGW told Girouard that his proposed coalition would be represented in the executive council, with leading French Canadians in important offices. 'I should consider such a combination to be a mere delusion or cheat, unless it were based . . . upon . . . justice for the Canadians . . . not merely nominal justice . . . but that real practical justice which in this present case could not exist without large allowances for the peculiar language, laws, and customs of half the population of the colony.' The Upper Canada Reformers, with 'their condition to propose', would seek 'the working of the Union, honestly and cordially, but not so as to preclude the combined party from endeavouring . . . to get an alteration of those parts of the Union Act which are obviously unjust and foolish'.[38] EGW counselled that an understanding should be reached with the Upper Canada Reformers before the start of the forthcoming session of the assembly. Too much could go wrong if it were left to wheeling and dealing on the floor of the House.

The letter was marked 'confidential' and 'intended for equally confidential communication to any of your friends' and it is evident that EGW had talked with Girouard on the subject before. Less than a week later, on 26 August, EGW met the acknowledged leader of the French party in the assembly, La Fontaine, whom he had first dealt with during the Durham mission, and it seems likely that EGW's letter to Girouard had been the prompt. Since 1839 La Fontaine had been discussing with Upper Canada Reformers how they and the French Canadians might achieve their aims by working together under the new union. He had close political and personal links with Robert Baldwin, the reform leader. But there was strong resistance within his own ranks to any compact with English Canadians, reformers or not, and La Fontaine had been working long and hard to bring them round. It is likely that La Fontaine met EGW on the basis that he was a declared French Canadian supporter and appeared to have influence with the governor at a critical moment for the political future of the union.

The next day EGW wrote to La Fontaine and the letter is worth quoting in full because it throws good light on EGW's attitude and methods.[39]

> Though I wish to go to Quebec to night, I wish still more to have an opportunity of conversing with you after having reflected on the subject of our last night's conversation.
>
> Upon principles & policy there is, I think, no difference of opinion between us – unless it be that I may go somewhat further than you with respect to the conditions upon which any leading [French] Canadian ought to take office, & also with respect to the share of influence in the Government which ought to be awarded to the Canadian party. But on the question of the means of giving effect to such views, we are both without a settled opinion. I should be very glad if we could agree on this point.
>
> Supposing that we had so agreed, I should be ready to act, wherever action by me might promise to be of use, in helping to provide the results which we equally desire. But I am so thoroughly afraid of becoming a party in any negociations by which the Canadians might be misled or disappointed, that I will not take the part of a Go-between between them & the Governor or any body else. If I act at all, it shall be as the avowed friend of the Canadian party, as one of themselves, bound never to take any step without their full knowledge & approval, & to communicate to them without the least reserve whatever may in my way come to my knowledge in the course of events. I could easily explain to you how in this way, I might be able to exert an influence powerful for good: and this explanation, I wish, my hand being crippled, to give you by word of mouth, after coming to an understanding about immediate objects.

> Will you therefore be so good as to say when & where it would suit your convenience that we should meet.[40]

The letter confirms EGW's commitment to the French Canadian cause and the willingness of its leader to meet him over ways and means. These are clearly indicated where EGW promises to tell 'them without the least reserve whatever may in my way come to my knowledge'. This suggests not only that EGW was privy to Bagot's dealings and discussions but also that he had the ear of someone close to Bagot. Provincial Secretary Dominick Daly is again a likely candidate but J. W. Dunscomb was also always active on EGW's behalf.

There is no evidence that EGW did meet La Fontaine again at the end of August but it is likely. If EGW then went to Quebec, he did not stay long before travelling back west to be in Kingston for the opening session of the assembly on 8 September. Bagot had not received the reply to his 28 July letter to Stanley that he had hoped for. But mail took about three weeks each way across the Atlantic and Stanley had been on summer holiday in Scotland when the letter arrived in London: the reply left England only on 4 September.

Bagot could delay no longer and on 10 September he called in La Fontaine to discuss terms for his support in the assembly. La Fontaine immediately consulted his long-time ally and Upper Canada reform leader Robert Baldwin, the most determined and outspoken proponent of responsible self-government – an executive council of elected representatives to govern the new Canada without direction from the governor. On 11 September, La Fontaine told Bagot that he wanted four places on the eleven-member council, including Baldwin. But Bagot offered only three and, not wanting to make any concession that appeared to be condoning self-government, said he would accept Baldwin only if he were considered part of the French Canadian party.

The talks broke down and executive councillor William Draper, concerned that the impasse would lead to an alliance of the French and British Tories, both of whom opposed the union, offered to resign if this helped to make way for a La Fontaine-Baldwin group of four. He threatened Bagot with mass resignations if he did not take his advice. On the 13th Bagot went back to La Fontaine and offered him four seats but, to his surprise, La Fontaine now refused. Later that day, Baldwin introduced a motion of no confidence into the assembly, demanding responsible government and it was now clear that Baldwin and La Fontaine were trying to force a reconstruction of the executive council along reform lines.

There now occurred the 'stroke of genius' that many have attributed to the hand of EGW, remembering his action in leaking the full Durham Report to *The Times* in February 1839. EGW was certainly at the debate, either in the press or public gallery, and would have spoken to or had messages relayed to Dunscomb, if no one else. He would also have been aware of the French Canadian position and aware that La Fontaine had been dealing only with Baldwin during the previous days, and not other members of their parties. Bagot later wrote Stanley that he had taken 'scrupulous care . . . to avoid all communication whatever with [EGW] during my negotiations with the French Canadians. . .' but Dunscomb had 'supported me manfully in my French Canadian move'.[41] It is inconceivable that EGW, in the urgency of the no-confidence debate, would not have pressed Dunscomb to tell Bagot, Daly or Draper to call Baldwin and La Fontaine's bluff by reading out to the assembly the terms Bagot had offered La Fontaine that morning. Draper did so and in the ensuing debate Baldwin and La Fontaine had to give way to the pressure of their followers and accept Bagot's offer.

The next day a newly reconstituted executive council was sworn in: La Fontaine and two other French Canadians; Baldwin and a reform colleague; three 'moderate' English Canadian reformers; one Tory and two 'non-partisan' councillors, Killaly and Daly. Although the council was not formed along party lines and Bagot appeared to have staved off responsible self-government, he admitted to Stanley that 'whether the doctrine of responsible government is openly acknowledged, or is only tacitly acquiesced in, virtually it exists'.[42]

Stanley's and Peel's letters of 4 September arrived too late and Tories abed in England in a dull October awoke to 'a more absurd, a more scandalous and a more suicidal step, so far as hitherto appears, has seldom, we think, been taken by a statesman who calls himself Conservative'.[43] The Duke of Wellington railed against Bagot, his nephew-in-law, 'What a fool the man must have been to act as he has done!'[44] There were fears that with the executive council now in the hands of 'ultra radicals', the Canadians would sever links with Britain.

Canadian Tories were beside themselves and, in search of a radical conspiracy, fixed on EGW as the culprit. The local press became thoroughly convinced that EGW had been playing a machiavellian role in the governor's affairs. On 18 October the *Montreal Gazette*, in reporting political events, asked if EGW would now unmake the ministry he had made; and a few weeks later *The Church* declaimed, 'this felon has exercised a mysterious influence in our affairs'.

The world did not split asunder, Canada did not leave the empire and the union survived with a proper French Canadian role. But the stress of events throughout the summer and autumn had dealt Bagot a fatal blow and, as his final illness deepened, he increasingly left the responsibility of government to La Fontaine and Baldwin until self-government virtually existed.

EGW now wanted to be a part of that government. On 12 October, Bagot wrote to Stanley,

> What annoys me most at this moment is a manoeuvre of Gibbon Wakefield's to get himself into The House of Assembly – I am well aware of his very superior talents, and am confident that he would be as much disposed as he is certainly able to give me very effective support – but by taking this step, at this particular instant, he will endanger the complexion of my whole measure and give colour to the report that . . . he was the real

> mover, and contriver of all – Nothing, so far as I am concerned, can be more unfounded . . . or more inconvenient. . . . He suggested to me a very few days ago, in a very circuitous manner, to put Mr. Dunscomb into the Legislative Council [Upper House] – evidently that he might succeed to his seat . . . . I refused – declaring that I would not interfere in Elections in any way – much less in the way of job . . . . He has however since persuaded Mr Dunscomb to resign . . . and I have no doubt he will declare himself a candidate. . . . All this has vexed me sorely; but I have no means of helping myself.[45]

At that time 'Bear' Ellice received a letter from his lawyer in Montreal: 'Mr Wakefield is the reputed head of our government and is said to lead His Excellency as he pleases: the public prints assert that he is to have a valuable appointment in reward for his services, and to qualify himself for it he is going to get himself elected member for Beauharnois. . . . He probably will fail . . . as he has disgusted all the English but he may find refuge in some of the other counties. . . .'[46]

In the same issue of the *Colonial Gazette* that included EGW's 17 October address to the electors of Beauharnois, there were extracts from the *Kingston Chronicle*, reporting an announcement, in a Toronto paper, that EGW was to be the new Commissioner of Crown Lands. 'This falsehood was evidently *coined* for the purpose of furnishing a pretext for the pouring out of a fresh torrent of abuse against Mr. Wakefield and the Government. Its baseness was of course detected as soon as Mr. Morin accepted of that office, and it again became necessary to set the *mint* in motion for a fresh supply of *base metal* to replace the detected counterfeit. Accordingly it was asserted that Mr. Wakefield was to be Secretary East; and we believe that this rap is still in circulation. A few days will also see it nailed to the counter. . . . Mr. Wakefield never sought for or expected office, and . . . Sir Charles Bagot never even contemplated such an event.'[47] Clearly, many of the rumours circulating about EGW's role in Canadian politics had been put about by Tory opponents of EGW's influential support for French Canadian participation in government and the principles of self-government, coloured no doubt by his part in the Beauharnois canal project.

In his address to the electors, EGW made much of his work in promoting the canal, and dealt with tenure, agricultural and seigneurial matters as 'the son of a farmer and a farmer's daughter, brought up myself in the midst of farming', though anyone less rustic would be hard to imagine. The three main points of his electoral platform were, typically, consistent with past beliefs yet tuned to the ears of those he wished to persuade. Nowhere did he claim to have directly influenced the formation of the new La Fontaine-Baldwin government.

First, EGW stated, 'I am strongly attached to the measure of the Union of the Provinces; being of opinion that it is calculated to insure justice for all.' Second, 'I am no less attached to the dependence of this country on Great Britain; being convinced that it is for the advantage of every colonist that Canada should continue to form part of the great empire to which it is our boast to belong'. Third,

'I am warmly in favour of what has been termed responsible government. I should as soon expect to be elected for the county by a minority of the constituency, as to see the government of Canada happily carried on in opposition to the wishes of the majority of the people. I know of no way in which the wishes . . . of the people can be properly made known except through their representatives in Parliament.'[48] In the parlance of the time, this made EGW an ultra radical and, though he was certainly acknowledging the influence of the noisy and rampant democracy across the border just 20 miles away, it was of a piece with his last electoral address – to the citizens of Birmingham in 1836 – when he paid allegiance to Attwood and the Chartists. He had certainly changed his view on democracy since *England and America* but if his interpretations would always be shaped to suit his current political ends, he never loosened his grip on the principle.

On 11 November, Bagot wrote to Stanley, 'Wakefield has gained his election by a large majority – His language on the hustings was neither intemperate, nor mischievous – I wish you could continue to keep him at home, or tell him that he is sadly wanted in Australia'.[49] On 1 December *The Times* reported tartly, 'Mr E. G. Wakefield has carried his election. . . by a majority of 737 . . . entirely made up of the votes of the three parishes of St Martine, St Clement and St Timothy, where the population is exclusively French Canadians.' The implication was clear: this was another EGW 'job' with a traitorous reliance on the votes of second-class citizens.

EGW left Canada a few days after his election and sailed from New York on the *Great Western* steamer on 17 November. If he had planned on an interview with Lord Stanley after arriving in England, he was disappointed. Bagot wrote to Stanley on 12 December, 'I am rejoiced that you are resolved not to see Cacodæmon [evil spirit, malignant person] – nothing will more effectually contradict the lie that he has been in my confidence and that I desire to employ him – but it may be as well not to affront him overtly, as he is a vindictive, as well as subtle serpent, and like Col. Charteris "would not give a fig for fortune if he could only get character".'[50]

'Bear' Ellice identified the paradox of character and ability in EGW in a letter to Joseph Parkes at the end of November: 'He is clever, smooth, plausible, & designing – & one cannot pay a greater tribute to his abilities, than in the admission, that with his character against him, he has still been able to band with honest, & [discerning?] men against all their better feelings. . . . So far as I was satisfied his own interest ran in the same current with mine – I have trusted him with the utmost caution and circumspection – but always with hesitation. . . .'[51]

In the same letter, Ellice's vituperation about EGW's behaviour was extensive. Whereas Bagot's complaint seems just, from a man of unquestionable public probity, Ellice's unending ire seems to spring from envy of someone who played a better hand in a game that used any means to achieve self-justified ends. Ellice undoubtedly regarded himself as one of the 'honest' men, yet his interest in EGW was also almost entirely commercial: he overlooked the fact that men like Durham banded with EGW not merely for profit but for the value and power of his ideas and his ability to project them. Bagot and Stanley's shunning of him was testimony of that.

Bagot's last reference to the Cacodæmon EGW preceded his resignation by scarcely a month. He was terminally ill and from late November the government of Canada was effectively in the hands of La Fontaine and Baldwin. Aware of this, EGW kept up a correspondence with the French camp, rendering advice and information from London that he considered would help keep the reformers in power, despite the antipathies of the imperial government.

Writing from New Zealand House in the new year, EGW told La Fontaine, 'People in general here know absolutely nothing about the state of parties in Canada. The [common] impression is that Sir Charles Bagot has foolishly discouraged the loyal & given strength to the spirit of rebellion' – and that Peel and Stanley's acceptance of Bagot's actions had offended the bulk of the Tory party, let alone the Whigs. He urged La Fontaine to ensure his government took no steps that could be seen as 'hostile to any part of the Union Act' and to avoid 'the giving of weapons to your enemies to wound you with here. Any error of judgment in this matter by the present [Canadian] Government party would enable your Opposition to excite the public mind here against you.' Calm and sensible government, creating loyalty and peace, would be the best advertisement for self-government and allow later alterations to the Union Act that 'wisdom & justice require'.

EGW went on to write of the successor to 'Poor Sir Charles Bagot!' and suggested ('it is rumoured') that Sir Charles Metcalfe would be the next governor, following his 'complete victory over great difficulties as Governor of Jamaica'.[52] EGW knew of Metcalfe's appointment even before Metcalfe did, from Charles Buller who had the confidence of Prime Minister Peel, and on 19 January 1843 the new governor accepted his post 'without being sure that I have done right'.[53] Metcalfe arrived in Kingston on 30 March, six weeks before Bagot's death. EGW thought that Peel and Stanley, in appointing this Whig liberal, had chosen someone who would not 'endeavour to restore the old system of governing'. But though Metcalfe approved of vote by ballot and 'equal rights to all men in civil matters', he had been so long in imperial service, in India and Jamaica, that Peel and Stanley knew that he would bring a more conservative and determined hand to Canadian affairs than kind and ailing Bagot. Personal habit gave the key to his character and style of governing. Before facing fourteen-hour days of work and service, Metcalfe was in the habit of taking a cold bath after sleeping in an unheated room, even in the middle of a Canadian winter.

EGW showed no sign of wishing to return to Canada to further his political career. To La Fontaine at the beginning of February 1843 he wrote, 'I intend to sail from England on the 4th of April, but shall certainly not be able to remain in

Canada over the session of Parliament: so there will be a vacancy for Beauharnois.'[54] In the event, New Zealand affairs and politics at home took precedence. On 6 April, Charles Buller made one of his most powerful speeches to Parliament on the need for systematic colonisation as a remedy for economic distress in Britain. He strongly supported the Wakefield system which had, within the previous few years, 'entirely altered' the character of colonisation: 'a Colonial career is now looked upon as one of the careers open to a gentleman'.[55]

In August, at EGW's behest, Buller again addressed Parliament on colonial affairs, stating that emigration to Canada needed control and co-operation with the Canadian government. It was on this issue, closely connected to NACAI's interests, that EGW left London again on 5 September, aiming to reach Kingston for the start of the new parliamentary session on the 28th. He intended to return home after its conclusion: 'I have written to Lafontaine desiring him to look out for my successor at Beauharnois, and have engaged myself to dine at Mile End on Xmas Day.'[56]

His chief purpose was to have legislation passed enabling the NACAI to operate as a mortgage and trust company and to continue pushing for the Beauharnois colonisation scheme, following Buller's political boost at home. But the government of Canada was again approaching crisis point and EGW's self-interested plans once more became entangled with the continuing struggle for responsible self-government that would not be resolved for another half-dozen years. Given his role at the beginning of this process with Durham, he could scarcely leave it alone. But his position and role in the ensuing constitutional debate was conditioned by his failure to gain the support of La Fontaine and Baldwin, and other executive council members, for his NACAI schemes. One of them, Francis Hincks, a moderate Upper Canada reform member and Inspector General of Accounts, later wrote, 'From a warm professing friend of the Ministers, he became their bitter enemy when he found that they refused to support his project.'[57] And EGW was forced to seek support from a member of the opposition in setting up a committee to examine the Beauharnois scheme.

In his own writings about the events in Canada between September 1843 and January 1844, EGW barely mentioned NACAI affairs; nor did he reply to Hincks's criticisms in letters to the London *Morning Chronicle*, lending support to Hincks's implications that EGW's motives in the entire affair were self-serving. Yet an examination of both men's versions of events reveals workaday political wrangling and some self-serving on Hincks's behalf, too. Certainly, EGW was mortified by what he saw as La Fontaine's betrayal after the efforts he had made to help the French Canadians into power, whether self-interest was involved or not.

La Fontaine struck a Napoleonic pose, down to hairstyle and hand in jacket, and even his 'closest friends admit that his temper is suspicious, haughty and overbearing', though EGW gave him 'credit for patriotism and honesty'. Baldwin he considered as 'remarkable for a blind self-esteem in public, as for respectability of character in private life'.[58] Both probably considered they no longer needed EGW's support in the denouement of the crisis that was looming by the end of October. 'I now *know* that Messrs. Lafontaine and Baldwin have got thoroughly into the Governor General's bad graces. So they have into mine, by reason of various follies, and above all, by a course of treachery towards a colleague who greatly helped to bring them into power.'[59] This referred to a move in the assembly to impeach Dominick Daly for improper appropriation of public funds. EGW described how, in the House, he had been shocked at La Fontaine and Baldwin's treachery towards Daly: 'I upbraided them with it, and insisted on a full inquiry into the subject.'[60] An immediate select committee inquiry cleared Daly. But the details of this affair reveal the enmities that had now developed between the majority La Fontaine-Baldwin reform party, running the executive as a cabinet, and Daly, the sole councillor who continued to support Metcalfe as head of state. It also becomes clear that EGW had close liaison with Daly during the two months before the resignations, lending more weight to the likelihood that Daly had been EGW's chief mole over the previous years.

EGW's style in the assembly was said to be 'argumentative and able. . . . As a public speaker he appealed to the reason rather than to the imagination, and there was little of the *ad captandum* [appealing to the emotions] orator about him. He was better calculated to impress educated men than the public at large, and by consequence was not well fitted for the labours of an electoral campaign, although he possessed many rare qualifications for a legislator.'[61] EGW brought some of these qualifications to bear as the government threatened to split apart.

The tension between the La Fontaine-Baldwin executive and governor Metcalfe had been deepening from the moment he arrived. Following his brief from Lord Stanley, Metcalfe was determined to restore the governor's role as effective head of the administration, consulting the executive council but taking ultimate responsibility. But after months of self-government, La Fontaine and Baldwin had become convinced of party government, and had strengthened their support by the distribution of patronage. By the end of October, EGW observed that, 'they have not only, not treated the Governor General as the head of the Council, but have also denied him the equal position of a Councillor'.[62] EGW thought that La Fontaine and Baldwin were now failing to support a vital principle of responsible government where the elected executive had both the confidence of the House and the governor and regarded the governor as head of state.

EGW has been criticised for supporting only the narrowest version of responsible government, chiefly as a way of justifying his newly acquired opposition to La Fontaine and Baldwin. By late November he saw '[t]he rigid and exacting spirit in which they administer power' which had 'become intolerable, and will be their ruin'. His published views, later in 1844, of the principles of responsible self-government are more expansive than those he expounded in Canada at the end of 1843, but this was essentially the difference between practice and theory.

At the beginning of the year he had cautioned La Fontaine against making any moves that might provoke the hostility of the imperial government and set back the reforms that had been achieved. At the end of the year, he still saw the clear and present danger of which La Fontaine and Baldwin, corrupted by the hubris of power, had become careless. Correspondingly, they had become uninterested in EGW's views and advice, and it was this, as much as their failure to support his NACAI schemes, that reinforced his determination to support the governor in the version of self-government sanctioned by Westminster. EGW feared the collapse of the union and a revolutionary conflict between the old provinces that would be 'fatal to the people of Canada, and especially to the French-Canadians, whose position in *English* America subjects them to dangers as a peculiar people which nothing but *British* protection can avert'.[63] They were, after all, his constituents.

The rupture came at the end of November on the issue of patronage. In a letter dated the 25th to British MP R. D. Mangles, EGW added a postscript:

> P.S. – Sunday, 26th. I was just going to seal this, when information reached me to the effect that all the Ministers, with the exception of Daly, after a Council held this morning, have resigned their offices; the ground of resignation being that Sir Charles refused to comply with a demand of theirs that no appointment should be made by him without first submitting to them his intention to make it, or, in fact, getting their assent. The ground is *not* good for him . . . nor for them . . . because there can be no doubt that it is not a true ground, but a pretext made for the occasion when they found that he was resolved to get rid of them at all events. There will be 'explanations' in the assembly to-morrow. I am very glad to be here.[64]

Indeed he must have been: his greatest political opportunity now presented itself and there would be no Christmas dinner at Mile End.

La Fontaine and Hincks had intended the threat of resignation to force 'Old Square Toes' or 'Charles the Simple', as they disparagingly called Metcalfe, to accede to their wishes. But Metcalfe was made of sterner stuff and had long mastered the art of holding out until he had won or irretrievably lost. He accepted the resignations and in the fiery debate on the 27th EGW claimed that La Fontaine and Baldwin had forced the rupture because they had lost popularity and were afraid of being turned out by the assembly. EGW had allowed his new antagonisms to cloud his political judgement: the assembly voted two to one in favour of the ex-ministers. Despite this, Metcalfe prorogued Parliament on 9 December and persuaded two conservative politicians to come out of retirement and make up a reduced three-man council with Daly. It was the beginning of a long and bitter struggle for power.

Metcalfe could not call EGW on to the council since, given his radical and controversial record, this would upset his plan to people it with moderates who would bring some stability to the volatile political situation. But he accepted

EGW's offer of help as an adviser in actively proselytising for his government. By 22 December MP J. H. Dunn was telling La Fontaine of rumours that EGW was 'the Governor-General in fact and in deed . . . . He appears to have taken possession of the Public Office. I find him in and out the whole day long.'[65] The mole was finally redundant.

It is not known whether his new position had begun to persuade EGW of the virtues of staying on in Canada with an expanding political career in view. It is likely that he would have wished to see the crisis through and perhaps assist Metcalfe until the outcome of the next general elections. But on the knell of the new year came news that was both larger in his own life and more critical to the fulfilment of his political and theoretical thinking than any crisis in Canada. More than six months after the event, the news of Arthur's death at the Wairau finally reached Kingston after voyaging halfway round the world to Charles Torlesse in England and then starting the journey back again across the Atlantic.

EGW returned to England immediately and abandoned Canada forever, an action disapproved of by those unconscious of the depth of his feelings. He reached London 'in a state of the deepest depression. His personal fascination, so potent with all, was most deeply felt by children and the young. Mrs Storr, then little Miss [Amy] Allom, who, in her own words, would have been glad of an opportunity of dying for him, remembers him as he sat lost in gloom at the end of the drawing-room in Hart Street, Bloomsbury. She nestled against him trying to sooth [*sic*] him, and her mother called her away. "Let her be," answered Wakefield, "let her be!"'[66]

Arthur's death caused EGW to leave Canada with both his political and business work incomplete. Although he wrote in support of Sir Charles Metcalfe's policies and actions throughout the first half of 1844, and bolstered the governor's reputation at home, he had no bearing on the outcomes in Canada. Metcalfe governed unhappily with an awkwardly mixed council until September when he called an election. La Fontaine won most of the seats in Lower Canada but members supporting the governor won most in Upper Canada and Metcalfe had his majority in the council. Then, like his two predecessors, Metcalfe began slowly to succumb to a fatal illness. By the end of 1845 a cancerous tumour on his cheek had left him blind and scarcely able to speak or eat. Inevitably, as it had under Bagot, power shifted from the governor to his executive council.

After Metcalfe's departure and death, the abolition of the Corn Laws in Britain in 1846 contributed to the returning Whig government's acceptance of the principle of colonial self-government. Lord Durham's son-in-law, Lord Elgin, arrived in Canada as the new governor-general early in 1847, and wrote to his wife that achieving self-government there would be the 'real and effectual vindication' of her father's memory – and of EGW's and Charles Buller's continued campaigns since his death.

EGW had brought some success to the NACAI Beauharnois project by ensuring the construction of the canal, but his settlement schemes had proved a financial failure and everyone except EGW suffered a loss. On 24 May 1844, Edward 'Bear' Ellice wrote to the secretary of NACAI, John Dewar,

> Sir, I think it right . . . to restate to you for the information of the Governor and Board of Directors, the opinion I have before expressed . . . of the great disproportion between the remuneration, as it actually appears given by them to Mr. Wakefield, & any results which have yet been realized, or are . . . prospectively secured to the shareholders of the association, by his agency in their affairs.
>
> I was not aware of the amount proposed to be paid to him, till I heard it stated in the report. Whatever may be the issue of this speculation to the association, or to the seller, or purchase of the Beauharnois property, it appears that Mr. Wakefield will have received . . . exactly the sum of £20,000 – within 5 or 6000 as much as has been received by principal by me, and two thirds of a whole cash paid up by the proprietors – before they have realized at their Bankers the least benefit from his agency.[67]

As a creditor of the company and a leading shareholder, Ellice was justly aggrieved at the disproportion of EGW's commission; though he had contributed to EGW's expectations by his own ambiguous role in the original dealing and his inflated view of the value of the Beauharnois estate. The project was a failure but Ellice recovered his position by repossessing the property about ten years later, and it is unlikely that other businessmen involved in the project suffered any serious losses. The entire affair had been a speculation, a risky bid that did not come off.

The amount of money received by EGW was enormous but it is impossible to know how much of the £20,000 was used in the cause of the company's interests, including the payment of considerable election expenses for Beauharnois County and the remuneration of his moles in government. The NACAI affair, and the later crisis with the New Zealand Company, proved to the City that EGW's skills lay not in the management of money and business but in the management of men and ideas. After 1844, he was not entrusted with company agency or management again. EGW's cavalier attitude towards acquiring cash and his ability to misuse and lose it was consistent with a Wakefield family trait that infected his entire generation, as well as two generations before it, and at least a generation to come.

EGW's official Canadian biographer wrote that the outcome of his disjointed and abruptly ended Canadian career between 1838 and 1844 was that 'His reputation among Canadians was no higher when he left than it had been when he first came'.[68] This echoes Bagot's disparagement of his character. Given that, in this judgement, EGW was described as 'author and politician' this is praise indeed when neither type can expect any reputation at all. EGW would probably have approved of Henry St John's anecdote,[69] 'The greatest art of a politician is to render vice serviceable to the cause of virtue', and he understood that authors, like philosopher David Hume's poets, 'though liars by profession, always endeavour to give an air of truth to their fictions'.

Despite his perceived shortcomings in character and reputation, it is hard to see what damage EGW caused during his political activities in Canada. He played a seminal role in Durham's mission, contributing in both Canada and England to the union of the two provinces. By later changing his mind about the French Canadians, he did them a service in assisting them into power during Bagot's term. By changing his mind about La Fontaine and Baldwin he helped avert a potentially catastrophic crisis between imperial and colonial governments. Ready-made theory and structure of responsible self-government for British colonies is a product only of hindsight. In the early 1840s it was a new and radical concept in a developing imperial world. It was easy for the crusaders, like Robert Baldwin, to fight for autonomy on a platform of provincial righteousness, or for home reactionaries, like Lord Stanley, to defend the imperial fort. It took skill to have a foot in both camps, averting revolution in the cause of inevitable and just political evolution. But men such as EGW, who possess this skill, leave both camps with no friends.

EGW's involvement in Canadian affairs had given him the extra experience and insight to produce his most important, yet often overlooked, essay on imperial and colonial government. It appeared in Fisher's *Colonial Magazine* in July 1844, misleadingly entitled 'A View of Sir Charles Metcalfe's Government in Canada'; it is not included in EGW's collected works; and when reprinted in 1926 it was included in a book principally about Charles Buller (though it comprised half the contents). This 45,000-word work, the size of a small book in its own right, certainly covered the contemporary constitutional problems in Canada; but it also provided a powerful overview of the constitutional position at home and abroad and the questions facing Britain and its empire. EGW ranged over the different possibilities for future colonial governments, including the American republican model, federalism and representation in the imperial Parliament as well as responsible self-government at a provincial level. Much of this work is now of interest only to students of Commonwealth constitutional history, but two passages reveal the democracy at the heart of EGW's thinking and his remarkable vision of the future for the British Empire and Commonwealth.

In delineating the character of British colonies he wrote,

> It is clear enough, then, that in attempting to give to our Colonies political institutions essentially modelled upon our own, it is idle to think of their adopting all our aristocratic peculiarities, be they ever so cherished or venerable, whether in Church or State. In the one or two of our most recently-planted settlements, where pains have been taken in the first instance to transplant an organized society of rich and poor, landholders,

> merchants, tradesmen, artisans, and labourers, all together, and to have them carry at once with them from home into the wilderness their church and school-house, a state of things promises to grow up more like our own than is to be found in our older colonial possessions. But no such marked inequalities of rank as prevail at home can by any chance be made a lasting feature of the social state, even in colonies so founded. As to hereditary rank, with here and there perhaps a solitary exception, it is a thing not to be thought of. The political franchise, too, must be more extended, and representation more nearly apportioned to population, than with us. And as regards privileged church-establishments, every Colony had need be allowed altogether its own way. If it want them, they are easily to be had. If not, it will be worse than folly to try and force it to put up with them.[70]

Tennyson's 'Locksley Hall' had been published just a couple of years before EGW's essay and its visionary phrases may have touched his imagination as he 'dipped into the future, far as human eye could see', thought of 'the Parliament of man, the Federation of the world', while he scrawled the final paragraph of his essay.

> True it is, that the wide Continents we are colonizing promise at some distant day to maintain communities too powerful for the precise colonial relation, even as I have been describing it, to continue for ever to subsist between them and the people of these Islands. But that period is distant, though inevitable. All we can certainly know is that it will come; that at some future time our Colonies, powerful as the Parent State or more so, must either, thanks to mismanagement, have become independent states more likely to be its enemies than its hearty friends, or else, through a wise foresight, have been kept closely bound to it, – confederacy in some shape, by degrees taking the place of the old bond of union, – the British nation continuing still united, so far as perpetual peace, mutual good understanding, freedom of commerce, and identity of foreign policy, can unite it,– these Islands still its Metropolis, though their people be no longer the admitted holders of its whole Imperial power. All we can do is to take care of the present and near future. The future that is far off will take good care of itself. For this age and the next it is enough to know that Colonies, built up by its own people and gifted with our own free institutions, must be bound, alike by the natural feelings and the commercial wants of their people, to ourselves and our policy, no less than to our trade; that neither the one tie nor the other need we, nor yet if we are wise shall we, ever let go or loosen.[71]

Britain began to loosen those ties 130 years after EGW wrote his essay, but his vision of the British Commonwealth of Nations still holds true. Here, EGW's writing has an almost elegiac tone: in submitting to the task of such a substantial work, he may have found some refuge from his grief for Arthur, and been moved to affirm that his sacrifice at the colonial altar would not be in vain.

CHAPTER TWENTY-ONE

Utu Postponed

AT THE BEGINNING OF 1844, EDWARD Wakefield, in his seventieth year, wrote to a friend from Blois, 'I feel it my duty to rouse myself from a sort of lethargic state of misery to which I could readily fall but I am not so selfish as to solely deplore the loss of my dear son although he was the pride of my life. his whole naval career for 30 years having been one of exultation. and I am sure he will be regretted by the whole naval service.'[1]

Throughout 1843, Edward had unwittingly continued to send Arthur the detailed, sometimes eccentric, advice he had gleaned from his studies and travels. A letter sent ten days before Arthur's death offered opinions about farming techniques, sheep and types of emigrants. Arthur was exhorted to read the letters and articles in the *New Zealand Journal* to which his father was a regular contributor. In October, still ignorant of the terrible news, Edward wrote with awful unconscious irony, 'I am worried to pieces with your Maori names. They are as bad as the Celtic in North Wales . . . . pray give names to those places of the best men in England such as Scrope, Slaney, Ashley, Buller, Egerton.'[2] But Wairau would forever remain Wairau.

The effect of Arthur's death on his father, EGW and William was profound, and William anticipated the shock and grief in England when he wrote to Catherine, 'The intelligence of poor Arthur's fate must have been a cruel blow to you all but I fear to think how it must have affected my father . . . . I can find no will and conclude my father is his heir. There are clothes, furniture, a horse & some balance at the Bank, after paying his small debts. . . .' Three months after the Wairau, William could still say, 'I can yet scarcely realize the great loss we have had.'[3] He assured Catherine of her son Charley's safety and assumed that she would wish him returned home at the end of his engagement the following year. Christmas 1843 at Stoke was marked by the absence of all Catherine's brothers. Beyond her own immediate family, her grief at Arthur's death could be shared only with younger sister Priscilla, who had returned to England from

India in May. Father Edward considered Pris to have 'an excellent husband who is as attentive and as fond of her as if they had not been married a week'.[4] Pris had brought home two sons and added a daughter in July. Her next son, born in 1845, was christened Arthur Wakefield.

From Wellington in July 1843, William had written Catherine, 'For myself, having been four years here and having fought an uphill game with some success, I should be glad to finish my work and see the settlement established prosperously, but the loss of poor Arthur and the disgusting opposition of the Government, which has led to it, have nearly upset me, and incline me to go home myself.'[5] Two months later he told her that the natives were 'much disturbed as to the land question; having been tampered with by a host of missionaries, protectors, magistrates & commissioners'. But fleeing to England in grief would have been an admission of defeat, leaving the field to his enemies, abandoning the chance for retribution against Te Rauparaha and Te Rangihaeata. To honour Arthur's memory he should stay to see it through. And now that Emily was with him, what was there for William to return to in England?

The impact of the Wairau clash on Maori, settler and government was both immediate and far-reaching. It had been the almost inevitable outcome of company settlers 'walking the land' in defiance of Maori claims to possession of unsold, or 'unleased', territory. Land Commissioner Spain's report echoed the view of Acting Governor Willoughby Shortland that the company's representatives had tried to 'set British law at defiance'. In alleging to have purchased one-third of New Zealand, they had then 'selected the most available districts within their imaginary boundaries, without the slightest reference as to whether they had purchased them of the aborigines or not'.[6] William covered his tracks with his superiors in London by declaring that opposition to settlement of the Wairau had arisen only recently and had been fomented by Europeans cohabiting with Ngati Toa women who had claimed land there. And the Wairau had been included in the document that Te Rauparaha signed in October 1839.

The Nelson and Wellington settlements were in an uproar of fear and anger, expectant – even eager – that war should settle accounts with Te Rauparaha and Te Rangihaeata. William, driven by grief, outrage, self-righteousness and self-interest, could advocate and encourage only one course of action: to demand that the government bring the Ngati Toa chiefs to justice and prepare the settlements for armed conflict. Volunteer corps were formed in Wellington, William leading the élite cavalry; cannon were dug in on the headlands and daily drilling and shooting practice instituted. At the end of July, Major Mathew Richmond, appointed police magistrate for Wellington, arrived from Auckland with 53 grenadiers of the 96th Regiment and ordered the disbanding of the volunteers. He resisted the settlers' insistence on maintaining the militias and they now became convinced that the troops had been sent, not as a defence against the Maori, but to police local Pakeha.

Jerningham, filled with the excitement of the moment, wrote, 'The settlers, though they forbore from drilling, began to practise rifle-shooting in their own gardens, and kept stands of arms and ammunition always ready in their houses. For no one could say, from hour to hour, when he might hear the news that some settler's forbearance had been exhausted by the increasing licence and insolence of the natives, and that every man was required to do his best in defence of the women and children. No one believed that the 53 soldiers alone would be able to defend the broad line occupied by the town for an hour, should a general attack be made.'[7] In Nelson, a Public Committee of Safety was formed, special constables were sworn in and a wooden 'Fort Wakefield' with musket loopholes was erected above Trafalgar Square. Military protection by the government was demanded.

William went across Cook Strait with Richmond on the government brig on 25 July 1843, calling first at Port Underwood where he engaged some Maori to fence the graves at Tuamarina. They arrived at Nelson on 1 August where Richmond read Shortland's 12 July proclamation prohibiting settler occupation of land in dispute with Maori until claims had been heard by Spain's commission. The proclamation was intended to avoid another Wairau by preventing premature settler occupation. But it also had the effect of emboldening local Maori who had feared Pakeha retaliation but now saw the proclamation as an approval of Te Rauparaha's actions. In Nelson, as in the other company settlements, Maori 'resisted the encroachment of the Europeans, halting surveys, disputing boundaries, and in some cases actually driving settlers from lands which they had cultivated for a considerable time'.[8]

William stayed at Nelson for two weeks, attending to Arthur's small estate, seeing that Charley Torlesse was in good hands and advising in the re-establishment of some kind of order and purpose. Immediate depression had followed the Wairau disaster and, with an excess of labourers to landowners and capitalists, an increasing number were dependent directly on the company for work and money, both of which were running out. Chief Surveyor Frederick Tuckett, still under emotional stress following his escape from near death at the Wairau, struggled to manage the settlement as acting Company agent. On 15 July, he had been threatened with guns and sticks by drunken labourers after he tried to make their wage payments fortnightly rather than weekly. On his August visit, William's solution to the crisis was to order that the many small dispersed parties of labourers should be concentrated into larger groups working under close supervision, in order to 'screw them down'. This was the complete reverse of Arthur's careful management of an always volatile situation and simply gave labourers more opportunity to organise and protest as work and money dwindled.

The loss of all the small community's leaders and the fear of further aggressive acts from Maori had left it with a sense of both isolation and siege. Arthur's death, in particular, 'had left a void, a hiatus in the settlement, which to us, it appears vain to hope to see adequately supplied . . . The life he had lived . . . had developed in him all that one most desired to see in a man occupying the post he did.'[9] After the loss of their paragon, William was small beer. He came only to meddle and promptly objected to a suggestion that, now the Wairau was denied to settlers, the company should make sections in Taranaki available instead. It could well have occurred to a number of Nelsonians that the wrong Wakefield had been tomahawked.

Te Rauparaha and Te Rangihaeata had fully expected retribution – utu – after their killing of Nelson's leaders at Tuamarina. Both had recrossed Cook Strait without delay, Te Rangihaeata pushing on to the Manawatu, where he built a fighting pa in the bush among the reaches of the lower river. The Pakeha might cut his throat but they would 'never make a tie' of him. Te Rauparaha employed all his practised theatre of oratory and generalship. At Waikanae he played the infirm kaumatua and, with the prop of a pair of handcuffs, held up his tied hands in appeal to suspicious Ati Awa, 'Why should they seek to fetter me? I am old and weak; I must soon pass away . . . . No; that is not what they seek. It is because through my person they hope to dishonour you. If they can enslave me, they think they can degrade the whole Maori race.' Ati Awa had no reason to trust the 'Old Sarpint', but his oratory stirred them to anger and indignation which was cooled only when missionary Octavius Hadfield cut him short by ringing the church bell and calling them to worship. Te Rauparaha moved up the coast to Otaki and his Ngati Raukawa kin where he played the great Napoleonic chief: 'Now is the time to strike. You see the deceit of the white people . . . . you know what they mean in their hearts . . . . you can expect nothing but tyranny and injustices at their hands. Come forward and sweep them from the land. . . .' As the Wellington militia drilled and continued target practice across the hills, the potential for a catastrophic confrontation was high.

Hadfield's influence among Ati Awa and his hurried journey to Wellington to warn of Te Rauparaha's rabble-rousing saved the day. Commissioner Spain was sent to assure the Kapiti coast Maori that the Wellington authorities would do nothing to avenge the Wairau and convinced the majority of coast Maori of the government's best intentions in settling the matter. But Te Rauparaha demanded of Spain, 'If the Governor should decide upon sending soldiers to take me and Rangihaeata, will you send and let us know when they arrive; because you need not take the trouble to come up here for us . . . . I will go down to Wellington with a thousand warriors and have a fight with the white men. If they beat us they shall have New Zealand and we will be their slaves; but if we beat them; they must stand clear!'[10]

When the British 26-gun frigate *North Star* arrived in Wellington at the end of August, in response to the Wellington settlers' appeal to the Governor of New South Wales for protection, William was foremost in advocating a 'demonstration on the coast which might strike terror into the tribes and lead to the disbanding of Rauparaha's forces now mustered within 15 miles of us at Porerua'.[11] He had in mind a fierce reprisal against Ngati Toa in the order of HMS *Alligator*'s bloody reduction of Taranaki's Waimate pa in 1834. But the *North Star* had called in at Auckland before reaching Wellington and her captain was quite clear that his role was to keep the peace, not make war. When Nelson magistrates in October issued warrants for the arrest of Te Rauparaha and Te Rangihaeata, he firmly declined to carry them out.

Missionaries and government officials persuaded the Maori and the settlers to an uneasy peace. Te Rauparaha also found he did not have the support of 1000 warriors and modified his position. But he still warned George Clarke Jnr in September, 'We look to the government for protection but if they cannot defend us we must stand up for ourselves.'[12] Te Rangihaeata, though he knew little of the Pakeha's plans, understood very well that utu would one day be exacted.

In the same letter to the company that advised reprisal by the *North Star*, William had added, 'The time is not far distant when the rising generation of Anglo-Saxons will neither want the nerve nor the skill to hold their ground against the savage, and take ample and just vengeance for their opposition we are now encountering.'[13] Taking his cue from that, Jerningham later expressed similar sentiments in his book, writing that a new generation would grow up with a hatred towards the Maori 'instead of a generous eagerness to befriend and cherish them as feeble brothers. And the leading settlers, who had fondly hoped to afford real protection to the inferior race, shuddered lest even in their day the law respecting forbearance of the Englishman should be exhausted, and the mutual distrust of the races should break forth into general warfare; which could only end in the more or less speedy extermination of the natives, crushed like a wasp in the iron gauntlet of armed civilization.'[14] Whatever its name, this was the kind of utu for the spilt blood of kin that Te Rangihaeata expected. The Wairau had been the match to start the burning of a long and sputtering fuse.

When he first heard of his uncle's death at the Wairau, Jerningham had been at Wanganui, working at his flax trade. He sent a message to William that he could assemble a force of men to come down the coast and, with an armed Wellington party, round up Te Rauparaha at Otaki. William wisely turned down the idea, but Jerningham travelled up and down the coast armed with rifle, cutlass and dagger, declaring what should be done to those who had killed his uncle.

His bluff was finally called at the end of December at Otaki. As he sat exchanging niceties with Te Rauparaha at Katihiku pa, Te Rangihaeata emerged from a hut into an adjoining 'court-yard' and made a 'furious oration . . . . he foamed at the mouth, leaped high into the air at the end of each run up and down, and made frightful grimaces at me through the fence . . . . He taunted me with being a spy, hiding about . . . to watch his doings . . . . He applied the most insulting expressions to the Queen, to all the Governors, and to all the White people. He got to his highest pitch of excitement, when he at length challenged me to stand out and fight him manfully, hand to hand.' As Jerningham blanched at Te Rangihaeata's challenge, Te Rauparaha whispered, 'Don't listen to him! Don't answer! Don't be afraid, they're only words!' Jerningham stoutly recorded that Te Rangihaeata 'at length appeared to get tired, or to be convinced that I would not be intimidated'.

But Te Rauparaha now had a shaken Jerningham in the palm of his hand and told him of all the spies he had around Wellington, of murders committed that the authorities knew nothing about and of a plan of attack on Wellington by Ati Awa. He told him that 'in private [they] swore at the missionaries as the principal cause of their disasters, and were perfectly ready at any time to sing the war-song with their old fury'.[15] Jerningham then did exactly what the old conniver had been expecting: he returned to Wellington and spread the news of Te Rauparaha's supposed murders and plot, principally in a colourful letter to the *Gazette*. This caused considerable alarm in the settlement and enraged Ati Awa, threatening the uneasy truce. Now both settler and Maori waited anxiously upon the judgements and action of the new governor, Robert FitzRoy, who had just arrived in Auckland.

Aristocrat and naval captain, FitzRoy was distinguished by the success of his command of the *Beagle*'s survey voyages around southern South America. During his second voyage in 1835 he had visited the Bay of Islands with Charles Darwin aboard and, from his observations in Patagonia, Tierra del Fuego and northern New Zealand, had developed views on the government of native peoples that accorded with the CMS lobby at the Colonial Office. Dandeson Coates had put forward his name as a potential lieutenant-governor as early as February 1838. FitzRoy wrote and edited two of the three volumes of *Narrative of the surveying voyages of His Majesty's ships* Adventure *and* Beagle *between the years 1826 and 1836* (Darwin wrote the third), establishing strong scientific credentials that were marked by the award of a gold medal from the Royal Geographical Society and which led, later, to his establishment of the first scientifically based meteorological office in England.

As commander, navigator, surveyor and scientist FitzRoy seemed the logical successor to a New Zealand governorship in the best traditions of Cook and Hobson. But the tyranny of time and distance in the British managing of New Zealand meant that FitzRoy's ship of state began taking water from the start. He was appointed in April 1843; the Wairau clash occurred in June. News of his appointment reached New Zealand in September; news of the Wairau reached England in December; FitzRoy arrived on the eve of Christmas. The settlers expected great things of their new and distinguished 38-year-old governor but the resources he had been given in money, men and matériel were utterly inadequate to deal with the crisis generated by land disputes and the Wairau. 'All that FitzRoy was given was his commission, all that he had was his integrity, training, ability to work, and determination to succeed to the satisfaction of both races.'[16]

Unlike Spain, FitzRoy wasted no time at all. Just a month after reaching Auckland, he arrived in Wellington on the *North Star* and arranged a levée for the afternoon of 27 January 1844. According to Jerningham, 'The Governor was greeted with cordial acclamations of welcome from a large assemblage of the best settlers in the colony. They appeared determined to prove their confidence in his favourable intentions towards them.' But a 'sort of chill or damp' descended on the assemblage as FitzRoy made his position and intentions clear. He deprecated 'in the strongest terms, the feelings displayed by the settlers . . . against the native population . . . . he considered the opposition to the natives to have emanated from young, indiscreet men'. *Gazette* editor Sam Revans had printed 'most pernicious statements . . . . The native should be protected. Justice should be done . . . . he would settle the land question . . . "Mistake me not; not an acre, not an inch of land belonging to the natives shall be touched without their consent; and none of their *pas*, cultivated grounds, or sacred burial places, shall be taken from them". '[17]

Following his speech, members of the Wellington community were presented to Governor FitzRoy by Major Richmond. Jerningham presented his card, bowed to the governor and moved on, only to be called back and addressed by FitzRoy in the 'tone of the commander of a frigate reprimanding his youngest midshipman'. Before the assembled worthies of the settlement, Jerningham suffered the mortification of being told: 'When you are twenty years older, you will have a great deal more prudence and discretion. Your conduct has been most indiscreet. In the observations which I made to this assembly just now, I referred almost entirely to you. I strongly disapprove and very much regret everything you have written and done regarding the missionaries and natives in New Zealand.'[18]

FitzRoy's attention had been drawn to Jerningham's immoral behaviour at Wanganui, his rash vituperation during the land commission hearings and his armed swaggering up and down the coast since the Wairau. FitzRoy's crushing public humiliation was not spontaneous. He had thought Jerningham planned to leave Wellington directly after the levée and had chosen that occasion for a calculated reprimand. FitzRoy knew that there would be little personal sympathy for Jerningham among the settlers and that attacking him would be an effective way of striking at all the Wakefields, the company and the anti-government and anti-Maori sentiment among the settlers.

Jerningham's ordeal was not over. After the levée he was jeered at by Maori for not having anything to say to FitzRoy in defence while others simply cried out, 'Wairau! Wairau!' Two days after the levée, Jerningham sought a private interview with FitzRoy in order to represent his case, but the harangue continued. FitzRoy cited letters by Jerningham in the *New Zealand Journal* that were 'filled with sneers and sarcasms levelled at the missionaries' showing that he was a 'decided enemy to their proceedings *and to religion*!' In Sydney he had become known as the 'leader of the devil's missionaries'. He would be struck off as a justice of the peace 'on account of the bad example I had set the natives, and on account of my being known as one of those who entertained an especial hatred and animosity towards them'. When Jerningham attempted to defend himself, FitzRoy browbeat him further, declaring, 'he knew his duty and he would do it, without caring for public feeling. . . .'[19]

All this was a good headmaster's wigging, a moral caning that was excessive when most of Jerningham's extravagant or immoral behaviour damaged no one but himself. He could not set a 'bad example to the natives' when his nickname 'Tiraureka' went before him. It was 'Teddiwake', not 'Wideawake', for him. Accusations of 'hatred and animosity' towards Maori were inappropriate when Jerningham's dealings with them had been more accepting of their condition and custom than any missionary's condescending patronage.

FitzRoy proved the best vessel yet for a missionary community that had been largely unable to register official censure of those settlers who ridiculed them, broke the Sabbath and, as one later described Jerningham's shocking practices, went 'sauntering about in a blanket – singing lewd *hakas* and *waiatas* – galloping about with the females on horseback – and squatting in the warm baths of Taupo, with both sexes, in a state of nudity, for hours together. . . .'[20] The missionary scolder continued, 'If we compute the number of females whom [Jerningham] has debauched at the awful amount of *half-a-hundred*, we believe our calculation will be found too low . . . . with reference to his libidinous propensities [he] obtained for himself the disreputable cognomen "Toa".' It was also a cognomen of mana.

The missionaries and their FitzRoy figurehead could confidently preach a kind of protection of Maori land while possessing no compunction at all about alienating their customs and beliefs. Jerningham's attitude to the Maori was even-handed and it is arguable who was corrupting whom. But he set an atrocious Pakeha example in the eyes of a missionary governor who told 200 Auckland chiefs soon after his arrival that he did not intend to interfere with their customs among themselves, but hoped they would 'eliminate nakedness and "the strange contortions of face" that were so offensive, and become more like Europeans. . . .'[21]

Jerningham was left with nowhere to go but home: 'I could stay no more in the country with comfort under this Government; for so long as Captain Fitzroy ruled, I must always appear to a certain degree as a disgraced member of the society' and he had lost considerable mana with the Maori following his being 'degraded' by the governor as their 'bitter enemy'.[22] Jerningham took ship for England a month later, on a voyage towards revenge.

William probably felt some shame and disquiet at the way his nephew had been treated, but he may also have felt some relief at his departure and deep satisfaction at FitzRoy's bull-headed approach to the settlers, which could only serve to assure him of allies. Although Jerningham's humiliation at the levée would have given pleasure to many of those present, FitzRoy's manner and intentions garnered him no friends; the presence-room was empty soon after the wigging, cards unpresented.

As FitzRoy prepared to leave for Nelson, the *Himalaya* entered Wellington Harbour, ex New Plymouth and Nelson, with another arrival of significance to

William. After a separation of more than five years, William had the opportunity to discreetly welcome his older brother Daniel to the turbulent New Zealand frontier. Probably in response to a note that William sent to his father announcing Dan's arrival, Edward replied from Blois, 'I cannot imagine what will become of Dan and what EGW's object can have been in sending him out, perhaps he may get employed on one of the newspapers.'[23]

In April 1843, EGW had written to Catherine, 'I mean to try and spend a few days with you in Easter week. Should you object to my bringing poor Dodo, who leads a miserably monotonous & melancholy life?'[24] It must have been during this sojourn at Stoke that EGW decided to send Dan out to New Zealand, but the reason was never later disclosed to father Edward for fear of the effect it would have had on him following Arthur's death. Dan had separated from his wife Angela 'for giving her a loathsome disease'[25] and, as the sporting paper *Bell's Life for London* reported, he had defaulted at the Newmarket races to the tune of £4,000. So that Dan could escape his creditors and tormentors, EGW despatched him, under the pseudonym of 'Mr Bowler', to New Plymouth, where he stayed for a few months before moving on to Wellington under his own name. The timing was not good for William, but he could find some company employment for his brother's rusting legal skills.

Undeterred by his reception in Wellington, FitzRoy crossed the strait to reprimand the Nelson settlers. At a public meeting he declared that the Wairau expedition had been illegal. 'Great allowance was certainly to be made for feelings arising from the loss of friends so highly esteemed, but they were not justified in suffering themselves to be hurried into courses which the law could not sanction.' He saw the Maori as an 'oppressed people, and standing so much in need of peculiar protection that his chief business in New Zealand was to shield them from the aggressions of his countrymen'.[26] His words would have appalled all those who knew that FitzRoy had been a naval colleague of god-fearing Arthur Wakefield and with whom he had discussed the entire Nelson enterprise before the expedition's departure.

Later, FitzRoy told a private meeting with magistrates that those who had signed the warrant for the arrest of Te Rauparaha would not be included in the new commission of the peace. Some resigned immediately, another with such a flourish at a public meeting on 8 February that FitzRoy exploded in a violent temper, accusing the Nelsonians of republican ideas and ranting, 'I am come to dictate and not be dictated to, to govern and not be governed, to rule and not be ruled.' He would take no advice from any of them.

FitzRoy's final meeting in Nelson was with a deputation of settlers who asked him to take action against the Maori over the killing of the settlers at the Wairau. Alfred Domett had already led a deputation to Acting Governor Shortland the previous August which had also requested government assistance for the dependants of the dead men. Shortland had refused the deputation's case on the grounds that the settlers' action at the Wairau had been illegal and he would not express an opinion regarding criminality since the affair might become the subject of a judicial inquiry. He ignored any claims on behalf of the widows and orphans. FitzRoy now stated unequivocally that there would be no judicial inquiry: he was satisfied the settlers had been in the wrong and that any attempt to apprehend the Maori offenders could only result in a war that would bring about the destruction of the British settlements.

No one in Nelson accompanied FitzRoy to his boat as he left on 11 February, 'nor did a soul who met him take off their hat or bow to him'.[27] Domett the poet drew up in verse a 'Petition from the Gentleman and Inhabitants of Nelson to the High and Mighty Prince Fitzgig the First', a ballad that was soon quoted all around the colony:

> Thus we see in your method to civilise savages,
> By giving them licence to murder and thieve,
> And then hanging up all who resist their wild ravages,
> A scheme which it needed *your* brain to conceive!
> For 'tis doubtless but democrat pride that embitters
> The pleasant dilemma to which it consigns us,
> Before us the savage's Tomahawk glitters,
> Yourself and the gallows stand frowning behind us![28]

The qualities of Arthur Wakefield, though, were engraved in the heart of his friend and ardent admirer, who wrote of him:

> Yet there was a Scot's cap and an old shooting jacket
> That by all of us once were beloved and revered;
> And authority needing no gold lace to back it,
> Was felt and acknowledged where'er they appeared.

FitzRoy's aristocratic dismissal of the Nelson settlers' claim for some kind of justice and humanity in the Wairau affair created deep grievance and bitterness that would, in time, inevitably discover their own form of retribution. Twenty years later, about the time that FitzRoy died by his own hand, Alfred Domett, as both politician and senior bureaucrat in charge of Crown lands, set his face against the Maori in recommending punitive land confiscations in Taranaki and the Waikato. Briefly premier of the colony, he suggested early in 1863 that money voted by the imperial government for 'civilisation of the natives' would be better spent on their conquest.

Having dealt with the Nelson settlers, FitzRoy recrossed Cook Strait to meet with Te Rauparaha. On 12 February, when he went ashore with his officers at Waikanae to address about 500 Ati Awa and Ngati Toa people, Te Rauparaha squatted close to the governor but Te Rangihaeata kept his distance beyond the edge of the crowd. FitzRoy declared that when he had first heard about the Wairau at Sydney, 'my heart was very dark, and my mind was filled with gloom; my first thought was to revenge the deaths of my friends and the other Pakehas who had been killed; and for that purpose to bring many ships of war, sailing vessels and vessels moving by fire, with many soldiers; and had I done so you would have been sacrificed, and your pahs destroyed'.[29]

But FitzRoy then found that the Pakeha had been very much to blame; he had been to Nelson to hear their side of the story and now wanted the Maori's. In response, Te Rauparaha gave his version of events which stated that the settlers at Wairau had fired first and killed several Ngati Toa before they had responded. FitzRoy thereupon gave a show of deliberation and consultation before coming to the judgement he had prepared on board the *North Star* some days before. He announced that since the Pakeha had been in the wrong he would not avenge their deaths. But 'I have to tell you that you have committed a horrible crime, in murdering men who had surrendered themselves in reliance on your honour as chiefs. White men never kill their prisoners. For the future let us live peaceably and amicably . . . and let there be no more bloodshed.'

The chiefs were not impressed. FitzRoy had not greeted Te Rauparaha with the ceremony and protocol that should have attended such a momentous meeting – he had not even sought an introduction to him – and there had been only three speeches, two from FitzRoy. Te Rauparaha was deeply offended and considered that FitzRoy, in truth, wanted utu for the death of the Nelson settlers but did not have the courage or the soldiers to take it. Te Rangihaeata considered Ngati Toa had been shamed by FitzRoy's lack of respect, that he had spoken to them as their master and yet was unable to exact utu. Later in the year on a visit to Waikanae, Bishop of New Zealand, George Selwyn, compounded the offence when he refused to acknowledge Te Rangihaeata, as killer of those who surrendered at Wairau, but shook hands with Te Rauparaha, who would have spared them.

FitzRoy departed Waikanae thinking he had found a just and expedient solution to the Wairau question, but the manner in which he had administered it was intemperate, arbitrary and almost completely lacking in political nous. In bringing down a humane judgement in the context of the Treaty of Waitangi, and within the constraints of the resources and forces at his immediate disposal, FitzRoy succeeded in patronising and alienating both Pakeha and Maori, earning the contempt of both, and helped to prepare the ground for armed conflict. While visiting British Christian justice upon the Wairau affair, ostensibly in the cause of the Maori by excepting them from its consequences, he also demonstrated an utter failure to understand the Maori world. Wanganui missionary Richard Taylor, who was in the region at that time, wrote ten years later: 'It was a pity the Governor was not acquainted with native customs; otherwise he would have claimed the [Wairau] district as having been paid for with blood; this was what the chiefs themselves expected; it would have asserted our power, and made a salutary impression on the native mind, for it is a fixed custom among themselves. . . .'[30] Te Rangihaeata spoke for both sides in the conflict when he said, 'The Governor is soft, he is a pumpkin.' FitzRoy's weakness, exacerbated by economic crisis, was soon taken advantage of. Within months Hone Heke began his challenge to British authority in the Bay of Islands with his symbolic felling of the flagstaff; and in the Wellington district, Ngati Toa and their allies moved to test the resolve of the settlers and their 'pumpkin' governor in the Hutt Valley.

On his voyage out from England, FitzRoy had been accompanied by H. S. Chapman. By 1840, Chapman had progressed from being editor of Montreal's *Daily Advertiser* to becoming EGW's chosen editor for the company-sponsored *New Zealand Journal*. In 1840 he had also married and been admitted to the bar at the Middle Temple. Chapman's interest in New Zealand had led to his being appointed the first puisne judge of the Supreme Court of New Zealand for the southern district, which included the three company settlements at Wellington, Nelson and New Plymouth. His arrival in Wellington brought the number of ex-Canadians there to three. Chapman could reminisce with R. D. Hanson, EGW's Crown Lands assistant during the Durham mission, but more especially with his old friend, *Gazette* editor Sam Revans. The surviving correspondence between Revans and Chapman from 1839 to 1843 casts much light on the politics of early Wellington; the voluminous correspondence that Chapman sent to his father from 1843 to 1851 gives even more insight into Wellington life and politics of that period. It includes the kind of comments on the Wakefields that could be entrusted only to private communication and which were, therefore, both uninhibited and untempered. Chapman was a distinguished Supreme Court judge and legislator (in Australia), but it is worth recalling, too, Charlotte Godley's description of him in 1851, when he was 48: 'I do not like him at all, though he is certainly clever . . . . he talks, Oh! so grandly – plainly telling you that he considers himself too good for his present position.'[31]

Chapman was sworn in at Auckland on the same occasion as FitzRoy whom, he was to conclude, suffered from a 'sort of monomania: – a notion that the Europeans were bent on destroying the natives and that the natives could do no wrong'.[32] Chapman, arriving in Wellington with the new governor, found that 'A great many merchants and others were keeping their business for me, especially Colonel Wakefield'.[33] Within three months he had come to the conclusion that the company would not 'long stand the effects of their own mismanagement. They are in bad odours with their own settlers partly owing to the apathy of their agent here Wakefields brother.'[34]

FitzRoy's adamant position regarding Maori and the company's land claims, stated so forcibly at his first levée in Wellington, had had a salutary effect on

William. After the Wairau, he had persisted in his obstructive tactics with Commissioner Spain who had responded by closing his court in August 1843 and returning to Auckland where he prepared a detailed report pending FitzRoy's arrival. Now William knew the game was up – FitzRoy's treatment of Jerningham was warning enough – and at a meeting two days after the levée he agreed to FitzRoy's terms for reopening negotiations. As conditions of the Crown grants for Port Nicholson lands the company would pay further compensation to Maori to the sum of £1,500 – the figure arrived at by George Clarke Jnr – while areas incorporating Maori pa, cultivations or burial grounds were not to be occupied. Any settlers who could not take up their balloted sections because of this provision would be compensated by the company.

Although it might have appeared that William had finally lost the battle he had, in fact, won the war: his compromise on behalf of the company was nothing as compared with the compromise of the Maori. When discussions with the inhabitants of the various Wellington pa began on 24 February, the money offered was rejected as paltry and only pressure from FitzRoy, who threatened to leave Wellington unless the Maori accepted his terms, brought about their reluctant agreement. By April, meagre payments had been spread about the pa bordering Port Nicholson. The real validity of William's purchases of 1839 was no longer being tested; compensation in English shillings was now seen as the solution for negligence and a cure for faulty title by Commissioner Spain, Governor FitzRoy and Protector Clarke. Even so, the Crown grant issue was still not settled: William would not accept it on behalf of the company until concomitant Maori reserves had been properly defined by size and location. The resolution of this had to wait another four years and for another governor.[35]

Now that the Crown's agents would admit of simple compensation as the key to company claims, William's long-standing intransigence turned to warm co-operation and he travelled north with Spain and young Clarke in May 1844, carrying £3,000 in gold and silver to settle the Wanganui and Taranaki claims. At Wanganui, Spain proposed to settle the company's dubious title to land negotiated by Jerningham with a sum of £1,300 plus four blocks of reserves. When most chiefs refused to accept William's distribution of coin, Spain arbitrarily decreed that their refusal to accept payment would not prevent land going to the settlers. More grounds were now provided for future violent conflict.

Spain's attitude towards settling the land claims seemed to have changed from one of plodding, fair deliberation to one of impatience at the endless hostile wrangling by both Maori and Pakeha, and perhaps resignation that the settlers would get the land one day, one way or another. Take it or leave it compensation was the quickest way out. It is possible that William's new spirit of co-operation (with doses of flattery) may have also encouraged in him a new bias towards the settlers.

When Spain travelled on with William to New Plymouth he swiftly ruled that returning Ati Awa claims to land there were forfeit by reason of exile or slavery, and that the company purchase in 1839 from the 47 resident Maori of that time was valid. He gave the company 60,000 acres stretching from just south of New Plymouth north to Waitara. Ati Awa were in immediate uproar and 50 warriors prepared to lay waste to the settlement. Only Clarke's intervention prevented another Wairau. He persuaded the chiefs to petition FitzRoy and wrote urgently himself in its support. Hone Heke had just cut down the flagstaff for the first time at Kororareka when FitzRoy received Clarke's letter. After sending a request to Sydney for more troops, he hurried to New Plymouth and reversed Spain's decision – now outraging the settlers – and worked to find a compromise that included an offer of free passage to any settlers who wished to shift north. William was furious.

John Wicksteed, the company agent at New Plymouth, wrote to William at the end of October that, unless he advised to the contrary, he would insist on Spain's award for the settlement. Wicksteed and William saw eye to eye. Two years before, in the early days of the settlement, when Ati Awa and other Maori had begun returning to ancestral homes after release from Waikato slavery, he had used a demonstration of armed constables, plus a few blankets and tobacco, to assert the settlers' right to the prime site of Waitara. With that episode in mind, William told Wicksteed that he would 'sanction and co-operate in any steps you may find necessary under the extraordinary and pertinacious disallowance of Commissioner Spain's award by the Governor to ensure peaceable possession of the land by the settlers'.[36]

Renegotiation with Maori brought a temporary settlement in the new year when a block of 3500 acres around New Plymouth was allowed to the company for its colony. At this, William reverted to his old technique: he told Wicksteed that the company's policy with FitzRoy was now non-co-operation, trusting to 'time and some future Governor to repair the mischief done by the present one'. But nothing would undo the mischief started in Taranaki by Jerningham, William and Wicksteed. Waitara would prove the flashpoint for the ultimate conflict between Maori and Pakeha in the Land Wars of the 1860s.

Less incendiary was William's purchase of South Island land for the Free Church of Scotland's proposed settlement. FitzRoy had brought with him authorisation to assign to the Scots promoters, under the auspices of the New Zealand Company, an area of land adjacent to Port Cooper on Banks Peninsula, provided no better site in the south could be found. Remembering Hobson's obstruction of Arthur over the Port Cooper settlement, William quickly assented to FitzRoy's key proviso that a government officer, John Jermyn Symonds, should travel with the company's agent, Frederick Tuckett, to safeguard Maori interests during a purchase. In September 1843, William had replaced Tuckett as company agent in Nelson. Tuckett's experiences at the Wairau, combined with the wanton abuse he continued to suffer from rebellious Nelson labourers, 'evidently unhinged his mind, and rendered his continual residence' in Nelson 'very distasteful to him'.[37]

At the end of August he had written to William, 'I am worn out with vexatious oppositions and endless importunities, and would rather be confined to solitary imprisonment for twelve months than endure such sort of existence for another twelve months.'[38] Despairing of finding any resolution to the multiple problems facing the Nelson survey, he also resigned his post as chief surveyor in February 1844, planning to return to England just as William needed an agent with surveying skills to go south and find the site for 'New Edinburgh'.

Notoriously tactless and stubborn, Tuckett was even more cantankerous after his experiences during the preceding year. He demanded complete freedom of action in choosing the Free Church settlement block, strongly doubting the choice of the Port Cooper region designated in the New Edinburgh prospectus. In the face of such obduracy, William gave way, assuming that the superior qualities of Port Cooper and its plains would become self-evident. In April 1844, Tuckett's exploration of Banks Peninsula and the plains gave him the proof to assert that the area's light soils and lack of timber made it unsuitable for the kind of smallholdings for Scots farmer-proprietors that the New Edinburgh scheme had in mind. It was better suited, he decided, for 'landed proprietors' who needed large acreages for grazing.

Tuckett sailed on south to Otago where he found pasture lands he considered the best he had encountered in New Zealand. In his enthusiasm to begin a survey, Tuckett fell into acrimonious dispute with Symonds who maintained that purchase from the Maori must be completed first. Neither man gave ground and Symonds returned to Wellington to register an official complaint. But Tuckett's services were too valuable to dispense with and Symonds was sent back with Dan Wakefield to act as mediator. Dan found the task of establishing common ground between the obdurate Tuckett and the righteous Symonds beyond him and returned to Wellington in disgust.

By the middle of June Tuckett, by dint of prodigious energy and determination, had completed a reconnaissance survey of all the coastal regions of Otago and had decided that the area from Nugget Point north to Otago Harbour was just what the promoters of the New Edinburgh scheme desired. It encompassed fertile land, a good harbour, plentiful timber and coal, an invigorating climate, all of a 'character that would attract a humble, labouring class of emigrant from their Scottish homeland'.[39] But by the time Tuckett began the negotiations with Otago chiefs for purchase of 400,000 acres, he had again quarrelled with Symonds who again returned to Wellington in protest.

To settle matters, William set sail for Otago with William Spain and George Clarke Jnr. Before the sale was legally completed, William wished to familiarise himself with the land and, with Clarke, Symonds and six Maori, he travelled for ten days around the boundaries of the Otago block, across densely wooded, virtually uninhabited country. On 31 July, the deed was signed. Tuhawaiki, a 'shrewd, straightforward and highly intelligent chief' according to William, played a leading role. This generous description may well have been coloured by hearing that the Otago Maori wished to dispose of their land because their race would soon be extinct and it would no longer be of use to them. The statement to the assembled Otago Maori by their protector, before the signing of the deed, also reveals how clearly Clarke complied with Crown interpretation of the Treaty of Waitangi, viewing informed sale of land by Maori as irrevocable alienation. He told them that 'they were about to part with the land described in the deed . . . with all growing on it or under it – that it would be gone from them and their children for ever – that they must respect the white man's land, and that the white man would not touch that reserved by the natives'.[40] This was Crown-sanctioned alienation of Maori land to the Company at the currently acceptable going rate (£2,400 or a penny halfpenny an acre). This was an improvement on the deals that William had struck nearly five years before in the Cook Strait region, and it may be that Otago Maori now better understood the reality of alienation, but the intentions of the purchasers had not changed.

William's journey south to settle the Otago purchase gave him some respite from the stresses and disputes – to the point of armed conflict and blood-letting – that continually beset him in Wellington. For four years he had tried to make the ill-planned and ill-organised Cook Strait settlements work but, if H. S. Chapman is to be believed, William was the most ill-equipped of leaders for the task.

> He has only just energy enough to sit down and write an excuse for not having shown energy, he has not only no activity but rather affects the half military lounger. He is not absolutely without intellect but it is without boldness and therefore exhibits itself in cunning and a disposition for low intrigue; his manner is reserved and suspicious both of which are stamped upon his countenance, and kindliness of feeling is an emotion which he never betrayed. But for his craft, cunning and want of boldness of intellect he might perhaps have been as hot as his brother but those low qualities have robbed his temper of its impetuosity without improving it. Cleverness he has; for he has shown skill in playing with the passions and weaknesses of others – a sort of skill of very little use in the world at large but which has been of service to him up to a point in this small community.[41]

Chapman thought, with some accuracy, that the only reason William had been given the job as principal agent of the Company was because 'Wakefield [EGW] may feel that he has been the cause of the ruin of his brother's prospects and hence he thinks he ought to sustain him through thick and thin. He had far better pension him which he can afford . . . for this man [WW] will ruin the ambitious prospects of the family. E.G.W.'s grand scheme has been by the force of his ability – and he would have done it but for the stupid inactivity of this man.' Chapman felt there could be no 'greater contrast' between the two men: 'Edward Gibbon Wakefield is a man of extraordinary energy, activity, boldness of intellect and frankness of manner with much kindness of disposition united with a rather passionate temper. William Wakefield has none of these qualities.'[42]

Chapman was not the only new settler to convey this opinion of William. A year or more before Chapman's arrival, Lieutenant John Wood had come to the conclusion that William constantly shifted 'responsibility from the Company to the Government. He is powerless for good, and his lethargic conduct is anything but satisfactory to the colonists unconnected with the Company.'[43]

Chapman's and Wood's view of William is borne out by the evidence of his perpetual dilatoriness over settling land claims, his reluctance to make decisions without instructions from London, and the compulsive deceit, blaming and self-justification that invest his missives to the company. His authoritarian and vindictive way of dealing with subordinates is shown by the consistently acrimonious and unproductive relationships he had with all the company's surveyors.[44] In a private letter to Company secretary Ward in April 1843, he wrote, 'They are a troublesome race, these surveyors – either hard working and ill conditioned, or gentlemen and idlers.' He blamed these expert messengers who told him that the survey ballot plan devised in London for a flat or gently undulating countryside could not be imposed on the jumped-up landscape of Wellington. Rather than confront with energy and sagacity the reality of the settlement's physical circumstance, he persisted in assuring the company that their instructions and plan could be fulfilled, ascribing all failures to his surveying staff, and that proverbial 'host of missionaries, protectors, magistrates & commissioners'. He worked hardest, and was most successful, at convincing the company of his good administration despite all the odds thrown against him; a dose of the truth might have worked better for all concerned. What he told EGW is unknown since no correspondence between them from this time survives, but William knew that EGW would do nothing less than continue to back him in London.

William's disputes and poor relations with Maori, Crown officials and his own surveyors meant that clarity over colonists' land titles was interminably delayed, causing frustration and conflict within the settlements. Add absentee ownership, inadequate investment and economic uncertainty and the mood in Wellington, Nelson and New Plymouth was often close to rebellion. The plight of labourers, overbundant in all the company settlements, steadily worsened with lack of capitalisation and slow movement of land sales in London. The company had guaranteed all labourers work and wages if private capitalists could not, but as resources dwindled, William was told to employ only labourers who were indispensable to the company's activities. He received these instructions at the time of the Wairau, compounding Nelson's crisis. Tuckett could not cope but his successor as company agent, William Fox, introduced a 'Half Week' system that paid labourers for piece work, allowing them time to cultivate their own patches of land as cottiers.

In Wellington, William cut the number of men on relief work and sent 50 families off to work their own smallholdings in the Hutt Valley bush. The distress and misery this caused prompted a protest meeting in October 1843 to resolve 'that the alarming conditions of the labouring classes in this settlement requires on their part the most strenuous exertions to maintain the means of subsistence during the depressed and cheerless state of the colony, to prevent the well-disposed and industrious workman from becoming a pauper or felon in this distant land, to procure food for himself and his family, as the cry of bread from a hungry family is an irresistible appeal that no man of humanity, however well-disposed, can resist'.[45] But resist William did. A labourers' deputation to him asking the company to honour its pledge of employment brought them no comfort. William had nothing to offer them.

The situation in the settlements steadily worsened. Some working people were able to leave altogether, such as the 40 men, women and children who shipped out from Nelson to Valparaiso early in 1844; but most were forced to 'encounter the labours of the bush', as William reported to the company directors, whose answer seemed to be more new schemes, such as New Edinburgh, to raise more capital.

William was caught in the vice of having to prosecute the company's deluded plans with inadequate resources that were reducing rapidly by the day, a situation that exacerbated his natural propensity for inertia and delay. He showed no sense of enterprise, hindering the proposal of settlers to open up the Wairarapa for sheepfarming – one of the few economic ways forward – because he was unwilling to depart from the company plan. Finally, the settlers forced his hand and drove the first sheep into the Wairarapa in May 1844.

William seemed temperamentally unable to provide cogent leadership during these critical times; nor did he have the initiative to resign and pursue a career more compatible with his limited credentials. Instead, he muddled through, warding off criticism and attack with disdain and malice, employing a practised charm and flattery where this might yield him influence with those wielding an authority greater than his own.

He had lost almost all his local support. Sam Revans who, though privately critical, had largely continued to support him in print, finally went for the jugular in April 1844: 'The baneful influence of Colonel Wakefield has almost ruined every settler, and the settlement of Port Nicholson . . . . How different would the position of the Company and its settlers have been if a master mind in an active body, with warm-hearted and conciliatory manners, had presided over their affairs.'[46] Revans and Chapman had clearly been conferring and this public comparison of William with the attributes of his elder brother smarted. Revans kept up the attacks. In May he blamed William for the Wairau; in June he described settlers as 'sad victims' and in July wrote of the company's 'gross public fraud'. These prompted secret meetings at the Wakefield Club to establish another newspaper. Revans finally tired of the whole business and threw up the *Gazette* at the end of September. The first edition of its successor, the *New Zealand Spectator*, took the company line and blamed all the woes of the Cook Strait settlements on

FitzRoy and the government in Auckland. It was a tired ploy. William had long been able to deflect settler discontent and hostility on to the governor and his establishment in Auckland but he could continue to use this tactic only while a misguided and under-resourced governorship persisted in New Zealand.

Increasingly, William withdrew into the social protection of a close circle of friends that were connected by family, company or soldierly association. This circle centred on the Wakefield Club, established at Barrett's Hotel late in 1840. Jerningham described it as an institution established for the élite with strict screening for membership to exclude the 'grumblers' and 'sots' and those who had committed some 'disgraceful act at home'. The hypocrisy of these criteria was not lost on any of those refused membership when the histories of Jerningham's uncles Will and Dan were canvassed, let alone his own baronial debaucheries in Wanganui. Rather than a club for virtuous gentlemen, it was a 'favourite haunt for the indolent', and a 'small gambling hell'.[47]

Jerningham was wont to describe Auckland as in a 'wretched state', and in a 'most disagreeable state of ferment' compared with the 'peaceable society' of Wellington. But the Wakefield ideal of Wellington as a planned settlement with services for a balanced cross-section of the best people from every class of English society was a joke four years after the first emigrant ships arrived. The population of Wellington were said to comprise 'some refugees of parishes, who are for the most part an idle set; a few rural labourers; an undue proportion of petty shopkeepers; some settlers of enterprise and talent; and a sprinkling of young gentlemen adventurers who gamble in billiards and land'.[48] Jerningham was not without confrères who hoped to make a quick fortune from land speculation or trade and return Home. But many became derelicts from grog and gambling and financial loss in a settlement that lurched along with no economic or political direction, beset by uncertainty over land development, the company's future and threats of war. In 1845, FitzRoy observed that active and educated young men had become 'destitute of profitable occupation, totally disappointed – perhaps ruined – and with the world's diameter separating them from their homes'.[49] Broken dreams lay in the broken grog bottles and human ordure that made the Wellington beach a dangerous place for an evening stroll.

There were more pubs than churches in early Wellington; no hospital until 1847; no fire services to fight the frequent blazes such as the mid-1842 calamity when 40 structures were destroyed along the waterfront. Lunatics were incarcerated in a wooden building alongside the gaol, which fell into such a ruinous state that prisoners had to be locked up in the police barracks. Throughout the 1840s children depended mostly on dame schools for their education: one had a simple, if broad-ranging, curriculum that entailed working through Dr Johnson's English dictionary.

Wellington was no decorous country market town for the close-knit agricultural settlement of the Wakefield dream. It was a rough and ready frontier port that somehow worked, despite its lack of a substantial hinterland and despite William's mediocre management and lack of vision. It did have the finest harbour in the country, was central to all the British settlements, had a stirring climate and the energy of a core of dedicated colonists. And though forcing labourers prematurely on to the land caused privation, it also created an independent group of robust smallholders who established the market gardens and farms in the Hutt Valley that came to sustain the town. For this was, as Lieutenant Wood acutely observed, 'in truth, a stubborn country, which only the nerve of a peasant's arm will subdue'.[50] The settlement inexorably developed according, not to plan, but to local needs and conditions. And signals of British civilisation such as the Pickwick Club, cricket and the races, balls at Barrett's and melodrama at the Royal Victoria theatre now formed a luminous edge to the dark harbour at the end of the world. It was vivid testimony to the enterprise and creativity that were producing the most durable colonists the world had ever seen.

William built his house on a hill above the hoi polloi, on the site that has been the ruler's perch from that day to this, and Emily made it a home. From the verandah, the broken glass on the beach winked only distantly in the sun, yet the house lay within easy walking distance of Barrett's Hotel and the Wakefield Club. Francis Molesworth, Sir William's darling youngest brother, was a regular at the club when he was in town from his farm 9 miles away in the Hutt Valley. Young Molesworth had arrived in Wellington on the *Oriental* in 1840 and with Henry Petre and Edward Hopper had set to with a will to establish the first sawmill and flour mill in the settlement. Molesworth's success on his 120-acre farm was touted far and wide as an example of what could be achieved in one of the company's Cook Strait settlements. The Wellington *Spectator* reported that Molesworth's potatoes would produce a 100 per cent profit 'for the first outlay' and more like 250 per cent for the second crop. 'This is a pretty good proof that the often commiserated wretches of Port Nicholson will not be able to pursue agriculture with profit!'[51] At the settlement's first Horticultural Show Molesworth's spuds measured all of 9 inches in length and in May 1842, Revans in the *Gazette* made much of the 20 tons of Molesworth potatoes that were being exported to Sydney.

Emily arrived in Wellington that same month and of all the suitors for that delicate beauty's hand, none could be more eligible, in William's eyes, than young Francis. The pair became engaged before she was 16 but plans for a wedding ball at Barrett's were dashed a few months later when Molesworth fell and fractured his skull. He did not mend well, suffering from brain fever, and he left for England at the end of 1843 in the hope that medical treatment in London would effect a cure. At this time, William wrote to Catherine of Emily that she was 'nearly a woman now, & much improved in appearance',[52] but he did not mention her fiancé's accident: there had been enough New Zealand tragedies in the family. Belatedly, Edward wrote to William from Blois, 'I am truly glad that you have Emily with you and that she has a poney and can gallop about with you.'[53] Still in ignorance of Arthur's death, Edward was equally ignorant of New Zealand, which he regarded as a kind of English country idyll.

By June 1844, Emily loitered palely in the house above the port, waiting for news of the man to whom she was inextricably betrothed. And though her father would not have bothered her with the details, his manner and disturbed comings and goings must have conveyed the crisis of the company on the verge of bankruptcy. The decision to suspend its activities did not reach William until 26 August, as he attended a session of William Spain's land court in Nelson. The directors realised the 'most appalling difficulties' to which he would now be exposed, but they could offer nothing other than advice to discharge all labourers and cut his establishment.

William immediately reduced the Nelson staff to two and the office and barracks were sold in November. He made similar reductions in Wellington on his return and suspended all surveys, including Tuckett's in the south. William considered himself fortunate to be in Nelson when the bad news came because he was on the spot to deal with any trouble from the 300 labourers on public works who had to be put off with only a week's notice. But the collapse of the company had been anticipated for months and the labourers knew that riot and looting would achieve nothing. 'We must all make the best of the business we can,' said the *Examiner*, '. . . all of us are in the mess together.'[54] Landowners did what they could, taking on some labourers at 10s a week or paying wages wholly or partly in provisions and produce. Young surveyors or improvers, like Thomas Brunner, who had been with the colony from the outset, were reduced to odd jobs and subsistence farming on smallholdings. The months that followed were desperate for many. One who survived that time wrote, 'Food was so scarce that the seed potatoes were dug up, but found to be uneatable . . . I kept the family in fish and in meat by killing wild pigs. I wore no boots for years, and we grew up like wild people.'[55]

William may have sympathised with the plight of the labouring people and smallholders but he could expect no reciprocal sympathy for being placed in an impossible position by the company. More than ever, he was the cold and stony public face of an inept capitalist speculation that had misled many into this dire situation. And like all capitalists before and since, William, while remaining comfortable in his house on the hill, knew very well how good a sharp dose of economic reality would be for the health of the settlements. Ten days after receiving the bad news he wrote to the company secretary about Nelson, 'Although it may create a sharp pinch for a short time, it seems likely that the compulsory reduction of the Company's expenditure will be the means . . . to restore the settlement to a wholesome and natural condition after the long duration of an artificial and injurious system.'[56] In a prefiguring of economic decisions a century and more later, William's young cousin Francis Dillon Bell observed that despite the misery involved, the end of public works was '"one of the greatest benefits that could be conferred upon the settlement", because it brought labour within reach of the capitalists'.[57]

In October, William wrote a long letter to a Mr Gowan at the Natural History Museum in London for whom he was collecting moa bones: 'I am afraid I must have expressed myself too sanguinely about procuring a skeleton of the Dinornis. I was lately down in the south where they used to live; but, like the human race in that part of the world, they have gradually disappeared. Is there not some theory of some one animal disappearing every thousand years and may not our friend the Moa have fallen a victim to this Fate?'[58]

Natural history was a distraction and hobby that might keep up both his own and Emily's spirits as the company was threatened with extinction, and hundreds of its settlers became endangered species, either from starvation or at the hands of Maori who increasingly rattled their muskets and taiaha in the Hutt Valley.

CHAPTER TWENTY-TWO

The New Zealand War

EDWARD JERNINGHAM WAKEFIELD REACHED Europe via Valparaiso on 7 August 1844, disembarking at Bordeaux so that he could spend three days with his grandfather at Blois en route to London. Edward complained to William, 'I . . . only regret that the importance of seeing his father rendered it necessary for him to quit me so soon'. Jerningham's short stay with his grandfather probably had less to do with the importance of meeting EGW than with an urgent need to indulge in the sensual and gourmet delights of Paris after his protracted time at sea: he took a month to reach England after leaving Bordeaux. Edward's letter continued, 'I have no good news to tell you. Catherine writes that EGW had about 3 weeks since a dangerous attack from a determination of blood to the head – he is better but I fear in anything but a satisfactory state.'[1]

Full of five years of New Zealand news and adventures, Jerningham arrived home on 7 September to find his father severely weakened and distracted from the effects of a stroke. At 48, overweight and careless of health and diet, EGW had predictably become a victim of his own relentless lifestyle, especially after the stress of the preceding year. He had been deeply embroiled in the Canadian constitutional crisis during the latter months of 1843; he had been emotionally shattered by Arthur's death in the new year of 1844; and, still distressed, he had been engaged since February in a life and death struggle with Lord Stanley and the Colonial Office to save the New Zealand Company and its settlements.

There is no record of how delighted or otherwise EGW was to see his errant son, effectively sent home by FitzRoy, but he undoubtedly stood by his own against the missionary governor and, in the tales that Jerningham had to tell, he recognised a powerful tool they could both use against their mutual enemies. He immediately set the young man before a desk, pen and paper. Through the vehicle of an exciting and colourful narrative of adventures on the savage Pacific frontier, the Wakefields could reach a wide public, making their case for the theory, the vision and the company, and provoking sympathy for the family and exoneration for the lost Arthur. Jerningham set to with an unusual will. Drawing from his diaries and New Zealand Company material, he wrote 300,000 words within six months. Before the end of April 1845, Byron's old publisher, John Murray, had the two-volume saga, *Adventure in New Zealand*, in the shops.

The financial position of the company had been deteriorating during 1843. It was brought close to insolvency when news of the Wairau was broadcast in England at Christmas, severely depressing land sales and interest in emigration to New Zealand. On 17 February 1844, EGW accompanied other directors, including Joseph Somes and William Hutt, to a meeting with Colonial Secretary Lord Stanley at which they sought a government loan of £100,000 'to preserve from ruin the Capitalists in the Colony, and from starvation the Emigrant Labourers'. The local colonial government was blamed for the troubles. At the end of March, the company teetered as the government first agreed to advance £40,000 towards paying its costs and then promptly withdrew it when the Colonial Office discovered it already owed more than £9,000. The directors had no alternative but to suspend operations in early April, sending the news that reached William at Nelson in late August.

On 26 April a special court of the directors formally sought the establishment of a select committee of inquiry, seeking a 'redress of the wrongs inflicted on the Company, assured that the Proprietors may rely on receiving from that Tribunal the justice which has been denied them by the Colonial Department of the Executive Government'.[2] The next day, EGW wrote to Catherine, 'Yesterday the N.Z. Co. proprietors learnt all the truth about their affairs – which is a great relief to me. We declared war to the knife with the Colonial Office: and last night the House of Commons, on Aglionby's [Henry Aglionby, MP and company director] motion, appointed a Select Committee to enquire into the whole subject.' The truth EGW wrote of was an appendix to the report he had compiled as detailed evidence of the company's activities over the previous five years. His postscript to Catherine added, 'You may guess how busy I have been, when I tell you that our Evidence . . . occupies 800 or 900 pages of print.'[3]

The vast appendix that became attached to one of the 'most formidable Blue Books ever produced as regards weight and size'[4] incorporated all of William's reports, correspondence and despatches; Dieffenbach's natural history reports; a detailed account of the Wairau affair and FitzRoy's judgements; the company's accounts; and the correspondence between the company and Lord Stanley and James Stephen. This, with the committee's minutes of evidence, was the printed resource that Jerningham was able to call upon when he began compiling his book in September.[5]

EGW threw himself into managing and manipulating the select committee's proceedings. 'All the labour of Edward Gibbon Wakefield of which it is possible to take cognisance would probably appear insignificant in comparison with his exertions in originating, organising, coaching, cramming, sometimes, perhaps, coaxing or mystifying the various Parliamentary Committees convened to further his projects.'[6] Wakefield family lore tells that EGW used to buy tins of boiled sweets called suckers from Mrs Boggis's little shop in Stoke and take them away to committee meetings in London. 'He declared that when he wanted to carry a point . . . he handed round the tin, and the various Committee men found it so hard to speak while engaged on a "sucker" that he could carry his own point.'[7]

On 9 July, after more than two months of battling, EGW could report to Charles Torlesse from the House of Commons, 'The Resolutions have all passed, after a desperate fight, together with one proposed by Ld. F. Egerton speaking in the handsomest terms of poor Arthur.' The report, based on these resolutions 'will be drawn by Ld Howick, & presented to the Committee in a fortnight. There is no doubt of its passing.'[8] The 'desperate fight' had been to have Howick's draft resolutions accepted in the face of an alternative draft presented by the Colonial Office.

About a week later, EGW wrote to Catherine,

> As London secrets are very safe at Stoke, I write to tell you that we know what the Report . . . will be, having seen a draft of it. It goes to exculpate us and condemn the Colonial Office upon almost every point of difference, and will be, I think, a complete exculpation of poor Arthur's memory, and of William's and my boy's conduct throughout. This concerns ourselves and might not have been mentioned first. As to the Company, and what I care more about, the colony, measures will be recommended for putting all to rights without delay. I expect the Report will be carried by a large majority . . . . FitzRoy must, I think, resign; and the animals who governed in Hobson's name, and afterwards with Shortland, will be sent about their business. This is not a too sanguine account.[9]

The first resolution of the report condemned the company for sending settlers out to New Zealand in defiance of the Crown. But EGW no doubt approved this minor concession, this nugatory rap over the knuckles, when the report's remaining seventeen resolutions fitted the company's requirements almost perfectly. For Howick's report also condemned the Treaty of Waitangi as 'part of a series of injudicious proceedings' with Maori, asserting that acknowledging their rights to 'all wild lands' in New Zealand 'was not essential to the true construction' of the treaty. It went on to recommend measures to obtain Crown title to all lands not actually occupied or enjoyed by Maori. The report also declared that the company had the right to land previously awarded to it by the government 'without reference to the validity or otherwise of its supposed purchase from the Natives'.

Flushed by the success of achieving such a public triumph for the company and his family, EGW understandably expected too much as a result of the report. Neither FitzRoy nor anyone else resigned or was recalled. Howick's resolutions had not only been adopted in the select committee by only a narrow majority but were directly contrary to the Colonial Office's interpretation of the government's obligations under the Treaty of Waitangi.

When it became clear that the government proposed to do little in response to the report, Charles Buller was asked to go over Stanley's head and appeal direct to the prime minister, Sir Robert Peel. This had no effect and nor, it seems, did the letter campaign led by EGW against the Colonial Office. 'The N.Z. war waxes hotter every week,' he wrote to Charles Torlesse. 'The correspondence with Ld. Stanley has now got to a ludicrous pitch of Billingsgate on both sides. Cheat, liar, fool, are not common words in the letters, but express ideas commonly found there. There is little to chuse between the parties as to fierceness, but we have the great advantage of truth on our side. The correspondence rolls the proud Stanley in the dirt; and how he will ever bring himself to let the public see it passes my comprehension. His part in it is a series of tricks and falsehoods, which our part remorselessly exposes.'[10]

In December, Stanley explained his position to Peel in a long letter, declaring that while he wished to assist the company in their difficulties, 'I must own that I have been disgusted by the perpetual small trickery which from first to last has characterised their proceedings.' He explained that the independence of Maori chiefs had been recognised in the Treaty, yet admitted that the Company had a right to Crown property – but 'what is the property of the Crown?' The meaning of 'wild lands' had concerned him in the past but he considered Maori understood very well their own form of title to the land. Besides they were 'well armed and warlike' and outnumbered settlers by ten to one. 'Even setting aside considerations of justice and good faith, I *dare* not act on the principles laid down by the Company and apparently supported by the Committee.' He finished by stating that the company had been 'from the first a great bubble, the bursting of which but for the immediate consequences to their Settlers I should rejoice at, and consider eminently advantageous to New Zealand; though, had their affairs been differently conducted, I think they might have been a most efficient instrument of colonisation'.[11]

There was chronic government confusion over the occupancy, use and title of waste lands in New Zealand, as well as the exact obligations of the Crown under the treaty and which lands belonged to it. In the 1844 report, the company had rightly pointed out that 'neither the Company nor Lord John Russell, nor indeed Lord Stanley, down to the time when difficulties arose through the operation of the Court of Claims [Spain Commission], contemplated the interpretation of the Treaty of Waitangi which is now the occasion of great and unexpected embarrassment to the Government'.

One product of the confusion was that, despite his concern for Maori, Stanley was prepared to accept the select committee's recommendation of instituting taxes on uncultivated land with confiscation in the case of default. He thought this would be an 'easy mode' of getting plenty of land from Maori for the settlers. When Charles Buller attacked the government during a three-day parliamentary debate in June 1845, he exposed Stanley's hypocrisy with devastating sarcasm. How could the Right Honourable Secretary for War and the Colonies propose to defraud the Maori of their land through a tax scheme while still claiming to honour the promises of the Treaty of Waitangi?

When the government had failed to respond to the company's demands by the end of 1844, Buller gave Peel notice in February 1845 of its intention to petition the House. It was the beginning of another relentless campaign of letter-writing, personal lobbying and propaganda through a press largely favourable to the company's position. The sizeable petition, signed by many leading London bankers and merchants, was presented to the government by Aglionby in early April. It declared that the 1844 report had satisfied the petitioners that the 'New Zealand Company and the colonists who emigrated under their auspices have been exposed to hardships and difficulties, the result of the policy on the part of the Colonial Office and the local authorities'. It called for prompt reparation and security for the company's future.

EGW was closely involved with the resumed 1845 campaign although, following his stroke at the end of August and minor recurrences, he had been forced to rest and withdraw from day-to-day battling. The exact state of his health during the winter of 1844–45 is hard to determine. In February, Edward was writing to William, 'I hear much of the state EGW was in which, I fear, is at times a falling into a sort of imbecility.'[12] In late April he added, 'I fear that EGW is no better. The slightest excitement renders him so giddy that he cannot stand. It is to be dreaded that he may fall into a state of perfect imbecility.'[13] Yet EGW wrote a long letter to Catherine on 23 March recounting the latest moves in the war with the Colonial Office and making detailed arrangements for her visit to him. And on 1 May, Jerningham recorded an outing with his father to the Haymarket Theatre.[14]

But EGW's March letter was written from Burstow Park, near Reigate in Surrey. Catherine was travelling south in order to meet her son Charley, who was due back from Nelson. EGW urged her to stay with him at Burstow 'whilst at the worst of your waiting . . . I think this plan would be good for us both, and the longer you may stay the better I shall be pleased – being very dull when I manage to resist the temptation to go to London during this crisis'.[15] Clearly, though Reigate was still within range of 'London smoke',[16] he had to stay away as much as possible from the stresses of Westminster and New Zealand House and take the country air while riding and walking. And when Charley finally arrived in May, EGW had his company for a while as secretary.

Edward's exaggerated depiction of EGW's incipient imbecility arose not simply from a tendency to hyperbole shared with his son, or from gaining only second-hand news of events in England. Direct association remained virtually impossible while the estrangement between EGW and Frances Wakefield, now into its twentieth year, continued. Lack of personal contact increased Edward's resentment of EGW's attempts to keep him from participating in the drama of New Zealand politics. He finally wrote to William, 'The conclusion that I draw is that he is in a very uncertain state, crotchety, and not liking that anybody should act but himself'[17] and that EGW was jealous of his own 'continued interference' in parliamentary affairs.

Driven by grief and helpless outrage, Edward persisted in writing to Prime Minister Peel, seeking retribution for Arthur's death. In August 1844, he attacked the missionary influence in New Zealand and FitzRoy's lack of action over the Wairau: 'I the father of one of the slaughtered sufferers assert my solemn conviction that my son has been murdered by the vindictive hostility of the local government . . . the colonial minister was their natural and legal protector and to his wilful negligence do I attribute the death of my dear son. . . .'[18] In June 1845, 'There is not one letter that does not describe Governor FitzRoy as insane.'[19] When he wrote to William in March 1846, he praised Alfred Domett's work on the Nelson petition against FitzRoy and complained, 'EGW and Jerningham are against it saying bygones must be bygones.'[20] A week later he was writing that he wanted Te Rauparaha and Te Rangihaeata sent to Bermuda as convicts.

Edward confided in the silent William that his sons were a disappointment to him: EGW was overbearing and distant, Felix never wrote and 'As for Dan, I can form no opinion about him. I have a father's feeling towards him, but he has flung away life and the chances of success so many times that I cannot foresee what may be his ultimate fate.'[21] His grief for the lost flower of his field was unending: 'Poor Arthur, how his figure is constantly before me, lamenting that he was cut off instead of living to see the success of his work.'[22]

Burstow Park farmhouse was not only good for EGW's health; it was also strategically placed, within walking distance of Reigate station on the London to Brighton railway. Jerningham recounted on 5 May 1845 how fast the journey from country to town had become. In company with *Spectator* editor Robert Rintoul, he walked from Burstow Park to Reigate Station, 'got into the Brighton fast . . . . started at 20 min. to 10, & arrived viâ cab etc. at Wellington Street in an hour'.[23] From this time on, EGW resided chiefly in the Reigate-Redhill area, for peace and quiet when he chose it, yet convenient for rapid forays to town and visits from family and colleagues. Ah, the railway! On the way home to Burstow from London on 20 May, EGW expatiated to Jerningham 'on taste – of Greeks – of monks in England – reasons for all pinnacles on Gothic churches,' but above all on what a 'man of last century waking in a railway tunnel' would make of this marvel of the age.[24] Many already wide awake were to lose money in that year of railroad boom and bust.

Jerningham's London diary, which begins soon after the publication of *Adventure in New Zealand*, records reactions to the book and the literary and social connections that it generated. There was some truth in Edward's assertion, when he delightedly received his own copy, that 'this book will I expect make him quite a lion . . . . he appears to be destined to play a great card in life'.[25] Jerningham was certainly the man about town, invited here and there, calling on all and sundry, pursuing unsuccessfully the mysterious 'MAB', patronising theatre with a passion born of his own amateur talents, attending exhibitions – scorning J. M. W. Turner's 'wild daubs' – and hobnobbing with publishers and the literary set. One May Wednesday's entry from his diary provides a good index to his activities and connections that year:

> Breakfasted at Gowen's – 2 or 3 members – Lawson and 2 others. Fitzroy's recall. Carelessness of one man as to who shd be Govr – his friend. . . .walked to Chowne's & got physicked – Few's – still delaying.– home.– /Cab at 1/2 p.12 to Milnes's;/at 3 to Ld Petre's – Doyle's – 13 Up Seymour St – Saw Rosabel [Attwood], who is not so much changed as I expected – pity she has not a better bust.– I still prefer la cousine decidedly.– thence to Mrs Pelichet's – Murray's –Thackeray's – Exhibition – Not a single person looking at his portrait . . . . dined at Dubourg's – exct Bouilli aux choux – Drove to Lady Mth's – Francis much better, talking about his departure – Mesmerism, opera – , ticket for Hortl Society – 24th May . . . . to Princess's – Love in livery very good farce. Compton.– Club – Cockerell & dramatic discussion.[26]

Jerningham had come to know William Makepeace Thackeray not simply from literary interest in *Adventure*. As a mutual friend of William Molesworth and Charles Buller, Thackeray had met EGW in 1840: 'a rogue if ever there was one', he had decided from his looks and voice. He was also familiar with the Pattle girls, daughters of Thomas Pattle's younger brother James and, therefore, Jerningham's cousins, although he makes no mention of them in his diary.[27] Thirty-four-year-old Thackeray was in his 'last year of Bohemian life', earning a living as a journalist, including writing for *Punch*, and indulging in 'too much dining and pleasuring . . . hob and nob [with] companions over the bottle'.[28] Jerningham – Teddy – the wild colonial boy nine years his junior, made for an amusing and suitably dissolute companion. In a satirical article from this time, it is easy to see Teddy at the table as Thackeray eulogises the English dinner: 'I am a diner-out, and live in London. I protest, as I look back at the men and diners I have seen in the last week, my mind is filled with manly respect and pleasure. How good they have been! how admirable the entertainments! how worthy the men!' Partaking of the English dinner, a 'man flourishes under that generous and robust regimen; the healthy energies of society are kept up by it; our friendly intercourse is maintained; our intellect ripens with the good cheer, and throws off surprising crops, like the fields about Edinburgh, under the influence of that admirable liquid, Claret'.[29]

Thackeray had begun to draft his masterpiece *Vanity Fair*, to be published throughout 1847 and 1848, and, though the novel is set 'while the present century was in its teens', it is a portrayal of English society as Thackeray knew it in the 1830s and 1840s. An early draft of Chapter Six described Vauxhall, the famous pleasure gardens across the river from Chelsea, as 'passed away as much as the Gardens of Babylon'. Vauxhall Gardens had been closed since 1841 but on 12 May 1845, Jerningham recorded a visit on the night of their reopening and he visited with Thackeray several times, notably on Derby Day. Outsider Merry Monarch was the winner that year and well-known punter Ginger Stubbs won £7,000. Thackeray's experience with Teddy on that Derby night out surely influenced his revision of *Vanity Fair*'s description of

> all the delights of the Gardens; of the hundred thousand extra lamps, which were always lighted; the fiddlers in cocked-hats, who played ravishing melodies under the gilded cockle-shell in the midst of the Gardens; the singers, both of comic and sentimental ballads, who charmed the ears there; the country dances, formed by bouncing cockneys and cockneyesses, and executed amidst jumping, thumping, and laughter; the signal which announced that Madame Saqui was about to mount skyward on a slack rope ascending to the stars; the hermit that always sat in the illuminated hermitage; the dark walks, so favourable to the interviews of young lovers.

This was Teddy's London of 1845.

Jerningham had noted on 7 May that Francis Molesworth was 'much better' and talking about his return to Wellington and Emily, whom he had last seen almost eighteen months before. But this was merely a temporary remission from the effects of the brain damage he had suffered in his fall. Neither medical treatment nor self-healing had made him well and the Molesworth family was willing to try any avenue for a cure, including mesmerism. The Molesworths were friends and patients of the chief proponent of hypnosis – principally as an anaesthetic device – Dr John Elliotson, Professor of Medicine at University College, London. The Wakefields, *père et fils*, were well-known practitioners and it is unexceptional that Jerningham should have been invited on several occasions to put Francis under hypnosis, though whether in pursuit of cure or relief is unknown. He mesmerised Francis on five occasions during the second half of May, but there was 'little progress – still more deep inspirations, and winking. – eyelids also, discoloured'.[30] At the end of August Francis Molesworth was 'much better' but then Jerningham's diary is silent on the subject until, almost a year later, on 4 August 1846, 'At 9 found at home a note from Lady Molesworth, informing me of the death of poor Francis at 1/2 p.1. this morning.'[31] Edward wrote to William that Jerningham had told him of Francis's 'incipient insanity' and that his death had saved Emily from a 'dreadful misfortune'. But Emily had long since been free of her commitment. A fortnight before Francis's death she had become newly engaged, to Nelson's most eligible bachelor, Edward Stafford.

Jerningham's journal entry of 7 May referred to Governor FitzRoy's recall from New Zealand, which had been announced in Parliament two days before.

The reasons given for his recall, after just two years in the post, were that he had issued debentures against instructions (to avoid bankruptcy), had not raised a militia to meet the northern insurrections of Hone Heke (he had no resources) and had not kept the Colonial Office properly informed. Since the office did not appear to know what was going on, his reticence was understandable. A leading, but unadmitted, reason for his recall was that, owing largely to the relentless propaganda and lobbying of EGW, Charles Buller and the company directors, the government had been persuaded of the inefficacy of its New Zealand policies. FitzRoy's weak communication made Peel's insecure government vulnerable to deadly attacks in the house, led by Buller who was armed with up-to-date New Zealand information provided by the company.

The failure of the government's New Zealand policies was admitted by the instructions and provisions made for FitzRoy's successor, Captain George Grey. His salary and parliamentary grant would be double FitzRoy's and he would be provided with an effective military and naval establishment. Grey was an ex-army captain, still only 33 years old, who had brought financial discipline and order to the tangled affairs of South Australia over the previous four years. He had also impressed the 'Saints' at the Colonial Office with a memorandum on racial amalgamation in the new colonies.

Despatches to Grey from Stanley, following the new governor's departure for New Zealand, show the government's first consideration of the notion, stirred by Buller and EGW, that the colony should eventually move towards self-government. Local administration and appointed councils, combined with the preponderance of European population in the rapidly growing new settlements, meant that the power of decision over interpretations of treaty and land ownership shifted steadily into the hands of settlers. Although Lord Stanley was inclined to protect Maori land interests, he secretly gave Governor Grey a £10,000 slush fund to be spent on buying waste lands from the Maori, either to meet the company's requirements under Lord John Russell's 1840 award or to be sold on. Over the next eight years, Grey purchased for a pittance much of the Wairarapa and over 30 million acres of the South Island, including the Wairau in 1847. The alienation of most New Zealand land, into Crown or private ownership, had now become inexorable.

The company's struggle to gain compensation and security from the government continued throughout 1845 and 1846 in concert with the larger ideological campaign in Parliament and the press. On 23 March 1845, EGW told Catherine that

> the recent debates about N. Z. have had the desired effect; the Govt.– not Ld. Stanley alone – having made us an overture of reconciliation. We have said 'Yes' on the understanding that we are not to patch up the old arrangement which is too vague, and makes us too dependent on the goodwill of Govt. – but have a new one, which,

> subject to certain well defined checks, shall render us independent. We require in short, security for the future as well as indemnity for the past; and the reply has been 'Very well; it is best to make an effectual and lasting arrangement whilst we are about it'. The negociation is now in full swing.[32]

On 1 May, Charles Buller withdrew his notice of motion for a debate on New Zealand on the understanding that confidential negotiations would continue between the Colonial Office and a secret committee of the company that included Somes, Aglionby, Buller and EGW. On 5 May this committee put forward the extraordinary proposal, probably EGW's brainchild, that New Zealand be split in two, with the portion north of a line from the Mokau River to Cape Kidnappers in the North Island reserved for the Maori and their missionaries; and the rest of the country turned into a self-governing province, 'New Victoria', open to colonisation by a company formed for that purpose.

On 6 June, EGW reported to his sister, 'The negociation is over and has not resulted in any agreement. Our proposal is rejected by Stanley; and we have rejected an offer from him to pay off the shareholders of the Company. The whole must come out next week . . . I am better than might have been expected, and have been able to take all the part I wished in the negociation.'[33] By this time, Buller had renewed his notice of motion amid accusations of bad faith and trickery between the company and the Colonial Office.

The company and its friends threw themselves into an intense lobbying campaign before the debate began on 17 June 1845. On 3 June, Jerningham 'Commenced the work of the Deputation. Wrote & despatched 44 letters to M.P.s.' Two days later he visited Edward 'Bear' Ellice who, remarkably, 'spoke as EGW could have done upon self-government for colonists, & gave us to understand that we should have it if he were connected with the Colonial Office'.[34] The debate, led by Buller at the height of his powers, centred on the proposal that the House should turn itself into a committee to consider the case of the company; the government opposed this on the grounds that it would amount to a vote of censure on the Colonial Secretary, Lord Stanley. The government was made to feel uncomfortable, its prevarications and inconsistencies exposed, but Peel could not afford to lose Stanley's support as government leader in the House of Lords and feared war with the Maori if the company had its way. (News of Stanley's land tax proposal the year before had helped to provoke Hone Heke's second demolition of the flagstaff at Russell.) Peel made the division a party matter and the government defeated the motion, but its majority was reduced from 90 to 51, a victory of sorts for the company. And when news arrived in early July of the start of the war in the north against Hone Heke and Kawiti, Buller raised the issue in the House again. The motion was defeated again, this time by 66 votes.

The result of the first debate had put EGW 'in good spirits, and thinking how to make the most of the N.Z. victory'.[35] On 20 July, Edward was reporting to

William that EGW was 'seriously ill' again but on the eve of the second vote, EGW wrote to Catherine,

> All my power of writing and even thinking, is so thoroughly engaged with the N.Z. affairs, that I really have been unable to write to you: nor can I say more than a few words now. We shall be beaten in the Commons by a larger majority than before, as Peel has staked his Government on the issue, and people would send New Zealand not to mention all Polynesia to the bottom of the sea, rather than turn him out for such a cause. But Stanley is gradually ruining himself, and everybody says he will retire when things are quiet. We mean to fight to the last, even on our stumps. I suffer from the excitement, & now talk of going abroad after the Session for 3 months, with C. Buller. If I could keep out of business in England, it would please me better; but of that I see no chance.[36]

Despite the defeat of Buller's motions in the house, EGW's and the company's 'war to the knife' had drawn blood. On 7 August the Colonial Office advised the company that each of its settlements would become a municipality, with powers to send members to the New Zealand legislative council and the Crown would waive its pre-emption purchase right in the company's districts. Three weeks later, Stanley promised to ask Parliament for a loan of £100,000 to ensure the continuance of the company's operations and, at the end of the year, Governor Grey was told that a competent person would be sent out to help the company select land. In December, Lord Stanley finally resigned, ostensibly in opposition to Peel's free trade policies, but many a knowing glass was raised in celebration at New Zealand House. 'Mr Over Secretary' James Stephen had long given up the fight and withdrawn as far as possible from New Zealand affairs. In May he wrote to a colleague, 'Of course nothing remains but to leave them in indisputed possession of the field.'[37]

At the end of August 1845, EGW travelled to France for a much needed holiday but in a letter to Jerningham from Paris on 3 September he reported that he was '*much worse* for travelling and very feeble'.[38] He went with a Canadian friend to Dieppe where, Edward told William, it was 'determined to try what 3 months entire absence from all knowledge of New Zealand affairs will do for EGW.– no papers are to be forwarded to him or even letters'.[39] But, finding no advantage to his health in France, EGW returned to London two months later, travelling in easy stages.

The lengthy separation from England and politics had, however, given him time to reflect on the company's plight and the state of the settlements in New Zealand.[40] Amid the smog of Paris and the autumnal Channel fogs of Dieppe, EGW became confirmed in his belief that the company, strait-jacketed by its financial crisis, was no longer the appropriate agent for his colonial ideals. He already placed more hope on the nascent Free Church of Scotland and Church of England schemes, which depended on land transactions involving the company's South Island titles but would be independent of the company's management. Both were in the early stages of planning but the Scottish 'New Edinburgh' scheme was the more advanced. In December, EGW sent Jerningham north to Glasgow and Edinburgh to assist in the negotiations that led to the Lay Association of the Free Church approving arrangements with the company at Christmas. The continuing disputes between the company and the Crown delayed the scheme during 1846 but the first ships sailed for Otago later in 1847.

After EGW returned to London, William Ewart Gladstone replaced Stanley as colonial secretary. Gladstone, then 36, was in the early stages of a parliamentary career that was to span six decades and include eight years as chancellor of the exchequer and more than a dozen as prime minister. EGW had marked him early as a politician to have on side and in 1836 had sent him a personally inscribed circular when seeking nominations for working-class free emigrants to South Australia,[41] as well as a copy of *England and America* in 1837. EGW had also worked to gain Gladstone's support when he had been a member of select committees on New Zealand.

At New Year 1846, EGW decided to approach Gladstone directly, without consulting the company, to propose a new scheme for New Zealand, developed from the two-province plan rejected the previous April. In an elaborate memoir, EGW outlined the problems besetting the colony, which he attributed to the 'placing of colonization in one set of hands and leaving all the rest of government in another set' like 'a pair of legs directed by different volitions, which would inevitably try to go different ways, and thus come to a standstill'.[42] He suggested that the company should withdraw from New Zealand affairs, after being compensated by the government; that the powers of the governor be curtailed and provinces set up for settlers with municipal self-government and regulation. Areas outside these would be left to Maori to manage their own domestic affairs until they were ready to accept English law and government. EGW saw this separation as a 'defensive policy' aimed at a gradual merging of the races, rather than resolutions through conflict, towards which New Zealand now seemed headed. His plan was designed to rid settlers in New Zealand of both the company and the Colonial Office, as well as leaving Maori relatively free of Crown interference.

Like the street plans for Wellington the company had laid out on a drawing board in London, EGW's new scheme made some ideological sense but was impractical on the ground. It was ahead of its time with its ideas of self-government, revolutionary in leaving parts of the country to Maori self-determination and contrary to all current notions of Crown colonial management. EGW did not maintain that it was the best plan, but it was more acceptable than allowing government of the country by a chartered company. EGW's attitude towards

Maori seems to have been paternal rather than patronising: though sharing the almost universal British view of their eventual civilised assimilation, he was consistent in his belief that they should share in the benefits of British settlement. There is contemporary evidence of this approach. At the time he was preparing his plan, EGW rented a cottage at Stoke for Pirikawau, a Christian Ngati Toa chief from Waikanae who was visiting England, and provided for his schooling there.

Although the core ideas of EGW's new scheme had some merit, some of the intemperate language he used in presenting them gained him no favours at the Colonial Office. He could not resist this opportunity to attack James Stephen yet again, as well as the past 'disastrous' policies of the Colonial Office and the 'great original error' of the Treaty of Waitangi. This had become the language of endless frustration, of a sick man approaching the end of his tether. He played games with Gladstone when the colonial secretary asked for details of offending articles written by Stephen for the *Edinburgh Review*. The previous June, timed for the day before the first debate on New Zealand, Stephen had written his famous note to Earl Grey (Lord Howick)[43] about having long treated EGW as a 'declared enemy' who wanted for truth and honour. He now wrote to Gladstone stating that EGW 'could not rationally expect to be considered a man of honour, integrity or truth'.[44]

Gladstone had soon become aware of the vituperative warring between EGW and Stephen that had echoed about the 'Sighing rooms' of the Colonial Office for the past dozen years; he began his ministerial career there as an under-secretary in 1835. If EGW's language was the public screech of a peacock then Stephen's was a much subtler hiss in the grass, judging Gladstone as 'wanting pugnacity' for success in public life. Vituperation or hostility in correspondence affected Gladstone not a whit. Rintoul commented, '"Willie is like that door" – perfectly passionless & imperturbable – "let us proceed to business, without regard to feelings".'[45]

EGW gave the company a copy of his memorandum on 13 February and the directors cautiously approved it, with modifications. Jerningham wrote to grandfather Edward, passing on the news and EGW's instructions not to write press articles or letters to politicians while matters were under negotiation – whereupon Edward promptly wrote to Gladstone.

In March the directors set up a committee to consider 'the detailed plan which at your [Gladstone's] suggestion, had been prepared by Mr Wakefield'. Gladstone sent a despatch to Governor Grey in which he recommended to him EGW's communications regarding the 'institutions of N.Z. . . . these should not be regarded by you in any other light than as . . . entitled to that degree of careful attention which the ability of their author and his known application to such inquiries may appear to demand'. He told Grey, 'The signal ability of Mr Wakefield and the time and care which he has devoted to almost every subject connected with the foundations of Colonies have made it my duty to peruse with great attention the letters to which I refer.'[46] EGW's ideas on self-government, at least, appealed to a politician who would eventually stake his career on Home Rule for Ireland.[47]

On 2 April a modified scheme was sent to Gladstone in which the directors reclaimed the company's role as taking over the 'entire business of colonising New Zealand'. It was accompanied by a map of the proposed seven municipalities, delineated and described by Jerningham. There was silence for three weeks before Gladstone replied, firmly denying that he had given any encouragement to the plan, and stating that he could not possibly make a decision until he had received Governor Grey's views. This effectively postponed any consideration of the project for a year. It is likely that Gladstone had been prevailed upon by Peel to shelve it. The government had enough on its plate as it moved to repeal the Corn Laws, and it could not afford to antagonise Stanley any further in the Lords.

On 26 April, Jerningham recorded, 'My poor father is very downcast & ill again at the result, so unexpected, of three months' hard labour. He still hopes to have the plan adopted this session; or rather *does not despair of it*.– Yesterday he was trying to get C.B. [Buller] up to the mark again for Colonisation.'[48] So it was back to political sparring. Letters were exchanged during May and Buller raised the matter in the house again on the 21st. Having made no progress, the company published the entire correspondence over the issue in a special 24-page supplement to the *Spectator* on 6 June.

A little over three weeks later, Sir Robert Peel resigned, the Tories went out and Lord John Russell led the Whigs in with Earl Grey, the ex-Lord Howick, as colonial secretary and Benjamin Hawes, an ex-New Zealand Company director, as his under-secretary. Best of all, Charles Buller was given the post of judge-advocate-general with special responsibility to the Colonial Office. Russell, Grey, Buller and Hawes: at last EGW and the company might have their right combination for New Zealand. But a fortnight before Peel's resignation, Jerningham recorded the unwillingness of 'Bear' Ellice and Russell to attack Peel on New Zealand issues: 'It is now said that John [Russell] is to be *in* in a week: and it appears of vital importance to get him to approve the Short Bill *before* he comes in. I am very fearful lest C.B. [Buller] should let this slip away. If he does, Stephen & Co. will beat us after Johnny's advent.'[49]

Jerningham's fears were realised. On 4 August EGW called on him on his way to meet Earl Grey at Charles Buller's house. No doubt echoing his father's sentiments, Jerningham wrote, 'Lord Grey's perverse disposition seems about to prevent him from taking that high place to which his talents would give him a right, if he would be a great Colonial Reformer. He is a coward, afraid either to acknowledge and profit by my fathers superior knowledge . . . or to enter into contest with him in which he knows he must succumb . . . . C.B. is funked; almost as prostrate as he was during the crisis of Ld Durham's reign in Canada. – Hawes, they say, completely mastered by Stephen. – was there ever such an example of "Official fever"? Fresh men, of whom so much was expected, afraid *within a week* to grapple manfully with the subject!'[50]

The next day, EGW told him that the meeting with Grey had gone badly and described Grey as having 'all Stephen's errors added to his own fractiousness'. On 8 August, Jerningham wrote, 'My poor father *very much* shaken by the great disappointment of Grey's most shameful backsliding – How can Lord Grey be such a fool as not to see the reputation he might gain by adopting EGW's views – Why he has publicly advocated them, and almost promised to promote them . . . . we are doomed to add his name to those who have disappointed us as well as the promise of their own fair fame.'[51]

Doubt has been expressed about the veracity of EGW's accounts of his meeting with Earl Grey who recorded in his own journal that 'Our conversation was very amicable, but it did not lead to much conclusion'.[52] Yet Jerningham's contemporary and spontaneous description of EGW's condition and feelings gives the lie to this view. Two years later, EGW set down his version of the meeting in his last major work, *The Art of Colonization*:

> Considering how his [Earl Grey's] rank and official station placed me greatly at his mercy, and that I could hardly stand or speak from illness, his reception of me was perfectly brutal. Bearing this with outward meekness at least (for I had promised not to quarrel with him), I endeavoured to perform my allotted task, but without the least success. He listened to me with impatience . . . and, addressing himself rather to Mr. Buller than to me, talked in angry and contemptuous terms of the principal suggestions contained in my letter to Mr. Gladstone . . . . I now saw that the attempt to make an impression on him was utterly hopeless.[53]

A contemporary letter from EGW concluded: 'I begged and prayed in vain; and the interview was concluded by Lord Grey's flinging out of the room in a pet, whilst I sank exhausted by the effort and agitation of the meeting.'[54]

EGW's account has the air of truth. Earl Grey was well known for his aristocratic hauteur and unpredictable behaviour and he was not prepared to accede in his policies to the influence of an individual without official status, whose social reputation and political methods were widely considered dubious. EGW had also been tactically careless in not keeping Grey abreast of developments during the first half of 1846, when the fall of the Peel government had become increasingly likely, and after Grey had proved such a strong parliamentary ally in past years.

Also, the attitudes of the new government men towards change and reform had changed from the passion of opposition to the conservatism of power. As Bertrand Russell wrote of his grandfather, Lord John, he 'subscribed to democracy as an ideal, but was by no means anxious that the approach to it should be in any way precipitate'.[55] Jerningham brilliantly captured this attitude, and EGW's position, in a three-act comedy that he wrote and had printed for private circulation in

1848. John Redtape MP in *Jack-In-Office or Prigs in Place* declares, 'The courage to acknowledge and forsake absurd errors is the most noble quality of a statesman, and I have been convinced how much need there is for prudence and discretion, in order to avoid the fearful anarchy into which we might be whirled by the Utopian dreams of certain reckless and empirical imaginations.'[56]

EGW's shock at Earl Grey's brutal rebuff was exacerbated by the news of Francis Molesworth's death on the same day; and both events followed the grief caused by the death of EGW's Uncle Daniel just two weeks before. The 70-year-old philanthropic QC had been found dead in his shower bath on the morning of Sunday 19 July. Both EGW and Jerningham assisted with his funeral on the 24th, when he was buried in the crypt of Lincoln's Inn Chapel. Feckless in youth and benevolent in maturity, Dan had been a model Wakefield, and as unpredictable as any of them. His sole legatee was his companion in old age, Sarah 'Sally' Clarke. 'Sally turns out to be his daughter at least so she fully believes and has believed a long time and the will seems to confirm her supposition.'[57] Jerningham met her several times and 'She kindly offered to let me take anything I wished. I shall confine myself to his Literary Journals & an old Book or two.'[58]

The stress of these events, in combination with unrelenting ill health over the previous year, caused EGW to suffer a near fatal stroke on 14 August, while he was at his hairdresser's on The Strand. Three days later, Jerningham wrote to Catherine:

> The only chance for my father is perfect tranquillity for some days . . . . he had a repetition of his attack of Friday – which tho' not so severe lasted longer. It was determined to bleed him a little, and he had two leeches on each temple. This has done him, I think, some good . . . . He is still very feeble but I hope in a fair way of recovery, provided he remain positively free from agitation . . . . Should there be anything to consult about, write to me . . . as I, and no one else, decide what is to be told him and what not. At present, I tell him nothing whatever; and nobody, besides his kind nurses the Allom family, communicates with him in any way.[59]

The Alloms had been close friends of the Wakefields since the 1830s and their house at 14 Hart Street, Bloomsbury had become a home away from home for EGW. It was here that he retreated after Arthur's death and here that he was nursed during this critical illness. Thomas Allom (1804–1872) was a noted engraver and his wife Mary Ann had become a 'zealous Anglo-New Zealander', supplying Edward in Blois with the news and material that he used in bombarding politicians and the press. H. S. Chapman found her thirst for news 'monstrous' and political intrigue 'prurient' but she remained a loyal and zealous supporter of the Wakefields. She had a practical interest in the settlement of New Zealand: in 1842, she sent out with Emily the first hive of bees to be successfully established in Nelson.

Thomas and Mary's eldest son Charles was EGW's secretary between 1840 and 1843 but it was their younger son, Albert (1825–1909), who was destined to play a larger role in EGW's work. In 1841, the year after being smitten by Emily on a visit to Richmond Park, he had gone to Wellington as a survey cadet and accompanied Tuckett on the Otago survey in 1844.

EGW's most persistent request was that Jerningham 'write to Catherine'. After 50 years this remained his deepest bond. On 19 August, Jerningham reported to her that Dr Tod of King's College thought EGW would recover 'with care and perfect quiet' and with the application of the 'new treatment . . . . This consists of raising the system, which was too low, and keeping down the local determination of blood to the head . . . he is to eat animal food twice a day, and frequently of arrow-root, gruel etc. besides – They are giving him quinine at the same time, and continuing the ice to the head, as well as counter-irritation by blisters behind the ear, mustard poultices on the back and stomach.'[60] If nothing else, all this would have surely distracted him from his underlying condition.

By 22 August, Jerningham told Catherine that EGW was eating well and 'His whole appearance is changed – He looks cheerful and animated' but 'There is no chance of your being allowed to see him for some days. We must not think of risking a relapse.' Jerningham was constantly at his side while Mrs Allom sat up sixteen nights in a row to minister to him. By the 25th EGW was strong enough to write Catherine a note and on the 27th dictated a letter in which he advised her that he was 'going to a Hotel in the fields established for invalids at Norwood. It would be a great satisfaction if you could come and pass a few days with me there: the sooner, the better . . . . I am considered better, but in need of the smell of mother earth in order to be able to sleep.'[61]

After Norwood, EGW went to Stoke and travelled a little in the country, removed from all contact with political affairs. Now he constantly carried a card inscribed 'Do not bleed me' in case he suffered another sudden attack. At the beginning of October he repaired to a cottage on one of John Abel Smith's farms at South Stoke, near Arundel, where he took little Amy Allom, also recovering from illness, as well as nephew Charley Torlesse to look after his correspondence. EGW considered he had become a 'very conceited young man'. EGW stayed at South Stoke for the entire winter, in a regime of full convalescence.

There had been a touch of *Schadenfreude* in Edward's report to William of EGW's August stroke and in the new year he wrote him that as far as New Zealand was concerned 'without him everything is in abeyance'.[62] But this time Mary Allom had her gossip wrong. The torch continued to be carried by Charles Buller. In a strongly argued memorandum to Earl Grey, Buller urged him to establish a clear and active colonisation policy. This should be based on Wakefield principles and local self-government as well as continued support of the New Zealand Company: 'I say still, "Keep it up at almost any cost: for in that Company . . . are contained the seeds of innumerable similar companies, & of much colonization through their agency."' He even argued that it might be possible to 'form the Southern Island into a third N.Z. Govt on a Proprietory footing'.[63]

But Grey was determined to do it his own way. Before the end of 1846, he had drafted a complicated constitution for New Zealand which, while providing for self-governing municipalities within two provinces and an overarching national general assembly, was pronounced mostly unworkable by Governor Grey because it focused entirely on settler government. Most Maori, still in a clear majority of population, would have been disenfranchised by a literacy criterion. The gradualism of EGW's proposed separate Maori province would have overcome this deficiency.

And then, in May 1847, before receiving Governor Grey's advice, Earl Grey proposed a settlement to the company. He advised the directors that the government would advance the sum of £236,000 (which included Stanley's promised £100,000). If, after three years, the company was still in a position to continue operation, then it would repay the entire principal without interest; if it could not, then the government would remit the advances made and, in addition, buy back all the company's land in New Zealand to a value fixed at £268,000. The charge would be made not on the British Treasury but on the colony's finances. During the three-year period, the company would take over the disposal of Crown lands and the Crown's pre-emption rights in the 'southern government of New Zealand'. But there was a major catch. Under the deal, a Colonial Office commissioner with the power of veto would sit on the board.

The directors accepted the offer with almost unseemly haste and expressed their appreciation of the efforts of Buller, Earl Grey and Governor Grey. Buller declined their appreciation. Despite the incorporation of several of his proposals, he 'cordially disapproved' of Grey's compromising measures. In a subordinate sinecure position in government, he was effectively powerless and yet was held at least partially responsible for Grey's actions. He resigned later in the year.

When EGW came to learn of the deal he declared that the directors had 'made a bargain. The Directors sold the honour of the Company and the interests of the colony for money, to come through a Parliamentary obligation upon New Zealand to recompense the Company for its losses; and with this purchase money Lord Grey bought exemption from the obligations of rectitude and honour.'[64] The company had been founded by 'men with great souls and little pockets' but had fallen into the hands of 'men with great pockets and little souls'. With a Colonial Office commissioner on the board, it would be 'so tightly muzzled that it was henceforth incapable, not only of biting, but even of barking!'[65] But EGW himself no longer had any bite, on the government or the company, and his bark sounded as distant and lonely as that of a chained and distempered dog.

CHAPTER TWENTY-THREE

'He is but cold earth'

ON 9 OCTOBER 1845, JERNINGHAM WAKEFIELD noted in his journal that he had received letters from friends in Wellington, sent more than five months before: 'All the *pakeha* in good spirits, altho they have not yet recd their good news. – Poor W. wants to follow me to London.'[1] But as Jerningham took 'MAB' to Drury Lane Theatre that night, the 'good news' of FitzRoy's recall was about to reach New Zealand, marking the beginning of an end to William's campaign for the company that was better than its acrimonious and inconclusive beginnings.

At the time he wrote to Jerningham, William was entirely on the defensive in Wellington, coping with the anger, entreaties and threats of petition and litigation resulting from the unfulfilled contracts colonists had made with the company in England for satisfactory land and title, and labourers for work. He argued, postponed and prevaricated with FitzRoy and his officials and staged a holding action with settler claimants until news came through from London.

He gained private comfort from his close military friends, from the enjoyment of his first home with Emily and from the company and career of young cousin Francis Dillon Bell, his 22-year-old protégé and, perhaps, a surrogate for the son that he had never had. Bell was described as tall and good-looking, vain, clever and hard-working but also 'shallow and unstable',[2] which suggests why he and William had a basis for mutual affection. It seems surprising that Bell and Emily did not make a match when, somewhere in the middle of 1845, her engagement with Francis Molesworth was dissolved. But Emily must not have taken to him and Bell's well-known promiscuity, with Maori and Pakeha women alike, may have been a bar to the respectable marriage that William sought for his daughter. Of William's own intimate life there is not a trace; although this very absence has led to the inference that he was covertly homosexual.[3] This is based largely on the fact that he frequented the Wellington bath house, though this was probably a symptom of his 'abstemiousness, remarkable personal cleanliness and general regularity of living'.[4]

There was nothing regular about the physical threat and uncertainty that assailed the Wellington settlement from all quarters – another cause for William's wish to be in England. Despite FitzRoy's and Spain's agreement with local Maori a year before, the latter continued to dispute settler farmers' rights to take possession of the Hutt Valley. Hutt Maori paid tribute to Ngati Toa so that Te Rangihaeata and Te Rauparaha still acted as power brokers in the region, though their positions towards the settlers, each other and local hapu shifted according to changing circumstances. Raids on farmers in the Hutt late in 1844 led to appeals to FitzRoy for military aid. Preoccupied with Hone Heke's raids in the north, FitzRoy could spare only two companies of soldiers while news of the sacking of Kororareka in the Bay of Islands stiffened Te Rangihaeata's resolve.

Frustrated by Maori intransigence and threat, Police Magistrate and Superintendent of the Southern Division Major Richmond concluded that local Maori needed a 'check'. He augmented his tiny professional force by raising a militia of 220 settlers who drilled daily throughout April 1845, using the old muskets that William had brought out for land purchase. Forts and redoubts were built at Te Aro, Thorndon and Kaiwharawhara to defend Wellington and provide refuge for women and children. More soldiers arrived from the north in April and a show of force was made in the occupation of Fort Richmond in the Hutt Valley. There were now three detachments of regular soldiers, each 50 strong, based at Te Aro, Thorndon and Fort Richmond, backed by the four militia companies and a cavalry company to patrol the roads and provide communications. William was of the strong opinion that the show of force had thoroughly alarmed the valley Maori and that another military demonstration would see them off. But FitzRoy had given orders that the soldiers were to be used only in a defensive capacity and Richmond, after news of the Heke disturbances, did not consider he was in a strong enough position to force the issue. Instead he authorised a failed attempt to pay off Hutt Maori. William condemned this as a 'lamentable and feeble measure of expediency'.[5]

William consistently espoused the demonstration of armed courage and nerve against unco-operative Maori, a trait that had marked Arthur's actions at the Wairau. This approach was based not on recklessness but on his considered judgement as an experienced military commander and on the knowledge that any significant reverse in a justified confrontation with Maori would be met with considerable retributive force. Both Richmond and FitzRoy had been goaded into action by strong-willed Maori chiefs, but had hesitated and stumbled because they lacked military backing. William's desire to see a firm check to Maori resistance and aggression would have to await a new governor.

When news of FitzRoy's recall reached New Zealand in October, there was jubilation in the southern settlements. There were illuminations at Wellington and in Nelson 'effigies of FitzRoy and the two Clarkes were paraded about the town and consumed in a grand *auto-da-fé* which was celebrated with tumultuous outbursts of applause'.[6] New governor George Grey arrived in Auckland on 14 November to find that the conflict in the north was unresolved after the destruction of Kororareka and the humiliating defeat by Kawiti of Colonel Henry Despard's force at Ohaeawai. Utter defeat had been avoided by FitzRoy's diplomatic ability to gain the trust and support of powerful Maori allies such as Waka Nene in a war complicated by old inter-tribal enmities.

Grey moved quickly to turn FitzRoy's truce with Kawiti and Hone Heke into lasting peace. He put a short deadline on a negotiated settlement and, when this was not met, moved with the increased resources that had been put at his disposal. With an overwhelming, and expensive, force of more than 1000 troops, hundreds of 'loyal' Maori warriors, and with cannon, mortars and rockets, Grey overcame the innovation, bravery and persistence of the 'rebels'. The fighting stopped and Grey declared victory: Hone Heke was a 'broken man' and 'peace and tranquillity' had been restored. In fact the fighting had stopped largely because opposing Maori felt they had achieved their war aims. In October 1846, Henry Williams wrote, 'It cannot be said that we have peace of a healthy character . . . . [Hone] Heke's cause is by no means extinguished, he is at large and could command as large a force as ever.'[7] But Grey's propaganda and diplomacy projected a legend of victory that most Pakeha wanted to hear, including his superiors. And by mid-January 1846 Grey had achieved victory enough in the north to turn his attention to the south.

On 12 February he made a grand arrival at Wellington with the paddle sloop HMS *Driver*, the first steamer to enter Wellington harbour, as well as the frigates HMS *Castor* and HMS *Calliope* and two merchantmen transporting 600 troops and military materiel. There was still time for negotiation, compensation and a peaceful settlement but, egged on by William and most of the settlers, Grey miscalculated and used the application, rather than the show, of his considerable force. He declared martial law, after Hutt Maori burned settlers' homes and drove them off the land in retaliation for the occupation of their potato grounds and damage to their houses. The final struggle for possession of the Wellington district had begun.

Now William was glad that he had not succumbed to his natural desire to leave the struggle behind and join Jerningham in London. He and Grey shared a military background; autocratic, ambitious and less scrupulous than FitzRoy, Grey could be as flattering and devious as William, though altogether more charming and subtle, and possessed an intellectual range that, among the Wakefield brothers, could be matched only by EGW. Grey's interest in colonial settlement could be traced back to his membership of the New Zealand Association in 1837. A year before that, witnessing the impoverishment of the Irish peasantry while on service as a young soldier, he had become convinced of the value of emigration as a way of ameliorating the degradation of the poor. He saw 'the hope there was in the new lands, and the greatness of the work of attempting to do something for the hopeless poor'.[8] In this he had a good deal in common with EGW, but he did not subscribe to the latter's theory of transporting the English class structure to new colonies. Just before leaving to take over the governorship of South Australia, Grey had met both EGW and Arthur when they were planning the Nelson expedition. Grey's success in solving the problems of the first Wakefield planned settlement between 1841 and 1845 caused Prime Minister Peel to consider him ideal to solve the 'yet greater difficulties' of New Zealand. It is not surprising, therefore, that William told Catherine, 'No two people can be on better terms personally than Capt. Grey and I am. He talks familiarly to me about all our family whom he seems to know. I even talk to him, whilst we walk the deck, of your parsonage & inclination to come to New Zealand.'[9] Grey even promised Dodo a job. William could do business with this 'prodigy of a governor'.

Threat, skirmish and sporadic killing continued, as did a great deal of tactical manoeuvring by Grey, Te Rauparaha – who had now adopted the role of peacemaker – and Te Rangihaeata who wanted no part of a fight but staunchly defended the rights of hapu under his patronage. But as Grey extended his control of the region with such moves as constructing a redoubt at Paremata and a military road from Wellington to Porirua, he slowly provoked Te Rangihaeata into active resistance. The chief refused Grey's invitation to go aboard HMS *Castor* for a korero, suspecting a plot for his capture. The company rag, the *Spectator*, assumed it was for fear of being punished for the Wairau.

Grey returned to Auckland in late April where he engineered the dismissal of Henry Williams from the Church Missionary Society on the grounds of suspect land deals and provoked the resignations from the Protectorate Department of the Clarkes, father and son. Where FitzRoy had been a missionary governor, Grey was clearly the settlers' governor.

While Grey was in the north, fighting broke out again in the Hutt. William and his co-magistrates called out the militia, issued small arms and authorised the arming of friendly Maori with muskets from company stocks. The *Spectator* blamed Richmond for the new attacks and a public meeting argued his 'incompetence'. R. D. Hanson in the *Independent* accused William of playing the old game of keeping up the quarrel between settlers and government with the idea of scoring political points to the Company's advantage in the House of Commons. Both papers told some truth.

Grey returned to Wellington at the beginning of July and the *Spectator*, echoing William's wishes, demanded the arrest of Te Rangihaeata, who had now constructed a fortified pa at Pauatahanui. Grey decided it was time to settle the suppurating conflict and that the most effective way was to neutralise the power of both Ngati Toa chiefs. He considered it too risky to assault Pauatahanui with Te Rauparaha unaccounted for behind him and with the threat of a Wanganui war party coming down the coast to assist Te Rangihaeata.

With an armed detachment Grey steamed up the west coast in the *Driver* on 20 July, intending a 'combined operations' landing at the Ohau to disperse the Wanganui warriors. A heavy surf prevented this so he put the detachment ashore further south at Otaki and Waikanae to block the Wanganui taua's progress. Grey had been given information that Te Rauparaha was playing his familiar devious games and planned to assist the Wanganui, despite protestations of peace over the previous months. Grey had no hard evidence but he took Te Rauparaha's history as moral justification enough to make a move that would destroy a mana and fatally injure the old system of tribal power in the region. Politically, Grey knew that he would judged only by his success or failure, not by his scruples. 'What is certain is that Te Rauparaha was now matched by one whose guile exceeded his own.'[10]

On the evening of 22 July, Grey took the *Driver* south past Te Rauparaha's Taupo pa, to give the 'Old Sarpint' the impression that he was returning to Wellington. Grey returned during the night and at daybreak put ashore an armed party to seize him. Te Rauparaha was surprised as he slept, naked between his two wives and coated with red ochre and oil. One man 'grabbed him by the neck and the bluejackets by the arms and legs. Shouting "Ngati Toa! Ngati Toa!" and biting a bluejacket's arm, the naked and well anointed old cannibal twisted like a basket of eels. Even at four to one, his kidnappers were not able to make him fast until one of them grabbed his privates and held on.'[11]

The company settlers felt 'universal satisfaction' at Grey's action.[12] But unless he had evidence to prove conspiracy or treason, the governor had no right to hold Te Rauparaha prisoner. Judge Chapman told Grey that if Te Rauparaha came to his court for a writ of habeas corpus, he would have to give it – but neglected to explain this cornerstone point of English law to Te Rauparaha or any other Maori.

Grey now proposed to dispose of Te Rangihaeata by blockading his pa at Pauatahanui. But six days after Te Rauparaha's capture, it was discovered empty: Te Rangihaeata was retreating north with his Ngati Toa party of about 100 men plus women and children. Grey sent hundreds of soldiers, seamen and allied Maori after Te Rangihaeata as, over the following month of deep winter, he fought his way to the safety of his refuge among the Poroutawao swamps north of the Manawatu River. It was the most amazing rearguard action in New Zealand's land war history. Te Rangihaeata had always said that no Pakeha would 'make a tie' of him, and though William was triumphant over the destruction of his old enemies, and the delivery of a kind of justice for Arthur, Te Rangihaeata had not been overcome.

Yet Grey could now safely leave Te Rangihaeata to his swampy hideaway. He had finished in a few months the struggle that William had started seven years before: 'Before 1846 the Pakeha at Port Nicholson had been living, even if they did not quite know it, in a Maori world. After 1846 Maori were living in a Pakeha one.'[13] But the wider struggle over land had only begun.

The following year William took his chance to participate personally in Grey's military expeditions. He had handled the purchase and settlement of Wanganui land in the same cursory manner as he had other settlements, and with the same arrogant certainty that the company would prevail. In January 1842 he had written to a Wanganui settler, 'Above all, I calculate on the increased and daily increasing power of the Company. The hostility of the local Government must either give way or be removed and no distant day will reward the patience and courage of the Settlers with ensured prospects of Security and wealth.'[14]

In May 1844 he had considered that, with more payments and William Spain's support, the Wanganui land purchase could be settled, but local Maori refused to accept William's £1,000 in gold. Two years later he accompanied Grey to Wanganui on HMS *Castor* and some progress was made on land settlement in the months that followed, though the £1,000 shuttled back and forth between Wellington and Wanganui until William finally spent it on company wages and expenses. Another year on, the increasing tangle of Wanganui affairs was brought to a knot by the murder of the Gilfillan family at Putiki and government military intervention became inevitable. Coincidentally, Te Rangihaeata had ventured from his Manawatu stronghold to raid Kapiti Island for gunpowder. Grey feared a general conspiracy.

On 19 May the small town of Wanganui was attacked by 300 Maori warriors. Four days later, Major Richmond sent military reinforcements from Wellington on HMS *Calliope*. For ten months Te Rauparaha had been held prisoner aboard this vessel. In February, William described 'a grand fête' on board, which began at 11 a.m. and lasted till midnight. 'All the ladies except Mrs Petre and Mrs Crawford and some occasionally invisible ones were present. The ship sailed round the harbour, during which time some very bad shots were fired at some rocks . . . . During the day Ld C. Butler had the bad taste to introduce Rauperaha on deck in the dress of an Officer in the Navy, which so much distressed Mrs McDonald that she almost fainted. As this was repeated in the evening, it has created great disgust but otherwise the party was first rate. . . .'[15] In this most humiliating of circumtances, the great Ngati Toa chief, the 'Maori Napoleon', had become a colonial trophy to excite the ladies.

On HMS *Inflexible*, however, Governor Grey treated his Maori guests with the courtesy due to their mana, but they were nonetheless trophies of his success as he set out from Auckland for the Wanganui on 20 May. His guest, with a retinue of 30, was the great Waikato chief Te Wherowhero, known throughout Maoridom. He had guaranteed the security of Auckland during the war in the north and his presence beside the Queen's kawana could only have a salutary effect on recalcitrant Wanganui Maori; as would that of Waka Nene, the other chiefly ally whom Grey picked up from Kororareka en route. Also aboard were Grey's bodyguard, 100 men of the Grenadier Company 65th Regiment, his wife Eliza and William, who was bunking down in steerage with Wanganui missionary Richard Taylor.

William had already been aboard the *Inflexible* for three weeks in March, on a trip to Nelson and New Plymouth when he had found it 'very arguably . . . one of the most powerful & well fitted up of H.M.'s steam vessels'.[16]

William had rejoined the *Inflexible* in Wellington and made the journey to Auckland to join Grey's party in just 63 hours. It was, he wrote to Emily, the 'best sea travel' he had experienced. He enjoyed the sightseeing excursion to the Bay of Islands where, with George and Eliza Grey, he had visited the sites of the battles. On the way south to Wellington the *Inflexible* arrived at Wanganui in concert with the *Calliope*.

> On arriving off the mouth of the river we perceived the British ensign flying on the sandhills and upon a boat going to the place we had soon a signal made to let us know on board the Steamer that the Maoris had attacked the Town and destroyed the buildings at all the outstations. A great bustle followed in the ship. Every body seemed to be as warlike as possible. Mrs Grey's eyes sparkled as if she would not have been backward if she had been allowed to go. The boats, six in number, were quickly lowered and all the men on board, with the exception of one officer and 40 men and boys, started for the river. The two paddlebox boats carried 100 of the 65th Regt whom we had brought from Auckland. The next morning the Gov made a sortie from the stockade in which we had slept, and people expected a fight . . . . the affair ended in nothing but a few shots fired . . . and I must say I was a good deal vexed at returning to the Stockade so soon – particularly as I had gone to the extent of rigging myself in one of Tommy Pedder's blue worsted shirts and of carrying his 2 barrelled gun, with ammunition enough to exterminate all the natives, amounting to 50 or 60, that I could discover with a telescope.[17]

William wrote as if he had returned with an empty bag from grouse-shooting, a day of blood sport ruined.

The Wanganui disturbances dragged on into 1848 before peace and land payments were finally made. But the potential conflict at Wellington, Wanganui, New Plymouth and in the north always bubbled just below the surface, kept in check only while enough Maori maintained control over enough land, and the material benefits of Pakeha settlement offset the loss and indignities that this brought. And also while Grey successfully maintained a balance between negotiation and armed strength, alliance with key chiefs and manipulation of the news, especially that reaching the Colonial Office.

William was as susceptible as anyone to Grey's flattering manipulation and enjoyed taking part in the governor's seaborne military parades. But the government was still the government and William was objective enough to continue seeing through the company's aims and to take advantage of his relationship with

Grey. Chapman may have thought him a 'military lounger' but William was more politically effective than this dismissive soubriquet allows. Justice Chapman himself, at the beginning of 1847 and after just three years in New Zealand, began seeking Charles Buller's influence to find him a new job that was better paid and not too onerous, preferably an 'office at home' that would allow him to practise law privately. But not the office of a parliamentary under-secretary, which paid only £1,000 a year and meant 'very hard work. I have a salary equal to that [here] with certainty of increase and moderate work.'[18]

In the same letter, Chapman described the effect of the news of EGW's seven provinces plan when it reached Wellington just before Christmas 1846: 'This little community has been for some time in a state of great turmoil in consequence of certain reports industriously set about by the Company's agent and his friends.' The governor had come down at Christmas, but rumours 'set afloat . . . sent him back to Auckland for his despatches'. Chapman reported that the company's solicitor 'wrote out – "We are preparing a Bill with powers as extensive as those of the E.I. Co [East India Company]". Another letter said – "E.G. Wakefield is coming out as Governor". A passenger by the *Hope* related that Wakefield had said to him "I shall soon follow you either in an official or private capacity".' Unsurprisingly, 'All this alarmed the public, for I hardly know anything more dreaded than a proprietary Government – especially with Colonel Wakefield as Governor . . . . If it was meant as a feeler it has succeeded . . . . for it has produced a burst of public indignation that can never be quelled. Colonel Wakefield's unpopularity is excessive. It partly arises from his complete incompetency and partly from his nasty little intriguing habit of setting people together by the ears.'

By August of 1847, where William was concerned, Chapman's often astute assessment of character and situation had become deeply coloured by personal animosity. 'He is cowardly, suspicious and mean to a degree I have scarcely ever met with. No generous sympathy ever enters his breast. It is impossible to conceive the universal detestation in which he is held here by every one except a few toadies as base as himself, who will abandon him the instant they find his power is over.'[19] Chapman ascribed all the company's failures to William and, by contrast, continued to praise the qualities of EGW and to rehearse the superior ways in which the man he had once described as a 'clever scoundrel' would have handled matters. The learned judge did protest too much. It became known that in 'private conversations and in correspondence his comments were trenchant and he showed intolerance towards many of his contemporaries. He described FitzRoy as "ignorant" and "thoroughly selfish", George Grey as insincere, and Edward Eyre as "totally unfit" for his office'.[20] Edward Jerningham Wakefield was 'that drinking little blackguard Tiraweka'.[21]

The threat of EGW and William's proprietary government of southern New Zealand faded and then disappeared once information came through of Earl Grey's appointment as colonial secretary, and his dismissal of EGW's plan. This was followed by news of EGW's serious illness. Later, in May, Earl Grey's complicated constitutional proposals arrived. Although the prospect of a Wakefield governorship proved a bubble soon pricked, Governor Grey could not predict the outcome of the company's negotiations with the government and he kept William on side with regular opportunities to promenade along the decks of the *Inflexible*.

With a kind of peace established in the Cook Strait region, Grey moved to settle the Wairau dispute. Negotiations with Ngati Toa chiefs began in February 1847 and in Wellington on 18 March the deed of sale was signed with a payment of £3,000. Grey drove a hard bargain for rights to 3 million acres of what was to become the province of Marlborough: 80,000 acres were agricultural land and 240,000 good pastoral country. Grey refused to release Te Rauparaha unless the other Ngati Toa chiefs signed and when 'he was told that the bargain was incomplete without the consent of Te Rangihaeata the Govr. said he was a rebel and would not treat with him'.[22] Partly at the urging of William, the money was paid out in annual instalments of £600. Both he and Grey considered this would promote a better use of the money by Ngati Toa and it also allowed Grey an extended influence over the tribe. William had pointed out, too, that some of the signatories to this deed were also signatories to the £2,000 settlement for the sale of Porirua and, therefore, recipients of double payments.

Grey told William that the company could now purchase whatever Wairau land it needed to fulfil its obligations to the settlers, at a price the imperial government might direct. A week earlier, when William had accompanied Grey to Nelson during land settlement negotiations, he had broken down in grief when a dinner toast to the Wairau fallen had been raised. When it had been proposed to make this toast before that to Governor Grey, Dr J. D. Greenwood had declared he would immediately propose 'Perdition to the New Zealand Company'.[23]

Understandably, William strongly objected to Grey's deal to release Te Rauparaha. A week after the deed of sale, with realisation that the company would have to pay for the Wairau, he wrote a letter to Grey in which his conflicting emotions showed through the surface of his practised officialese.

> When I find not only that district [Wairau] included as part for which a very large sum of money is paid by the Crown, but the Company desired to repay the proportionate amount for it, I cannot but remind His Excellency that the Company's claim to the whole district has never been investigated, as the late Commissioner of Claims, Mr Spain, has publically [*sic*] admitted in his Official Report, but respectfully and earnestly submit that the payment of this sum, not to resident natives in actual enjoyment of the land, but to the very men who savagely murdered our countrymen at Wairao now nearly four years ago, is tantamount to a declaration of the invalidity of that claim without investigating it, and therefore to a justification of the perpetrators of that dreadful tragedy. I cannot but contemplate that after all the struggles the Company

> have made to vindicate their claim to the Wairao and the memory of those who fell in supporting it against unlawful violence, they will regard in the same light the arrangement which His Excellency has been pleased to make. . . .[24]

William's heartfelt plaint brought no result. Grey upheld Spain's disallowance of the original Wairau purchase, saying that to do other would destroy Ngati Toa's, and every other tribe's, trust in British justice and again 'plunge the country into an expensive war'.[25] The *Spectator* expressed the feeling of the majority about the events of four years before: 'Our sentiments with regard to the Wairau Massacre remain unchanged, and we think we best show our respect for the memory of its unfortunate victims by allowing them to rest in honour – and in peace.'[26] But at least the Wairau Valley could now be opened for Nelson settlers and by November William received news of the company's deal with Earl Grey and the financial wherewithal to settle all the claims on the company. By August 1848, Dr Greenwood could no longer justify his toast of 'Perdition!'

William continued to dabble in natural history as a diversion from the stress of politics. In August 1845 he wrote to London palaeontologist Richard Owen, thanking him for sending copies of his book on Apteryx (Kiwi) and Dinornis (Moa). One would go to the Nelson Literary Institute, whose rooms were much frequented, but 'At present the community at Waikowaite [Waikouaiti, Otago] is not of a reading class'. But he would give it to whaler and trader Johnny Jones and 'request him to show it to any intelligent visitors'. Many of the moa bones collected for Owen had come from North Otago. He also advised Owen that 'Some time ago I gave Sir Everard Home [of HMS *North Star*], who told me he was collecting for you, a curious species of lizard, about 18 inches long and having a row of white spikes along its back, caught on Somes Island, Port Nicholson.'[27] It was the first specimen of a tuatara to be sent off for scientific examination. A couple of years later he sent J. R. Gowan a mixed collection of moa bones, both large and small, commenting accurately, 'I can only account for the admixture by supposing that the natives formerly killed and ate the flesh of these birds indiscriminately at their pahs . . . which have been time out of mind near the mouths of rivers. . . .'[28]

The new year of 1848 brought a change of governance in New Zealand, when part of Earl Grey's constitution was implemented. On 10 March, the two provinces of New Ulster and New Munster were officially proclaimed, north and south respectively of a line running due east of the mouth of the Patea River. Grey, now Governor-in-Chief, continued to reside in Auckland but New Munster's Lieutenant-Governor, Edward John Eyre, had his capital in Wellington. Eyre was less successful as a governor, both in New Munster and later in Jamaica, than as an explorer of the desert wastes of central and west Australia. Determined to continue his adventurous career, he began exploring inland mountain routes between Marlborough and Canterbury. During the course of this he made the first ascent of Mount Tapuaenuku, 9465 feet high, but lost one of his Maori companions in a fatal fall. Grey prevailed upon him to confine his explorations to the wilder reaches of political and social life in the southern settlements.

Grey also prevailed upon Eyre to consider Dan for a job in the New Munster government, as he had promised William. H. S. Chapman was at his vituperative best as Dan was being considered for provincial appointments. When asked for his advice as puisne judge, he said that Dan was as 'well fitted as other practitioners to fill the office of Crown Solicitor – I do not think there is much choice among them'. As for the 'new and more important post of Attorney-General Dan. Wakefield is very unfit. His knowledge of law is very so-so – if he ever had much it has grown rusty through non-use. His want of principle will render him a bad counsellor. . . .' Chapman considered him 'mendacious and so slanderous: a mere spy of the Colonel's that almost every house is closed against him'.[29]

Chapman's comment probably referred to a public altercation that had occurred between Dan and Sam Revans. During his first three years in Wellington, Dan kept a generally low profile while finding work as a barrister and solicitor. In March 1845, he had represented a party opposed to Revans and outside the court, during the course of the case, told Revans that he had obtained a *rule nisi*. 'Revans said "Oh a Rule Nisi is nothing", upon which I said, "It is a first step". Mr Revans immediately said, "Well I will bet five to one, I win it. I know Chapman . . . I can trust him, or he will take care of it. I know Chapman; we kept two sisters together for three years . . .".'[30] Indignant at 'such an outrage' on the administration of justice, Dan repeated and recorded what Revans had said and the question was referred to the chief justice. In the *Spectator* of 29 March, Dan took out an advertisement on the front page to recount what happened next: 'Last evening about ten o'clock, I was in the Billiard Room at Barrett's Hotel, when Mr Samuel Revans came into the room and in the presence of several persons said – "I have long sought to tell you that you are a liar, a scoundrel, and a coward. I made him no reply, and he shortly afterwards left the room. I have since been informed that [he] intends to assault me, and I fear some bodily injury from him; and I therefore pray that the said Samuel Revans may be bound in recognizance to keep the peace.' Revans's behaviour was consistent with his 'rough' and 'easy' morals[31] and Chapman would have been mortified at his revelation of what they had got up to in their earlier days in Montreal.

Dan was appointed a Crown solicitor and public prosecutor on 1 September 1847 and redesignated Crown solicitor, legal adviser and Standing Counsel for Natives on 1 February 1848. The last post may indicate how low legal counsel for Maori lay on the government's list of priorities. William Fox, the company's agent in Nelson, was appointed New Munster's attorney-general but soon resigned over political differences with Grey. Despite Chapman's opposition,

Dan was advised at the end of the year by Alfred Domett, now colonial secretary for New Munster, that he had been appointed attorney-general. This was in a temporary capacity because of the 'delicate state' of his health; if necessary he could fall back on his existing post at £400 per annum. Eventually Dan became well enough and in February 1850, Chapman told his father: 'I have sworn in Dan. Wakefield the Attorney General . . . . There'll be a row to a certainty. Dan Wakefield is always in a funk on these occasions – for at public meetings his having come out under a false name is always brought up – and lately the reason is said to have been discovered.'[32] Whatever the reason, Dan's five-year estrangement from his wife Angela ended after she took ship for Wellington with their two children, Selina Elizabeth and Charles Marcus, at the end of September 1847. Their departure had been delayed some months by ten-year-old Selina's ill health but the family was finally together again by March 1848.

By this time, William's short experience of family was well over. In November 1845, when he visited Nelson with Bishop Selwyn, he had taken eighteen-year-old Emily and two of her friends with him and during their five-day stay she had met Edward Stafford, 'so much Nelson's leading young bachelor and, for the present, the friend of her affectionate, excitable but rather unreliable cousin, Francis Dillon Bell'.[33] Stafford, 26, was the son of Anglo-Irish gentry and had arrived in Nelson in January 1843 where he managed Aldourie Station, in the Waimea Valley, for Tytler family cousins. He was a fine horseman and a successful pastoralist. Intelligent and energetic, he had indicated his political ambitions early by moving Nelson's vote of no confidence in FitzRoy in September 1843. Short on capital, he was long on prospects, and William was warmed by his consistent support and sympathy over Arthur's death at the Wairau. When William visited Nelson again with Governor Grey in March 1846 he invited young Stafford to visit him when he was next in Wellington.

Stafford wasted no time and was across the strait within a month. Although his visit to Wellington coincided with the war alarums in the Hutt Valley, he was less interested in calls to arms than calls on the colonel and paying assiduous court to Emily. In July it was reported, 'Stafford has just concluded a treaty of marriage with Miss Emily Wakefield to come off as soon as Stafford can get his house in order.'[34] The pairing seems to have been a love match but Stafford would not have been unaware of the material advantages attached to the marriage. William had no wealth, but he had influence and Stafford would return to Nelson with the 'Colonel in one pocket and the Company in the other'.[35] On her mother's side, Emily had an interest in the Sidney family fortune. But Stafford had to somehow provide a home in keeping with such an eminent bride and he sold his prized thoroughbred stallion to raise funds for the equipping of a superior household. Also, 'Colonel Wakefield would never let his beloved daughter want if he could afford otherwise, so, in spite of his own rumoured financial difficulties he raised £100 and bought them a piano and other furniture'.[36]

Before the wedding ceremony on 24 September, Stafford became so excited that the 'necessity of putting a strait waistcoat on him had been thought of'.[37] The wedding party was large and Emily was attended by six of her Wellington friends, including Major Richmond's daughter (also Emily) and little Georgina Thompson, the daughter of Henry Thompson who had been killed at the Wairau. Justice Chapman was there too: 'There was a breakfast to which most people of any station and respectability were invited. In the evening there was a tag rag and bobtail ball which ended in a drunken row. [Dr Isaac] Featherston – though his [William's] daughter's medical attendant – and although his conduct against the Company had been singularly free from every personal feeling was excluded from the breakfast. The stupid paltry folly of this was apparent to every one. Featherston and especially his charming and most amiable wife were hurt . . . .'[38] The consequences were to prove almost fatal.

The Staffords honeymooned in Wellington and then stayed with William Fox and his wife in Nelson until their own house was ready. John Saxton went to visit them there and found Emily 'rather shy and grave though kind. [W. O.] Cautley said he "had never been so disappointed in any woman as in Mrs Stafford . . . . [he] could only obtain from her 'Yes' or 'No,' that it was all cold and dead and impossible to get any conversation. She was either unhappy or had been deceived as to Stafford's circumstances, perhaps both".'[39] Stafford was an extrovert, voluble and excitable; Emily, eight years his junior, was withdrawn, grave and delicate. It was noted within a year of the marriage that Emily showed no signs of becoming pregnant.

Perhaps Emily missed her papa. Certainly William missed her. In November he wrote, 'This house looks very melancholy notwithstanding it is beautiful weather. The dogs run in and out. Poor Fly is very solicitous about her family and often invites me to her kennel with the most affectionate whines.'[40] But there was compensation. He told Catherine, 'Francis Bell has been staying with me, since Emily's marriage and renders my bachelor home tolerable. He is a most delightful companion & assistant in times of hard work.'[41] William did his best domestically: 'After fitting up the bathroom [*sic*] with your four poster and making sundry other preparations for Mrs Grey she has not accompanied the Governor – so that unless I take it into my head to look out for some one to avail herself of what I have done by accepting my vows I shall cut a very ridiculous figure with all the paraphernalia of a married life – except a wife.'[42] This rare humorous self-deprecation was afforded Emily alone. In the same letter, he gives paternal comfort in reply to her unhappiness at fending for herself in Nelson: 'I can imagine the life you must lead when he [Stafford] is absent to be very dull, but this cannot often occur and the anticipation of his return is something gained'. Early in the new year he recounted for Emily the details of the Christmas party she had missed: 'Miss Richmond took your place in the dance; but I looked several times around the room for you and missed you very much. It made me regret more than ever our separation by Cook's Strait. Your old apartments look quite cheerful the bathroom being occupied by the Fox's (the Ohiro four-poster figuring there in chintz) and the two little bedrooms are converted into dressing rooms. F. Bell lives where he did and I have again retired to my den . . . . I must not tell you of our pastimes or you will be wishing to run away from home.'[43]

When William visited Nelson again in March 1847 with Grey during the negotiations for the Wairau purchase, the Staffords had been accorded the status of being part of the 'official clique', christened 'The Count' and 'The Countess' as they dined in full dress at the Fox's with Grey, Domett and William. John Saxton complained about how supercilious Stafford had become and how Emily 'sat in state and did not rise to shake hands but merely suffered her raised hand to be taken and was evidently inflated by the presence of her papa'.[44] Saxton, like Justice Chapman, was a great private critic and later complained about a hard bed at Aldourie, which he also suspected had fleas.

Back in Wellington, William reported to Catherine that he had 'found Emily very comfortably established in the "Waimea". She & her husband appear to be as cooing as six months ago when they were married. He is one of the best tempered men I ever knew – which suits her admirably, for it is impossible to displease him by any ordinary domestic irritation, & I must say I never saw so young a wife behave so like a grave matron as she does.' He told Catherine of his visit to see Naomi Songer and her family, immigrants from Stoke on one of the first ships. Naomi had for many years ruled the Torlesse nursery with a 'Spartan discipline'[45] but she now 'squeezed out a tear' and sent by him 'a thousand good wishes for your children who might be hers for the love she bears them'. She had even nursed Charley Torlesse through an illness during his time in Nelson.[46] William did not tell his sister that, just four days before, he had fought a duel.

Dr Isaac Featherston had arrived in Wellington in May 1841 and had ministered to the Wakefields since. 'The Little Doctor' became the first editor of the *Wellington Independent* in 1845 and was involved in many community projects, including the founding of the Wellington Savings Bank. Justice Chapman said that he had turned against the company because 'he invested money in land in 1840 and has got a useless swamp worth nothing'.[47] On behalf of all land purchasers who thought they had been duped, he began to fight the company for compensation – and William responded by freezing the Featherstons out at Emily's wedding.

Six months later, on 24 March 1847, Featherston published an editorial in the *Wellington Independent* that savaged the company and, by association, William. With the government about to finally purchase the Wairarapa and build a road there from the Wellington settlement, the editorial asked whether the land would be 'granted to the New Zealand Company without first exacting security for performance of their actual contracts with land purchasers, and implied contracts with labourers?' It called for a petition to the governor, asking him to ensure that the company fulfilled its contracts and also to set aside some Wairarapa land for purchase at a reasonable price. The editorial asserted that in its agreement with the government, the company had been required to 'fulfil all contracts they had made for sale of land . . . . that condition remains unfulfilled to this day. No attempt has been made, no desire manifested, to fulfil it. It has been broken or evaded, and remains with its results a fitting illustration of corporate faith . . . . their zeal for the settler's interest was only a cloak put on to enable them more easily to promote their own. . . .' The government's promise of a £100,000 loan to the company was a 'misappropriation of sympathy which, in the degree of tact displayed, was only approached by the thief who at the close of a Missionary meeting stole the money which had been collected, while one of its ministers present was engaged in prayer'.[48]

This was altogether too much for William. It was one thing to attack the company's mismanagement but quite another to impugn his honour by accusing him, indirectly or no, of being a thief. Awkward, unco-operative, dilatory and manipulative maybe – dishonest never. William immediately challenged Featherston to a duel and the pair met with pistols the next morning at Te Aro flat. Dr John Dorset was second for Featherston, Francis Dillon Bell for William. Featherston fired first and missed; then William 'fired into the air with the comment that he would not shoot a man who had seven daughters'.[49] William's action accords with his sense of honour but the story of it grew in the telling. Featherston was to have eight daughters (and four sons) but at the time of the duel he had fathered only three, so that the account credits William with an uncharacteristic degree of prescience.

A few weeks later, William responded with his old insouciance to Emily's alarm on hearing of the event: 'I cannot tell you how much I felt affected by your affectionate fears for my safety via à vis mon voisin, le medecin. Now know how irritable he is, poor man, and that there are certain bounds to language beyond which the world says that a man cannot permit another to go without drawing upon himself disgrace for the rest of his life. The Dr and I have both benefitted by our morning rencontre and are now as good friends as ever.'[50]

Perhaps in case rumour of the duel reached Catherine, he advised her that

> the colony is perfectly tranquil. Numerous troops, working on the roads in concert & friendship with the natives, are opening our communications in all directions. An immense expenditure by the Government keeps everyone employed & the country is filling with flocks and herds. Our politics are nevertheless as agitated as ever, & the Governor and I do not always agree – besides now the Company has to economize, I get the ill-will & opposition of a considerable number of the settlers who prefer a Government that spends a deal of money. But I came prepared for all this and have

> many sincere friends. My tenure of occupation by the Company must be uncertain, & it is not impossible that I may see you in England again, if you do not come here.[51]

A few weeks later he told Emily that the company was likely to be finished by the end of the year and he was thinking of going to England with her, but not to plan too much for the future: 'I much own . . . that the loneliness of the Waimea is not what I wish you to enjoy forever.'[52] A propos his 'friendship with the natives' he had told her of the 'beautiful silver cup' he had ordered from England with a 'Maori inscription' to present to Te Puni 'for his alliance with the Militia in the fights of May last year. . . . the old gentleman comes nearly every day to enquire about it'.[53] Later Te Puni stayed with William and 'conversed with us till near midnight and displayed the same intelligence, honesty and want of selfishness I have always seen him do'.[54]

William's relationship with disgruntled settlers began to improve after news of the company's deal with the government came through at the end of 1847. But a sense of loneliness began to invest his letters to Emily. After May he was no longer able to act as host to the governor and his wife, for he had been prevailed upon to sell his home in order to provide an official residence for the incoming Lieutenant-Governor Eyre. After six months he told Emily that he was planning to move 'as soon as Mr and Mrs Hay leave the Hanson's old house. The one I am in is too ricketty and exposed. I shall be in the other I think within a month and shall not forget to have a spare room added for your visits.'[55]

In the new year of 1848, William bought Emily a phaeton so that she could get about better and visit her Nelson friends. Stafford's father had died and she wanted him to return with her to England as she was dull for want of society. But Stafford had too much to do in Nelson and affairs were too unsettled at Home. Partly to alleviate Emily's dullness, he purchased Fox's old house above Nelson port and they moved into town.

When writing to Catherine about EGW's illness in March 1847, William had counselled her, 'Pray him to eschew doctors & their medicaments. In this climate we know them not. A salt-water shower-bath, every morning winter & summer, moderation in living & a good share of exercise & employment out of doors, have given me robust health & calm nerves, with which I was never blessed before.'[56] Justice Chapman considered that William's idea of exercise was 'strolling up the hills with his dogs' or 'a rotten-row sort of ride on a good hack'.[57]

Whatever the extent of his exercise regimen, William suffered a minor stroke in January 1848, further evidence of the apoplectic tendency that would affect almost all the men of this Wakefield generation. After bleeding and rest, William soon recovered and he did not bother to tell Emily. After a second and more severe attack in August, Dr Featherston prescribed abstemiousness and exercise.

William had better live out at the Hutt, riding in and out to Wellington each day, sometimes walking all the way. It was impossible for William to be more abstemious and it was impracticable for him to move out of town. Early in September, William wrote Emily, 'My health has been rather out of order of late from being overworked during the visit of Captn Grey and nothing but copious bleeding saved my life. I am now, however, all right again and only mention the subject lest you should hear some exaggerated reports.'[58]

Of more extended concern for the family had been the steadily deteriorating condition of Dan and Angela's daughter Selina. In May, soon after her arrival in Wellington, William had written to Emily, 'I wish you were here for her [Angela's] sake, for she is kept at home nearly all day by the illness of her daughter who cannot, I think, live long. She has a disease of the spine. Tell me when you propose to pay me a visit.'[59] There is no evidence that Emily did so. Four months later, William was reporting to her that 'Dan's little girl is at death's door. Not expected to survive the day. Her father and mother are in a great state of affliction.'[60] At the beginning of September, in the letter telling Emily of his illness, he wrote, 'Uncle Dan and Angela lost their daughter on Sunday 20th August at 3 in the morning . . . . she had been insensible for several days . . . . Poor Aunt Angela is very much end up at her loss.'[61]

The next news Emily had of her father was from Stafford in Nelson, after he had received a packet of letters sent from Wellington. Notes to him from Dan and Bell covered letters to Emily from Angela and from Bell breaking the news of William's death. 'Read the enclosed,' Bell advised Stafford, '& when dear Emily is sufficiently composed give it to her. To you it will be a consolation to know I never left the Colonel, & that he died in my arms.'[62]

William had been a regular user of the Russian Vapour Bath house. On the afternoon of Friday 15 September, he had a warm bath, 'imprudently took it too hot', according to Justice Chapman and, about five o'clock, 'on leaving the bathroom he was observed to stagger and fall – he was caught by the attendant before he reached the ground. A Dr Muirhead, surgeon of H.M.S. *Dido* was at hand and attended at once – Featherston followed him at scarce an interval.'[63] Dr John Dorset, William's old comrade from Spain, was also soon on the scene and did not leave his side until the end.

For Emily, Angela Wakefield began her account of William's last hours on the Monday morning, and recorded that he could not be moved home. 'Though able to raise himself once in bed & once to walk supported . . . across the room, he has never recovered the use of his voice . . . . When your Uncle [Dan] was fetched, I followed as fast as I could, to see if I could be of any use, & it will comfort you to know that he was lying quite quietly & apparently without pain, neither is he believed to suffer anything except when the fits come on.' Dorset, Bell and a servant stayed beside William constantly; 'indeed your Uncle only goes in occasionally, though nearly all the day in the next room'.[64] As usual, Dan was of little use and took ill himself as a consequence of the event; his chief protector was slipping away before his eyes.

Francis Bell told Emily that her father 'suffered no pain the whole time . . . . He was perfectly conscious till within a short time . . . of his death, and knew me perfectly well . . . . He listened with tender pleasure to your name & anything about you.' At 9 a.m. on Tuesday 19 September, William 'breathed his last sigh in the arms of one who loved him well and closed his eyes with affectionate care'.[65]

William's funeral, by far the grandest accorded any of the Wakefields, took place on the following Friday. More than 1000 mourners followed his coffin to the cemetery. One of the pallbearers was Te Puni, Francis Dillon Bell was chief mourner and the procession was headed by Governor Grey and Lieutenant-Governor Eyre. There were 'three to four hundred native men and one hundred native women. Independent of those who walked in procession, were hundreds of the inhabitants in attendance near the cemetery . . . . The whole of the shops and public houses were closed during the day, and every mark of respect was exhibited by all classes in the settlement . . . . a stranger, ignorant of the lamentable event which had occurred might well have imagined that the inhabitants had turned Friday into the Sabbath.'[66]

Justice Chapman took a more cynical view of the funeral, writing that William, with his 'last official act' of finally settling the land claims against the company, had behaved well enough so that the 'settlers gave him a funeral . . . a peace offering . . . which certainly would not have been made a month before'. Governor Grey had also happened to be in town and had gazetted the closure of public offices, allowing the attendance of officials and the military. Yet Chapman had to admit that the 'real tribute was in the numerous attendance of the settlers and natives. The day was fine and I have rarely seen (perhaps never) a larger funeral procession even in a larger Colony.'[67] About a third of the Wellington population, Maori and Pakeha, had turned out: a remarkable number. But William had founded this town and, in the end, the settlers had perceived that many of the New Zealand Company's deficiencies had been beyond William's control and that he had struggled for nine years to manage the competing demands of settler, Maori, company director and government official. Maori came to pay respect to a man whose ideas and actions they may have opposed but who carried the mana of a chief, had shown unwavering belief in his mission and had been a warrior of undoubted physical courage.

Behind the scenes there was a 'sad contretemps'. For Grey, prompting a grand funeral for William was useful politically in bringing all factions of the settlement together; and he could never resist a colourful show. But he overreached himself when, to complete the funeral procession, he proposed to invite Te Rauparaha and Te Rangihaeata. When Dan heard of it he protested strongly and the 'scheme was abandoned. It would indeed have been a very indecent one, and I believe most of the settlers would have kept away. . . .'[68]

Te Rauparaha had been returned to his people at Otaki in January. After his confinement on the *Calliope*, he had been kept by Grey under a kind of house arrest in Auckland until the troubles around the North Island had been settled. He had been escorted home by Grey and his wife and Te Wherowhero. But 'It was a shamed Rauparaha who was put ashore. For two hours he sat alone on the sand crying and gazing out to sea.'[69] When he joined his people for the waiting feast, Grey was warned to stay away and Te Rangihaeata would not meet him. Te Rauparaha was to die a year after William, in November 1849, aged about 85. In the night following his demeaning Christian burial, Te Rangihaeata led 100 men to his grave. They removed his body from the Pakeha's coffin and ferried it by canoe to Kapiti Island where it was secreted in a cave that looked out towards his old home in Kawhia.

Te Rangihaeata continued to resist Pakeha settlement of the Manawatu and to cause trouble along the Kapiti coast but in September 1848, just before William's death, he finally agreed to meet with Grey. In his oration at Otaki he claimed to be still a free man and that the land between Waikanae and Wanganui remained with his people. 'The way of the white people is not mine; I want nothing of theirs, nothing!' Te Rangihaeata wore not a stitch of European clothing but he had a peacock's feather in his hair and Grey smiled and asked to whom that belonged. Te Rangihaeata plucked out the feather and let it flutter slowly to the ground. 'True,' Rangihaeata said, his finger pointing down, but his eyes still on Grey. 'True, that is the white man's.'[70]

Te Rangihaeata finally made peace with Grey a few years before he died in 1855, in his early seventies. He had not ceased, he had remained true to his heart and mana. And though Ngati Toa had been subdued, the Pakeha had never made a tie of him, nor extracted utu from him for the Wairau. And he had outlived his old enemy Wideawake.

Francis Dillon Bell had assumed that Stafford would cross to Wellington immediately upon hearing of William's death in order to settle his father-in-law's affairs but Emily was so shocked that he could not leave her. Dan took out letters of administration and, with Bell, wound up the estate; they could find no will and William had left only about £1,200 plus furniture and personal effects. His work on behalf of the company and their settlements had gained him no landed estates. Bell told Stafford, 'I have one favour to beg of Emily – that she will let me keep the ring he used to wear. His hand that wore it was coldly lying in mine for long before he died, and I took off the ring after I closed his eyes, & put it on my own finger . . . . it is a plain signet ring – but he and I have so often used it together during the last five years that I look upon it as the most vivid memento of him I could have . . . . Little did I think that my watch would ever come into my possession again! Emily will remember his exchanging with me, with the bantering condition that the one who died or went to England first should keep the other's.'[71] William had 'intended to go home as soon as possible after settling the land claims and intended to leave Bell as principal agent'.[72] But he had not been able to fulfil either intention; William Fox, as senior company officer in the colony, had claimed the job and its salary of £1,000 a year.

There is no written or reported record of Emily's thoughts and feelings following the death of her father but Francis Dillon Bell, in an emotional letter to Stafford in October, spoke for her:

> Daily I miss more & more the man who was so constantly, so kindly, so considerately my friend & confidant . . . . How much more, I often say, must dear Emily suffer, whose affections from childhood were so thoroughly centred in him, that kindness of others, & separation from him, could never attach her to any one else! For it was a remarkable feature in her young girl's history that notwithstanding the persecution of him by people of many classes & families, & the many efforts which were often made to estrange her from him, she seemed to cling still more fondly ever to that one love, and to reject even the semblance of it towards others. But alas, what avail all these recollections? He is but cold earth who awakens them, & cannot even know that his memory is held dear.[73]

As he put the letter down, Stafford perhaps recognised an emotional truth he had long avoided: Emily's deepest love would always be reserved for her father. For Stafford, there would now be no more 'cooing' with Emily. In the new year of 1849, John Saxton recorded that Stafford 'used his wife shamefully. She sometimes said simple things and instead of hiding it, he exposed it always by saying, "What is that Emily, my love?" in derision.'[74] Emily mourned William for months and this was scarcely ended when she received news of the death of her maternal grandfather, Sir James Shelley Sidney. Her mourning was deepened and extended, but for Stafford this was excellent news. Sidney had left Emily £5,000 in consols and because, under the legal system of the day, a wife's property was her husband's, Emily was required to sign a deed settling all the interest from this legacy on Stafford. He had serious financial problems and the legacy saved his estate. 'In a real sense Emily had been Edward's most profitable gain so far.'[75] And as the months, and then the years, went by, there continued to be no sign of children.

Above left: Sam Revans, editor of the first newspaper in Wellington, later a Wairarapa runholder and MP. At first a supporter but later an outspoken opponent of William Wakefield and EGW. ATL F-38720-1/2

Above right: H. S. (Henry) Chapman, first judge of the Supreme Court based in Wellington. His friendship with Revans dated from their founding of a newspaper in Montreal in the late 1830s. He was editor of the *New Zealand Journal* in London before arriving in New Zealand with Governor Robert FitzRoy. ATL B-039-010

Left: Alfred Domett as poet in 1836, five years before he emigrated to the Nelson settlement. George Lance watercolour. ATL PUBL-0154-032

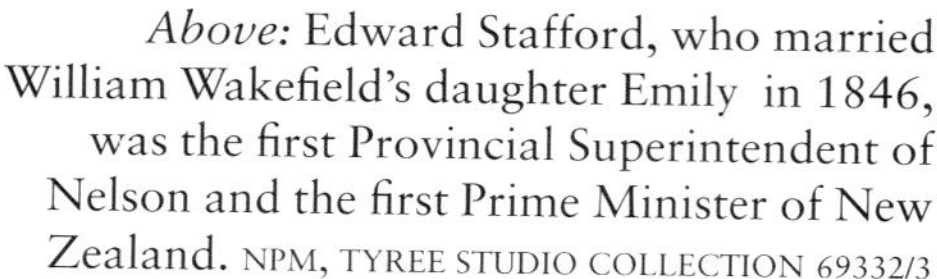

Above: Edward Stafford, who married William Wakefield's daughter Emily in 1846, was the first Provincial Superintendent of Nelson and the first Prime Minister of New Zealand. NPM, TYREE STUDIO COLLECTION 69332/3

Above right: John Robert Godley developed the Canterbury Association plan with EGW and founded the settlement. ATL F-5079-1/2

Right: James Edward FitzGerald, first editor of the *Lyttelton Times* and first Canterbury Provincial Superintendent. His political struggle with EGW wrecked the first General Assembly. The earliest known photograph, taken in Christchurch by A.C. Barker in the late 1850s. CM 17132

Above: Lord Lyttelton, chairman of the Canterbury Association after the forced resignation of John Hutt. Photograph taken in Christchurch when he visited Canterbury in 1868. CM, D. L. MUNDY 2223

Above right: William Ewart Gladstone. The leading British prime minister of the late Victorian era, he was, earlier in his career, a supporter of EGW's theories of colonial settlement and self-government. ATL F-103648-1/2

Right: Henry Sewell, deputy chairman of the Canterbury Association and leading provincial and national politician in New Zealand. A close associate of EGW until the 1854 General Assembly. ATL F-1710-1/1

Above: Felix's son Edward Wakefield, journalist and editor. Later Edward Stafford's private secretary and a Member of Parliament. NPM, TYREE STUDIO COLLECTION 67925/3

Top right: Felix Wakefield. The only known portrait or photograph, probably taken in Nelson, early 1870s. NPM, MISC. COLL 4X5, BOX 5

Right: Edward Gibbon Wakefield (with talbot hounds) in 1850. This oil painting by J. Edgill Collins was commissioned by the New Zealand Company and now hangs in the Canterbury Museum, Christchurch. CM 321A

Left: Edward Jerningham Wakefield. The only photograph, probably taken some time during the 1860s. IRMA O'CONNOR COLLECTION, ATL, PACOLL-6987-1

Below left: Robert Henry Wynyard, acting governor during the term of the first New Zealand General Assembly in 1854. H. J. SCHMIDT COLLECTION, ATL, G-1829-1/1

Below right: William Fox. As a young man he was a strong supporter of EGW's theories of colonial settlement and self-government. He was the agent for the New Zealand Company in Nelson after 1843 and Principal Agent after William Wakefield's death. Later, he was an MP for 25 years and several times prime minister. ATL F-84708-1/2

Above: The only photograph of Edward Gibbon Wakefield, taken not long before his death in 1862. ATL F-31744-1/2

Left: Marble bust of Edward Gibbon Wakefield, sculpted by Joseph Durham from the photograph above and exhibited at the Royal Academy in 1876. It was displayed in London's Colonial Office for many years but is now held by the Art Gallery of South Australia, Adelaide. FROM IRMA O'CONNOR, *EDWARD GIBBON WAKEFIELD*

CHAPTER TWENTY-FOUR

A Highly Excitable Temperament

AT THE END OF MAY 1847, EGW'S outrage at the New Zealand Company for literally selling out to the Colonial Office was quickly overwhelmed by a family crisis of a proportion greater than any he had faced since Newgate 20 years before. Without warning, his youngest brother Felix, now 40, arrived in England with eight of his nine children, having abandoned his wife and youngest child in Van Diemen's Land (Tasmania). Felix was 'so penniless and friendless that an account of his state would be one of complete destitution'.[1] EGW's shock and dismay would have been ameliorated by the curiosity of seeing his brother again after an absence of sixteen years, in which he had penned few lines of correspondence, and by receiving such a sudden and colourful enlargement to the Wakefield tribe.

John Howard in India had produced four children but Felix had outdone all his siblings. With a creative flourish he had named his three eldest sons Murat, after Napoleon's ill-starred brother-in-law, Joseph Murat, King of Naples; Salvator Rosa, after an Italian romantic artist and poet who had worked for the Medicis; and Ariosto, for a Ferraran Renaissance poet. Felix's passion for romantic Italian names may have been compensation for the cultural shortcomings he had experienced in the Hobart and Launceston of the 1830s and 1840s, or merely a sign of the eccentricity that led a later historian to describe Felix as 'not bad; he was only rather mad'.[2] How mad and how bad was yet to be discovered by the world outside Van Diemen's Land.

EGW immediately found Felix so 'weighed down and partly crazed by the dreadful misfortune of his wife, and his ruin through her' that he could not bring himself to ask him a 'question about his wife, or allude to her in any way, though I greatly longed to know whether she was dead, or insane'. She was neither but EGW was unable to discover this until four years after Felix's arrival. Whether EGW ever unearthed the truth about Felix's life in Tasmania is impossible to know. The person most likely to tell him, Felix's fifteen-year-old eldest child,

Constance, spent much time in her uncle's company after the family returned to England but it seems she conveyed little of the causes of the family's situation or the reality of her mother's condition.

When Felix and Marie Wakefield arrived in Hobart Town on 26 April 1832, Constance, the cause of her parents' precipitate marriage and departure from France at the end of 1831, was nine months old. Felix was 24; Marie's age is unknown. The country they arrived in had the reputation of being the most notorious penal colony in the world. A census in 1837 showed that of a total population of just 43,000, only a little more than half were counted as 'free'; the rest were convicts or probationers (on 'ticket of leave'). There were only 12,000 females in Van Diemen's Land (most of them free), proportionally even fewer at the time Felix arrived, and this deficiency had promoted the procurement of women by the shipload. In August 1832, the *Princess Royal* arrived with women who were 'quite immoral and who exerted a baneful influence over the others . . . at least half the complement were more depraved than convict women'.[3] Women on the later *Strathfieldsay* were publicly ogled and abused on arrival. Van Diemen's Land was also an extremely violent society: public flagellation and executions were common, and escaped convicts turned to bushranging and terrorised the country districts. And in one of the most infamous events of the early nineteenth century, the Aboriginal population had been hunted to extermination. The enchanting shores and the lovely hill and bush landscapes of temperate Van Diemen's Land harboured the worst human depravities of the colonial frontier.

At the beginning, Felix struck it lucky. He had arrived in Hobart with Marie and Constance just two months after the introduction of the Ripon Regulations, which required that all land be purchased from the Crown at a minimum upset price of 5s an acre. Large numbers of sections had to be surveyed quickly for auction to settlers and Surveyor-General George Frankland was in desperate need of competent survey staff. Because of Felix's training with the English Ordnance Survey Frankland recommended him for appointment as an assistant surveyor but Lieutenant-Governor George Arthur discovered that Felix also had training as an engineer and, while approving the appointment, had Felix attached to the Roads Department. His first conflict with his superiors occurred in October 1832 when a senior surveyor disapproved of his recommendations for improving the line of Hobart's Constitution Hill Road, then under construction. The lieutenant-governor's sanction of Felix's new plan in December created enemies, while his continued appeals for a greater forage allowance caused conflict between the survey and roads offices. To escape an increasingly uncomfortable situation, Felix obtained a transfer to the northern Launceston district, which had a population of about 5200, in October 1833. Felix and Marie's first son, Murat, had been born two months earlier.

For the next two years, Felix continued working principally for the survey department in the Meander District and also bought a 65-acre farm at Longford, south of Launceston, which he named Chateau Rais after his father's home in Blois. Here a second son, Salvator Rosa, was born in March 1836. By this time, Felix and Marie's world had begun to creak. Immigration had slackened off and the northern survey office was closed in November 1835. Rather than leave Chateau Rais and transfer south again Felix resigned, and endeavoured to make a living from farming and occasional survey jobs. In August 1836, a public notice in the *Launceston Courier*, seeking comments on his roading plan for Perth parish, showed that he was still listed as an assistant surveyor with the Survey Department.

EGW reported in 1837 to Catherine that he had heard 'Felix is rapidly growing rich',[4] but by August 1838 the combination of farming and occasional work for the survey was not proving a success. Felix moved to Charles Street, Launceston and set up as a land agent and surveyor, soliciting work from a variety of lawyers; the farm was advertised for sale. The slow decline in the Tasmanian Wakefields' fortunes did not inhibit family growth: Ariosto had been born in October 1837. When calamity followed the death of Surveyor-General Frankland at the end of 1838, Felix's plaints on behalf of his large family were a moral card that he played without inhibition.

At the beginning of 1839 the new surveyor-general, Captain Edward Boyd, accused Felix of making a measurement error of 10 chains in the boundary between two properties where the course of the River Meander had changed and pointed to other discrepancies in his surveys. Boyd said that these had forced him to withdraw 'any confidence from you as a surveyor for whom I could be responsible'. In May, he gave further example of errors made by Felix that had brought about claims upon the department for compensation in one case and a loss to the public of £100 in another.[5] Boyd struck him off the list of authorised surveyors. This was unmitigated disaster for Felix, whose career and family depended on his work as a surveyor.

The only way that Felix could rehabilitate his reputation was by disproving Boyd's claims. He collected technical evidence and witnesses to support his case, but also chose to attack Boyd's character and capacity. This is the first clear evidence of erratic and vituperative behaviour that could, at times, border on physical violence. Felix had become a fierce temperance advocate, a wowser of the first water, and Boyd's enjoyment of a tipple became his prime target when he wrote to the colonial secretary, Captain Forster. He told him that when he called on Boyd 'with a highly respectable individual' early one Saturday evening, he had 'found him far from sober and his indulgence in this may have an effect on his personal conduct and produce imbecility in his mind'. He alleged that Boyd's animosity towards him had been stirred by his questioning him on the employment of a surveyor who had been in hospital for some time suffering from alcoholism.[6] 'It is a duty I owe to myself – as well as to my numerous family – to exert myself to the utmost to defend my character and interests against a person so maliciously inclined as Captain Boyd', while enduring the 'hardship of having the means of existence for one's family held in the hands of one whose intellects are clouded by the degrading effects of intoxication'.[7] When Boyd denied receiving particular letters, Felix told Forster that, 'as a man who is capable of taking the chair of a meeting to establish a Temperance Society at one – and of getting so intoxicated at ten – as to require assistance to crawl to his den', Boyd was capable of destroying letters 'or any other such act abhorred in civilised life'.[8] Felix finally declared, 'I can distinctly prove [Boyd] is an imbecile sot and a Liar. . . . After my sufferings Captain Boyd need not be astonished at any conduct I may pursue – the scabbard is thrown away and I will dog him to the grave.'[9] Colonial Secretary Forster was provoked to minute, 'Mr Wakefield's correspondence . . . has been marked by a contempt of the usages of all courtesy and propriety of language . . . . to reply to Mr. Wakefield's letters is exposing officers to weekly insult'.[10]

Boyd, naturally, defended himself, pointing to documented errors that Felix had made, the chief one by his own admission: 'As for the survey of the Meander I am liable to error and perhaps from not paying sufficient attention I am open to censure but I trust in this matter I may be dealt leniently with as I will take very good care you shall have no future cause to regret your having authorized me to act under your orders.'[11] Both Boyd and Forster tried to ignore Felix, deliberately taking weeks over each reply to his letters, driving him to greater heights of fury and despair.

By the end of 1839, child number five, Josephine, had been added to the family and Felix was almost out of money. The family removed to cheap rented accommodation and, to raise cash quickly, Felix resorted to gambling. The *Hobart Town Advertiser* of 24 January 1840, reported, 'Pedestrianism. The long-talked of match between Mr Stillwell, solicitor, and Mr Wakefield, surveyor . . . to walk 120 miles successively came off this week, and was decided in favor of Mr Wakefield, who accomplished his task in forty hours and three quarters, including stoppages amounting to 9 hours and 53 minutes, having arrived at the Exchange, Launceston . . . in fine style and excellent condition.' How much money Felix won on the wager is not known but he readily accepted a second challenge for £100 a few days after this report and won that, too. Indigence had been denied at the door.

In an effort to find justice, Felix now put his case to Lieutenant-Governor Sir John Franklin, with the support of a damning letter from a Major Wentworth who had accompanied Surveyor-General Boyd on his inspection of the Meander survey. This revealed that Boyd had supported Felix's survey, although it was out by 3 or 4 chains, in comparison with measurements taken by two other survey officers, but had then reversed his opinion for no apparent reason after discussing the question with one of the affected property owners. Finally, in June and July 1840, justice was done. Colonial Secretary Forster wrote to Boyd under Franklin's instructions, telling him that the observations he had made to Wentworth respecting Felix's survey had been 'inconsiderate and uncalled for' and that his behaviour in the matter 'cannot but tend to shake the confidence which it is essential the Public Service should have in your decisions'. Franklin also considered it 'highly reprehensible' that Boyd had failed to supply government commissioners with all the papers relevant to the case. Boyd lost his job within the year and Felix gained a measure of exoneration.

The case had, nevertheless, laid open to question the stability of Felix's personality and his reliability as a surveyor. He found it almost impossible to secure professional rehabilitation and scratched a living from the farm and the occasional survey job. News reached Arthur in London at the beginning of 1841 that he planned on going to New Zealand,[12] but he clearly did not have the resources to make the move. Two years later, after Arthur had established the Nelson settlement, he and William received an appeal for help from Felix. Arthur advised William, 'I told him we would help if we could, but begged him to consider the best means, I doubted the practicability of removing his large family [now six with the arrival of Priscilla] and the prospect of success here in farming without capital'. While Arthur was willing to somehow 'keep him above water' with £50 a quarter, prospects in Van Diemen's Land seemed better for Felix, although the state of the family appeared desperate: 'His wife's letter is disturbing, if literally the case, but I cannot understand the degree of poverty on so large a farm which must be stocked. I heard some time ago from a Launceston skipper that he [Felix] was over-rented and not doing well. . . .[13] I cannot see any hopes for a man with his numerous family doing anything here with less than £500.'[14]

Trying everything to earn a living, Felix offered to victual shipping and applied unsuccessfully for a job with the Department of Roads and Bridges. Refused this, he appealed to the new colonial secretary, James Bicheno, for any kind of work that would help him support his large family. A referee, Sheriff W. G. Sams, told Bicheno, 'I know of no one in this island of general talent or business habits, superior or of preferable conduct as a husband and father, or who has more sincerely endeavoured to maintain his family by the most persevering and untiring assiduity, though unfortunately without success.'[15] Felix's situation was not helped by the economic depression of the 1840s: while convicts continued to be shipped out from Britain in their thousands, Van Diemen's Land received just 26 free immigrants in 1843 and only one in 1844.

Felix's luck seemed to change in 1845 when he was paid £20 to prepare plans for the Launceston water supply. This money would not go far following the arrival of two more mouths to feed – Oliver in October 1843 and Edward in May 1845 – bringing the number of children to eight. No wonder there were signs of Marie Wakefield approaching her wits' end.

Felix's first plan required a weir 180 feet deep to be formed by dumping large quantities of rock into a gorge; water would be fed into existing town piping by way of aerial chutes. The Northern Commandant approved of Felix's scheme and reported to the colonial secretary that Felix's earlier 'lack of soundness and application had been counteracted by experience and misfortune'.[16] Deputy Surveyor-General Major Hugh Cotton disagreed: 'A dam or rather weir formed of loose masses of Rock . . . could never resist the overfall of a River flood precipitated from a height of 180 feet.'[17] Felix's alternative scheme, involving a dam, a tunnel, aqueducts and a reservoir, was never attempted, probably because it could not be financed. Yet the commandant's faith remained undiminished; for he now recommended Felix as just the engineer to be put in charge of draining Launceston's swamps. But Felix had entered a deep swamp of his own making, engaging in another vituperative correspondence with the colonial secretary over Cotton's damning report that was exacerbated by news of Cotton's appointment as 'irrigation engineer'. Felix's incorrigible behaviour had now placed him beyond all chance of official employment.

By mid-1846, Marie Wakefield was six months pregnant with her ninth child. The other eight ranged in age from one to barely fifteen and only the eldest, Constance, was capable of offering much practical assistance in the management of the family. In these circumstances, having lived for years on the bread line and in the company of an erratic husband, it is unsurprising that Marie became increasingly hysterical and unstable: at the end of June 1846, 'The poor woman . . . took away what little money Wakefield had and all the children's clothes etc. . . etc. . . and returned destitute a few days after. Wakefield has now to attend to his eight little ones, is consequently prevented leaving home to obtain food for them.'[18] This was part of a letter from Sheriff Sams to Marie Wakefield's doctor, seeking his support for Felix's petition to the lieutenant-governor in which he prayed that his wife, 'Eliza Marie Felicie Wakefield may be admitted into the Hospital for Lunatics at New Norfolk – she being totally unfit to be at large, her own life and those of her children being at times in danger from her mental aberration'.[19]

Felix's petition went forward with Sams's and Dr Paton's support and a three-man medical board dealt with the case promptly. Ten days later, Felix received its judgement: 'Mrs Wakefield is not of unsound mind, although of a highly excitable temperament with feelings much harassed by misfortune and poverty, she is yet capable of performing the ordinary duties of life.' The governor declined to support the petition, however much he regretted the circumstances in which Felix was placed.[20] The implications were clear: if Marie Wakefield was suffering from a kind of madness, it was caused mostly by Felix.

Sams told Paton at the time that he had a 'plan in view' by which he hoped to relieve Felix and his children from 'their present wretched position'. But nothing worked to solve the family's dire financial situation or to temper the estrangement between Felix and Marie. By the end of 1846, Felix could see no way forward and made a decision sprung from utter desperation. He abandoned Marie with three-month-old Percy and took ship for England on 23 December with the other eight children, in order to throw them all on the mercy of his family.

Felix never saw his wife again. Shipping records indicate that she departed Launceston with little Percy for Adelaide in October 1847. The movements of three of her sons in the years that followed suggest that she remained in South Australia. Genealogical records show that Murat, Salvator and Ariosto had all arrived in South Australia by 1853–54,[21] aged respectively about 20, seventeen and sixteen. They presumably established contact with their mother and perhaps helped support her: both Ariosto and Percy later went to New Zealand but the others stayed and Salvator, in particular, was successful in business. But the true circumstances of Marie Wakefield's life after 1846, and the date and place of her death, remain unknown.

When Felix and his children arrived in England, EGW was still 'very ill' from the after-effects of his stroke and 'could be of no service to him except by supplying his family with the means of subsistence. Some of our relations, who knew more of him than I did, would not assist; and the whole charge fell upon me.'[22] In June, father Edward imparted to William that EGW had hired a lodging for Felix and family in Hackney. 'Felix seems in high spirits at having got rid of his wife'[23] – at escaping a marriage that his father had insisted upon in the first place. A month later the relations did assist and Felix's seven youngest children were 'satisfactorily placed at a school in Ipswich, supported by the Friends [Quakers]'. The Head family, the children of Edward's late sister 'dear Bell', were to the fore. Sixteen-year-old Constance, described by Edward as a 'useful, clever girl', went to 'some family from Van Diemen's Land . . . near Uxbridge. Felix is lodging himself in my old house in Pall Mall.' Edward, as always, waxed expansive about his youngest son's prospects, telling William that he had a new plan for an immense reservoir in a valley north of Derby to bring in a water supply to London along the rail roads. It would be the 'making of him'.[24]

Felix seems to have resigned much of his responsibility for his offspring. One account tells that, 'The eldest son Murat went to sea; Ariosto and Salvator went to school at Ipswich; Constance, a girl of remarkable character and ability, taking charge of the four youngest children, was settled in a farmhouse not far from Stoke, where their aunt CT watched over them. The clergyman of the parish of Wiston, Mr Birch and his family, proved devoted friends and Mr Fenn the doctor at Nayland and his family also showed every care and kindness to these children.'[25] This arrangement lasted for about a year until a more restored EGW took full charge as a willing surrogate father to his newly extended family.

The stress of coping with Felix's arrival made no improvement to EGW's physical condition. To escape from the distractions and pressures of family and colonial politics, and to take some positive steps towards restoring his health, he went to Great Malvern at the beginning of September and 'submitted with good results to a course of hydropathic treatment under Dr Wilson'.[26] There he encountered Dan's father-in-law, the grand reformer Thomas Attwood and his daughter Rosabel, long-dead Nina's childhood friend. Angela, too, visited them with her children before she took ship to join Dan in Wellington. Her son Charles Marcus, then just nine years old, and destined to become Attwood's biographer, recorded that at Malvern he had the 'privilege of seeing these extraordinary men together. Though both ranked as Radicals, or at least as extreme Liberals, they differed greatly in other respects. Attwood was utterly incapable of understanding the magnificent and far-sighted views of Wakefield on colonial subjects.'[27] Attwood was not the only one.

Someone who did understand those views was John Robert Godley and on 27 November 1847, EGW wrote to him from Malvern: 'I hope you have not changed your mind about coming here; as I have a suggestion to make . . . relating to yourself and a very pleasant colonising object . . . . If you come do not let us be cut short for time.'[28] The fresh air and pure spring waters of the Malvern Hills had revivified the instincts of the political animal. EGW sensed that the time was right and that he had discovered the right disciple to build the best colonial castle in the air yet. But he needed plenty of time to effect a conversion.

The plan had been growing in EGW's mind for years. He had long perceived the value, to the social acceptance and success of his colonial ventures, of Church of England association and endowments. Ten years earlier, Dr Samuel Hinds, then simply the vicar of Yardley, had contributed a chapter on 'Religious Establishment' to EGW's *The British Colonization of New Zealand* and with Hinds's aid and advice EGW had been influential in the appointment of George Selwyn as first Bishop of New Zealand in 1841. He attempted to find church endowments for the first company colonies and in November of that year told Catherine, 'I think, if matters proceed as they promise, New Zealand will be the most Church of England colony in the world.'[29]

By May 1843, he could write to Catherine: 'The project of a new colony in N.Z. is so ripe, that I want to talk to you and Charles about it. It will be a Church of England colony: that is, the foundation fund of the colony will contain ample endowments for religious and educational purposes in connection with our church exclusively.' The Church of England was certainly 'ours' for Catherine and Charles Torlesse but more expediently, it seems, for EGW. His creed has been nicely described as a 'masculine Theism; but to get his plans adopted in influential quarters, and to secure desirable emigrants for his beloved colony, he would have transplanted the Grand Lama of Tibet with all his praying wheels, and did actually nibble at the Chief Rabbi'.[30] In the pursuit of capital, character and capacity for his new colony, ecclesiastical support, investment and moral discipline might achieve the ideal planned settlement better than any of the New Zealand Company schemes to date.

EGW told Hinds years later that he was responsible for his 'conversion to a belief of the great importance of good religious provision in colonizing'.[31] By 1848 he firmly believed that no reputable emigration scheme could be successful unless its provisions appealed to women. 'Women are more religious than men; or, at all events, there are more religious women than religious men: I need not stop to prove that. There is another proposition which I think you will adopt as readily: it is, that in every rank the best sort of women for colonists are those to whom religion is a rule, a guide, a stay, and a comfort . . . . As respects morals and manners, it is of little importance what colonial fathers are, in comparison with what the mothers are.' He averred that the early colonisation of America had been 'more or less a religious colonization: the parts of it that prospered the most, were the most religious parts: the prosperity was chiefly occasioned by the respectability of the emigration: and the respectability of the emigration to each colony had a close relation to the force of the religious attraction'.[32] The Church of England project was to be 'an experiment of that politico-religious principle in colonizing which I long to see fairly tried'.[33]

There remained 'a sort of conscience' in all of this, a tacit acknowledgement that though EGW could lay claim to little religious morality himself, he should provide the scope for others, in an increasingly pious age, to exert its power for order and social discipline. Catherine remained his surrogate religious conscience and, during his lifelong bond with her, it always pricked him to satisfy her expectations. She was the 'colonial mother' to his 'colonial father'; and there is no reason to suspect that his letters to her on the subject were anything other than sincere. Most sincere of all was his endeavour to find a place for Catherine and her family somewhere in his plans.

In May 1843 EGW told Catherine, 'A body of colonists will be formed . . . in conjunction with eminent clergymen and laymen of the Church of England not intending to emigrate: and this body will mature the plan and offer it to the N.Z. Company by whom it will be accepted.' The plan included a place for Charles as archdeacon with money, land, passage and parsonage, and he also saw a place for pious younger sister Pris and her husband Henry Chapman. 'So here is something for you to think about' – and quickly, too. If Charles should 'lay himself open to this offer' he would have to spend much time in London over the following six weeks. EGW travelled down to Stoke by train two days later to discuss the whole matter.[34]

The company expanded on the plan over the following year but it developed no real weigh as the company's fortunes began to sink, and when EGW became distracted again by Canadian affairs. His dreams of an antipodean ecclesiastical heaven were then overwhelmed by the tragedy of Arthur's death, the battles for the company's very survival and his chronic illness. The Free Church of Scotland settlement in Otago went ahead with Wakefield assistance, a whisky with water imitation of the grand plan; but it may have been the transfer of the Otago block to the Free Church Lay Association in June 1847, following the New Zealand Company's settlement with the government, that seriously revived EGW's thoughts of a Church of England colony. He must have been greatly stirred by reports of the Lay Association meeting on 10 August in Glasgow where it was declared that 'in place of the random emigration that has prevailed the people are to be accompanied by their institutions, and to present . . . a complete section of the Home Society with its social comforts and economic combinations of capital and labour'.[35] He could hardly have put it better himself. When he wrote to Godley at the end of November, the first Free Church ships had just left for Otago.

John Robert Godley began to move within EGW's orbit in the spring of 1847. A son of Anglo-Irish High Church Protestant gentry, he had devoted his energies, since returning from America in 1844, to helping solve the vicious and recurrent Irish political and economic crises that had brought the island to near revolution and ultimately to the ghastly famine of 1846. A million died after the potato crop failed, fulfilling Edward Wakefield's prophecy 34 years before. Early in 1845, Godley first suggested to a government commission that organised Irish settlements in Upper Canada, along Wakefield principles, would help to alleviate Ireland's problems. Two years later, at the height of the famine, Godley was able to press his plan again and with the encouragement of EGW and Robert Rintoul, published an open letter to Lord John Russell in the *Spectator* of 31 March 1847. Five long Godley articles on Ireland followed in the autumn and it is likely that EGW and Godley met for the first time in Rintoul's office.

EGW recognised in Godley a zealot and potential leader in the colonial field and when he got him alone at Malvern, not 'cut short for time', he began the successful diversion of Godley's considerable energies away from Ireland and Canada and towards England and New Zealand. They were very different men. EGW was heavily built, a semi-invalid and, as an ageing lion at 51, almost old enough to be father to the 33-year-old. Where EGW was loquacious, persuasive and charming, infinitely wise and weary in the ways of the world, the tall and lean Godley was reserved, serious and passionate with religious moral purpose. Yet their contrasting qualities were useful in complement and Godley fully shared EGW's views on colonisation. On 30 November, EGW wrote to his old supporter John Abel Smith, MP and director of the company, 'I find that my notion of a distinct settlement in New Zealand . . . desirous of spreading the Church of England, stands a good chance of being realised sooner than I expected. The subject has been fully considered, and at length something like practical conclusions have been arrived at. Mr. Godley left me this morning for Ireland; and I have undertaken to ascertain how far the Company is disposed to act. . . .'

The settlement was to consist of 300,000 acres (with right of pasturage attached), which would be purchased from the company for 10s per acre, or £150,000. The site, 'if possible', was to be the Wairarapa. The land purchasers, 'whether colonists or absentees', would pay the company, as a trustee for them,

£2.10s per acre on top of their 10s an acre and the total amount of £750,000 would be used by the company ' in public objects, such as emigration, roads, and church and school endowments'. The 'plan of the colony' would be carried out by 'a society outside of the Company, consisting of bishops and clergymen, peers, members of parliament, and intending colonists of the highest class'. But then came 'the all important practical question, By whose exertions is the whole scheme to be realised?' EGW had persuaded Godley to 'think of devoting himself to the work. A good deal might be done by my son, according to your late suggestion to me . . . Godley . . . must be remunerated. He ought to become a Director of the Company, with a view of giving confidence in us to his friends and others who are expected to join the outside Society, of which my son would be a working member and intending colonist.'

EGW had fastened on Godley not only for his zeal and devotion to Wakefield theory but also for his High Church connections and circle of friends who had attended Christ Church College, Oxford. EGW promoted Godley's qualities to Abel Smith, adding that he should be offered a salary of £500 a year 'which would induce him to settle in London and think of nothing but business until it is completed . . . . He will not proceed further . . . without some security that the Company would not, by rejecting the proposal hereafter, expose him to the annoyance of having enlisted his friends and others in a fruitless project.'[36] A week later, EGW told Abel Smith that he was travelling to London and wanted, on 10 December, 'some decision on the Church Settlement proposal for the information of Godley and his friends. If that iron is to be struck at all with effect, it must be while it is hot . . . .The dead Company may and must be brought to life again: or, if not, let us bury and have done with it.'[37]

EGW was clearly feeling a good deal better. He pressed and pressed throughout December, writing two or three dozen letters to MPs, to company directors and to Godley, keeping him constantly up-to-date with progress and arrangements and urging him to encourage all his well-placed friends and colleagues to take an active interest in the new plan. Just before Christmas 1847, EGW began renting a house, Warwick Lodge, at Redhill, within five minutes walk of the station 'for the sole purpose of being accessible' to Godley and others.

Now he also began to see a 'good deal' of Felix, whose welfare during his Malvern convalescence had been in the 'compassionate' hands of William Bowler, a company employee. EGW now

> became satisfied that [Felix] possessed talents which, if well directed, would enable him to take care of himself, but that there were also deficiencies of capacity and some defects of character which need careful handling. For instance, he could not write decent English, or rather was incapable of writing a letter upon any matter of business that would be fit to be seen, and he was so devoid of the sense of the value of money as to be capable of independence . . . . I taught him English; no easy task at his age; and

> otherwise qualified him to make use of his ability as a surveyor and engineer, which was unquestionable . . . . I also restrained him by constant vigilance and counsel from all sorts of flighty doings, more especially with regard to expense, a proneness to which I attributed to habits of thought and conduct acquired by a 'bush' life in V.D. Land. At length, after he was, by degrees, apparently civilized, a relation in Suffolk, who has political influence and who was struck by his professional ability, thought of getting him appointed to the Sanitary Commission.[38]

EGW worked hard to conceal Felix's deficiencies of capacity from the world at large, both for his brother's sake and from concern about their effect on his own and the family's reputation. EGW's statement that Felix was semi-literate, however, is not supported by the evidence of his Tasmanian reports and letters – unless he was referring to Felix's writing style and the arrangement of his material.

By 11 January 1848, EGW had eased the way for Godley to become a director of the company by providing him with stock to the value of £500, and he was placed in charge of the Church of England plan at a salary of £500 per annum, this for a duration of at least two to three years. The new Church of England association was formed on 27 March 1848 under the presidency of the Archbishop of Canterbury. The vast committee of the association included another archbishop (of Dublin); seven bishops who became eight when EGW's old ecclesiastical friend, Samuel Hinds, became Bishop of Norwich in 1849; a duke, a marquess, two viscounts, three earls, six lords and several knights. The business of the association was undertaken by a management committee, initially chaired by John Hutt and later Lord Lyttelton. At its first meeting, it was decided that the proposed settlement would be known as Canterbury and its chief town as Christchurch. Godley later wrote, 'I hope that my old College is grateful to me for naming the future capital of New Zealand after it.'[39]

The character of the association, with all its mitres and coronets, is usually taken as ultimate evidence that EGW was besotted by noble rank, the clearest indication that he wished to transplant the old English class society into a new world. It is, rather, evidence that, in making what he knew would be his last attempt at establishing the ideal colonial settlement, EGW was determined the association must have sufficient character to transcend the commercial and speculative imperatives that had vitiated the New Zealand Company. Such an association would have the credentials to reassure a cynical Colonial Office and to attract settlers with means and serious intent – and its members would have enough capital resources to maintain its solvency. It would have both Godliness and Godleyness, in the form of rich friends.

EGW's name was nowhere to be spied among the articles of association, minutes or prospectus of the Canterbury Association, but his advice, guidance and writing were essential to its operation and all its officers would take the train to Redhill for consultation. As an asthmatic, he complained of feeling 'half dead' amid the smoke and noise of London. The uncertainties of his chronic coronary condition and his now fluctuating energies had resigned him to his back room, or country cottage, role. But whenever it was politically necessary he would take the train to London Bridge, and a cab to New Zealand House. And he soon had Jerningham on the management committee to provide him with off-the-record reports of what was going on.

Jerningham had continued to live the life of a man about town but with steadily decreasing resources. The Alloms had endeavoured to get him out of London for his health's sake in 1847, and to put some distance between him and those means of squandering his money – the club, the theatre and the bawdy house. Grandfather Edward described him in July 1847 as being 'much harassed as to the means of existing'.[40] Having him compile *The Hand-book for New Zealand*, and finding a place for Jerningham on the Canterbury Association's management committee in May 1848, were probably moves by EGW to give him useful occupation and income. Jerningham's theatrical interests and literary ability also led him that year to write his play, *Jack-In-Office or Prigs in Place*. An upstairs-downstairs comedy of matchmaking and political patronage, the play is full of the current vernacular and reflects Jerningham's first-hand Wakefield experience. As servants prepare to assist the lady heroine to elope towards the end of the play one asks, 'But to-morrow? What am I to do for things if we're off to Gretna Green?' to which the other replies, 'Gretna Green?– grandmother's tales! Common sense and the rail is knocked that up long ago. We marries in town, my dear; license and glass coach all ready.'[41] But Jerningham's dissolute behaviour and poor prospects meant there was still no prospective bride or glass coach in view.

Godley began preparing the Canterbury prospectus and started negotiations with Lord Grey at the Colonial Office. An early task was to select a reliable surveyor who would go out to New Zealand well in advance of the first emigrants, to choose and lay out the settlement site. Felix Wakefield was asked early in 1848 to undertake this task but EGW prevented him, 'partly from distrust of the Company . . . partly from distrust of his ability to manage the diplomatic questions of choice of site with the Governor and Bishop'.[42] So Felix declined but then undertook, after the formation of the association, to draw up instructions for surveying methods, based on his extensive experience in Tasmania.[43] He completed these on 25 May and they were given to Captain Joseph Thomas, who sailed for New Zealand at the beginning of July as the New Zealand Company agent authorised to select and survey the Canterbury site, subject to the approval of Grey and Selwyn. Thomas had already spent seven years in New Zealand, surveying Wanganui, exploring the Wairarapa and working on the Otago surveys and probably knew as much as Felix did. He was armed with £20,000 and two assistants, one of them Charley Torlesse.

EGW was mightily upset when Charley informed him. 'I feel bound to say,' wrote EGW to Thomas, 'that if you had consulted me . . . . I should not have advised you to confide largely in his fitness for an office of importance under you; and, even as it is, I cannot help putting you on your guard against his defects of character. The chief of these is conceit. He has far too high an opinion of himself. In the next place . . . he is not tractable, but, on the contrary, difficult to manage. And lastly, his temper is not amiable. I say nothing about his good qualities, which it is your business to find out.' He advised Thomas to 'never give him rein' and to keep a 'tight hand' on him. EGW knew that this account of Charley would likely be counted as severe, 'especially by his partial mother', but considered that, in warning Thomas, he was doing Charley a service.[44]

The motivations for this admonitory letter are unclear, although EGW had already complained of Charley's conceit a year earlier at Abel Smith's Stoke farm. His dudgeon was high mostly because Charley had been chosen without consulting him, probably under the influence of Charles Torlesse, who was on the management committee. Any nepotism should be under his control, calculated and weighed for effect. EGW did not let the matter rest there. He told Godley of it and after the *Bernicia* set sail from London for New Zealand with the survey team, he had the ship intercepted off the Kent coast with a message on 9 July, requesting Thomas to go ashore and meet him for a final briefing. EGW no doubt reinforced his strictures about Charley and also ensured that he was the last to give Thomas advice and instruction on what to do when he arrived in New Zealand. The key question was probably the point that he raised in a letter to Godley three days later: 'There are obstacles; and I fear that the absolute dependence of Thomas's mission for success on the good-will of the Bishop may prove a formidable one.'[45]

He also urged Godley to get a body of intending colonists together as soon as possible: 'This is the one thing needful: it is indispensable; and all the rest would follow.' The project was threatening to grind to a halt. Despite his approval, Lord Grey had logically declined to grant the association a charter, or any kind of specific support, until the site of Canterbury had been established. Thomas's survey reports could not possibly reach England before the middle of 1849 and, since no one could buy land before that, interest in the venture had naturally begun to wane. In establishing New Zealand colonies, you were damned if you did and damned if you didn't make the survey in advance of sales and emigration.

Thomas had gone ashore at Boulogne to meet EGW who had travelled to France to be 'out of the way of distractions for a few months' – unsuccessfully at first – 'to use my present strength for the purpose of completing my long intended book on A View of the Art of Colonization'.[46] EGW had begun work on this last testament some time during 1847 and its composition occupied much of his stay at Great Malvern. At the end of November he told John Abel Smith that the book 'advances to completion' but then the distractions of Canterbury halted progress. Early in 1848, John Stuart Mill wrote EGW that he was 'glad to hear that you are writing the book you speak of. I have long regretted that there does not exist a systematic treatise . . . from your hand and with your name, in which the whole subject of colonization is treated . . . . at present people have to pick up your doctrines both theoretical and practical.'[47] Godley had begun to refer to EGW's long-announced book as 'Mrs Harris', the friend of Mrs Gamp in Dickens's *Martin Chuzzlewit* whom no one had ever seen and was thought to be a 'phantom' of Mrs Gamp's brain 'created for the express purpose of holding visionary dialogues with her on all manner of subjects and invariably winding up with a compliment to the excellence of her nature'. EGW played up to the sharp irony of Godley's comment and, as the book approached completion, told him that 'My Mrs Harris is in a bad way; and I feel pretty confident in seeing the last of her'.[48]

Determined to finish the volume, EGW had repaired in June with his dogs to the Chateau Mabille, on the heights above Boulogne. He also took Constance and Felix's four youngest with him, now making full provision for their care and instruction. But progress on the book had continued to be slow. After the Thomas distractions, EGW decided he needed an amanuensis and sent to London for 22-year-old Albert Allom. He had recently returned to England from New Zealand after being laid off as a survey cadet consequent on the company's retrenchments, and following a fire in which he had lost most of his possessions. He had been able to return home only with the financial assistance of Judge Chapman who had paid his bills to the tune of £90.[49] With EGW's help, Allom was later able to find recompense from the company to pay his debt.

Albert Allom arrived at Boulogne in September and the final stages of EGW's book were put in train. Allom recorded that EGW's health

> did not permit him to work more than four or five hours a day, and this only was accomplished by extreme regularity in taking morning and evening exercise. As the winter approached we often sallied forth before daylight, regardless of the weather, our pockets filled with ripe pears, and scoured the country with his fine, well-known Talbot hounds and beautiful little beagles, whose alternate deep baying and yelping in the darkness of the morning the farmers and others have good reason to remember. When at work, he would slowly pace up and down the room, dictating to me the copy, pausing occasionally the more carefully to frame a sentence or to choose a particular word. He seldom made a correction. The day's work had generally been well thought out previously.[50]

In writing a memoir and vindication of theory, was EGW acknowledging the death of a vision that had been the chief focus of his life and work over the preceding 20 years? Or did he feel that he had little life and energy left and that Canterbury would be his last throw of the colonial dice? EGW's accurate vision of the future for Britain's commonwealth of nations, in his 1844 Canadian essay, and his opinion that self-government for British-settled colonies would be accomplished within a decade or so, show he understood that the future for planned colonial expeditions was strictly limited. It would be not long before colonial governments decided on their own immigration plans. Allom faithfully recorded that, 'Plodding on steadily day by day, the work was finished on Christmas Eve, 1848. I had only just enough time to pack up the manuscript and hurry with it on board the steamer leaving at midnight for London. The next morning the manuscript was delivered to Mr Rintoul.' A separate message to Rintoul from EGW told him that 'the coffin holding Mrs. Harris's remains was put on board the Albion steamer'.

EGW had intended to have his manuscript 'revised critically' by Charles Buller, who had visited him at the Chateau Mabille twice during the autumn. But after leaving EGW a second time, Buller had gone to London for an operation and had contracted erysipelas (a streptococcal infection) and then typhus, through the 'blundering of an unskilful surgeon', and he died on 29 November, aged just 42. His bust was placed in Westminster Abbey, Carlyle eulogised him as 'the genialist radical I have ever met' and Bulwer Lytton wrote

> Farewell, fine humorist, finer reasoner still,
> Lively as Luttrell, logical as Mill.[51]

The loss for EGW was severe – a good friend, another of the 1830s radicals gone, another supporter and devoted campaigner for the colonial cause; and, just at that moment, EGW had lost the editor who, knowing his 'rash and fanciful' nature, would have toned down any excess of opinion or digression in the text. His loss was 'great indeed'. EGW wrote no special eulogy for Buller but, as a lasting tribute, included as a 35-page appendix to *A View of the Art of Colonization* his masterly April 1843 speech to the House of Commons on systematic colonisation.

Soon EGW also received news of William's death. There is no record of how this affected him although months later, in a letter to Dillon Bell, he stated simply, 'I cannot write about my brother William.'[52] H. S. Chapman, in July, received news that showed 'EGW bears his brother's death better than was expected. My own notion is that Wakefield must feel that his brother's death removes an Incubus out of his way.'[53] EGW may have felt that William's death was well timed to leave him with a measure of honour before the collapse of the company, and its rancorous aftermath, during which William would have been a focus of vilification. Whether EGW felt relief or grief or a mixture of both, he would have certainly become conscious that the ranks of both family and the faithful had begun to thin. Only Molesworth of the old guard was left.

PART FOUR

A Suicide of the Affections

1849–1879

CHAPTER TWENTY-FIVE

Flying with a Broken Wing

WHEN EGW SENT THE MANUSCRIPT OF *A View of the Art of Colonization* to Rintoul for publication at Christmas 1848 he said, 'My object has been . . . to now *establish* my claim to the real authorship of most of what has been done with respect to colonization during that long period. Many, doubtless, have shared my labours, and done much independently of me; but more have made profit and reputation out of my slavery, without offering me a share. So now I claim my own; and having resolved to do it, I have not done it by halves. The large space allotted to this purpose was deliberately given to it; and I wrote without a thought about the exhibition of egotism, intending to say all that seemed likely to serve my purpose, and taking care only to keep within the truth.'[1] In a February letter to Rintoul he railed at even greater length against Lord Grey, perhaps in response to criticism of the work.

It is easy to remark, in long hindsight, that EGW had made a fatal mistake in taking this approach to what John Stuart Mill had expected to be a systematic treatise of the Wakefield theory and vision. A work without egotism, in the character of the fine 1844 essay, would have gained him more recognition and reputation than a text aimed at settling old scores and arguments. This was not the way to seek the rehabilitation that critics of EGW describe as his chief motivation in life. But the rashness and petulance of EGW's personality, and his sense of impending death, produced a cry for recognition, for some justice for all the work, effort and money he had put into the colonisation cause.

EGW did his best to stage manage the effect of the book's publication, planned for 5 February 1849. He moved back from Boulogne to Reigate in the new year and rented a cottage in the grounds of the White Hart Inn. His father visited London from time to time, and stayed with the Alloms in Bloomsbury – the year before he had given evidence to the House of Lords Monteagle Committee on Ireland – but there is no evidence that father and son met up, in London, Reigate or Boulogne: the long estrangement continued. Edward's continued attempts to belittle EGW culminated in his writing to Lord Grey after the publication of *A View of the Art of Colonization*, apologising for his son's offensive comments.

EGW told Godley a few weeks before publication that 'the book is *awfully* personal as regards Lord Grey. Now suppose that this does not fail in its object, which is to raise myself from the slough into which he has trampled me; the effect would be to damage him: and then, after he was damaged, those who moved in Parliament would seem to attack the wounded.' Rintoul had assured EGW that after the book was published, 'there can be no stir in Parliament about colonization without reference to it.'[2] EGW tried to convince Godley to circulate unbound pre-publication copies to key politicians, particularly ex-Secretary for War and Colonies Gladstone, so they might use its contents to attack Lord Grey in a debate over colonisation. EGW was willing to delay publication if that promised to be the case.

He had also decided that this was the propitious moment to resign from the company and in writing to secretary T. C. Harington on 29 January, gave three reasons. First, the book might revive in 'Lord Grey's mind certain feelings [and] a new irritation of his passions might be hurtfully visited on the Company in some way or other, if I continued a Director'. Second, he disagreed with the company's arrangement with Lord Grey and publication of his opinions on that matter dictated that he should retire. Third, because this arrangement placed the company on a 'footing of complete dependence on the Colonial Office' and given that his book related in 'great measure to the defects and vices of the Colonial Office' he should also cease to be a director.[3]

A View of the Art of Colonization appeared as planned. It comprised a series of 71 letters between a 'Statesman' and a 'Colonist' in which the former is instructed in the 'art' of colonisation, including a history of past events. Early on, in Letter VI, EGW attacks Lord Grey personally. The letter form helps to disguise a rambling diffuseness to the text that was, perhaps, a consequence of the ambulatory dictation to Allom, with little revision or correction. EGW's first biographer, Richard Garnett, thought the book 'ill fitted to attract novices, and those who had already attended to the subject can only say, "We knew this before"'. The satire on obstructive bureaucracy through that old *bête noire* 'Mr Mother Country', Garnett saw as 'deadly in so far as it strikes the abuses of the only system of government which no one defends, and at the same time the only system of which it is impossible to get rid'. But Garnett saw the personal attack on James Stephen as 'most unjust': where the former colonial secretary 'represents the opponents of the vital principles of Wakefield's system, he is entirely in place, but where he merely personifies the general spirit of obstructiveness he is an excrescence upon a book whose sole aim should have been to instruct in the art and mystery of planting colonies. Misled into polemics, the author left this unwritten.'[4] EGW's friends were disappointed, even in the face of justifying personal explanations such as those he sent to John Abel Smith on publication day: 'Many will object, on the score of bad taste, to the personal matter that is mixed with the disquisitions on public topics. To them, if I had the opportunity, I would say, that it was not a question of taste, but of self-defence against intolerable wrong.' The best of his friends could acknowledge his lingering sense of humiliation, yet regret its damaging expression.

The book was greeted, at best with tolerance and, at worst, with vituperation. Gladstone kept his discreet distance and it seems as if even Godley kept away at the time of publication, ignoring EGW's sneers at the political inaction of his friends. By 22 February, EGW complained to him, 'I am getting concerned at not hearing from you or of you, fearing that you may be unwell.' There is a hint of disingenuousness in EGW's concern for Godley's health, an echo of the pathetic appeal for sympathy in the second letter of his book: 'My health, instead of improving, has got worse lately, and will probably never mend. It is a disorder of the nerves which has long hindered, and now absolutely precludes me from engaging in the oral discussion of subjects that deeply interest me, more especially if they are subjects involving argument and continuous thought. You must have observed how I suffered towards the end of our last conversation. At length, I cannot disobey the doctor's injunction to stay at home and be quiet, without effects that remind me of a bird trying to fly with a broken wing, and knocking itself to pieces in the vain exertion.'[5] This appeal to the reader's indulgence may have seemed to many of his audience, and all of his enemies, as evidence simply of a man who had shot his bolt.

After H. S. Chapman read *A View of the Art of Colonization*, he commented, 'It is a great exposure of the obstructive character of the Colonial Office, and besides that it is calculated to excite the animosity of so many persons . . . that I am quite prepared to find it made the subject of some savage and recriminative criticism. Wakefield forgets that "they who live in glass houses should not throw stones" . . . ought Wakefield to be surprised if some of the persons attacked give him as good as he gives them?'[6]

The book proved a failure as an adequate history and treatise of Wakefield colonial theory and experience. But its declaration of hostility against Lord Grey and the Colonial Office provided a springboard for the colonial reformers to attack the government's failure to grant the Canterbury Association a charter or New Zealand a self-governing constitution. By the spring of 1849 there was still no news from New Zealand of a site for Canterbury and there were no signs of co-operation from a government that had become distracted by turbulence and revolution at home and abroad. The French revolution of 1848 had sparked revolution across the states of Germany, Italy and Austria-Hungary, as the Hungarian nationalist poet Petöfi had prophesied:

I dream of days of bloodshed
In which an old world dies,

And see from smoking ruins
A phoenix world arise.

The class-based republican struggles prompted insurrection in Ireland and the 79-year-old Duke of Wellington was called out of retirement to organise a force of special constables to contain a gathering of Chartists on Kennington Common. As revolutionary outbreaks recurred in 1849, and a would-be assassin attempted to shoot Queen Victoria, proposed Church of England colonies on the other side of the world were scarcely a government priority.

During the first parliamentary session of 1849, the reformers attacked from several salients. Godley persuaded his close friend Charles Adderley to take up the South African constitutional cause in the House; Molesworth tried to organise a general vote of censure on Grey's colonial policies; and Gladstone attacked over problems in Ceylon, Canada and Vancouver. In July, Godley and Adderley held a public dinner to organise a Society for the Reform of Colonial Government (soon the Colonial Reform Society) and another campaign against Grey. EGW manoeuvred Adderley into doing most of the work and, ever the publicist, advised both men to make sure newspaper editors were invited to the society's meetings. Godley enthused, 'What a battle we shall make next session for colonial self-government if we are still alive!'[7] EGW worked ceaselessly with both younger men in framing resolutions for an Australian constitution bill that presaged self-government in New Zealand.

Adderley attracted to the society not only radical opponents of the government but Whigs, too. The Tories were circumspect. Sir Robert Peel told Adderley that, in respect to Canterbury, 'I will not conceal from you my opinion that the experiment you are about to make is a hazardous one'; and Benjamin Disraeli stood back, telling Lord Stanley, 'Clearly, instead of more Wakefieldism, we want less: and it appears to me that the real key to Lord Grey's position is that he talked too much Wakefieldism out of office, and found, when at length Secretary of State for the Colonies, that his theoretical Colonial Reform was a delusion.'[8] Disraeli had been quick to purloin EGW's notion of Britain as the workshop of the world when a novice parliamentarian and was later the champion of empire; just now the reformers did not suit his political ends.

The formation of the Colonial Reform Society by EGW, Godley and Adderley had been prompted partly by news, received in June, of Captain Thomas's preferred site for Canterbury and the now urgent need to harry Lord Grey into granting the association a charter. Thomas had arrived in New Zealand in late November and within three weeks advised the New Zealand Company that he intended to give priority to a survey of the plains adjacent to Banks Peninsula in the South Island. Governor Grey and Bishop Selwyn would have preferred him to consider North Island sites, such as Hawke's Bay, anxious to keep new settlements within easy governance. But Thomas, from his surveying knowledge of the lower half of the North Island and the Otago block, and all earlier reports of the middle South Island, was not to be deflected.

Thomas's party undertook an intensive two-month exploration of the plains and downlands between the foothills of the Southern Alps and the sea, as far north as the Waipara River and as far south as the Ashburton. Charley Torlesse led the party that surveyed the block between the Waimakariri and the Rakaia and on New Year's Day 1849 climbed the 7000-foot peak overlooking the central plains that today bears his name. In April, Charley pushed further south to the Rangitata but by mid-February Thomas had already decided to seek the approval of Grey and Selwyn for the plains and peninsula site. On 28 February, by the *Cornelia*, he sent a despatch to the company that included a full report and maps.

The *Cornelia* made a fast passage. Four months later, EGW was telling Godley that Felix had 'seen the Reports and Maps from New Zealand, and, after carefully examining them, is of opinion that the place chosen is *excellent* for the purpose. He has no doubt that it is one of the finest spots in the world for a new settlement on a great scale.' EGW was giving heart to Godley who had begun to despair of the company's commitment to the enterprise: 'They don't care a straw for Canterbury.' EGW confirmed that some of the directors wanted rid of the association and to sell off Thomas's southern plains elsewhere. This was bringing 'Canterbury affairs to a crisis. You will be presently required to "go on" or "be off".'[9] He worked at stiffening the younger man's resolve, in the face of both lack of company interest and also the slow deterioration of Godley's health.

EGW's work on bills for colonial self-government was an attack on Governor Grey's reluctance to grant New Zealand's southern settlements some form of political independence. It was a continuation of the old New Zealand Company v. Colonial Office and Wellington v. Auckland fight, of EGW's continual struggle to gain political pre-eminence for the settlements created through his own vision, but it would also help to parry any attempts by Grey to upset the Canterbury plan. EGW also wished to counter any moves by Bishop Selwyn and the Church Missionary Society, declared enemies of the company's activities, that would cause problems for the association. In July he initiated the plan to create a separate bishopric for Canterbury, thus removing it from Selwyn's demesne and lending the association more power in fighting the Low Church CMS evangelists who wielded such influence at the Colonial Office. This move reinforced criticism of the Canterbury Association as a High Church enterprise led by 'Tractarians' or 'Puseyites'.

It is difficult now to appreciate the power of the religious revival that affected every part of English society in the early Victorian age. No party or movement could ignore the political significance of the debate between the evangelical and traditionalist factions of the Church of England and, further, between it and the non-conforming Methodists. The breakaway evangelicals had considered that 'Church and State, political power and ecclesiastical patronage, were throughout the whole structure of English social life so interwoven that the Church had almost ceased to have a corporate identity and a corporate will.'[10] The evangelical movement had been one response to what was seen as vitiation of the church's spiritual vigour and doctrinal leadership. But in the 1830s a series of publications, *Tracts for the Times*, written by the Vicar of St Mary's, Oxford, John Henry Newman, signalled the start of a new movement designed to return the church to its role as a divinely inspired national force, with restoration of its ritual, doctrine and catholicity. Newman published 90 tracts between 1833 and 1841 before his conversion to Roman Catholicism. Followers of the intellectual leader of the Oxford 'Tractarians', Canon E. B. Pusey of Christ Church, were labelled 'Puseyites', a pejorative term indicating extremism in religious thought.

Godley rejected its application to him, yet he and his friends, such as Charles Adderley, were at Oxford in 1833 when the first tract appeared. They sympathised with Newman and Pusey and with the movement's thrust to re-emphasise the catholicity of the church. And support for the Canterbury project, with its proposal to transport an entire diocesan establishment, came from Tractarian supporters who saw an opportunity to renew the church in the Antipodes. EGW's move to find Canterbury a bishop was a shrewd political move to reinforce this support, not least from the High Church reformers in Parliament, friends of Godley and Gladstone. But the Tractarian connection began to backfire on EGW during 1850 when English society slipped into one of its periodic anti-Catholic moods and he found himself exhorting Godley to stick to 'safe' clergy.

Although not complete, EGW's surviving correspondence from this 1849–52 Canterbury period remains the most comprehensive record of his mature political method. He may have been based at Reigate but, through a steady flow of letters and visitors, he kept a finger on the day-to-day pulse of London politics. He exhorted, advised and lectured, maintaining an unbroken influence on everything relating to the association, the company and colonial affairs in Parliament. At the same time he drew much joy and vitality from Felix's children. In order to keep them close to him, EGW rented nearby Woodhatch for Constance and the sisters and brothers in her care, Josephine, Priscilla, Oliver and Edward.

Constance became EGW's secretary, 'an office also sometimes discharged by his nephew George, the son of his brother Howard, and afterwards an Indian civil servant'. George had been sent home from India for schooling. All her life, Constance vividly remembered her first impression of her uncle, 'as of one superior to all men she had ever seen or imagined'. To her, he was like a lion, 'with massive head, magnificent brow, sanguine complexion, somewhat too full habit of body, long floating hair, the token of the enthusiast, and brilliant blue eyes, indescribably tender when in gentle mood, but frequently blazing with passion and excitement . . .'. In personality, too, he was a man of contrasts: 'in general the kindest of men – continually performing generous actions, and affectionate and tender-hearted to a fault – he had moods of perverseness, and could be bitterly resentful and vindictive when his plans were thwarted . . . .' She recalled his kindness to and interest in young people: he saw that Constance had French and dancing lessons and she remembered, with gratitude, 'his constant admonitions on punctuality, method, good handwriting, and the other valuable habits whose importance is so often undiscerned by the young'. He loved 'contriving parties and picnics for the amusement of his young people' and delighted especially in exuberant 'practical joking, especially by alterations of apparel. He so effectually disguised the daughter of a friend as to impose on her own parents.' In this there was sweet nostalgia for his own Edinburgh youth and the pranks of Nina and Jerningham when they were young. EGW would 'sometimes calm the perturbed nerves by the anodyne of a new novel, and he read *The Vicar of Wakefield* through regularly once a year', perhaps for reassurance that, despite vicissitudes, good will always out. And ever present at Reigate were 'the enormous Talbot hounds, the awful delight of the neighbourhood . . . and . . . a good cat, demonstrative in her affection to her master'.

Constance 'copied documents and letters for him, and wrote abundantly to his dictation'. She was often 'fetched in haste' when her uncle was closeted with 'some leading public man, such as Sir William Molesworth or Mr Aglionby', to take down 'an oration or disquisition from his lips, which frequently reappeared in the proceedings of the House of Commons'. She remembered, too, Robert Rintoul, 'the large-browed, gentle-mannered editor of the *Spectator*, who must never be spoken to upon a Friday'.[11]

In mid-July 1849, the Colonial Office received its first report from Governor Grey on the site for the Canterbury settlement. EGW saw that the company and association must now move decisively if the plan was to come off. Since he was an officer of neither, Godley, with the help of Adderley, must lead the way. But Godley's chronic laryngitis had caused a steady deterioration in his health. Following his own treatment at Malvern, EGW had recommended hydropathy – cold water and fresh air – and had avoided disturbing Godley during the summer as he undertook the cure. But in early August, EGW wrote to John Hutt asking after Godley's health and a month later learned Godley's condition had worsened to such an extent that he had been ordered to spend the winter in a milder climate, at Madeira or Naples. This was disastrous news; without Godley the association would collapse. And then EGW saw how to pluck the flower of Canterbury from the nettle of Godley's illness.

On 23 September, EGW told Godley,

> My brother [Felix] came here last night. He speaks of the climate of Hobart in Van Diemen's Land (the very parallel of Akaroa) as most favourable to delicate lungs. He knows several cases of grown men given over in England, who are now in perfect

> health. He says it is the dryness of the southern hemisphere which is so good – consumption being the rarest of complaints thereabouts. He knew one case of a lady, 70 years of age, who left England with a cruel asthma, and lived in Van Diemen's Land ten years without a trace of the complaint – that is, lived to 80, free of asthma . . . . the climate of New Zealand is more like that of Van Diemen's Land than any other, but better, as it is free of the hot winds which sometimes get to Van Diemen's Land from Australia.[12]

Only the exclamation marks are missing.

The very next day, EGW wrote to Adderley – 'It seems essential that Godley should not breathe English air after the month of October'– And to the company's Henry Aglionby: 'Within a fortnight it must be *on* or *off* with the whole matter [Canterbury]'. He told William Baring of the association that Godley was the 'life and soul of the Canterbury Association. I am moving heaven and earth to induce him to go to New Zealand, rather than Madeira or Naples . . . . the climate of New Zealand is most fit to cure him entirely. His going to New Zealand would have excellent effects in promoting the Canterbury settlement.'[13]

Over the following month, EGW fought trenchantly on three fronts: to persuade Godley to go to New Zealand, for his health and for Canterbury; to secure his appointment as leader of the settlement; and to find a bishop while parrying attempts at interference by Bishop Selwyn's friends in the association. One idea was to fob Selwyn off with a colony of his own.

EGW became almost brutally manipulative: if he could get Godley away, then Adderley and Godley's other friends would stay committed to Canterbury. 'I hope you won't agree with any make-shift, such as Adderley *now* proposes, for going to Italy and keeping up New Zealand or any other political relations in England. It is just the thing you ought *not* to do with a view to your recovery – which is the main point. Either New Zealand at once, properly and pleasantly; or else, cut politics, and England, and everything that could in the least interfere with the rest which is needful for recovery. The proposal of this *mezzo termine* [half measure] seems to me childish, not to say cruel. It would save them trouble: that is all.'[14]

Adderley had been countering EGW's pressure, distrustful of the man he would call 'the most amazing genius I ever knew' yet 'sulky', 'satanic' and 'Machiavellian'.[15] But Godley reassured him:

> I really think, taking all things . . . into consideration, you ought to see him. I think you may trust me when your interests are concerned; and I would most scrupulously avoid advising anything which would injure or compromise you. But I know that Wakefield is most anxious to place his great knowledge and abilities at the service of gentlemen and Conservatives; and he is most especially devoted to you personally. Do not therefore let any scruples dissuade you from acting with him, so far as you agree with him. Depend

> upon it, he is very valuable, and, to you very manageable. Pray see him before you settle anything about the colonial campaign, and, if possible, before I go.[16]

Godley himself was not only concerned about his health and the Canterbury situation but also with filial duties to his aged father, his wife Charlotte's pregnancy and the desire of his friends not to lose him on some long-term project on the other side of the world. Godley's father gave his consent for a journey to New Zealand, Charlotte's confinement passed (the child was stillborn) and both he and the association succumbed to EGW's pressure. On 10 October, the management committee of the association recorded their approval of Godley's agreement to go to New Zealand as their resident chief agent (for a term of two years). EGW concurred with Adderley's suggestion that Godley should now receive an honour, a baronetcy or somesuch, but a Whig government with Lord Grey in the cabinet dismissed *that* idea promptly.

Bouncing a bishop into office meant opposition on complex constitutional and canonical grounds, quite apart from acquiring Selwyn's approval. Godley met with EGW at Reigate to devise the strategy that would launch a bishop and a charter for the association before he left for New Zealand at Christmas. By this time EGW had probably also heard from his mole at the Colonial Office that it had recently received Governor Grey's official despatch confirming the southern plains site for Canterbury. The key to the bishopric was the surety of an endowment of £10,000, which was usually enough to prompt the Colonial Office to recommend that the Crown issue letters-patent for a colonial bishop. EGW and Godley decided that it was time they invoked the aid of the Canterbury Association's titular president, the Archbishop of Canterbury. On 25 October, EGW wrote Godley, 'By all means go with Lord Courtenay [a member of the association committee]: for the object is that *you* should inform the Archbishop by conversation. He evidently does not understand the matter. Of course, the appointment of a Bishop is to depend on the endowment. But the present object it to have it settled now, that *when* the endowment shall be provided, there will be a Bishopric and that Mr. So-and-So will be the Bishop.'[17] EGW's current prospective Mr So-and-So was the Reverend J. C. Wynter, Rector of Gatton, near Reigate; over the last months of 1849 he pursued him relentlessly.

Courtenay and Godley obtained the archbishop's support but he would not personally solicit Lord Grey on the matter. EGW commented, 'His Grace is not singular in avoiding the risk of being snubbed, which everybody must run who prefers a request or makes a suggestion to Lord Grey. But an Archbishop of Canterbury ought to be singularly free from moral timidity.'[18] Courtenay decided not to approach Lord Grey in the overheated environs of Westminster but to catch the earl in calmer circumstances, at his country house; and he came away with Grey's approval to carve another bishopric from Selwyn's diocese, provided the endowment were found. At this news, the association launched the Canterbury settlement and on 13 November its charter was sealed. Godley was due to sail within the month and all the practical arrangements for land sales, shipping and emigration were immediately set in train. Ever conscious of finding a place for family, EGW arranged that Jerningham would accompany Godley to New Zealand as an aide. Was there a job for Felix?

In April 1849, Felix had been offered the post of surveyor-general to the New Zealand Company. Before he could answer Godley wrote to him, 'Pray don't decide without considering your brother's strong *prejudice* against the existing state of things both at the Colonial Office and at New Zealand House. I am not going to brag of either, but they are not so bad as he thinks . . . . I shall be very much grieved if you refuse.'[19] The offer was immensely attractive to Felix, much more than the opportunity to work for the Sanitary Commission. But decline Felix did, under pressure from EGW, and Godley had to wait another two years for a satisfactory explanation. EGW told him in 1851,

> I would not let him go for three reasons: first, because I believed the Co. . . . would merely send him out, and then leave him in the lurch, if his appointment did not revive their land sales; secondly because, though I thought his appointment, by reconnecting me with the Direction, might enable them to sell some land, or rather to obtain some money. I knew that they had not got the land to deliver, and I would not be a party, however indirectly, to the sort of delusion which they were willing to attempt; and thirdly, because, I doubted of his being fit to be trusted alone, at that distance, in a position of great responsibility.[20]

Soon after Felix turned down the surveyor-general offer, he was asked to compile a report on the management of the company's surveys in New Zealand, an amplification of his earlier instructions to Captain Thomas. Felix completed this, without pay, by 12 September and there were immediate doubts about who had written the report because of the marked difference in the quality of writing between the narrative and technical parts of the report. EGW admitted off-handedly to Godley, 'Of course, I had a good deal to do with the literary composition of Felix's Report; but though the exposition of the ideas may be regarded as in good measure mine, the ideas were not mine last year, and I still dissent from some of them.'[21] Felix admitted that EGW 'assisted me not a little',[22] but his 'deficiencies of capacities' now appeared to be exposed for the first time, despite EGW's firm management.

Payment for his report was to be awarded on its merit by Captain Robert Dawson of the Royal Engineers. On 7 November, Dawson wrote to Felix: 'As I feel confident that the system of surveying described and recommended by you will never be carried out, I must guard myself against being supposed to acquiesce in it.'[23] He could not bring himself to approve it; yet the Canterbury Association adopted Felix's report and sent a draft proof of it to Captain Thomas in New

Zealand soon afterwards. It was published as an 88-page booklet, *Colonial Surveying With A View to the Disposal of Waste Land*, in time for Godley's departure in December. Yet Dawson's letter debarred payment to Felix and he had to wait until 1851 for recompense from the Crown. It is hard to see what Dawson's objections were since the triangulation methods described had already been employed successfully during the Otago surveys, and would be in Canterbury, but it may be that he disapproved of the methods of sale, selection and possession of title.

In any event, the application of Felix's recommendations and instructions for the survey of Canterbury saw the colony 'more rapidly and more accurately' laid out than any other new settlement 'known in any new country'.[24] One of Felix's key recommendations was that country sections should not be surveyed until purchasers or their agents had made their selections on site. This both encouraged genuine settlers and also entailed much less survey work before migrants arrived, saving time and money. But the most important contribution Felix made to the planning of Canterbury, drawn from his Tasmanian experience, was his insistence on the importance of pastoralists – sheep graziers – to the development of settlements and the need to make pasturage available at the outset. He believed that pastoralists would in time want to freehold their land and become permanent settlers. He also considered that anyone should be able to purchase pastoral land after due notice.

It is on this point, at least, that EGW would have disagreed: the encouragement of unrestricted pastoralism mitigated against the Wakefieldian fixed-price, close-knit agricultural settlement. But as both a realist and a theorist he would have acknowledged Felix's reasoning from hard experience. The widespread belief that EGW was against pastoralism or proposed the application of the sufficient price for pastoral lands is received opinion without secure foundation. On 11 November 1849, he wrote to E. H. W. (William) Bellairs, a rich Norfolk landowner he was approaching to lead the new colony, 'The Canterbury Plains are now ascertained to be eminently fit for pastoral husbandry, which is the only sort, in countries where labour for hire is scarce, that yields quick and large returns.'[25] Both EGW's statement and the character of his correspondent accorded with his views in *A View of the Art of Colonization*: 'The theorists of 1830 never thought of compelling settlers to pay for the use of natural pasturage. According to their theory [i.e. EGW's], it is the extreme cheapness, not of natural pasturage, but of land for cultivation, which occasions scarcity of labour for hire. Labourers could not become landowners by using natural pasturage. The use of it requires, in order to be profitable, the employment of a considerable capital, of numerous servants, and of very superior skill . . . . it is a business altogether unsuitable to the common labourer or small capitalist.'[26]

EGW had prevented Felix from becoming surveyor-general to the company and from taking up the agent's post filled by Thomas. After seeing Felix's report,

Godley now proposed that he become the sole agent for Canterbury land sales in England. EGW acceded, though with some reluctance. He told Godley eighteen months later that though they were 'about equally responsible' for the appointment, 'knowing more of him [Felix] than you could, or rather having a sort of lurking distrust of him which you could not have, I was less keen for it than you were. But I really thought he would do the work well – better than anybody else we could find, if I could retain a complete control over him. I was also very glad of a prospect of his earning some money, both on his own account, and in order that he might be able to pay the heavy debt to me.'[27] With that in view, EGW had assured Godley on the eve of his departure from England that Felix 'for steadiness and fidelity cannot be surpassed',[28] and agreed to bankroll all the advertising, administrative and travel expenses of the land agency, which Felix was expected to meet from his commission.

As 1849 neared its end and the winter deepened, the stresses of managing the Canterbury project and coping with Felix began to affect EGW's health and to stimulate a rising fear that his enemies, real or imagined, would upset his plans yet again. This fear verged on a paranoia that he frankly admitted to John Abel Smith. He wrote of a

> suspicion which has lately got possession of me, and from which I cannot escape. It is founded on a great deal of circumstantial evidence, too long for recital here. It is that both in Downing Street and Broad Street Buildings, the project is entertained of putting an end to the Canterbury Association, and perhaps to the Company, with the view of securing the Southern Plains near Banks Promontory for *exploitation* by the Colonial Office and Governor Grey. It is by this suspicion only, that I can account for a number of things that have happened lately. . . . If the suspicion should turn out to be unfounded, let it be attributed to my state of health, which is apt to be attended by an insanity of suspicion. If it should turn out to be true, you will indignantly join those who will have to defend the colony and Company from the treason.

Abel Smith was entitled to EGW's 'frankness' and concealing his suspicion would be a 'kind of treachery similar to that which I suspect and will denounce if my fears should be confirmed . . . If I am wrong, call me mad.'[29] Two weeks later, on 13 December 1849, Godley sailed from Plymouth with his wife and small son for New Zealand. Although it was still not too late for determined opponents to scupper Canterbury, they would now face the wrath of Godley's friends, such as Adderley and Lord Lyttelton, in whose hands he had left the ultimate security of the association. EGW's alarums continued, if on a lower note, and the real crisis, that had nothing to do with treason and plot, was yet to come.

CHAPTER TWENTY-SIX

A Slice of England

EGW'S STRENGTH FLUCTUATED. On 6 December 1849, he told Godley that he did 'not dare to face the journey to Plymouth' to see him and Jerningham off to New Zealand and a week later he was exhausted by 'business and disturbance of mind arising from my son's departure'.[1] Yet he somehow garnered the energy to organise a key meeting of the Colonial Reform Society at his Reigate home. His memorandum dated 15 December recorded that 'Rintoul, Adderley, Molesworth and FitzGerald passed the day here; when we settled programme of Society for the Reform of Colonial Government, with list of persons to be asked to become members of the Council; also heads of intended Bill for N.S. Wales, to be brought in by Molesworth; also terms of notice of motion to be given on first day of session'.[2] FitzGerald was appointed the society's secretary and under EGW's advice wrote its manifesto.

Born of Irish gentry, James Edward FitzGerald was then 31 years old, a Cambridge scholar who had been employed for five years in the Antiquities Department of the British Museum. Since becoming assistant secretary to the trustees in 1848 he had been so efficient in reorganising the museum's internal administrative structures 'that there was the strong probability that his own post might be abolished'.[3] His work at the museum led to friendships and connections among the artistic and political milieux in London and he discovered a talent for writing and debating on topics of the day, ranging from music criticism to Irish improvement. In this latter arena he eventually came under the influence of the Oxford Movement and Godley, whom he almost hero-worshipped. Yet their characters had little in common: Godley was serious, humourless and class-conscious; FitzGerald exuberant, extrovert, hot-headed and something of a Renaissance man in his range of talents. 'He charmed, annoyed and fascinated people, but was never ignored.'[4]

By September 1849, FitzGerald was bored with his job. Frustrated in his attempts to become one of the first settlers in a proposed colony on Vancouver

Island, he decided to become a Canterbury colonist instead. He discussed this idea with Gladstone, who gave him guarded support, but EGW responded: 'I don't fancy your project at all: I mean that for yourself. Without a specific object, a man of your qualities would be lost in a Colony like New Zealand. It is not the place for trusting "that something will turn up". This *is* – of all the places in the world [London]. However disagreeable your position may be, it is one of independence for the present; and it gives you time to wait and watch. What would not many give for that? Sooner or later something will occur to suit you: meanwhile patience!'[5] FitzGerald promptly came up with a specific object: he would found the first newspaper in the colony. EGW did not warm to that idea either: where was his capital?

EGW was thinking only partly of FitzGerald's welfare; after all, he would make an ideal Canterbury settler. Although lacking capital, he was educated, intelligent, enthusiastic and from the right social group. But EGW, that consummate judge of character, would have divined quickly that the mercurial and energetic young Irishman, with his unpredictable passions, would be difficult to direct and manage, especially as the editor of a newspaper. FitzGerald, though, was also almost impossible to divert. At the 15 December meeting for the Colonial Reform Society, FitzGerald again solicited EGW's support for his plan to emigrate to Canterbury, and EGW again tried to put him off, insisting that he act as his public mouthpiece in society and association matters. EGW genuinely liked FitzGerald and had respect for his ability as a writer and speaker – 'I hear your article . . . very well spoken of. It has been much read in the clubs.'[6] But FitzGerald proved immune to EGW's flattery and manipulation. They were too much alike: this was the beginning of a struggle of wills between lion and cub that would not be settled for five years.

EGW had not been well enough even to travel to Catherine's at Stoke for Christmas and, by the new year of 1850, was desperate for a rest. On 8 January, he wrote Rintoul: 'What can *I* do any more than you? Your letter is like spurring the flanks of a broken-winded horse . . . . I am trying to make holyday as far as possible this week: but next week I will endeavour to proceed with New Zealand.'[7] He needed breathing space before attempting to solve the pressing problems of finding a bishop and a leader for the Canterbury colony ahead of the first emigrants' departure about mid-year. To complicate matters, there were signs that John Hutt was no longer up to the job of chairing the management committee. With time running out, expediency began to take precedence over ideals.

By late February, there was still no sign of a bishop: Wynter was keen but Mrs Wynter was not. On Wynter's suggestion, the association now tried the Reverend W. Maddock, but there was a mix-up in arrangements and a formal offer of the bishopric was made to Maddock before he had made up his mind. His refusal of a widely known offer seriously damaged the association's prospects. A bishop had to be found quickly or the enterprise would lose all credibility. With some desperation, the association lit upon the Reverend Thomas Jackson, who had been principal of the Battersea Training College. At the end of April, EGW reported to Abel Smith that his trusted colleague Samuel Hinds, Bishop of Norwich, was 'perfectly satisfied by his enquiries; thinks the gentleman unexceptionable'. But if there had been any time left for reflection, EGW might have reached the conclusion that, though Jackson was a good public speaker, and something of a theologian, 'a man less suited to be a colonizing bishop it would be difficult to imagine. He was not a man of business; he was not born to be a leader; and he was excessively touchy in matters affecting his dignity.'[8] But the choosers had become beggars and EGW set about using Jackson's speaking abilities to encourage investors and emigrants.

EGW and the association had no luck either in finding an appropriate leader for the colony. He thought they had found their man in William Bellairs, to whom he promised a baronetcy obtained through the association's political connections, flattering him with the notion that he would 'thus emulate Raleigh and the other noble adventurers of the Elizabethan era'. But Bellairs played hard to get. First he demanded a position for his eldest son and EGW agreed that he should be emigration agent, provided he led the first group of emigrants. Then just when matters seemed settled, Bellairs demanded the baronetcy *before* he left for New Zealand. EGW made an attempt on his behalf by asking Hinds to use his influence with Prime Minister Lord John Russell, but this came to nothing and the arrangement collapsed.

When FitzGerald heard of the difficulties with Bellairs, he decided he was the man for the job. EGW responded:

> I am worn out to-day, and cannot answer your letter. Nor indeed have I any power to answer its main question. But I may say that I think you have not been made aware of the part that Bellairs was to have taken . . . . Bellairs and his father together (this in strict confidence) would have taken some £70,000 to the colony . . . . I believe the Canterbury Committee have offered the post of Leader . . . to more than one person . . . . they desire to find somebody resembling Bellairs as respects property and the sacrifice . . . he would make by emigrating . . . . I dare not seem to lecture you; but your sudden resolve to give up Colonial Reform for emigration any how, has disturbed and fretted me on your account.[9]

EGW invited FitzGerald down to Reigate a few days later and wrote to John Hutt: 'I shall tell him that in my opinion, which is Godley's . . . he wants some of the essential qualifications. The main objection is, that he has not position enough in this country. He is a younger brother without property and looking for a provision. He has uncommon abilities, is a very good fellow and I like him very much. But if I gave way to a strong liking for him it would be jobbing for a friend.'[10]

FitzGerald continued to lobby hard and seemed about to persuade Hutt of his eminent suitability. EGW continued to try talking them both out of it: 'Can you think of anything else that would meet your objects, except taking what was intended for Bellairs. . . ? I wish you would tell me *precisely* what your objects are, and what you require or desire. I am sure that all Godley's friends, and none more than myself, would be glad to see you pleased, and embarked in a good career. Neither can they doubt that you have talents that might be of great service to the colony.'[11]

EGW found the solution when the Bellairs plan finally collapsed; FitzGerald could replace Bellairs junior as emigration agent. He told Hutt that 'The office which we rather cooked-up . . . to enlist the Bellairs family, may now enlist somebody else; and there is nobody whom I consider more fit for it than FitzGerald. He will do the work of Emigration Agent well . . . and will be a great acquisition to the colony as regards talents.'[12] All this was largely true, but would it be enough to satisfy FitzGerald?

The next pressing problem was the slow rate of land sales. Felix had been travelling the country, setting up sub-agencies under EGW's fairly explicit instructions: 'Keep in mind that there is no *time* for you doing more than cram *one* intelligent and respected man at each place; and that you can do this better with the individual alone than by talking to numbers. . . . You are not a missionary, but only a setter-up of missionaries.'[13] Felix was on a commission of 5 per cent, if he sold £100,000 worth of land before the end of April 1850: the company had reserved 2.5 million acres to the association provided this target was met, otherwise the land would revert to the Company. Felix recorded, 'During the whole time I held the appointment, as I received the commission from the Association I paid it into [EGW's] banker's, he paying all expenses . . . . the first three months' advertisements cost £500.'[14] Felix remained in EGW's keep.

The land price was high at £3 an acre and potential emigrants not fully in sympathy with the High Church ideals of the project baulked at a third of that being set aside for church objects. Then there came the publicly known troubles with the bishop and failure to announce a leader. When it became known that land sales were slow, prospective buyers held back for fear the total required by the company would not be met and the scheme would collapse. In early March, EGW even attempted to arrange for Prince Albert to chair a public meeting in favour of the Canterbury plan, knowing that this would generate more interest and sales than any amount of advertising.

By late March, FitzGerald and Charles Wynne, Godley's brother-in-law and a member of the Canterbury management committee, were becoming alarmed at the slow land sales and the inaction of chairman John Hutt. They met with Hutt to establish exactly how matters stood and Wynne wrote to Godley, 'We pressed him hard, and he lost his temper and allowed the truth to escape him – that he has for some time considered the thing as gone, and that he for his part did not intend to make any attempt to save it.'[15] On the 25th, EGW wrote to Rintoul: 'John Hutt was intended to fill the gap created by Godley's departure. Godley and I were conscious of his deficiencies, but hoped that they might be effectually counteracted by *my* constant advice, and the doing of some other people.' The problem was, 'Hutt has never taken my advice without reluctance, has often disregarded it wholly, and has prevented others from supplying his want of action . . . . I have reluctantly concluded that his intellect and temper are in a state of decay or disease. His wrongheadedness, stupidity, jealousy of his own consequence, and irritability of temper, have been forced on my most reluctant belief by his conduct for nearly three months . . . . He is an old and close friend of mine: but I have for some weeks almost ceased to communicate with him, because I thought his brains dried up, and his temper incurably soured.'[16]

In consultation with FitzGerald and Wynne, EGW arranged for the first Canterbury land purchaser and chairman of the Society of Canterbury Colonists, William Guise Brittan, to write a letter to the association, asking it to make a firm commitment to go ahead with Canterbury, irrespective of the amount of land sold, and claiming that a public statement to that effect would encourage many families to buy. On the same date Felix, probably at EGW's prompting, made a similar request and suggested that the closing date for land applications should be put back to the end of June. EGW himself proposed that the association should ask the company to remove the 'contingency of failure' clause from the agreement and drafted an appropriate letter, in consultation with Rintoul. With Wynne and FitzGerald, he presented this to the management committee on 26 March and carried it against Hutt's opposition.

The next day Hutt resigned on the grounds of ill health. 'What can I say?' EGW wrote to the man who had, as the dedication to his last book put it, 'more than any other individual known to me . . . combined study and experience in learning A View of the Art of Colonization'. 'It is a distressing affair altogether, but is somewhat redeemed by your most becoming resolution to resign nothing but the Chairmanship. Let us still do all we can to save poor Godley's scheme. If we succeed, all personal disagreeables will soon be forgotten . . . . my respect for your virtues and my personal affection for you, remain as they were before this unhappy business; not to say that they are increased by your conduct in it.'[17] As EGW told Godley, 'It is very distressing . . . the necessity for knocking him out of the Chair: but if you saw your own child boring a hole in the bottom of a ship full of passengers, and you could not stop him in any other way, you would shoot him, would you not?'[18]

On Hutt's resignation, EGW lost no time in manoeuvring Lord Lyttelton into the position of chairman. Having got Godley to New Zealand, EGW now had the 'melancholic' Lyttelton, Gladstone's brother-in-law, in charge of the association. No sooner had Lyttelton become chairman than a make-or-break crisis struck. In response to its letter, the New Zealand Company agreed to revise its arrangements with the Canterbury Association, provided there was a personal guarantee of funds due to the company. EGW considered this grossly unfair but was persuaded by Lyttelton to agree and Abel Smith drew up a memorandum of guarantee whereby payment of up to £15,000 was underwritten equally by EGW, Lyttelton and two other association members. This guarantee (payable if necessary by the end of 1851), plus the money received from land sales, made up the £50,000 required to put the association in possession of the Canterbury block. On 22 April, the association took the final plunge and announced publicly that the registered list of applicants for land would close on 30 June and the first colonising ships would leave for Canterbury by the first week of September. At the same time, revised terms of purchase were announced, allowing the first purchasers a pre-emptive right over their pasture lands. Plans were published for 'Christchurch College', the prime Church of England school planned for the new Christchurch, and Jackson's appointment as bishop-designate was announced.

Land sales picked up, but by mid-year it was revealed that only 8650 acres had been purchased, yielding just £25,950, little more than the company had advanced the association for Thomas's survey. And now the company itself collapsed, after a dozen years of speculation and false promise, failing to repay its three-year loan to the government by the end of June. 'Their last word in expiring,' EGW wrote to Godley, 'was to cast upon C. Buller the blame due to somebody for the defects and frauds of the agreement of 1847 . . . . I longed to expose the ineffable meanness . . . but I had only strength to propose and carry a Committee of Inquiry, which however had not the courage to report the truth though I informed them of it. I cannot recollect to have been ever so much disgusted as by the unworthy, contemptible manner of the Company's death; but the death itself is a great satisfaction.'[19]

The company collapse, the cash crisis, Lyttelton's other commitments and the inadequacies of its current secretary meant that the association needed a manager. 'The gentleman selected is Mr. Henry Sewell, a brother of William of Exeter College; a conscientious and able man of business, of high character, with his heart in the thing as an intending colonist, and with no defect that I know of unless his Puseyite name should prove hurtful.'[20] Solicitor Sewell, 42, was appointed deputy chairman on 16 July. The post promised to improve his difficult personal circumstances. His family's Isle of Wight law firm had become saddled with considerable debts upon his father's death in 1842 and after his wife died in 1844, he had been left to provide not only for four young children but also for his mother and three unmarried sisters. Sewell had remarried early in 1850 and bought a 50-acre section in the new Canterbury settlement with the hope of restoring his fortunes through emigration.

Sewell, as the full-time day-to-day manager, brought the association's affairs under some measure of control, achieved considerable power within the entire colonising enterprise and exerted much influence over Lyttelton, who was to write to Godley only four months later: 'No words can exaggerate the value of Sewell's services. The whole plan would undoubtedly have smashed long ago but for him. All the admirable dispatches which you have got are written by him. I am only a foolish sort of ultimate court of appeal, and nobody else is anything, always excepting Wakefield.'[21] Sewell's immediate task, following the collapse of the company, of which the association was a kind of subsidiary, was to prepare and rush through Parliament the Canterbury Settlement Land Bill in order to establish the association's independent footing. When this was passed on 14 August, final preparations could be made to despatch what would become known as the first four ships, carrying the vanguard of what *The Times* had now dubbed the 'Canterbury Pilgrims'.

The campaign was stepped up to sell more land to colonists and to enlist suitable emigrant labourers and small tradesmen. Public meetings were held in London, Birmingham, Reading, the Isle of Wight and Ipswich where Bishop-designate Jackson excelled himself, evoking a new spirit of colonisation: 'In Canterbury the wines may be scanty, but Homer and Milton may be invited to the board.' It would not be a colony 'where slang will be substituted for conversation . . . where the English language has lost its nerve and purity . . . where men drink and do not dress for dinner'.[22] His audience were so impressed that they filled his colonising collection box with £385. But Jackson then left without arranging to pay for the hire of the Ipswich Town Hall and the expenses of the meeting. It was the first sign of his financial incompetence.

EGW attended this meeting in Suffolk and continued to keep a close watch on Felix's progress. He reported enthusiastically to Godley,

> I am not acquainted with a single emigrant who goes as a money-grubbing speculator, though of course there must be some. We are sure that nearly all go to do something of a steady pursuit – most of them to cultivate the earth, breed horses and cattle, and grow wool. This is chiefly owing to the nature of the people whom the plan attracts, who are steady, prudent people, of quiet moderate tastes, and simple habits; but it is also a good deal owing to the agricultural and pastoral enthusiasm of Felix Van Diemen, who has infected many with his Tasmanian tastes. Besides teaching the Canterbury plan of colonization, he preaches getting up with the sun, gardening, farming, dining at one o'clock, teetotalism, and going to bed before night-time.

EGW pandered to Godley's class discrimination with the most unctuous of reassurances: 'I believe you will see, not merely a nice, but a choice society of English people assembled there. Not that more than a very few of the really bettermost class in habits and manners have already declared themselves, but many of that sort – families of the very nicest description (or shall I say after your own fancy) are preparing slowly, and not without pain, to take the step which will commit them. At present there is certainly too large a proportion of people who, however estimable, are deficient as respects manners – good and satisfactory, but not refined and polished people.'

'However courage!' EGW exhorted Godley, knowing that his New Zealand 'money destitution' meant he could not complete the full survey, roads and accommodation in time for the arrival of the first settlers. This was an 'unavoidable misfortune, unless you and I are to blame for having thought of founding with twenty-five thousand pounds a colony whose proper foundation . . . requires a capital of two or three hundred thousand'. But, EGW insisted, 'It is a good plan; there is a good colony of people; an excellent prospect, on this side, of the largest and best emigration that we ever hoped for; and we Englishmen are not apt to faint. I rely on your English blood. I often say to Felix, it is well Godley is not Irish, meaning faint-hearted Celtic.'[23] EGW might have been able to get away with this eugenic humbug in bantering face-to-face conversation; but to Godley, standing on the edge of the uncultured, largely uninhabited Canterbury Plains, battling with the practical and political problems of establishing a new colony, this element of typical balderdash would have been at its most obvious.

If EGW regarded Godley as the 'only Irishman he ever knew who was not in the least Irish', he thought FitzGerald was a parody of an Irishman, 'wild enough to hunt his own sheep'. The tension between them increased in concert with the succession of crises affecting the association. In mid-April EGW saw FitzGerald as meddling in business that was no concern of his, questioning his own actions. EGW scolded him: 'I am old and experienced, you young and quite without experience in such things . . . . It will be difficult enough to get the thing done, but it may be if I am let alone, and cheerfully helped as much as possible. You must not lecture me.'[24]

By early August, EGW was becoming alarmed at FitzGerald's slow recruitment of emigrants and appalled at his plan to pay agents: 'The *paying* of Emigration Agents is murder as respects the quality of the emigrants. It always succeeds as respects numbers – always breaks down as respects quality.'[25] On the same day, EGW wrote to Sewell as a first step in moving the emigration agency away from FitzGerald, to William Bowler and Felix.

Then EGW heard that the Society of Colonists had decided to establish a newspaper on arrival in Canterbury, bankrolled by an Oxford printer, and that FitzGerald had quickly volunteered to be its first editor without pay. Outmanoeuvred, EGW wrote to Lyttelton, complaining about the actions of FitzGerald and Brittan as leaders of the Society of Colonists, alleging that they had wanted Godley home as soon as possible and the whole machinery of the association transferred to the Canterbury colony. EGW had convinced Brittan of the absurdity of the plan, given that there *was* no colony in New Zealand yet. 'But that notion was not abandoned by FitzGerald,' he told Lyttelton, 'until he discovered at the end of last week, that his Emigration Agency had entirely broken down in consequence . . . of having been quite neglected for all these matters relating to politics and government, and the return of Godley, and a grand dream of his fertile imagination which pictured himself as the Lord Baltimore of the

Canterbury Settlement.' EGW had decided to go for the jugular: 'He is *all* imagination and *no* action – an immense promiser, quite sincerely; *ready* to undertake every thing, but for performance, except in writing or talking, singularly feeble and heedless.'[26] EGW insisted that the emigration agency be shifted, and the break between the two men became complete.

Aware that FitzGerald would have Godley's ear when he arrived in the new Canterbury, and have immense influence among the first settlers as editor of the first newspaper, EGW sent a letter to Godley on one of the first four ships. After warning him of Brittan's shortcomings, which were offset by his 'strongheartedness' and from being the 'most useful business man' among the first colonists, he started in on FitzGerald who had been 'up and down all along like the steam-engine piston. . . . He is nearly the most provoking man I have ever had to do with . . . . He is immensely presumptuous, believing himself that he can do every-thing better than any body; and when it comes to the *doing,* he is a very child . . . . FitzGerald's utter break-down in the collection of emigrants has been remedied by great exertion and considerable cost in money.' He warned Godley that he might find FitzGerald 'in less than three months after landing, at the head of a party at war with the Association' for 'his worst behaviour has been the endeavour to instill his own jealousy and dislike of me into others'.[27]

EGW had read the tea leaves well; but his attempts to manipulate Godley from such a distance were bound to be of limited effect, especially given FitzGerald's admiration for Godley and Godley's growing disaffection with the association as it both failed to communicate or provide enough money. And EGW would not have been aware of the contents of letters to Godley from his old Oxford friends such as Wynne, who had told him, during the crisis over John Hutt, 'If the scheme succeeds it will be to FitzGerald that it will be due! He first sounded the alarm – and of his exertions during the last week I can give you no idea.'[28] By now, those associated with the Canterbury project had become more than familiar with EGW's tactics and behaviour – his experience, astuteness and brilliance coupled with unstable emotions bubbling beneath a very thin skin and a proclivity to be, as he accused FitzGerald, 'immensely presumptuous, believing himself that he can do everything better than any body'.

While admiring his capacities, indeed relying on them, Lyttelton also grew to discriminate the valuable and useful from the immoderate and self-serving in EGW's proposals and demands. In the margin of one EGW letter he noted 'another of Wakefield's queer delusions' and, simply, 'falsehood'. Under the neutral eye of Lyttelton, the protagonists for Canterbury were now shifting into two political camps: the group of friends and admirers clustered about Godley and those beholden to EGW, and more under his direct influence, such as Sewell.

On 7 and 8 September, the first four ships departed Plymouth for Canterbury with 127 cabin passengers at £42 a berth, 85 intermediate passengers at £25 a berth and 534 steerage passengers at £15. *The Times* nicely caught the character of the moment:

> A slice of England cut from top to bottom . . . . a complete sample of Christian civilization, weary of the difficult fight for breath within the compass of these narrow isles, took ship . . . in search of less crowded markets . . . . a deliberate, long-considered, solemn and devoted pilgrimage to a temple erected by nature for the good of all comers.
>
> At the head of the pilgrims stood an actual bishop, behind him were working clergy, working schoolmasters, working landlords, working labourers, workers every one. Between deck and keel were the elements of a college, the contents of a public library, the machinery for a bank, yea, the constituent parts of a constitutional government. The adventurers stepped on board British subjects with British failings, British associations, and British habits and, let them be drowned or disembarked where they might, they would carry to the bottom or any other landing-place the British character, as emphatically expressed upon their persons as the effigy of Britannia on their familiar halfpence.[29]

The mocking edge to the editorial could not disguise the paper's reluctant admiration, even pride. There remained something heroic and, indeed, very British about setting out for the far side of the world with such solemn and thoroughly organised intent. *The Times* did not mention it, but the colony's Britishness was already on the map. In adhering to one of Felix's key recommendations, native title to the Canterbury land – both ownership and name – had been thoroughly extinguished and, even more than William's Wellington of 1839, the new settlement had been made British by name. From Captain Thomas's sketch map of Canterbury, received before they left, the pilgrims saw that when they sailed into Port Victoria, between Godley and Adderley Heads, they would disembark at Port Lyttelton and settle in the towns of Christchurch, Stratford, Oxford or Lincoln; ply the rivers Cholmondeley, Courtenay or Ashley; farm the plains of Whateley, Sumner or Wilberforce; make summer excursions to Alford or Harewood forests, perhaps to Lake Coleridge, while the more adventurous might scale Mount Hutt or Mount Somers. In trying to imagine themselves in England they would be constantly reminded of their betters who had founded the colony, and the politics that had made one river Selwyn and a mountain Grey. Some of these names would disappear or shift and a few Maori names would be restored, but Canterbury now had the titles for its future British tales. One name, as ever, was missing – though it had briefly been assigned to the Southern Alps – and it would appear only belatedly in a suburb and not in memory of EGW.

This was the last of New Zealand's planned settlements, and also the last of any significance anywhere. During the second half of the nineteenth century, as steamship, rail and the telegraph shrank time and distance, as colonies became self-governing within or without the British Empire, the days of self-sufficient pioneers voyaging into the unknown under sail, with all the elements of a working society 'between deck and keel', were rapidly consigned to history. But if this was the last, would it also turn out to be the best?

Canterbury was certainly the best provided for in terms of facilities for the first settlers. Thomas had, almost lavishly, created a small town at Port Lyttelton with a jetty and a custom house, an agent's house, stores, a six-room house with verandah for the Godley family among its 60 wooden buildings. There was also the start of a cart road over the steep hills that separated the harbour from the plains. Because of the expense and time needed to complete this Godley ordered Thomas to cut a steep bridle track to the saddle directly above the town to provide immediate access for the first arrivals. The artisan Thomas, who had made such a superb job of laying out and preparing the settlement over the previous year or more, fell out with the aristocratic Godley who now accused him of extravagance.

After he arrived in New Zealand in late March 1850, Godley had spent most of his time in Wellington, 'really a vortex of dissipation', Charlotte Godley told her mother. 'Fancy our being overrun with morning visitors, when we take it in turns to sit down.' But the 'town surpassed my expectations in every way. It is really uncommonly pretty, and with very good comfortable houses' in one of which she discovered attorney-general 'Mr. D. Wakefield'. His house had 'very civilized looking rooms, but quite unfinished; it is not his own, but belongs to man who is gone to Sydney to get married'. Dan rescued the Godleys on a dark and stormy night as they groped their way down the slippery unlit streets to visit Archdeacon Hadfield but later fell victim to the weather himself when the worst storm since settlement struck the town in June 1850. By now, Dan was living in the Hutt Valley. 'Mr. Wakefield told me he tried to ride in on the worst day (it lasted four), but *could not.* He got on some miles, and then, at a pass in the road where the spray was quite flying over the hills, he thought he would wait behind a fence . . . till the gust was over. However, the next puff sent over the fence, and his horse, and himself, and they were blown thirty or forty feet up the gully, the horse down on his side, so he thought it wisest to go home.' At least Dodo had not fallen over a cliff again.

Along with storm and earthquake there was 'gaiety' to offset Godley's strict cold water and fresh air régime as he worked to complete a cure: 'One or two complete shower baths are enough, in the day, and the other times for exercise are spent in hopping and jumping about his room', imitated by his son, 'at the imminent peril of breaking his head against the ceiling. All done with the greatest earnestness *to obtain an end,* as he would write an article, and eat his dinner.'[30]

By November, Godley had recovered sufficiently to lead the charge for Wellington's Constitutional Association against Grey's proposed nominated council for

New Munster. With each ship came news about the war of attrition being waged against Lord Grey's inadequate Australian Constitution Bill in Parliament by Gladstone, Molesworth, Lyttelton and Adderley, constantly aided and abetted by EGW. Godley's calls for local self-government provoked Governor Grey's enmity and marked the start of an independent campaign that would eventually provoke EGW's wrath.

On arriving in Wellington, Charlotte Godley had reported, 'The Lieut.-Governor [Eyre] who lives here is very unpopular and the great gossip of the place now is about his marriage. A young lady, Miss Ormond, came out to be married to him . . . and stopped at New Plymouth with Lady Grey; when Mr. Eyre immediately rushed, in the Government brig, with Chaplain, licence, etc., all complete, and then the lady would not have him!'[31] The bishop himself was needed to persuade her into matrimony.

Another attempt at marriage was of more intimate interest to Mrs Godley. On the Godleys' voyage out in the *Lady Nugent*, Edward Jerningham Wakefield had begun acting as her husband's aide. As they ran through the southern Indian Ocean towards Van Diemen's Land in March, Jerningham was in his element when he organised a stage on the poop deck for theatricals. '"The Mock Doctor" was the first piece and then we had "Bombastes". It was really a very creditable performance; Mr. Wakefield, who is half a foreigner, is a capital actor.' Jerningham would have been also capital at organising endless games of whist and backgammon and passing around Thackeray's latest works, including *Vanity Fair* and *The Book of Snobs*, which may not have amused Mrs Godley at all. She wrote to her mother, 'We suspect him [EJW] of designs upon Miss Borton', a passenger whom she had earlier described as 'quite young and rather pretty, though neither aristocratic nor very bright'. She went on, 'There is certainly a strong flirtation, in spite of a rumour that she is engaged to someone at home.'[32] And despite the chaperoning eye of her elder brother, Fred.

It was more than a shipboard romance. Jerningham, now turning 30, pursued nineteen-year-old Emily Borton with considerable passion and determination. On board ship, he became 'aware that she remained under an engagement to a gentleman named Harris', who had travelled to New Zealand with her eldest sister. Jerningham did not, therefore, ask for her hand although he was sure she returned his feelings. But he persuaded her, when she went ashore at Dunedin in April, to enlist the support of her sister and two brothers, in order to break off her engagement to Harris. This was accomplished and in September, by now in Wellington, Jerningham sailed for Dunedin with Charley Torlesse, believing that Emily was 'perfectly free . . . and to ask her to give me leave to prepare a home for her, and to ensure my future happiness by consenting to become my wife. To my extreme grief and astonishment, I found that she had, five days before, accepted a proposal of the same kind, made to her by a gentleman resident here, Mr Strode, who had already been once refused by her before the arrival of Mr

Harris, and who had not waited, like myself, until she was positively free. . . .'[33] Jerningham poured out his woes in a letter to Emily's mother, a Mrs Campbell in Lincolnshire, informing her that brother Fred had turned her against him, saying that he intended not marriage but only to 'trifle with her affections'. Fred had told Emily 'that the best way of removing any obloquy which envious persons might attempt to cast upon her in consequence of her rejection of Mr Harris, would be to accept the first offer of marriage made to her by any person not positively repulsive to her, whether she might feel any love for him or not . . . I was confirmed by her tears, words and bitter expressions of regret, in my belief that she had no feeling for Mr Strode beyond esteem, and that principally founded on the fact that I had, on our first arrival here, introduced him to her as my friend.' Jerningham had known Alfred Strode in Wellington in the early 1840s; in 1848 he had been appointed Dunedin's sub-inspector of police and was now resident magistrate. Charlotte Godley's judgement of Emily Borton as not 'very bright' may have been correct but then Jerningham had not been very clever either in precipitating a romantic melodrama better played out on the boards. This affair also illustrates the demand for attractive young women, however bright or aristocratic, in the male-dominated early settlements.

In the absence of Fred, Jerningham persuaded Emily and her other brother John, who had been in Dunedin for a couple of years, to allow him to make an appeal to Strode, who thereupon gave up his claim on Emily, though 'overwhelmed with affliction'. Fred then returned and reluctantly accepted Jerningham's 'solemn engagement to make dear Emily my wife as soon as she should choose after I had been enabled to settle my affairs and prepare a home for her'. But when Fred went to see Strode he was so affected by his grief that he censured Emily for her 'want of feeling' and showed a 'revival of all his prejudices against me'. Pathetically, Jerningham said he could not think what these could be based on. The upshot was that Emily decided to accept neither suitor but to 'remain perfectly unengaged to anyone for a whole twelvemonth' during which time there would be no communication between the parties. Since Jerningham would be 200 miles off in Canterbury, he knew that this would give Fred more than enough time to work up Emily's feelings against him, and Strode an opportunity to promote his prospects. Hence Jerningham's long, flattering and appealing letter to Emily's mother, in hope that she would exert her influence in his favour. As character referees, he cited John Abel Smith, the Bishop of Norwich, and grandfather Edward, who had now returned to England to live with Frances at her old home of Macclesfield.

In the new year of 1851 Jerningham wrote again to Mrs Campbell and to EGW, asking him to buy all kinds of goods and equipment including gifts and outfitting for Emily. In February he journeyed back to Dunedin and, from the Royal Hotel, wrote in vain to Strode and Fred Borton. He was not granted a meeting and he did not see Emily again. The following month she was married to Strode. Jerningham's diary jottings at the time indicate a considerable perturbation of mind, yet in July

Charlotte Godley could write to her mother that Jerningham had 'apparently quite recovered his little disappointment about the young lady . . . who came out in our ship'.[34]

Jerningham had told Mrs Campbell that he expected EGW, the Torlesse family and his Aunt Priscilla's family among the first Canterbury settlers. 'I shall then be able to learn in what state my pecuniary affairs are, for they were in some confusion when I sailed from England and I left my Father full powers to deal with and arrange them for me.' In fact Jerningham had debts of about £3,000 and EGW had been required to take a 'bold step . . . with regard to the residue of his property' in the hopes that this would effect a 'revolution in his habits with regard to expense'.[35] As long as EGW was able to hold the reins of his affairs, Jerningham's life continued to find some kind of order.

EGW understood well the dangers for the single man in the colonies. When he wrote to intending Canterbury settler R. J. S. Harman in April 1850, Jerningham must have been at the forefront of his mind:

> A new colony is a bad place for a young single man . . . . The hospitality is so great that a young man who can make himself agreeable, may live in idleness . . . till he becomes unfit for marriage by becoming wedded to his pipe and his bottle, not to mention the billiard-table. Whereas if he is nicely married, he has a sweet home to go to after his day's work, and his mind is kept tranquil enough to bear without injury the intense excitement of sharing in the creation of society . . . . The success of a young colonist who remains single is a rare exception . . . . the same capital goes further with a wife than without one. It is her moral influence that both saves the money, and stimulates her husband's energy and prudence.[36]

But in matters of matrimony, both father and son were dogged by their reputations; opinion and gossip continued to work against Jerningham finding a wife.

During the time he pursued Emily Borton, Jerningham appears to have remained mostly in the service of the Godleys, though he took time off for hunting and exploring, including a journey overland to the Clutha Valley with Charley Torlesse during his sojourn in Otago. In early December 1850 he accompanied the Godley party on an expedition across the Canterbury Plains as far as the forests in the Oxford district. In early February 1851, after the Canterbury pilgrims arrived, Jerningham, in his element, organised the first dance in the settlement, 'intended as a kind of friendly meeting, before the people all separate to go to their selections of land on the plain next month . . .'.[37] In September, Jerningham also organised a 'Bachelors' Ball' in the first, almost complete, hotel in Lyttelton. 'Some of the bachelors . . . thought that they had not been sufficiently consulted, after originating the idea. Mr. E. J. Wakefield did the whole of it, and was supposed to take too much upon himself, the fact being, I think, only that he has so little tact that he does sometimes offend people.'[38]

Charley Torlesse also took part in the plains expedition and reported to his sister Emily that, during their times together, his older cousin had been kind to him and given 'valuable advice on one or two occasions'. Although Jerningham had written expectantly of a large family contingent on one of the first four ships, and Charley looked 'forward to a grand family reunion', he knew in his heart that there was not 'much probability of such an event, except in my mother's strong determination and unceasing efforts to make the move . . . . I wish to see them all here, as I have no doubt the move would be conducive to their happiness & prosperity.'[39] Charley continued to encourage his parents to sail for Canterbury and in 1854 made a particularly determined effort to persuade his father,[40] but Charles Torlesse never would 'see his way clear' to making the great move.

In June 1850, however, EGW had optimistically told Godley that the emigration of his younger sister Priscilla's family was 'the more probable because at last Torlesse has been fixed'. Suffolk clergy who had wanted Charles Torlesse to stay at Stoke had turned him against Jackson as bishop-designate but 'this prejudice has been overcome by Jackson himself'. EGW considered that Torlesse's decision to finally go to Canterbury would overcome the opposition of Priscilla's husband, Henry Chapman, whose Low Church family had 'frightened him with Papist Bugaboos' spurred by the Puseyite connections of the association. Priscilla was 'sure in the long run to bring him round to her view' of emigrating.[41] But no matter how persuasive Priscilla might be or how 'unceasing' Catherine's efforts, both women were bound by their husbands' ultimate power of decision. Over the following months, Torlesse's doubts about Jackson returned, for good reason, and Henry Chapman could not be turned.

Each family was soon struck by tragedies that proved a major deterrence. In October 1851, Catherine's third daughter Louisa died aged 23 and, just six months later, her sixth, sixteen-year-old Catherine. The health of the Torlesses' second son, Henry, became seriously affected and later in 1852, at the age of eighteen, he sailed for the recuperative climate of New Zealand rather than going to university at Cambridge. Of the nine children born to her, just three daughters remained with Catherine at Stoke. 'Neither father nor mother were the same after that fatal year, but on father the change was more marked. Mother had had so many great sorrows and troubles in her previous life that these bereavements did not change her as they did father.'[42] Three years later, when Priscilla was 46, her husband Henry Chapman died suddenly and she was left to bring up nine children alone, remaining a widow until her own death 32 years later.

Charley Torlesse was deeply impressed by the principles governing the Canterbury plan and, despite his uncle's past personal strictures, thought EGW a 'great man, and must be a good man: for his whole scheme is intended for the general benefit of his countrymen; and the more one studies it practically, the more is one struck by its wisdom and practical applicability to the character of Englishmen and the nature of the country they are to adopt'.[43] The trouble was, as Charley already knew, less than 10 per cent of the expected land sales had been made and the settlement would remain chronically short for many years of the cash essential to its planned development and endowments.

Both Charley and Jerningham had also been expecting EGW among the first pilgrims. Since the launch of the Canterbury enterprise he had confidently told all and sundry that he would be among the leading settlers. Having lectured Godley on going for his health, he could hardly deny the likely benefits to his own. In June 1849 he wrote Francis Dillon Bell, 'It is quite *settled* that I go to New Zealand as soon as ever the aforesaid [preparatory] work shall be crowned with success.'[44] A year later, he told Godley that he had 'fully intended' to sail on one of the first four ships but now hesitated because he thought that if he did he would 'scarcely keep my engagement with you by which I am pledged'.[45] When Lyttelton praised EGW's efforts on behalf of Canterbury, he told him that 'having been drawn into Canterbury work altogether against my will, and with the knowledge that every time I go to London I risk incurring paralysis of the brain . . . I was impelled by a motive strong enough to keep me at work so long as it shall last; the motive being a pledge to Godley that I would at all risks devote myself to the work he would have done had he remained, provided he would take the only means of saving his life by going away'.[46]

As the first four ships were leaving, he told Godley, 'It is my firm purpose to depart for New Zealand within six weeks after the time when I shall see Canterbury is fairly launched. The ideas of stopping for the chance of participating in the settlement of the question of *government,* though still pleasing, has less hold of me than it had two months ago: and my present intention is to see Canterbury safe – so safe that it would not be unsafe to transfer the Charter to the colony – and then to take my passage'.[47] He hoped that this would be before the end of the year. Unfortunately, the question of government remained unsafe, as did the government of the association. Soon there was the problem of an unsafe bishop – and a *very* unsafe brother.

CHAPTER TWENTY-SEVEN

Noodles

TEN DAYS AFTER THE FIRST FOUR SHIPS departed for Canterbury, EGW complained in a letter to Godley about the incapacity of the association when Lord Lyttelton was absent. 'The only Committee men besides Sewell who now attend, are Cocks, when sent for to make a quorum or sign a check, Hutt and Halswell. Thus Messrs. Hutt, Halswell and Alston, one cracked, one a mere jobber in the smallest line, and the third an imbecile in desperate circumstances with one foot in the grave . . . I get seriously ill at Cockspur Street, and make a daily resolution not to go there again, but am led to break it by the fear that something horrid may be done if I do not keep an eye on these noodles.'[1]

And now there was another noodle, one who disliked 'all positions but that of cock of his own dunghill' and who 'instead of courting, as he ought to do, the order of men, both lay and clerical' for the Canterbury settlement, 'actually repels them', including the Reverend Charles Torlesse. As a preacher and platform orator bishop-designate Jackson may have had 'no living superior', but he was overweening. He concurred with Lord Grey's ruling that his bishopric must encompass the entire South Island (and Stewart Island). Therefore, according to EGW, Jackson had no real interest in Canterbury but was using the scheme as an elevation to a more extensive bishopric that New Zealand Bishop Selwyn was bound to deny. The purpose of Jackson's imminent voyage to New Zealand was to settle the diocesan business with Selwyn, settle his clergy and schoolmasters, choose land for his home and the college, before returning to England to be consecrated and undertake more promotional work for the association. EGW complained that the future bishop surrounded himself with 'very dull, or very crawling people' and 'in one word, he is not, and never can be, a gentleman'.[2] Much worse was to come.

On 2 October, EGW wrote to Wynter, '*Very* disagreeable Jacksonian money-matters at Cockspur Street to-day. John Hutt talking about the Bishop being *arrested* at Plymouth',[3] as he was about to set sail for Canterbury. But sail Jackson did and Godley would field the entire problem when Jackson landed. As EGW told Godley in a letter that would reach him in the first post after Jackson's arrival, 'There will be nothing uncommon if it should fall to my lot to stand alone in telling you fully of the most disagreeable circumstance that has yet happened in the Canterbury affair. This is the discovery that Mr. Jackson is as loose and reckless about money-matters as can well be imagined . . . . there are facts which you ought to know, that will not be communicated officially . . . after Jackson left town for Plymouth, his check for over £300 was dishonoured . . . . Perhaps not less than 50 people [know].' The matter had become 'what may be termed public, short of appearing in the newspapers'. An outfitting firm in the City was also out of pocket for over £300 and there were other smaller unpaid debts. Jackson had not accounted for a collection at a public meeting and even Rintoul now told EGW he had heard that the 'Battersea Training College (which is dead) died of Finance and Jackson'.[4] Clearly Jackson was quite unfit to be responsible for the ecclesiastical and educational funds for Canterbury.

With the management committee 'PARALYZED' by the situation, EGW and Sewell led the way to avoiding the kind of 'public discredit and disgrace which must ruin both Mr. Jackson and the Association'. As the association attempted to keep the lid on the scandal in London and Jackson's debts were settled, Sewell advised Godley to persuade Jackson to quietly resign and take up another post more suited to his temperament and talents. Sewell suggested that instead of splitting the existing New Zealand diocese into two, a tripartite division would be a better idea: 'Mr Jackson's powers, which are very great, would be turned to useful account in any of the northern parts, especially amongst the Natives'.

Jackson arrived at Lyttelton with his wife and two sons on 7 February 1851. Charlotte Godley was already apprehensive and 'then judge of our mortification and sorrow on seeing Mr. Jackson, a little fussy upstanding man, whose very bow and style of greeting, tone, manner, words, all have on them the very stamp of humbug . . . . I was ready to cry with shame at having to show Dr. Selwyn such a man as the Bishop who we are desiring in his stead; and he could not, and did not, conceal his contempt and even dislike.'[5] Nor did Godley.

A few weeks later Godley received the letters from EGW, Sewell and secretary Alston who requested him to obtain from Jackson explanations of a list of obscure or irregular financial transactions. Godley and Selwyn handled Jackson with firmness and diplomacy. When he left New Zealand six weeks after his arrival, Jackson was confident that he had reached an understanding with Selwyn over his diocese and had fulfilled all the duties incumbent on his journey. But after considering Godley's report on the financial transactions, the association notified the Archbishop of Canterbury that Jackson was 'unfit for business' and, on the primate's advice, Jackson withdrew. He was found a living at Stoke Newington, just outside London, where he was the incumbent for 34 years, sustaining his reputation as a pulpit orator until his death. Canterbury would have to wait almost another six years for its first bishop. The turmoil created by the Jackson affair meant that EGW was still not free to leave for New Zealand. And there was a financial crisis much closer to home.

As the association's land sales agent, Felix Wakefield had felt 'inferior' to other members, such as FitzGerald, and to his purchasing clients because he was financially incapable of purchasing land himself. He pressured EGW to buy him some land and EGW 'resisted much importunity on this point' but Felix became 'so fractious and violent in his manner, that I gave way in order to pacify him'. EGW gave him the money to buy two Canterbury sections but, because Felix was already so deeply in debt to him, EGW 'required of him that he should buy as Trustee for me' and he arranged for two of the first settlers to select Felix's land. EGW was 'pleased to see that the gratification of Felix's pride or vanity in figuring as a land owner seemed to restore his good humour and usefulness'.[6] Felix later maintained that EGW had paid for the sections 'out of my commission in order to make me a *bona fide* colonist'.[7] EGW wrote that the 'mere possession of money had an intoxicating effect upon my brother, and I did my best to keep him in check and subjection by making him hand over to me, on the very day he received it, all money paid to him by the Association on the score of commission . . . I really believe at that time, he was not only desirous of cancelling his heavy debt to me, but that he felt the need to himself of being under my control with respect to all outlay as well as for the Association as for his family.'

But it was not long before Felix moved to assert his independence. His version of events was that in December 1850 a pamphlet prepared by EGW and Bowler, the association shipping agent, gave a false gloss to the performance of the Canterbury migrant vessels. Writing of this in January, EGW reported to Godley that the 'shipping business of the association has been better managed than any other body's'.[8] Felix declared that he knew the ships had been sent out at a 'great loss' and was 'so much annoyed' at the pamphlet that his previously 'cordial relations' with Bowler and EGW were suspended. 'From that time my occupation became particularly disagreeable, being in daily communication with Mr. E.G. Wakefield', especially since Felix's work as land sales agent had been proceeding informally (but satisfactorily) since his contract ended in August. Felix lobbied Sewell hard for a new formal contract, but the deputy chairman resisted, and Felix then persuaded his brother to take his part to the point where EGW had 'nearly a mortal quarrel' with Sewell. EGW confided to Godley, 'Even at the times when Felix plagued me most by his wildness, I felt such a compassion for him, and, if you can understand me, such a respect for his misfortunes . . . that I have invariably had a tenderness for his infirmities . . . thus I have been in the habit of humouring Felix a good deal . . . .'

On 19 April, Lord Lyttelton wrote to Felix confirming that he should continue as land sales agent at a rate of 5 per cent commission, for 'as long as you like to remain, and to hold the office'. According to EGW, Felix now went his own way and avoided consulting with him. 'The effects soon became visible in a neglected state of the business at the Adelphi, and in emptiness of the Colonists' Rooms . . . . I could not but see that he was going on badly with his work . . . doing it in a manner rather to drive away colonists than attract them.' The brothers now began to quarrel about everything. Felix behaved 'unhandsomely to visitors at my house, and gave way to fits of violent ill temper, alledging when I complained of his unreasonableness, that he was distressed by care, and that he felt the approaches of insanity. Again I humoured him from motives of true pity.'

Eventually EGW moved to put an end to the wrangling and conflict and decided to communicate with Felix only by letter or through third parties. Felix now resorted to blackmail. He demanded the Canterbury sections in his own name, as well as money to establish himself as a leading colonist in Canterbury, or he would compel EGW and the association to 'meet his views by availing himself of Ld. Lyttelton's letter which entitled him to a commission on future sales to a large amount, and by making a public disturbance if we did not yield'. EGW told Godley that all this 'nearly killed me; and the wonder is it did not quite'.

To save himself, and the association's reputation, EGW decided to submit to his demands provided he could sever Felix's connection to the association and get him out of the country as soon as possible. Bowler engineered a settlement of the land to ensure that, though Felix had a life tenancy, he could not sell it and his family would benefit after his death. Felix agreed but insisted that Godley should be one of its trustees; hence EGW's elaborate explanations to him.

Before Felix would resign his position in favour of Bowler, he demanded £500 as an advance on account of his future land sales commission. But not before Bowler discovered irregularities in his dealings with emigrants. When Sewell wrote suggesting that he correct these, Felix threatened to 'accuse Sewell of having set him the example of wrong-doing if it be wrong' and taking the issue before the management committee. Bowler countered threat with threat, saying he would not execute the land settlement if 'he took so outrageous a course'. Felix mentioned none of this in his self-justifying 1853 pamphlet, *The Mutual Relations between the Canterbury Association and the Purchasers of Land*, stating simply that in July 1851 he was 'advanced £320 on my commission accruing upon land sales after my departure and I got away quickly in the *Sir George Pollock* with my family, for Canterbury'. Again Godley had to cope with an errant servant of the association, this time a genuine remittance man, to the accompaniment of EGW's insinuating, pleading and palpitating narrative of events.

One of the most remarkable aspects of EGW's July 1851 letter to Godley is his description of Felix's character, which also projects something of EGW's own personality. 'He is not the deliberate, designing villain, which some of his acts would indicate,' he told Godley.

> I fully believe that in the early part of our connection in this matter . . . he meant to do all that is right; and that evil thoughts and projects grew up in him only when his head was turned by a prosperity and flattery which it was not strong enough to bear. His love of consequence is a passion, latent when starved by adversity, but ungovernable when indulged; so that he is really modest and winning, really ambitious and dangerous, at different times. In many other things he is full of contradiction – very fond of his children, and yet unjust to them, and frightfully severe when the evil humour is on him – highly capable in several ways, and yet sure to break down in any business if left to his own guidance – amiable when poor, imperious and tyrannical when rich or fancying that he shall be so – cunning and soft – misleading with facility on first knowledge, and yet most easily misled by flatterers of his dominant passion – appearing in self-contradiction at different times . . . .

EGW referred to a former letter in which he had spoken as if he Felix 'might go out of his mind' but he now judges that talk 'insincere; only intended to move me to let him have his own way. . . . the devils of conceit and ambition . . . have led him towards destruction'.

EGW's feelings about Felix were also transmitted to Catherine who, in turn, wrote to her son Charley concerning Felix's shortcomings. But by this time, Charley had become fully aware of EGW's criticism of him to Captain Thomas. He replied to his mother, 'You must remember that the impression you have received of his [Felix's] character . . . if it is derived from my uncle Edward's statements, ought not receive implicit credence, for I cannot refrain from saying that his statements about me to Thomas were false and iniquitous, as they had no foundation whatever. You know his unscrupulousness in his mode of carrying out his plans. Then just consider whether Felix has thwarted him in some way.'[9] Catherine's loyalties would have been torn by this letter but she may have perceived that, with some justification, Charley was seeking retribution for his uncle's criticism. And though EGW undoubtedly put his own gloss on his dealings with Felix, his judgement of his brother seemed soon borne out by Charlotte Godley's description of Felix as a 'most unsatisfactory man' and the 'worst character we have had' in Canterbury.[10]

Felix and six of his children arrived at Lyttelton on 10 November 1851. In the land ballot that had taken place early in the year, his agents had drawn Rural Section 2 and selected 100 acres for him at Sumner, beside the line of the road planned to connect Lyttelton with Christchurch via Evans Pass. The commercial possibilities for such land seemed high but Felix was angered to find that the road was far from complete and all heavy goods for Christchurch from the port were being transported by sea and up the Avon-Heathcote estuary, past Sumner. He immediately blamed Godley for stopping Thomas's work on the road and also for telling intending settlers in England that the road was complete.

Felix's arrival had been accompanied by EGW's long damning letter to Godley which concluded with a footnote on 16 July: 'The last few days have produced disclosures which aggravate the necessity for getting Felix away at all sacrifices . . . . in several cases of trust reposed in him I have been unable to interfere, lest he should get into a frantic state, and let the ship go without him.'[11] To Jerningham, on the same date and by the same ship, he sent a copy of this letter and added, 'First, as you will be safe yourself from being led into mischief by any intimacy with Felix, so I beg of you to make other people whom you may see likely to suffer by confiding in him. He is utterly dangerous.'[12] EGW told Jerningham that Felix had induced an intending emigrant to pay for the greater part of his own outfit by 'frightening her into the belief that he should destroy himself if she withstood his demand. He has worked me for some time with the same sort of threatening. I tell you this in order that you may not be moved by the acting.'

Felix arrived to other accusations that he had kept money given him for a zoological fund, a cricket fund and for a widow in the colony. He denied receiving the funds or said that he had passed them on as required. Felix was in Canterbury less than two months and in that time satisfied no one either with his views and opinions or explanations of his expenditure and activities. FitzGerald said, 'he has not ventured to show his face publicly here and . . . he is regarded by the community generally as a man whose word is not to be believed'.[13]

It is tedious to attempt to extract truth and untruth from the cycle of accusation and denial that followed Felix wherever he went. His undoubted abilities as a surveyor and engineer, and perfectly innocent actions on his part, were continually in the shadow of his misrepresentations, his dubious transactions and his coercive and unhinged behaviour towards those who questioned him. In some ways, this was EGW's character writ large but with few of his compensating traits such as personal generosity and intellectual power. Dan, and to a lesser extent William, also exhibited the duplicity or dishonesty that forever tainted their better qualities.

True to form, Felix left Canterbury early in 1852 determined to bring down Godley and his supporters. He leased the Canterbury Association store at Clifton (Redcliffs) for £3 a month and left his children there for nearly three years in the care of 20-year-old Constance and her friend Miss Laws. In old age, son Edward recalled that, as a six-year-old, he and his siblings grew up 'amid wild surroundings . . . struggling against the hardships and dangers that beset the pioneers. . .'.[14] Constance would have had the practical help of brother Salvator, then aged fifteen, but Murat, eighteen, was away at sea and fourteen-year-old Ariosto had been left in England, presumably at school. The other children were all younger.

In Wellington, Felix landed on Dan's doorstep and launched into details about his quarrel with EGW, reiterating that he 'refused to tell any more lies'.[15] He also went about abusing Godley, Brittan, FitzGerald and anything to do with the Canterbury settlement. When Governor Grey returned to Wellington from a visit to Canterbury in March, Felix and Dan met with him and Felix made much of Godley's failure to accept Grey's offered loan of £5,000 to finish the Lyttelton-Sumner road. At the end of March, before he left for England again, he wrote a voluminous report on Canterbury for the benefit of Lyttelton and the association: according to Felix, almost everything about the settlement was wrong, but especially the roading. Anticipating Felix's stories, FitzGerald reminded friends in England that Felix's land was at Sumner and its whole value consisted in the 'road being completed in which case he would realise a large fortune. . . . I strongly suspect that his object is to get himself appointed engineer of the road so that he may reap as large a percentage of the loan for the road as he has already done out of the land sales.'[16] This was a telling blow in revenge for Felix replacing him as association land agent. There would be no quarter given in the FitzGerald-Wakefield war.

Felix's description of Canterbury reveals the laughable hyperbole, far exceeding EGW's, he was prepared to use to justify himself and his arguments: 'Four thousand helpless Christian people on an uncultivated waste, surrounded on all sides by impassable rock and bar; no church, no bishop, no ecclesiastical or educational establishment of the meanest kind; no preparation beyond a barrack for the labouring classes, and a wharf subject to dues; no roads, nothing but the hard earth and shapeless rock as it was from the earliest ages; – such and such only was the disastrous issue of the greatest religious delusion that could disgrace the intelligent sanctity of modern days'.[17] And EGW said that Felix could not write!

When he arrived back in London in August 1852, Felix handed his report to Lyttelton but its exaggeration and intent were abundantly clear and it was passed over, chiefly because the Canterbury Association was winding up. At the end of November, Sewell received a letter from Godley asking the association committee to inquire into the questions hanging over Felix's head in connection with the zoological and cricket money and the fund subscribed for the widow Waller. In requesting explanations of Felix, Lyttelton told him that the Waller funds had already been accounted for and in reply Felix cleared himself convincingly over the other matters.

But Godley's letter, and the noncommittal filing of his report, redoubled his fury and on 1 February 1853 he organised a meeting of absentee landowners in London, under the chair of Dr Henry Savage, to prosecute his cause and publish his pamphlet, *Mutual Relations*. The meeting passed a resolution claiming the association had misinformed prospective settlers and that funds had been misused. One of their number called on Lyttelton who calmly referred their complaints to the association's accountant. The disappearance of the association would soon transfer the dispute back to New Zealand where Felix would eventually be forced to face the people he accused.

Godley would not be among them. He had returned to London on 18 June 1853, after his two years in Canterbury as the association's agent. Felix wasted no time in confronting him over the contents of his letter to Sewell. He first asked Dr Savage to request an interview. Godley declined but agreed to answer questions by letter. On 4 July, Felix wrote to him, asking by 'whose authority' he had made the statements in his letter to Sewell.[18] Godley replied the same day, quoting a questionable source for his information. On the 5th, Felix wrote again, vigorously and effectively refuting the accusations against him, but then concluding: 'The fact is, that, in a dastardly manner you propagated scandals against me during my absence, when you knew I had no chance of meeting them, with the truth or untruth of which . . . you might have easily satisfied yourself before you wrote them. I have no hesitation in branding you, therefore, as a shocking scoundrel & I now give you fair notice that I will thrash you soundly the first moment I can meet you, which I shall immediately make every effort to do.'[19]

From within the secure walls of the Carlton Club, Godley laid a complaint with the police. Felix and he faced each other only in the Westminster Police Court where, for sending a threatening letter, Felix was ordered to find two sureties in £200 each to keep the peace for twelve months. Before that time was up, Felix was back in Canterbury.

Neither Felix nor Godley emerge from this episode with much credit; as in the Boyd case in Tasmania, Felix had managed to partially clear his name but nullified this with threats and slander. Godley, that much-lauded paragon of church and colony, had shown extremely bad judgement in accusing Felix of misdemeanours for which he had no evidence. He had allowed his earlier approval and support of Felix to be corrupted by both EGW's criticisms and hearsay in the colony; perhaps FitzGerald had poured a little poison in his ear. When faced with evidence of his mistake, Godley took cover behind the pillars of his club. Reckless Felix may have been, but at least he showed courage. After this, Godley steered clear of anyone called Wakefield.

Godley is reputed to have frequently regretted leaving Canterbury so soon. In just two years from the arrival of the first four ships in December 1850, the colony had been soundly established under his autocratic but principled good management, and had prospered despite shortage of funds. And he had led it towards self-government in defiance of Governor Grey's attempts to check him. The respect and admiration of many of his fellow settlers saw a bronze statue to his memory erected in Christchurch's Cathedral Square in 1867, six years after his death; it has remained there ever since.

One of Godley's most important achievements was to promptly remedy a key flaw in the Canterbury plan. Before the settlers arrived he accepted the truth in Felix's 1849 report that pastoralism must form the economic base for new settlements by providing wool for an export trade; and he concurred with surveyor Frederick Tuckett's conclusion, back in 1844, that the Canterbury Plains were ideally suited for sheep graziers. This news reached entrepreneurial graziers in Australia and in Nelson and squatters with flocks moved in outside the boundaries of the Canterbury Block. Conflicts quickly arose between Canterbury land purchasers, who were governed by regulations and had paid for their pre-emptive rights over pastoral land, and squatters who could graze vast acreages outside the block at low government rents, while taking advantage of the port and town facilities being developed at the settlers' expense. Defying both the letter of the governor's law, and the association's own long-distance instructions, Godley made *ad hoc* arrangements that suited both settlers and squatters in order to get the colony moving. Eventually, the association reluctantly gave Godley the right to make his own pasturage regulations and, in February 1852, he introduced a three-tier system of pastoral licences that met everyone's requirements and led to a sheepfarming explosion. By the end of 1852 all the plains had been taken up, and the first slopes of the foothills of the Southern Alps. At the beginning of 1851 there were fewer than 15,000 sheep in Canterbury; three years later this number had increased to 100,000 and, by 1861, to nearly 900,000, a third of New Zealand's entire flock. Godley had ensured that Canterbury rode into its future on the sheep's back.

When Godley took matters into his own hands, this offended not only Governor Grey but also the principals of the Canterbury Association. EGW became bewildered and then angry at Godley's failure to communicate with London and, when he did, his tendency to treat the committee members as imbeciles. EGW's expressions of concern to chairman Lyttelton about both Godley's health and state of mind have been taken as evidence of EGW's malice and poor judgement.[20] But an examination of EGW's 1851 correspondence to Godley shows that he, and other association members, had good reason to be concerned. The dispute between EGW and Godley is worth examining at greater length than it has been in past accounts, where EGW has generally been cast as the unscrupulous villain and Godley as the principled, if irritable, hero. The reality is a good deal more complex.

In January, EGW wrote a long and friendly letter to Godley, enclosing three months' copies of the *Morning Chronicle*, and pointed out that though Godley had sent a long letter home to his father, the association suffered 'seriously from the want of reports' from Canterbury: 'let us know immediately the bent of your own inclinations and purposes'. He reassured Godley that 'we all, I think, see that probably the powers of the Association will have to be transferred to the colony as soon as there shall be men in the colony fit to exercise them'.[21]

A month later EGW wrote, 'The total lack of intelligence is a sad drawback. Your letter to Hutt of the 15th August is our only news since your first dispatch & private journal, & we have not a scrap from Thomas but a letter to his brother . . . . It is really surprising that the land should sell in England without a map of the country. We always suppose that a ship bearing surveys & full reports, must have gone to the bottom.' EGW *had* received a letter from Godley but it was 'unfit to be shown by reason of its personalities [Wellington social and political figures]; but these personalities are so informing that I resolved to send the letter to Ld. Lyttelton with a request that he will burn it'. Of more interest now is that in this letter, which Godley sent from Wellington months before the first four ships arrived, he had begun to question the validity of the sufficient price, suggesting that what made good theory may not be true in practice. EGW naturally argued to the contrary: 'Let us see the high price once fairly tried; and then we will determine whether or not it will work in practice. If it won't work in practice, the theory is rubbish.'[22] This might show EGW's overbearing confidence in his idea but it also demonstrated a willing pragmatism. The sufficient price was, after all, a device, not a law; an 'elastic belt' not a 'wall of brass'.[23]

In early May, EGW scolded Godley, 'Here we are, a full twelvemonth after you reached the Colony, without one scrap of topographical information beyond the meagre & crude report from Thomas, which had reached England before you left . . . . I should deserve to be scolded by you, if I had not told you the plain truth, as to the evil we have suffered from this cause, & the really angry feelings to which it has given occasion.' While EGW and the association in London grew angry from lack of information and consideration on Godley's part, Godley grew furious at Sewell's interminable despatches giving him instructions without having any idea of what was happening on the spot. The bad feelings and conflicts over these years were caused by communication difficulties and the need of powerful personalities on opposite sides of the world to exert control. Yet Godley at first continued to have EGW's warm support: 'Your two dispatches about money – one announcing that you have incurred a private debt of £5000, & the other proposing a decrease of your salary – have been received as they deserved.'[24] The debt would be met and the proposed cut in salary refused. Altruistically, Godley thereupon charged himself rent on his Lyttelton house.

EGW could not persuade a 'hog of a shipowner' to name one of the emigrant ships after Godley, one whose sailing to Canterbury had been delayed for various reasons, including the fact that Prince Albert's 'Great Exhibition really does occupy a good deal of people's thoughts, not excepting the people who contemplate emigration'. Not only British people but British goods and British technology were flooding out to the world. Much of the latter was being proudly displayed by 13,000 exhibitors to the six million people who visited Joseph Paxton's Crystal Palace in Hyde Park, opened by the 82-year-old Duke of Wellington, a year before he died. Eighteen fifty-one was also the year in which Britain had become the first country in the world where most of the burgeoning populace lived in cities and towns. In seeking to escape these polluted cityscapes of brick terraces and chimneys, and the limitations of hope and ambition, hundreds of thousands of migrants were heading for the promise of freedom and opportunity in North America. By contrast, most of the mere thousands who emigrated to Canterbury initially went there from a countryside that was changing rapidly under the effects of industrialisation. They sought space, peace and a fresh start in a colony where prosperity would be founded on agriculture and pastoral farming.

As more of Godley's despatches arrived in London, their language became stronger although, ironically, EGW and Godley were not essentially far apart in their goals. In his haste to get Canterbury going, Godley seemed oblivious to the effect on land sales in England if pastoral preferences could not be guaranteed. How many would buy at the high £3 price if prospective emigrants were told, '"What the quantity [of pastoral land] thus placed out of your reach may be, we cannot tell; it may be half a million acres; all depends on what the demand may have been, arising from the influx of people with flocks and herds from other places."' Emigrants would then say, '"The charm of this settlement was its promise of social propinquity and appliances: I do not fancy the life of a pastoral squatter; I had rather stay at home, or as soon go to New South Wales".'[25] Yet EGW, ever the pragmatist, understood the reality facing Godley: 'Let me again admit . . . that you ought to have been properly authorised to encourage squatting as much as possible, short of discouraging sales here'.

The very next day, EGW chided Godley for a critical and unsympathetic letter to Lyttelton: 'If you had known what Ld. L. and Sewell have gone through in the way of trouble and anxiety, and what an utter failure the whole thing would have been but for their devotion to it, you would not have written so blamefully. The asperity of your letter towards Sewell made cold water run down my back; and I am sure that he, who is of a sensitive nature, felt it deeply.' EGW was convinced that the 'complaining tartness of your letter, as well as the peremptory tone of your dispatch about squatting, was occasioned by the impatience of over fatigue and excitement in proportion to your strength; and the expressions in your letter to Ld. Lyttelton about your health are very grievous to me . . . . For I judge of you by myself. When much worse than usual, I cannot help writing and speaking savagely. I am very sorry afterwards; but at the time, illness overcomes philosophy.'[26]

If Godley had been not well at the beginning of the year, he was now telling Charles Adderley that he had 'not been so vigorous for twenty years'.[27] And a little later, on the question of the disputes with the association, 'Wakefield and Sewell, both of whom, I suspect, are fond of power, will doubtless abuse me heartily, but I trust to Lyttelton, and you, and Simeon.'[28]

In response to Godley's complaints about low land sales, EGW pointed out, 'If we had taken a quarter of the pains to rouse and cultivate mere speculation in land, the sales might have been very much greater. We deliberately discouraged what had heretofore been the main spring of colonizing enterprises. We did this for the sake of that goodness of colonization on which your heart was set.' While Godley coped with building a community from scratch at the end of the world, EGW continued to battle for the vision.

He soon wrote to Lyttelton about Godley's 'unpleasant' despatches. 'I am seriously afraid that Godley's health is gone.' And by early August, after receiving more strong letters from Canterbury, EGW became 'seriously and painfully afraid that Godley's mind *has* got into a bad state'. EGW did not mean 'out of his mind', as Godley's biographer claimed,[29] but in the bad state he sometimes admitted was caused by his own fevered brain, or as he claimed of John Hutt before his resignation. EGW told Lyttelton, 'It is really very difficult for me to think in disparagement of anybody of whom I have once got to admire and like, so that I shut my eyes to their unfavourable aspects: but at last, of course, the truth prevails . . . . I think he is ill and longing to get home . . . . If so, it seems most expedient that he should be set free as soon as possible by the sending out of a successor.'[30]

With his usual perspicacity, EGW had sensed Godley's next move: already at sea was a letter proposing that he resign the following March or April and return to England. Tired of coping with Governor Grey's hostile intents and utterly frustrated at what he saw as the association denying Canterbury self-government, Godley wrote, 'The form of a constitution might be a question for discussion, but it must be *localized*. I would rather be governed by a Nero on the spot than by a board of Angels in London, because we could, if the worst came to the worst, cut off Nero's head, but we could not get at the Board in London at all.'[31] Godley held the guillotine above the association's head by saying that he would resign if they did not 'make at once that radical change in the system which I believe is imperatively required'; he would, of course, stay on to see it through if they did.[32] The irony is that the 'Board in London' was mostly made up of the same friends who were battling away with the Colonial Office to achieve a satisfactory form of self-government for New Zealand and its disparate settlements.

In September, even the diplomatic and level-headed Lyttelton was moved to write to Godley regretting the controversial character of the communications with the association. At the same time, EGW wrote to Godley, expressing concern about the state of Godley's mind and body: every day he thought, '"Would to God that he were here, or I with him well enough myself to be of help to him"'. Such empathy did not prevent EGW from listing for Godley his errors in relationship to the association. EGW was particularly grieved about Godley's demand for local self-government that would have effectively given control of Canterbury to the Colonial Office and also his indifference to the 'heavy pecuniary liabilities into which your friends here entered from motives of sympathy towards you' and the 'pecuniary obligations of the Association to the Company as to repayment of the advances by means of which the foundation of the Settlement was laid'.[33] As he explained, the Colonial Office and company were pressing for payment of the monies due to them on account of land sales. Once again the association faced disaster; and once again, Lyttelton, EGW and two others came to the rescue by guaranteeing a bank loan of £12,000. Godley was reputed to have presumptuously commented that his friends were prepared to lose money on behalf of his cause.

The misunderstanding and bad feeling continued as both men stayed where they were in Canterbury and England – while both stating the contrary – and then news of their altered decisions took the usual four months to filter through. When EGW and Godley finally sailed for their new destinations at the end of 1852, they crossed en route – a key letter from Godley to EGW written in June 1852 did not reach him until July 1853, and his reply did not reach Godley until the following Christmas. When Godley opened it, he read, in reference to his letter of eighteen months before, 'You will not have forgotten its contents. They had instantly upon me the effect which you desired – that of obliterating from my mind all past causes of difference between us, & causing me to undo in my thoughts every word of complaint that I have uttered about you . . . . it is best that we should say nothing more about the past. According to the spirit of your letter, I discharge it all from my mind, & shall do this with such a will that all disagreeables will soon be with me as if they had never been.'[34] EGW would never see Godley again: this was a generous reconciliation between two very different men who, nevertheless, shared a vision of Canterbury that would never have been fulfilled had either been absent from its plan and execution.

Apart from his continuing work with the Canterbury Association throughout 1851 and 1852, EGW had become more deeply embroiled with the activities of the Colonial Reform Society and the matter of colonial self-government. Domestic life for EGW at Reigate was lonelier now that Constance and the family were gone, and with Charley Torlesse too far away to be of either help or irritation, Albert Allom fulfilled the role of faithful secretary. Allom also assisted Frederick Young, who had taken over management of the association's shipping department. Young, later chairman of the Royal Colonial Institute, had been 22 when he first met EGW in 1839. He recalled that EGW 'exercised a powerful influence over all who came within his sphere, and especially over young men. His manner was striking, and most persuasive. There was peculiar fascination about the way in which he put everything before one, which seldom failed to inspire confidence . . . In my own case he quite captivated me.'[35] During his time as shipping manager, Young said that EGW was 'daily in attendance' at the association offices at the Adelphi in The Strand. This seems unlikely since EGW was still living in the Reigate cottage. 'It was a comfortable and commodious little residence, with a large dining-room. Here he every now and then invited me to stay with him for a day or two.' Henry Sewell was there sometimes, too, and evenings, inevitably, were spent discussing colonial matters. 'I remember one night, just after Sewell had retired, and Wakefield and I were leaving the room to do the same, Wakefield, candle in hand, turned to me and said: "What a good fellow he is! It is a pity he is such a Puseyite!"'

Young recalled, too, EGW's 'rare dogs, the Talbot hounds. He had two magnificent specimens, who were his constant companions, both in and out of doors . . . . He also had a strong cob, on which he used to ride every morning before breakfast. When I was at Reigate, I always accompanied him on foot, as he only rode at a walking pace, listening to his sage remarks . . . .' When Young knew him, EGW was 'between fifty and sixty, about five feet six inches in height, stout and burly in figure, with a round, smooth, fair face, looking very like a prosperous English farmer'. Young believed that, but for 'his unfortunate escapade in early life he would have attained a very high place in public estimation. Still, among politicians, and especially those in any way feeling an interest in colonial questions, he was undoubtedly a great power. One day he said to me, "Young, I had thirty-six members of Parliament in this room yesterday." They had travelled down to Reigate to consult him on some important colonial subject then on the tapis [under consideration].'

When Young knew EGW, 'His personal habits . . . were of the simplest kind. He was most temperate, and never indulged in any of the pleasures of the table. He rose very early and went to bed early. He lived on the simplest food and scarcely touched wine. He had an especial dislike to the vulgar snobbery of the *nouveaux riches*, of whom there were many specimens around him. As he was a person with a name they desired to have him at their tables, but they could never succeed in getting him. One of them said, "If you will come I will have fish down from London and dine at six." "Thank you," was the reply, "I always dine at one, on a leg of mutton and a rice pudding".'

When William Fox arrived from New Zealand in June 1851, he met EGW for the first time and provoked the final campaign for a New Zealand constitution. Fox had been New Zealand Company agent in Nelson from 1843 to 1848. When William Wakefield died in September 1848, Fox was holding his power of attorney and swiftly took over company affairs as William's nominated successor. The devoted Francis Dillon Bell had expected the job, after carrying much of the burden of William's work in the months before his death and because of his close Wakefield family connections. The resulting acrimony caused EGW to write to his young cousin to calm his feelings: Fox was too valuable an ally.

Fox presided over the end of the company's activities in New Zealand and continued William's battles against the political establishment, especially against Governor Grey for his continued suspension of the 1846 constitution. In Wellington, along with Godley, he 'denounced Grey's nominee councils, and, as he saw them, the spineless and devious Colonial Office and incompetent administration in New Zealand'.[36] He might have taken his cue from *The Art of Colonization*. At the end of 1850, Wellington settlers appointed him their political agent to visit England and to lobby for political and constitutional reform. On arrival he immediately clashed with Earl Grey who refused to see him officially. Unsurprisingly, Fox and EGW hit it off, to the point where EGW recommended Fox as the replacement for Godley after his resignation. Fox also recounted for EGW the details of Godley's constitutional battles with Governor Grey, and the new enthusiasm that Fox brought to the debate sparked a meeting of the reformers to focus on a new constitution for New Zealand.

Charles Adderley recounted that in July 1851, he had 'got on with the New Zealand Bill and Constitution which had been drafted on the terrace at Hams [his country seat] with Gibbon Wakefield . . . Fox, Sewell and Lord Lyttelton assisting'.[37] It has been observed that 'The chief architect of the New Zealand constitution of 1852 was Governor Grey himself. He had differed from the settlers on little more than the question of timing.'[38] But at the time of the Hams meeting, Governor Grey had not finally formulated his thoughts on a new bill to replace the suspended and unwieldy 1846 constitution and these did not reach Earl Grey until the end of the year.[39] By that time, the reformers had 'made it their great object to hound him out of office'.[40]

Earl Grey's unpopularity was now irredeemable: his policies were seen as failing everywhere, in South Africa, Canada and Australia, as well as New Zealand. *The Times* moved into opposition: 'From the first moment of his colonial rule, he has in every colony resisted to the utmost every attempt on the part of the colonists to manage their own affairs'.[41] In December of 1851 Palmerston was pushed from the Foreign Office by Prime Minister Russell after Queen Victoria complained of his 'personal arbitrary perversion' of the principles of policy, and, after five and a half years in office, the government began to list seriously. Palmerston engineered its sinking in February 1852, and in the weak administration of the Earl of Derby that followed the reformers saw their chance as Grey left the Colonial Office at last, and ministerial office for good.

'Who is Sir John Pakington?' asked the Duke of Wellington querulously. The new colonial secretary was a Worcestershire squire, a neighbour of Lyttelton and a friend of Adderley but 'far from being a man of sufficiency for the office'.[42] Just what the reformers needed. EGW and other reformers – Adderley and Sewell – had their first meeting with him on 18 March 1852, after working in 'close concert' with Gladstone. The reformers knew that Earl Grey, before leaving office, had sent out to Governor Grey a new draft constitution that contained most of the elements they desired. EGW reported to Lyttelton, 'Sir John told us of his wish, or rather intention, to suspend again the Constitution of 1846, urging as his reason his own incapacity for sudden action on a matter of so much importance, and the little importance to the colonists of only one year's more delay.' Pakington also told them that he had written to the governor, asking him not to publish the proposed new bill. 'We insisted on a measure now or the revival of the constitution of 1846, to which the colonists have never objected . . . . Mr Gladstone had told us to be very importunate; and so we were.' But the colonists' arguments 'were quite without effect' until they made it clear that they intended to oppose another suspension bill. Then Pakington 'altered his tone' and asked EGW and the others to send him a draft of the bill, which he intimated that he would support, 'with a view to immediate legislation'.[43]

EGW had a considerable hand in modifying the constitution prepared by the two Greys. The new bill provided for a governor, a General Assembly with an elected House of Representatives, six elected provincial councils and elected provincial superintendents; the provincial provisions could be abolished by a simple majority of the General Assembly. Members of the Legislative Council, or upper house, of the General Assembly were to be nominated for life by the governor, whereas Governor Grey had recommended that the provincial councils elect the upper house members. The property qualification for the franchise (men only) was low but still excluded most Maori because they rarely possessed individual landed property (Maori finally gained separate representation fifteen years later).

On 21 May, Gladstone delivered a powerful speech which, while criticising parts of it, urged the passage of the bill as a whole. This appeal was backed by EGW's petition to the House on 2 June, occasioned by unexpected opposition from his old ally Molesworth, who attacked the bill's provisions for provincial government. EGW petitioned, 'Evil happens when the area of the colony is so large, and its means of communications so deficient, that the seat of government is what London has been as the seat of government for many remote dependencies. In such cases the benefits of government . . . are confined to the seat of government and its immediate neighbourhood.' The bill recognised the current separation and isolation of New Zealand's settlements and the reality that it might, for example, take weeks by sea to travel between Otago and Auckland. This concurred with Governor Grey's observations. If New Zealand's demography and communications changed, the act could be changed: 'Your Petitioner humbly prays that your Honorable House may be pleased to pass the Bill . . . for the sake of its merits, and without regard to its obvious defects, because there is not time for amendment by present legislation here, whilst the whole measure is open to future amendment by legislation in the colony.'[44] Three days later, the bill completed its passage through the House and the New Zealand Constitution Act received the royal assent on 30 June. 'All the New Zealanders in London are in high spirits.'[45]

The act was extremely democratic for the times and provincial government served a useful life from 1853 to 1876, when government was centralised in Wellington. The franchise was progressively liberalised over the years and the core provision of an elected House of Representatives remains today. The major flaw in the act, the nominated Legislative Council, was not abolished until 1950; but 100 years before that H. S. Chapman, and many others, had criticised EGW's plan to have a New Zealand 'house of Peers' where place might be found for friends and family such as Francis Dillon Bell.[46] In this context, Chapman also criticised EGW for his loyalty to the concept of constitutional monarchy and New Zealand's allegiance to the British Crown through a governor. EGW conjectured that Lyttelton might one day become New Zealand's governor, helping to ensure 'monarchy will be preserved in the Southern world: if not we must be content with democratic republics'.[47] This statement has been taken to mean that EGW was no democrat, but he read well the inclination and mood of the people, early in Victoria's reign, when the practice of constitutional monarchy was by no means secure. Constitutional monarchy has, though modified, remained popular in New Zealand for 150 years: the 1852 constitution was replaced only in 1986.

Attracting even more criticism, indeed anger and vituperation, was the British government's decision, as a provision of the bill, to attach the remaining New Zealand Company debt of more than £268,000 to the New Zealand land fund. The outrage was general, but the government would not be moved.

Godley had been persuaded to withdraw his resignation and stay on in Canterbury until the reformers carried the Constitution Act and news of their success prompted his preparations for departure at the end of 1852. He disliked several aspects of the act, especially the considerable powers still left to the governor, the nominated Legislative Council and the power of the General Assembly to overrule the provincial councils. But, as he told Adderley, 'on the whole it is workable, and as coming, in a certain way, from our friends, and couched in a friendly spirit, we will try to make the best of it thankfully and cheerfully'.[48]

The legislation cleared the way for governance of the settlement to be transferred to Canterbury's first provincial council, and the association wasted no time. As soon as the final reading of the act had been completed, the association's committee resolved to discontinue their operations from 30 September and Sewell was deputed to travel out to New Zealand to manage the difficult task of transferring the association's assets and liabilities.

EGW decided to leave for Canterbury with Sewell. He had, for years, asserted his intention of going to New Zealand once his work with colonising projects was complete, and once he had helped to steer through an adequate constitution. The New Zealand constitution, and other colonial self-government developments, precluded any more colonising projects on the model settlement principle. His work was done, there was nothing more to write about and, at 56, he was reaching the end of his physical tether. But was emigration to Canterbury his best option? Why undertake a voyage around the world to construct an entirely new life, with all its difficulties and stresses, cut off from a familiar social and political environment that was filled with close friends such as Robert Rintoul and his daughter Henrietta, and key members of his family such as Catherine? On the other hand, Jerningham, Dan and his family, Felix's children, Charley Torlesse and other family connections such as Emily and Francis Dillon Bell were all in New Zealand. He could also cite many friends and acquaintances in the colony: 'I am personally acquainted with more people in New Zealand than anybody else can be, having known them at home as intending colonists.'[49]

But there were also enemies. He had told Godley, 'The ingratitude of colonists if not proverbial, is an old story. Penn and Baltimore felt it deeply. I have never known or heard of colonial gratitude . . . towards its founders. There is not one of the settlements which I have had so much part in founding, from South Australia to Canterbury, but would roast me alive if they thought that my dripping would enrich their land.' But he had qualified this: 'Knowing how this colonial state of mind is caused, I do not quarrel with it; nor has it ever deterred me from going on with the sort of work, and finding it full of charms. The feeling, or want of feeling, is a natural product of being engaged in the acquisition of a new country and a new nationality.'[50]

Doubtless, EGW thought the sea voyage and the New Zealand climate would be good for his health, and he longed to see the country that must have seemed, in its new society, to be almost his own – and to which Arthur and William had given their lives. But all of this could have been accomplished by an extended visit. Perhaps, in the end, he felt compelled to go as a settler to the country he had persuaded, cajoled and willed so many others to embrace, to show by his own commitment a real faith in his vision. Despite his misgivings, he may well have decided, too, that it was time to glory in his success, win some public praise and recognition and, despite his disavowals, find a role in the new self-government of New Zealand.

EGW's journeys to Canada had always been made with a clear or implicit intention to return; his departure for New Zealand meant he would almost certainly *never* return. On 29 September 1852 he left London for Plymouth and was seen off by friends and family; he was especially grieved to farewell Rintoul and his daughter Henrietta, with whom he had lately formed a warm relationship. From Plymouth he wrote to her, 'It was so very painful to part, that I said I would write, but without knowing what there would be to say, and only from an impulse which suggested procrastination of the eternal adieu. You may believe it or not; but I assure you that the only real sharp pain I felt in taking leave, was . . . when your tears and your father's last grasp of the hand completely upset me. You cannot imagine how I have longed that you had both come with us. But I shall not say Good Bye any more; it is too hateful.'[51]

His departure was marked by an event that was even more poignant. Mrs Allom, father Edward's indispensable correspondent, could not countenance the thought that the 26-year breach between Frances Wakefield and EGW would remain unhealed before he left England forever. She arranged for Frances to come down to London from Macclesfield with 78-year-old Edward. Her unexpected presence at a time of such heightened emotions brought about 'scenes surpassed for dramatic intensity by nothing off the stage, and little upon it'.[52] EGW sank to his knees, took her hand and wept, asking and receiving her forgiveness. It is not recorded if she finally acknowledged her part in the madness of 1826.

Both Charles Torlesse and Catherine made the journey to Plymouth with EGW, to farewell not only him, but also their nineteen-year-old son Henry who was going out with his uncle in hopes of recovering his health; he would join Charley in Canterbury. Storms delayed the sailing of the *Minerva* and Charles had to leave for home but Catherine was determined to stay until the end. In his letter to Henrietta Rintoul EGW said, 'The place is full of emigrants waiting for ships from London, and we have got lodgings at a Temperance Hotel . . . a fortunate accident for my sister; for the other hotels are crammed with moustachioed young bloods.' He implored Henrietta to meet Catherine at Paddington Station when she returned to London: 'Keep her away from her house, if you possibly can, for a few days.'

EGW sent Catherine a last note from the ship. It was the end of a long life together, a final separation. The deepest sense of loss was, perhaps, Catherine's, but for EGW there was now the knowledge that Stoke would be no more a refuge from tribulation. From the *Minerva* at 11 a.m. on 12 October he wrote,

> We have just got an anchor from the Government Dock Yard, and shall sail in an hour. Henry was cast down, of course, yesterday; but he slept all night, and devoured his breakfast this morning with a chaw-bacon appetite. At this moment he is, to all appearance, in the best of health. Every body slept on board last night; and all seem cheerful this morning, except only poor Mrs Sewell who has yet to part from her sister . . . . This morning at six, Henslow, Sewell, Bogey, Thring, Violet and I went onto the breakwater and walked there for an hour. The wind is most fair, and the weather not less promising. The seaweed seems a perfect truth-teller.
>
> With kindest love to all and one more parting kiss.
>
> Ever your most affectionate, E.G. Wakefield.[53]

He would confide to Henrietta Rintoul, but never to Catherine, of a long letter he wrote later, but burned, because 'it was a curiosity, being all sentiment and almost passion as excited by the strange event of committing suicide with respect to the affections. I felt that in going away, I had morally stepped into a grave, and must remain there, dead to the past, and also dead to the future until born again' in New Zealand.[54]

CHAPTER TWENTY-EIGHT

Dead to the Past

LIFE AT SEA WAS TEDIOUS, EACH DAY LIKE the next, without land or another passing ship to send mail Home. In the enervating atmosphere and rhythm of shipboard life EGW could not bring himself to write anything substantive. He had no theatrical skills, like Jerningham, to entertain the *Minerva*'s passengers and crew, although he produced plenty of talk at the captain's table. John Deans, homeward bound to his farm at Riccarton Bush, did not think EGW the clever man that 'I have often heard him called. He has an excellent memory and a large stock of brass and impudence, and these seem to carry him through.'[1] If the other passengers tired of his talk, he could always bore Henry Sewell and there was young Henry Torlesse to keep an eye on, a bull and a heifer to care for and, of course, the Talbot bloodhounds.

If EGW could not bring himself to write anything social or political, he was at least inclined to write letters. As England receded further and further in the *Minerva*'s wake, he wrote to Henrietta Rintoul: 'Has the Derby fraud exploded? How did you get on with my sister, and how did she bear the separation at last? Does your father miss his call at the Adelphi? Has Robert been drilled? Has your mother quite forgiven my supposed purpose of making him a colonist? How is poor Lucy? Is the fog very thick? Here's but a sample of the thousand questions that I am continually asking about home. . . .'[2] Regret and nostalgia were eased by having a pair of cabins and the care of two servants. He had not been seasick, 'thanks to the Double Action Bed of Mr Brown . . . . the inventor is a poor man, with twelve children alive of twenty four by one wife – honest and industrious – but totally ignorant of the art of pushing. So I have written to him what may get him custom, by way of repaying him something more than the mere price of the bed for the immense comfort it has afforded me.' In a perfect advertising slogan EGW concluded: 'Getting into it is like going on shore.'

On 2 February 1853, 112 days out from England, EGW woke Sewell at two in the morning: land had been sighted. Sewell wrote in his journal, 'safe arrival at one's destination with the prodigious interest about the future before us are sufficient excuses for intoxication. All the Telescopes were brought into use.'[3] He thought the panorama of wooded Banks Peninsula 'more beautiful than any thing I can remember', but he was not impressed by the 'newness and unfinishedness' of Lyttelton: 'Streets laid out without pavements – Roads unmacadamised. Small low Sheds serving for Shops and dwellings – Gardens only half cultivated – rough palings . . . .' Christchurch he found 'an odd straggling place. Small wooden buildings dotted about with little pretension to regularity . . . . a few gardens but except Riccarton bush not a tree near it – Every body therefore can see what every body else does in the open air.'[4]

Sewell's disapproving tone reflected well his stuffy and pessimistic personality; though worthy, thorough and honest, he was also a terrible vacillator and a snob. He sniffed at EGW's 'intense excitement about the Colony and every thing in it. Every thing was ultra *couleur de rose*.' EGW's accounts to Catherine and Rintoul gave full rein to his sheer pleasure and enthusiasm at finding that the colony he had worked so hard for exceeded his expectations. There was rarely a middle ground for EGW – people and places were either wonderful or wicked. Less than a week after his arrival, he wrote to Catherine from Charley's farm at Rangiora. Canterbury far surpassed his 'pre-conceptions as respects hearty natural capabilities, and progress of settlement. Its civilization in respect of drawing-rooms and ladies elegancies is quite surprising. I am charmed with the climate so far.'[5] Henry was in 'perfect and whole health', Charley was 'well and as happy as anyone can be in this world' and, as for himself, he had 'never been ill at all'.

To Rintoul, a couple of months later, he expanded on the question of health: 'I have not had . . . a moment of that depression & feebleness which used to make me such a cripple at home . . . . perhaps it is from having been so long ill that I value so much the constant feeling of health which this climate produces', something he had not felt for at least seven years, since before his stroke. But this was not remarkable: 'Fine health is general in old & young . . . some ladies . . . appeared ten years younger than when I parted from them in London.' Even the 'creole' children he encountered were 'plump & ruddy', he wrote, reminding Rintoul, 'you know how I examine the children & dogs wherever I may be'. His bloodhound Bogey, which had landed 'like a rake in a bag', was now in the 'rudest & handsomest health'.[6]

Farm produce and animals were similarly a source of wonder. The productiveness of soil and climate was 'really tropical in quantity & rapidity of growth'. The yield from one Canterbury wheat crop was amazing and horses 'which are never housed, & which never get any thing to eat but the grass . . . of their paddock . . .' were as fat and sleek as 'animals fed for the Smithfield show'. Sewell may have disparaged EGW's excessive excitement, but EGW told Rintoul that Sewell, '(you know his dislike to strong expressions) has been caught saying first . . . "exquisitely beautiful" and then "intensely lovely"' about a country that EGW thought 'less

Italian and more English' than he had expected. After the smoke of London, the squalor of the new industrial towns and the often impoverished English countryside, New Zealand was proving to be the Arcadia that he had always imagined.

Socially and politically, however, it was not yet Utopia. Socially there was 'much to like & much to dislike'. He thought, of course, that the best people were in the newest settlements. In Canterbury 'I would have fancied myself in England, except for the hard-working industry of the upper classes and the luxurious independence of the common people'. In Wellington, however, Governor Sir George Grey – 'Double G' – had

> made trickery & cajolery fashionable . . . . To his example mainly I likewise attribute a greedy selfishness which pervades society here. Still the upper classes are very hospitable & very deficient in the pride of mere purse or station, & the common people are remarkably honest . . . . Their entire independence is not disagreeable to me who am accustomed to America & like it. There is absolutely no servility . . . . I get on famously with the 'unwashed' & like them. Sewell as yet is incapable of understanding them, thinks them rude & disagreeable. His Oxford & Isle of Wight habits of thought are shocked by the democratic ways of a carpenter here, who speaks of him as 'Sewell' without the Mister & calls a brother carpenter 'Mister' Smith.

Thirteen years after the first ships arrived in Wellington, egalitarianism was entrenched.

But there was something rotten in the state of Arcadia and its source was local politics. EGW found a 'general narrow-mindedness. Every body's ideas seem to be localized to his own part of the country. I have not met with one person as well acquainted as I am myself with New Zealand in general.' This was partly a result of the 'want of inter-communication between the settlements'. Until there was steam navigation they would remain 'cut off from each other as if separated by a thousand miles of ocean'. But the real problem was the lack of responsible government, the 'total absence of popular power & responsibility' caused by the jealous despotism of Governor Grey, who had not only caused the suspension of the 1846 constitution but was now trying to impede the introduction of the new 1852 arrangement. His character was a 'cross between the foreign political police agent, and the low English attorney'. The 'total want of political liberty produces a stagnant frame of mind, except as regards getting money or spending it. I can't find one person who has it in his head to contemplate the prosperity & greatness of this country . . . . it is a miserable state of things . . . & you will think I must be very unhappy. But I am not so at all. On the contrary I am sure that there is a good foundation to work upon in the best set of colonists that have ever left England in modern times.' The people would be 'changed by the coming responsibilities of political power. Only there is heavy work for me, if I can but keep health for doing it. At present I am not in the least down-hearted.'

Before EGW could take on his self-appointed task as the only true governor of New Zealand, he and Sewell had to cope with the initial ungratefulness and hostility of the Canterbury settlers. Neither knew that Godley had quit Canterbury only six weeks before they arrived. For Sewell, 'The news of Godley's departure fell upon me like a Cloud.'[7] EGW became convinced that his own coming had driven him away. Godley had deputed Captain Charles Simeon to be acting association agent but FitzGerald was quickly becoming the most politically influential figure in the 3000-strong colony as sub-inspector of police, association immigration agent and editor of the *Lyttelton Times*. EGW sent messages to him, asking for a meeting, but FitzGerald lay low at his Springs farm, 15 miles from Christchurch, and did not venture into town or port for three weeks after the *Minerva*'s arrival.

Although EGW knew well how jealous settlers treated their colony's founders, he was injured and offended by his cold reception. He told Rintoul that, 'Godley and Fitzgerald taught the colonists . . . to distrust and hate the Association . . . . Othello has almost killed his Desdemona: that is Godley and his colony. Fitzgerald is the Iago, I am the Cassio of the piece.'[8] EGW reserved his greatest venom for FitzGerald, whom he accused of overweening ambition and jealousy: 'I was insinuated to be a self-seeking intriguer, leading Lord Lyttelton by the nose for my own purposes'.

Both EGW and Sewell found it especially galling that both FitzGerald and Godley seemed to have fostered opposition to the plan for the settlement to take over the association's debts. EGW was offended by the reluctance of the Canterbury community to repay the debt of honour they owed to EGW, Lyttelton and the other association members who had guaranteed loans and maintained the association's solvency. On the other hand, it was understandable that hard-working settlers, struggling to earn a living and make a new society, would not take kindly to men just arrived from London, one frequently perceived as an untrustworthy and unscrupulous know-all and the other as a slippery lawyer.

Charles Bowen, Godley's young private secretary from the time of his arrival until Godley's departure, vividly described the feeling in a letter to Godley who was then holidaying in Australia, en route for England:

> Messrs Wakefield and Sewell . . . were immediately attacked for accounts. A rumour had gone abroad that the town reserves were to be sold which created a great ferment. They gave no explicit answer but resorted to the dodge of palaver – which went down very badly . . . . Every one was disgusted especially by the way they spoke of you – not attacking your policy openly but trying to disparage it by insinuations . . . . The truth is they were so overjoyed at not finding you here on their arrival, that they were hurried into overcalculating their power to lead people by the nose. I assure you that two more unpopular men could not have been sent out by the Assocn. in the critical situation of their affairs. Mr Wakefield especially has given great offence by his style of

writing . . . by the domineering manner in which he has pretended to instruct them and has openly spoken of their ignorance.

FitzGerald looks upon Sewell as an unprincipled pettifogger, the tool of Wakefield, and the mismanager of the Assocn.'s affairs . . . the general opinion here among all classes is that Lord Lyttelton and others are the victims of Mr Wakefield and Sewell who led them on, when they knew that the Assocn. was bankrupt. . . .'[9]

John Deans regretted Godley's absence as the enmities deepened and the wrangles worsened, for he 'would have been the colonists' best champion' against EGW and Sewell. Yet Sewell commented accurately that Godley had 'left nothing behind him but the prestige of personal and social popularity – no policy, no plans for the future, no organisation'.[10] As the settlers had always wanted, and as he was to admit himself, Godley should have stayed on, at least for another year until the election of the first provincial council. Then the enmities and misunderstandings would have been rapidly cleared away. EGW was quick to take offence and to attack perceived enemies, but he was just as quick to frankly clear the air and move on. Outspoken and aware of his own frailties, EGW considered his relationship with Sewell warm enough that 'We call each other names, between which perhaps the truth may be found. He is "timid and desponding", I "rash and over-sanguine." Acting together we get on famously.'[11]

Although some judged Sewell to have 'no fixity of purpose' and to be 'fertile in resource and skilful in evasion',[12] he was able, over the following two years, to settle the debt problems to the settlers' satisfaction. The new province agreed to pay the association's debt of around £29,000 in return for its public reserves (including Hagley Park). It was Sewell who revived the church college plan so that a third of association lands were assigned to endow Christ's College in 1855. 'By his financial and legal acumen Sewell salvaged many of the ecclesiastical and educational aspects of the Canterbury plan.'[13]

This process should have also cleared away suspicions of EGW's role in Canterbury as simply a self-serving intriguer. But the hostility and resistance he found in 1853 never quite disappeared. It lingers to this day: Christchurch has its statues to Godley and FitzGerald but quite recent offers to fund one for EGW have been firmly turned down. Godley made it work and FitzGerald carried it on, after his fashion, but Canterbury was EGW's idea and he worked hard to realise it. It was the apotheosis of his castle in the air, the planned settlement based on a sufficient price. That Canterbury worked better than any other settlement could be attributed largely to the quality of the colonists that EGW had been at such pains to ensure, despite FitzGerald's carelessness. Although the returns from extensive pastoralism outside the Canterbury Block were essential to its early economic prosperity, maintenance of a high sufficient price within the block meant that Canterbury cleared its debts early and accumulated the funds for its social and educational development.

The sufficiently high price in Canterbury was evidence of the twist to EGW's theory. In 1858, William Fox reported to Godley that it had prevented the land from passing 'into the hands of large capitalists, speculating runholders etc . . . so that the day labourer would not be able to get an acre. Therefore, the price is maintained for exactly the reverse reason to that for which it was imposed.'[14] But, EGW might have said, though the sufficient price had been intended to give the small capitalist landowner security and availability of labour, it had also been intended to give labour a chance. The sufficient price still did: God and the theory moved in mysterious ways.

EGW finally met up with FitzGerald in the Mitre Hotel in Lyttelton on 22 February. EGW said that FitzGerald regarded him with 'looks of shame and fear. I let him off, almost without reproach. It was not worth while to scold him.' EGW floated his proposal of preparing a public address from the people of Canterbury to Governor Grey which supported his doctrine, as Sewell put it, 'that the wisdom of the Colony would be to make peace with the Governor, and work the Constitution for the best, the Governor putting himself in the hands of the Colonists, and they supporting him'. It might also deliver the governor into the hands of EGW. According to Sewell, 'FitzGerald hardly knew what to make of it. He handled the question like a hotplate afraid to burn his fingers . . . . He approved of the principle, but seemed afraid to commit himself to anything Wakefieldian.'[15] EGW failed to get too much support for his address. His self-interest was too clear and, though he told Rintoul that he had been asked by some to stand as first superintendent of the pending Canterbury Province, in opposition to FitzGerald's declared candidacy, it was he who had 'not a chance of success' and not the man who, as editor of the *Lyttelton Times*, had control of the propaganda.

The day after their meeting with FitzGerald, Sewell recorded that EGW had persuaded Simeon and his wife to go with them both to 'carry the Olive branch' to the governor, and a week later they all set sail for Wellington on the *Minerva*. Despite his brave claims to the contrary, after precisely a month in Canterbury EGW had been roundly rejected and seen off. The only service that he had rendered the settlement was in lodging his prize bull and heifer at Charley Torlesse's Rangiora farm. FitzGerald had warned him before he came, 'This place is but a village. Its politics are not large enough for you.'[16] But EGW had showed no sign of being able to adapt to his new colonial circumstances. The opportunity for real political power at last was too much to resist.

There was also the problem that, 'Cut off from Sewell, I have no friendship here'.[17] EGW had the lawyer's companionship and support during his short stay in Canterbury and his first few months in Wellington, but Sewell was soon deeply embroiled with Canterbury affairs. EGW had no Rintoul to turn to, no one he saw 'as cool and wary as I may be imaginative and impetuous' and who would edit his more extravagant statements or actions. There was no powerful guiding force such as Lyttelton or Durham, whose judgements he would be willing to defer to; and no equal intellect such as Buller's to challenge and modify his arguments. Clearly, he did not see George Grey in either light as he sailed off for Wellington, restored in health and hubris, confident that he would work hand in glove with the highest officer in the land to implement the new constitution as it should be.

The weather should have warned him. The *Minerva* made good progress up the east coast of the South Island on Tuesday 1 March but contrary winds and bad weather in the Cook Strait region meant that by Friday, as Sewell recorded, 'we were knocking about in a state of perfect blindness' and then there 'came a hubble bubble of a sea in which we danced about madly . . . sending the water up to and over our stern windows . . . . This climate of New Zealand seems made up of nothing but gales, with little momentary lulls in between . . . . I hold with the grumblers that the climate is "dreadful healthy" but extremely disagreeable.'[18]

With the aid of a pilot, the *Minerva* was worked into Wellington harbour in the early hours of 7 March but a nor'west gale meant that 'Boats could scarcely come off – at all events nobody could get on Shore without risk of a wetting'. The gentlemen stood on their dignity and decided not to risk it but younger, hardier souls moved back and forth between ship and shore. The bad weather meant that the government brig, and Governor Grey, were still in Wellington. When Sewell sent a message asking for an interview, Grey's private secretary came off to tell them that the governor was on the point of leaving overland for Hawke's Bay. Grey suggested, 'Either that we should go in the Brig to Auckland or follow him a two days' journey into the interior' to meet him and Bishop Selwyn 'at some place . . . beyond the Wairarapa'. This was a clever move on Grey's part, designed to throw them off balance. EGW saw it as 'a Manoeuvre to entrap us away from the proper place of business, into the bush where real business could not be transacted, and no witnesses would be present to ensure a truthful version of what might take place, or to get us on board the brig where he would out-general us'.[19]

EGW elected to stay aboard the *Minerva* and send the governor messages, until he was accorded the kind of reception he considered should dignify his arrival. That very day, 7 March, Grey proclaimed self-government under the 1852 Constitution Act and, just three days before, he had also issued a proclamation reducing the price of land throughout New Zealand to 10s an acre (5s for poorer land), thus effectively scuppering any further application of the Wakefield sufficient price. EGW could have been forgiven for believing that Grey had seen him coming.

In his first letter to Grey, on 9 March, EGW wrote, 'After landing in Canterbury, I discovered that there are great difficulties in the way of your establishing the new Constitution with advantage to the country and credit to yourself . . . you have received the address from some Canterbury people . . . intended to assist you in getting your past differences with the colonists to be laid aside by them, so that . . . all parties might sincerely co-operate in giving effect to the objects of the Parliament in granting powers of self-government to the colony. In the same spirit I now tender you my further services towards the same end.' Shifting into statesman mode, EGW went on,

> But let me not be misunderstood. There is no favour which it is possible for the Governor of New Zealand to bestow upon me in a personal sense, though he may bind me to him in eternal gratitude by giving real and full effect to the new Constitutional Act. My object is single and unmistakable: it is the prosperity and greatness of New Zealand which, come when it may, will be my glory and a personal reward surpassing in value any that the power of Government could bestow upon me; which will be your glory here and at home, if you establish the Constitution in peace. I wish to help you in that rather difficult task. My experience in this sort of work, at least in regard to colonies, is greater than any other man's.[20]

This was precisely the help Grey did not want and he did not take kindly to EGW standing regally offshore in the hope of a deferential reception. Sewell had gone ashore to speak with him the day before; EGW could do the same. Grey replied, by return, that just as EGW's letter arrived he was 'preparing to . . . join my party who have been waiting for me since Friday last . . . . I have indeed delayed here for two days, partly in the hope of seeing you onshore . . . . I shall however, I trust, be again at Wellington in less than two months when we shall meet before even the electoral lists can be fully formed.' He continued:

> I think whoever has informed you that any differences exist between myself and the inhabitants of this country generally has misled you. I can only say that I am sincerely attached to them and to their interests and that whenever I move amongst them I find warm and attached friends and that I am entirely unconscious of the existence of such difficulties as you allude to and notwithstanding the manner in which my actions and intentions have been so misrepresented by a few persons who (you must pardon me for saying so) have I think invariably been friends of yours and acting with you and have at least in some instances been assisted by your published letters; of course I cannot approve of such misrepresentations or of the means by which they were in some cases supported but even in the case of the persons who made them (although I cannot avoid a sense of wrong done me) I have not the slightest ill-will towards them or any such sense of difference existing between them and myself as would prevent me from gladly seeing them engage in any work for the public good and from cordially co-operating with them in such work and I shall be very glad indeed if you will set them such an example as you propose and if you will afford the Government such assistance as you offer.[21]

EGW could hardly mistake Grey's sarcasm and disingenuousness or his notification that he had no intention of becoming another Charles Metcalfe. Grey could not have been 'entirely unconscious' of difficulties he had with some settlers, the worst of them to be found the further south he travelled. He had been fiercely opposed by southern settlement leaders for his constitutional manipulations since 1846, and they now believed, accurately, that he would delay implementation of the new constitution for as long as possible. He was genuinely hostile towards the whole Canterbury plan, with its aristocratic credentials and, therefore, its creators. It was nothing less than a downright lie when Grey advised the Colonial Office in May 1854 that 'no complaint has yet reached me of any partiality or unfairness on my part'.[22]

Grey and EGW should have been allies: ostensibly, their objects sprang from a desire to improve the lot of the disadvantaged through enlightened colonisation. But Grey wished to '"keep the Old World out of the New World', to prevent its defilement',[23] whereas EGW wished to transplant the best of the old for the mutual benefit of both. If that was indeed Grey's ideal then it was more Utopian than anything EGW dreamed up. And if EGW could be accused of bending the knee to aristocracy a little more often than was necessary, then Grey could be accused of being instinctively 'autocratic by temperament'.[24] He was in no hurry to grant a democracy in New Zealand that was beyond the control of his grace and favour. Throughout 1853, his despatches to London disguised the fact that the constitution was not being implemented with the intent or the speed that the Colonial Office expected.[25]

Grey had other good reasons for treating EGW with asperity: the imperial government had landed the company debt around his ears and EGW could be accused of at least partially creating it; and he saw EGW as one of those responsible for making the Legislative Council nominative and the provincial councils fully elective. The constitution was both less and more democratic in the ways that EGW wanted, giving more power to the provinces. Given all this, Grey and EGW could only be rivals for the implementation of the new constitution.

Replying to Grey's letter the next day, EGW effectively declared war: 'The differences between yourself and the colonists to which I alluded were so many that I will not attempt to describe them'. But he did remind Grey of his 'attack on the Canterbury settlement and the ill-will towards you which it notoriously produced . . . of the numerous refusals by most respectable settlers of the offers which you made to them of seats in the [General Legislative] Council and lastly of the petitions for your recall'. He had not met anybody 'who questions your unpopularity or that your position with a free constitution coming to work is highly dangerous'. Admitting that it was well known he had opposed Grey's style of government for years he said that Grey had then apologised to him 'for noticing the assistance which I have given to the Colonial opposition. This is so odd that I really cannot make out satisfactorily what you intend me to understand.'

Grey's offer of help with the constitution was 'wholly conditional on my obtaining satisfactory assurances that you were anxious to really and fully give effect' to the new act. But now he had discovered that Grey's proclamation on waste lands, making them freely available at a low price, ran contrary to the act, which was to place the disposal of such lands in the hands of the people through their new forms of government. Grey had been smart enough to proclaim the land sales regulations before proclaiming self-government. 'It seems to me,' wrote EGW, 'that you tear off and trample upon a great piece of the Constitutional Act in its integrity.'[26] Grey did not respond to EGW's second letter and left for the Wairarapa. EGW now determined, with Sewell's help, to challenge the land proclamation in the courts; brother Dan, whom he had not seen for ten years, was attorney-general for New Munster and could make himself useful.

Sewell, who had gone ashore on the 8th, had also been incensed at Grey's land proclamation. He had a noncommittal audience with the governor, whose 'manner at first was like that of a Cat pawing hot chestnuts'[27] and who 'alluded to Godley now and then with evident dislike'. Sewell met Dan Wakefield and next day visited his house, a 'pretty looking cottage pervious to rain, as all sorts of things seemed to be in requisition in the entrance passage to catch the descending streams'. Sewell's descriptions touched nicely on the architectural facade that was Wellington: Dan's house was 'one of those nice looking and somewhat deceptive Tenements which one admired from the Ship. Being on shore is like going behind the scenes at a Theatre.' Dan showed Sewell various acts and incomplete government papers: 'indeed his legal apparatus of books seemed deficient almost to the degree of "nil"'. On the 11th Sewell attended a trial and 'Mr Attorney General Wakefield was there in proper costume of wig and gown' overseeing proceedings that were 'altogether decorous and a very fair copy of our English Courts'.

Later in the day, an address was brought to Sewell welcoming EGW to Wellington. It had been prepared for public signature by Isaac Featherston, William's old duelling opponent and now leader of the Constitutionalist party. It recognised EGW as 'the Founder of this Colony . . . but, above all, appreciating most warmly your strenuous and untiring exertions towards the procuring for us the Constitutional Act'.[28] Sewell thought this well merited: 'Whatever differences there may be on theoretical points it is clear that all the good which people are enjoying is mainly owing to him. As to that it is impossible to deny that on the whole people are doing remarkably well, and are far more prosperous than they could have hoped to be in England. Is this no cause for gratitude?' What Sewell did not record is that this address for a potential political rival was prepared with no enthusiasm by Featherston and that 'the thing was done with as bad a grace as possible'.[29]

EGW finally went ashore on 12 March. He had dismissed his two servants for drunkenness and insolence and temporarily employed Sewell's man Henwood. But he was to find a new and loyal manservant in Wilhelm Schmidt, a Holstein sailor who had broken his leg in a fall from the mast of the *Minerva* and who was befriended by EGW as he was recovering in Wellington's hospital. 'Preceded by carts of luggage' and accompanied by Henwood, Captain Henslow, his little nephew Charles Marcus (Dan's son) and his dogs, EGW climbed the hill above the shoreline of Lambton Quay to take up residence in a cottage on the Tinakori Road. He was soon reunited with son Jerningham and with Dan, who was apprehensive and anxious in the presence of his elder brother's authoritative personality and intellect; impotent before this keeper of his worst secrets. EGW found his wife Angela a 'charming woman' but 'Dan is oldish in his ways; far more so than either of us; & lives only to vegetate'.[30] He would soon be uprooted.

The next day was Sunday and EGW probably walked down for a social worship at St Paul's Church with Dan's family where he would have been warmly reunited with John and Liocadia (di Oliveira) Taine and the children for whom he had provided a cradle a dozen years before. Liocadia and Angela were now close friends. After the service they may have walked the short distance to pause at William's grave in the Bolton Street cemetery. Among family, close friends and the company immigrants who had found good fortune, EGW had a small crowd of well-wishers about him, encouraging him in his political ambitions.

Within a week of stepping ashore EGW, with Sewell, opened the attack on Grey's land regulations. They sent open letters to their allies in Canterbury that were published in most newspapers. On 22 March, Sewell applied for an injunction in the Supreme Court to restrain the local commissioner of Crown lands from selling land under the new regulations. The commissioner was Francis Dillon Bell whom EGW was soon to denounce as corrupted beyond hope by Grey. He told Rintoul, 'You will remember what a nice clever well-conducted young fellow [he] was . . . he is now a brazen faced trickster in jobbery and corruption; and perfectly irreclaimable.' Nearly all of Grey's officials were tarred by the same brush: Alfred Domett, according to EGW, was 'so degraded in private life as to be wholly excluded from association with decent families'.[31] Such dire faults may well have been overlooked if they had pledged some kind of allegiance to EGW.

Sewell wrote to Gladstone and, later, the new Secretary for War and Colonies, the Duke of Newcastle, and EGW wrote to Lyttelton, railing against Grey, and telling him that 'I am going to throw myself on the people by means of an address which shall tell the whole truth about the land question, and shall necessitate a deliberate choice between Swanriverism and what I have always designed for New Zealand.' He added, 'If you send us out a good Governor, Sewell may be Attorney General if he should please!! He is all you could wish; as acute as ever, constant in labour, and wonderfully bold. Canterbury would have been a perfect smash if he had not come out. We are capital friends, and not in the least downhearted. . . .'[32]

In April, EGW wrote to Catherine, 'You will see what a turmoil our politics are in. Though up to my ears in it, I feel none the worse for the excitement . . . .[33] The other day, I attended a public meeting, and spoke, without any preparation an hour and a half – actually spouted – as I have not done since 1843 in the Canadian House of Assembly.' To Catherine, he admitted his principal goal:

'There is an immense task for me to get through; in consequence of the rotten state of public matters . . . . But all looks well for the future, so far as the future may be affected by my attaining an influence in the country greater than that of anybody else.' By this he did not necessarily mean high political office; he had long grown to accept the realities of his reputation and to understand that there was more real power – and little responsibility – in being the power behind the throne. He considered that his influence was increasing already, 'by means of straightforwardness, boldness & assiduity'.

And now he had a trusty extra hand: 'I work like a horse, much aided by Jerningham who is a faithful and diligent Lieutenant. If, as seems probable, he should be able to conquer some colonial habits, he will be a leading person in this country.' He expected him to be a Canterbury member of the General Assembly, although this was far from being established. Jerningham's 'colonial habits' he told Catherine, were 'nothing bad, in the really bad sense; only habits of desultory application . . . with respect to thought, as well as somewhat of a turn for wrangling. But he is improving daily . . . . he is very amiable and is now living entirely with me.'[34] EGW naturally put a gloss on Jerningham's behaviour for Catherine's sake and it is possible that Jerningham disguised, for EGW's benefit, his growing penchant for hard liquor as well as continuing sexual liaisons which suggested a life at least as degraded as the one EGW ascribed to Domett.

The Constitutionalist camp, led by Featherston, could only relish EGW's savage attacks on their old enemy Grey, but they had no wish to support his bid for retaining high sufficient prices on land under the Wakefield theory. Nor had many of the settlers any illusions about the moral tone of the Wakefield clan. EGW might hope to bluff his way past the abduction, claiming a sentence long served out, and expect that no one in Wellington knew more than a hint of the earlier Pattle will case, but he would sooner or later have to face his accusers over the bad practices of the New Zealand Company and a legacy of antagonism resulting from past antipathies to William. His case would not be assisted by the sniggering esteem in which Jerningham was held and a general contempt for Dan's cowardice and limited competence. Any admiration and respect for EGW's work and ideas were countered by distrust of his motives and methods and, among politicians, fear of what havoc his intellectual brilliance and political experience might wreak if directed to dubious ends. Few were capable of matching him in debate and propaganda. Despite the quality of many settlement leaders, such as Stafford, this was scarcely surprising in a country where the entire male franchise did not number 10,000.

EGW's legal challenge to Grey's proclamation was merely the first salvo in a long campaign that he saw culminating in power at both provincial and national levels, with Jerningham becoming his cipher in the General Assembly. Meanwhile Jerningham was able to make his own inimitable contribution to the injunction debate with a piece of satire aimed at Grey:

Whereas I, the Governor, still have the right
    To make laws, and give orders for every known thing,
And Acts are mere cobwebs while mine is the might!
    Now this is the will of your Deputy-King! . . . .
I myself wear chain-mail, as a sign of my reign,
    The bold leader and chief of this glittering band;
And the King of six Provinces still shall obtain
    His throne from dear rule, and his crowns from cheap land.[35]

On 30 March, Justice Stephen granted EGW's and Sewell's injunction, surprising the settlement, and also placing Dan, as Attorney-General of New Munster, under intense scrutiny and pressure. As a Grey-appointed official, he had not opposed the introduction of the land regulations, and had indeed been convinced of the proclamation's legality. But now EGW persuaded him to advise the New Munster Executive Council against an attempt to dissolve the injunction, and to suggest that the case be referred to Chief Justice Martin in Auckland. EGW's hand can also be seen in Justice Stephen's opinion that the Constitution Act should be put into immediate effect and the whole question of land policy left to the new General Assembly. Dan followed up with a memorandum to Grey saying that, because there could be delays in achieving an acceptable nominated Legislative Council, and thus a full General Assembly, the governor should show evidence of good faith by immediately including popular representatives in the Executive Council. This would mean the resignation of its current members and EGW set about lobbying those councillors he had known in England, asking them to resign without official prompting. One wonders if EGW would have achieved even half of this had H. S. Chapman been presiding judge, but he had left for Tasmania the year before to become its colonial secretary.

Although the Executive Council became split, it held firm under Wakefield pressure and Dan resigned, protesting against any further proceedings under Grey's proclamation and claiming that the General Assembly should be called. Contrarily, at the last meeting of the council he attended on 8 April, Dan advised that the best way for them to state the government case was to oppose the injunction. A month later, Grey compounded the absurdity of Dan's contortions by informing him that, 'as your appointment as Attorney-General of New Munster expired some time since with the existence of that Province, it is unnecessary for me formally to accept your resignation of an office which has ceased to exist'.[36]

As Francis Dillon Bell was to comment later, Dan had again 'made an ass of himself' by resigning and by allowing himself to be manipulated by EGW into departing from the requirements of his official position. When Grey took control of the injunction affair, he peremptorily told officials the proclamation was valid and to act on its provisions, provoking Sewell's cry of 'Tyranny!' The injunction was also attacked on technical irregularities and Justice Stephen was eventually forced to concede that Dan should have been a party to the suit in the first place. Although the case staggered on until late May, EGW let it drop under the law of diminishing returns. He had caused Grey some damage by advertising his unprincipled proclamation but realised that he could not win the case.

The injunction had also been a useful issue when, on 10 April, news arrived that the Duke of Newcastle, a friend of the colonial reformers, had become colonial secretary; EGW started a letter campaign to stir allies in London to work for Grey's recall on the platform of the land proclamation. The culmination was a sustained attack on Grey in Parliament in May and June of 1854 which the government was able to eventually sidestep, largely because Newcastle needed to use Grey's talents in South Africa, and also because the country was too distracted by the outbreak of the Crimean War to care. In July, Godley expressed publicly, in the *Morning Chronicle*, Newcastle's private belief that Grey should not have second-guessed a General Assembly's policy on land, nor have treated a Supreme Court injunction with such contempt. But this made no difference to what was happening in New Zealand, and the stain on the reputation of Grey, the career governor, was slight.

EGW-directed efforts to have Grey recalled proved to be a complete waste of paper, ink and postage; in July 1852 Grey had applied for an eighteen-month leave of absence and he received confirmation of a year's break – and thus the end of his New Zealand governorship – at the end of May. First news of this may have also influenced EGW's decision to lose interest in the injunction case. In any case, throughout EGW's struggle with Grey in 1853, the governor almost invariably outwitted EGW politically: he had been too long in the colony, knew its people and methods too well and had much greater resources at his disposal.

Grey had been granted leave on the condition that he did not 'avail himself of it till the Act conferring the New Constitution has been brought into full operation'.[37] Grey had begun to implement the constitution but, 'incorrigibly self-willed', he would make it conform 'as closely as possible to his original conception of what it ought to be, namely a provincial system of government operating under the authoritative supervision of the Governor, supplemented by a general legislature meeting infrequently as required'.[38] After his constitutional declaration at the beginning of March, Grey had begun the legal processes necessary for the August elections of the provincial councils and superintendents and General Assembly members. But it became apparent that he had no intention of calling a meeting of the national parliament during his term of office. He would remain king until the end.

As Grey's intentions became clear, and EGW realised he would not be able to fight him from a parliamentary platform, his expressions of loathing exceeded any he had earlier reserved for Lord Stanley or Earl Grey. A taste of his acid pen in the course of another 'monster' letter to Rintoul in June will serve as illustration. It was in Grey's character 'to have an ardent and most jealous love of the use of power, if not for its own sake . . . then for the sake of his own ambition, which prompts him to work all his power in this country in such a way as to represent himself at home as a man capable of being himself a government both legislative and executive'. He was like Sydenham but with 'more concentrated selfishness of ambition, and far less ability . . . Yet as a managing intriguer, a simulator, and a deceiver, he has rare talents, comprising assiduous industry, great circumspection, perfect command of temper, a keen appreciation of individual character, and a thorough contempt for mankind. I have never known a man so devoid of generous sentiments . . . As a corrupter of honest men he has no rival . . . . he is most skilful at the business of corrupting the public mind, and moulding it to serve his own ends.'[39] This letter brings to mind EGW's 1851 letter to Godley describing Felix's character as the pot-and-kettle reflection of his own. And EGW's hatred of Grey was provoked by the frustrating truth that the governor, and not he, was in the position to be the 'government both legislative and executive' of New Zealand, with the power to conduct a 'sustained campaign' which had been 'patient and restrained at first' but had now become 'urgent and imperative . . . to substitute his own more radical designs for those of Wakefield and the Company. . .'.[40] There could be no truce.

EGW's injunction case had proved a diversion, a political ploy, and was regarded as such in the Wellington community. Although the sufficient price now survived only within the Canterbury and Otago blocks, EGW did not cease to point out the adverse consequences of Grey's cheap land policies elsewhere as he moved to secure a new power base for his election to both the Wellington Provincial Council and the House of Representatives. The sufficient price became the central plank to EGW's political campaign: 'Everybody will cry out against [the regulations] by-and-bye, when all will feel its hurtful effects, and none more than the working classes, whom it may delude for a time by holding out to them the bait of cheap land, though their class will be really unable to acquire land except by purchasing from the speculators at a high price'.[41] EGW's predictions were to prove right: the government's revenue base from the control of steady sales at a sufficiently high price was destroyed, the returns for Maori from sale of their land were greatly diminished and increasing speculation placed vast areas of land into the hands of rich pastoralists and speculators.

At first, however, even the working classes saw their salvation in Grey's cheap land and few concurred with EGW's views. As Sewell wrote in May, 'At Wellington, being with Wakefield we should be in a minority of two.'[42] Yet EGW's political future now lay in championing the cause of the small man on the land, 'the 'blue shirts', the 'unwashed' with whom he claimed to get along so well. Both the new land regulations, and the government compensation provided for those purchasers injured by the New Zealand Company's mismanagement, favoured the larger capitalists. The labourers who had come out under the company's schemes had received nothing but unemployment and hardship. But, in taking up the working man's cause, EGW had somehow to dissociate himself from the company's bad reputation, its expensive land policy, the 'compensation jobbery' and his failure to take action on behalf of labouring immigrants while he was a company director.

This was a tall order but, seeing no political power base among the Constitutionalists and landowners, he must appeal to the neglected smallholders, the men with their hands in the soil, just as he had appealed to their French Canadian counterparts in Beauharnois ten years before. Yet this was more than expediency: it was the only way he could find to prosecute his ideas under Grey's despotic political control. Grey might deny it, but EGW had always known democracy was inevitable, and he saw now that this was where New Zealand's future lay.

One of EGW's first moves was to detach himself from the odium of New Zealand Company jobbing and to declare himself in favour of compensation for the workers as well as the landowners. He had invested heavily in Wellington land under the company scheme and owned 22 town sections and 25 country sections (nine under compensation scrip), comprising 2500 acres. His English farm holdings and investment of his Canadian earnings had given him the resources for these purchases, allowed him to help underwrite the Canterbury Association and made him financially independent for the past six or seven years. Now he could focus all his energies on political campaigning.

On 5 April, Sewell recorded, 'I am setting in motion a plan to make use of Wakefield's Compensation Scrip to give land to the working classes upon fair arrangements, which will give him return for his money, and stifle all the clamour about working men not being able to get on the land.' Sewell's plan meant using EGW's nine compensation scrip country sections for purchase of a large block of land (about 675 acres) that would be developed into a community of smallholders with the village of Wakefield as its centre. But it did not work and EGW eventually sold his scrip to Wellington's biggest landowner. This scheme has been dismissed as 'simply another version (on a smaller scale) of the grateful and dependent New Zealand community pictured by Wakefield as a setting for his old age'.[43] It was also seen as a 'crib' of the Wairarapa Small Farms Association scheme, where Grey's regulations enabled settlers to buy one acre of village land and 40 acres of rural land for little more than £20 and created the lasting settlements of Greytown, Masterton, Featherston and Carterton between 1853 and 1857.

EGW now attempted to sell his other land holdings, to small cultivators only, on terms of 8 to 10 per cent over seven years. Only a little was sold this way but the offer gave him the basis to appeal politically to the working settlers of the Hutt Valley who, ironically, had been Grey loyalists. EGW campaigned brilliantly, notably at a lively Friday afternoon meeting in the Hutt's Aglionby Arms which lasted from one in the afternoon until eight in the evening. He first gave his audience a lecture on the principles of colonisation and declared that he had been misrepresented by the jealous and malicious as being, through advocating a high sufficient price, as the 'promoter of impediments to the acquisition of freehold land by the industrious classes' but he could feel pride at 'having done more than any other man has done or attempted, in the work of giving effect' to successful colonisation. He was no villain. The real villains were a government that had neither the money nor the capability to secure more land from the Maori, or provide money for the essential surveys, and the self-interested land-jobbers of Wellington who had divided among themselves most of the Crown land sold since the first sales of the Company. He depicted himself as the conscience of the company. Seven years before, he reminded his listeners, he had quarrelled with the company when they had continued to offer land for sale when it was highly probable they 'would not be able to fulfil their engagements'. At an earlier meeting, he had proclaimed his altruism and disinterestedness. The *Independent* reported that for EGW, the 'possession of a great private estate in New Zealand would afford him no gratification. The whole colony was the object of his attachment. He regarded it, if he might say so without boasting or presumption, as something in which he had a sort of property (cheers). The prosperity and greatness of New Zealand were dearer objects to him than the finest estate in the world (cheers).'[44]

EGW eloquently laid all the blame for the working man's landlessness and impecuniosity on a corrupt government controlled by an unscrupulous governor, on absentee landlords, speculators and monopoly by the wealthy. Working men should have compensation, too, he declared: 'they are justly entitled to redress'. A government commissioner should be appointed to award worthy workers 100 acres of land, cost free. He also declared it likely that grants of land already made for compensation scrip were unlawful and would be set aside. A Constitutionalist candidate at the meeting, William Fitzherbert, was outraged at the idea that he and other compensation beneficiaries would lose their land but EGW's 'blue shirt' audience,[45] each with a vision of their own free 100-acre block shouted, 'Turn him out!' When Fitzherbert tried to counter EGW's offer with the prospect of auction land available at a reserve of half a crown an acre, EGW's old compatriot company colleague, Dr George Evans, ridiculed him for turning the meeting into a Dutch auction. When Sewell heard of the meeting and EGW's proposals, he wrote, 'What an inimitable dodge! As Dr Evans said . . . it takes one's breath away.'[46]

'The hundred-acre grant-in-compensation was a brilliant electioneering device,' as Peter Stuart has noted. 'It skilfully combined an attractive material bait, an appeal to class solidarity and an attack on long-festering grievances. It beat the Governor at his own game and detached his supporters without driving them into the Constitutionalist camp.'[47] EGW now had the Hutt in his electoral pocket and had declared war on the Constitutionalists. By political sleight of hand he had also managed to keep the theory of the sufficient price alive in a modified form. But he still had to evade responsibility for company mismanagements and this would require more than political promises.

Less than a fortnight later, EGW was endorsed as a Hutt candidate for the forthcoming elections and ten days after that, on 20 June, the largest meeting ever held in the valley endorsed EGW's petition to the Governor asking for the workers land compensation scheme. A committee of four, led by EGW, was appointed to present the petition to Governor Grey and the only meeting between the two men took place in Wellington on 23 June.

Grey immediately attacked EGW for his role as a company director: if any compensation was due the labourers it should come from the company, not the colonial government. Why had EGW not brought this matter before the court of directors and why had he not taken action on behalf of the labourers before? EGW replied that he had been 'dead to the Company' following his stroke in 1846 and had not heard of the labourers' problems until he arrived in New Zealand. EGW reported to Rintoul that Grey's aim at the meeting was to 'evade the question submitted to him and to cast the blame of what the deputation complained of upon me individually as a Director of the Company. Four times he repeated the accusation, and four times I showed that it was utterly unfounded . . . . He kept his temper admirably in words and tone of voice, but became white as paper with rage at being foiled by a downrightness to which he is wholly unaccustomed'. EGW described the behaviour of Grey and his staff as intimidatory: the 'fear which he inspires is a great means of influence'. Given that New Zealand was divided into six very separate communities and that the 'Governor has on his side, time, money and command, you will only wonder as I do, how these people ever resisted him as they have done almost continually throughout his reign'.[48]

But Grey had exposed publicly EGW's admission that the company, of which he was a guiding force, had let the labouring migrants down and done nothing about it; that he was one of the compensation holders of whom he complained; and also that, far from being 'dead to the Company' after 1846, he had been well enough to attend some company meetings after that time. EGW was now more vulnerable to attack by his political enemies. Indiscreetly, he told Featherston that he had been in the House of Commons in 1845 when the situation of the labouring migrants in New Zealand had been revealed in an address; Featherston passed this on to his friends and political allies. At the beginning of July the gloves came off and Wellington's first election campaign turned into a nasty brawl, centred almost entirely on EGW's plans, theories and reputation.

The Constitutionalist party found it hard to attack EGW's compensation plan for fear of being accused of class greed so they decided to attack the man. On 1 July EGW reported to a Hutt meeting on the compensation committee's unsatisfactory meeting with Grey and recommended that the issue be taken forward to the new General Assembly or the Provincial Council if that became responsible for waste lands. In the meantime the committee should work to find election candidates who favoured compensation. Constitutionalist Captain Edward Daniell, one of the first Wellington settlers, thereupon attacked EGW, using Grey's arguments. EGW strenuously denied that he had known of workers' demands for compensation until he had attended meetings in the Hutt. He denied he had told Featherston about his attendance at the House of Commons in 1845. According to FitzGerald this filled Featherston with such fury that he determined to drive EGW out of the colony.[49] EGW felt a lie was justified in the face of Featherston's malicious gossip.

EGW also told the meeting he had not received 'one farthing from the New Zealand Company as either compensation or pay . . . . On the contrary, he had expended a very considerable fortune of his own . . . in order that New Zealand should be colonised . . . in publications, in journies, in help of various kinds to emigrants, sometimes in actual money, sometimes in outfits for emigrants who could not afford to buy them.' He had given his health, his strength and his fortune.[50] This was substantially true and though EGW made money from his land purchases, it can be viewed as reward for his time, energy and investment.

The Constitutionalists returned to the attack in force four days later in a Hutt candidates meeting.[51] Daniell moved the motion, 'That we feel the deepest regret for the sufferings of those individuals who have been betrayed by the false promises of the New Zealand Company and their Agents', and read an extract from a company report that showed EGW had been at a meeting when more than £5,000 in directors' fees had been distributed. The meeting broke into cheers when EGW loudly seconded the motion and challenged Daniell to wager that he had been a party to that transaction. After 1846, he said, he always left the directors' court when business other than Canterbury was being discussed. Fitzherbert then arrived at the meeting and similarly accused EGW of profiteering through the company and electoral bribery with his 100-acre compensation scheme. This was rich coming from someone who had received more than 2000 acres of company compensation land. EGW reminded Fitzherbert that he had also agreed compensation claims should be investigated; and said he would lay his £1,500 to Fitzherbert's £500 that he had never received money from the Company. Fitzherbert backed off in confusion and Daniell stalked out of the meeting, refusing to shake EGW's proffered hand. Soon afterwards, EGW wrote to Godley, 'You were right in saying people here would be very jealous of me. It is so with a vengeance. But that will wear out with time. Its very intensity will hasten its death.'[52]

Truth is the first casualty of such a war but the fact that EGW emerged largely unscathed from these exchanges can be put down to more than 'incautious statements' by the Constitutionalists and 'fast talking' by EGW.[53] There was the ring of sincerity and the evidence to support EGW's claim of relative disinterest in any pecuniary advantage from the company. Also, he had been largely absent from its management: he had been deeply involved in Canadian affairs from early 1841 to the beginning of 1844; frequently ill from September 1844 and largely incapacitated after his major stroke in August 1846 and until he resigned from the company at the beginning of 1849. Except at the beginning, he had rarely been involved in the detail of the company: his energy had gone into the politics of the thing, leading the charge against the Colonial Office, attending to the philosophical framework of the enterprise, struggling against the propensity of the City men to turn the company into a purely commercial operation. He had been, unashamedly, its greatest publicist, overselling in the best propagandist tradition, but had he not wanted to make it succeed, persuade others to share the dream? Grey was right, however, in one major respect: if EGW blamed the company for the workers' ills, why did he not, even now, put the onus on the company, whose massive debt was being borne by the colony? But the Company no longer existed and, in the politics of the moment, the free 100-acre block was a hammer against Grey and the Constitutionalists.

Despite his success with the Hutt electors, EGW felt isolated and powerless against Grey's aloof autocracy. It was quite clear that Grey would not call together the first General Assembly before his departure at the end of the year. And was Grey just taking leave or would a new governor be appointed? Would he be the 'just Governor' that EGW had exhorted of everyone in England?

In the middle of July he imparted his secret anxieties to Henrietta Rintoul: 'I assure you that, feeling myself utterly helpless here; that all power for good to New Zealand resides in London; I pass hours every day, and some every night, in imagining all sort of things as happening there; and in these scenes your father's broad and indignant forehead often figures, not seldom expressing his disappointment and frustration similar to my own. In short, I vegetate here, but live in London still; and not a day passes but I go with somebody, generally your father, to the Duke of Newcastle or Gladstone, to talk about New Zealand and Governor Grey. . . .'[54]

Earlier, he had written to her saying how much he wished her father would 'cut the Spectator, and you would all come here. I am sure there is nothing on earth that would be [more] agreeable to me. But agreeable is not the right word; but I leave it for fear you should laugh at me; or rather for fear the critic-censor should; for the softness of the amorous heart would not think the biggest word an exaggeration. The recollection of the evidence of yours when we parted, often unmans me; but I do not tell that to any who will laugh at it.'[55]

Without close understanding friends, distant from an unrequited – perhaps unanswered – love, EGW must have come close to abandoning New Zealand when, after he had been elected in the Hutt for the Provincial Council (and soon after, the General Assembly), Captain Daniell presented a petition against his return on the grounds of his being a convicted felon. EGW wrote to Sewell about it, 'evidently in soreness and pain'. Yet he should have been prepared for this; he had known very well what would happen if he entered the fray of New Zealand politics. Five years before, in *The Art of Colonization*, he had written: 'It is a general custom in the colonies, when your antagonist withstands abuse, to hurt him seriously if you can, and even to do him a mortal injury. . . . In every walk of colonial life, everybody strikes at his opponent's heart . . . . they will attack each other's credit at the bank, rake up ugly old stories about each other, get two newspapers to be the instruments of their bitter animosity, perhaps ruin each other in a desperate litigation. . . . Colonists at variance resemble the Kilkenny cats.'[56]

Sewell, who believed his friend would return to England, considered it was a 'Distressing position for [EGW], but he cannot help it. There it is sticking to him. The attack is mere malice, for the effect of the conviction has been purged by punishment. Morally and socially he has to appeal to valuable public Services for years past on behalf of the Colonies, especially New Zealand as virtual absolution. It has been accepted as such by people at home. For the people here to set up that old scandal is monstrous; for in truth New Zealand itself is a creation of Wakefield's. The spirit of the Wellington people is narrow, factious and virulent . . . .'[57]

Despite his 'criminal' reputation, the doubt surrounding some of his company activities, his often unscrupulous politicking and the bait of the 100-acre block, EGW had been elected by people who recognised what Sewell described as 'public Services' and his 'creation'. If he could be saddled with some responsibility for the iniquities of the company's activities, he could also claim the greater share of its triumph: several colonies of settlers who were mostly considerably better off than if they had stayed in England.

He did not go back, he could not go back. He was 'dead to the past', as he wrote to Henrietta. But would he be born again in New Zealand?

CHAPTER TWENTY-NINE

'That Old Giant Spider'

WHEN FITZGERALD HEARD OF EGW'S successes in the Wellington election campaign, he told Godley of 'that Old Giant Spider . . . weaving his spells in the Hutt Valley. . .'.[1] But at first EGW seemed at a loss to know what to do with his new powers as the senior member of the new Wellington Provincial Council and the elected, but still notional, House of Representatives. After his meeting with Governor Grey in June, EGW had written to Edward Stafford, saying, '. . . my most ardent wish is to avoid all public responsibilities in this country. Only I cannot sit still & see Grey ruin all without trying to circumvent him.'[2] After the elections, this chief motive for seeking political office continued to be frustrated, for if Grey did not call the General Assembly before he left – and he was really to be gone only on a year's leave of absence – then EGW was effectively neutered. At the end of August he told Rintoul that constitutions were no good unless governors effected them 'in strict good faith . . . though elected a member both of the Provincial Council . . . and of the General Assembly, I feel that it is wholly out of my power to do any real good for the country. In fact, the constitution as mutilated and violated by Grey, has no substantial existence.'[3]

When Stafford, now Superintendent of Nelson, visited Wellington at the end of August, EGW worked hard to bring him into his political camp. Stafford was certainly in favour of pushing Grey for a General Assembly but he was too circumspect to be seen taking sides with EGW, despite his family connection. In June 1853, EGW had told Stafford that his Emily 'shall have a Talbot blood-hound; a young dog, the handsomest I ever saw, & of drawing-room manners'.[4] There is no record of what Emily thought of her uncle's gift; perhaps because of Stafford's need for political distance, she never crossed the strait to see him, despite the care he had taken of her in England, and he visited Nelson only once, and then briefly.

In another letter at the end of August,[5] EGW wrote of the constitutional mess caused by Grey but said that the members of the provincial councils (except

Auckland) were largely anti-Greyites, as well as all the southern superintendents: Charles Brown in New Plymouth, Featherston in Wellington, Stafford in Nelson, FitzGerald in Canterbury and William Cargill in Otago. Only the last was pro-Wakefield though all subscribed to his campaign for representative self-government. EGW wrote despairingly about the quality of the members elected for the House of Representatives. In Wellington 'the best men did not come forward . . . the refuse of the first [provincial] elections were deemed good enough for the second'. All eight Wellington members had been elected 'without a contest . . . . It was plain to a few close observers that the cause of this indifference was a common belief either that the General Assembly would not meet at all, or that, meeting at Auckland, it would be a mere instrument of the Governor.' In his familiar complaint about there now being six separate democratic governments overseen by a despot, he failed to accept that provincial self-government was what the settlers most wanted, with as much power and money as possible accrued to them. Of course, he gave Grey no credit for recognising this or for his desire to see the constitution built from the bottom up and not from the top down. And what was the point in attempting to call a General Assembly in Auckland before he left the country in the new year? In the spring of 1853, EGW continued to lament that he was 'utterly at a loss' to know what to do to make the constitution work. 'Many apply to me for counsel, and I know not what to say.' But EGW was never at a loss for words for long.

When Featherston formally opened the first Wellington Provincial Council on 25 October and then ceremoniously withdrew to allow it to begin its proceedings, he left the stage vacant for a bravura performance that EGW could not resist. Claiming his role as the pioneer of colonial self-government, and taking his seat as the elder of the eighteen-man council in age, intellect and knowledge of parliamentary procedure, EGW set about making the new council a model of responsible government. It has been said that EGW, having used the 100-acre compensation 'dodge' as a 'tool' to gain his double election, now allowed the land question to slide and picked up the mantle of constitutional expert in order to 'consolidate his claim to be regarded as the "founding father" of New Zealand'.[6] And that all his 'political somersaults were in one direction – towards power for himself'.[7] Such views ascribe all EGW's motives and actions to his desire for social rehabilitation and status. Yet there were few in the council who were not at least partially motivated by vanity and thoughts of posterity – and these motives alone were too shallow to have sustained EGW's efforts to create parliamentary democracy over the following twelve months.

First EGW sought the establishment of a sound legal basis for electing an executive responsible to the council. Although aimed at reducing Featherston's power as a potentially dictatorial superintendent, such a move also shifted the real power, democratically, to the floor of the council chamber and the electors' representatives. Fitzherbert as nominee provincial secretary, and leader of Featherston's party, and Alfred de Bathe Brandon as nominee provincial solicitor, managed to make asses of themselves in the face of EGW's deep knowledge of constitutional law and protocol. Sewell, who was in Wellington during the first sessions of the council, described Fitzherbert as a 'man of ability and reading but <of bad temper, very bad judgment, and exceedingly> disliked. <Brandon the lawyer of the party is a mere nobody>.'[8] Against the wishes of Fitzherbert's and Featherston's Constitutionalists, EGW's insistence that the law providing for the election of an executive must be passed before any other business could be dealt with, led to a month-long adjournment of the council for such an election to take place.

During all this, Sewell considered that, 'Wakefield has behaved admirably . . . with an excellent spirit towards Featherston, with an earnest and sincere desire to allay party hostility . . . but Featherston rejects it all. Jealousy and dislike of Wakefield are an insuperable bar and Featherston's implacable and inflexible temper renders it quite hopeless to attempt to bring matters right.'[9] Against such hostility, and in leading the disparate elements of the opposition, EGW needed considerable energy and a degree of self-belief that was now beginning to harden into a bull-headed determination to have his way. In the first session of the council EGW's political reputation was enhanced and the incompetence of Fitzherbert and Brandon demonstrated to the point where a sarcastic correspondent to the *Spectator* suggested they pay over part of their salaries to EGW in recognition of his services as the 'only executive officer in the Council'.[10] EGW wrote to Stafford that Sam Revans (now a Wairarapa runholder), a declared Wakefield foe and in the Constitutionalist camp, 'told Featherston that Fitzherbert's mismanagement has caused all the mischief'. FitzGerald moaned to Godley that EGW 'will smash Featherstons Govt. to pieces and then he will be Suptdt. of Wellington'.[11]

EGW had no such ambition. When the council resumed at the beginning of December, he continued to devote most of his attention to constitutional matters relating to both provincial and central government and the appointment and responsibilities of officials, seeking to set up a system of checks and balances and to assert the overriding authority of a central government. In this context, he used revenue appropriation as another stick with which to beat Grey. The old Appropriation Act governing the country's finances had expired at the end of September and Grey subsequently awarded revenues to the new provincial councils unilaterally, without consultation and without calling the General Assembly that held the appropriation authority under the new constitution. But EGW could not overcome the Constitutionalists' desire for as much provincial money and power as they could garner, regardless of the legalities. EGW's real fear was that the country would split into warring enclaves: Grey's inaction, an Auckland petition for separation and Wellington's parochial greed appeared to threaten the formation of a central national government.

EGW was not entirely preoccupied with constitutional matters. The Constitutionalists' carelessness with the law meant that he chipped in whenever he detected shortcomings in proposed legislation and continued to score political points off the executive. When he pointed out a flaw in the Contractors Bill, Brandon acknowledged this but complained that it was, after all, 'only a little illegality'. EGW brought the house down when he replied that the provincial solicitor reminded him of the 'unfortunate girl who had a child she ought not to have had, and excused herself by saying that it was a very little one'.[12]

EGW also demonstrated much interest in improving relations with Maori, so that more land could be bought under the continuing management of Chief Land Purchase Officer, Donald McLean. He praised Featherston's efforts to bring the races together with such measures as his new year dinner to which both Maori and Pakeha leaders were invited. He worked for Maori to have the right to present petitions in their own language, an intelligent gesture of support for racial equality. But though EGW accurately criticised Grey's Maori policy of military strength, personal influence and a little bribery as being unsustainable and likely to lead to war, his own well-meaning belief in the assimilation of Maori into the Pakeha economic and social system was paternalistic and showed no understanding of its likely effect on Maori social structures and culture.

The first session of the Wellington Provincial Council was prorogued on 17 February 1854 and from it EGW had emerged as the 'most able man in Wellington'. The Wellington *Spectator*, once his fiercest critic, commented that, 'The establishment of Responsible Government in the General Government of the Colony is mainly owing to the course pursued by the independent members of the Provincial Council of Wellington. Through their exertions and those of Mr. Wakefield, it was forced on the Provincial Government, who adopted it, it must be confessed with considerable reluctance. Its admission by the General Government will as a matter of course cause the principle to be acted upon in all the Provinces of New Zealand.'[13] Until his departure, Grey had contemptuously avoided the tendentious and fraught task of calling the first General Assembly, and left this to Lieutenant-Colonel Robert Wynyard, senior military officer in the colony and superintendent of Auckland Province, who took office as acting governor on 3 January 1854. Within a month, he responded to the demands of EGW and most of the country's other political leaders by calling for the General Assembly at the end of May. EGW's speeches and letters on the subject had failed to move Grey but had helped build up a level of demand that his successor could not deny.

At the end of February, EGW's idea of a 'Founders' Festival' was held at Petone. Maori constructed a whare on the foreshore 240 feet long by 30 feet wide, thatched with raupo and partly floored for dancing. Two dinner tables provided seating space for 300 people, including 60 Maori, attired in European dress and with the venerable Te Puni at their head. All the Wakefields were there: EGW, Jerningham, Dan and Angela. The occasion was a triumph for EGW as Francis Dillon Bell proposed the premier toast, 'to the original founders of the Colony and Mr. Edward Gibbon Wakefield'. In reply, EGW first waxed jingoistic, declaring a 'feeling of satisfaction and pride at belonging to the race and nation which have conquered a third of the earth, and seem destined to possess the whole of it'. He recounted an anecdote from his time in Canada with Durham when, at a dinner for visiting Americans, Joseph Gurney had protested to them about the United States' annexation of Texas. They were, Gurney said, just like the English who 'never missed an opportunity of appropriating any part of the world which they could manage to grasp for themselves'. Where would it all end? '"Probably, Mr Gurney," Lord Durham replied. "It will end somewhere about Cape Horn."'[14]

EGW also recalled how Sir Robert Peel had been the first to suggest that New Zealand would become the 'Britain of the South'. And told his (at least half) adoring audience that New Zealand had become the 'favourite' colony in England because it had featured so much in political debate and because the 'press of England had produced a greater number of separate publications about New Zealand than about any other colony' and probably about as many for 'all the other colonies put together. I counted them two or three years ago, when they amounted, I think, to about 180.' He neglected to observe how many of those he had written, edited or sponsored himself.

After a puff for the new constitution, EGW sat down to prolonged cheering and Jerningham rose and spoke entirely about the Maori, their welcome, their generosity and their assistance when the first settlers arrived. His toast was 'To the natives who received them as brothers'. Te Puni spoke briefly in reply; there was a sombre toast to the departed William, and before long the tables were drawn back and the floor prepared for dancing to the band of the 65th regiment. The settlers, their wives, daughters and even some Maori women joined in the polkas and quadrilles, and they danced their way through until dawn at five the following morning.[15]

The Founders' Festival confirmed that, although Featherston was superintendent, EGW had become his political equal in the settlement. Both his allies and opponents looked forward with some apprehension to his performance on a national stage. Dramatically, FitzGerald wrote to Godley, 'Wakefield stands alone, looking portentous like an ill-omened meteor amidst the Wellington politicians. He is the only man who sees his way clearly amidst the shoals and quicksands into which Sir George Grey has plunged the colony.'[16]

In the hiatus between the end of the first session of the provincial council and the beginning of the first session of the General Assembly, Felix reappeared. Having failed to make any headway with his disputes in England, he had taken ship again for New Zealand in the new year of 1854, presumably eager to see his land and his children again and to continue prosecuting his various arguments with the Canterbury settlers. When he arrived at Nelson in the *Eagle* on 7 May he brought two new and very influential migrants: a pair of red deer.

Felix had long taken an interest in natural history. He had been a member of the Linnean Society since 1827, and in 1845 had donated his copies of its transactions to the Mechanics Institute in Launceston. Now he had become an acclimatisation enthusiast, anxious to enliven the New Zealand landscape with new animals that would help assure the settlers they really did live in a home away from Home. His son Edward, 70 years later, waxed eloquent over these red deer, the first to be introduced to the country's unsuspecting forests, saying that they had since 'grown into perhaps the most splendid herds in the world. These deer, which came from Richmond Park as a gift from Lord John Russell, the Ranger, to my father, were kept in the Stafford racing stables until they had recovered from the effects of the voyage, and were then driven into the hills by a party of horsemen.'[17] The progeny of those deer went on to destroy many of New Zealand's forests.

A few days before Felix reached Nelson, EGW had arrived on the government brig *Victoria*, on his way to Auckland. There is no record of whether the two brothers met for what would have been the last time, but it seems possible, given that, as Edward Wakefield recorded, a 'family council' took place to determine that Felix would revisit Canterbury and 'send my sister, Josephine, to stay with the Staffords, and then, after settling my other sisters under the care of my uncles, Edward Gibbon and Daniel, and my aunt, Angela, at Wellington, should again sail for England with my brother Oliver and myself'.[18] That left Murat, presumably still at sea; Ariosto, presumably still in England; and Salvator, who may now have gone to join his mother in South Australia. It seems unlikely, in the event, that Constance went to Nelson since she had established a school in Lyttelton with her friend Miss Laws.

Felix arrived in Canterbury again to a hostile reception. The *Lyttelton Times* reported: 'This town has been astonished by the arrival of Mr Felix Wakefield. It is strange that such an advent has not been properly appreciated by our fellow colonists. On going into an auction store on Thursday last, Mr Wakefield was received with loud hootings, upon which he thought it prudent to retire. Several gentlemen it is said, have declined the honour of his acquaintance. It is rumoured that he intends to seek a more congenial atmosphere.'[19] The arrival, the previous December, of Felix's pamphlet *Mutual Relations*, attacking the conditions and management of Canterbury, had provoked heated public meetings. On 16 January, members of the Christchurch Colonists Society had given it short shrift: 'Mr Bishop said we should disabuse our friends at home of the injurious statements in the pamphlet . . . . Mr Ollivier felt there needed to be an emphatic denial . . . . Mr Wilson said that . . . it might be nothing more than an ex parte statement got up by the only two names that appeared on it viz Dr Savage and Mr Felix Wakefield.'[20]

Felix tried to humour the hostile by writing a letter to the provincial secretary, published in the *Lyttelton Times*, in which he offered to pay £100 towards preparing plans for improving navigation across the Sumner bar into the Avon-

Heathcote estuary and so to Christchurch. He admitted his own interest in the scheme, 'as my children have 100 acres of land at Sumner . . . . But I am also one of a large community who are not blind to our present dilemma' and he could see what was 'likely to happen by the lamentable want of unanimity and action in striving to get out of our difficulties'. But, being 'too much of an Englishman to sit down crying in the rut and call on Hercules to help me', he believed '[W]e should forgive and forget our injuries, whether of omission or commission, in short we should let bygones be bygones and set to work energetically to make a beginning: by only aiming at a little first, we may effect a great deal at last'.[21] Settlers who had been working hard to build the settlement for more than three years can only have been riled by this blandishing lecture and found Felix's humble pie altogether too lumpy to swallow.

The provincial secretary was happy enough to take up Felix's offer of a plan if it did not cost the council any cash. But the Sumner bar and steam navigation up the Avon were the subject of all kinds of surveys and opinion and, at this time, Felix's plans were ignored. His name appeared in the *Lyttelton Times* again in August, when the newspaper reported he had lost a case where he had tried to eject the occupier of a building to which he 'had no right or title'. But it was disclosed that the occupier had indeed leased it from a Mr Wakefield – Jerningham. After this little debacle, Felix collected up his remaining children and left an ungrateful Canterbury.

His youngest daughter Priscilla, now about thirteen, presumably went to Wellington to live with her Aunt Angela, but there is no record of her fate save that she 'died as a girl'.[22] Felix arrived in Nelson sometime in September with Oliver and Edward and they 'received a hearty welcome from the Staffords, with whom Josephine was now almost on the footing of a daughter'. After eight years of marriage, the Staffords remained childless. The Staffords lived in an imposing brick house on Waimea Road, 'in a plantation of very large blue gums and wattles, and there were fine stables, containing beautiful racehorses, and a pony' on which Stafford taught the boys to ride. They were also taken on picnics in the nearby bush to which members of 'upper class' families took 'their own particular contribution to the feast'. Passages to Victoria were hard to find in these gold rush days, but Felix and the boys finally found berths on a small brig and sailed away in November on a 'stormy and perilous voyage lasting thirty-five days'.[23] They waited another month in Melbourne before leaving for England in the new year.

EGW's prodigious letter-writing and speaking campaign reached a new pitch in the three months preceding the first General Assembly. He was aided by the fact that Jerningham, as his private secretary and personal representative, had also been elected a member of the House of Representatives (MHR) for Christchurch Country. The tedious work of copying and distributing EGW's letters and tracts was undertaken by his amanuensis, John Knowles. The substance of EGW's objectives for the first Parliament was clearly set out in the resolutions he drafted for a meeting of local MHRs held in Wellington on 6 March 1854. Chaired by William Fox, who had recently returned to New Zealand, the meeting unanimously passed the resolutions that had been earlier agreed to in EGW's private discussions. All MHRs should attend the first session in Auckland (a necessary admonishment, given the time and difficulties attached to travelling). They must press for responsible government in the form of ministers elected to the executive by and responsible to Parliament, for the assignation to each province of an appropriate proportion of the revenues each raised and for the transfer of control over waste lands – that is, lands for farming development – to the provincial governments. EGW did, however, wish this question to be left open to central government legislation because he 'trusted that the General Assembly would make rules to deprive the speculator of all advantage over the working settler'.[24] He even declared himself willing to support the prices included in Grey's legislation, saying that he had never denied that 10s and 5s might be a sufficient price 'under the present circumstances of the colony'. The theory had become malleable indeed under the exigencies of everyday colonial politics.

He was also anxious to head off any northern separatism and proposed that Auckland should bear no burden of the New Zealand Company's debt. A more obvious bait to secure the support of the northern members was his suggestion that Auckland settlers might be allowed to buy land direct from the Maori. And he stated that he was 'most anxiously desirous that the House of Representatives should not begin its intercourse with the Governor by anything like a declaration of war against him'.[25] The southern face of the new Parliament must show that the propaganda war had been against Grey, not against Wynyard and the officials. By this time, EGW had also become in favour of an elected Legislative Council, seeing the real dangers of a second House stacked with a Grey-like governor's nominated favourites. The 6 March meeting also urged MHRs from other provinces to support these resolutions. Jerningham answered already for the Canterbury members and EGW announced that he had received a letter from Otago pledging its support.

It was now important to present Wynyard and the administration with a united front on the issues of responsible self-government, waste lands and appropriation. EGW damped down a fight between Wellington's *Independent* and *Spectator* which proclaimed continuing factionalism and took every opportunity to bend the ear of anyone with likely influence at the forthcoming General Assembly. When the Otago MHRs arrived in Wellington in April, en route to Auckland, they found themselves exposed to weeks of persuasive Wakefield hospitality and exhortation until they were firmly in his camp. He did the same with Nelson members as the government brig *Victoria* continued on its way to Auckland. When he arrived in Auckland EGW urged New Plymouth men to join forces in self-interest with Otago and worked unceasingly to allay the suspicions and fears of Auckland members in the face of this mass arrival of members from the south.

It was an exciting moment: the first gathering of men from all over New Zealand concerned with finding a way to govern a nascent nation. 'Out of the chaos of clashing personalities, rival sectional interests and wavering political loyalties emerged an almost unanimous demand for responsible government. The strength of this demand was almost entirely due to the efforts of [EGW], whose management of the campaign was masterly.'[26] It also masked the fact that the new constitution did not actually provide for responsible ministerial government. EGW was pushing a dream that had been fermenting since his first days in Canada. New Zealand would be the model for his concept of a commonwealth of self-governing nations bonded by their loyalty to the Crown.

When Acting Governor Wynyard opened the first General Assembly on 27 May – in a hastily constructed, graceless building dubbed 'The Shedifice' – EGW was again the senior member of the gathering in terms of age, expertise and experience, though not in official status: FitzGerald, MHR for Lyttelton and the only provincial superintendent present, was top of the political pecking order. Henry Sewell described well the position of the two men during the opening days of the assembly.[27] 'The whole of the present state of affairs has been brought about by [EGW]. He regards Responsible Government as his own child and must pet and nurse it into being. Then however comes the question who is to be the Tutor and Manager of the young bantling. He, the natural Parent, feels his paramount title, and is . . . sore at his parental claim being superseded by men who are mere accidents. I see the painfulness of this position, but not how it is to be avoided.' This was the story of EGW's entire political life: the stigma of the abduction and his past unscrupulousness forever barred him from appointed leadership. In April, FitzGerald had written to Godley with a nice metaphor from the new steam age: EGW 'may be the screw under the stern but wont do for the figurehead'.

On the question of leadership, Sewell continued, '<FitzGerald, with nothing like the power has higher social claims, and is free from personal objection, which Wakefield is not.> So FitzGerald steps into the first place. Then comes into play all the dislike and distrust mutually felt between the two. FitzGerald will not work *under* Wakefield, and with difficulty *with* him. Wakefield distrusts and depreciates FitzGerald . . . . The truth is, the men here in general distrust Wakefield. He is too politic, too diplomatic, too secret, and too powerful. They have almost an ignorant superstitious terror of him.' The situation placed Sewell in a difficult position. EGW was not generally acceptable, although Sewell had a 'great personal regard for him . . . . I am persuaded of his patriotism, his wisdom in general affairs, and his great power; and if I must needs have a leader, let me have one whom I can respect.' And there was no one else within a country mile of him.[28] 'FitzGerald is very talented, very honest, a gentleman, an agreeable speaker, and by no means a contemptible debater; but his flightiness spoils him for leadership.' The apparently irresolvable enmity between EGW and FitzGerald, and their conflicting ambitions, would dictate the course of the first General Assembly.

Wynyard's opening address made no mention of responsible government; after all, he had no instructions on the matter from London. FitzGerald now held a 'snug meeting', which excluded EGW and the governor's supporters, and drafted a formal address-in-reply that was then presented to a larger meeting. At this, EGW prevailed upon the others to exclude any reference to responsible government and to agree that, though FitzGerald would move the address-in-reply, the opening address on responsible government, the 'question of questions', would be left to him.

EGW spoke for three hours on the nature of and reasons for responsible government. He had mulled over the difficulties of its introduction with an inexperienced House and an acting governor who would not sanction a radical interpretation of the constitution on his own authority. An executive of ministers fully responsible to the House was not possible iunitially, and there was also the problem of dealing with the existing executive appointees who would have to resign to make way for newcomers. '[S]peaking for myself alone,' said EGW, 'I shall be content with a small reality at present', meaning one or two MHRs included in the executive. His imprecise compromise was aimed at getting responsible government started while giving Wynyard time to consult with London. It also gave EGW plenty of room to influence the course of events, but left too much room for others to do the same. EGW had not been able to reach the Auckland executive officials, especially Attorney-General William Swainson, upon whom Wynyard depended heavily for guidance. Swainson had worked for years under Grey and, though well versed in Crown colony politics, was not fitted to the turbulent world of parliamentary politics. He decided early on, without showing his hand, that real responsible government must not be granted without approval from London.

At first, however, Swainson told Speaker of the House, Charles Clifford (Wellington), privately that responsible government was conceded. Clifford then held secret discussions, at Swainson's behest, with EGW and Frederick Weld (Wairau) about who should be suggested to Wynyard for the new executive. During these, Clifford told EGW that Swainson had said, 'one great personal difficulty would be removed if [EGW] would not be expecting to be called in the matter'. This angered EGW, who 'ridiculed the idea . . . that it was possible for anybody's notice to hinder me from taking an influential part in the government of this colony'.[29]

Soon after, EGW met FitzGerald in the street and urged him to stand for office, but FitzGerald said that he could not take office as colonial secretary and act as Canterbury superintendent at the same time. FitzGerald reported to Godley that he had asked EGW 'to tell me distinctly and truly whether he would not take part in a Govt, he told me *upon his honour* nothing should induce him to take office . . . . he thought he had a right to be consulted but he would never take office'.[30] A nice exchange of mutual disingenuousness. EGW was waiting for the call, for a demand that he take office, to be dragged unwilling to the executive table. It would be his greatest triumph – and bring acceptance at last. As for FitzGerald, he might not be colonial secretary, but he could still be the leading minister.

On 7 June, Wynyard told the House, on Swainson's recommendation, that EGW's compromise proposal would be given effect and sent for FitzGerald and Dr David Monro (Nelson), as the mover and seconder of the address-in-reply, to help form the first ministry. FitzGerald became, in effect, prime minister and Weld would become the colonial secretary once the older appointees on the executive retired on pensions. FitzGerald took no steps to include EGW in the discussions that immediately followed, until he found that he could not do without Sewell as notional solicitor-general, and Sewell insisted that EGW be consulted. Left out himself, EGW condoned Sewell's acceptance of office – at least he would have an ally on the executive – but, unwisely, vanity caused him to accede to Sewell's request to explain the workings of the ministerial arrangements to a meeting of most of the members. This gave the false impression that EGW approved of the ministry's formation.

On 10 June, some clerks were turned out of the local survey office so that FitzGerald, Weld and Sewell could sit down at their desks and together 'make a Government'. As Sewell wrote, 'I can hardly help rubbing my eyes, and asking whether it is not all a dream.'[31] Attorney-General Swainson remained a member of the executive along with appointees Dr Andrew Sinclair, continuing in the meantime as colonial secretary, and Alexander Shepherd, as colonial treasurer, who had been members of the administration since the early 1840s.

They set to with a will but, three days later, Sewell recorded, 'In the evening came Wakefield, fretful, dissatisfied, and I am afraid brewing a storm. He is affronted at being left out of active participation in the Government work. The fact is so, and it is unfortunate.' Sewell knew what would follow. 'Wakefield's intensity must have its object and if it cannot help, will be sure to employ itself in marring . . . . now accident seems to have divided us. I am now one of FitzGerald's Cabinet, and in good faith to him must keep myself aloof from one whom we all fear as dangerous. This estrangement will I foresee in a short time produce want of confidence, and probably lead to absolute schism. Wakefield in his readiness to damage an enemy, will have little scruple in shooting down a friend.'[32]

EGW suddenly found himself powerless. The fulfilment of his hopes had brought the disappointment of his expectations. He had not been, and would not be, called to be part of a ministry; and it was difficult for him to pull strings effectively in such a small capital of about 9000 people and within a Parliament of only 37 members. He had a choice. He could now confine his parliamentary work to the role of a constructive leader of the opposition, as he had done so effectively in the Wellington Provincial Council: this would improve his standing and reputation, allay the old suspicions and eventually lead to office. Or he could take a destructive opposition role in an attempt to take control of the executive in whatever manner was needed, and destroy FitzGerald in the process. On 13 June, Sewell forecast that he would inevitably take the latter course, yet, in two letters that EGW wrote the following day, there was only a hint of such an approach.

To Lyttelton, he wrote, 'Events come so fast that one cannot hold the same position for a week. I, who was in the van of the attack, am now a moderator and holder-back; sure that all is gained', but added the curious, even ominous, rider 'and only afraid of losing by intolerance and violence'. His own or others'? He gave Lyttelton a thumbnail account of what had happened and wrote fulsomely of the piece of plate worth more than £1,000 that was going to be inscribed and presented to Wynyard as a testimonial to his promptitude in enacting the constitution after Grey's 'wicked work'. The letter shows EGW's continued determination to see that Grey never returned to New Zealand: he did not know that Grey had taken up the governorship of South Africa. Although he told Lyttelton that he was now taking a lesser role, his attitude to the new ministry was dismissive: 'It is a patched-up, make-shift affair, and cannot – indeed it is not intended to – last' and 'The <u>composition</u> of the new Government was almost accidental, by reason of the hurry.'[33]

In his last surviving letter to Catherine, of the same date, he is almost euphoric: 'New Zealand has undergone neither more nor less than a revolution! Do not be alarmed. The change though enormous, has been peaceful, & will be very conservative in its results. Nothing is overturned, except Governor Grey's wicked policy and false reputation.' He could not admit, to her, his failure to be part of the new government:

> Mr Sewell is a Cabinet Minister, as I might also have been had I pleased. You will open your eyes, & ask what all this means. It means . . . that after trouble, & annoyance & disappointment & real suffering without end, I am now as happy as anyone can be in this world, having a full realization of what I have hoped, & longed and striven for, during so many years. The only drawback is a kind of apprehension arising from the greatness & suddenness of the success. My health & strength are wonderful. The greater the danger, the louder, the raging of the storm, the more important the crisis, & the larger my own share of responsibility & labour the more I have been capable of doing whatever I wished to do. Neither effort nor the highest excitement, have disturbed or fatigued me. Throughout the struggle I have been as cool as you could wish, & have slept like a pig. This is all about myself, but you will like it the better for that.[34]

Although delighted by such ecstatic news from her dear brother, Catherine would have been apprehensive about the possible consequences. Accustomed to his hyperbole, she knew that such heights had their corresponding depths. In this letter there is a sense of bravado as he rides the crest of a great wave that, inevitably, must break.

The makeshift quality of the new executive was soon apparent: FitzGerald had failed to clarify the lines of responsibility so that the appointees – Swainson, Sinclair and Shepherd – considered themselves accountable only to the governor and the others to the House. Wynyard began to show himself a puppet to Swainson's manipulative hand. The attorney-general mischievously allowed it to be known that ten minutes' discussion with EGW would have solved the responsibility problem, implying that FitzGerald's jealousy had prevented it. EGW's resentment deepened.

EGW opened his attack on 20 June in a long speech that occupied three-quarters of the House's time. He declared that he had now taken a position of 'entire independence of thought and speech' and then pointed out that, 'Instead of one homogeneous Government, we have two Governments in one – the old and new systems bound together in an unnatural alliance.' He attacked FitzGerald's (and Sewell's) uncertain tenure of office since both planned to return to Canterbury at the end of the session, and hoist FitzGerald on his own petard by stating that it was inappropriate for a provincial superintendent to hold central government office. Attacking the ministry wherever he could find a cause, he appealed to sectional and class interests and, as he had done in Wellington, worked to reduce the power of the executive. But the personal pique and enmity that invested his speech were plain. As FitzGerald said, 'His best supporter Hart immediately attacked it as the most ungenerous speech he had ever heard.'[35] EGW was voted down.

He returned to the attack with attempts to reduce the southern members' power on the executive. He moved for a select committee to enquire into the justice of Auckland meeting any part of the New Zealand Company debt, and then a notice of motion requiring that any central government administration 'should comprise a special representation of each Province in the Executive Council'. Jerningham brought in a notice of motion that legislation should be on 'principles to be the subject of debate and resolution by the whole House in Committee'.[36]

The real threat to FitzGerald came with the second reading of the ministry's Waste Lands Bill, which made the central executive responsible for land regulations subject to a provincial veto and a minimum price of 5s an acre. The upper house, the Legislative Council, now came into play and FitzGerald increased his ministry's power by making Auckland MHR Thomas Bartley a member of it and also giving him a place on the executive. When he appeared unexpectedly in the House with the other ministers, this unsettled EGW, who had decided to make the bill a full trial of strength: it had been conveyed to him that Wynyard 'would have no objection to send for him' if he obtained a majority.[37] Confident of success, the MHRs in EGW's camp vigorously attacked the bill. Colonial Secretary Weld replied with an unexpectedly strong and expert counter-attack. He reminded the

House that EGW, as a self-proclaimed framer of the constitution, had always been in favour of giving control over waste lands to the provinces. Had not he and his close colleague Sewell always been of a like mind on this issue? Without flinching, EGW denied Weld and, worse, denied Sewell.

Weld then moved on to EGW's role as the author of systematic colonisation and held up a copy of *The Art of Colonization*, reminding everyone of its idea of the sufficient price, presented as a means of preventing labourers from becoming landowners too soon. How did EGW square that with his pledge in Wellington to vote for the lowest price proposed in the General Assembly? 'Sir, he owes it to his own great reputation to answer these questions . . . and I must tell my honourable friend that his silence will be a triumph for all who have opposed the principles he has enunciated in his book.'[38]

EGW replied with some justification that this issue was 'foreign to the objects' of the bill, but he had been neatly skewered on this vexed point, and he lamely went on to say, 'In the present circumstances of New Zealand, as they are influenced by the neighbouring [Victorian] gold fields, I do not attach much importance to the subject of price . . . . it might perhaps be safely left to the Provincial governments.' This was worse than Weld's triumph of silence. It seemed to be a public abandonment of the sufficient price, a tacit admission to the House that EGW would do anything for the sake of power.

After Weld's attack, EGW's speech, according to FitzGerald, was 'full of undisguised malice and spleen. It was captious and wearisome and more than all it proposed no other policy. That was its great blunder . . . The feeling was one of utter disappointment and disgust. When he sat down Sewell rose. His reply was really a master piece. It was the first time Wakefield had betrayed him – misrepresented their private opinions held together and long talked over. I never saw a man more wounded than Sewell. He said to me whilst Wakefield was speaking, "I'm afraid after all he is a very great scoundrel".'[39]

Sewell wrote, 'To me the affair was painful, as making the final split between me and Wakefield but it is I fear irremediable . . . . Granting some cause he might have had for annoyance at not being asked to join the Government, he had given me his express pledge to support us – an assurance without which I told him that I would not join the government. Then at the very first measure he turns round with fierce opposition to turn us out. One cannot work with a man from whom one is in such peril.'[40] In his unscrupulous bid for power, EGW had lost his one true ally. When Sewell had finished his speech, Sam Revans sprang to his feet and moved the division: EGW was beaten by 20 votes to ten.

Years before, Charles Buller had said of EGW that 'one must be on one's guard against his rashness & fancy'.[41] EGW had never learnt to be on guard against them himself. He had now crossed his Rubicon and left his chief-of-staff behind; retreat was impossible, except in admission of defeat and retirement from the field. As he had done nearly 30 years before in the Turner abduction, he had committed himself too far to give up. It would be victory or exile to another 'black place'.

EGW had alienated most of the southern members, except those from Otago, and he set about finding new allies in the north and to exert influence in the Legislative Council.[42] Also, he returned to the land issues that had seen him elected so enthusiastically by the small farmers of the Hutt. On 18 July, he introduced working settler amendments to the Waste Lands Bill. His proposed new regulations stipulated that a third of all land would be set aside for working settlers in lots of not more than 200 acres, these to be sold at the lowest possible price on a deferred payment basis. Provincial waste land boards would manage the scheme publicly and openly. FitzGerald immediately denounced it as 'class legislation', showing clearly which class he represented. EGW's motives, as usual, were ambiguous. The scheme has been described as no 'brainchild of a Utilitarian intellectual. It was a bit of hard-headed colonial politics.'[43] And as a 'last desperate lunge for popularity'.[44] But there was still heart to it.

The far-reaching implications of EGW's challenge to the Waste Lands Bill helped to precipitate the inevitable crisis over ministerial responsibility in the two-faced executive. FitzGerald, Weld and Sewell now insisted that the older appointees resign and take their pensions so that the executive became fully responsible to the elected house in its actions and expenditure. Wynyard wavered. Just when it seemed likely he would concede, he chose the conservative option. He followed Attorney-General Swainson's deeply self-interested advice and refused to ask his officials to resign. When FitzGerald, Weld and Sewell consequently resigned, Wynyard, continuing to heed Swainson's advice, sent for EGW. Swainson knew that this could only keep the House in permanent division, prevent the early introduction of fully responsible government and safeguard his own position. The first General Assembly was turning into a fiasco.

Stafford, who had come to Auckland to observe the assembly proceedings, wagered £50 that EGW would not take up a role as adviser to Wynyard but would stand by the House and the principle of responsible government. 'Had he done that,' FitzGerald told Godley, 'he must have been at the head of party, because he might have always thrown it on us that we had spoiled his policy and that if he had been called in all would have gone right and so on. That was his clear game. But he could not resist the charms of advising whilst he would not take the responsibility of office.'[45] An Auckland ally of EGW, Thomas Forsaith, commented with both humour and accuracy that EGW's attitude towards FitzGerald and responsible government was 'akin to that of Frankenstein when the result of his occult labours suddenly started up before him'.[46]

In his statement to the House on 3 August, EGW said that he had undertaken to assist Wynyard, provided he did not have to take office, or head a ministry, and that the acting governor acted on his advice alone. This last proviso was designed partly to isolate Swainson. His main object, he declared, was to restore responsible government, perhaps with improvements over what had occurred during the past eight weeks, or to find some mode of carrying on government that was acceptable to the House. He was not optimistic, given the last ministry's demand for the resignation of the old officials from the executive and that the southern members wanted to go home. He warned the House against attacking the executive or persecuting Wynyard. Should this occur, he would 'at once accept office, and, if it became necessary to prorogue the House, he would stand by [Wynyard]'. The threat was clear: if his opponents were not careful, the House would be dismissed and EGW would be left in Auckland in charge of the central government.

On 6 August, Sewell wrote, 'Nothing but sheer insanity can excuse the course he is taking. First he allows Col. Wynyard to place himself in the position of calling him in as *sole adviser*. He declares he will be *sole adviser* or *not at all* . . . . It is impossible not to feel pity and shame when one thinks of him, mixed in my own mind with yearnings of old friendship and admiration of his strangely misapplied powers.'[47] But there was no insanity involved. EGW planned to use the same management methods he had used with Sir Charles Metcalfe in Canada ten years earlier: get Wynyard to appoint a pliant minority government, and then, on grounds that would favour his aims, go to the country.

The first communication from Wynyard under EGW's advice arrived in the House on 5 August. As the speaker was reading it, he discovered that a page was missing. EGW stepped over to him and quietly handed him a duplicate sheet from his own pocket. EGW explained that he was merely correcting a clerical error, but this action highlighted his anomalous position and suggested that Wynyard had not known what he was signing. It was a skilful attack on the FitzGerald ministry, casting the blame for its collapse on their hasty arrangements in a bid for power, their attempted coercion of Wynyard, their general inadequacy.

The statement, intended to alienate the House from FitzGerald, Sewell and Weld, was clearly meant to be propaganda for wider dissemination, appealing over the heads of the members to the voters. The proceedings of the assembly were being reported in Auckland newspapers and despatched to the southern settlements. The recent advent of a steamer service meant that readers in Wellington, for example, could read of assembly events within a few days. EGW and Jerningham had stolen a march in the propaganda war with their biased and cleverly contrived articles in the *New-Zealander*, but FitzGerald and Sewell were determined to effectively counter-attack through the pages of the *Southern Cross*. FitzGerald might be the nominal leader of the opposition to EGW, but the slighted Sewell was the shrewd planner of a strategy that aimed to ensure EGW would not gain ministerial power during the life of the Assembly.

The wrangling continued over the next days, when it was revealed that EGW did not have sole access to Wynyard and that much of his advice was filtered through Swainson. The House prepared an address that presented its own version of executive council events and called upon Wynyard to establish fully responsible government and promised pensions to the retiring officials. This, the complete answer to EGW's story, was printed and despatched south by steamer before the House had even approved it. EGW tried to discredit the address by saying that Wynyard could not possibly grant full responsible government without the approval of London. But the address was passed, again by a majority of two to one, in a balance of forces that EGW seemed unable to alter.

His only chance now was to prolong the length of the assembly, knowing that many of the southern members would soon be forced to return home for political and personal reasons. Then the balance of power might shift as he worked to achieve the support of Auckland members. On 17 August, under EGW's advice, Wynyard sent two messages to the House. The first stated that the differences between the executive and the legislature had become irreconcilable and the session had to all intents and purposes come to an end. It proposed a fortnight's prorogation of the House to let tempers cool; when it reconvened he promised to include members of the House on the executive 'as shall give all the provinces an effectual voice'. Meanwhile, he was requesting the imperial government's approval of responsible government.

Before the House could debate this, a second message arrived with a copy of the official government *Gazette* announcing the assembly prorogued. Sewell, who spotted the manoeuvre, quickly moved that the first message be considered while the second was left unopened on the table. EGW's supporters then tried to break up proceedings by withdrawing from the House and acting as though prorogation had taken place. James Mackay from Nelson walked into the chamber with his hat on, umbrella in one hand, *Gazette* in the other, loudly proclaiming that the House had been dismissed. Sewell grabbed his umbrella and, with another member, 'rather indecorously proceeded to eject him'. The House got its discussion on the first message but could not upset prorogation. The shambles continued. Stafford left Auckland in disgust – and £50 the lighter.

In the hiatus between sessions, Swainson insinuated that there was really not much point in having a second session, given the chaos of the first and the violence at its end. EGW strongly objected. Extending the prorogation would leave the government in the hands of the old officials; exactly as Swainson wanted. Suspecting that the executive and Wynyard were about to act outside his advice, EGW resigned his position. It would no longer be useful in achieving his own ministry. In the end, Wynyard was forced to call the second session in order for the House to grant money supply and pass some necessary legislation. And somehow EGW prevailed upon him to form a ministry that represented all the provinces. The majority of the members resisted Wynyard's overtures to form this new ministry without the promise of responsible government. When the assembly met again on 31 August, EGW was 'back into Council in disguise'. EGW's supporters were sworn into the executive: Thomas Forsaith (Auckland), James Macandrew (Otago), William Travers (Nelson) and Jerningham Wakefield (Canterbury).

Wynyard's opening address included an extraordinarily radical legislative programme that was obviously of EGW's making. It proposed complete ministerial responsibility; to transfer all power over waste lands to the provinces and consequently allow fresh local elections if required; to issue working settler land regulations and establish boards to administer them; to give Auckland a degree of self-government if the seat of government changed (as the southern members wanted); to undertake currency reform (an Otago request); to set up compensation commissions to hear claims from labourers in Wellington, New Plymouth and Nelson; to make the Legislative Council elective (a senate); to give provincial superintendents the power to dissolve their councils; and to make provision for equal representation in all electorates. Its democratic underpinning was demonstrated by the measure to pay General Assembly members adequately so that working-class men would not be prevented from holding political office.

The programme has been described as 'an attempt to fashion a radically democratic state on an economic basis of small-scale intensive farming'.[48] Sewell, recognising this, wrote that, if the programme was implemented, it would be a 'signal of war between classes, and for men of education and capital to leave the Country'. EGW had drawn the first line between Tory and Radical, Conservative and Liberal, National and Labour, that would distinguish the country's future party politics. In bringing together such a programme, EGW appeared, in a bout of demagogic opportunism, to have repudiated most of the colonial theories he had long campaigned for. And yet, in what he may have understood was his last, best chance, he was giving full rein to his instincts in moving towards a democracy.

It was clear to his opponents that EGW was the *de facto* head of this new ministry, and that he was seeking to manouvre the house into violent clashes over his radical programme in order to bring about a dissolution and a fresh bout of elections. Sewell 'saw what the game was, and preached moderation and a crafty wariness; our object being, now that we are met, to do what can be done, so as to satisfy the Colony, and to go away with the satisfaction that our Meeting has not been wholly fruitless. Another thing is to get rid of this horrid Monster of a Government, and the terrible danger to the Colony of a dissolution upon Wakefield's Agrarian policy.'[49] Sewell drafted a careful address-in-reply, entrusted to Monro to deliver, which pointed out that the new ministry did not have the confidence of the House and it would grant supply only to the old executive. Wynyard gave way and the ministry collapsed within days. EGW's immediate bid for power was over. Swainson must have smiled as the old appointees remained in control of the executive.

The remaining two weeks of the second session were given over to a rush of necessary legislation. As FitzGerald pushed ahead with his original Waste Lands Bill, EGW used his influence in the Legislative Council to have it modified in favour of working settlers. He still brought his regulations before the House and raised a petition around Auckland asking for them to be introduced. They had no chance of success but it was all good propaganda for his cause as the champion of the working man. Influenced by EGW, but on his own authority, Wynyard established compensation commissions to investigate labourers' claims in Wellington, Nelson and New Plymouth. In another move to further his political standing, EGW presented temperance petitions and a resolution calling for liquor reform that the House could hardly disapprove. On 13 September, to Sewell's disgust, EGW carried the House on the question of wages for members. 'It ended in our voting ourselves the monstrous allowance of £1 a day.'[50] For Sewell, this was the fulfilment of an infamous Chartist pledge yet, though British politicians of the modern era did not receive salaries until 1912, Canadian parliamentarians had been paid since before the Durham mission.

FitzGerald 'lived through these days in a sustained rage. Determined to strike a lethal blow against Wakefield – and Auckland for its apparent conversion to Wakefield's mesmeric visions – he proposed on 15 September that the seat of government be moved.'[51] FitzGerald, increasingly erratic and irrational, failed to ensure enough southern members were in the House and EGW and his men walked out before the vote could be taken, ensuring there could not be a quorum.

The next day, the first General Assembly was all over and the southern members headed at once for the steamer to take them home; but FitzGerald could not leave Auckland without a final slash at EGW, stung by his charge that he been too precipitate in taking office. In a letter to the *Southern Cross*, he described EGW as a man known in England as 'incapable of speaking the truth when he has an object in view . . . . I am quite content that I have been the means . . . . of saving the colony from the hands of a man who no one has ever yet walked with in any of his numerous schemes without being damaged in reputation or pocket.'[52]

In reply, EGW wound himself up to his best pitch of vituperation. Feinting with sarcastic compliments – 'in private life, few are more accomplished and agreeable . . . . in public life, he is very quick and clever . . .' – EGW savaged FitzGerald with the kind of prose caricature that again revealed the novelist manqué: 'In prosperity, boastful, overbearing, supercilious, and blind to danger; in difficulties, fretful, impatient, very spiteful, and often pale with the fear of failing; in settled adversity either low-spirited and helpless, or reckless as the maniac; fickle as well as versatile; readily inflated, and as easily depressed: without magnanimity, fortitude, caution, or patience, but envious, jealous, treacherous and vindictive; such is the broken-down hero of the first meeting of the New Zealand Parliament.'[53] The *Southern Cross* editorialised that FitzGerald's character 'is that of a gentleman. Mr Wakefield should also endeavour to get a character before he offers to give one'.

On the evening before he took the steamer, Sewell went to see EGW, 'if possible to put an end to personal unkindness of feeling'. They spent three hours together and 'talked of the past and the future . . . . The one great motive which has guided him throughout his late career has been palpably hatred of FitzGerald. This has blinded him and led him into a succession of errors . . . . We parted in a friendly way, but my conclusion is absolutely formed, that between him and me there never could be co-operation again. <I regard him as utterly untrustworthy.> Pity that so much natural benevolence, and so much intellectual power should be so wasted, or indeed turned to evil.'[54]

The southern members returned to their provinces, mostly to acclaim and the Wakefield supporters to disapprobation. At the beginning of October, Sewell recorded that, in Canterbury, 'The almost universal feeling here is approval of our conduct, and a most intense bitterness against Wakefield. <At Christchurch, the Colonists' Society, Jerningham Wakefield's own creation, had passed strong resolutions condemnatory of him; but these are as yet early days. Jerningham Wakefield is active and unscrupulous, and frequents the Public Houses to get influence among the lower classes. The Wakefields are still and must be always formidable from those very qualities which detach the better class of men from them.>'[55]

EGW stayed in Auckland – the place he had so often reviled as contrary to his precepts of colonial settlement – for another two months, endeavouring to build a new power base among its numerous working-class settlers. His health was now said to be suffering from the strains of the past hectic five months. Dan later commented, 'What he went through in Auckland . . . was enough to break up the constitution of a very strong man . . . too much for one in feeble health.'[56] Yet this was contrary to EGW's continued protestations of glowing health. At about this time, also, he may have been affected by the news of his father Edward's death in England on 18 May, not far short of his eightieth birthday. Edward had retained an interest in colonial matters until the end, attending a London dinner in November 1853 at which Godley had extolled the success of Canterbury.

Before returning to Wellington, EGW helped to prepare the working settler regulations and the details of the compensation commissions with Wynyard, and had himself appointed to the one for Wellington. He attended a variety of public meetings, accepted an address acknowledging his services on behalf of Auckland and, at Onehunga, gave a speech that attributed the failures of the first General Assembly to a bid for power by the 'squattocracy of the South'. An anti-squattocracy cry soon gathered force throughout the colony and EGW's clever use of this began to counter the triumphalism of FitzGerald, Sewell and their allies in the south. A celebratory public dinner put on by the Constitutionalists in Wellington proved a disaster and a cold public meeting failed to pass a resolution in their support. Sewell, Featherston and Fox conferred on how to counter the very real danger of a Wakefield party as a growing provincial crisis, centred on the new land regulations, threatened fresh elections.

EGW arrived back in Wellington in late November to face his constituents, well aware that the colony was waiting to see what would happen when he appeared before them. On 30 November, he drove out to the Hutt and the familiar hustings of the Aglionby Arms for the first of three planned meetings. Scores attended: those who could not get on to the floor of the room either perched in the loft or peered through the windows. EGW was given a warm reception but said little that first evening, which was largely given over to Alfred Ludlam, his fellow member for the Hutt, and William Fox, both of whom took the stand for the prosecution. EGW effortlessly handled Fox who, for his attack on him, 'earned a hostile barrage of groans and jeers. As [Donald] McLean later remarked, Fox was lucky to escape a ducking in the nearby river.'[57]

At the second meeting on 4 December, EGW gave a masterly five-hour speech in which he took credit for all the important initiatives taken at the General Assembly. He suppressed his role in initially supporting the FitzGerald ministry and glossed over his ambiguous role as adviser to Wynyard. Everything was the fault of FitzGerald who, with Sewell and Weld, represented the 'Squattocracy of Wellington, Nelson and Canterbury . . . . I declare that the North helped me to prevent the Southern representatives from establishing a system of land monopoly which would have been fatal to the interests of the colony.'[58] The Hutt voters gave him a vote of confidence.

When Sewell heard of the meeting, he wrote gloomily, 'Wakefield has made a demonstration at the Hutt, and as I gather from sundry people, rather successfully than not. He is sure of a large amount of success. He has a wonderful art in leading men to follow his opinions, and his plausible representations of facts are some of the most remarkable works of fiction I know. The Political future of the Colony is all under a cloud, and nobody can predict or guess what it is to be.'[59] EGW's opponents waited anxiously for the third meeting and the new Wakefield campaign cry. But it never came.

CHAPTER THIRTY

Dead to the Future

AFTER HIS 4 DECEMBER SPEECH IN THE HUTT, 'In order, I suppose, to get away from the noise and excitement consequent on such a political meeting, [EGW] drove home in an open chaise, nine miles in the face of a cold south-easterly gale, at two o'clock in the morning. Although he began to feel ill, he accepted an invitation a day or two afterwards to dine with the members of an Oddfellows' Lodge . . . and sat in a hot room with an open window at his back. The next day he was attacked with rheumatic fever, and suffered acute pain. This turned . . . into neuralgia, every nerve in his body being affected.'[1] Desperately ill, EGW withdrew to the darkened seclusion of his house on Tinakori Road.

Apprehensively, as Christmas came and went, the political leaders of the country waited for him to reappear. Featherston told Stafford, 'He has taken to his bed in disgust, and I doubt much whether he will shew fight . . . . every atom of his influence has gone.'[2] As the weeks turned into months and EGW did not emerge from seclusion, his relieved political opponents ascribed his non-appearance to an admission of defeat. In February 1855, Fox wrote to Godley, 'Excessive excitement, and disappointment at the reception he met with among his Constituents at the Hutt, broke him down, and for some three months past he has not been out of his room. I doubt from what I hear if he will reappear on the political stage. It will be no loss to N.Zd. as he is utterly unmanageable, unprincipled, and as reckless as a lunatic.'[3]

Three months later, Fox added, 'So far he has not reappeared on the political stage . . . how far really ill I cannot learn, but from what I can gather he is so shaken that he will never again be able to take part in public life. You know his impetuous temper and will easily understand that the position he took at Auckland has estranged him personally from most of his private friends . . . . Indeed he sees no one, not even I believe the members of his brothers family though he lives in his house. Jerningham W is here at present – he oscillates between here and

Canterbury, but has not much weight in either, though sufficient sometimes to do mischief by turning the scale.'[4]

Jerningham wrote to Catherine in May, 'For a long time he would let no one know how ill he was, and would see no one. But then he wrote to me at Canterbury, asking me to come to him. I arrived about the first week in January. I found the pains were going off, but that he was dreadfully weak, very nervous, and at times desponding, with no appetite, and irregular circulation.' At first, EGW had been attended by a doctor but then had resorted to complete peace and quiet and occasional radiation treatment with an oil lamp. Jerningham 'remonstrated against the rejection of the drug system without substituting his own panacea of "packing" [wrapping the body in a wet sheet or blanket] in which he used to have such faith. But he always replies that he feels a presentiment that the effort would be too much for him, that he has an idea it would choke him, and so on. So that he positively does nothing but rest, opens no letters, reads no local papers, indeed, tries to think about nothing on which his thoughts can have any influence.' Jerningham concurred: 'He has sadly overtasked both his bodily and his mental powers during the past two years, and complete rest . . . will, I have no doubt, do much to restore him in course of time. My being here, of course, saves him from attending to any business, public or private, and I pass an hour or two with him nearly every day.' Although he hoped and believed his father to be 'out of all danger', Jerningham knew 'his recovery must necessarily be slow and tedious, and perhaps never perfect. My great desire is to see him strong enough to get a change of air, such as up to Charles's sheep station at Rangiora, perhaps to Sydney, and I also trust that he may make up his mind to give up the idea of any more active political labour. But I confess to a dread lest, as soon as he feels at all strong, he should again endeavour, by his own efforts in public life to arrest the progress of what he may think evil in the colony. At present he cannot walk across the room.'[5]

Although EGW was also attended continually by his manservant, Schmidt, Jerningham decided to stay by his father and not travel to Auckland to attend the next General Assembly. This opened in early August after Wynyard had received approval from London to introduce responsible government and pension off the old officials. This assembly lasted just a month, was attended by only five southern members, none from Otago and only Sewell from Canterbury. As he prepared for the long trip from Lyttelton, Sewell discussed in his journal who might lead the House. He discounted FitzGerald, for loss of prestige and 'uncertainty of purpose', and wrote *finis* to EGW's career: 'Wakefield we must put out of calculation. He is hors de combat from illness of body and mind and I do not think will rise again. Of Wakefield's party there is no man capable of leading but himself.'[6]

In April Sewell had written, with sympathy and understanding 'Wakefield is ill – worse I think both in mind and body. Poor fellow! I grieve when I think of him, eating his big heart up with disappointment and disgust of himself and others.'[7]

Perhaps EGW did see how he had destroyed himself in the mortal combat with FitzGerald who, though badly wounded, was young enough to recover and go on in political life. Perhaps he was disgusted with himself at abandoning all principle in a ruinous bid for power. Perhaps he did regret not succeeding in his last throw. Perhaps he had sensed, at the age of 58, that his strength was going, that he had the energy and time for only one last attempt at control, in order to fulfil some of his political aims. Perhaps, most of all, he regretted losing friends through behaviour and actions he had believed necessary; and now wished to make amends with some of them, personally at least.

But EGW's thoughts will never be known. More than a century ago biographer Richard Garnett wrote, with an access to information long gone, 'Wakefield could never again have appeared upon a platform, but some thought that his pen would still have been active if he could have felt more confidence in the political future of his son.' Garnett believed that EGW's 'great mistake . . . was to have taken any part in politics except as a writer'. The buoyant health of which he wrote to Catherine was the 'effect of an unnatural stimulus, and was to be expiated by a reaction which secluded him from the world'. Garnett doubted that EGW would have even begun to write again: his 'intellectual faculties were not in themselves impaired, but he appeared to feel that his grasp upon them had become uncertain, and that a slight shock might dissolve it altogether'.[8] No written word by EGW from after December 1854 survives – not a letter, an article, a journal entry or an unfinished manuscript. The last seven years of his life were silent. He became 'dead to the future' of New Zealand. Although it has been stated that EGW 'lapsed into a deep depression',[9] the very course of his life during these last years would also be unknowable, but for the friendship of a little girl.

Dan and Angela Wakefield had suffered deeply from the premature death of their eleven-year-old daughter Selina in August 1848. Although Dan was then 50 and Angela nearing 40, they conceived another child soon afterwards and Angela was delivered of Alice Mary, without complications, in October 1849. More robust than either of her parents or sole sibling, brother Charles Marcus, Alice was to live well into the next century, to tell tales of her first years in Wellington, and of EGW in particular. Alice's first memory of her uncle came from the 'night of the great earthquake'. The massive tremor that struck Wellington in January 1855 was the biggest earthquake ever to have affected the city and 'For fourteen hours the town trembled like a shaken jelly'. There was little loss of life but many buildings were destroyed and the settlement was subject to after-shocks for months. Its long-term effects were, in fact, highly beneficial: it raised the harbour foreshore by an average of 5 feet, instantly reclaiming land, and creating a shelf for road and rail between Wellington and the Hutt Valley.

Alice remembered that, as a five year-old, 'I was carried out of my bed, and found myself amongst a number of frightened people, who had come from the houses around and were all passing the night out of doors. In the middle of the group was my uncle seated in an arm-chair, and he was of much interest to me, for, though we lived in the same house, I do not recall having seen him before. My father and mother had left their home in Wellington Terrace and come to live with him at his house in the [Tinakori] Road. . . . At the earthquake my uncle's attention was drawn to me, and from that time until his death . . . I was a great deal with him.'[10] Nina, Liocadia, Frances, Amy, Constance and now Alice. 'The feelings of love and admiration that I had for him it is impossible to describe; my greatest pleasure was to be in his company; his slightest wish was my law, at any sacrifice of my own pleasure. It is only fair to my mother to say that she encouraged this devotion to my uncle, feeling that in his solitary life, often seeing no one but his man-servant . . . I was the only pleasure that was left to him.' As the years went by, 'All was done for me according to my uncle's views of making a child strong. I had a cold bath in the morning, then walked with him for half an hour before breakfast, then had porridge.' Schmidt 'proved most faithful; he was always at hand, and looked upon his master with the greatest affection and respect . . . . He was very fond of carpentering, and made very pretty boxes and frames out of the honeysuckle and other fine New Zealand woods. In his workshop I passed many hours with my uncle. We walked up and down a very small space, our companions . . . being "Powder" and "Blucher", two bull dogs considered very fierce, but perfectly gentle with us.'

Alice remained convinced that 'I have never met any man with the power that E. G. Wakefield had, and I have never come across anyone who cared for young people and their improvement in the way that he did. I used to read books with my mother, and then repeat them chapter by chapter to my uncle. I read the whole of the Waverley novels through twice over this way, except *Castle Dangerous* and *Count Robert of Paris*, which he did not think worth my reading; his favourites were *Guy Mannering*, *Rob Roy*, *Waverley*, and *Old Mortality*' – as he had probably told Ellen Turner all those years before on the way to Gretna Green.

'My uncle was not able to bear any noise, so that we never went on his side of the house, or used the rooms nearest to him . . . .' Family tradition has it that Dan was so afraid of disturbing his brother that he would pace the hall anxiously before summoning up the courage to even knock on his door. Neither did Alice's 'little playfellows' come to visit her. 'I went to see them and they would say, "Do you not dislike having to go back every day at four to walk with your uncle?" I know the very question astonished me, and I warmly replied there was nothing else I enjoyed so much.' Although she did not remember her uncle seeing any visitors, she recalled 'a friend to whom he used to give lessons in the open air to cure his stammering, and another who lent him books on the Millennium. . . . I have a prayer book with his name in his own writing, and he once said that he should have gone to church, only from fear of disturbing people with his breathing from asthma. . . .'

This life of 'complete seclusion' was broken once or twice. '[T]here was an election in which he was interested; our walks then were beyond our own gates, and I listened to my uncle persuading a man to vote; that, ill though he was, he would rather be carried to the poll in his bed than not give his vote.' This must have been the occasion, in November 1857, marked by William Richmond when he wrote to Sewell, 'I must not omit to notice a great sign and portent in the Wellington sky. E.G. Wakefield is out again and walked down to poll. . . .'[11] Even after three years' complete absence from the political scene, EGW's very appearance caused apprehension. On 9 December, the *Spectator* commented, 'Even in 1857 the mention of his name on public occasions produced cheers from the workers.'

Many of EGW's sayings remained in Alice's mind from

> memory of the impressive way in which he said everything. Once when my mother was very anxious about something he said, 'Throw it aside, forget. I should have been in a lunatic asylum before now if I had not been able to put a subject out of my mind.' Then he would say, 'It is a blessing that women love needlework; it has the same soothing effect upon their minds that a pipe has upon men's.' He told us once that years ago a doctor had told him that he ought to become a monk of La Trappe, talking was so bad for him;[12] the last years of his life he might almost have belonged to this order. His mother was, I am sure, often in his thoughts, for he used to look at me and say, 'Alice, I believe that you are growing like my mother,' and when I wanted to name my favourite parrot he said, 'Call it Susan; it was my mother's name.' I never heard him mention his wife or Nina; I think he was too fond of them to talk about them.

Or the memories were so painful that they were among the subjects he must still put 'out of mind'.

Another subject that EGW had to put partly out of mind was his 'bitter disappointment' at Jerningham's failure to marry. He 'believed that the right wife would be his salvation'[13] from the bad 'colonial habits' that were increasingly taking a hold on him as he moved through his thirties. He drank and ate to some excess, growing rather portly, and followed no line of business, living off the interest of his inheritance. His capacity for wrangling, often under the influence, and his absence from Parliament saw him lose the 1855 General Assembly election; he was unable to regain a seat in the 1858 and 1861 elections. Spending most of his time in Wellington, partly on attendance of EGW's affairs, he did find a seat and office in the Wellington Provincial Council from 1857 to 1861. His term was notable for his obdurate opposition to Featherston, which often brought about deadlock in council business.

Jerningham was much happier, and more successful, when he was able to indulge his theatrical talents. During the winter of 1857, he was 'Wellington's stage manager, star actor, and on several occasions, dramatist'.[14] In June at the Lyceum, the Wellington Amateur Dramatic Society presented his three-act vaudeville,

Playing for the Odd Trick; the next month his farce, *The Widow Rescued*, proved 'eminently successful'. He played starring roles in other productions, including that of Sir Charles Coldstream in Boucicault's *Used Up*, 'with great ability'. He named his Fendalton property in Christchurch Coldstream and spent a good deal of his money there in establishing a thoroughbred racehorse stud and importing a world-famous stallion, The Peer. In November 1854 he was one of those responsible for founding the Canterbury Jockey Club, acting as secretary or a member of the committee on several occasions over the following ten years.

While Jerningham enjoyed his racehorses as a gentleman profligate, his cousin by marriage, Edward Stafford, enjoyed them equally while building a successful political career. Stafford bided his time as the chaos of the early general assemblies settled down and, in June 1856, after both Sewell and Fox had failed, he formed the first successful ministry under responsible government and became New Zealand's first prime minister during a term that lasted five years. Emily and Josephine travelled with him to Auckland in the autumn of 1856 and then south again to Nelson when Stafford resigned his superintendency. The house, contents and horses were sold up as the Staffords shifted permanently to the seat of government in October. William Richmond, from New Plymouth, had become colonial secretary, and Emily was able to renew her friendship with his family, especially his sister Emily.

Emily Richmond thought her a 'handsome stately creature'. From her new home, as Stafford became deeply embroiled in the business of being prime minister, Emily enjoyed the social and shopping round with the Richmonds, Bartleys and Bells. Also, the wife of the new governor Sir Thomas Gore Browne was an 'outstanding hostess of real charm and tact, and her musical evenings quickly became very popular. As the wife of a Premier whom Harriet Browne very much liked . . . Emily would have received particular attention. After all those years in gossipy and introverted Nelson she was at last able to enjoy a new and more extensive society.'[15] Perhaps it was this that made the difference. In the new year of 1857, Emily found herself pregnant after ten years of marriage.

Stafford went to Nelson again in January, leaving Emily in good health and spirits, and won over 200 guineas in prize money at the annual races from running the last of his horses. He stayed on to be a steward at the Race Ball and to attend a public dinner in his honour before returning to Auckland on 25 March. There he found Emily seriously and inexplicably ill. He railed against the doctors to take action but a fortnight passed before she was diagnosed as suffering from pleurisy. By then, treatment was ineffective and Emily died on 18 April, just a month after her thirtieth birthday.

Stafford's grief was shot through with anger at the doctors and he requested a post mortem. This prompted 'odious reports', put about by Stafford's enemies, that he had not properly cared for his wife. But Emily's friends had long known that, like her mother, she was of a delicate, even frail, disposition. William Richmond wrote that he had 'always feared for her'. During the previous years there may have been miscarriage or menstrual irregularities that had become known only to her closest women friends, or fears of cancer. Richmond's sister Jane wrote that Stafford's 'grief must be more bitter if he imagines that more skilful treatment might have saved her life. For her own sake I really believe if she was at all likely to [remain] a lifelong sufferer from one of those dreadful internal complaints, it is really a blessing that mistaken treatment has shortened her period of suffering.'[16]

Stafford was also accused of callousness because he took no time to mourn and continued with his hectic round of public work, but it was his way of coping. Emily Richmond seemed to feel Emily's loss the most and also hinted at the stress that had developed between the couple during their childless years of marriage: 'If God had seen fit to spare her a son would have been sent them in five months from the time she was taken away. And now all her beauty is gone, and she lies beside the little wooden church [St Stephen's Chapel in Parnell] where William and I had often promised to take her and to the majestic and haughty as well as the best are laid low, and we sail on over the waters where a sister has gone down, how soon forgetting. How mysterious it seems that the desire of their lives should have been almost granted, and a bond which might have bound them to bear together, they had as it seemed just begun to know what married life might be when she was called away, what a blooming stately creature she was not three months ago. I must always consider her sacrificed to ignorance. . . .'[17] Angela, too, must have been deeply affected by Emily's death, given how much care she had taken to comfort her after her father's death in 1848. And now, as 1857 wore on, Angela had to prepare herself for an impending loss that would have more drastic consequences for her and her children.

In June 1855, after two years jobbing at the bar, Dan agreed to the colonial secretary's request to 'temporarily fill the office of Puisne Judge during the absence of Mr Justice Stephen on account of ill health'.[18] He was sworn in as acting judge on 1 November, the first man to be appointed a judge from among those who had practised at the New Zealand Bar. He was also 'unique among New Zealand judges in being, so far as is known, the only one who has emigrated to this country under an assumed name'.[19] Otherwise, Dan's tenure as acting puisne judge was undistinguished and unremarkable. The stress of the job soon began to tell and by October 1857 he was unable to hold a court in Lyttelton because of ill health. He resigned at the end of that month and died in the new year, aged 59. As he had always done, EGW took charge. He gave directions for Dan's funeral and burial beside his brother William and daughter Selina in the Bolton Street Cemetery; and then shifted with Angela and her children – and with Schmidt and the bulldogs – to the house on The Terrace, taking care that Angela was financially secure.

Felix made a move to shorten his life by volunteering to serve in the Crimean War soon after his return to England in May 1855. Sir Joseph Paxton, creator of the Crystal Palace, had been put in charge of works and engineering for the army after the disastrous blunders and inefficiencies of the opening months of the war, epitomised by the notorious Charge of the Light Brigade. The privations of the savage winter of 1854–55 had caused terrible loss of life from inadequate provision of food, basic supplies of matériel and care of the sick and wounded. A war that was to last barely two years, and was confined to one small theatre, cost Britain more than 22,000 dead. In order to bring order, efficiency and expertise to engineering works, Paxton set up the Army Works Corps, which operated in the Crimea from 1 July 1855 until after the end of the war in the spring of 1856. The corps of 1000 men and staff were under the supervision of a chief superintendent of works and six assistant superintendents, one of whom was Felix. The main works force of 900 labourers and tradesmen was largely drawn from the group of men who had just completed the Balaklava railway under dreadful winter and spring conditions. During the life of the corps, 48 of these deserted, 45 were invalided home and 151 died.

Felix arrived at Balaklava in July to help supervise the construction of roads, the improvement of the railway and the building of stone stores, huts, jetties and piers in the military build-up to the successful assault on Sevastopol. He was paid £33 6s 8d a month (an annual rate of £400), most of which was 'allotted' to his cousin Benjamin Head in Kensington, who was presumably caring for his sons.[20] There was much criticism of the corps' operation and the behaviour of its workforce from military commanders: 'they were always drunk, insubordinate and mutinous . . . and after all were of very little use, while their presence was bad for discipline at large and excited natural discontent among the soldiers who did far more work, were punished for drunkenness, and received much lower pay.'[21] In April 1856 criticism of the corps was thoroughly defended by its superintendent-general, who provided a catalogue of its engineering and construction achievements after the experience of the 1854–55 winter 'had proved to the English people that the Army "per se" was unequal to the task of supporting itself'.[22]

How much Felix contributed to the achievement of the Army Works Corps is unknown, but its pay books show that he did not last the full course of its operation. His employment finished after about four months, on 12 November 1855. It is not hard to imagine that Felix might have fallen out with his superiors or colleagues over some survey or engineering question. Over the following eight years Felix is said to have travelled, and presumably worked, in Russia, Turkey, Syria and Egypt; his son Edward wrote that he was 'employed on special service' during the Indian Mutiny of 1857–58. By 1859 he was back in London, living in Benjamin Head's Kensington home and borrowing his money. Young Edward was educated in France and at King's College, London; he described his life in Kensington as being 'surrounded by the literary, artistic and scientific company his father kept'.[23] Certainly Edward was in the company of Thackeray towards the end of his life and wrote a small pamphlet entitled 'Walks with Thackeray'. Felix continued to pursue his natural history enthusiasms and in July 1863, not long before he took ship again for New Zealand at the age of 56, he wrote to Richard Owen, now Director of the Natural History Museum, to obtain a copy of his pamphlet about the moa: 'I am just about to become a permanent resident in New Zealand with my children and intend to devote what literary leisure I can snatch from public works to compile a sort of "White's Selborne" or "Fauna of New Zealand". If the Moa exists my sons shall give an account of his whereabouts.'[24] Encouraged by Stafford during a trip to England as prime minister, Felix was, at least, about to become a 'permanent resident of New Zealand'.

At the time of Emily's death in April 1857, her surrogate daughter, Felix's Josephine, was seventeen years old. Her adoptive household gone, she was sent to England. Her entire long life she remained unmarried and she seems to have acted as companion or housekeeper for her father or in other Wakefield and Torlesse households. For a time she was with the family of John Howard Wakefield, who had retired from the Indian Army as a lieutenant-colonel at the age of 53, and returned to England in 1856. His son George, educated in England under EGW's notice, remained in India but his two surviving daughters, Lucy and Julie – famous Anglo-Indian beauties – travelled home with him.[25] On a trip to the Rhineland with Sir Henry Havelock, Josephine watched as the beautiful Lucy was secretly courted beneath a Bad Godesberg oak tree by a Polish student at Bonn, Hugo de Radolin, Count Radolinski.

The family returned to England where Howard lectured in Hindustani at Oxford. In 1861, he became a convinced abstainer and an active member of the National Temperance League and 'laboured to advance the cause, with a degree of ability, disinterestedness, and zeal that have rarely been equalled'.[26] In this activity, he would have found common cause and sympathy with Felix and Catherine. On 25 February 1862, Howard travelled up to London to attend an evening 'meeting for the promotion of female education in the East'. He went to the house of a friend in Islington, then for an afternoon walk, but on his return was called to a 'higher meeting, even to Himself'. On retiring to his room, he had 'scarcely got inside the door when a heavy fall was heard, and on hastening to assist him his friends found him dying'.[27] Yet another Wakefield man of this generation had succumbed to a heart attack. When the news reached Count Radolinski, now a Prussian diplomat, he rushed over from Berlin and proposed to sweet Lucy. They were married the next year in London and she left for a high society life among the diplomatic and court circles of Berlin and Potsdam: Radolinski was a close friend of the future Emperor Friedrich III of Germany.

Despite the mail now reaching New Zealand with the aid of steam, it is unlikely that EGW heard of his younger brother's death. Sometime in April 1862, Alice Wakefield, now twelve years old, was alarmed by the sound of violent barking. The two bulldogs had escaped on to the Wellington Terrace roadway and begun 'fighting with another dog. William [Schmidt] went out to separate them, and Blucher flew at him and bit him in the face. I carried off Powder, and shut him up in the stable. William went to my uncle and asked permission to have both dogs shot. This was allowed, to my great grief; and my mother said she was sure [EGW] must be feeling much worse to have consented.' This proved to be the case. On the night of 16 May 1862, EGW woke his manservant, who slept in his room, 'with the words, "William, this is death." William woke up my mother and myself; we hurried to the room. My uncle held my hand with a tight clasp, and looked in my face with an expression that I shall never forget; he could not speak. When Jerningham entered the room in answer to a hasty summons, his father struggled hard to speak, but nothing more than the name Jerningham was distinguished.'

Alice could no longer remember who came to the funeral on 19 May, but she knew that 'two Maoris came to follow after the funeral had started'. EGW was buried beside William, Dan and Selina: the four graves can still be seen in the lower part of the preserved Bolton Street cemetery, just off Wellington's Bowen Street. The *Spectator* reported that 'the funeral was private, and only the immediate friends of the deceased were invited, but several persons attended at the Church and joined the mournful procession to the grave from a desire to pay their tribute of respect to his memory; – among others the Superintendent [Featherston] and several members of the Provincial Government, his Honor the Judge, the Bishop of Wellington, several members of the Provincial Council, and many of the old settlers in Wellington'.[28] Sir George Grey had returned to New Zealand in September 1861, to begin his second term as governor, and was in Wellington at the time. There had been some advantage to his making an event of William's funeral fourteen years before, but he perceived none in attending EGW's. The *Spectator* showed more generosity in its obituary by saying that EGW would be buried 'in that settlement which he was chiefly instrumental in founding, and which will be an enduring monument to after times of his ability and energy. . . .'[29]

Young Alice recalled that, 'On one occasion my uncle spoke before me with bitterness of the quick way in which people were forgotten after death, and I burst forth with the assurance that I should never forget him.' For the right and the wrong reasons, EGW could rest in peace. He would never be forgotten. Generously, Lyttelton would say of him, 'The man in these latter days beyond comparison of the most genius and the widest influence in the great science of colonization, both as a thinker, a writer, and a worker; whose name is like a spell to all interested in the subject.'[30] When Lyttelton finally visited Canterbury in 1868, even FitzGerald was moved to give EGW a graceful tribute at a commemorative dinner. Godley was not alive to comment, having died a year before EGW; nor his arch enemy James Stephen, who died in 1859; nor his old friend William Molesworth, who was only 45 when he died in 1855, just a few months after becoming colonial secretary in Lord Palmerston's first government, 'a position for which he had specially qualified himself' in his long alliance with EGW.[31]

As soon as he heard in London of EGW's death, Felix began litigation to retrieve control from Jerningham of his Canterbury land. In 1853 Jerningham had paid EGW £1,483 to take possession of the land that his father had bought for Felix in 1851, but Felix continued to claim that EGW had taken the purchase money from his commission as Canterbury land sales agent. Legal action continued throughout 1863 and, in the process, Felix attempted to besmirch Jerningham's reputation in both London and Christchurch. Charley Torlesse wrote his father in protest: 'You have my full authority for refuting Felix's statement as to E. J. W.'s sottish habits . . . . Felix ought to be the last man to cast up anybody's sins . . . . Bad as he may have been, I have never heard a word against [EJW's] honesty whereas Felix is put upon as a swindler here – whether he deserves it or not. It is the greatest mistake in the world his coming out here. Let him remain in London where nobody knows him. Ben Head clearly wants to get rid of him.'[32] But come he did, with Edward, Oliver, Josephine and 85 birds, including 25 English skylarks.

Ariosto had travelled to New Zealand some years earlier, and suffered the common colonial death of drowning when attempting to cross South Canterbury's Tekapo River in 1862. Curiously, there is no word of Constance in contemporary correspondence. Yet she had married in Canterbury and been widowed before the age of 30, left with three children under ten. It is not clear if she was still there when Felix returned. Constance eventually returned to England where she remarried, bearing another four children; six of her seven offspring were boys.

When Felix arrived back in New Zealand in January 1864, he discovered that Jerningham had married Ellen Roe, 20 years his junior, at Christchurch the previous October. She was the daughter of Edward Roe, an early Wellington settler who had been printer, builder, farmer and, finally, proprietor of Barrett's Hotel, where Jerningham often stayed when he was in Wellington. He had first encountered Ellen when she was a pretty child and he always jokingly called her his 'little wife'. 'Joke became earnest, however, when in due course the family retired to their farm at Karori and Ellen developed into a beautiful girl of seventeen. Jerningham constantly rode out to the homestead, always announcing his arrival at the gate by vigorously blowing his hunting horn . . . . But Ellen had many suitors . . . and his mode of life did not inspire her with confidence. It was not until she paid a long visit to her sister in Christchurch that she became engaged to him.'[33]

Jerningham was attempting to reform: in August 1863, Charley Torlesse wrote to his father, 'E.J.W. continues quite steady & a total abstainer & really he is a quite different man'.[34] Jerningham and Ellen made their first home at Coldstream and 'At first all went well. The Wakefields entertained lavishly, and their house was always full of guests. Their first child, Catherine Alice [Cassie], was born there in 1864.'[35] Released by his father's death, Jerningham now had full control of his property and inheritances. EGW had left no will and his disposable assets at death amounted in value to less than £500.[36] But before he died, EGW had divided his town acre on The Terrace, given half to Angela[37] and left the other half to Jerningham who sold this in September 1864.

Felix bought a 'very nice property close to Nelson' and, according to son Edward, 'we made our permanent home there'.[38] It was relatively permanent for eighteen-year-old Edward, who began his journalistic career on the Nelson *Examiner*; Oliver, 21, went to work on a Marlborough sheep station. Felix travelled to Christchurch in March upon receiving news of the settlement of the land dispute with Jerningham: the Canterbury properties had been split with a balance in Felix's favour. Charley Torlesse, working now in business that included land agency, considered that Jerningham had acted generously in the affair. He wrote to sister Fanny in April: 'Uncle Felix is tremendously excited about his property which really promises to yield a comfortable provision for the family if they are moderate in their ideas. We can manage his property if he will keep out of the way but he now proposes to come down with Josephine and live at Sumner.' Admitting that his uncle had 'gone through enough to drive him crazy', Charley realised that 'a life of inactivity will be much worse for him. He is looking well and strong & has started to ride overland to Nelson . . . .' Charley knew Fanny would be 'surprized that we have come into such intimate connection with [Felix] again after what I said I should do when he arrived', but he 'could not pass [his] mother's brother' in the street. 'As to the business connection, he walked into our office one day and said, "You might as well have the letting of my property as anyone else". We do not refuse any reasonable business and consequently undertook it.'

Charley added, 'I have two pleasant objects in life to interest me in the midst of all sorts of harass and anxiety – my children and Henry [brother].' The chief anxiety was his own health and in the same letter he writes of 'suffering from diarrhoea during the last fortnight'.[39] His decline was steady from this time and the whole family returned to England in 1865 by which time Charley was 'entirely an invalid'. He died at Stoke in November 1866 at the age of 41. His brother Henry died less than four years later, aged 37.

By the spring of 1873, in her eightieth year, 'My dear Catherine' was still in the Stoke vicarage, where she had lived for almost half a century, with just two of her children left alive. Both were unmarried daughters devoted to the care of their aged parents: Priscilla, the eldest of Catherine's children, was now nearing 50 and

Fanny, the youngest, was in her thirties. Fanny recorded that in the summer before Catherine had been 'so curiously happy . . . telling me that she no longer had the wearing anxiety about her sons; she thought of them in peace and happiness, she felt them so much nearer to her than when seas divided, and she was always on the rack of "waiting for the mail." She was confident of soon rejoining them in the Unseen World.'

Directly after Easter in 1873 Catherine became ill and sank into a terminal delirium. 'She was unconscious except for one interval . . . when she began to say the Te Deum. Although I do not think she was unconscious when she began it, yet the words seemed to bring recognition, and as she said verse after verse her eyes lightened with triumph till in a full clear tone her voice rang out, "In Thee Oh Lord have I trusted: let me never be confounded".'[40] These are the words inscribed on the cross atop the Torlesse family grave monument in the Stoke-by-Nayland churchyard where Catherine lies with husband Charles, who outlived her by eight years; Charley, his wife and two daughters, Priscilla, and Fanny, who outlived all of her own and most of the next generation, to die in 1935 at the age of 96.

In the years following Felix's return to New Zealand, nothing went quite right for the last surviving Wakefield brother. The road from Lyttelton to Sumner had been completed in 1857 but, because of its precipitous, narrow and winding nature, it did not bring the traffic and commerce he had expected across his Sumner land; heavy goods continued to be freighted up the Heathcote and Avon Rivers to Christchurch. In an attempt to raise the importance and value of land at Sumner, Felix now turned his feverish energies towards promoting the construction of 'Port Wakefield' at the Sumner bar. He drew up plans for a 500-foot wide artificial channel into the estuary contained by two massive rubble walls, one approaching a mile in length. The scheme, which included docks, a wharf and roads, would have cost tens of thousands of pounds. Felix pushed the plan for ten years but, like all his other major engineering projects, it came to nothing.[41] It was finally made redundant when the Lyttelton railway tunnel was opened in 1867, providing a fast and reliable freight and passenger service between the port and city.

Canterbury did not prove profitable for him and in that year, turning 60, he took up the first of a number of bureaucratic appointments in Wellington. Over the following three years he acted as secretary to various committees, commissions and boards of inquiry and, during this time, designed the plaque fixed to the Tuamarina monument to the Nelson men killed in the Wairau incident. In July 1870, he returned to Nelson and was employed as a clerk in the post office. He soon felt this demeaning both to him and the Wakefield reputation. Incorrigible to the end, he wrote to Donald McLean, now native and defence minister, asking him to use his influence to have the Nelson chief postmaster transferred so that he might take over his position. 'It is not either decorous or just that I should hold such an inferior position when I could hold a higher one with credit, in a Province that my brother Arthur lost his life in founding, and where our family is universally popular.'[42] The entreaty brought no result and Felix continued to labour behind a clerk's counter until he retired to Sumner in 1874.

Felix's last years were lonely, with none of his children close by. He took lodgings in Sumner and spent most of his days tending his 2-acre garden near Cave Rock, where he pursued his lifelong interest in natural history and horticulture. In 1870 he had published a 'small book on horticulture in which he . . . described the cultivation of shrubs and other plants under New Zealand conditions and included a gardener's calendar'.[43] It is not quite Gilbert White's *Selborne*, and his sons did not chase and find the moa for Richard Owen, but the booklet remains a rare horticultural record from the early days of British settlement.

Just before Christmas 1875, on his way home from the garden to his lodgings, Felix had a Wakefield heart attack and dropped dead in the street. He was 68, the longest lived of all the brothers. The *Lyttelton Times* obituary included no word about his contribution to the founding of Canterbury and few attended his burial in Christchurch's Barbadoes Street cemetery. His headstone bears an apt inscription, taken from *Macbeth*. As the tormented king reflects on Duncan's death, he says, 'After life's fitful fever he sleeps well.' Whoever chose this line for Felix would have also had in mind those that followed: 'Treason has done his worst: nor steel, nor poison,/Malice domestic, foreign levy, nothing,/Can touch him further.'[44]

There is no evidence that Jerningham Wakefield attended the funeral of his last uncle. He had just attended his own political funeral and was likely to have been drowning his sorrows.

Jerningham's high life continued for a year or so after his marriage. At the Canterbury Jockey Club meeting in 1864 he presented a handsome cup for competition and won it himself with a horse called Creepmouse. But his high spending and gambling were already beginning to tell. At the time of his wedding he sold The Peer for £2,600, after it had won the thoroughbred stallion prize at the Canterbury A & P shows of 1862 and 1863, and within a year he sold off the rest of his thoroughbred stable and his Wellington land-holdings in an attempt to stave off financial collapse. But in February 1865 he was forced to assign his estate to trustees; Coldstream was sold and the family's furniture, remaining horses and equipment were auctioned. With Ellen and little Cassie, he moved into a small house in Worcester Street. Socially he was on the edge of respectability: he was forced to give up his bid to become a captain in the new voluntary Canterbury Yeomanry Cavalry when all the other officers resigned at the prospect.

Jerningham and his family led a precarious existence as he scratched an income from journalism and pamphleteering. In 1866, the year his second daughter was born – and named Nina for his long-dead sister – he stood for election to the

Canterbury Provincial Council but received only 59 votes. In 1867 he was active in local theatre and gave a series of public lectures on 'The History and Geography of New Zealand', but the audiences were small and his income slight. He did a little better the next year with the subscribed publication of his father's Canterbury Association letters in *The Founders of Canterbury*, but a planned second volume never appeared. There are no details of the privations that the family endured during these years, compounded by Jerningham's evident alcoholism, and the arrival of a third daughter, Lilly, in 1869.

In September 1870, Jerningham spoke at meetings of the unemployed, which may have been part of his campaign plan for the parliamentary elections in January 1871, the first to be held under a secret ballot. Both factors may have contributed to the fact that, against all expectations, Jerningham beat his chief opponent in Christchurch East by 169 votes to 154. When the result was announced at the town hall, Jerningham shouted, 'Won by a head! Won by a head!' The *Lyttelton Times*, which had given him virtually no space during the electioneering, hoped 'that his promotion to a seat in the Assembly would have the effect of reforming the man and giving him another chance in life'. At the age of 50 he went to Wellington, which had been the capital since 1864, with a renewed political role, and an income; and he still had some Christchurch land in trust. In middle age, perhaps he could at last find stability and respectability for his family.

The *Otago Daily Times* reported on his first speech to the new House of Representatives. It was a 'carefully prepared one and was evidently an attempt to regain the ear of the House and the reputation he once enjoyed as the best public speaker in the Colony. Rising after Mr Stafford he had the advantage of a full house, but before he had spoken ten minutes, members started to leave their seats and he was soon left to speak to almost empty benches. His speech was, in fact, a miserable failure.'[45] The humiliation was scarring. Personal disaster followed: in December 1871, Jerningham's eldest daughter, Cassie, died, aged only seven. Soon afterwards he was found comatose on a Christchurch street and charged with being drunk and disorderly.

His parliamentary career turned into a fiasco as, despite often proposing worthy motions, he sometimes appeared intoxicated in the House. He simultaneously supported and attacked William Fox's government in print, and improperly 'puffed' a railway contractor in whom he had an interest. By 1875, 'his reputation had sunk so low that he could never get a seconder' for anything he moved in Parliament. 'He had been sent to Coventry by the House.' In August, a meeting of Christchurch East electors passed a resolution 'that it is the duty of the electors to use every means to prevent the constituency being again represented by E. J. Wakefield'.[46] The next month, in some desperation, Jerningham joined the Good Templars lodge, saying that though he 'did not agree with their aims', he had become a 'total abstainer'. Few believed him and in the December election he came fifth on the ballot.

The following April, Jerningham was again found hopelessly drunk on the footpath outside the Clarendon Hotel. Fined 5s, he asked if he could be given time to find the money. He was now completely destitute – no money, no land, no assets and few friends. He persuaded Ellen to take Nina and Lilly to her brother's home in Palmerston North until he had the wherewithal to provide for her again. As he scavenged a living and tried to cope with his alcoholism, Jerningham kept up a regular correspondence with his young daughters, sending them books and music. Ellen eventually established a boarding house in order to make a living.

By the middle of 1878 there were some signs of recovery. Jerningham issued a useful pamphlet, 'The Taxes in N.Z. Who pays? Who doesn't? Who ought to pay?', and told his family that he was embarking on a tour to lecture on the topic. As he was about to begin, he was taken seriously ill and in early September went to recuperate with farming friends at Ashburton Forks. From there he wrote to Nina, telling her that he would soon start his tour in Ashburton: it would take him around the country, culminating with his arrival in Palmerston North.

On 20 September in Ashburton, Jerningham gave 'Readings! Classical and Political . . . With Interludes by a skilled Pianist'. He read from Longfellow, Macaulay, Byron, Scott and Shakespeare and, in part two of the evening, 'The Taxes in New Zealand. As they affect the Ladies!' plus 'A Land of Our Own!', a national hymn he had written for the departing Canterbury colonists in 1849. The next day, he read excerpts from EGW's writings, as well as Scott, and gave an address titled 'The Taxes in New Zealand, as they affect Wealthy Men and Working Men!!' Entrance prices were 2s 6d and 1s. The lecture tour did not continue. Jerningham was taken ill again and returned to Ashburton Forks where he wrote his last letter to Nina on 7 November, enclosing a printed copy of 'A Land of Our Own!'

Just before Christmas, in what must have been an act of utter desperation, Jerningham wrote a begging, and fruitless, letter to Governor George Grey: he was ill and destitute, his clothes had been seized and he had been arrested and fined for stealing flowers from the Ashburton government domain.[47] Ellen and the girls heard nothing of him for months, until a letter reached them from cousin Edward Wakefield, now editor of the *Timaru Herald* and MHR for Geraldine.[48] With his condolences, Edward sent Ellen a clipping from the *Ashburton Mail* of 4 March 1879. It announced that

> Edward Jerningham Wakefield died at the Old Men's Home, Ashburton, at a quarter to 5 o'clock yesterday morning [Monday] . . . . The immediate cause of his death was, we believe, diarrhoea. He had been confined to his bed for several days before the end came, of which he did not appear to have any apprehension. He remained quite sensible and conscious to the last moment. During Sunday afternoon he would not hear of any word being sent to his relatives, but after it was too late to get a telegram away he expressed a wish that his state might be communicated to his cousin in

> Timaru. His last words were, 'I would give the whole world **** Cassie' – the words indicated by the asterisks could not be heard – and then, after two long-drawn breathings, he lay still and dead.

According to the *Ashburton Mail*, Jerningham's career had been 'a chequered one. Born, if not to affluence, at least to abundance, and an enviable position in English society, he has died in an asylum for the aged and indigent in this little colonial town . . . . he certainly possessed one of the most potential intellects in the colony, but in the language of Burns he was

> *A man whose judgment clear*
> *Could others teach the course to steer*
> *Yet ran himself life's mad career*
> *Wild as the wave . . .'*

After 40 years, Jerningham's Adventure in New Zealand – and the Wakefield Family Tour Through the British Empire – were over.

EPILOGUE

THIS STORY OF A GENERATION OF THE Wakefield family has shown how the siblings' lives revolved around the career of its most dynamic individual. Edward Gibbon Wakefield, EGW, reached independent adulthood in the year of Waterloo, the beginning of British imperial domination of world affairs that lasted for over 100 years. His social and political consciousness had developed during revolutionary times and under the influence of family elders directly involved in reform movements that were gathering momentum with the new century.

EGW's character was shaped by a disruptive upbringing when he began 'life ten years too early',[1] given adult responsibilities by his mother during his father's absences and infidelities. He was also witness to events within his family that caused his grandmother Priscilla to say of his closest sibling, twelve-year-old Catherine, 'Some conversation . . . made me very uneasy and proved that her understanding and observation are beyond her years.' Although conclusions are necessarily speculative, these suggestive statements and the evidence of family conflicts, illnesses and financial difficulties all point to what would be described, in today's parlance, as a 'dysfunctional family'.

Most of the siblings seemed to have suffered from their disruptive upbringing, apart from Arthur who was given away early to the navy. He moves in and out of the Wakefield story, returning from noble deeds on behalf of empire and humanity, as if from another hemisphere, another moral dimension – what all the Wakefield boys might have been, perhaps, had they been equally exposed to the duties and disciplines of England's senior service. Yet Arthur always seems to have had character and later sublimated any personal desires in his vows to the navy and the religion that Catherine also took to as the opium for her temperamental ills.

There were two key turning points for the family, both initiated by EGW. The first came in 1816 when he eloped with Eliza Pattle and her fortune. From that time, he increasingly became father to his generation, the main source of direction and employment for his brothers. EGW's abduction of Ellen Turner, the second turning point ten years later, fractured the family and ruined their reputation, but increased rather than reduced EGW's role. As H. S. Chapman observed regarding

William, this was partly due to EGW's need to compensate for spoiling his brothers' prospects. John Howard escaped all this by rejecting EGW's control and going off to India but, progressively, William, Arthur, Dan and Felix (and son Jerningham) were all found significant employment in EGW's colonisation ventures. Between 1839 and 1855, New Zealand was very much a family business; and this ran down rapidly once EGW became inactive.

It is important to analyse EGW's character and behaviour further, not only because he was the guiding force for his Wakefield generation, but also because of his role in colonial politics between 1830 and 1855. After the start of his diplomatic career at the age of 20, EGW soon developed a well-formed ambition to obtain a seat in the House of Commons and become a force in British politics. Eliza's premature death in 1820 compromised his fortune and thus his political prospects: a career in politics was impossible without a substantial private income. His dealings with Mrs Pattle over the will settlement in Italy, while he was just 21 and 22, were an early revelation of his unscrupulousness, especially where money was concerned, and his attempts to restore both fortune and career led to the will cause and the Turner abduction. Yet it should be remembered that, though he preferred to live in reasonable comfort, money for EGW was always principally the lubricant means to political ends. He ended his life with no fortune or great estates. None of these Wakefields sought or acquired great wealth – a career and status, maybe, but not as landed gentry.

EGW's unscrupulous tendency was probably exacerbated by the corrupting influence of the European diplomatic world he inhabited from 1815 to 1826. Even after the salutary effect of imprisonment, EGW could still be importunate about money, as his dealings with Edward Ellice in the early 1840s attest; and often unscrupulous in attacking character, as Charley Torlesse understood well in the 1850s. But eloquent vilification of one's opponents in correspondence, politics and the 'public prints' was part of the period's style. EGW's saving grace was a widely appreciated kindness and generosity, not only with his money but also in spirit; he was quick to make amends and let bygones be bygones, even over Arthur's death.

Nevertheless, death and grief played an important, if imperfectly understood, role in the shaping and shading of EGW's character and behaviour. He would tell Angela Wakefield late in life that 'I should have been in a lunatic asylum before now if I had not been able to put a subject out of my mind', but his letters to Catherine following Eliza's death in 1820 and Nina's in 1835 reveal his deep grief. The loss of those closest to him inevitably caused him to think worse of this 'incongruous, contradictory, mottled world'. His unscrupulousness may have been grounded in a scepticism and lack of confidence in the morality and reliability of adult behaviour developed in childhood and youth and confirmed by his later worldly experience and arbitrary personal losses.

An appreciation of EGW's behaviour from the mid-1840s must also take into account his ill health. The grief and stress arising from news of Arthur's death at the end of 1843 are likely to have been at least partially responsible for his first stroke in September 1844. From then until his departure for New Zealand, he was never entirely well and he was close to death in August 1846. He admitted to John Abel Smith in 1849 that, when he was at his lowest in health, he was subject to paranoia about the motives and actions of even his friends and became irrational in his judgements. 'If I am wrong,' he declared, 'call me mad.' Plenty of his critics have responded to this invitation without examining the causes of his behaviour and actions, but it is worth looking at what evidence there is for any mental instability in the family.

Mother Susannah's helplessness and, later, irrational behaviour I have ascribed to stress caused by malaria and its aftermath, continual pregnancies, impecuniosity and her husband Edward's neglect. But there is a possibility that Susannah's unstable mental state may have been constitutional rather than inflicted. Felix was to later demonstrate irrationality and lack of control, and the behaviour of EGW could be volatile and unpredictable. Referring to EGW's actions before his final illness, historian David Herron wrote that, 'It would not be uncharitable to question his mental condition'.[2] L. C. Webb in *A History of Canterbury* commented, 'The letters he wrote at this period are so violent as to suggest that already he was under the shadow of mental illness.'[3] Webb seems to be alluding to EGW's final illness and seclusion, as well as contemporary views of him such as Fox's belief that EGW was 'as reckless as a lunatic'.[4] Webb would have been unaware of MP Joseph Parkes's 1839 description of EGW's 'insane physical tendency' (see Chapter Twenty). Recently, Graham Butterworth has suggested more moderately that there were 'elements of a nervous breakdown' in EGW's final illness.[5]

Without having the patients on a couch, and in the best psychiatric hands, it is impossible to make accurate diagnoses. But the surviving evidence does suggest a level of instability in both EGW's and Felix's behaviour that might be ascribed to a bi-polar or manic-depressive tendency. In EGW, the euphoric highs and gloomy lows, and the wild swings from warm praise to violent attack of friends and associates, are well documented in his correspondence. His brilliance, energy and vision are also consistent with the bi-polar personality.

Most commentators, however, have not adduced mental instability as the guiding factor in EGW's personality. When his first biographer, Richard Garnett, interviewed Felix's daughter Constance – then in her late sixties – she frequently used the word 'complex' when discussing EGW's character and behaviour. Lord Lyttelton put it another way: 'A man of much vicissitude of fortune and much inequality of character.' One who knew him well, that trenchant and perspicacious critic Justice H. S. Chapman, wrote, 'Wakefield is a man of great ability, and is endowed with many good qualities, among others I believe he is of a very kindly nature and has a natural and constitutional tendency to do acts of kindness to others. When he has an end in view he is unscrupulous as to means, and that has been his ruin. He is also vindictive, but he has no meannesses.'[6]

EGW's less discerning contemporaries tended to either overpraise him, or to condemn him out of hand. Yet those with whom EGW had the best political relationship – Durham, Lyttelton and Buller, for example – understood the dualities of his character and did not allow disapproval to prevent them appreciating and employing his vision and skills. Like historian Miles Fairburn, they saw that the 'qualities which allowed Wakefield to deviate from the norms of acceptable conduct also enabled him to be an intellectual innovator'.[7] It is noticeable that the men who trusted EGW and gave him rein were rewarded with unqualified service and friendship.

Charismatic and energetic, EGW has tended to be seen as either visionary and inspirational or machiavellian and self-serving. If one scholar from the Wakefield Appreciation Society can write, 'He acquired . . . the kind of influence which a great mind can always exercise upon an able though lesser one',[8] another from the Wakefield Demonising Club will counter with EGW being 'frequently activated by that "motiveless malignity" which a great Shakespearean critic ascribed to Iago'.[9]

EGW's means of achieving ends were often questionable, or often hard to perceive because force of circumstance required him to work incognito. The only way he might obtain credit for whatever he achieved was self-publicity, regarded as vulgar and reprehensible by the already privileged or rewarded. That he could be malign or vindictive is unquestionable, but the extreme view that 'Practically everyone who came into contact with Wakefield was eventually anathematised for disloyalty, heterodoxy or simply malicious refusal to obey'[10] is a predication for the hypothesis that it was 'not that Wakefield founded South Australia or Canterbury, but rather that these projects offered opportunities for the refounding of Wakefield'.[11] Simplistic hypotheses do not work with Edward Gibbon Wakefield. If, like Byron, he was 'mad, bad and dangerous to know', then he was mad with ideas – some fanciful and some brave, some useless and some visionary; sometimes bad in the ways he worked amorally among politicians, bureaucrats and businessmen to realise his ideas; and dangerous as only someone so dynamic and unpredictable can be when excluded from the corridors of power. The preoccupation with EGW's character has consistently confused or obscured dispassionate analysis and review of his work. And the tendency to accord him the status of hero or villain has led most recently to caricature: 'E. G. Wakefield himself did not come down to us until 1852 [*sic*], although He did send His Son', and when he did come it was as a 'convicted kidnapper, who hypnotised people into frothing fits as a party trick. . .'.[12] Or as the 'ludicrous figure in a fantasy world' seeking only to 'recover from his past'. This is surely historical reductionism at its worst.

Rehabilitation was, naturally, always a motive for EGW. The experience and ignominy of Newgate prison forced him to turn from a diplomatic and overtly political career to social and political causes that were in harmony with those he had grown up with. Following in the tradition of his grandmother and father, he used outstanding literary skills, which he was to pass on to his son. Richard Garnett felt that EGW made the mistake of not confining his work in the colonial field to writing for he was, as one reviewer of the time put it, 'that very rare thing, a theorist in politics'.[13] Another has written, 'The history of the theory of colonization without Gibbon Wakefield would indeed be Hamlet without the Prince of Denmark.'[14] The volume of his written work testifies to his talents for bringing together ideas and information, his own and others, and promoting them with an unusual persuasiveness. Storytelling and metaphor are powerful elements of EGW's writing: if he had felt the enthusiasm and inclination for it, he might have been a successful social novelist in the age of Dickens and Thackeray.

But EGW could never have limited himself to a purely literary or editorial career. He was driven too hard by the political ambitions he harboured all his adult life. And it is not too much to say that some of his reviled behaviour was simply common to politics. Yet when EGW achieved his goal of parliamentary prominence at last, in Auckland in 1854, he could not overcome the ingrained habits of 25 years of lobbying and wire-pulling. He also believed, rightly if arrogantly, that no one in the colony was his political equal and that, since it had been so much his own creation, he had a right to power. Add a weakened physical constitution with increasing age, and disaster was inevitable. During those last weeks of the first New Zealand Parliament he was running on adrenalin.

After Newgate had blocked his parliamentary ambitions, therefore, EGW mostly promoted his policies in books, journals and private chambers rather than on the hustings or on the floor of the House. As he told his father in 1841, he was 'only a generalizer or theorizer' and left 'all the filling-up of the details' to others. He never took any ultimate responsibility for his views, actions and propaganda, largely because he was not required to. Rarely holding any kind of official office after Newgate, he was not often publicly accountable. Yet he made it plain that he did not consider his ideas valid beyond his immediate era, and that the tenets of his colonial schemes were flexible enough to suit current circumstances both at home and abroad. The 'sufficient price', for example, was not a 'wall of brass', as he told Godley, but 'an elastic belt'. And if it did not work, throw it out. If you needed pastoralists to make it work, get pastoralists. The planned settlements were never set up or worked quite as EGW planned and the faults have been almost all laid at his door, but he was only one among the directors of the New Zealand Company and he was its philosopher rather than its sole manager. Its drift away from his philosophy towards pure speculation and profit provoked his ire and eventual disassociation.

Erik Olssen wrote in 1996, 'For more than a generation, historians have dedicated themselves to assessing Wakefield and the systematic colonisers either in terms of individual character, or the lack thereof, or by intensively analysing the gap between Wakefield's planned ideal and the muddy reality.'[15] And there have been continuing attacks on any belief that EGW was more than a 'successful pamphleteer and lobbyist'. Political scientist Mark Francis wrote in 2001, 'Compared to other colonial radicals, he was less original as a writer or theorist, his serious statements about constitutional issues were more conventional and less republican than theirs . . . he had little social credibility [and] little influence with the major politicians of his era . . . He was a tiny figure overshadowed by the giants of classical economics.'[16] The shades of Durham, Gladstone, J. S. Mill and Marx might disagree with at least some of this. And such a sweeping dismissal takes no account of the power of myth in a nation's understanding of itself. Or of such realities as EGW's direct hand, with his brothers – for this was, after all, a family business – in the establishment of the Wellington and Nelson settlements. Such was not achieved by pamphleteering and lobbying alone.

But much of the received criticism of EGW in association with the New Zealand Company 'Bubble', led off by Michael Turnbull, John Miller and Keith Sinclair in the 1950s, has tended to ease in the face of a reconsideration of the longer term success of his colonial ideas. Acknowledging EGW's grasp of the future, Fairburn wrote in 1990 that he 'brilliantly anticipated the manner in which settler societies such as Argentina, New Zealand, South Africa, and Australia actually developed later in the century by importing investment capital and people from the Old World'.[17] More recently, Eric Richards wrote that 'Wakefieldianism' in the 'first twenty years [from the mid-1830s] had been pivotal in the peopling of Australia, and it is in this that Wakefield's peculiar achievement must be registered'. He designed a 'mechanism which, despite all its defects, conveyed tens of thousands of ordinary people across the oceans'.[18] In a late-twentieth-century climate of freer markets and globalisation, Olssen pointed to EGW as an heir to Adam Smith in the tradition whereby the 'creation of wealth – still the major goal of economic thought – was analysed as the outcome of complex social and cultural practices which were captured in the notion of an advancing civilisation. Europeans, and especially Britons, had imagined New Zealand before colonisation began as a scientific experiment in constructing a new civilisation.'[19]

Although Herron would say in 1959 that it was 'straining credibility to intolerable lengths to discern generous infusions of idealism or altruistic ends' in EGW's New Zealand political manoeuvrings,[20] by 1996 John E. Martin would speak of the major contributions EGW made in New Zealand provincial and national politics, in particular land policies, within a burst of activity that lasted only eighteen months. He also pointed out that his 'influence on the very constitution of this country was absolutely fundamental . . . self representation and democracy are integral parts of nationhood taken for granted in the twentieth century. In the mid-nineteenth, they were radical ideas indeed.'[21] A reluctant democrat at first, EGW was to end by frightening the nascent ruling class in New Zealand with a kind of socialism.

So is EGW finally achieving his rehabilitation? Not a chance. His posthumous reputation will always bear the cross of moral turpitude: no age has found fraud and abduction acceptable behaviour. And his reputation will continue to be smeared by exaggerations such as the statement that he 'ruthlessly terrified Ellen Turner'[22] when he patently did not. It does seem, however, that some historians are now more willing to separate EGW's pre-1830 personal behaviour from his later work in colonial politics and to look more dispassionately at its results, finding some of it worthwhile. But here there is another dark shadow over EGW's reputation: 'Much criticism, too, has been directed at Wakefield's neglect of the rights and welfare of indigenous peoples'.[23] For, 'Where do Maori see the foundation of all this hurt, this loss of mana, this loss of wairua, our very souls? It is in the visions of this ambitious man, this charlatan, this politician extraordinaire, in his ambition for a land he could not create in his own homeland.'[24] Again, EGW is seen as chief villain, in this case of Maori loss of land and rights. His doubtful personal morals make him the perfect fall guy for the evils of colonisation. Yet, as long as 40 years ago, W. H. Oliver observed accurately that EGW was a 'characteristic and leading figure of the troubled English generation after 1815' and had 'influenced a great number of . . . men of greater contemporary eminence than he'[25] – men who had no difficulty in believing in the force and validity of EGW's ideas. Such a man, such a tohunga, found in the whakapapa of any Maori iwi or hapu would be accorded great reverence for what he had achieved for his people. And in the Wellington region, at least, EGW's provision of reserving land for Maori in the section ballots survives today in the Wellington Tenths Association, an effective force in achieving redress and compensation over land claims dating back to 1840.

The achievements and values of New Zealand's Pakeha ancestors – colonists almost all – are sometimes accorded limited respect in prevailing political, intellectual and judicial circles at the beginning of the twenty-first century. They are portrayed often as people to be ashamed of, with EGW the worst of them all. Yet, flawed as he and they were, clumsy and arrogant though some of their behaviour and actions may have been, they founded settlements with civic and social institutions that have produced arguably the most open, democratic and humanitarian nation in the world. As far as EGW is concerned, Canadians probably still place some value on the Durham Report as a founding constitutional document; he still has standing as a political economist in Britain; and even Australians find merit in some aspects of 'Wakefieldianism'.

Alive and dead, EGW (with his brothers) has been on the rack for 175 years now and for New Zealanders he has become rather like King Richard III for the English. It took 500 years, after the Battle of Bosworth, for the arms of Richard III to be fixed in an obscure window at the eastern end of York Minster. Will it take as long for EGW to be discreetly honoured in New Zealand? It is often said that Pakeha New Zealanders have much to learn from Maori. One useful lesson may be to understand and assimilate the Maori way of valuing ancestors for the good, useful or powerful things they achieved for their people, regardless of their sometimes reprehensible behaviour: Te Rauparaha is a case in point. Then, like Maori, Pakeha may walk confidently with their ancestors through the present and into the future.

EXTENDED NOTES

A

EGW and Mrs Rocke

In 1825, there was a curious sequel to the will case. The defendant in the 1824 case had been Mrs Sarah Susanna Rocke (*née* Pattle), Thomas Pattle's sister, a considerable beneficiary of his will. She had become rich in her own right upon the death of her husband, the Senior Judge of the Court of Appeal in Calcutta. After the trial, she married Thomas Berkeley Bond, who then attempted to take over her entire fortune. On 1 April 1825, EGW, again at the British Embassy in Paris, wrote an extraordinary letter to the Parisian Director of Police, claiming to represent the interests of the woman he had taken his case against the previous year. 'Her fortune,' he wrote,

> rests under the protection of an English Court but Bond has instituted proceedings to seize it.
>
> Mrs Bond (i.e. the former Mrs Rocke), who has suffered much from the infamous conduct of her husband, is opposing him in this suit; but she could not but lose were it not that she has learnt that she is not Bond's wife, but that Bond has been married for some years to a widow named Love . . . .
>
> I have learnt that Mrs Love confided to several persons the secret of her marriage, that she is at present carefully hidden in the vicinity of Paris and that she plans to remain hidden there until Bond shall have laid hold of the fortune of Mrs Rocke.

According to EGW, Bond already had possession of her Parisian 'town house with furniture, very precious jewellery and large sums of money'.[1]

Parisian police investigations discovered that Mrs Love had indeed lived 'maritally' with Bond for some years but no formal marriage had taken place. Bond returned to Paris in July, flush with money to pay off old debts and was harassed by the police on suspicion of being involved in 'political intrigue'; but he was eventually cleared of this and of any marital impropriety. On 25 August, Sarah Susanna Bond wrote to the Director of Police in her husband's defence, signing herself as his 'very distressed and very humble servant'.

EGW gained nothing from this exercise and his only possible motive could have been that, if his allegations had been proved correct, then Mrs Rocke may have rewarded him for saving her from a bigamist: that, or simple malice for having been defeated and exposed as a fraud himself in the Prerogative Court.

B

Rebellion in Canada

The political and social difficulties between and within the separate provinces of French Lower Canada and British Upper Canada had been pushed to outright rebellion by severe economic depression. British Canada had been the chief receptacle for the massive movement of British immigrant poor into the country since the 1820s – 66,000 in 1832 alone – but control over government and land had remained in the hands of early established families. The self-interested political behaviour of the 'Family Compact', allied to inconsistent policy directives from an often uninterested Colonial Office, created growing unrest throughout the 1830s.

The relationship between the two Canadas had become increasingly difficult as the frontier of trade extended steadily west. The flow of goods via the natural east-west St Lawrence waterway remained under the control of businessmen in Montreal and both tariffs and vital canal development was subject to the political jurisdiction of the Lower Canada legislature. Upper Canada relied heavily on imports up the St Lawrence system but in 1822 received only 20 per cent of customs revenue levied in Quebec and Montreal. This prompted an attempt at union that year that was scuttled by French Canadians who saw that the Union Bill provided for an English majority in government. Also, most anglophone farmers and small businessmen decided that the bill provided mostly to boost the power and line the pockets of the old oligarchic networks of Montreal and Toronto.

Economic growth was sluggish compared to the United States. From 1830, the example of the robust and bank-reforming democracy of Andrew Jackson's America inspired reformers in Upper Canada to call for the elimination of old privilege, government based on a broad electorate, and the extension of credit facilities to small businessmen and farmers. Leader of the reformers was William Lyon Mackenzie whose attacks on the establishment so incensed the Tory majority that he was four times expelled from the Upper Canada Assembly and had the presses for his scourging newspaper, *Colonial Advocate*, thrown into Lake Ontario. By the mid-1830s, in the face of unyielding Tory privilege among the political hierarchies of Toronto and London, Mackenzie increasingly advocated the virtues of the American republican system. But for this he had little support from a populace that still valued British political and constitutional traditions. They also feared the overwhelming effect on their lives and businesses – perhaps ultimate absorption – from too close an association with the American democratic experiment.

Mackenzie's counterpart in Lower Canada was Louis-Joseph Papineau. A conservative seigneur,[2] Papineau was the long-serving speaker of the Lower Canada Assembly and had come to embrace, like many French Canadians, the British form of representative government. But he was also thoroughly acquainted with the ideas of the French and American revolutions and came to oppose the oligarchic collusion of higher Roman Catholic clergy with the French official class and what was called the 'Chateau Clique' – the English-speaking mercantile hierarchy in Montreal. Like Mackenzie, Papineau's calls for more democracy were a way of pushing the establishment towards more moderate reforms. His radicalism was mostly propaganda: he knew well that to make an alliance, let alone union, with the United States would soon spell the end of a separate French Canadian identity.

C

EGW, Dr Evans and Liocadia

From May 1845, EGW was harassed not only by the battle with the government, but also by the demands of a deputation of settlers from Wellington seeking financial relief from the directors of the company. They were led by Dr George Samuel Evans who had been

EGW's first secretary of the company in 1837. Edward Jerningham Wakefield recorded that Evans arrived at Burstow on the evening of 4 May when there was an 'Escape of bitterness and bile' and that the next morning he left EGW and Evans to 'confabulate and have it out'.[3] Ten days later, Evans was at Burstow again – an 'inconsistent & flighty soul' according to Jerningham. On 5 June, Jerningham accompanied Evans to a conference with the company directors which sought to find the 'best means of protecting the interests of the Colonists and the company' in view of the pending debate in Parliament. They came away with letters and promises of introductions to MPs. On 22 June, Jerningham noted, 'I have been struck more than ever with the fearful impracticability of old Evans.'[4]

Evans's 'impracticability' led him on 7 August to send a letter to the directors staking 'the claim of the Colonists to be indemnified, either by the Company or the Government, for the delay that has occurred, in the fulfilment of the Company's contract with them'. He was rebuffed by the directors who 'considered that, from the part he took in the early proceedings of the Company, he was more identified with the responsibilities it had incurred, than almost any other person'.[5] The company sent a copy of the correspondence to Lord Stanley to scupper any approach he might make to the Colonial Office.

The reply to Evans had EGW stamped all over it, and it is certain that he and Evans had fallen out. By 1845, EGW must have learnt of Evans's treatment of Liocadia di Oliveira during the voyage out and the early days of the Wellington settlement; and stories of his obstreperous behaviour on board the *Adelaide* had become notorious. In 1843 he had prepared a report on the Wairau for Acting New Zealand Governor Willoughby Shortland that condemned Arthur's actions with faint praise. It is likely that William Wakefield had sent EGW word in advance of Evans's turncoat behaviour.

In January 1846, Evans approached the directors again with a new tactic, proposing that they buy his Wellington properties. With a sarcastic flourish, the company appointed a special 'select committee' to examine the proposal. A month later they agreed to buy but on the condition that he sell his entire property, including the three town sections on which his own and his daughter-in-law's houses had been built. Evans wanted his original purchase price plus 5 per cent for six years, a bargain for the directors. EGW and George Young pointedly opposed the interest but were overruled by the others. Evans was left with little choice and pathetically asked that his wife and daughter, still in Wellington, not be deprived of any rents they had received. EGW and the other directors agreed and instructed William Wakefield 'to afford Mrs Evans all accommodation in his power'. EGW had obtained satisfaction, at least on Liocadia's and Arthur's behalf.

D

Swainson and the Art of Colonization

The fiercest critic of *A View of the Art of Colonization* was Wellington settler William Swainson, who had arrived in the colony in 1841 with his family, aged 52, having purchased farm land in the Porirua district. The family had lost most of their household goods in a shipwreck. Swainson had been unable to take possession of his land because of Te Rangihaeata's opposition and while he waited for title to be settled had rented 300 acres of land in the Hutt Valley. After expending hundreds of pounds on clearing and improving that land, most of it had been taken by the Maori during the 1844–45 conflict; later he had been required to pay rent to the absentee owners when it was no longer in his possession. A natural historian of some standing, Swainson had also been disappointed in his attempts to obtain an official position in the colony as zoologist and botanist. By the end of 1849, EGW's book provided the perfect target for Swainson to vent his considerable spleen, both on the theory and the man. Swainson's extensive review appeared in the first and only two issues of Wellington's *New Zealand Magazine* in 1850. By the time it had circulated throughout the country and reached England, the company was no more and Canterbury was well in hand. But this tirade of the disappointed settler articulated much of the anger and frustrations of the early company settlers, and added much to the debit sheet of criticism that lay in wait for EGW in New Zealand.

ACKNOWLEDGEMENTS

This book would never have been written without the generous support and encouragement of many people and institutions over the past eleven years. It was set firmly on its way in 1994 by the award of a Non-Fiction Bursary by the Queen Elizabeth II Arts Council (re-established as Creative New Zealand). The Historical Branch of the Department of Internal Affairs gave me a grant towards the cost of research in England and, later, a grant to assist completion of the manuscript. In 1996–97, I was awarded the National Library Fellowship in Wellington, domiciled within the Alexander Turnbull Library, and for a year enjoyed the most supportive working environment of my career.

My alphabetically ordered list of those institutions that assisted this project, therefore, begins appropriately with the Alexander Turnbull Library and, though it seems invidious to single out any staff member for particular praise, I should acknowledge the long-term interest and assistance of David Colquhoun, Marsha Donaldson, Marian Minson, Phil Parkinson and David Retter. I also used the supportive services of Archives New Zealand, Wellington; the Archives Office of Tasmania, Hobart (Margaret Parkes); the British Library, London; the Canterbury Museum, Christchurch; the Canterbury Public Library, Christchurch (Richard Greenaway); the Dunedin Public Library (McNab Collection); the Harry Ransom Humanities Research Center, University of Texas at Austin; the Hocken Library, Dunedin (the late David McDonald, Stuart Strachan and Beverley Booth); the Local History Section, Edmonton Town Hall, London; Mitchell Library, Sydney; the National Army Museum Library, London; the National Library of New Zealand, Wellington; the National Library of Scotland, Edinburgh; the National Maritime Museum Library, Greenwich, London; the National Portrait Gallery, London; the Natural History Museum Library, London; the Nelson Provincial Museum (Anne McEwan); the New Zealand Parliamentary Library, Wellington; the Public Archives of Canada, Ottawa (Patricia Kennedy); the Public Record Office, Kew and Chancery Lane, London; the Royal New Zealand Navy Museum, Auckland (Lieutenant Commander Peter Dennerly); Le Service de la Bibliothèque, Assemblée Nationale, Paris (Jeanine Dodu); the University of Otago Central Library and Law Library, Dunedin (Alan Edwards); the Victoria University of Wellington Library, Beaglehole Room (Kathleen Coleridge); the Wellington Public Library (Hilda McDonnell).

Other people who helped with valuable research material or advice were Brian Baldwin (Adelaide); George Barton (Wellington); Edmund Bohan (Christchurch); Keith Borrow (Adelaide); Tom Brooking (Dunedin); Ronald A. Chapman (Christchurch); Roger Collins (Dunedin); Gaile Douglas (Nelson); Chris Else (Wellington); Gerald Fischer (Adelaide); Michael Fitzgerald (Wellington); Ray Grover (Wellington); Mary Hammonds (Dunedin); Michael Harlow (Christchurch); Alan Horsman (Dunedin); Philip Houghton (Auckland); Richard King (Christchurch); Sara Joynes (London, initially with Australian Joint Copying Project); Geoff Park (Wellington); Harry Poole (Devon); Eric Richards (Adelaide); Paul Schimmel (Sydney); Tony Simpson (Wellington); David Small (London); Geoffrey Taylor

(Nottingham); Jane Thomson (Dunedin); Christine Vivien (USIS, Wellington); Sir Humphry Wakefield (London); Lois Witherow (Dunedin). For her encouragement and support in the closing stages of this marathon, especial thanks to my partner, Diane Brown.

In conclusion, there are two people who have been as good as godparents to the project: Professor Erik Olssen, University of Otago, who tracked my manuscript all the way and gave me the vital advice and reassurances I needed over such a long haul; and Priscilla Mitchell (*née* Wakefield) of Totnes in Devon who, with the same philanthropic virtues of her illustrious eponymous ancestor, generously shared with me her collection of Wakefield family papers. Priscilla Mitchell also gave me the most direct link to this book's generation of Wakefields. The last surviving descendant of Daniel Wakefield, she told me how, as a young woman, she spoke with the great-aunt who, as a young girl, gave Edward Gibbon Wakefield such comfort in his dying days. Ancestors are never as distant as we think.

BIBLIOGRAPHY

Abbreviations

ADM	Admiralty
ANZ	Archives New Zealand, Wellington
ATL	Alexander Turnbull Library, Wellington
AW	Arthur Wakefield
BL	British Library, London
BPP	*British Parliamentary Papers* (Irish University Press)
CM	Canterbury Museum, Christchurch
CO	Colonial Office
CPL	Canterbury Public Library, Christchurch
CT	Catherine Torlesse
CW	Catherine Wakefield
DCB	*Dictionary of Canadian Biography*
DNB	*Dictionary of National Biography* (UK)
DNZB	*Dictionary of New Zealand Biography*
DW	Daniel Wakefield
EGW	Edward Gibbon Wakefield
EJW	Edward Jerningham Wakefield
EW	Edward Wakefield
FW	Felix Wakefield
HL	Hocken Library, Dunedin
ML	Mitchell Library, Sydney
MP	Mitchell (Wakefield Family) Papers, Devon
NAM	National Army Museum, London
NPG	National Portrait Gallery, London
NPM	Nelson Provincial Museum
PAC	Public Archives of Canada, Ottawa
PRO	Public Record Office, London
PW	Priscilla Wakefield
WW	William Wakefield

MANUSCRIPT COLLECTIONS

ALEXANDER TURNBULL LIBRARY, WELLINGTON

Allom Papers
Bett Papers
Canterbury Papers
Chapman Letters
Edward Betts Hopper Diary
Lambton Papers
New Zealand Company records
O'Connor Papers
Partridge Letters
Revans Letters
Stafford Papers
Wakefield Family Papers

ARCHIVES NEW ZEALAND, WELLINGTON
Colonial Office records
Internal Affairs records
New Zealand Company records

BRITISH LIBRARY, LONDON
Gladstone Papers
Hardwicke Papers
Hone Papers
Leigh Hunt Papers
Peel Papers
Place Papers
Russell Papers
Young Papers
Add. MSS

CANTERBURY MUSEUM, CHRISTCHURCH
J. R. Godley Papers
Lyttelton Papers
McDonald Biographies
O'Connor Papers
Selfe Papers
Chas O. Torlesse Letters
E. G. Wakefield Papers
E. J. Wakefield Papers

CANTERBURY PUBLIC LIBRARY, CHRISTCHURCH
Sir John Hall Collection

HOCKEN LIBRARY, DUNEDIN
F. R. Chapman Papers
New Zealand Company records
E. G. Wakefield Letters

MITCHELL LIBRARY, SYDNEY
Sir John George Lefèvre Papers
Ward Family Papers

NATURAL HISTORY MUSEUM, LONDON
Owen Collection

NELSON PROVINCIAL MUSEUM
John Barnicoat Journal

PUBLIC ARCHIVES OF CANADA, OTTAWA
Sir Charles Bagot Papers
Charles Buller Papers
Elgin-Grey Papers
Ellice Family Papers*
La Fontaine Papers
John George Lambton Papers
Papineau Papers
Denis-Benjamin Viger Papers
** Note: Ellice Papers from PAC are facsimiles used by permission of the National Library of Scotland, Edinburgh.*

PUBLIC RECORD OFFICE, LONDON
Admiralty records
Chancery records

HARRY RANSOM HUMANITIES RESEARCH CENTER, UNIVERSITY OF TEXAS AT AUSTIN
Richard Garnett Collection

WAKEFIELD FAMILY, DEVON
Mitchell Papers

NEWSPAPERS AND JOURNALS

Blackwood's Edinburgh Magazine
Colonial Gazette
English Chronicle
Evening Post (New Zealand)
Independent (New Zealand)
Liverpool Mercury
Lyttelton Times (New Zealand)
Monthly Review
Morning Chronicle
Morning Post
Naval Chronicle
Nelson Examiner (New Zealand)
New Zealand Gazette
New Zealand Journal
Spectator (London)
Spectator (New Zealand)
The Times

THESES, ARTICLES, PAMPHLETS

Baldwin, B. S., 'Edward Gibbon Wakefield in Paris, 1825, and the fortune of Sarah Susanna Rocke', *Historical Facts and Events*, Vol. 8, No. 3, pp. 44-51 and Vol. 9, No. 3, p. 62.
Beaglehole, J. C., 'Captain Hobson and the New Zealand Company: A Study in Colonial Administration', *Smith College Studies in History*, Vol. XIII, Nos 1–3, October 1927–April 1928, Northampton, Mass.
Buller, Charles, 'Responsible Government for the Colonies', London, 1840.
Chapman, Ronald A.,'Felix Wakefield, A Life of Fitful Fever', Christchurch, 1996.
Collie, Margerita, 'Quakers of Tottenham 1775–1825', Edmonton Hundred Historical Society Occasional Papers, NS 37, 1978.
Dewar, James, 'Colonization of the County of Beauharnois', London, 1840 (Pamphlet for North American Colonial Association of Ireland and possibly written by EGW).
Edwards, Douglas George, 'The Voyage of the Barque Tory', MA Thesis, 1939 ATL 993.1.
Francis, Mark, 'Settler Historiography in New Zealand: Politics and Biography in the Early Colonial Period', *Political Science*, Vol. 52, No. 2, December 2000.
Gilbert, Arthur N., 'Buggery and the British Navy 1700–1861', *Journal of Social History*, 10, 1977.
Herron, D. G., 'The Structure and Course of New Zealand Politics, 1853–58', PhD Thesis 1959, HL.
Howell, P. A., 'Clearing the cobwebs: a reconsideration of the beginnings of the province of South Australia', *Journal of the History Teachers Association of South Australia*, Vol. 13, No. 1, July 1991.
Hussey, H., 'New Zealand and How It Became a British Province', ATL MS Hus 133, 560, 1868.
Lloyd Prichard, M. F., 'Wakefield Changes His Mind About the Sufficient Price', *International Review of Social History*, Vol. 8, No. 2, 1963.

Lower, A. R. M., 'Edward Gibbon Wakefield and the Beauharnois Canal', *Canadian Historical Review*, Vol. XIII, 1932.
MacDonnell, Ursilla, 'Gibbon Wakefield and Canada subsequent to the Durham Mission, 1839–1842', Bulletin No. 49, Departments of History and Political and Economic Science, Queens University, Kingston, 1924–25.
Manning, Helen Taft, 'Edward Gibbon Wakefield and the Beauharnois Canal,' *Canadian Historical Review*, Vol. XLVIII, 1967.
Monteagle, Thomas Spring-Rice, 'The Necessity and Consequences of Colonization', London, 1848.
Norman, John, 'Edward Gibbon Wakefield: a Political Reappraisal', Fairfield, Conn., 1963.
Palmer, Leonard Russell, 'Captain Arthur Wakefield,' MA Thesis, 1929, ATL Micro 275b.
Pike, Douglas, 'Wakefield, Waste Land and Empire', *Proceedings of Tasmanian Historical Research Association*, Vol. 12, 1965.
Pollock, Josephine, 'Tottenham 1800–1850', Edmonton Hundred Historical Society, Occasional Papers, NS 29, 1974.
Pretty, Graeme, 'Edward Gibbon Wakefield and New Zealand 1846–52', Department of History, University of Sydney, 1960.
Ritchie, John, 'Towards Ending an Unclean Thing: the Molesworth Committee', *Journal of the Historical Society of Australia and New Zealand*, Vol. XVII.
Shteir, Ann B., 'Priscilla Wakefield's Natural History Books,' *From Linnaeus to Darwin*, Society for the History of Natural History, London, 1985.
Wakefield, Edward Gibbon, *The Hangman and the Judge*, London, 1833.
Wakefield, Edward Gibbon, *Householders in Danger from the Populace*, London, 1831.
Wakefield, Edward Gibbon, *Popular Politics*, London, 1837.
Wakefield, Edward Gibbon, *Statement of Facts Regarding the Marriage of Edward G. Wakefield Esq., with Miss Turner*, London, 6 May 1826.
Wakefield, Edward Gibbon, *Swing Unmasked or the Causes of Rural Incendiarism*, London, 1831.
Wakefield, Edward Gibbon, 'A View of Sir Charles Metcalfe's Government of Canada', London, 1844.
(Wakefield, Edward Gibbon) 'Instructions from the New Zealand Land Company to Colonel Wakefield, Principal Agent of the Company', London, 1839.
Wakefield, Felix, *The Mutual Relations Between the Canterbury Association and the Purchasers of Land*, London, 1853.
White, William, *Letter to Edward Gibbon Wakefield*, London, 1838.

BOOKS

Ackroyd, Peter, *Dickens*, London, 1990.
Adams, Peter, *Fatal Necessity*, Auckland, 1977.
Adderley, Charles (ed.), *Extracts from Letters of John Robert Godley to C. B. Adderley*, London, 1863.
Allan, Ruth M., *Nelson, A History of Early Settlement*, Wellington, 1965.
Allington, Margaret H., *Unquiet Earth*, Wellington, 1978.
Andrew, J. L., *The Wairau Massacre*, Blenheim, 1999.
Austen, Jane, *Persuasion*, London, 1930.
Austen, Jane, *Sense and Sensibility*, Oxford, 1990.
Babington, Anthony, *The English Bastille*, London, 1971.
Balzac, Honoré de, *Père Goriot*, Paris, 1835.
Beecham, John, *Colonization*, London, 1838.
Belich, James, *Making Peoples*, Auckland, 1996.
Belich, James, *The New Zealand Wars*, Auckland, 1986.
Bell, Gerda, *Ernest Dieffenbach*, Palmerston North, 1976.
Bell K. N. and Morrell W. S., *Select Documents on British Colonial Policy 1830–60*, Oxford, 1928.
Birmingham, David, *A Concise History of Portugal*, Cambridge, 1993.
Bloomfield, Paul, *Edward Gibbon Wakefield*, London, 1961.
Bohan, Edmund, *'Blest Madman', FitzGerald of Canterbury*, Christchurch, 1998.
Bohan, Edmund, *Edward Stafford*, Christchurch, 1994.
Bridges, Reverend C. (ed.), *A Selection from the Correspondence of the Rev. J. T. Nottidge*, London, 1849.

Briggs, Asa, *The Age of Improvement, 1783–1867*, London, 1959.
Burns, Patricia (ed. Henry Richardson), *Fatal Success, A History of the New Zealand Company*, Auckland, 1989.
Burns, Patricia, *Te Rauparaha, A New Perspective*, Wellington, 1980.
Bury, J. P. T., *France 1814–1840*, London, 1949.
Carleton, Hugh, *The Life of Henry Williams*, Auckland, 1874.
Carrington, C. E., *John Robert Godley*, Christchurch, 1950.
Caughey, Angela, *The Interpreter, The Biography of Richard 'Dicky' Barrett*,Auckland, 1998.
Clarke, George Jr, *Notes on Early Life in New Zealand*, Hobart, 1903.
Clowes, Wm Laird, *The Royal Navy, A History*, Vols V and VI, London, 1901.
Colley, Linda, *Britons, Forging the Nation 1707–1837*, London, 1994.
Collins, Philip, *Dickens and Crime*, London, 1962.
Cooke, Robin, *Portrait of a Profession*, Wellington, 1969.
Couchman, Harriet, *Reminiscences of Tottenham*, London, 1909.
Currey, C. H., *British Colonial Policy 1783–1915*, Oxford, 1924.
Dalby, John, *Tottenham Parish Church and Parish*, London, 1980.
Davy, Humphry, *Collected Works of Humphry Davy*, London, 1839.
Deans, J. (ed.), *Pioneers of Canterbury*, Wellington, 1937.
Dickens, Charles, *David Copperfield*, London, 1850.
Dickens, Charles, *Dombey and Son*, London, 1848.
Dickens, Charles, *Martin Chuzzlewit*, London, 1844.
Dickens, Charles, *Sketches by Boz*, London, 1957.
Dieffenbach, Ernest, *Travels in New Zealand*, London, 1843.
Durham, Earl of, *Lord Durham's Report on the Affairs of British North America*, Oxford, 1912.
Edward Gibbon Wakefield and the Colonial Dream: A Reconsideration, Wellington, 1997 (various contributors).
Edwards, Doug, *Put Him in the Longboat*, Wellington, 1989.
Egan, Pierce, *Life in London: The day and night scenes of Jerry Hawthorn Esq and his elegant friend Corinthian Tom*, London, 1821.
Farr, Reverend Thomas, *A Traveller's Rambling Reminiscences of the Spanish War*, London, 1838.
Fawcett, Millicent, *Life of the Rt. Hon. Sir William Molesworth*, London, 1901.
Fenton, James, *A History of Tasmania*, Hobart, 1884.
Fisk, Frederic, *History of the Ancient Parish of Tottenham*, Tottenham, 1923.
FitzGerald, James Edward (ed.), *Writings and Speeches by John Robert Godley*, Christchurch, 1863.
Fortescue, Hon. J. W., *History of the British Army*, Vol. XIII, London, 1930.
Fox, William, *The Colonisation of New Zealand*, London, 1842.
Garnett, Richard, *Edward Gibbon Wakefield*, London, 1898.
Gisborne, William, *New Zealand Rulers and Statesmen*, Wellington, 1886.
Godley, Charlotte, *Letters from Early New Zealand*, Christchurch, 1951.
Godsell, Patricia (ed.), *Letters and Diaries of Lady Durham*, Toronto, 1979.
Graham Gerald S. and Humphreys R. A., *The Navy and South America 1807–1823*, London, 1962.
Grey, Alan H., *Aotearoa and New Zealand*, Christchurch, 1994.
Griffiths, Arthur George Frederick, *The Chronicles of Newgate*, London, 1883.
Grover, Ray, *Cork of War*, Dunedin, 1982.
Hamer, David and Nicholls, Roberta (eds), *The Making of Wellington 1800–1914*, Wellington, 1990.
Harrop, A. J., *The Amazing Career of Edward Gibbon Wakefield*, London, 1928.
Heaphy, Charles, *Narrative of a Residence in Various Parts of New Zealand*, London, 1842.
Hight, James and Straubel, C. R., *A History of Canterbury*, Vol. 1, Christchurch, 1957.
Hincks, Sir Francis, *Reminiscences in the Life of Sir Francis Hincks*, Montreal, 1884.
Hodder, Edwin, *History of South Australia*, London, 1893.
Holloway, John and Black, Joan (eds), *Later English Broadside Ballads*, Vol. 2, London, 1979.
Hollingsworth, Keith, *The Newgate Novel 1830–47: Bulwer, Ainsworth, Dickens & Thackeray*, Detroit, 1963.
Holt, Edgar, *The Carlist Wars in Spain*, London, 1967.
Huelin, Gordon, *King's College 1828–1978*, London, 1978.
Hyde, Ralph, *Panoramania*, London, 1988.
James,Wm., *The Naval History of Great Britain 1793–1820*, Vol. VI, London, 1826.

Jardin, André and Tudesq, André-Jean, *Restoration & Reaction 1815–1848*, Cambridge, 1973.
Jones, Alan, *Backsight, A History of Surveying in Colonial Tasmania*, Hobart, 1989.
Legget, Robert F., *Canals of Canada*, Vancouver, 1976.
Lewis, Michael, *A Social History of the Navy, 1793–1815*, London, 1960.
Lewis Michael, *The Navy in Transition, 1814–1864*, London, 1965.
Livermore, H. V., *A New History of Portugal*, Cambridge, 1966.
Lloyd, Christopher, *The Nation and the Navy*, London, 1954.
Lloyd, Christopher, *The Navy and the Slave Trade*, London, 1949.
Lloyd Prichard, M. F., *The Collected Works of Edward Gibbon Wakefield*, London, 1968 (see Wakefield, Edward Gibbon, below).
Lyon, David, *The Sailing Navy List*, London, 1993.
McIntyre, W. David (ed.), *The Journal of Henry Sewell 1853–7*, Vols 1 & 2, Christchurch, 1980.
McKinnon, Malcolm (ed.), *New Zealand Historical Atlas*, Wellington, 1997.
McLean, Gavin, *Wellington, the First Years of European Settlement 1840–1850*, Auckland, 2000.
McLintock, A. H., *The History of Otago*, Dunedin, 1949.
McLintock, A. H. (ed.), *New Zealand Encyclopedia*, Wellington, 1966.
McNaught, Kenneth, *The History of Canada*, London, 1970.
Mandler, Peter, *Aristocratic Government in the Age of Reform*, Oxford, 1990.
Marais, J. S., *The Colonization of New Zealand*, London, 1927.
Marjoribanks, Alexander, *Travels in New Zealand*, London, 1846.
Marryat, Captain, *Peter Simple*, London, 1907.
Marshall's Naval Biography, Supplement 1, I/2, II/1, III/2, London (1820–40).
Marx, Karl, *Capital*, Vol. 1, Moscow, 1958.
Merivale, Herman, *Lectures on Colonization and Colonies*, Oxford, 1861.
Mill, John Stuart, *The Principles of Political Economy*, London, 1900.
Miller, John, *Early Victorian New Zealand*, London, 1958.
Mills, R. C., *The Colonisation of Australia*, London, 1915.
Moon, Paul, *FitzRoy, Governor in Crisis*, Auckland, 2000.
Morrell, W. P., *British Colonial Policy in the Age of Peel and Russell*, Oxford, 1930.
The Navy List, 1818–1842, London.
Neale, June E., *Pioneer Passengers*, Nelson, 1982.
New, Chester, *Durham*, Oxford, 1929.
New, Chester, *Lord Durham's Mission to Canada*, edited H.W. MCready, Toronto, 1963.
O'Brian, Patrick, *Master and Commander*, London, 1970.
O'Connor, Irma, *Edward Gibbon Wakefield, The Man Himself*, London, 1929.
Olssen, Erik, *A History of Otago*, Dunedin, 1984.
Orange, Claudia, *The Treaty of Waitangi*, Wellington, 1987.
Ormsby, Wm.(ed.), *The Grey Letters and Journals*, London, 1965.
Outhwaite, R. B. (ed.), *Marriage and Society*, London, 1981.
Park, Geoff, *Nga Uruora, the Groves of Life*, Wellington, 1995.
Petre, Hon. H. W., *An Account of the Settlements of the NZ Company*, London, 1842.
Philipp, June, *A Great View of Things*, Melbourne, 1971.
Pike, Douglas, *Paradise of Dissent*, Melbourne, 1957.
Price, A. Grenfell, *Founders and Pioneers of South Australia*, Adelaide, 1929.
Read, Colin, *The Rising in Western Upper Canada 1837–38*, Toronto, 1982.
Reid, J.C., *Bucks and Bruisers,* Pierce Egan and Regency England, London, 1971.
Richardson, Len and McIntyre, W. David (eds), *Provincial Perspectives, Essays in Honour of W. J. Gardner*, Christchurch, 1980.
Roach, John, *A History of Secondary Education in England 1800–1870*, London, 1986.
Robbins, Lionel, *Robert Torrens and the Evolution of Classical Economics*, London, 1958.
Robinson, William,*The History and Antiquities of Tottenham, Middlesex*, London, 1840.
Robson, Lloyd, *A History of Tasmania*, Vol. 1, Melbourne, 1983.
Rodger, N. A. M., *Articles of War*, Havant, 1982.
Roebuck, J. A., *The Colonies of England*, London, 1849.
Rumbelow, Donald, *The Triple Tree*, London, 1982.
Russell, Paul F., *Man's Mastery of Malaria*, London, 1955.
Russell, W. H., *The British Expedition to the Crimea*, London, 1858.

Rutherford, J., *Sir George Grey*, London, 1961.
Ryan, William and Guinness, Desmond, *The White House*, New York, 1980.
Salmond, Anne, *Between Worlds*, Auckland, 1997.
Sharp, Andrew and McHugh, Paul (eds), *Histories, Power and Loss*, Wellington, 2001.
Shaw, Sir Charles, *Personal Memoirs and Correspondence of Colonel Charles Shaw*, London, 1837.
Sheppard, Francis Henry Wollaston, *London 1808–70: The Infernal Wen*, London, 1971.
Simpson, Tony, *The Immigrants*, Auckland, 1997.
Sinclair, Keith, *A History of New Zealand*, Auckland, 1959.
Somerville, Alexander, *History of the British Legion and War in Spain*, London, 1839.
Spiller, P., Finn, J. and Boast, R., *A New Zealand Legal History*, Wellington, 1995.
Stevens, Joan (ed.), *The London Journal of Edward Jerningham Wakefield, 1845–1846*, Wellington, 1972.
Stuart, Peter, *Edward Gibbon Wakefield in New Zealand*, Wellington, 1971.
Swainson, Wm, *A Review of the Art of Colonization*, Auckland, 1987.
Taylor, Nancy M. (ed.), *The Journal of Ensign Best*, Wellington, 1966.
Taylor, Richard, *Te Ika a Maui*, London, 1855.
Thackeray, William Makepeace, *Sketches and Travels in London (1853)*, Gloucester, 1989.
Thackeray, William Makepeace, *Vanity Fair*, London, 1848.
Thale, Mary (ed.), *The Autobiography of Francis Place*, Cambridge, 1972.
Thompson, C. W., *Twelve Months in the British Legion*, London, 1836.
Thompson, E. P., *The Making of the English Working Class*, London, 1968.
Thomson, Arthur S., *The Story of New Zealand*, London, 1859.
Torlesse, Frances, *Bygone Days*, London, 1914.
Townsend, William C., *Modern State Trials*, Vol. 2, London, 1850.
The Trial of Edward Gibbon Wakefield, William Wakefield and Frances Wakefield indicted with one Edward Thevenot, A Servant for A Conspiracy and for the Abduction of Miss Ellen Turner, London, 1827.
Trollope, Anthony, *New Zealand*, London, 1874.
Turnbull, Michael, *The New Zealand Bubble, Wakefield Theory in Practice*, Wellington, 1959.
Wakefield, Charles Marcus, *The Life of Thomas Attwood*, London, 1885.
Wakefield, Edward, *An Account of Ireland, Statistical and Political*, London, 1812.
Wakefield, Edward, *Sir Edward William Stafford, A Memoir*, London, 1922.
Note: Page references to the following four major works by EGW, and also to his pamphlet, A View of Sir Charles Metcalfe's Government of Canada, *are for the* Collected Works of EGW, *ed. M. F. Lloyd Prichard (see above).*
Wakefield, Edward Gibbon, *England and America*, London, 1833.
Wakefield, Edward Gibbon, *Facts Relating to the Punishment of Death in the Metropolis*, London, 1831.
Wakefield, Edward Gibbon, *A Letter from Sydney*, London, 1829.
Wakefield, Edward Gibbon, *A View of the Art of Colonization*, London, 1849.
Wakefield, Edward Gibbon (ed.), Adam Smith, *Wealth of Nations*, London, 1835.
Wakefield, Edward Gibbon and Ward, John, *The British Colonisation of New Zealand*, London, 1837.
Wakefield, Edward Jerningham, *Adventure in New Zealand*, London, 1845.
Wakefield, Edward Jerningham (ed.), *The Founders of Canterbury*, Christchurch, 1868.
Wakefield, Priscilla, *A Family Tour Through the British Empire*, London, 1804.
Wakefield, Priscilla, *Reflections on the Present Condition of the Female Sex*, London, 1798.
Wallas, Graham, *The Life of Francis Place*, London, 1918.
Ward, W. E. F., *The Royal Navy and the Slavers*, London, 1969.
Wards, Ian, *The Shadow of the Land*, Wellington, 1968.
Watson, J. Stevan, *The Reign of George III*, Oxford, 1960.
Whipple, A. B. C., *Fighting Sail*, Amsterdam, 1978.
White, G. F., *A Century of Spain and Portugal*, London, 1909.
Wood, Lieutenant John, *Twelve Months in Wellington*, London, 1843.
Woodward, E. L., *The Age of Reform 1815–70*, Oxford, 1962.
Writings and Speeches of John Robert Godley, Christchurch, 1863.
Wrong, E. M., *Charles Buller and Responsible Government*, Oxford, 1926.
Ziegler, Philip, *Melbourne*, London, 1976.

NOTES

Chapter One: The Matriarch and Her Sons

1 Harrop, p. 13.
2 Garnett, p. 5.
3 Essex Record Office, pers. comm., H. D. Poole.
4 Garnett, p. 5.
5 EW to Frances Davies, 7 Apr. 1823, MP.
6 All quotes from Priscilla Wakefield's journal 1796–1816 are from the TS version in Mitchell Papers (and ATL) unless otherwise noted.
7 EW to Frances Davies, 5 Nov. 1823, MP.
8 Collie, p. 23.
9 *Ibid.*
10 *Ibid.*
11 Robinson, p. 281.
12 Pollock, p. 7.
13 Jeremy Bentham (1748–1832), philosopher and reformer, believed that all legislation should be measured against its 'utility' in promoting the pleasure, good and happiness of the people concerned.
14 Arthur Young (1741–1820), agricultural journalist and publicist who edited 47 volumes of the *Annals of Agriculture* from 1784 to 1809. First secretary of the Board of Agriculture 1793.
15 Extract from an account of a Female Benefit Club at Tottenham by Mrs Wakefield, Reports of the Society for Bettering the Condition, and Increasing the Comforts of the Poor, London, 1801.
16 Thompson, E .P., p. 33.
17 Fisk, p. 222.
18 PW Diary hand-transcription, 24 Jul. 1799, MP.
19 PW in Journal TS, MP.
20 A good education for a girl was an 'appropriate' one; girls should not be brought up 'above their expectations', in one of the four classes: the nobility, the professional class, the tradesman class and the 'labouring poor'. Raised expectations could lead only to personal disaster, even descent to prostitution as a way to maintain an affected lifestyle. And 'the knowledge of things that are in themselves useful can only be injurious when it has a tendency to break down the distinctions of society'.
21 PW, *A Family Tour,* Chap. 1.
22 PW, *Reflections,* p. 34.
23 PW Diary hand-transcription, 27 Jul., 17 Aug. 1799, MP.
24 PW Diary hand-transcription, 29 Jan., 24 Apr. 1799, MP.
25 PW Diary hand-transcription, 14 Oct. 1799, MP.
26 The whole cost of the wars from 1793 to 1815 was £1,657,854,518, about $NZ350 billion in today's currency (Paul Kennedy, *The Rise and Fall of the Great Powers*, London, 1988, p. 105).
27 EW, *A Letter to the Land Owners and Other Contributors to the Poor's Rates, in the Hundred of Dangye in Essex*, 1802, ATL.
28 Daniel Bell to David Barclay, 7 Mar. 1804, MP.
29 EGW to PW, 27 Feb. 1828, MP.
30 EW to Frances Davies, Dec. 1823, MP.
31 PW to Daniel Wakefield, 19 Apr. 1800, ATL Family Papers 88–144, O'Connor 2.
32 *Monthly Review*, Oct. 1806.
33 Pollock, p. 3.
34 EW to Frances Davies, Oct. 1823, MP.
35 EW to Frances Davies, 1823, MP.
36 EW to Frances Davies, Nov. 1823, MP.
37 PW Diary hand-transcription, 21 Dec. 1807, MP.
38 Priscilla Wakefield's separate 'literary diary' shows that she read, summarised and commented on a vast range of contemporary books – a major resource for her own instructional volumes (MP).
39 James Mill (1773–1836): a Scots philosopher who developed his friend Jeremy Bentham's theory of Utilitarianism (actions are morally right if they lead to happiness) and who had a particular interest in education. He and Bentham helped to found the University of London in 1828.
40 EW, Intro.
41 PW Journal TS, p. 51, MP.
42 EW, Intro.
43 *Liverpool Mercury*, 2 Jun. 1826.
44 Francis Place (1771–1854), son of a bailiff and publican, was apprenticed to a leather breeches maker and set up as an independent journeyman in 1789 but was refused work by his masters after organising a strike in 1793. In 1799 he opened his own successful tailor's shop, which supported his large family and his wide-ranging political activities. He is seen as one of the fathers of trade unionism, especially because of his success in having the anti-union Combination Acts repealed in 1824.
45 Garnett, p. 7.

46 *The Works of Anna Laetitia Barbauld*, London, 1825, II, p. 107.
47 EW to Wm Hone, 28 Dec.1813, BL Hone Papers 40, 120, f. 20.
48 Francis Place Autobiography, BL 35,153, f. 171.
49 'Proposal for Establishing a London Asylum for the Care and Cure of the Insane', ATL EW MS Papers 849.
50 Francis Place Autobiography, *op. cit.*
51 Place to Jas Mill, BL Place Papers 35,152, f. 132.
52 EW to Francis Place, 27 Nov. 1814, BL Place Papers 35, 152, f. 114.
53 EW to Arthur Young, 18 Nov. 1812, BL Young Papers 35,131, f. 410.
54 EW to Arthur Young, 20 Jul. 1812, BL Young Papers 35,131, f. 377.
55 PW to EW, 6 Oct. 1809, MP.
56 PW to EW, 24 Oct. 1809, MP.
57 *Ibid.*
58 PW to EW, 11 Nov. 1809, MP.
59 EW to Frances Davies, 26 Nov. 1823, MP.
60 EW to Place, 29 Dec. 1814, BL Place Papers 37,949, f. 25.
61 EW to Frances Davies, 27 Nov. 1823, MP.
62 EW to Frances Davies, 7 Dec. 1823, MP.
63 EW to Arthur Young, 20 Jul. 1813, BL Young Papers 35,131, f. 497.
64 ATL Pam 330.942, 1802.
65 Francis Place to Jas Mill, 21 Sep. 1815, BL Place Papers 35,152, f. 172.
66 Garnett, p. 6 n.
67 EW to Francis Place, 29 Dec. 1814, BL Place Papers 37,949, f. 25.
68 EW to Place, 29 Dec. 1814, BL Place Papers 37, 949, f. 25.
69 EW to Arthur Young, 1 Dec. 1813, BL Young Papers 35,131, f. 561.

Chapter Two: Ten Years Too Early

1 O'Connor, p. 26.
2 Bloomfield, p. 27.
3 *Liverpool Mercury*, 2 Jun. 1826.
4 *Ibid.*
5 EW to Francis Place, 25 Aug. 1814, BL Place Papers 35,152, f. 81.
6 EGW, *Facts Relating to the Punishment of Death in the Metropolis*, p. 249.
7 EW to Francis Place, 6 Oct. 1814, BL Place Papers 35,152, f. 88.
8 PW to WW, 30 Sep. 1814, MP.
9 EW to Francis Place, 25 Aug. 1814, BL Place Papers 35,152, f. 81.
10 PW to WW, n.d., MP.
11 PW to DW, 30 Sep. 1814, MP.
12 PW to FW, 17 Mar. 1815, MP.
13 The Foreign Office in 1821 had only 28 staff; there were 21 unpaid and seven paid attachés abroad. In 1822 the Foreign Secretary, Viscount Castlereagh, committed suicide after 'his mind became deranged owing to overwork'.
14 Place to James Mill, 9 Dec. 1815, BL Place Papers 35,152, f. 187.
15 EGW, *A Letter from Sydney*, pp. 147–48.
16 Garnett, p. 16.
17 EGW, *A Letter from Sydney*, p. 147.
18 Garnett, p. 17.
19 EW to PW, 17 Oct. 1814, MP.
20 Francis Place to James Mill, 9 Sep. 1815, BL Place Papers 35,152, f. 187.
21 EGW, 27 Aug. 1815, BL Place Papers 35,152, f. 154.
22 Garnett, p. 18.
23 *Ibid.*
24 *Ibid.*
25 AW to CW, 26 Sep. 1815, BL Place Papers 35,261, f. 3.
26 AW to CW, 9 Feb. 1816, MP.
27 EGW to CW, Dec. 1821, MP.
28 EGW to PW, 27 Feb. 1828, MP.
29 Francis Place to James Mill, 21 Sept. 1815, BL Place Papers 35,152, f. 172.
30 EW to James Mill, 18 Jan. 1816, BL Place Papers 35,152, f. 195.
31 EW to Francis Place, 2 Aug. 1815, BL Place Papers 35,152, f. 144.
32 Francis Place to James Mill, 8 Aug. 1815, BL Place Papers 35,152, f. 143.
33 Francis Place to EW, 12 Aug. 1815, BL Place Papers 35,152, f. 146.
34 Francis Place to James Mill, 16 Aug. 1815, BL Place Papers 35,152, f. 148.
35 EW to Frances Davies, Oct. 1823, MP.
36 Francis Place to James Mill, 7 Sep. 1815, BL Place Papers 35,152, f. 166.
37 James Mill to Francis Place, 13 Sep. 1815, BL Place Papers 35,152, f. 162b.
38 Francis Place to James Mill, 18 Jan. 1816, BL Place Papers 35,152, f. 195.
39 Garnett, p. 5.

Chapter Three: The Best Boy in the World

1 AW to CW, 9 Feb. 1816, MP.
2 PW Journal TS 1810, p.104, MP.
3 Boys intended for a naval career were entered early: Nelson joined at twelve.
4 Arthur Wakefield's Memorial to Lord Minto, 28 Feb. 1837, ex Reports of the NZ Company, Vol. 1. H. No. 15.
5 Austen, *Sense and Sensibility*, p. 88.
6 Each gun was described by the weight of the shot it fired. A carronade was a short-barrelled cannon capable of firing heavy shot a short distance. Royal Navy tactics were based on close-quarters fire against an enemy's hull; French firing tactics concentrated on destroying masts and rigging.
7 O'Brian, p. 166.
8 Marryat, p. 21.
9 Articles of War, 22 Geo. II c.33 (1749), Clauses XIII and XXII.
10 O'Brian, p. 79.
11 Marryat, p. 59.
12 Articles of War, Clause XXIX.

13 AW to CW, 26 Sep. 1815, BL Place Papers 35,261, f. 3.
14 Whipple, p. 88.
15 AW's Memorial to Minto, *op. cit.*
16 Clowes, Vol. V, p. 300.
17 Naval Chronicle, Vol. XXVII, p. 76.
18 Wellington *Spectator*, 8 May 1847, ex *Chambers's Edinburgh Journal*, probably written by EW.
19 The *L'Étoile* was the last French frigate to be captured during the Napoleonic Wars.
20 *Marshall's*, Suppl.1, p. 216.
21 Naval Chronicle, Vol. XXXII, p. 250.
22 Clowes,Vol. VI, p. 144 (Theodore Roosevelt).
23 AW's Memorial to Minto, *op. cit.*
24 Naval Chronicle, Vol. XXXII, p. 250.
25 Tradition has it that the President's House became known as the White House only after this burning when, during the rebuilding, whitewash was used to hide the marks of the flames.
26 Naval Chronicle, Vol. XXXII, p. 249.
27 Clowes, Vol. VI, p. 146.
28 EW to Francis Place, 1 Oct. 1814, BL Place Papers 35,152, f. 85.
29 EW to Francis Place, 6 Oct. 1814, BL Place Papers 35,152, f. 88.
30 PW to DW, 30 Sep. 1814, MP.
31 AW to CW, 26 Sep. 1815, BL Place Papers 35,261, f. 3.
32 AW to CW, 9 Feb. 1816, MP.
33 Francis Place to James Mill, 9 Dec. 1815, BL Place Papers 35,152, f. 187.
34 Clowes, Vol. VI, p. 231.
35 *Hebrus* log, PRO, ADM 51/2379 (and other log quotes).
36 Naval Chronicle XXXVI, p. 290.
37 *Ibid.*, p. 288.
38 Naval Chronicle XXXVI, p. 290.
39 Edmund Palmer to EW, 29 Aug. 1816, MP.

Chapter Four: It Might Make One in Love with Death

1 Egan, pp. 9–10.
2 PRO C33/628.
3 EGW to CW, late 1820, MP.
4 *Liverpool Mercury*, 2 Jun. 1826.
5 Captain Tweeddale pursued the wrong chaise and four all the way to 46 Great Portland Street. There he searched the house and forced open a door to discover Clanton, the manservant and Charlotte Woodbine, the cook who then confessed their role in the elopement. PRO C33/628, p. 1246.
6 PRO C33/628, pp. 1246–47.
7 Garnett, p. 20.
8 Outhwaite, p. 206.
9 *Liverpool Mercury*, 2 Feb. 1827.
10 EGW to CW, late 1820, MP.
11 EGW to CW, late 1820, MP.
12 Francis Place to James Mill, 2 Aug. 1816, BL Place Papers 35,152, f. 199.
13 To partially contradict Place, there remains a letter fragment from a Wm Leake to either EW or Wm Hill dated 1 August which states, 'It is with real satisfaction I have the pleasure to inform you that Mr Templer has prevailed upon Mrs Pattle to consent to the young couple to being married. . . .' George Templer was one of the executors of Thomas Pattle's will.
14 PW to CW, 11 Aug. 1816, Journal TS, MP.
15 Francis Place to James Mill, 9 Aug. 1816, BL Place Papers 35,152, f. 201.
16 James Mill to Francis Place, 26 Aug. 1816, BL Place Papers 35,152, f. 206.
17 Francis Place to James Mill, 30 Oct. 1816, BL Place papers 35,152, f. 225.
18 Francis Place to James Mill, BL Place Papers 35,153, f. 25.
19 From about this time, Edward Gibbon Wakefield signed all correspondence to family and friends 'EGW' and was referred to as that (or sometimes 'E.G.') in their correspondence. EGW will be used throughout the rest of this book.
20 Phyllida Bathurst to Mrs Turner, 29 Mar. 1826, ATL qMS 2100.
21 PRO C33/638, p. 601.
22 O'Connor, *op. cit.*, p. 32.
23 EGW to EW, 18 Jun. 1817, MP.
24 EGW to EW, 11 Nov. 1816, MP.
25 EGW to EW, 16 Nov. 1816, MP.
26 EGW to EW, 23 Nov. 1816, MP.
27 EGW to EW, 16 Nov. 1816, MP.
28 EGW to EW, 28 Oct. 1816, MP.
29 EGW to EW, 23 Nov. 1816, MP.
30 EGW to EW, 7 Dec. 1816, MP.
31 EGW to EW, 18 Mar. 1817, MP.
32 EGW to EW, 1 Sep. 1817, MP.
33 EGW to EW, 30 Sep. 1817, MP.
34 EGW to PW, 20 Feb. 1817, MP.
35 EGW to EW, 30 Sep. 1817, MP.
36 EGW to EW, 4 Sep. 1817, MP.
37 EGW to EW, 14 Sep. 1817, MP.
38 EGW to EW, 3 Apr. 1817, MP.
39 EGW to EW, 1 Sep. 1817, MP.
40 EGW to EW, 4 Sep. 1817, MP.
41 PRO C33/650, p. 799.
42 Referring to P. Colquhoun's *A Treatise on the Wealth, Power and Resources of the British Empire* (1814), based on the 1801 census, EGW's life interest of, perhaps, £2,000 a year would have put him in the top 3 per cent of income earners and seen him described as rich when an average liveable income was about £1 a week. But he was not in the league of the landed aristocracy (who received five to 50 times as much from rents), or the great merchant and banking families with £4,000 a year and more, and in whose hands rested the levers of political and social power.
43 EGW to EW, 10 Dec. 1817. Writing to EW, Hill advised, 'It strikes me if the property bought is sufficiently near a borough to have an influence in it, Edward might have friends in Parliament who might possibly be of use to him and this

would be at first perhaps a better thing than being in Parlt himself, except he was sure to succeed as a public speaker.' Wm Hill to EW, 6 Sep. 1817, MP.
44 Bloomfield, p. 27.
45 EGW to EW, 25 Mar. 1819, MP.
46 EGW to EW, 18 Jun. 1817, MP.
47 EGW to EW, 2 Feb. 1818, MP.
48 EGW to EW, 19 Jan. 1818, MP.
49 CW to EW, 19 Oct. 1819, MP.
50 EGW to EW, 20 Oct. 1817, MP.
51 PRO FO 67/59, Jan. 1819. A full account of the Genoa fête and its consequences is included in Bloomfield, pp. 41–43.
52 EW to Frances Davies, 13 Sep. 1823, MP.
53 EGW to CW, late 1820, MP.
54 Diary of Eliza Wakefield, Jan. 1820, ATL Wakefield Family Papers, 88-144-4.
55 EGW to EW, 12 Sep. 1817, MP.
56 EGW to EW, 10 Dec. 1817, MP.
57 EGW to EW, 10 May 1817, MP.
58 AW to CW, 9 Feb. 1816, MP.
59 EGW to EW, 7 Oct. 1816, MP.
60 EGW to EW, 14 Sep. 1817, MP.
61 Edmund Palmer to EW (?), 7 Oct. 1816, MP.
62 AW's Memorial to Lord Minto, *op. cit.*
63 Admiral Earl St Vincent (then 84) had, since his tenure as First Lord of the Admiralty at the beginning of the century, been an opponent of interest in obtaining promotion and was the senior officer most likely to urge advancement for an officer on the basis of merit. But there was preferment involved, too. Palmer was writing from Rochetts, Lord St Vincent's home; he had recently married the daughter of St Vincent's nephew.
64 Edmund Palmer to AW, 8 Feb. 1818, MP.
65 EGW to EW, 25 Mar. 1819, MP.
66 EGW to EW, 11 Nov. 1816, MP.
67 EGW to EW, 16 Nov. 1816, MP.
68 EGW to EW, 2 Jan. 1817, MP.
69 EGW to EW, 1 Feb. 1817, MP.
70 EGW to EW, 3 Apr. 1817, MP.
71 EGW to EW, 10 May 1817, MP.
72 EGW to EW, 14 Sep. 1817, MP
73 DW to EW, 28 Jul. 1817, MP.
74 EGW to EW, 3 Apr. 1817, MP.
75 EGW to EW, 25 Mar. 1819, MP
76 CW to EW, 19 Oct. 1819, MP.
77 Diary of Eliza Wakefield 1820, *op. cit.*
78 EGW to CW, late 1820, MP.

Chapter Five: By Hook or by Crook

1 Torlesse, p. 63.
2 It is unclear if Major Robson was EGW's 'rotten carcase'.
3 EGW to CW, 26 Aug. 1821, MP.
4 Judgement – Sir John Nicholl: Robson (formerly Pattle) v. Rocke (1824) 2 Add. 53; 162 ER 215.
5 EGW to CW, 26 Aug. 1821.
6 EGW to CW, 23 Jan. 1822, MP.
7 EGW to CW, 26 Aug. 1821.
8 Torlesse, p. 65.
9 PW to CW, 3 Feb. 1810, MP.
10 PW to EW, 7 Nov. 1817, MP.
11 PW to EW, 10 Dec. 1817, MP.
12 Bridges, Preface p. xxiv.
13 Torlesse, p. 64. Much earlier, on 10 December 1817, PW had adjured EW not to 'disparage religion' in front of the boys and urged him to go to church with them on Sundays.
14 Torlesse, p. 78.
15 EGW to CW, 23 Jan. 1822, MP.
16 Notes and two letters from 26 July 1821 (MP) survive showing that Edward, for a while, was involved in secret negotiations with Lord Petre over the possible purchase of a property at Thetford in Norfolk, which had influence over a borough.
17 EGW to CW, Sep. (?) 1821, MP.
18 Stevens, pp. 65 and 138. Thirty years after the purchase EGW was still receiving £300 per year in rents from Cugley.
19 Pers. comm., Torlesse family, 1996.
20 Torlesse, p. 48.
21 *Ibid.*, pp. 49–50.
22 Torlesse, *op. cit.*, p. 203, CW to Charles Torlesse, 16 Dec. 1822.
23 EW to Frances Davies, 7 Apr. 1823, MP.
24 EW to Frances Davies, 1 Nov. 1823, MP.
25 EW to Frances Davies, 27 Nov. 1823, MP.
26 EW to Frances Davies, 26 Nov. 1823, MP.
27 PW to AW, 22 Jan. 1812, MP.
28 This school, under the headship of Dr B. H. Malkin (1809–28) 'stood very close in status to the major public schools . . . Malkin ran the school on an open system which allowed much freedom. Morally the tone was good; fagging was not allowed, and there was little bullying.' Roach, John, *A History of Secondary Education in England 1800–1870*, London, 1986, pp. 67, 77.
29 EGW to CW, 26 Aug. 1821, MP.
30 EGW to CW, 23 Jan. 1822, MP.
31 EW to Frances Davies, 26 Nov. 1823, MP.
32 PW to EW, 7 Nov. 1817, MP.
33 EW to Frances Davies, Oct. 1823, MP.
34 WW to EW, 30 May 1822, MP.
35 Mills's older brother had been at Westminster with EGW and at Algiers with Arthur.
36 London *Courier*, 30 Sep. 1823, p. 3.
37 EW to Frances Davies, 1 Oct. 1823, MP.
38 EW to Frances Davies, 26 Nov. 1823, MP.
39 Garnett, p. 23.
40 EW to Frances Davies, c. 8 Oct. 1823, 22 Nov. 1823, MP.
41 Nina Wakefield to CT, 22 Feb. 1824, MP.
42 Godfrey de Burgh to EW, 7 Feb. 1824, MP.
43 Francis Place to James Mill, 21 Oct. 1817, BL Place Papers, 35,153, f. 25.
44 EW to Frances Davies, 7 Apr. 1823, MP.
45 Garnett, p. 23.
46 EW to Frances Davies, 1822?, MP.
47 The bulk of the surviving journal-like letters come from the period September to December

1823 and their autobiographically self-justifying details inform much of this section of the narrative.

48 EW to Frances Davies, 27 Nov. 1823, MP.
49 EW to Frances Davies, early Nov. 1823, MP.
50 EW to Frances Davies, Oct. 1823, MP.
51 EW to Frances Davies, Nov. 1823, MP.
52 EW to Frances Davies, 7 Oct. 1823, MP.
53 EW to Frances Davies, Oct. 1823, MP.
54 EW to Frances Davies, 1 Nov. 1823, MP.
55 EW to Frances Davies, Dec. 1823, MP.
56 EW to Frances Davies, 22 Nov. 1823, MP.
57 EGW to CT, 22 Feb. 1824, MP.
58 Judgement – Sir John Nicholl, *op. cit.*, p. 215.
59 Judgement – Sir John Nicholl, *op. cit.*, p. 232.
60 *The Times,* 19 Feb. 1824.
61 See Extended Note A.
62 EW to Frances Davies, 26 Nov. 1823, MP.
63 EW to Frances Davies, 27 Nov. 1823, MP.
64 Garnett, p. 25.
65 EGW to CW, 26 Aug. 1821, MP.
66 Garnett, p. 26.
67 France at this time had a population of 24 million and the United States about 6 million.
68 Davy, p. 311.
69 Graham and Humphreys, p. xxiv.
70 *Marshall's*, II/I.
71 Graham and Humphreys, p. 91.
72 AW to EW, 27 May 1822, MP.
73 Wellington *Spectator*, 8 May 1847.
74 Ward, p. 101.
75 Parliamentary Papers 1828, Vol. XXVI, 89.
76 Commodore Chas Bullen to Secretary of Admiralty, 10 Nov. 1826, PRO ADM1/1574, Cap. B.12.
77 PRO ADM 51/3097.
78 PRO ADM 1/1574, Cap. B.116, 14 Feb. 1827.
79 EGW to PW, 27 Feb. 1828, MP.

Chapter Six: To Pick the Father's Pocket

1 EW to Wm Whitton (Sidney lawyer), 4 Mar. 1826, MP.
2 EW to Wm Whitton, 26 Feb. 1826, MP.
3 P. Bathurst to WW, 19 Mar. 1826, ATL qMS 2100.
4 The children had not been with Catherine for some time because of increasing conflict over their religious education. Edward had also removed young Priscilla from her care, for a time at least, because of the 'bigot' Nottidge. At the same time, EGW had not allowed his father to see Nina and Jerningham which for EW was a 'dagger to my heart'. The reasons are unknown.
5 Garnett, p. 33.
6 Balzac, p. 6.
7 P. Bathurst to WW, 19 Mar. 1826, *op. cit.*
8 EGW, *Statement of Facts*, p. 1. Unless otherwise stated, all quotes from EGW in this chapter are from this document.
9 P. Bathurst to WW, 19 Mar. 1826, *op. cit.*
10 Balzac, p. 21.
11 Affidavits sworn by EGW and WW, 14 May 1827, PRO KB1/50, Easter 8 Geo IV, No. 41.
12 *The Trial of Edward Gibbon Wakefield*, p. 16.
13 Affidavits EGW and WW, *op. cit.*
14 *Ibid.*
15 Wm Whitton to EW, 4 Mar. 1826, MP.
16 EW to Frances Davies, 27 Nov. 1823, MP.
17 *Trial*, p. 23.
18 *Trial*, p. 28 (Sergeant Cross, Prosecutor).
19 *The Times*, 26 May 1826.
20 *Ibid.*
21 *Trial*, p. 205.
22 The Wakefield family originated from the district.
23 *Trial*, p. 33.
24 *Ibid.*, p. 164.
25 *Ibid.*, p. 35.
26 *Ibid.*, p. 36.
27 Fanny Davies to WW, 12 Mar. 1826, ex *The Trial in Full of Ewd* [sic] *Gibbon Wakefield and Others for the Abduction of Miss Turner*, London, Knight and Lacey, 1827, p. 23.
28 EGW to Wm Turner, 13 Mar. 1826, *loc. cit. Minutes of Evidence Taken Upon the Second Reading of the Bill Intituled An Act to annul and declare void an alledged Marriage between Ellen Turner, an Infant, and Edward Gibbon Wakefield*, 30 May 1827, BL Coll.
29 Phyllida Bathurst to Mrs Turner, 29 Mar. 1826, ATL qMS 2100.
30 EGW to P. Bathurst, quoted Bathurst to Mrs Turner, *op. cit.*
31 *Statement.*
32 *The Times*, 28 Mar. 1826.
33 *Minutes of Evidence.*
34 *Trial*, p.131.
35 *The Times*, 27 May 1826.
36 Possibly Robert Mills.
37 *Minutes of Evidence.*
38 P. Bathurst to WW, 19 Mar. 1826, ATL qMS 2100.
39 A nineteenth-century legal commentator wrote that EGW had been 'under an erroneous but salutary terror of the law remaining capital in case of defilement', which explained why the marriage had not been consummated. The writer added that this old law had been repealed but 'marriage beyond the border had interposed a technical difficulty to any prosecution for felony, of which he was not aware'. William C. Townsend, *Modern State Trials*, London, 1850, p. 114. But EGW knew very well the provisions of Scottish marriage law from the circumstances of his first marriage. And he also saw non-consummation as proof for the Turner family of his 'honourable' intentions.
40 *Trial*, Appendix.
41 *The Times*, 3 Apr. 1826.
42 *Ibid.*, 26 May 1826.
43 *Ibid.*, 24 May 1826.
44 *Ibid.*, 6 May 1826.
45 Legal procedures of the time prevented EGW from giving evidence in his own defence at the trial.

46 *The English Chronicle*, 15–17 Aug. 1826, ATL.
47 One of the most damaging tabloid rumours was that EGW did not consummate his marriage because he was suffering from venereal disease. This was used against him for 100 years after the event though there is no shred of evidence or corroboration.
48 *Statement*.
49 P. Bathurst to Mrs Turner, 29 Mar. 1826, *op. cit*.
50 *Trial*, p. 37.
51 In 1869, Lord Colonsay, Lord President of the Court of Session in Scotland, who as a prominent young lawyer had been called as an expert witness for the 1827 trial, said that there had been a miscarriage of justice and an erroneous verdict returned against EGW: 'The case was pressed *not* to secure a just verdict but to render Edward Gibbon Wakefield ineligible as a member of Parliament'. ATL O'Connor Papers 81–173.
52 *The Times*, 4 Apr. 1826.
53 *Trial*, p. 329.
54 Garnett, pp. 36–37, this and following quotes.
55 *The English Chronicle*, 15–17 Aug. 1826.
56 *The Times*, 23 Aug. 1826.
57 From 'Odds and Ends', *Later English Broadside Ballads*, Vol. 2, ed. John Holloway and Joan Black, London, 1979.
58 *Manchester Guardian*, 8 Sep. 1826.
59 *An Accurate Report of the Trial of Mr Edward Gibbon Wakefield, etc.. etc.. for a conspiracy to effect the abduction of Miss Ellen Turner*, Liverpool, E. Smith and Co., 1827.
60 *Trial* (Knight and Lacey).
61 *The English Chronicle*, *op. cit*.
62 *Trial* (Knight and Lacey).
63 *The Times*, 21 Mar. 1827.
64 *Trial* (Knight and Lacey).
65 *Ibid*.
66 *Blackwood's Edinburgh Magazine*, Vol. XXI, No. CXXV, May 1827, p. 529.
67 *Ibid*., p. 522.
68 *The Times*, 31 May 1827.
69 Place to James Mill, 9 Dec. 1815, BL Place Papers 35,152, f. 187.
70 Torlesse, p. 97.
71 *The Times*, 26 Jun. 1827.
72 *Manchester Gazette*, 19 Sep. 1826.
73 *The Times*, 18 Jan. 1828.
74 *Blackburn Mail*, 18 Jan. 1828
75 *Macclesfield Courier*, 18 Jan. 1828.
76 *The Times*, 15 Aug. 1827.

Chapter Seven: This Black Place

1 Dickens, *Sketches by Boz*, p. 209.
2 EGW *Punishment*, pp. 255–56.
3 EGW *Punishment*, p. 194.
4 Dickens, *Sketches by Boz*, p. 196.
5 Griffiths, p. 5.
6 Rumbelow, p. 134.
7 Torlesse, p. 65.
8 'Jack Ketch' had become a synonym for hangmen in general, after the notorious seventeenth-century hangman of that name.
9 Griffiths, pp. 404–07.
10 *Ibid*., p. 418.
11 'Papa and I are very happy and we are often together, because I go there from 10.30 until two. On Sunday I go there from 4.30 until 8.' Nina Wakefield to CT, 15 Sep. 1827, MP.
12 EGW to CT, 15 Sep. 1827, MP.
13 EGW to PW, 27 Feb. 1828, MP.
14 *Ibid*.
15 *Ibid*.
16 EGW to CT, 1 Sep. 1828, Garnett, *loc. cit*., pp. 44–45.
17 *Ibid*.
18 *Ibid*.
19 EGW to PW, 27 Feb. 1828, *op. cit*.
20 Obit., *Morning Post*, 23 Jul. 1846.
21 Including abduction, of course. EGW's concern for capital reform may have been greater for the realisation that he had been too close to the gallows for comfort.
22 Garnett, p. 57.
23 EGW, *The Hangman and the Judge*, p. 16 blurb.
24 *Ibid*., p. 6.

Chapter Eight: A Castle in the Air

1 EGW, *Punishment*, p. 266.
2 *Ibid*., p. 267.
3 EGW, *A Letter from Sydney*, Preface, originally in *Quarterly Review*, No. l, xxvii, Art. 8.
4 EGW, *A Letter from Sydney*, p. 169.
5 John McVeagh, *loc. cit*., *Merchants*, London, 1981, p. 65.
6 EGW, *A Letter from Sydney*, p. 141.
7 Woodward, p. 213.
8 Adams, p. 81.
9 Robbins, p. 154.
10 Bell and Morrell, p. xxxiii.
11 EGW, *A Letter from Sydney*, p. 119.
12 *Ibid*., p. 134.
13 *Ibid*., p. 135.
14 Mill, p. 75.
15 EGW, *The Art of Colonization*, p. 830.
16 S. Maccoby, *loc. cit*., *English Radicalism 1832–52*, London, 1955, p. 349.
17 EGW, *A Letter from Sydney*, p. 165.
18 Mill, Book V, Chap. XI.
19 Marx, p. 766.
20 EGW, *England and America*, p. 467.
21 *Ibid*., p. 377.
22 EGW, *A Letter from Sydney*, p. 166.

Chapter Nine: Life as Propaganda

1 AW to EW, 5 Oct. 1830, MP.
2 Memorial to Lord Minto 1837, *op. cit*.
3 C. M. Wakefield Scrapbook, MP.
4 Memorial, *op. cit*.
5 Admiral Abbott to Charles Marcus Wakefield, 1 Jul. 1882, C. M. Wakefield Scrapbook, MP.
6 AW to EW, 5 Oct. 1830, *op. cit*.
7 Torlesse, p. 61.

8 Chapman, p. 5.
9 EGW to J. R. Godley, 8 Jul. 1851, Godley Papers, CM.
10 O'Connor, p. 219.
11 AW to EW, 13 Jul. 1833, MP.
12 *Ibid.*
13 *Ibid.*
14 Lewis, *The Navy in Transition*, p. 135. The *Excellent* was the old *Queen Charlotte* of Algiers fame.
15 Memorial, *op. cit.*
16 The last great battle under sail in 1827 in which British, French and Russian squadrons destroyed the Turkish and Egyptian fleets off the west coast of the Peloponnese.
17 Gisborne, p. 19.
18 It is possible that Catherine's October 1830 note, 'I had a letter from William lately: they were all well' means that he, and perhaps little Emily, were travelling with Edward and Frances who were in Austria also about this time.
19 EW to Frances Davies, Nov. 1823, MP.
20 Torlesse, p. 80.
21 AW to EW, 13 Jul. 1833, MP.
22 Richard Garnett to Alice Freeman, 25 Jul. 1898, ATL Allom Papers 11(b).
23 Garnett to Freeman, 16 Jul. 1898, ATL Allom Papers.
24 Garnett, p. 83.
25 Torlesse *op. cit.*, p. 83.
26 *Ibid.*, p. 87.
27 The village of Stoke has known a church since Saxon Times: Francis Engleheart, *The Church of St Mary the Virgin, Stoke-by-Nayland*, Gloucester, 1971.
28 Torlesse, pp. 89–91.
29 *Ibid.*, p. 78.
30 Catherine's longest lived child was family historian Frances Harriet (Fanny) who was born last in 1839 when she was 46. Frances lived until 1935.
31 EGW, *Swing Unmasked*, p. 26.
32 *Ibid.*, pp. 14–15.
33 William Cobbett (1763–1835) was a radical politician and journalist whose most well-known publication *Rural Rides* (1830) exposed and crusaded for improvement of the conditions of farmers and agricultural labourers.
34 *Swing Unmasked*, p. 16.
35 In fact the government sent out special commissions to try the labourers. Nine men and boys were hanged, 400 were imprisoned and 450 transported, almost 200 for life.
36 *Swing Unmasked*, p. 46.
37 Francis Place, *An Essay on the State of the Country in Respect to the Condition and Conduct of the Husbandry Labourers and to the Consequences likely to Result Therefrom*, Feb. 1831, NFS. BL Place Papers 35,146. Place concluded that with currently low profit margins farmers would be unable to pay more to labourers, given the other tithes, rents and taxes they had to pay. To tax the landlords significantly would have a deleterious flow-on effect by reducing their investment in business and manufacturing.
38 BL Place Papers 27,791, f. 79.
39 *Cobbett's Weekly Political Register*, 19 Nov. 1831.
40 BL Place Papers 35,146, f. 133.
41 Buller, Hume and others established the Reform Club in Pall Mall in 1836.
42 DNB, Vol. III, p. 247.
43 *Ibid.*, p. 248.
44 Robert Owen (1771–1858), radical factory owner, believed that the new form of society would be made up of producers owning the means of production and organised into small, self-directing communities: the first socialist. Henry 'Orator' Hunt (1773–1835), radical/revolutionary speaker and MP.
45 Bloomfield, *op. cit.*, p. 124, wrote that, at the height of unrest before the Reform Bill was passed in June 1832, 'Edward Wakefield senior came dashing over from his French silk factory and made a vibrant speech in Leicester Square in which he accused the King of being in the clutch of "female powers" and called the Tory bishops "reverend hypocrites" and "knaves in lawn"'. Francis Place urged people to make a run on the banks – 'Go for Gold' – to bring pressure to bear on parliament to push the bill through.
46 James Stephen to Viscount Howick, 16 Jun. 1845, Grey Papers, Univ. of Durham.
47 J. G. FitzGerald to J. R. Godley, 23 Apr. 1855,Godley Papers, CM.
48 Albert Allom, EGW's secretary, Garnett, *loc. cit.*, p. 283.

Chapter Ten: A Long and Sore Trial

1 Nina Wakefield to CT, Aug. 1834, MP.
2 The commission transmogrified into the London Emigration Committee in 1832, then the Office of the Agent General for Emigration in 1837 and, finally, the Colonial Land and Emigration Commission in 1840.
3 EGW, *The Art of Colonization*, p. 782.
4 *Ibid.*
5 The detailed story of the foundation of South Australia may be found in Chapter III of Douglas Pike's *Paradise of Dissent*. Note, however, that Pike made a hostile case against EGW which incorporated key factual errors: e.g. EGW 'took his invalid daughter to the Continent from October to March each winter' (p. 76). See also Lloyd-Prichard, p. 34.
6 'The colony of South Australia, devised by Mr Wakefield, was planted by me', Pike, *loc. cit.*, p. 94.
7 J. Stephen: Memorandum on the Draft Charter of the S.A. Land Company, 14 Jul. 1832, CO 13/1.
8 EGW, *The Art of Colonization*, p. 782.
9 Colonial Under-Secretary R. W. Hay to Col.

Robert Torrens, 6 Aug. 1832, BPP 1841, 394, App. p. 19.
10 EGW, *Art of Colonization*, *op. cit.*, p. 782.
11 Nina Wakefield to CT, Aug. 1834, MP.
12 EGW to CW, late 1820, MP.
13 EGW, *England and America*, p. 355.
14 *Ibid.*, p. 350.
15 *Ibid.*, pp. 346–47.
16 *Ibid.*, p. 353.
17 *Ibid.*, p. 400.
18 *Ibid.*, p. 406.
19 All reference works attribute the coining of this phrase to Benjamin Disraeli, uttered in a parliamentary speech on 15 March 1838. EGW's creation of it pre-dates Disraeli's use by more than four years.
20 EGW, *England and America*, *op. cit.*, p. 411.
21 *The Times*, 7 Dec. 1833.
22 EGW, *England and America*, p. 626.
23 For example, the family of James Stephen enjoyed much colonial patronage. His brother became solicitor-general and a judge of the Supreme Court in New South Wales while three other family members and a relation all held good posts there.
24 BL MS 46,612, f. 34.
25 EGW to R. S. Rintoul, Dec. 1841, Garnett, *loc. cit.*, p. 89.
26 DW, *Pledges Defended and Offered in a Letter to the Electors of Lambeth*, 23 Nov. 1832, MP.
27 *The Times*, 12 Nov. 1832.
28 *Morning Chronicle*, 8 Dec. 1832.
29 *Ibid.*
30 Pike, pp. 69–70.
31 *Ibid.*, p. 70.
32 *Morning Chronicle*, 1 Jul. 1834.
33 Robert Gouger to Duke of Wellington, 9 Aug. 1834, PRO, CO 386/10.
34 EGW to Charles Adderley, 24 Dec. 1849, EJW, *Founders of Canterbury*, *loc. cit.*, p. 176.
35 Rowland Hill (1795–1879) is chiefly remembered as the man who invented adhesive stamps and prompted the introduction of the prepaid penny post in 1840.
36 EGW to Rowland Hill, 18 Aug. 1834, BL Leigh Hunt Correspondence, 38,109, f. 132.
37 *Ibid.*, f. 134.
38 EGW, *The Art of Colonization* , p. 783.
39 Robert Gouger, diary 29 Apr. 1834, Harrop, *loc. cit.*, p. 71.
40 Gouger, 20 May 1834, Harrop, *loc. cit.*, p. 70.
41 Nina Wakefield to CT, late August 1834, MP.
42 Nina Wakefield to Rosabel Attwood, 4 Sep. 1834, MP.
43 With Lady Charlotte Bacon at Southsea: Thos Attwood to G. De B. Attwood, 14 Nov. 1834, Charles Marcus Wakefield, *loc. cit.*, p. 280.
44 EGW to Mrs Thomas Attwood, 18 Oct. 1834, Garnett, *loc. cit.*, pp. 116–17.
45 EGW to CT, 25 Nov. 1834, MP.
46 EGW to Mrs T. Attwood, 17 Jan. 1835, Garnett, *loc. cit.*, p. 118.
47 EGW to CT, 17 Jan. 1835, MP.
48 EGW to CT, 14 Apr. 1835, MP.
49 It is also possible, of course, that Nina picked up the bacteria by drinking infected raw milk from a Stoke or Hare Hatch dairy.
50 Alice Freeman, DW's daughter, to Richard Garnett, c.1897, Garnett, *loc. cit.*, pp. 336–37.
51 O'Connor, p.114.

Chapter Eleven: Down the Ringing Grooves of Change

1 EGW to CT, 14 Apr. 1835, MP.
2 O'Connor, p. 112.
3 Robinson, pp. 220–21.
4 Fisk, p. 168.
5 Huelin, p. 3.
6 Report from the Select Committee on the Disposal of Land in the British Colonies together with the Minutes of Evidence, 1 August 1836, BPP 1836, Par. 746.
7 Bloomfield, p. 138.
8 Harrop, p. 78.
9 *Ibid.*, p. 79.
10 EGW to South Australian Commissioners, 2 Jun. 1835, BPP 1841, 394, App. p. 332.
11 Robert Gouger, Journal 20 Jun.1835, Harrop, *loc. cit.*, p. 79.
12 EGW, *Wealth of Nations*, Vol.1, Preface.
13 Erik Olssen, 'Wakefield and the Scottish Enlightenment', in *Edward Gibbon Wakefield and the Colonial Dream*. Olssen discusses at length EGW as debtor and heir to Smith and the philosophers of the Scottish Enlightenment. 'This was Wakefield's central insight – a new international division of labour, where a colony blessed with an abundance of land and an economically efficient agriculture could exchange its produce for the manufactures and capital of an industrial society, a species of mercantilism based on freely given consent and self interest, would locate a space in evolutionary time where it might prove possible to achieve the best of both worlds.', p. 58.
14 Fawcett, p. 176.
15 *Spectator*, 23 Jan. 1836.
16 EGW to CT, 11 Dec. 1835, MP.
17 Pike, p. 114.
18 C. M. Wakefield, title page.
19 O'Connor, p. 118.
20 Bloomfield, p. 150.
21 L. Duckworth to J. G. Shaw-Lefèvre, 30 Jul. 1835, Sir John George Lefèvre Papers 1835–1841, House of Lords Record Office: ML Historical Coll., Micro Ref. Bks. 2.23/191. M1122.
22 Shaw-Lefèvre to Lord Glenelg, *ibid.*
23 EGW, *Letter from Sydney*, p. 119.
24 Report from the Select Committee on the Disposal of Land, *op. cit.*, Par. 944.
25 *Ibid.*, Par. 1159.
26 On 13 July 1836, EGW sent Gladstone a South Australian Association circular headed 'Emigration, cost free, for Young People of the

Working Class'. BL Gladstone Papers 44,355 f. 70.
27 Report from the Select Committee on the Disposal of Land, *op. cit.*, pp. iv–v.
28 Eric Richards, 'Wakefield and Australia', in *Edward Gibbon Wakefield*, p. 99.
29 EGW, *A Letter from Sydney*, p. 169.
30 Alfred Tennyson, *Locksley Hall*, 1837–38.
31 Taylor to Hindmarsh, 14 Jul. 1836, PRO, CO 13/4.
32 Allom Coll., ATL qMS-0056.
33 Fawcett, p. 137n.
34 WW to DW, Jan. 1837, MP.
35 Report, *op. cit.*, p. 108.

Chapter Twelve: Strangers to their Family
1 Memorial to Lord Minto 1837, *op. cit.*
2 *The Times,* 3 Aug. 1835.
3 There were seventeen British ships elsewhere in the Mediterranean, chiefly in the east.
4 *The Times,* 3 Aug. 1835.
5 Memorial to Lord Minto, *op. cit.*
6 Lewis, *The Navy in Transition*, p. 94.
7 WW to DW, 19 Jan. 1837, MP.
8 Memorial to Lord Minto, *op. cit.*
9 Thomas Attwood to Mrs Attwood, 17 Feb. 1837, C. M. Wakefield, *loc. cit.*, p. 315.
10 Memorial to Lord Minto, *op. cit.*
11 AW to Admiralty, 3 May 1837, PRO ADM1/2730, Cap W50.
12 Lewis, p. 194.
13 AW to CT, 3 Sep. 1837, MP.
14 Lloyd, p. 215.
15 AW to Admiralty, 4 Mar. 1839, PRO ADM 1/2731, Cap W21.
16 AW to Admiralty, Jan. 1839, PRO ADM1/2731, Cap W83.
17 WW to DW, 19 Jan. 1837, MP.
18 EGW to CT, 12 Oct. 1837, MP.
19 Shaw, Vol. 1, p. 336.
20 Shaw, Vol. 2, p. 6.
21 Farr, p. 75.
22 Holt, p. 113.
23 Thompson, C. W., pp. 4–5.
24 Evans had been on Wellington's staff in the Peninsular War, with Arthur Wakefield at the burning of the White House and had fought at Waterloo. For his service in those three instances he went from lieutenant to lieutenant-colonel during the first six months of 1815.
25 Holt, *loc. cit.*, p. 100.
26 Thompson, pp. 115–16.
27 Shaw, Vol. 2, p. 494.
28 Thompson, C.W., p. 119.
29 Somerville, pp. 47–48.
30 Somerville, p. 178.
31 *Ibid.*, pp. 141, 181.
32 *Ibid.*, p. 162.
33 *Ibid.*
34 WW to DW, 19 Jan. 1837, MP.
35 Col. Owen testimonial, 31 Jan. 1839, NA CO 208/185.
36 Somerville, p. 611.
37 *Ibid.*, p. 633.
38 The First Carlist War finally ended in October 1840, following Don Carlos's exile.
39 In 1838 EGW became a 'director of the Western Australia Co; its plans for a settlement, Australind, at Port Leschenault, were not carried out with marked success'. Graeme Pretty, *Australian Dictionary of Biography*, Vol. 2, 1788–1850, p. 561.
40 Sir George de Lacey Evans to WW, 16 Dec. 1838, ATL CO 208/185.

Chapter Thirteen: The Ingenious Protector
1 Sheppard, p. 18.
2 *Ibid.*, p. 117.
3 EGW to Dr G. S. Evans, 10 May 1837, ATL NZ Co. Papers, Micro MS 460/12.
4 CM, EGW Papers, Vol. 1, p. 25.
5 1840 Select Committee hearing, Garnett, *loc. cit.*, p. 141.
6 Burns, p. 44.
7 Edward Betts Hopper Diary, 13 Jul. 1837, ATL MS 1034.
8 Recollection of EGW's niece Constance, Felix's eldest daughter, in late 1890s, Garnett, *loc. cit.*, p. 322.
9 See Stevens, p. 110.
10 BL Place Papers 35, 261, f. 56, Albert Allom note.
11 Thomson, Vol. II, p. 14.
12 Fox, p. 6.
13 As European contact increased, native New Zealanders began to distinguish themselves from the new arrivals by calling themselves tangata maori (ordinary people). This soon became abbreviated to Maori.
14 *Statement of Objects*, p. 8.
15 Adams, p. 93.
16 EGW to Glenelg, Jun. 1837, Bloomfield, *loc. cit.*, p. 165.
17 Stephen to Glenelg, 16 Jun. 1837, PRO CO 209/2, pp. 386–87.
18 Adams, p. 96.
19 John Beecham (General Secretary Wesleyan Missionary Society), *Colonization: being Remarks on Colonization in General with an examination of the Proposals of the Association which has been formed for Colonizing New Zealand*, London, 1838.
20 EGW's *Wealth of Nations*, Vol. 1, p. vii.
21 Taylor, *loc. cit.*, p. 216.
22 A comfortable Anglicisation of Liocadia di Oliveira. The closest her relatives and friends ever came to the proper rendition of her name was Leocadia de Oliveira. Her marriage certificate provides evidence of the proper spelling (family comm.).
23 AW to CT, 3 Sep. 1837, MP.
24 EJW, *Adventure*, 1/221.
25 EGW, *British Colonization*, pp. 190–92.
26 *Ibid.*, Appendix A, p. 407.
27 EGW to CT, 12 Oct. 1837, MP.
28 John Ritchie, 'Towards Ending an Unclean

Thing: the Molesworth Committee', HSANZ Vol. XVII 1976, p. 152.
29 DNB, Vol. V, p. 465.
30 New, *Durham*, pp. 72–73.
31 Wm. Hutt to EGW, 9 Aug. 1837, New Zealand Association Minute Books, ATL Micro MS 459.
32 Durham to EGW, 9 Sep. 1837, ATL Lambton Papers, MS Copy Micro 0527.
33 Adams, p. 105.
34 Lambton Papers, ATL MS Copy Micro 0527.
35 Adams, *op. cit.*, pp. 5, 104.
36 Burns, *loc. cit.*, p. 59.
37 Handwritten copy of minutes of meeting of New Zealand Association, 28 Dec. 1837, HL F. R. Chapman Papers, MS 424/11. This and subsequent quotes.
38 Garnett, p. 150.
39 EGW to EW, 29 Sep. 1835, MP.
40 Open letter to EGW, William White, 4 Jan. 1838, ATL qPAM 1838.
41 *The Times,* 10 Feb. 1838.
42 See Extended Note B.
43 McNaught, p. 89.
44 Ziegler, *loc. cit.*, p. 283.
45 *Spectator*, 13 Jan. 1838.
46 New, *Durham*, p. 367.
47 Glenelg to Durham, 5 Feb. 1838, PRO CO 209/4, pp. 295–97.
48 Minutes of New Zealand Association Meeting, 13 Feb. 1838, ATL Micro MS, pp. 454–64.
49 Harrop, *loc. cit.*, p. 98.
50 Seven months later, Lord John Russell told Melbourne that Glenelg 'proposed nothing, asked nothing and decided nothing': Russell to Melbourne, 25 Oct. 1838, BL Russell Papers 3B, f. 332.
51 Report from the Select Committee of the House of Lords Appointed to Inquire into the Present State of New Zealand, 8 Aug. 1838, p. 115.
52 The evidence showed that the government's own supervised assisted passage scheme to New South Wales, funded by land sales revenue which had reached £130,000 in 1837, would see 5000 new migrants go to the colony that year, the implication being that no new schemes were needed. Report, p. 346.
53 Report.

Chapter Fourteen: 'I would die in your service'

1 Charles Buller, 'Sketch of Lord Durham's Mission to Canada in 1838', 1840. Charles Buller Papers, PAC MG 24, A26.
2 Bloomfield, p. 184.
3 Durham paid £10,000 of his own costs.
4 Bloomfield, p. 184.
5 E. J. Stanley to Durham, 30 Jun. 1838, PAC John George Lambton Papers, MG 24, A27, Reel C 1856, Vol. 26, pp. 692–95.
6 Chapman to O'Callaghan, 19 May 1838, PAC Papineau Papers, MG 24, B2, Vol. 2, pp. 2955–60. Micro C-15790.
7 Buller, 'Sketch', pp. 54–6.
8 Lady Durham to Countess Grey, 10 Aug. 1838, PAC John George Lambton Papers, MG 24, A27, Micro A 1219, and later references.
9 Edward Ellice to Edward Ellice Snr, 6 Oct. 1838, PAC Ellice Papers. MG 24, Micro A2, pp. 764–67.
10 DCB, Vol. IX, p. 818.
11 Bloomfield, p. 188.
12 *Ibid.*, p. 189.
13 *Ibid.*
14 Edward Ellice to Edward Ellice Senior, 28 Aug. 1838, PAC Ellice Family Papers, MG 24, Micro A1-19.
15 New, *Durham*, p. 422ff.
16 Fawcett, *loc. cit.*, p. 201.
17 Charles Grey to Earl Grey, 30 Sep. 1838, New, *Lord Durham's Mission*, *loc. cit.*, p. 130.
18 New, *Lord Durham's Mission*, *loc. cit.*, pp. 133–34.
19 Charles Grey to Earl Grey, 20 Oct. 1838, Ormsby, pp. 138–40.
20 Ormsby, pp. 186–87.
21 Bloomfield, p. 195.
22 Charles Buller to John Stuart Mill, 13 Oct. 1838, PAC MG 24, A26, Charles Buller Papers.
23 EGW to Durham, 24 Nov. 1838, PAC MG 24, A27, John George Lambton Papers, Reel C-1856, Vol. 27, pp. 466–71.
24 Fawcett, *loc. cit.*, p. 201.
25 EGW to Durham, 27 Nov. 1838, PAC MG 24, A27, John George Lambton Papers, Reel C-1856, Vol. 27, pp. 466–71.
26 EGW to Durham, 29 Nov. 1838, PAC MG 24, A27, John George Lambton Papers, Reel C-1854, Vol. 22, pp. 637–39.
27 New, *Lord Durham's Mission*, p. 155.
28 EGW to Durham, 3 Dec. 1838, PAC MG 24, A27, John George Lambton Papers, Reel C-1856, Vol. 27, pp. 503–14.
29 New, *Lord Durham's Mission*, p. 159.
30 Bloomfield, p. 198.
31 A letter from a Tory MP to EGW on the content of the report, and dated 31 January, was addressed to him at Cleveland Row, confirming that EGW was close to Durham as the report was prepared for printing.
32 Durham to Normanby, 28 Feb. 1839, PAC MG 27, A27, John George Lambton Papers, Reel C-1851, Vol. 15, pp. 10–13.
33 EGW to Durham, 26 Dec. 1839, PAC. MG 24, A 27, John George Lambton Papers. Micro C-1857, Vol. 28, pp. 410–13.
34 New, *Lord Durham's Mission*, p. 167.
35 New, *Lord Durham's Mission*, *loc. cit.*, p. 166.
36 EGW to Durham, n.d., PAC MG 24, A27, John George Lambton, Reel C-1857, Vol. 28, pp. 414–17.
37 Wm. Molesworth to Durham, May 1839, ATL Lambton Papers, MS Copy Micro 0527.

Chapter Fifteen: Possess Yourselves of the Soil

1 Adams, p. 140.
2 And which will be used from this point.
3 New Zealand Company Minutes, 5 Sep. 1838,

ANZ CO 208/185.
4 New Zealand Company Minutes, 31 Oct. 1838, ATL CO 208/185.
5 New Zealand Company Minutes, 28 Nov. 1838, ANZ CO 208/185.
6 *Ibid.*, New Zealand Company Minutes, 10 Dec. 1838.
7 D. G. Edwards, 'The Voyage of the Barque Tory'.
8 Adams, p. 132.
9 Hutt to Normanby, 20 Feb. 1839, ANZ CO209/4, pp. 301–02.
10 The eleven guests were Lord Petre, Hon. Henry Petre, William Hutt, John Ward, Dr G. S. Evans, Edmund Halswell, Daniel Riddiford, Messrs Boucher and Wardle (Waddell?), E. B. Hopper and EGW.
11 Edward Betts Hopper Diary, 20 Mar. 1839, ATL MS 1033.
12 *Ibid.*
13 *Ibid.*
14 *Ibid.*
15 ATL CO208/185:25
16 De Lacey Evans to WW, 25 Mar. 1839, ATL CO208/185, p. 227.
17 Samuel Evans to WW, 26 Mar. 1839, ANZ CO 208/185, p. 14.
18 CO Memo for Lord Normanby, ANZ CO 209/4:324.
19 Prospectus of the New Zealand Land Company, May 1839, ATL, p. 1.
20 Patrick Matthew, *Emigration Fields*, London, 1838 (?), quoted *Colonial Gazette*, Vol. 1, No. 20.
21 EJW, *Adventure*, 1/17.
22 Directors' Meeting 26 Apr. 1839, ATL CO 208/185.
23 This £84 plus means that the breakfast guests partied to the modern-day equivalent of about NZ$20,000.
24 *Colonial Gazette*, 4 May 1839, pp. 357–59, this and following quotes.
25 ATL CO 209/4:533.
26 The Directors' Minutes for 1 May 1839, for example, confirm that EGW drafted the second letter to the Colonial Office for Hutt's signature. ATL CO 208/185.
27 Burns, *loc. cit.*, p. 94.
28 EJW, *Adventure*, 1/20.
29 Also, on 4 May, William had received formal notification that the old 1825 New Zealand Company had been 'united under the designation of the New Zealand Land Company' and that he was required to 'sustain the property and rights of the Company in New Zealand'. ANZ CO 208/147.
30 WW, Journal, 6 May 1839, ATL qMS 2101.
31 Captain F. G. Moore, Journal and Correspondence 1840–1906, p. 124, ATL MS 1660.
32 *DNZB*, Vol. 1, p. 181 and Auckland Museum, Heaphy Papers, MS 141.
33 O'Connor, p. 163.
34 Garnett, p. 155. On the same page, EGW is described as 'the Hero as Company Promoter'.
35 See Bloomfield, p. 211.
36 *Morning Post*, 5 Feb. 1907; CM O'Connor ARC1988:92, Box 6/27.
37 *Ibid.*, O'Connor.
38 Edwards thesis, p. 69.
39 WW, Diary, 12 May 1839.

Chapter Sixteen: 'They would extort the masts out of the ship'

1 WW, Shipboard Journal, ATL qMS-2101.
2 WW, Journal 1839–42, CO 208/307, 17 Aug. 1839. This journal was written principally as a report for the company and with its directors in mind. WW sent the journal back to London in instalments, whenever he encountered a trading ship bound for England. The first part, for example, to 1 Sep. 1839, was sent home with the *Falcon*, bound for Sydney on 2 Sep.
3 EJW, *Adventure*, 1/24.
4 *Ibid.*, 1/25.
5 *Ibid.*, 1/33.
6 It is unclear how he formed this judgement, unless he was relaying observations by Chaffers who had earlier visited the Bay of Islands.
7 WW, Journal, 18 Aug. 1839.
8 WW, Journal, 19 Aug. 1839.
9 Dieffenbach, Vol. 1, p. 61.
10 Bell, p. 34.
11 'Most Europeans, for instance, saw themselves as having everything to offer, and Maori as having nothing to teach them.' Salmond, p. 509.
12 EJW, *Adventure*, 1/28.
13 WW, Journal, 27 Aug. 1839.
14 EJW, *Adventure*, 1/31.
15 Dieffenbach, II/19.
16 WW, Journal, 29 Aug. 1839.
17 Clarke, p. 46. George Clarke Jnr grew up in the Bay of Islands, son of missionary and Protector of Aborigines, George Clarke Snr, and was appointed a sub-protector at the age of nineteen.
18 WW, Shipboard Journal, 21 May 1839.
19 Henry Williams came through the region about a month after WW's departure and later claimed to have re-purchased all the land (in a kind of trust for Maori) that WW had purchased for the company.
20 EJW, *Adventure*, 1/35.
21 *Ibid.*, 1/36.
22 *Ibid.*, 1/222.
23 *Ibid.*, 1/42.
24 *Ibid.*, 1/43.
25 WW, Journal, 23 Sep. 1839.
26 For a full explication of the complicated movement of Maori throughout the Cook Strait area see Angela Ballara's essay, 'Te Whanganui-a-Tara: phases of Maori occupation of Wellington Harbour c.1800–1840', in Hamer and Nicholls, pp. 9–34.
27 WW, Journal, 20 Sep. 1839.

28 WW, Journal, 21 Sep. 1839. CMS missionaries had told Maori that all other white men were devils, which probably seemed as absurd as the idea that all missionaries were angels.
29 WW, Journal, 23 Sep. 1839.
30 *Ibid*., 26 Sep. 1839.
31 *Ibid*., 23 Sep. 1839.
32 BPP, Vol. 2, 1844, Appendix 26, F. No. 10.
33 Clarke, p. 49.
34 Burns, p. 125.
35 WW, Journal, 27 Sep. 1839.
36 *Ibid*., 13 Sep. 1839.
37 Dieffenbach, II/144.
38 EJW, *Adventure*, 1/96.
39 *Ibid*., 1/99.
40 *Ibid*., 1/100.
41 Tiraueke, tieke, saddleback – *Philesturnis carunculatus*.
42 EJW, *Adventure*, 1/91.
43 WW, Journal, 14 Oct. 1839.
44 Dieffenbach, 1/101.
45 'I once asked old Rauparaha how he made his way from the banks of the Thames to the neighbourhood of Otago, and he simply said: "Why, of course, I ate my way through," which was almost literally true.' Clarke, p. 17.
46 WW, Journal, 22 Oct. 1839.
47 Nopera Pana-kareao, referring to the Treaty of Waitangi, said in April 1840: 'What we have to say against the government, the shadow of the land will go to him but the substance will remain with us'. *DNZB* Vol. 1, p. 238.
48 WW, Journal, 23 Oct. 1839.
49 EJW, *Adventure*, 1/125.
50 Dicky Barrett pleaded his wife's illness as the reason for not assisting WW in the Kapiti negotiations. More likely, he did not fancy facing Te Rauparaha after his part in the Port Nicholson purchase.
51 WW, Journal, 23 Oct. 1839.
52 *Ibid*., 21 Oct. 1839.
53 EJW, *Adventure*, 1/127.
54 WW, Journal, 23 Oct. 1839.
55 *Ibid*.
56 *Ibid*., 27 Aug. 1839.
57 *Ibid*., 23 Oct. 1839.
58 EJW, *Adventure*, 1/131.
59 WW, Journal, 23 Oct. 1839.
60 *Ibid*., 24 Oct. 1839.
61 *Ibid*., 25 Oct. 1839.
62 EJW, *Adventure*, 1/202.
63 WW, Journal, 27 Oct. 1839.
64 *Ibid*., 26 Oct. 1839.
65 *Ibid*., 27 Oct. 1839.
66 EJW, *Adventure*, 1/132.
67 *Ibid*., 1/221.
68 *Ibid*., 1/223.
69 WW, Journal, 30 Oct. 1839.
70 EJW, *Adventure*, 1/136.
71 WW, Journal, 8 Nov. 1839.
72 *Ibid*., 12 Nov. 1839.
73 *Ibid*., 13 Nov. 1839.
74 EJW, *Adventure*, 1/143.
75 EGW to EW, 22 Oct. 1841, BL Place Papers 35,261, f. 57.
76 CO 208/2, 16 Jul.1839.
77 Taine Family Papers (Gaile Douglas, Nelson).
78 Sam. Revans to H. S. Chapman, 21 Dec. 1839, ATL qMS Rev 1687.
79 *Ibid*., 21 Dec. 1839.
80 *Ibid*., 25 Oct. 1840.
81 Taine Family Papers.
82 WW, Journal, 28 Nov. 1839, CO 208/307, HL Micro 215/196.
83 EJW, *Adventure*, 1/155.
84 *Ibid*., 1/154.
85 *Ibid*., 1/156.
86 *Ibid*., 1/159.
87 *Ibid*., 1/161.
88 WW, Journal, 2 Jan. 1840.
89 EJW, *Adventure*, 1/167.
90 WW, Journal, 11 Jan. 1840.

Chapter Seventeen: 'I am half a missionary myself'

1 WW to Ward, 26 Mar. 1840, HL CO 208/99; NZ Co. 40/2842.
2 Burns, p. 136.
3 Petre, p. 10.
4 WW, Journal, 15 Feb. 1840.
5 *New Zealand Journal*, Sept. 1840.
6 WW, Journal, 27 Jan. 1840.
7 EJW, *Adventure*, 1/197.
8 *Ibid*., 1/205.
9 Revans to Chapman, 15 Apr. 1840, ATL qMS REV 1687.
10 Petre, p.16.
11 EJW, *Adventure*, 1/214. See jacket picture.
12 John Miller, *loc. cit*., p. 46.
13 *Instructions from the New Zealand Land Company*, p. 2.
14 WW, Despatch, 10 Apr. 1840, HL CO 208/99; NZ Co. 40/2850.
15 Williams to Hobson, 29 Apr. 1840, ANZ IA 9/11.
16 WW, Despatch, 25 May 1840, HL CO 208/99; NZ Co. 40/2854.
17 BPP, Vol. 2, 1844, Appendix 26.
18 As native and defence minister Donald McLean would later say, 'Christianity is one of the principal causes of our easy conquest and retention of the New Zealand islands.' Journal 16 Jan. 1851, *loc. cit*., A. G. Bagnall and G. C. Petersen, *William Colenso*, Wellington, 1948, p. 353.
19 WW to CT, 25 Mar.1840, BL Place Papers 35,261, f. 13.
20 MP.
21 Gisborne, p. 19.
22 *Ibid*., p. 20.
23 *Ibid*.
24 Petre, p. 33.
25 Orange, p. 31.
26 Burns, p. 120.
27 AR MS 414, Auckland Institute and Museum.
28 *New Zealand Gazette*, 30 May 1840.
29 WW, Report 20, HL CO 208/99. In this, WW

suggests that the actions of one of his own council, Dudley Sinclair, on a visit to the Bay of Islands precipitated Hobson's action, not Pearson.
30 *New Zealand Gazette*, 6 Jun. 1840.
31 See J. C. Beaglehole, pp. 35-6.
32 WW, Report 20, *op. cit.*
33 T. Partridge to H. S. Chapman, 31 Jul. 1840, ATL qMS-0417.
34 *New Zealand Gazette*, 22 Aug. 1840.
35 WW, Report 20, *op. cit.*
36 *New Zealand Gazette,* 18 Jul. 1840.
37 Shortland to Hobson, 9 Oct. 1840, BPP, Vol. 3, pp. 242–43.
38 Wood, p. 20.
39 EJW, *Adventure,* 1/427-8.
40 Revans to Chapman, 6 Apr. 1841, ATL qMS REV1687.
41 *Ibid.*, 24 Feb. 1841.
42 T. Partridge to Chapman, 30 Apr. 1841, ATL qMS 0147.
43 Un-named emigrant to brother-in-law, dated Port Nicholson 29 Aug. 1840 and reprinted in *New Zealand Journal*, 10 Apr. 1841.
44 Revans to Chapman, 31 Jan. 1841, ATL qMS REV 1687.
45 *Ibid.*, 6 Apr. 1841.

Chapter Eighteen: Hobson's Choice
1 EGW to CT, Mar. 1843, BL Place Papers 35,261.
2 Burns, pp. 141–42
3 EGW to Molesworth, 26 Oct. 1840, MP.
4 AW to CT, 15 Feb. 1841, BL Place Papers 35,261, f. 16.
5 EGW to CT, 6 Oct. 1840, BL Place Papers, 35,261, f. 15.
6 The Nelson suburb of Stoke commemorates this.
7 AW to CT, 15 Feb. 1841, BL Place Papers 35,261, f. 16.
8 Torlesse, pp. 98–100.
9 *Ibid.*, pp. 212–3.
10 Charles Obins Torlesse was referred to as 'Charlie', 'Charley', 'Charly' (and even Charles).
11 EGW to CT, 30 Apr. 1841, BL Place Papers, 35,261, ff. 56–57.
12 EGW to Molesworth, 2 Jan. 1841, MP.
13 EGW to Molesworth, 4 Jan. 1841 *loc. cit.*, Fawcett, p. 170. Internal evidence proves Lady Fawcett has this correspondence wrongly dated 1840.
14 Molesworth to Woolcombe, 13 (prob.) Jan. 1841, *loc. cit.*, Fawcett, p. 176.
15 AW, Diary, 14 Jul. 1841, ATL qMS 2097.
16 *New Zealand Gazette*, 6 Feb. 1841.
17 Revans to Chapman, 18 Apr. 1841, ATL qMS REV 1687.
18 EJW, *Adventure*, II/44–45.
19 *Ibid.*, II/51, 52.
20 *Ibid.*, II/53.
21 Allan, p. 65.
22 AW to Hobson, 26 Sep. 1841, ATL qMS 2099.
23 Allan, *loc. cit.*, p. 65.
24 Burns, *loc. cit.*, p. 178.
25 *Ibid.*
26 C.O. Torlesse to CT, 1 Oct. 1841, CM EGW Papers, Vol. 1, p. 39.
27 Now the site of the Beehive.
28 EJW, *Adventure*, II/69.
29 Revans to Chapman, 2 Feb. 1842, ATL qMS REV 1688.
30 *Ibid.*, 18 Apr. 1841, ATL qMS REV 1687.
31 *Ibid.*, 26 May 1841.
32 *Ibid.*, 24 October 1841, ATL qMS REV 1688.
33 It is thought also that Dicky Barrett knew of the haven but had not told F. A. Carrington of it when he was looking for the site of New Plymouth, causing him to go to Taranaki.
34 Allan, p. 71.
35 Samuel Stephens to mother, 27 Jul. 1843, Allan, *loc cit.*, p. 262.
36 AW to EW, 23 Nov. 1841, MP.
37 W. C. Young to mother, 17 Jul. 1842, Allan, *loc. cit.*, p. 263.
38 AW, Diary 2, 27 Nov. 1841, ATL qMS 2096.
39 AW, Diary 3, 27 Jan. 1842, ATL MS Papers 3929.
40 AW, Diary 2, 25 Dec. 1841.
41 Stephens to mother, 10 Jan. 1842, Allan, *loc. cit.*, p. 82.
42 AW, Diary 3, 30 Jan. 1842.
43 AW to EGW, 1 Jan. 1842, ATL qMS 0417.
44 AW to WW, 22 Feb. 1842, ATL qMS 2099.
45 Bett Papers, ATL Micro 588, Reel 3.

Chapter Nineteen: Nursed in Blood
1 WW to CT, 3 Jun. 1842, BL Place Papers 35,261, f. 61.
2 EJW, *Adventure*, II/201.
3 Burns, *loc. cit.*, p. 208.
4 Burns, p. 209.
5 This was presumably an estimate of the Maori population from Taranaki to Nelson-Marlborough.
6 Clarke, p. 44.
7 *Ibid.*, p. 47.
8 EJW, *Adventure*, II/209.
9 Rosemarie Tonk, 'A Difficult and Complicated Question', in Hamer and Nicholls, p. 39.
10 Clarke, p. 48.
11 EJW, *Adventure*, II/206.
12 EJW, II/207.
13 *Ibid.*, II/209.
14 Clarke, p. 47.
15 EJW, *Adventure*, II/194.
16 Clarke, p. 38.
17 Revans to Chapman, 13 Jun. 1842, ATL qMS REV 1688.
18 Revans to Chapman, 6 Apr. 1841, ATL qMS REV 1687.
19 EJW, *Adventure*, II/180–181.
20 Young to father, 27 Apr. 1842, Allan, *loc. cit.*, p. 102.
21 Nelson *Examiner*, 22 Oct. 1842.

22 *Ibid.*, 3 Sep. 1842.
23 AW to WW, 23 Apr. 1842, ATL qMS 2099.
24 *Ibid.*, 13 May 1842.
25 *Ibid.*, 24 Jun. 1842.
26 *Ibid.*, 18 Oct. 1842.
27 Allan, p. 226 ex *Examiner* reports Nov. 1842.
28 Palmer thesis, pp. 137–45.
29 AW to WW, 24 Jun. 1842, ATL qMS 2099.
30 Clarke, pp. 52–3.
31 *Ibid.*, p. 52.
32 *Ibid.*, p. 54.
33 Caughey, p. 257.
34 Clarke, p. 49.
35 Burns, *loc. cit.*, p. 225.
36 *Ibid.*
37 Miller, *loc. cit.*, p. 68.
38 EJW, *Adventure*, II/222-23.
39 *Ibid.*, II/333–35.
40 Jollie to Blamire, 20 Dec. 1842, Bett Papers, Allan, *loc. cit.*, p. 239.
41 AW to WW, 16 Jan. 1843, ATL qMS 2099.
42 *Ibid.*, 17 Mar. 1843.
43 Fredk Tuckett to Francis Tuckett, 7 Jan. 1844, Allan, *loc. cit.*, p. 246.
44 F. Tuckett, 11 Jan. 1844, BPP Vol. 4, p. 187.
45 AW to WW, 17 Mar. 1843, ATL qMS 2099.
46 AW to W. Shortland, 2 May 1843, Allan, *loc. cit.*, p. 248.
47 Allan, p. 249.
48 *Ibid.*, p. 250.
49 John Barnicoat Journal, 14 Jun. 1843, TS Nelson Provincial Museum.
50 EJW, *Adventure*, II/385.
51 AW to WW, 7 Jun. 1843, ATL qMS 2099.
52 Barnicoat Journal, 28 Jun, 1843.
53 *Ibid.*, 16 Jun. 1843.
54 The most complete reconstruction of what happened on 17 Jun. 1843 may be found in Chapter 23 of Grover.
55 Fredk Tuckett at Magistrates Hearing, 18 Jun. 1843, BPP Series, Vol. 2, App. 4, p. 131.
56 Barnicoat Journal, 17 Jun. 1843.
57 *Ibid.*, 28 Jun. 1843.
58 'Tomahawk' is used freely in accounts of the time and can mean either European steel tomahawks or Maori greenstone mere and patiti.
59 BPP Papers, Vol. 2, App. 4, p. 155.
60 WW to Charles Torlesse, 29 Jun. 1843, BL Place Papers 35, 261, f. 64.
61 On 11 Mar. 1847, Allan, *loc. cit.*, p. 295.

Chapter Twenty: Cui bono?

1 Creating the small town that later became the federal capital, Ottawa, at the start of the Rideau Canal.
2 Joseph Parkes to Edward Ellice, 16 Aug. 1839, PAC Ellice Family Papers, MG 24, Micro A 19, pp. 4718–20.
3 Edward Ellice to Joseph Parkes, 1839; PAC Ellice Family Papers, MG 24, Micro A7, pp. 4995–96.
4 Parkes to Ellice, 4 Sep. 1839, PAC Ellice Family Papers, MG 24, Micro A 19, pp. 4770–04.
5 Parkes to Ellice, 3 Jan. 1840, PAC Ellice Family Papers, MG 24, Micro A 1, pp. 5002–07.
6 Parkes to Ellice, 4 Jan. 1840, *Ibid.*
7 Taft Manning, p. 5.
8 *Colonization of the County of Beauharnois*, NACAI, London, 1840, pp. 9–10, PAC.
9 Taft Manning, p. 9.
10 MacDonnell, p. 11.
11 *Ibid.*, p. 12.
12 Taft Manning, p. 10.
13 *DCB*, Vol. VII, p. 855.
14 Bloomfield, p. 245.
15 Lower, pp. 37–44.
16 MacDonnell, *loc. cit.*, pp. 14–15.
17 Abel Smith to Ellice, 30 Oct. 1841, PAC Ellice Family Papers, MG 24, Micro A4, pp. 5733–37.
18 Ellice to Parkes, 9 Nov. (?) 1841, PAC Ellice Family Papers, MG 24, Micro A7, pp. 4468–69.
19 *DCB*, Vol.VII, p. 32.
20 Taft Manning, p. 24.
21 MacDonnell, p. 37.
22 Probably Andrew Colville, Deputy Governor of NACAI and Hudson Bay Company luminary. Bloomfield, pp. 252–53.
23 Sir Charles Bagot Papers, PAC, MG 24, A13, Vol. 4, pp. 273–74.
24 Sir Charles Bagot Papers, PAC, MG 24, A13, Vol. 7, pp. 8–14.
25 EGW: 'To The Free and Independent Electors of the County of Beauharnois, 17 Oct. 1842, in *Colonial Gazette*, 21 Nov. 1842.
26 Bagot to Stanley, 11 Oct. 1842, PAC Sir Charles Bagot Papers, MG 24, A13, Vol. 7, p. 96.
27 *Colonial Gazette*, 30 Mar. 1842.
28 Taft Manning, p. 18.
29 Sir Charles Bagot Papers, PAC, MG 24, A13, Vol. 4, pp. 273–74.
30 EGW, *Metcalfe's Government of Canada*, pp. 731, 733.
31 See Taft Manning and *DCB* Vol. IX, p. 818.
32 Bagot was probably also right about EGW paying a mole at the Colonial Office. He probably had been since 1837 or 1838.
33 Chairman of the 1840 Select Committee on New Zealand and a director of the Plymouth Company.
34 Stanley to Bagot, 3 Sep. 1842, PAC Sir Charles Bagot Papers, MG 24, A13, Vol. 9. pp. 157–59.
35 Bagot to Stanley, 26 Sep. 1842, PAC Sir Charles Bagot Papers, MG 24, A13, Vol. 5, pp. 136–37.
36 Taft Manning, p.19.
37 EGW to J-J. Girouard, 20 Aug. 1842, PAC MG 24, B6, Denis-Benjamin Viger Papers, Vol. 5, pp. 2398–2416.
38 EGW to J-J. Girouard, 20 Aug. 1842, *loc. cit.*, Lloyd Prichard, p. 751.
39 This letter has not been quoted before, possibly because archival references give it the

wrong year of 1838. The letter, in EGW's own hand, is headed 'Saturday 27th August'. The 27th fell on a Saturday only in 1842 during the years 1838–44, the period when EGW visited Canada.
40 EGW to L-H La Fontaine, 27 Aug. 1842, PAC, La Fontaine Papers, M860, Item 000012.
41 Bagot to Stanley, 12 Oct. 1842, PAC Sir Charles Bagot Papers, MG 24, A13, Vol. 5, pp. 153–55.
42 DCB Vol. VII, p. 32.
43 *The Times*, 16 Oct. 1842.
44 Bloomfield, *loc. cit.*, p. 260.
45 Bagot to Stanley, 12 Oct. 1842, PAC. Sir Charles Bagot Papers, MG 24, A13, Vol. 5, pp.153–55.
46 Samuel Gerard to Edward Ellice, 11 Oct. 1842, PAC Ellice Family Papers, MG 24, A3, pp. 5915–57.
47 *Colonial Gazette*, 21 Nov.1842.
48 EGW: 'To The Free and Independent Electors of the County of Beauharnois', *op. cit.*
49 Bagot to Stanley, 11 Nov. 1842, PAC Sir Charles Bagot Papers, MG 24, A13, Vol. 5, pp. 187–88.
50 Bagot to Stanley, 12 Dec. 1842, PAC Sir Charles Bagot Papers, MG 24, A13, Vol. 5, p. 254.
51 Ellice to Parkes, 27 Nov. 1842, PAC Ellice Family Papers, MG 24, Micro A7, pp. 5931–35.
52 EGW to La Fontaine, 2 Jan.1843, PAC La Fontaine Papers, M860, Item 000230.
53 See Bloomfield, p. 263.
54 EGW to La Fontaine, 2 Feb. 1843, PAC La Fontaine Papers, M860, Item 000250.
55 EGW, *Art of Colonization*, p. 1023.
56 Bloomfield, p. 266.
57 Hincks, p.109.
58 EGW, *Charles Metcalfe's Government in Canada*, p. 741.
59 *Ibid.*, p. 737.
60 *Ibid.*, p. 738.
61 Garnett, p. 185.
62 EGW, *Metcalfe's Government*, p. 736.
63 *Ibid.*, p. 744.
64 *Ibid.*, p. 740.
65 Bloomfield, p. 270.
66 Garnett, p. 191.
67 Ellice to Dewar, 24 May 1844, PAC Ellice Family Papers, MG 24, Micro A4, pp. 5002–07.
68 H. J. M. Johnston in *DCB*, Vol. IX, p. 819.
69 First Viscount Bolingbroke 1678–1751, Tory statesman.
70 EGW, 'Sir Charles Metcalfe in Canada', *loc. cit.* Wrong, pp. 182–83.
71 *Ibid.*, pp. 351–52.

Chapter Twenty-one: Utu Postponed
1 EW to ??, 3 Jan. 1844, ATL 88-144 O'Connor 2, MS letter.
2 EW to AW, 30 Oct. 1843, ATL qMS 0056.
3 WW to CT, 29 Sep. 1843, MP.
4 EW to WW, 21 Jul. 1844, ATL, Allom Papers, qMS 0056-6.
5 Garnett, p. 230.
6 Burns, *loc. cit.*, p. 238.
7 EJW, *Adventure*, II/418.
8 Allan, p. 272.
9 Nelson *Examiner*, 8 Jul. 1843.
10 Grover, p. 193.
11 WW to Ward, 12 Sep. 1843, Ian Wards, *loc. cit.*, p. 83.
12 Miller, p. 76.
13 WW to Ward, 12 Sep. 1843, Wards, *op. cit.*
14 EJW, *Adventure*, II/468.
15 *Ibid.*, II/496–98.
16 *DNZB*,Vol. 1, p.131.
17 EJW, *Adventure*, II/505–07.
18 *Ibid.*, p. 508.
19 EJW, *Adventure*, II/510–12.
20 H. H. Turton in Wellington *Independent*, 4 Jul. 1846, Stevens, *loc. cit.*, p. 2.
21 Adams, p. 224.
22 EJW, *Adventure*, II/ 512, 528.
23 EW to WW, 21 Jul.1844, ATL Allom Papers, qMS 0056-6.
24 EGW to CT, n.d. but attributed Apr. 1843, ATL qMS-0387-1.
25 H. S. Chapman to father, 10 Jul. 1848, ATL qMS 0419.
26 Nelson *Examiner*, 10 Feb. 1844.
27 Constantine Dillon to his mother, 11 Feb.1844, Allan, *loc. cit.*, p. 291.
28 Allan, *loc. cit.*, p. 292.
29 BPP, Vol. 2, 1844, Minutes of Evidence, p. 197.
30 Taylor, p. 538.
31 Godley, pp. 238–39.
32 H. S. Chapman to father, 24 Dec. 1845, ATL qMS 0419.
33 H. S. Chapman to father, 10 Feb. 1844, ATL MS Papers 0053-22.
34 *Ibid.*, 26 Apr. 1844.
35 For a full explication of the issue see Rosemarie Tonk, 'A Difficult and Complicated Question', in Hamer and Nicholls, pp. 35–59.
36 WW to Wicksteed, 1 Nov. 1844, Burns, *loc. cit.*, p. 273.
37 Allan, p. 276.
38 Tuckett to WW, 31 Aug. 1843, Allan, *loc. cit.*, p. 279.
39 McLintock, p. 140.
40 *Ibid.*, pp. 142–43.
41 H. S. Chapman to father, 3 Feb. 1847, ATL MS Papers 0053-17B.
42 *Ibid.*
43 Wood, p. 17.
44 For full treatment of this subject, see Brad Patterson, 'A Queer Cantankerous Lot', in Hamer and Nicholls, pp. 61–87.
45 *New Zealand Gazette*, 18 Oct. 1843.
46 *New Zealand Gazette*, 17 Apr. 1844.
47 Miller, p. 117.
48 Marjoribanks, p. 49.
49 Miller *loc cit.*, p. 118.

50 Wood, p. 62.
51 Heaphy, p. 134.
52 WW to CT, 19 Sep. 1843, MP.
53 EW to WW, 5 Nov. 1843, ATL qMS 0056.
54 Nelson *Examiner*, 31 Aug. 1844.
55 I. Hewitson, Moutere, in Luther Broad's *Jubilee History of Nelson*, Nelson, 1892, p. 79.
56 WW to T. C. Harington, 5 Sep. 1844, HL CO 208/307.
57 Allan, *loc. cit.*, p. 363. Bell was the grandson of Priscilla Wakefield's brother Jonathan Bell.
58 WW to J. R. Gowan, 11 Oct. 1844, Natural History Museum, London, Owen Coll. Vol. XXVI.

Chapter Twenty-two: The New Zealand War

1 EW to WW 22 Sep. 1844, ATL Allom Papers, qMS 0056-6.
2 New Zealand Company Minutes, HL CO 208/179, p. 32.
3 EGW to CT, 27 Apr.1844, BL Place Papers 35,261, f. 69.
4 Garnett, p. 251.
5 BPP, Vol. 2, 1844, Report and Minutes of Evidence, Select Committee on New Zealand.
6 Garnett, p. 251.
7 Torlesse, p. 108.
8 EGW to Chas. Torlesse, 9 Jul. 1844, CM EGW Papers, Vol. 1, p. 58.
9 EGW to CT, [14] Jul. 1844, Garnett, *loc. cit.*, pp. 252–53.
10 EGW to Chas Torlesse, n.d.1844, BL Add. MSS 35,261, f. 71.
11 Stanley to Peel, 17 Dec. 1844, Burns, *loc. cit.*, p. 257.
12 EW to WW, 11 Feb. 1845, ML A3094, Micro CY 2870B. 'Imbecility' may indicate that the stroke affected EGW's speech.
13 EW to WW, 24 Apr. 1845, ML A3094, Micro CY 2870B.
14 Stevens, p. 25. Stevens's superb edition of Jerningham's cryptic London diary, which he kept from 1 May 1845 to 4 Sep. 1846, with breaks, provides invaluable detailed insights into activities and relationships during this time.
15 EGW to CT, 23 Mar. 1845, MP.
16 EJW, *Journal*, 15 May 1845.
17 EW to WW, 13 Apr. 1846, ML A3094, Micro CY 2870B.
18 EW to Sir Robert Peel, 19 Aug. 1844, BL MSS 40,550, f. 141.
19 EW to Sir Robert Peel, 13 Jun. 1845, BL MSS 40,569, f. 41-2.
20 EW to WW, 15 Mar. 1846, ML A3094, Micro CY 2870B.
21 *Ibid.*, 20 Dec. 1844.
22 *Ibid.*, 27 Feb. 1846.
23 Stevens, p. 28. The train journey entailed travelling to London Bridge Station because Waterloo and Victoria stations were yet to be built; the *Spectator* office was in Wellington Street which then connected The Strand and Waterloo Bridge.
24 Stevens, p. 37.
25 EW to WW, 24 Apr. 1845, ML A3094, Micro CY 2870B.
26 Stevens, pp. 30–31.
27 One of EJW's cousins, James Pattle's grand-daughter Julia Jackson, made a second marriage to Leslie Stephen (son of James Stephen and compiler of the *DNB*) and one of their children was Virginia Woolf.
28 Stevens, p. 18.
29 Thackeray, 'A Word About Dinners', in *Travels*.
30 Stevens, p. 39.
31 *Ibid.*, p. 93.
32 EGW to CT, 23 Mar. 1845, MP.
33 EGW to CT, Garnett, *loc. cit.*, p. 257.
34 Stevens, pp. 44, 46.
35 *Ibid.*, p. 49.
36 EGW to CT, 23 Jul. 1845, BL Place Papers, 35,261, f. 69.
37 Burns, *loc. cit.*, p. 266.
38 Stevens, p. 54.
39 EW to WW, 6 Oct. 1845, Stevens, *loc. cit.*, p. 10.
40 See Extended Note C.
41 EGW to Gladstone, 13 Jul. 1836, BL MSS 44,355, f.70.
42 Garnett, *loc. cit.*, p. 261.
43 Howick became the third Earl Grey upon his father's death in 1845.
44 Burns, *loc. cit.*, p. 284.
45 Stevens, pp. 87–88.
46 Gladstone to Grey, March 1846, CO Despatch 27/46, BL MSS 44,363, f. 359.
47 Nearly 50 years later, Gladstone said that he had derived the idea of Home Rule from the 'colonial reformers'. Hansard 6 Apr. 1893.
48 Stevens, p. 90.
49 *Ibid.*, p. 91.
50 *Ibid.*, p. 92.
51 *Ibid.*, p. 94.
52 Bloomfield, *loc. cit.*, p. 285.
53 EGW, *Art of Colonization*, p. 775.
54 Bloomfield, *loc. cit.*, p. 285.
55 *Ibid.*, p. 284
56 EJW, *Jack-In-Office*, Act II, Sc. IV, ML MSS 6927/14/1, Ward Family Papers 1831–1983. EJW's use of 'empirical' derives from the old definition of an 'empiric' = a charlatan.
57 WW to Emily, 29 Dec. 1846, ATL O'Connor 88-144-1.
58 Stevens, p. 92.
59 EJW to CT, 17 Aug. 1846, MP.
60 *Ibid.*, 19 Aug. 1846.
61 EGW to CT, 27 Aug. 1846, MP.
62 EW to WW, 2 Feb. 1847, ML A3094, Micro CY 2870B.
63 Buller to Grey, n.d. 1846, Elgin-Grey Papers, 1846–52, Vol. III, pp.1104–05, PAC 1937.
64 Harrop, *loc. cit.*, pp.147–48.
65 O'Connor, *loc. cit.*, p. 203.

Chapter Twenty-three: 'He is but cold earth'

1 Stevens, p. 57.
2 *DNZB*, Vol. 1, p. 25.
3 Phil Parkinson, 'Wideawake at the Wakefield', *Pink Triangle*, No. 47, May/June 1984.
4 H. S. Chapman to father, 10 Oct. 1848, ATL qMS 0419.
5 Wards, p. 236.
6 Miller, p. 91.
7 Belich, *Wars*, *loc. cit.*, p. 69.
8 Rutherford, p. 5.
9 WW to CT, 29 Mar. 1847, BL Place Papers 35, 261, f. 72. Commenting on this letter in 1898, Albert Allom wrote, 'I rather fancy Grey must have been what is vulgarly termed "poking borax" in his conversation with the Col. He would not have known much personally of the Wakefield family . . . He [Grey] was one of the cleverest men at "pumping" for information, and giving nothing in return, except perhaps something ambiguous, or purposely intended to be incorrect.' HL MS 508, p. 7.
10 Wards, p. 276.
11 Grover, p. 281.
12 *Spectator*, 25 Jul. 1846.
13 McKinnon, plate 32.
14 WW to P. Wilson, 24 Jan. 1842,Wards, *loc. cit.*, p. 307.
15 WW to Emily, 2 Feb. 1847, ATL O'Connor 88-144-1.
16 WW to CT, 29 Mar. 1847, BL Place Papers 35,261, f. 72.
17 WW to Emily, 9 Jun. 1847, ATL O'Connor 88-144-1.
18 H. S. Chapman to father, 3 Feb. 1847, ATL MS Papers 0053-17B.
19 H. S. Chapman to father, 19 Aug. 1847, ATL qMS 0419.
20 *DNZB*, Vol. 1, p. 79.
21 H. S. Chapman to father, 10 Jul. 1848, ATL qMS 0419.
22 Rutherford, p. 166.
23 Allan, p. 295.
24 WW to Superintendent of the Southern Province (Richmond), 25 Mar. 1847, HL CO208/308, p. 50.
25 Rutherford, p. 166.
26 *Spectator*, 31 Mar. 1847.
27 WW to Richard Owen, 1 Aug. 1845, Natural History Museum, Owen Coll., Vol. XXVI.
28 WW to J. R. Gowan, 12 Aug. 1847, Natural History Museum, Owen Coll., Vol. XXVI.
29 H. S. Chapman to father, 18 Jan. 1848, ATL qMS 0419.
30 *Spectator*, 4 Apr. 1845.
31 DNZB, Vol. 1, p. 360.
32 H. S. Chapman to father, 3 Feb. 1850, ATL qMS-4020.
33 Bohan, *Stafford*, p. 29.
34 John Saxton diary, Bohan, *loc. cit.*, p. 31.
35 *Ibid.*, p. 32.
36 *Ibid.*, p. 31.
37 *Ibid.*
38 H. S. Chapman to father, 19 Aug. 1847, ATL qMS 0419.
39 Bohan, *loc. cit.*, p. 32.
40 WW to Emily, 7 Nov. 1846, ATL O'Connor 88-144-1.
41 WW to CT, 29 Mar. 1847, BL Place Papers 35,261, f. 72.
42 WW to Emily, 29 Dec. 1846, ATL O'Connor 88-144-1.
43 *Ibid.*, 11 Jan. 1847.
44 Bohan, *loc. cit.*, p. 33.
45 Torlesse, p. 107.
46 WW to CT, 29 Mar. 1847, BL Place Papers 35,261, f. 72.
47 DNZB, Vol. 1, p. 120.
48 *Independent*, 24 Mar. 1847.
49 *New Zealand Encyclopedia* (1966), p. 500.
50 WW to Emily, 22 Apr. 1847, ATL O'Connor 88-144-1.
51 WW to CT, 29 Mar. 1847, BL Place Papers 35,261, f. 72.
52 WW to Emily, 22 Apr. 1847, ATL O'Connor 88-144-1.
53 *Ibid.*, 2 Feb. 1847.
54 *Ibid.*, 9 Jun. 1847, ATL O'Connor 88-144-1.
55 *Ibid.*, 9 Nov. 1847, ATL O'Connor 88-144-1.
56 WW to CT, 29 Mar. 1847, BL Place Papers 35,261, f. 72.
57 H. S. Chapman to father, 10 Oct. 1848, ATL qMS 0419.
58 WW to Emily, 2 Sep. 1848, ATL O'Connor 88-144-1.
59 *Ibid.*, 2 May 1848.
60 *Ibid.*, 6 Aug. 1848.
61 *Ibid.*, 2 Sep. 1848.
62 F. D. Bell to E. Stafford, 20 Sep. 1848, ATL MS 2045 Stafford Papers, Vol. 1.
63 H. S. Chapman to father, 10 Oct. 1848, ATL qMS 0419.
64 Angela Wakefield to Emily, 18 Sep. 1848, ATL MS 2045 Stafford Papers Vol. 1.
65 F. D. Bell to Emily, 20 Sep. 1848, ATL MS 2045 Stafford Papers Vol. 1.
66 Wellington *Independent*, 23 Sep. 1848.
67 H. S. Chapman to father, 10 Oct. 1848, ATL qMS 0419.
68 *Ibid.*
69 Grover, *op. cit.*, p. 317.
70 *Ibid.*, p. 319.
71 F. D. Bell to E. Stafford, 10 Oct. 1848, ATL MS 2045 Stafford Papers Vol. 1.
72 H. S. Chapman to father, 10 Oct. 1848, ATL qMs 0419.
73 F. D. Bell to E. Stafford, 10 Oct. 1848, ATL MS 2045 Stafford Papers Vol. 1.
74 Bohan, *loc. cit.*, p. 42.
75 Bohan, p. 45.

Chapter Twenty-four: A Highly Excitable Temperament

1 EGW to J. R. Godley, 8 Jul. 1851, Godley Papers, CM.
2 McDonald Biographies, W40, CM.

3 Robson, Vol. 1, p. 164.
4 EGW to CT, 12 Oct. 1837, MP.
5 Edw Boyd to FW, 31 May 1839, CSO 5/190, Archives Office of Tasmania.
6 FW to Capt Forster, Colonial Secretary, 26 Jun. 1839, CSO 5/190, Archives Office of Tasmania.
7 *Ibid.*, 11 Aug. 1839.
8 *Ibid.*, 4 Sept. 1839.
9 *Ibid.*, 2 Oct. 1839.
10 Pike, *Wakefield, Waste Land and Empire.*
11 FW to Edw Boyd, quoted Boyd to Colonial Secretary, 16 Apr. 1840, CSO 5/190, Archives Office of Tasmania.
12 AW to CT, 15 Feb. 1841, MP.
13 It is not clear if FW was paying a high mortgage over his old (unsold) property or high rent on a new one.
14 AW to WW, 13 Apr. 1843, ML A2226, Micro CY893.
15 W. G. Sams to J. E. Bicheno, 26 Aug. 1843, Pike, *Wakefield, loc. cit.*
16 Pike, *Wakefield.*
17 J. E. Bicheno to FW, 16 Jun. 1846, CSO 8/167, Archives Office of Tasmania.
18 W. G. Sams to Dr W. Paton, 6 Jul. 1846, CSO 20/32, Archives Office of Tasmania.
19 FW petition to Sir Eardley Eardley Wilmot, 6 Jul. 1846, CSO 20/32, Archives Office of Tasmania.
20 J. E. Bicheno to FW, 15 Jul. 1846, CSO 20/32, Archives Office of Tasmania.
21 *Biographical Index of South Australians*, Vol. IV, ed. J. Statton, Adelaide 1986.
22 EGW to Godley, 8 Jul. 1851, J. R. Godley Papers, CM.
23 EW to WW, 16 Jun. 1847, ML A3094, Micro CY2780B.
24 EW to WW, 30 Jul. 1847, ML A2226, Micro CY893.
25 O'Connor ARC 1988:92 Box 7/36, CM. Family memoir prob. written 1920s.
26 Garnett, p. 271.
27 *Ibid.*
28 EGW to Godley, 27 Nov. 1847, EJW, *Founders*, p. 1.
29 EGW to CT, 18 Nov. 1841, MP.
30 Garnett, p. 300.
31 EGW to Dr. S. Hinds, 26 Dec. 1848, EJW, *Founders*, p. 36.
32 EGW, *The Art of Colonization,* pp. 840–2.
33 EGW to J. R. Godley, 6 May 1851, Canterbury Papers, ATL qMS 3087-1.
34 EGW to CT, ?? May 1843, MP.
35 Olssen, p. 33.
36 EGW to J. A. Smith, 30 Nov. 1847, EJW, *Founders*, pp. 1–3.
37 *Ibid.*, 8 Dec. 1847, p. 4.
38 EGW to Godley, 8 Jul. 1851, J. R. Godley papers, CM.
39 Godley to his father, Feb. 1851, C. E. Carrington, *loc. cit.*, p. 69.
40 Stevens, p. 4.
41 ML Ward Family Papers, MSS 6927/14/1.
42 EGW to Godley, 8 Jul. 1851, J. R. Godley Papers, CM.
43 Chapman, p. 3.
44 EGW to Captain Thomas, 2 Jul. 1848, EJW, *Founders,* pp. 29-30.
45 EGW to Godley, 12 Jul. 1848, EJW, *Founders*, p. 30.
46 EGW to Dr S. Hinds, ?? May 1848, EJW, *Founders*, p. 29.
47 J. S. Mill to EGW, ?? 1848, BL MS 36,297, f. 23.
48 EGW to Godley, 9 Nov. 1848, EJW, *Founders*, p. 31.
49 H. S. Chapman to father, 2 Aug. 1848, ATL qMS 0419.
50 Garnett, *loc. cit.*, pp. 280–81.
51 *DNB*, Vol. II, p. 248.
52 EGW to Francis Dillon Bell, 29 Jun. 1849, EJW, *Founders*, p. 81.
53 H. S. Chapman to his father, 25 Jul. 1849, ATL MS Papers-0053-17B.

Chapter Twenty-five: Flying with a Broken Wing

1 EGW to Rintoul, 24 Dec. 1848, EJW, *Founders*, pp. 34–35.
2 EGW to Godley, 17 Jan. 1849, EJW, *Founders*, p. 40.
3 EGW to T. C. Harington, 29 Jan. 1849, EJW, *Founders*, p. 44.
4 Garnett, pp. 281–88.
5 EGW, *Art of Colonization*, p. 760.
6 *Ibid.*, see Extended Note D.
7 Bloomfield, *loc. cit.*, p. 307.
8 Bloomfield, *loc. cit.*, p. 308.
9 EGW to Godley, 28 Jun. 1849, EJW, *Founders*, p. 78.
10 L. C. Webb in Hight and Straubel, p. 139.
11 Garnett, pp. 321–24.
12 EGW to Godley, 23 Sep. 1849, EJW, *Founders*, p. 104.
13 EGW to Baring, 23 Sep. 1849, EJW, *Founders*, pp. 105–06.
14 EGW to Godley, 7 Oct. 1849, EJW, *Founders*, p. 120.
15 Carrington, p. 82.
16 Godley to Adderley, 12 Nov. 1849, Adderley, p. 132.
17 EGW to Godley, 25 Oct. 1849, EJW, *Founders*, p. 129.
18 EGW to Samuel Hinds, 30 Oct. 1849, EJW, *Founders*, p. 131.
19 Godley to FW, 5 Apr. 1849, FW, p. 86.
20 EGW to Godley, 8 Jul. 1851, J. R. Godley Papers, CM.
21 EGW to Godley, 27 Sep. 1849, EJW, *Founders*, p. 109.
22 FW to Rev. Dr J.D. Lang, 20 Nov. 1849, ML A2226 (Micro CY 893), p. 410.
23 FW, p. 87.
24 Carrington, p. 84.
25 EGW to Bellairs, 11 Nov. 1849, EJW, *Founders*, p. 139.

26 EGW, *Art of Colonization*, p. 975.
27 EGW to Godley, 8 Jul. 1851, J. R. Godley Papers, CM.
28 EGW's last letter to Godley before his departure, 6 Dec. 1849, EJW, *Founders*, p. 162.
29 EGW to John Abel Smith, 29 Nov. 1849, EJW, *Founders*, pp. 151–52.

Chapter Twenty-six: A Slice of England

1 EGW to J.E. FitzGerald, 12 Dec. 1849, EJW, *Founders*, p. 168.
2 EJW, *Founders*, p. 173.
3 Bohan, *FitzGerald*, p. 23.
4 *Ibid.*, p. 10.
5 EGW to FitzGerald, 3 Sep. 1849, EJW, *Founders*, p. 102.
6 EGW to FitzGerald, 2 Jan. 1850, EJW, *Founders*, p. 187.
7 EGW to Rintoul, 8 Jan. 1850, EJW, *Founders*, p. 191.
8 L. C. Webb in Hight and Straubel, p. 162.
9 EGW to FitzGerald, 21 and 22 Feb. 1850, EJW, *Founders*, pp. 219–20.
10 EGW to John Hutt, 25 Feb. 1850, EJW, *Founders*, p. 221.
11 EGW to FitzGerald, 1 Mar. 1850, EJW, *Founders*, p. 225.
12 EGW to John Hutt, 6 Mar. 1850, EJW, *Founders*, p. 228.
13 EGW to FW, 18 Jan. 1850, EJW, *Founders*, p. 203.
14 FW, p. 87.
15 L. C. Webb in Hight and Straubel, p. 164.
16 EGW to Rintoul, 25 Mar. 1850, EJW, *Founders*, p. 236.
17 EGW to John Hutt, 2 Apr. 1850, EJW, *Founders*, p. 242.
18 EGW to Godley, 4 Apr. 1850, EJW, *Founders*, p. 246.
19 EGW to Godley, 22 Jun. 1850 (not finished until at least 6 Jul.), EJW, *Founders*, p. 292.
20 *Ibid.*
21 Lyttelton to Godley, 24 Nov. 1850, L. C. Webb, in Hight and Straubel, *loc. cit.*, p.165.
22 Carrington, *loc. cit.*, p. 87.
23 EGW to Godley, 22 Jun. 1850, *op. cit.*
24 EGW to FitzGerald, 17 Apr. 1850, EJW, *Founders*, p. 262
25 EGW to FitzGerald, 3 Aug. 1850, EJW, *Founders*, p. 304.
26 EGW to Lyttelton, 9 Aug. 1850, EJW, *Founders*, pp. 308–09.
27 EGW to Godley, 17–24 Aug. 1850, EJW, *Founders*, pp. 318–19.
28 Charles Wynne to Godley, 29 Mar. 1850, J. R. Godley Papers, CM.
29 *The Times*, 5 Jul. 1851.
30 Godley, pp. 32–5.
31 *Ibid.*, p. 32.
32 *Ibid.*, p. 10.
33 EJW to Mrs Campbell, 16 Oct. 1850, E. J. Wakefield Letters 1850–64, CM.
34 Godley, p. 229.
35 EGW to CT, 29 Apr. 1853, MP.
36 EGW to R. J. S. Harman, 12 Apr. 1850, EJW, *Founders*, pp. 255–56.
37 Godley, p. 165.
38 *Ibid.*, p. 240.
39 Charley Torlesse to Emily Torlesse, 9 Nov. 1850, Chas. O. Torlesse Letters, CM.
40 Charley Torlesse to Chas Torlesse, 5 May 1854, Chas. O. Torlesse Letters, CM.
41 EGW to Godley, 22 Jun. 1850, ATL qMS 0387-1, Canterbury Papers.
42 Torlesse, p. 125.
43 Charley Torlesse to Emily Torlesse, 9 Nov. 1850, *op. cit.*
44 EGW to F. D. Bell, 29 Jun. 1849, EJW, *Founders*, p. 81.
45 EGW to Godley, 22 Jun. 1850, ATL qMS 0387-1, Canterbury Papers.
46 EGW to Lyttelton, 2 Feb. 1851, HL MS-0111.
47 EGW to Godley, 5 Sep. 1850, EJW, *Founders*, p. 323.

Chapter Twenty-seven: Noodles

1 EGW to Godley, 17 Sep. 1850, EJW, *Founders*, pp. 327–28.
2 *Ibid.*, pp. 330–32.
3 EGW to J.C. Wynter, 2 Oct. 1850, EJW, *Founders*, p. 337.
4 EGW to Godley, 19–21 Oct. 1850, ATL Canterbury Papers, qMS 0387-1.
5 Godley, pp. 172–3.
6 EGW to Godley, 8 Jul. 1851,Godley Papers, CM. Following EGW quotes about FW and his behaviour are from this letter.
7 FW to H. Savage, 22 Apr. 1853, FW, p. 86.
8 EGW to Godley, 9 Jan. 1851, ATL Canterbury Papers, qMS 0387-1.
9 Charley Torlesse to CT, 15 Nov. 1851, Box 2, Chas. O. Torlesse Papers, CM.
10 Godley, pp. 285, 336.
11 EGW to Godley, 8 Jul. 1851,Godley Papers, CM.
12 EGW to EJW, 16 Jul. 1851, ATL Canterbury Papers, qMS 3087-1.
13 FitzGerald to H. S. Selfe, 3 Feb. 1852, Selfe Papers, CM.
14 Edward Wakefield, *Stafford*.
15 F. D. Bell to E.W. Stafford, 21 Dec. 1851, Stafford Papers, ATL qMS 2045.
16 FitzGerald to H. S. Selfe, 18 Feb. 1852, Selfe Papers, CM.
17 FW, p. viii.
18 FW to Godley, 4 Jul. 1853, Godley Papers, Folder 1166, CM.
19 FW to Godley, 5 Jul. 1853, Godley Papers, CM.
20 Carrington, pp. 157–58.
21 EGW to Godley, 9 Jan. 1851, Canterbury Papers, ATL qMS 3087-1.
22 *Ibid.*, 9 Feb. 1851.
23 EGW, *England and America*, p. 541.
24 EGW to Godley, 6 May 1851, Canterbury Papers, ATL qMS 3087-1.

25 EGW to Godley, 6 Jun. 1851, HL MS- 505/7.
26 *Ibid.*, 7 Jun. 1851.
27 Godley to Adderley, 22 May 1851, Adderley.
28 *Ibid.*, 19 Jun. 1851.
29 Carrington, p. 157.
30 EGW to Lyttelton, 7 Aug. 1851, Carrington, *loc. cit.*, p. 157.
31 Carrington, p. 132.
32 Godley Despatch to Canterbury Association, 3 Jun. 1851, *Writings and Speeches*, p. 204.
33 EGW to Godley, 8 Sep. 1851, ATL qMS-0388.
34 *Ibid.*, 15 Jul. 1853.
35 Young quotes from Garnett, pp. 324–27.
36 *DNZB*, Vol. 1, p. 135.
37 Bloomfield, p. 322.
38 Sinclair, p. 87.
39 Bell and Morrell, dated 30 Aug. 1851.
40 Morrell, p. 499.
41 *The Times,* 12 Nov. 1851.
42 Bloomfield, p. 323.
43 EGW to Lyttelton, 19 Mar. 1852, HL MS-0111.
44 Garnett, *loc. cit.*, p. 332.
45 EGW to Lyttelton, 5 Jun. 1852, HL MS-0111.
46 H. S. Chapman to his father, 3 Feb. 1850, ATL MS Papers 0053, Folder 22. Chapman was referring to EGW's espousal of an hereditary chamber in *The Art of Colonization*. Bell was indeed appointed to the Legislative Council in 1877 after a long period as an elected member of the House of Representatives.
47 Lyttelton did not, but his great-grandson, the 10th Viscount Cobham, was governor-general from 1957 to 1962. EGW to Lyttelton, 8 Oct. 1852, HL MS-0111.
48 Godley to Adderley, 20 Sep. 1852, Adderley.
49 EGW to Rintoul, 22 Jun. 1853, HL MS-508.
50 EGW to Godley, 7 Jun. 1851, HL MS-505/7.
51 EGW to Henrietta Rintoul, 9 Oct. 1852, HL MS 508.
52 Garnett, p. 335.
53 EGW to CT, 12 Oct. 1852, MP.
54 EGW to Henrietta Rintoul, 19 Apr. 1853, ATL Canterbury Papers, qMS 3088-2.

Chapter Twenty-eight: Dead to the Past

1 John Deans to father, 21 Mar. 1853, Deans, p. 248.
2 EGW to Henrietta Rintoul, 1 Nov. 1852, HL MS-508.
3 McIntyre, Vol. 1, p. 121.
4 McIntyre, 1/122-4.
5 EGW to CT, 8 Feb. 1853, MP.
6 EGW to Rintoul, 16 Apr. 1853, HL MS-508. And following quotes.
7 McIntyre, 1/122.
8 EGW to Rintoul, 16 Apr. 1853, HL MS-508.
9 Bowen to Godley, 25 Apr. 1853, HL MS 505/1.
10 McIntyre, 1/171.
11 EGW to Rintoul, 16 Apr. 1853, HL MS-508.
12 Gisborne, p. 89.
13 *DNZB*, Vol. 1, p. 392.
14 Fox to Godley, 31 Dec. 1858, L. C. Webb in Hight and Straubel, p. 230.
15 McIntyre, 1/167.
16 Bloomfield, *loc. cit.*, p. 324.
17 EGW to Henrietta Rintoul, 13 Jul. 1853, ATL Canterbury Papers, qMS 3088-2.
18 McIntyre, 1/179.
19 *Ibid.*, 1/183.
20 EGW to Sir George Grey, 9 Mar. 1853, MP.
21 Grey to EGW, 9 Mar. 1853, MP.
22 Grey to Duke of Newcastle, 18 May 1854, ANZ CO 209/12.
23 Rutherford, p. 7.
24 *DNZB*, Vol. 1, p. 163.
25 Herron, Chapter XII, 'The Assembly Delayed', details Grey's delaying tactics.
26 EGW to Grey, 10 Mar. 1853, MP.
27 McIntyre, following quotes from Sewell journal entries of indicated dates.
28 *Independent*, 19 Mar. 1853, Peter Stuart, *loc. cit.*, p. 47n.
29 O'Connor, p. 238.
30 EGW to CT, 13 Jul. 1853, ATL Canterbury Papers, qMS 3088-2.
31 EGW to Rintoul, 22 Jun. 1853, HL MS-508.
32 EGW to Lyttelton, 24 Mar. 1853, HL MS-0111.
33 EGW to CT, 17 Apr. 1853, MP.
34 EGW to CT, 29 Apr. 1853, MP.
35 EJW, 'Proclamation', *Canterbury Rhymes*, Christchurch, 1853.
36 Grey to DW, 2 May 1853,Stuart, *loc. cit.*, p. 41n.
37 Rutherford, p. 252.
38 Rutherford, p. 253.
39 EGW to Rintoul, 22 Jun. 1853, HL MS-508.
40 Rutherford, p. 88.
41 EGW's open letter to H.J. Tancred, 15 Mar. 1853, published *Nelson Examiner*, 30 Apr. 1853.
42 McIntyre, 1/288.
43 Stuart, p. 49.
44 *Independent*, 30 Apr. 1853.
45 It was said that EGW even wore the blue serge shirt of the workers during his Hutt campaigning. R. Wakelin in *History and Politics* (1877), Herron, *loc. cit.*, p. 300.
46 McIntyre, 1/333.
47 Stuart, p. 55.
48 EGW to Rintoul, 22 Jun. 1853, HL MS-508.
49 Stuart, p. 63.
50 *Independent*, 6 Jul. 1853.
51 *Independent*, 9 and 13 Jul. 1853.
52 EGW to Godley, 15 Jul. 1853, ATL Canterbury Papers, qMS 3088-2.
53 Stuart, p. 67.
54 EGW to Henrietta Rintoul, 13 Jul. 1853, ATL Canterbury Papers, qMS 3088-2.
55 EGW to Henrietta Rintoul, 19 Apr. 1853, ATL Canterbury Papers, qMS 3088-2.
56 EGW, *Art of Colonization*, pp. 856–57.
57 McIntyre, 1/377.

Chapter Twenty-nine: 'That Old Giant Spider'

1 Stuart, *loc. cit.*, p. 103.
2 EGW to Stafford, 24 Jun. 1853, ATL Canterbury Papers, qMS 3088-2.
3 EGW to Rintoul, 31 Aug. 1853, HL MS-508.
4 EGW to Stafford, 24 Jun. 1853, ATL, Canterbury Papers, qMS 3088-2.
5 EGW, 24 Aug. 1853, HL MS-0111. The addressee is not known – probably Rintoul or Godley – but an edited copy made its way into Lyttelton's hands.
6 Stuart, pp. 89–90.
7 Herron, p. 313.
8 McIntyre, 1/392. < > indicates journal comments that Sewell later crossed out.
9 Sewell, *op. cit.*, 1/394.
10 Stuart, *op. cit.*, p. 102.
11 Stuart, *loc .cit.*, p. 93.
12 Stuart, *loc. cit.*, p. 94.
13 *Spectator*, 17 May 1854.
14 The *Independent*, 15 Mar. 1854, peevishly commented that EGW 'cannot make a speech without talking of his sayings and doings in Canada and quoting his friend Lord Durham . . .'.
15 *Spectator*, 4 Mar. 1854.
16 Stuart, *loc. cit.*, pp. 107–08.
17 Edward Wakefield, p. 4.
18 *Ibid.*
19 *Lyttelton Times*, 8 Jul. 1854.
20 *Lyttelton Times*, 21 Jan. 1854.
21 FW to H. G. Gouland, 16 Jul. 1854, *Lyttelton Times*, 5 Aug. 1854.
22 Torlesse, p. 71.
23 Edward Wakefield, pp. 4–5.
24 *Spectator*, 8 Mar. 1854.
25 *Ibid.*
26 Stuart, pp. 113–14.
27 McIntyre, II/39.
28 Neither Stafford nor Fox was yet a MHR.
29 Lloyd Prichard, p. 77.
30 FitzGerald to Godley, 23 Apr. 1855, McIntyre, *loc. cit.*, II/326.
31 McIntyre, II/37.
32 *Ibid.*, II/40.
33 EGW to Lyttelton, 14 Jun. 1854, HL MS-0111.
34 EGW to CT, 14 Jun. 1854, MP.
35 McIntyre, II/327.
36 Stuart, p. 137.
37 Fitzgerald to Godley, 23 Apr. 1855, McIntyre, *loc. cit.*, II/328.
38 Stuart, p. 39.
39 FitzGerald to Godley, 23 Apr. 1855, McIntyre, *loc. cit.*, II/328.
40 McIntyre, II/58-59.
41 Charles Buller to John Stuart Mill, 13 Oct. 1838, PAC MG24, A26, Charles Buller Papers.
42 Herron (p. 24) described Auckland members of the first General Assembly as part of an 'unrelieved stream of inarticulate mediocrities, palpably deficient in ministerial attributes'.
43 Stuart, p. 42.
44 Herron, p. 332.
45 FitzGerald to Godley, 23 Apr. 1855, McIntyre, *loc. cit.*, II/332.
46 Herron, *loc. cit.*, p. 323.
47 McIntyre, II/63–64.
48 Stuart, p. 160.
49 McIntyre, II/80.
50 *Ibid.*, II/85.
51 Bohan, *FitzGerald*, p. 130.
52 Bohan, *FitzGerald*, *loc. cit.*, pp. 132–32.
53 Garnett, p. 357n, described this as 'one of the most vigorous pieces of invective in the language'.
54 McIntyre, II/87–88.
55 *Ibid.*, II/99–100.
56 Garnett, *loc. cit.*, p. 358.
57 Stuart, p. 171.
58 *Ibid.*, pp. 171–72.
59 McIntyre, II/113.

Chapter Thirty: Dead to the Future

1 EJW to CT, 8 May 1855, Garnett, *loc. cit.*, p. 359.
2 Featherston to Stafford, 28 Dec. 1854, Stafford Papers, Vol. 2, ATL MS-2046.
3 Fox to Godley, 26 Feb. 1855, HL MS-505/7.
4 *Ibid.*, 9 Jun. 1855.
5 EJW to CT, 8 May 1855, Garnett, *loc. cit.*, pp. 359–61.
6 McIntyre, II/150.
7 *Ibid.*, II/138.
8 Garnett, pp. 358, 361.
9 *DNZB*, Vol. 1, p. 575.
10 All of this memoir is from Garnett, *loc. cit.*, pp. 362–68.Alice wrote her reminiscences for biographer Richard Garnett when she was about 48 years old.
11 Lloyd Prichard, *loc. cit.*, p. 90.
12 'And for us!' FitzGerald and Fox might have said. The idea of a silent EGW seems impossible.
13 Irma O'Connor, *Evening Post*, 24 Jun. 1939.
14 Stevens, p. 149.
15 Bohan, *Stafford*, p. 108.
16 Bohan, *ibid.*, p. 109.
17 *Loc. cit.*, p. 110.
18 DW to Col. Secretary, 15 Jun. 1855, ANZ IA 55/2061.
19 Cooke, p. 51.
20 Son of Edward Wakefield's sister 'Bell' (Isabella). Edward Wakefield described growing up in Kensington.
21 Fortescue,Vol. XIII, p. 225.
22 W. T. Doyne to Sir Joseph Paxton, 15 Apr.1856, NAM 6807/142-25.
23 Bohan, *Stafford*, p. 219.
24 FW to Richard Owen, 6 Jul. 1863, Natural History Museum, London, Owen Coll.,Vol. XXVI.
25 The fate of his wife is unclear but it seems as if she was dead by this time.
26 *The Times*, [1st week] Mar. 1862.
27 *Ibid.*
28 *Spectator*, 21 May 1862.

29 *Spectator*, 17 May 1862.
30 Garnett, *loc. cit.*, p. 375.
31 *DNB*, Vol. XIV, p. 571.
32 Charley Torlesse to C. M. Torlesse, 9 Aug. 1863, Chas. O. Torlesse Letters 1850s–1870s, CM. Charley and family had spent a year in England from May 1861.
33 Irma O'Connor, *Evening Post*, 24 Jun. 1939. O'Connor was Jerningham's granddaughter and heard first-hand stories from grandmother Ellen.
34 Charley Torlesse to Charles Torlesse, 9 Aug. 1863, *op. cit.*
35 O'Connor, *op. cit.*
36 Affidavits dated 12 Aug. 1862, Irma O'Connor ARC 1988.92, CM.
37 Angela returned to England with Alice soon after EGW's death but the section remained in Wakefield family hands until the 1980s. EGW also left land in Christchurch to his manservant Wilhelm Schmidt. Angela and Dan's son Charles Marcus spent most of his time 1857–72 in Canterbury, as a surveyor and also became a leading entomologist, before returning permanently to England.
38 Edward Wakefield, p. 13.
39 Charley Torlesse to Frances Torlesse, 7 Apr. 1864, Chas. O. Torlesse Letters 1850–1870, CM.
40 Torlesse, pp. 131–32.
41 Details of Felix's engineering schemes for Canterbury can be found in Chapman.
42 FW to Donald McLean, 10 Apr. 1871, Chapman, *loc. cit.*, p. 43.
43 Chapman, p. 38.
44 Shakespeare's *Macbeth*, Act III, Sc. ii.
45 McDonald Biographies, W 39, CM.
46 *Ibid.*
47 EJW to Grey, 23 Dec. 1878, Belich, *Making Peoples*, *loc. cit.*, p. 340.
48 Edward followed a controversial political and journalistic career before returning permanently to England in 1890. He published a survey of the country, *New Zealand After 50 years*, in 1889. Of Felix's other sons, Murat and Salvator settled in Australia; Oliver was killed in a Dunedin tram accident in 1884; and Percy lived and worked on the West Coast of the South Island and in Wellington where he died.

Epilogue

1 EGW to CW, Dec. 1821, MP.
2 Herron, p. 294 fn.
3 L. C. Webb in Hight and Straubel, p. 211.
4 Fox to Godley, 26 February 1855, MS-505/7, HL.
5 Graham Butterworth, 'Edward Gibbon Wakefield and the Quaker Tradition', *Edward Gibbon Wakefield*, p. 75.
6 H. S. Chapman to father, 19 Aug. 1847, ATL qMS 0419.
7 *DNZB*,Vol. 1, p. 575.
8 MacDonnell, p. 37.
9 Taft Manning, p. 23.
10 Ged Martin, 'Wakefield's Past and Futures', *Edward Gibbon Wakefield*, p. 30.
11 *Ibid.*, pp. 40–1.
12 Belich, *Making Peoples*, pp. 279-80.
13 London *Spectator*, 21 Jan. 1899.
14 Robbins, p. 154.
15 Erik Olssen, 'Wakefield and the Scottish Enlightenment', *Edward Gibbon Wakefield,* p. 62.
16 Mark Francis, 'Writings on Colonial New Zealand', in Sharp and McHugh, pp. 182–83.
17 *DNZB*, Vol. 1, p. 575.
18 Eric Richards, 'Wakefield and Australia,' *Edward Gibbon Wakefield*, p. 101.
19 Olssen, *op. cit.*, p. 63.
20 Herron, p. 340.
21 John E. Martin, 'A small nation on the move', *Edward Gibbon Wakefield*, p. 119.
22 Ged Martin, *op. cit.*, p. 40.
23 *DNZB*, Vol. 1, p. 573.
24 Ngatata Love, 'A Maori Perspective', *Edward Gibbon Wakefield*, p. 10.
25 W. H. Oliver, 'The Wakefield Myth', *Comment*, Jul. 1962, p. 6.

Extended Notes

1 B. S. Baldwin, 'Edward Gibbon Wakefield in Paris 1825', Facts and Events' (South Australia), Vol. 8, No. 3, pp. 44–51.
2 Much land in Lower Canada was held under a form of feudal tenure system imported from France. These landed estates were termed seigneuries.
3 EJW, *Journal*, *op cit.*, p. 28.
4 *Ibid.*, p. 47.
5 Burns, *loc. cit.*, p. 258.

INDEX

Note: Abbreviations for Wakefield family members are the same as those used in the notes: see the list of abbreviations on page 548. The use of *passim* after a range of pages, e.g. 335–45 *passim*, means that within those pages there is frequent mention but not continuous discussion of the relevant person or topic.